Treasures of Silver at Corpus Christi College, Cambridge

This is an acccount of the unique assemblage of silver and silver-mounted artefacts belonging to Corpus Christi College, Cambridge, some of them dating back to the College's foundation 650 years ago. They include extraordinary objects such as a thirteenth-century drinking vessel made of the horn of an extinct animal, as well as the everyday tools and utensils of past centuries. Although some of these objects are well known to art historians, they have never been published in detail.

A college's or other institution's history resides not only in its written records but in the buildings and historic artefacts which define its corporate identity. The objects in this book are especially significant for being documented in the College's archives from the fourteenth century onwards.

This book has more of an archaeological than an art-historical approach. It investigates the objects' construction, how the College came by them, their original meaning and context, how they came to survive the depredations of the Civil War, what happened to those that do not survive, evidence of wear and repair, and what they were (and still are) used for. The ultimate objective is to show how they illuminate the character and functioning of a still-flourishing medieval institution.

The book is illustrated comprehensively with photographs by Dr John Cleaver.

DR OLIVER RACKHAM O.B.E., F.B.A. has been a Fellow of Corpus Christi College, Cambridge, since 1964. He is an historical ecologist and historian of landscape with interests in Britain, southern Europe, North America, Japan and Australia. He holds an Honorary Doctorate from the University of Essex and is the author of *Trees and Woodland in the British Landscape*, *The History of the Countryside*, *The Illustrated History of the Countryside* and several other books and many articles.

DR JOHN CLEAVER is Assistant Director of Research at the Microelectronics Research Centre, Cavendish Laboratory, University of Cambridge, where his research interests are in the physics and fabrication of novel microelectronic devices. He is a Fellow of Fitzwilliam College, Cambridge.

Treasures of Silver at Corpus Christi College Cambridge

OLIVER RACKHAM

With photographs by JOHN CLEAVER

First published 2002

Printed in the United Kingdom at the University Press, Cambridge

Typeface Minion 9.75/12 pt *System* LaTeX 2ε [TB]

A catalogue record for this book is available from the British Library

ISBN 0 521 81880 X hardback

TO THE COLLEGE BUTLERS
WHO HAVE CARED FOR THE PLATE
DOWN THE CENTURIES

of whom I know the following by name:

1595–1626	ROBERT GILL (Butler or Promus)
1626–1643	PHILIP WILLIAMS (Promus)
1643–	THOMAS GRAVES (Promus)
1670	JOHN MORGAN (Promus)
1752/3	JACOB GODDARD
1757	WILLIAM KIDD
1761–1762	EDWARD GOODE
1795	JOHN ASHLEY
–1840	ASHBY (died 1840)
1840–1848	WILLIAM MILLER
1846–1864	JAMES CARELESS (Combination-room Man)
1864–1900	WILLIAM DOBBS, THE LITTLE DUKE (Combination-room Man)
1878–1928	HERMAN AUSTIN (cleaner of plate)
1900	Post of Butler created and offered to G. SHRUBB
*c.*1912–46	GEORGE MATTHEWS
1946–1958	L. E. FREEMAN
1958–1978	ALAN WILSON
1978–	RON STOREY

From Bury's *History*, miscellaneous references in College audit-books and inventories, and graffiti on plate. Undergraduate butlers, whose duties seem to have been nominal, are not listed.

Contents

Foreword

The prized heritage of Corpus Christi College, Cambridge includes a remarkable collection of silver treasures. Some of these date even from before the foundation of the College in 1352, being inherited from the Gilds that founded the College. Pride of place must be given to the ancient Drinking Horn which features prominently in this book and is believed to be more than 700 years old.

From that early beginning the collection has grown. Pieces have been added throughout the history of the College, and the collection continues to receive additions to this day. A particular boost was given by Archbishop Matthew Parker in the sixteenth century. He gave the College some of the finest pieces in the collection such as the great rosewater ewer and basin, his salt and tankard, and the magnificent apostle spoons.

This silver collection is famous for having survived the ravages of the English Civil War in the seventeenth century. As the College historian Patrick Bury wrote in 1952: '[when] various Colleges sacrificed their plate to the royal cause, or were compelled to surrender it to the other side, Corpus prudently distributed it for safe-keeping among the Fellows, who in July 1643 were given general leave of absence'.

This book re-investigates what happened: how Richard Love, the Master at that period, a man of good sense and political acumen, ensured that Corpus was not much affected by the unrest; how the College treasures were returned by Fellows or brought out of a secret store when the nation returned to peace; and what happened to them afterwards.

In this book the author has added much to the interest that these beautiful objects excite by giving us an account of their provenance, the manner of acquisition by the College, and the use to which they were put. Indeed the detailed accounts include fascinating information about the survival of the objects, not only through times of financial difficulty for the College, but also through times of inadequate care or inexpert repair. They are still in use today; even the finest pieces are displayed on Feast days or other special occasions.

This book will be of particular interest to Old Members of the College, who will recall some of the pieces, and particularly the Horn and loving-cups from which all College members drink at least once during their time here. It will also have a wider appeal for readers interested more generally in early English silver. Most of the artefacts have been in constant use over the centuries. The accounts of their usage provide a fascinating social history of a medieval establishment as it functioned over the years to its 650th anniversary, which this book commemorates.

The author, Dr Oliver Rackham, Senior Fellow of the College and Keeper of the College Records, is an acknowledged expert on the buildings and possessions of the College. He brings a scholarly and a pleasantly readable style to the book. His collaborator, Dr John Cleaver, has photographed the collection with meticulous care and brought to life the beauty of the pieces with great skill. The College owes a debt to both contributors, and hopes the book will provide a lasting symbol of its 650th anniversary.

HAROON AHMED
Master of the College, December 2001

Preface

The College of Corpus Christi and the Blessed Virgin Mary, over the 650 years of its existence, has accumulated what may be the the finest collection of silver artefacts, commonly called *plate,* of any college in Cambridge or Oxford. These form one of the College's three chief treasures, the others being its incomparable manuscript library and its surviving original buildings.

Over the centuries plate has passed from being a symbol of the status of a family or institution, to a symbol of continuity and stability, a definer of the owner's identity, a link with relatives and benefactors, as well as having a functional use on both ceremonial and ordinary occasions. Plate enters into most college functions, and is still in daily use: almost into the writer's own time every student handled some part of the College treasures every day.

The artefacts have been the material for scholarly study for some 230 years. Studies were concerned at first with their origin and use, and later with silver as a branch of art history and the development of style. The study of plate has now widened, especially through the work of Philippa Glanville, to investigate its functions, why institutions acquired particular objects and what they signified. Plate is a record of social history, especially when the pieces still belong to the original owner. As with any archaeological objects, context is all-important. The artefacts in isolation are of limited significance. Their meaning emerges when their inscriptions, alterations, and marks of wear are compared with archival records of their acquisition, use, and repair.

This book was inspired by the sumptuous volume, *Corpus Silver*, published in 1999 by the sister college of Corpus Christi, Oxford. But its objective is different. That book is a collection of essays by ten specialists on some of the most phenomenal treasures of that extraordinary college. It would hardly be possible to assemble such a brilliant team of scholars and art historians to repeat the research at Corpus Christi, Cambridge.

This book is a more modest and preliminary study. It does, however, cover the entire hoard, as does Douglas Bennett's on the plate of Trinity College, Dublin. Although the earlier and rare pieces are described in more detail, I have not tried to limit the scope to those objects now regarded as 'interesting'. Posterity would be baffled and frustrated by the exclusion of less interesting pieces. I have omitted most of the objects of silver-plated base metal, few of which tell much of a story: they rarely have dates, inscriptions, or graffiti.

It has long been a matter of regret that most Cambridge colleges, like those of Oxford and the monasteries of Mount Athos, lack the means of enabling the wider public to see and enjoy their treasures, except when a few grand pieces are lent to exhibitions. As Keeper of the Plate at Corpus, I have a duty to encourage appreciation of the hoard and research into what it has to say, and this book is a first attempt to discharge that obligation. I very much hope for a solution to the wider problem: Anglican cathedrals and London livery companies, with secure but transparent places for displaying their plate, have shown the way.

Some Explanations

Earlier pieces are arranged in roughly chronological order. After 1700, when many more pieces survive, this becomes impractical, and articles are arranged according to broad categories of type. There is a final chapter on Modernistic Plate, meaning pieces (mostly ceremonial) made in the self-consciously 'modern' styles that developed from 1920 onwards.

Uses and names of plate reflect changes in social habits. Generations pass away, and people forget what spiceplate and beryl, charger and argyle, salver and cuspidor, cruet and ashtray were used for. I have tried to identify pieces in neutral terms: Bowls, Two-Handled Cups, Giant Spoons.

Dates

Hallmarked pieces are dated by letters (p. 11), which were changed on arbitrary dates in the year. By convention, New Year's Day at the London Assay Office is taken to be 19 May down to 1697, 29 May from 1698 to 1974, and thereafter 1 January; thus the date 1830, identified by the letter **p**, means between 29 May 1830 and 28 May 1831.[1] The year begins in July at Birmingham and Sheffield, in October at Edinburgh, and in January at Dublin.

Before 1752 New Year's Day for most other purposes was 25 March: thus the date 14 February 1591 written on a document means 1592 in present reckoning. In this book it will be called 1591/2.

'The 1800s' means 1800–1809, the decade between the 1790s and the 1810s; it is not the same as 'the 19th century'.

Measures and Weights

The dimensions of objects are given in the order of greatest width × height, or length × width × height. With a cup or similar object having one or two handles, the length is taken to be the measurement along the handles, and the width at right angles to the handles.

Measuring plate is not easy: published dimensions can be in error by several millimetres. It is difficult to measure articles in metric units, since centimetres are too coarse a unit, while millimetres are impossibly fine and give a false impression of accuracy. (One can seldom be sure whether a cup is 176, 177, 178, or 179 mm high, especially if it is old and bent.) Quarters of centimetres would be a practical but unfamiliar metric unit, but rather than wrestle with these I shall use tenths of an inch.

Silver is weighed in troy ounces, 31.10 grams or 1.097 Anglo-American ounces. The ounce is divided into 24 pennyweights, each of 20 grains. Weights are often inscribed on articles in the form 15: 3, meaning 15 oz. 3 pennyweight. (Before 1700, ounces were usually divided into quarters: thus 15: 3 would mean $15\frac{3}{4}$ ounces.) I normally use decimals of an ounce, but give ounces and pennyweights (e.g. 17: 21) where comparing a present weight with an earlier weight which is so expressed.

A pound of money is divided into 20 shillings (*s.*) each of 12 pennies (*d.*); thus £3. 12*s.* 6*d.* = £3.625.

Pints and gallons have their English values: thus 1 English pint = 1.201 American pint = 0.568 litre; 1 English gallon = 8 pints = 1.201 American gallon = 4.55 litres.

Translations are mine unless otherwise stated.

Graffiti

I have transcribed the many graffiti which reveal something of the history of the piece or of the College. I omit most of the coded graffiti of letters and numbers which appear on pieces that have been sold or pawned.

Acknowledgements

I am not a specialist in plate. I first handled the Corpus treasures 43 years ago. My interest was stimulated by Geoffrey Bushnell, Keeper of Plate when I was elected a Fellow in 1964. In his later years I used to assist his failing steps at audits and exhibitions, and when he died in 1978 I became his successor. I here put on record the knowledge that he imparted to me: if this book has any pretensions to scholarship they are largely due to him.

I have received great help from Catherine Hall, Ancient Archivist of the College, and have drawn on her unrivalled knowledge of the medieval to Stuart records both of this College and of the closely linked college of Gonville & Caius. Robin Myers, Modern Archivist, has given similar help with post-1800 records. Among Fellows who have helped me I particularly mention Professor Geoffrey Woodhead and Dr Tom Faber.

I am greatly indebted to Ron Storey, for many years College Butler, and his assistants George Boulos, Mark Cox, and Pasquale Gargiulo. They have been unfailingly cheerful and prompt in getting out pieces from distant stores, even at the most awkward times of year.

Ray Symonds, of the University Museum of Zoology, has given practical help to my researches into aurochsen and griffins' eggs.

Biographical notes on donors are derived mainly from Venn & Venn, Masters, Lamb, Bury, Woodhead, the *Dictionary of National Biography*, the *Clergy List*,

1 JS Forbes has recently shown that the actual changeover date could vary by several weeks, especially before 1700 (*SSJ* **12** (2000) 82–4). This complication makes no difference in this book, and I shall ignore it.

or *Crockford's Clerical Directory*. They claim no originality or completeness. Likewise interpretations of hallmarks are from Grimwade, Jackson, and other standard works.

Among those who have helped out my ignorance of art history are Claude Blair, Marion Campbell, Dr Rolf Fritz, Paula Hardwick, and S.B.P. Perceval. I am indebted to Peter Waldron and Richard Came of Sotheby's, especially for interpreting difficult makers' marks. I was much encouraged by the varied interests of Tony Byrne, sometime College Director of Development.

Sir Tony Wrigley and Professor Haroon Ahmed, sucessive Masters of the College, have given their constant encouragement and support.

Photographs

John Cleaver, of Fitzwilliam College, took nearly all the photographs. I am most fortunate in securing his skills in this notoriously difficult field of photography.

Bayeux Tapestry

The two extracts from the Bayeux Tapestry are acknowledged thus:
<< The Bayeux Tapestry – 11th Century – By special permission of the City of Bayeux >>

Drawing of Parker Cup (p. 76)

Reproduced by kind permission of the Master & Fellows of Gonville & Caius College, Cambridge.

OLIVER RACKHAM
Corpus Christi College, Cambridge
December 2001

Contractions and acronyms

A.B. or B.A.: Bachelor of Arts.
A.M. or M.A.: Master of Arts.
BM: British Museum
B.M.V. or B.V.M.: Blessed Virgin Mary.
B. Mus.: Bachelor of Music.
C.C.C.: Corpus Christi College.
C.C.C.C.: Corpus Christi College, Cambridge.
Corp. Xti: Corpus Christi.
D.D.: Doctor of Divinity
D.D.: gave (*dono dedit*).
M.D.: Doctor of Medicine.
S.T.P.: Doctor of Divinity (*Sacræ Theologiæ Professor*).
U.C.: University of Cambridge.
V&A: Victoria & Albert Museum.

Archives and libraries

LCA: Corpus Association Letter
PCAS: Proceedings of Cambridge Antiquarian Society
CC(A): Corpus Christi College, Cambridge, Archives
CC(L): Corpus Christi College, Cambridge, Library
G&C: Gonville & Caius College

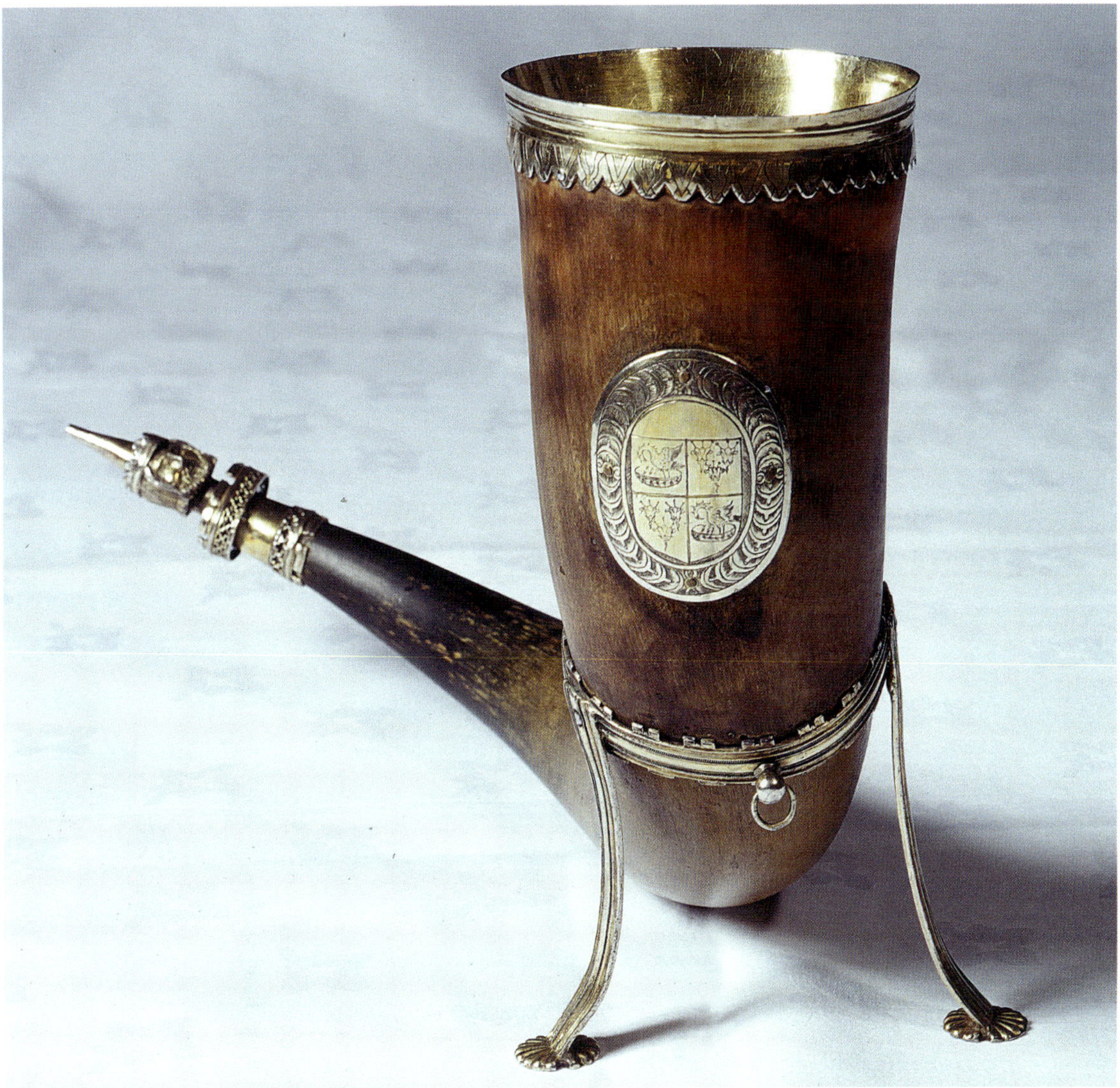

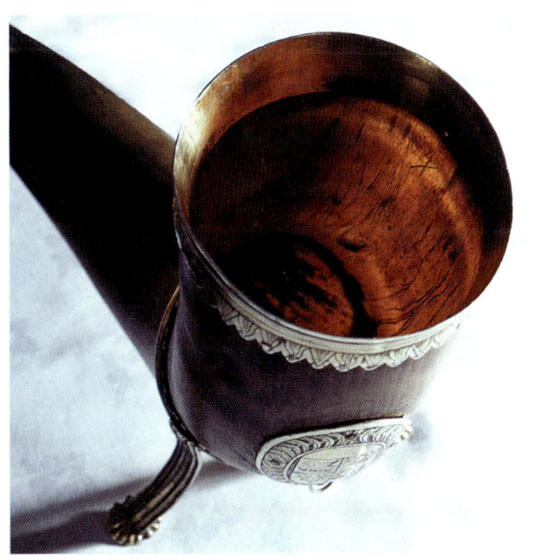

PLATE 1. The Great Horn (Chapter 4)

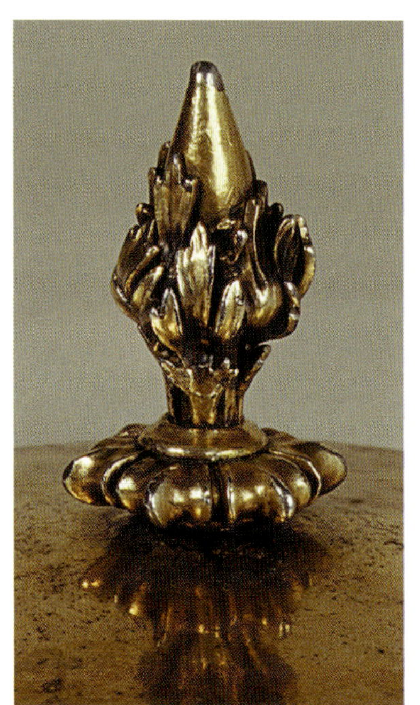

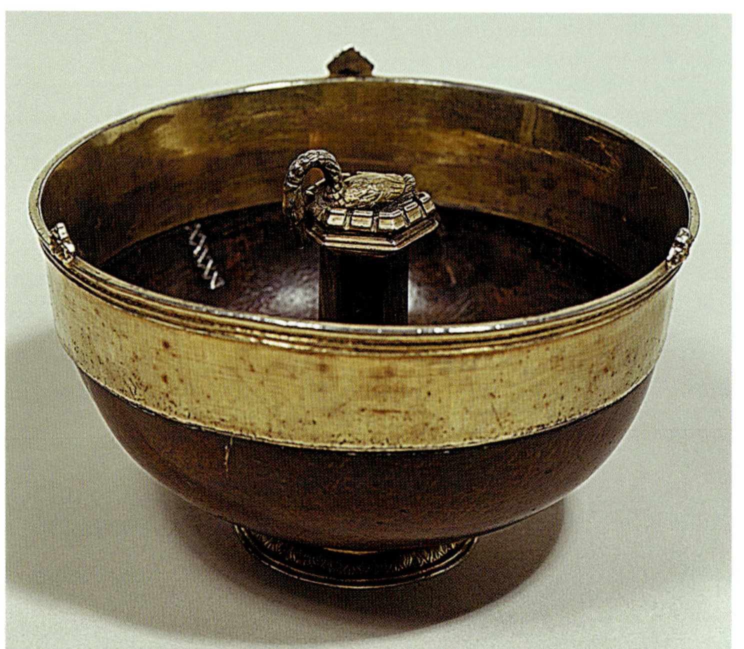

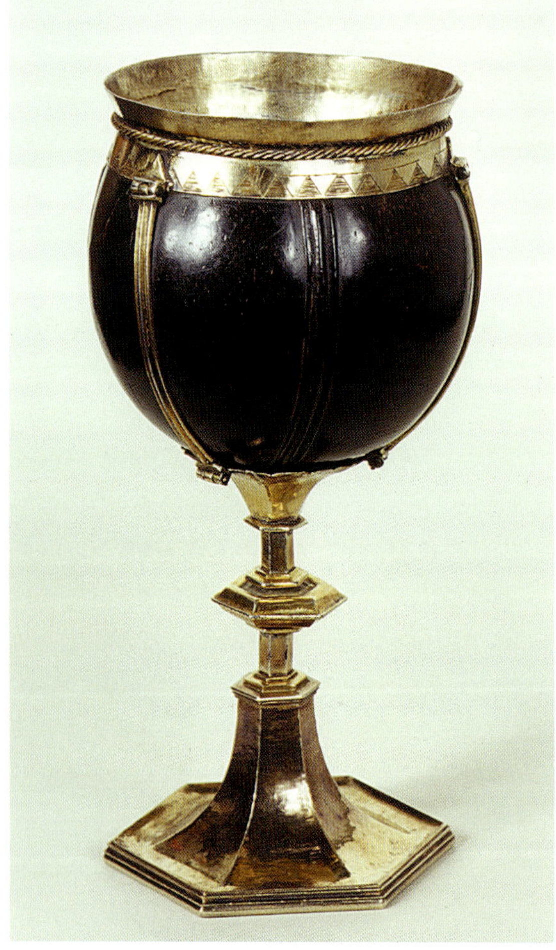

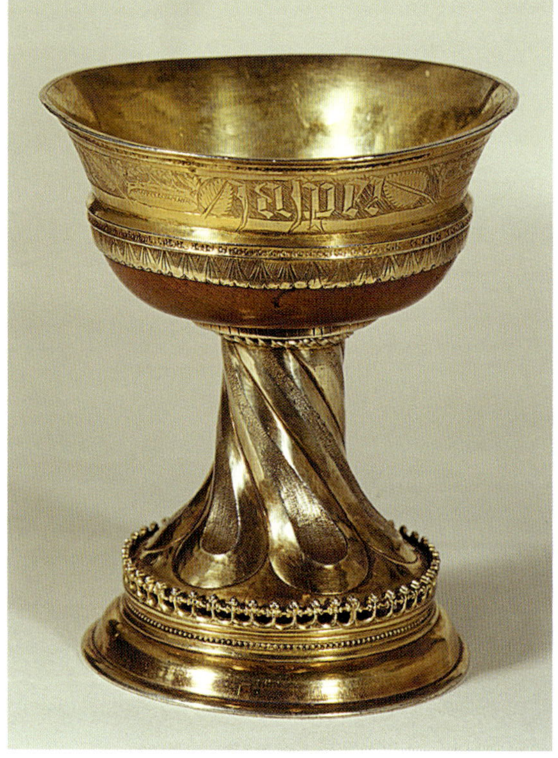

PLATE 2. The Knob (§6.5); Swan Mazer (§6.1); Coconut Cup (Chapter 5); Cup of the Three Kings (§6.2)

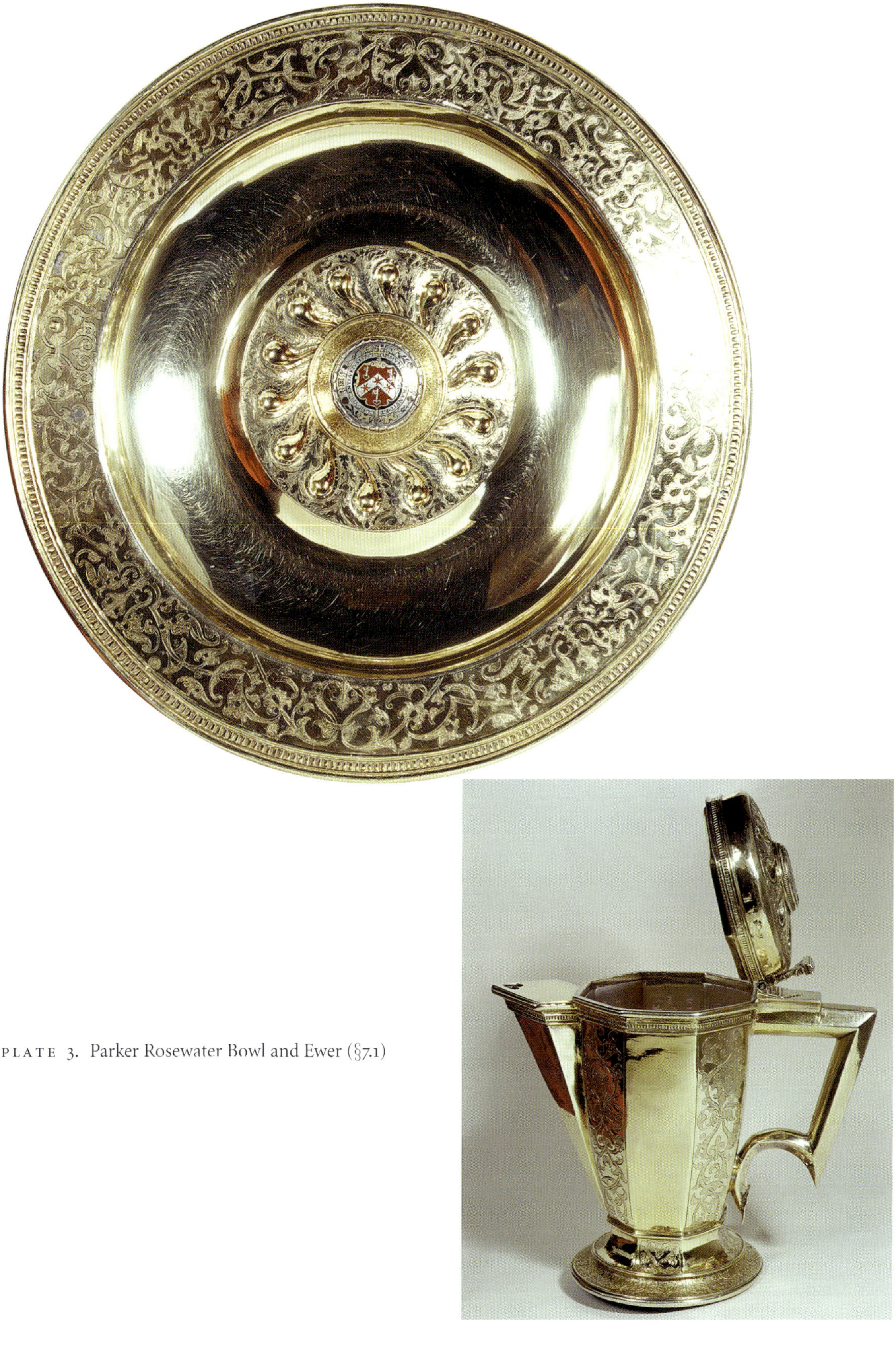

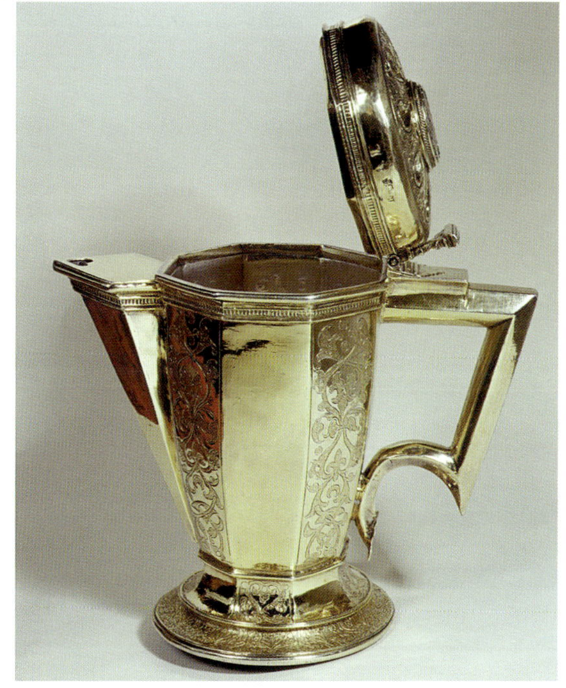

PLATE 3. Parker Rosewater Bowl and Ewer (§7.1)

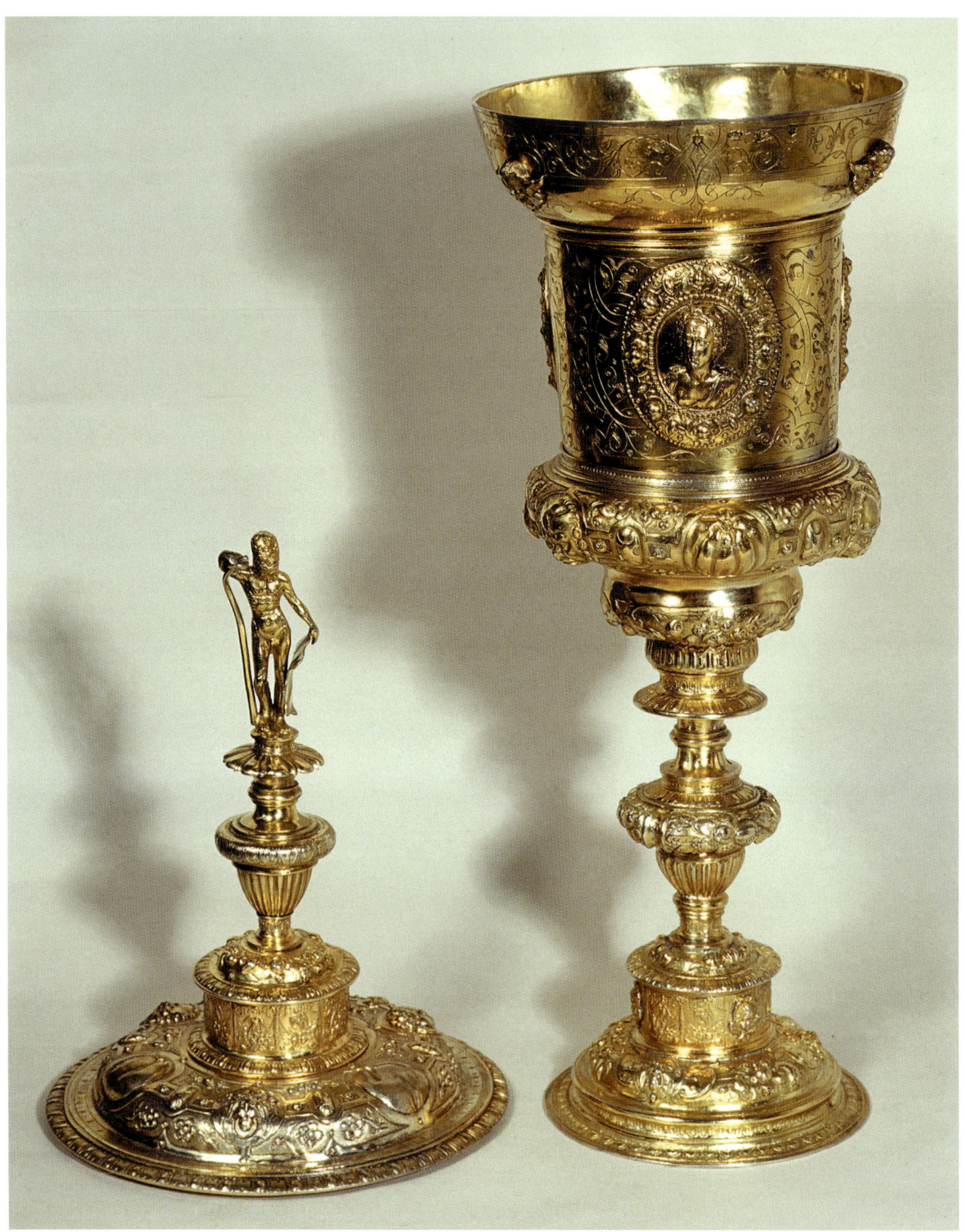

PLATE 4. Great Parker Cup (§7.2)

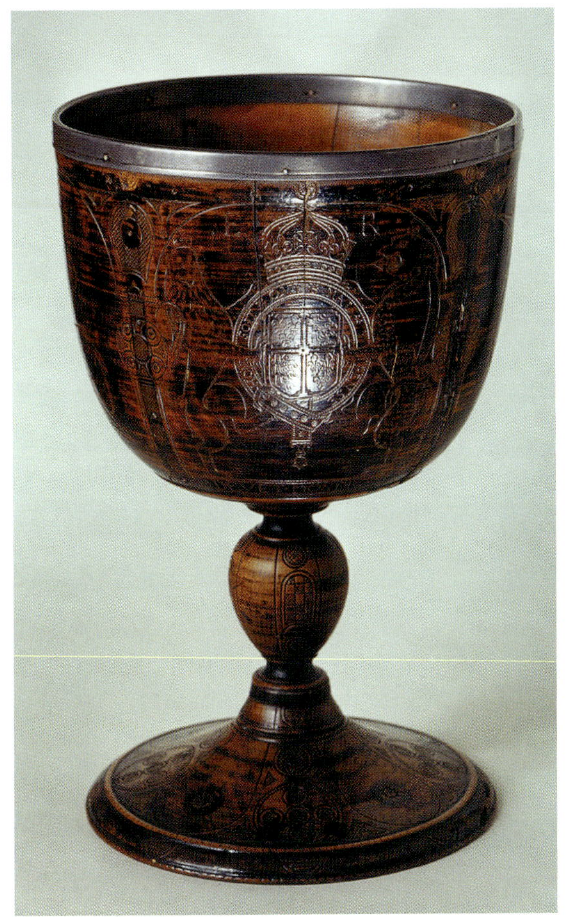

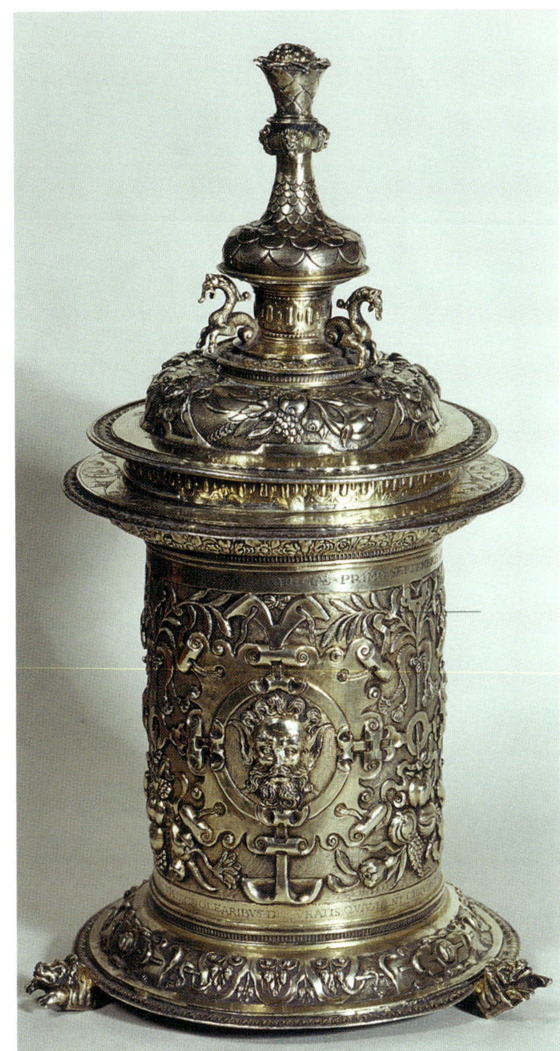

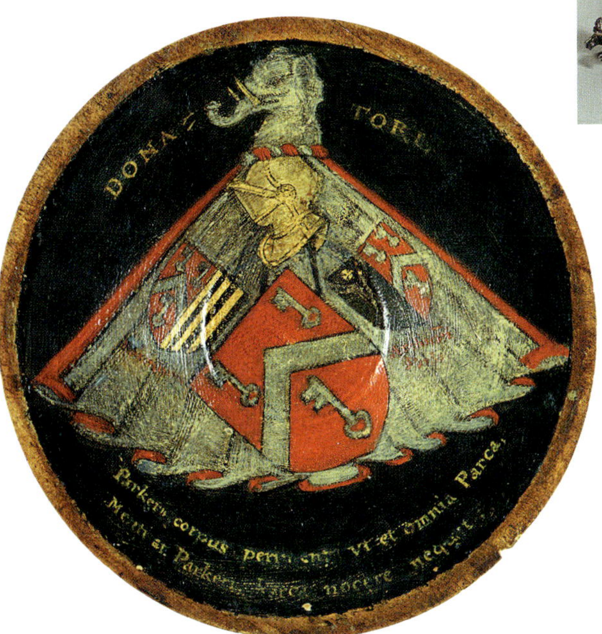

PLATE 5. Neame Cup (§7.8); Parker Salt (§7.3); Parker coat-of-arms under the Neame Cup

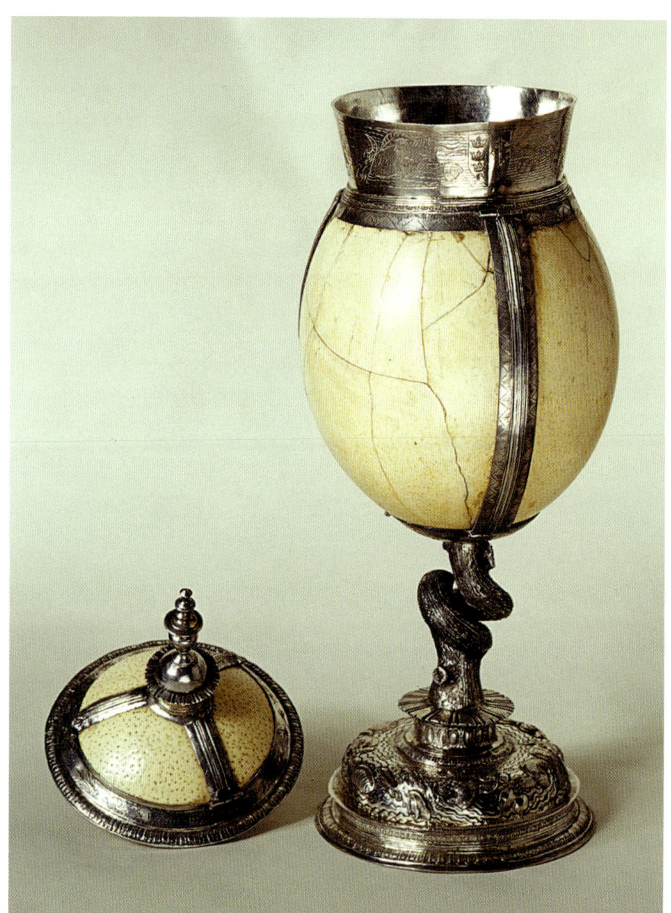

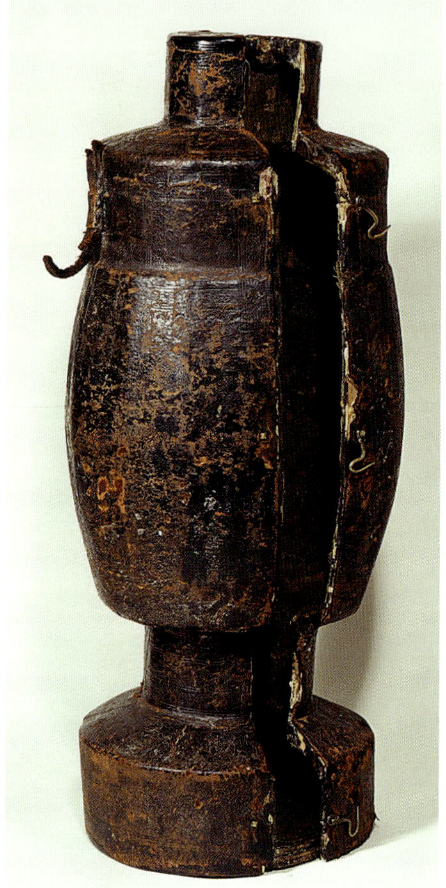

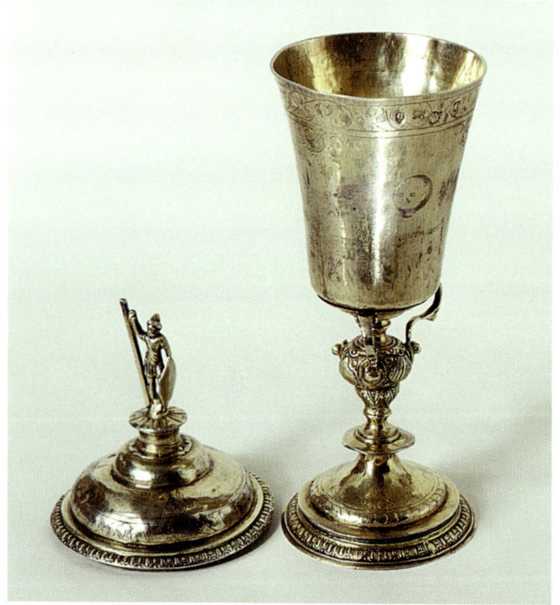

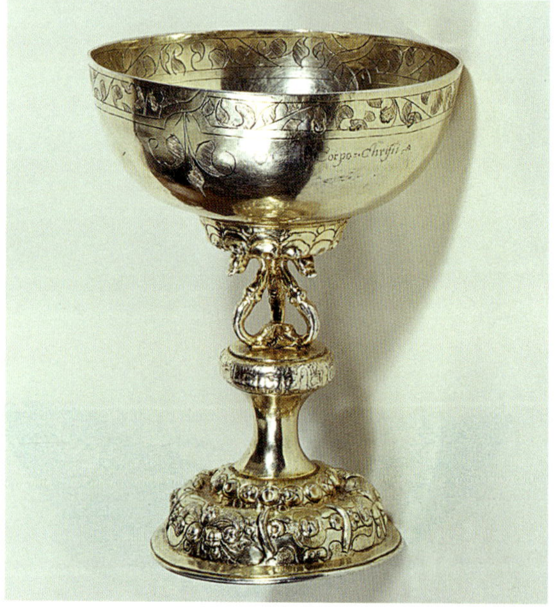

PLATE 6. Ostrich-Egg, lid, and its Case (§7.7); Champernowne Cup and lid (§8.1); Harrington Tazza (§8.2)

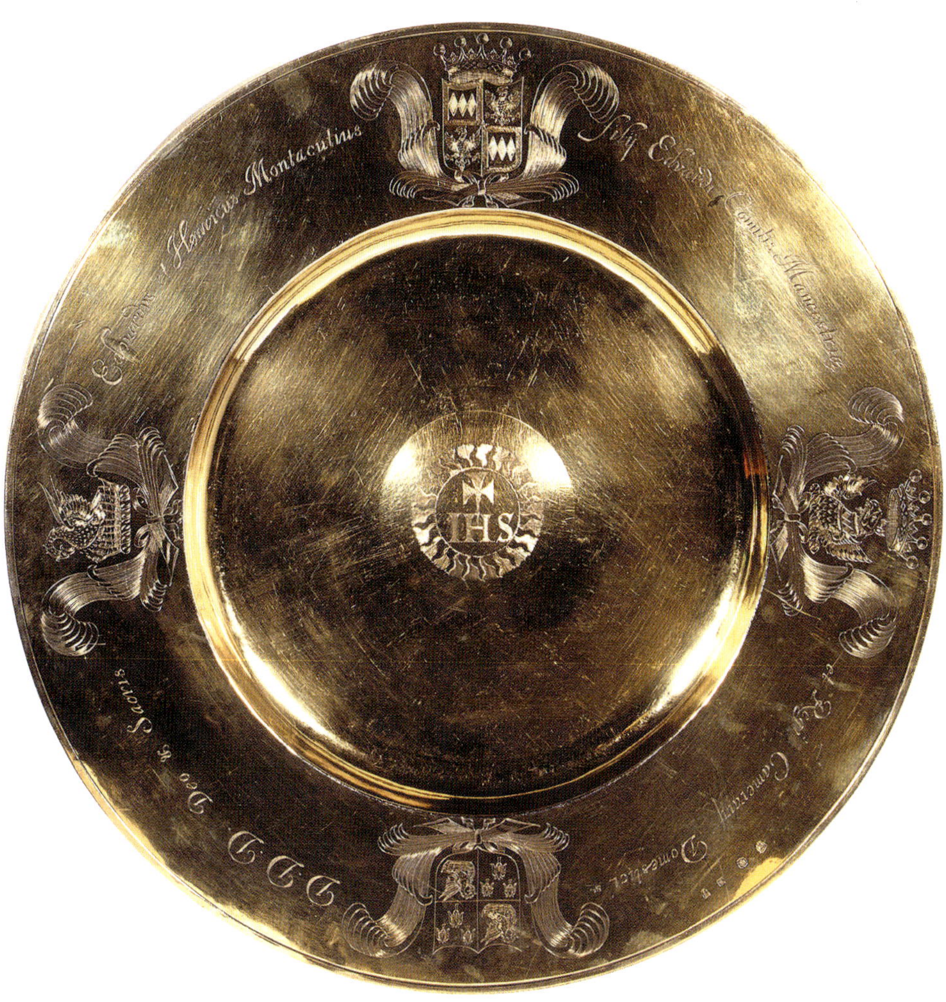

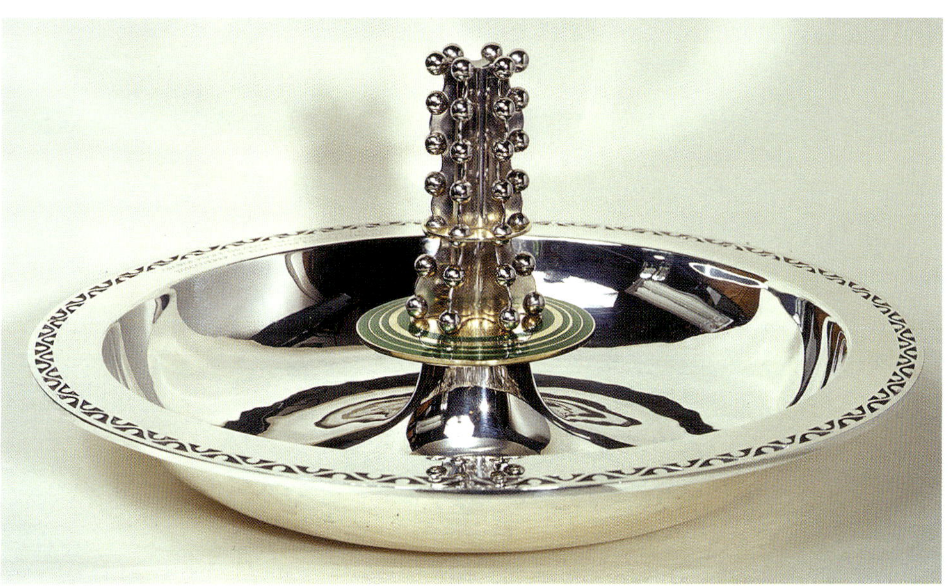

PLATE 7. Montacute Alms-dish (§9.1); Thomson Bowl (§22.6)

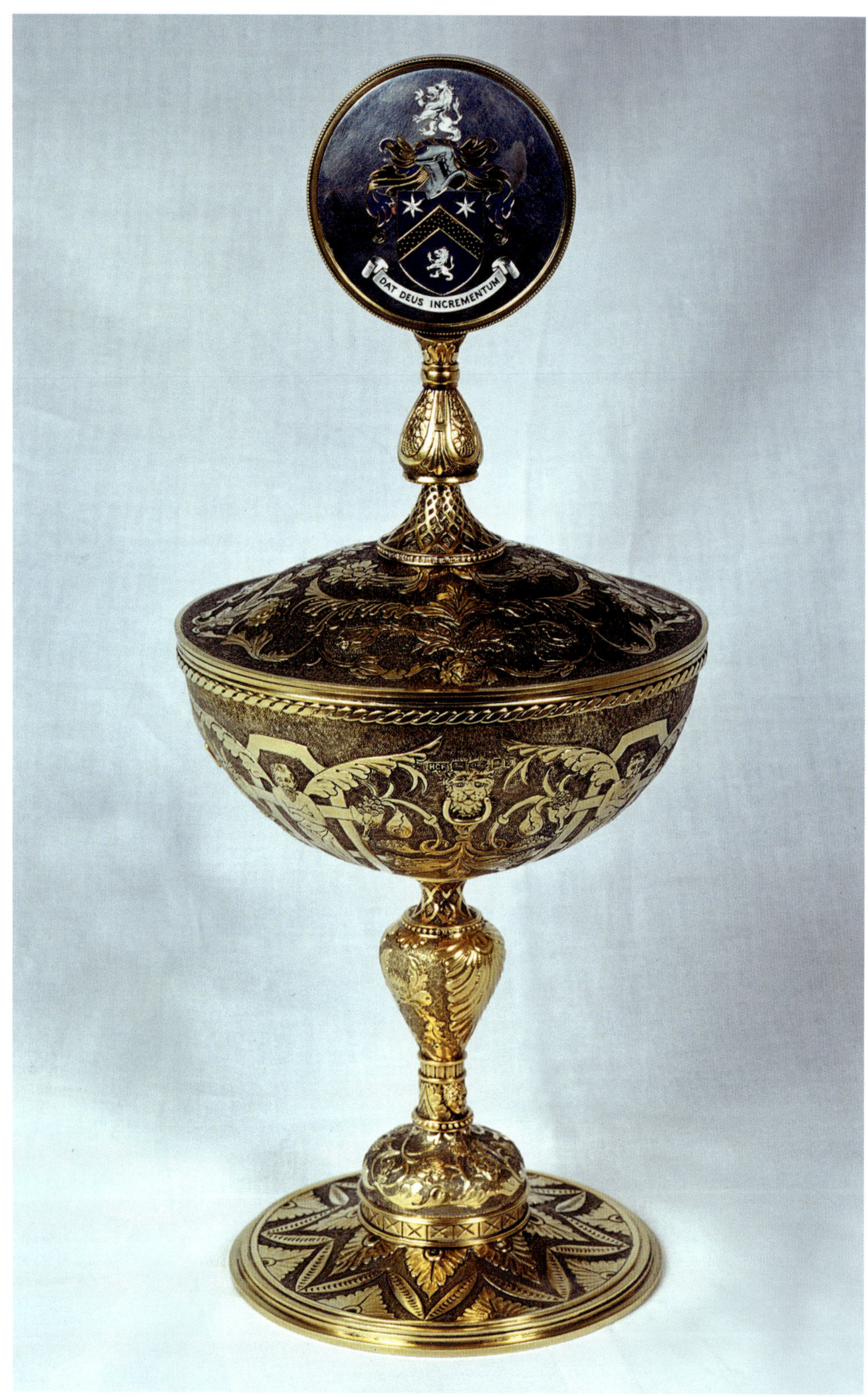

PLATE 8. Parker-Beldam Cup (§7.9)

1

Outline of the College's History

> The foundation of this College is very different from that of any other in either of our Universities; for whereas each of them were owing to the benevolence of one or two persons as original founders, this was the joint work of two several societies: ... the GILD of the BODY OF CHRIST and the GILD of the BLESSED VIRGIN MARY ...
>
> *Robert Masters, 1753*

The College of Corpus Christi and the Blessed Virgin Mary, otherwise called Bene't College, was founded in 1352. It is the sixth oldest of the thirty-one colleges in the University of Cambridge. It became the successor to the Gild of the Blessed Virgin Mary, the chief religious gild of 13th-century Cambridge. It lies next to the Church of St Benedict or Bene't, the oldest (Anglo-Saxon) standing building in the town.

Cambridge town was far older than the University, with origins in the Iron Age, developing civic functions from the late Anglo-Saxon period onwards; its best-known charter was in 1201. The Gild of St Mary was a large association of townspeople, with spiritual, charitable, convivial, and funerary functions; it was not commercial nor (at this stage) academic. It was an important civic body, whose patrons included two Lord Chancellors, but it included relatively poor people. Its functions were spread through the year, but once a year after Christmas the Alderman, Brethren, and Sisters solemnly met to commemorate departed members, and afterwards held a feast requiring ceremonial plate.[1]

The University of Cambridge had begun in the early 13th century and was probably somewhat older than the Gild. At first it functioned without colleges. In 1280 the Bishop of Ely founded the college now called Peterhouse; this was followed by Michaelhouse (now part of Trinity College) in 1324, University Hall (now Clare College) in 1326, King's Hall (now part of Trinity College) in 1337, Valence Marie Hall (now Pembroke College) in 1347, Gonville Hall (now Gonville & Caius College) in 1348, and Trinity Hall in 1350.

The period 1320–1350 was thus a time of extraordinary activity in Cambridge, parallel to the amazing building activities at Ely. It was the time when the cult of *Corpus Christi*, the Body of Christ, founded by Juliana de Cornillon, the 13th-century Belgian nun, spread through western Christendom: masses were sung, followed by processions and feasting, on the Thursday after Trinity Sunday (varying between 21 May and 24 June). It was not a pleasant time: the Little Ice Age brought cold and insecurity and the verge of famine, culminating in 1349 in the unimaginable grief and fear of the Black Death. People reacted to these disasters by increased devotion to the Body of Christ.[2] An immediate consequence seems to have been the founding of a Gild of Corpus Christi, planned during the Black Death, which held its first meeting in 1350.

There were fifty-odd gilds of Corpus Christi, including those of Shelford, Wisbech, and King's Lynn, but Cambridge's was an oddity among them. It was a small association of businessmen, with (it seems) only two functions: to hold a grand Corpus Christi procession, and to found another college. It lasted only 21 years. The brethren wasted no time: they took over the Gild of St Mary, found a noble patron in Henry Duke of Lancaster, got a licence from the king, secured equipment for brewing beer, appointed the Master and two Fellows, and began building. A large enough site to begin on had already been put together by Gonville Hall, who were persuaded to exchange it with another site belonging to members of the Gild. Its work done, the united Gild faded away; it is last heard of in 1371. The College inherited its assets and its duty of commemorating

1 Hall 1993.

2 M Rubin 1992 *Corpus Christi* Cambridge University Press.

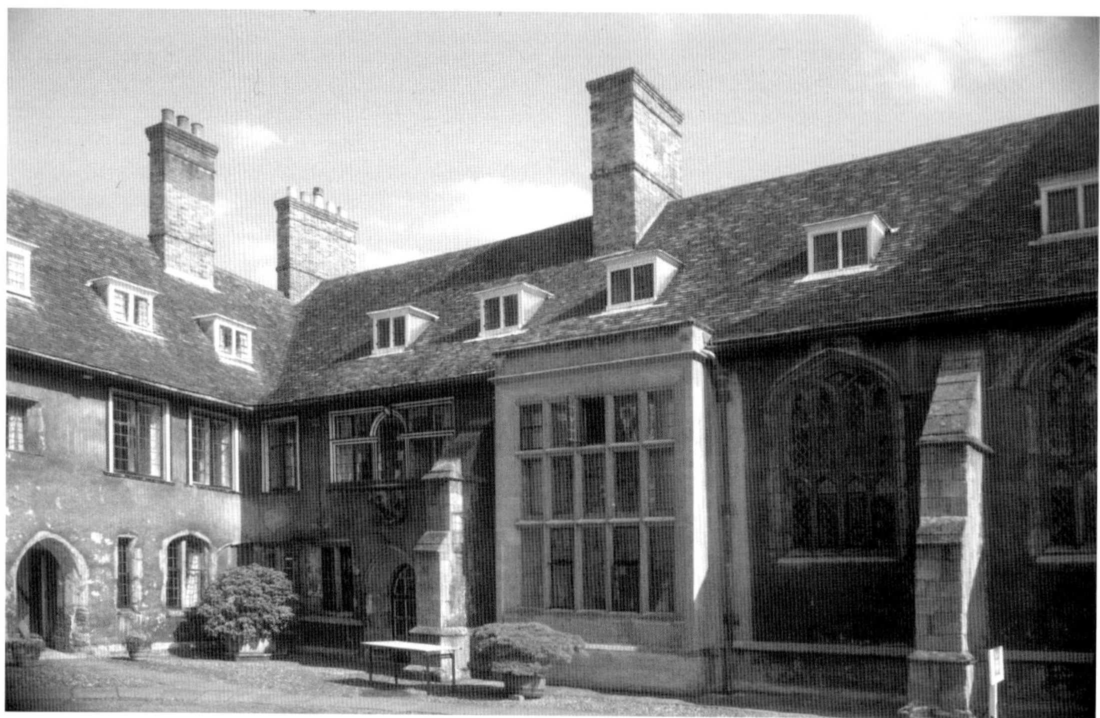

The earliest part of the College buildings. This picture shows the 14th-century structure, together with alterations in every century since.

departed members, which is still done at the Commemoration of Benefactors in December.[3]

The medieval College

The conventional date for founding the College is 7 November 1352, the date of the king's licence. The buildings are said to have been completed by 1378.[4]

Corpus, though it attracted many benefactions, was less well endowed than most colleges (and far less well endowed than almost any abbey). The original intention was probably to house and feed a Master and twelve Fellows, although medieval lists seldom have more than eight Fellows. The buildings were plain, serviceable, and robust, and are in use to this day. However, even the humblest college had to keep up appearances and show that it was not a mere Hall; the walls were of stone hauled from a distance, rather than timber-framed like ordinary Cambridge houses. It was adapted from the plan of a medieval house, with a hall, kitchen, buttery, and pantry, and living space which was expanded to form the earliest enclosed court in Cambridge. A chapel was unnecessary, since the College became linked to the adjacent church of St Benedict and shared in its services.

Corpus was designed to house students as well as Fellows. Although there were then no garrets in the roof, the Old Court is so spacious that at times each Fellow could have had a whole staircase. Many of the scholars were what would now be called graduate students. Undergraduates may not have existed in large numbers before the 16th century.[5] Other undergraduates might have been housed in various halls and inns which belonged to the College.

Fellows of the College were required to take Holy Orders, as most scholars did at that time. Corpus did not have a tendency towards law, like Trinity Hall, or medicine, like Gonville & Caius College.

3 CR Cheney 1984 'The gilds of the Blessed Virgin Mary and Corpus Christi' *LCA* **63** 24–35.

4 These dates need to be verified by tree-ring dating of the timbers.

5 For undergraduates in medieval Cambridge colleges see Cobban.

For a poor college Corpus was quick to accumulate treasure. The earliest inventory records plate, chalices, and a remarkable number of vestments as well as precious bedclothes and other secular textiles. The College had inherited the plate and precious goods of the two Gilds, as well as sharing the church vessels of St Bene't's. Two or three items, the Horn, the Coconut, and perhaps the Knob, survive from this remote age.

The inventory might have been even longer had not the townspeople in the Peasants' Revolt in 1381 – presumably townspeople whose parents had not been members of the Gilds – sacked the College and stolen £80 worth of plate, or so the Fellows said. The same nearly happened again in 1460, during a crisis of the Wars of the Roses. The College spent 12*d*. on 'the safeguard of the College plate and treasury, with title-deeds', and laid in saltpetre and sulphur, artillery, and twelve arrows.[6] These warlike precautions proved a sufficient deterrent, so that the 'tempestuous riot' did no harm. (The mob again broke in in 1689, but did not get as far as the plate.[7])

The 15th century is a story of the College slowly increasing in numbers and prosperity, of items such as the Cup of the Three Kings and Cup of the Three Bears being added to the plate, and of modest additions to the buildings. In *c*.1487[8] the first chapel was built as an annexe to St Bene't's church, having its own altar but communicating with the church by a squint.

The sixteenth century

The College was spared the wrath of Henry VIII, and avoided the worst of the religious disputes such as those which tore apart Corpus Christi, Oxford. The Corpus Christi procession, the great event of the year, was tamely given up in 1535 and weakly revived in 1554. Old members, however, included a Roman Catholic martyr, St Richard Reynolds, a Protestant martyr, George Wishart, and a heretic burnt by a Protestant bishop, Francis Kett.

All College history is overshadowed by the towering figure of Matthew Parker, Master 1544–53 and Queen Elizabeth's Archbishop of Canterbury 1559–75. He established the Church of England and gave Anglicanism the peculiar form in which it was to spread throughout the English-influenced world. Parker, besides his gifts of plate, bequeathed to the College an unrivalled manuscript library, his vast library of printed books, and his unique personal archive.

Numbers in the College were growing, helped by fellowships and scholarships endowed by Parker and other benefactors. This found expression in additions to the buildings; the only one to survive is the upper storey of garrets inserted under the medieval roof-timbers of Old Court. Distinguished members of the College included John Fletcher and Christopher Marlowe, dramatists, and Richard Fletcher, victim of smoking (p. 91).

The plate was steadily augmented by gifts, but some of these perished in two disasters. In or around the 1530s many of the medieval treasures disappeared rather mysteriously, partly because they were associated with popish-sounding ceremonies such as the Corpus Christi procession (p. 19). It was a much-depleted hoard to which Parker added his magnificent gifts, with stringent precautions lest the College again fritter them away.

The next disaster was inadvertent. In 1578 an old member, Sir Nicholas Bacon, Lord Keeper of the Great Seal, noted that the College needed a new chapel, and gave £200 towards the cost. Robert Norgate, Master and fund-raiser, persuaded the Queen, Edmund Grindal (Archbishop of Canterbury) and Francis Drake (maybe the Sir Francis 'of famous memory') to give money, loads of timber, and stone looted from the ruins of Thorney and Barnwell Abbeys. Even so, the project far outran its estimates and nearly bankrupted the College. The plate was plundered: the College pawned £47 worth of it to the University, and apparently never saw it again.[9] Only Parker's plate and those medieval pieces not worth melting (p. 25) were spared. Even this was not enough, and the chapel was not entirely finished until 1662. (Institutions never learn: similar mistakes are still made every year.)

From the late 16th to the early 19th century Cambridge was a class-ridden society. There were five classes of student: noblemen fellow-commoners, gentlemen fellow-commoners, scholars, pensioners, and sizars. Noblemen and Gentlemen – the distinction is often not made at Corpus – had special privileges in return for, among other things, giving plate to the College (Chapter 8). Scholars were undergraduates of academic distinction,

6 CC(A): *Liber Albus* part 2 ff 55, 57v, 58.

7 Lamb 196f.

8 *Accounts 1479–1534* f.44v. I am indebted to Catherine Hall for finding this.

9 CC (A): *Audits 1590–1678*, account for 1590, p.[19].

the beneficiaries of scholarships founded by particular benefactors. Pensioners comprised the majority of students. Sizars (in theory) were poor students working their way through college, being given jobs like porter or butler, although in practice a professional did most of the work. Scholars or pensioners did not often give plate, although even sizars occasionally did so (p. 155).

Another obvious distinction between this time and the present is the youth of the College personnel. Parker was typical in being an undergraduate at the age of 16, a Fellow at 23, and Master at 40. (18, 30, and 60 would now be more usual.) Only the Master was allowed to marry; most Fellows were young men awaiting a vacant living as a parish priest which would allow them to support a family.

The seventeenth century

The College's fortunes were revived in the Mastership of John Jegon, 1590–1602. Among other ways of raising money, he invited boys from well-to-do families to spend a year or two in the College as Gentlemen Fellow-Commoners; these were to be large contributors to the College plate for the next 250 years. Jegon was later Bishop of Norwich and the last English bishop to try to burn a heretic.

The 17th century brought hard times for Cambridge. The University was increasingly politicized. Plague took its toll every twenty years or so. The College lurched acrimoniously between Puritanism and the fringes of Popery. Two members, heroes of the plague, went on to be victims of politics: Henry Butts, the Master, driven to suicide in 1632, and St Henry Morse, an old member, executed for being a Roman Catholic priest shortly before Charles I's execution.[10] Butts's successor, Richard Love, took the College through the worst of times, the Civil War and the Commonwealth.

The Civil War (1642–7) has entered Corpus legend because of the story that Dr Love dispersed the ancient plate among the Fellows and thereby, uniquely among colleges, saved it from requisition by the King or confiscation by Parliament. The real events are related in Chapter 8. Suffice it to say that the Civil War did not bear hard on Cambridge. Corpus got off relatively lightly, although a number of Fellows were sacked by both sides. Love, though appointed by the King, was careful to be neutral; the College functioned normally during the conflict, and although there was a further meltdown of much of the plate this was done by the College itself, which needed money for repairs.

The Restoration and the eighteenth century

Dr Love saw the College through to the return of Charles II without great mishap. His successor, after a short interval, was the generous John Spencer, Hebrew scholar, who much increased the College's reputation and restored the buildings.

The College advanced in social circles to the political *demi-monde* of Prime Ministers' nephews and less-than-brilliant Parliamentary figures. Advancing in learning, it played a part in the beginnings of science and archaeology at Cambridge. Members included Thomas Tenison, hero of the last plague in 1665–6, and later King William's Archbishop of Canterbury; William Briggs, father of ophthalmology; William Sterne, Archbishop of York and benefactor; Richard Rigby, duellist, orgiast, and father of governmental corruption (p. 154); Thomas Herring, red Archbishop of Canterbury; William Stukeley, father of English archaeology, and several of his followers; Stephen Hales, animal experimenter and father of plant physiology; the second and third Professors of Chemistry; James De Lancey, father of the New York Turf; John Owen, father of the British & Foreign Bible Society; General Braddock, loser of his scalp on the way to Pittsburgh;[11] and Michael Tyson, father of the study of College plate (p. 41).

The nineteenth century

This century brought the two most momentous changes in the whole history of the College. The first was the building of the New Court. The idea of a second court had been discussed for centuries, but nothing came of it. All through the 18th century an increasing number of personnel had been spilling over from the College into town lodgings. Funds had been accumulating since 1758, and in 1822 John Lamb, the young Master, seized the opportunity, summoned William Wilkins the architect

10 M McCrum 1994 'Doctor Henry Butts' *LCA* **73** 42–53.
O Rackham 1992 'St Henry Morse, S.J.' *LCA* **71** 21–32.

11 JPC Roach 1993 'John Owen' *LCA* **72** 14–224.
Fenimore Cooper 1826 *The Last of the Mohicans* Philadelphia.

and built the whole New Court, then one of the biggest one-period courts in Cambridge, within five years.

Yet more momentous was the change of statute in 1882 allowing Fellows of Colleges to marry, which changed at a stroke the demography and housing structure of Cambridge. No longer was the typical don a young man doing, in effect, a few years of post-doctoral study; being a Fellow could now be a lifelong career. This introduced a new category of plate, the *wedding fine*, usually a piece of silver given by a newly married Fellow to the College in exchange for a wedding present subscribed by his colleagues.

Other general changes affected the College: the repeal of the Test Acts, which allowed non-Anglicans to join the University in theory as well as in practice; the spread of lay Fellows and University Lecturers (though it is still less than a hundred years since the first lay Master of Corpus); the growth of organized sport (beginning with the Boat Club) and sporting trophies as a *genre* of plate; the broadening of the syllabus and the introduction of sciences as undergraduate subjects; the gradual concentration of lectures into the hands of the University; the fading away of Gentleman Commoners; and the growth of drinking parties and of college societies.

The new building filled up and overflowed in turn. A monument to that period is the enlargement of Wilkins's Chapel in 1870. There was then a sharp decline, so that by the end of the century the College was half empty and looked neglected. It contained, however, such distinguished scholars as Edward Byles Cowell, Professor of Sanskrit (p. 225) and Samuel Savage Lewis, donor of the Lewis Collection of portable antiquities.

The twentieth century

From 1906 onwards the College's fortunes were revived in the Mastership of Colonel Caldwell (p. 234). With interruptions during the two World Wars, numbers rapidly increased: Corpus is among the few British institutions from which more men were killed in the Second than the First World War. This led to new buildings in almost every possible corner of the College, and even on top of the New Court. Other colleges had been increasing too, so that despite these increases Corpus long prided itself on being the smallest College in Cambridge.

The 1950s began with the restoration of the Old Court, regrettable by more recent standards, which destroyed many ancient interiors while not dispelling the dingy and institutional air which this wonderful building still wears. In 1960 there was the momentous decision to increase the College's numbers, not in undergraduates but in post-graduate students, and to house them in and around Leckhampton House a mile from the College.

Although numbers of Corpus undergraduates have risen little since 1950, Cambridge has become one of the richest cities in England and thus one of the least suitable for a university. Undergraduates can no longer hire rooms in town, and Colleges have had to build rooms for all their students. In Corpus this has been done on sites of ancient College possession one street away; Bene't Court and the adjacent Beldam Building on the north side, and Botolph Court, converted from old buildings in Botolph Lane on the south side.

The College was opened to female members in 1980. The electronic revolution in computers and data-handling has led to a great increase in numbers and cost of books and in the volume of office paper, so that more and more of the New Court has been taken over by offices and library.

Benefactors have been attracted on a scale not seen since Parker. The period 1960–2000 has been remarkably prolific in gifts of plate.

Although universities in general complain of hard times, Cambridge continues to flourish as never before. Soon the irresistible force of University expansion will meet the immovable obstacle of Cambridge running out of space. I wait to see what will happen then.

2

Introduction to Plate

And Solomon *made* all the vessels that *pertained* unto the house of the LORD: the altar of gold, and the table of gold, whereupon the shewbread *was*, and the candlesticks of pure gold, five on the right *side*, and five on the left, before the oracle, with the flowers, and the lamps, and the tongs *of* gold, and the bowls, and the snuffers, and the basons, and the spoons, and the censers *of* pure gold . . .

1 Kings **8** 48ff

And Nebuchadnezzar king of Babylon . . . carried out thence all the treasures of the house of the LORD, and the treasures of the king's house, and cut in pieces all the vessels of gold which Solomon king of Israel had made in the temple of the LORD . . .

2 *Kings* **25** 11ff

Belshazzar the king . . . whiles he tasted the wine, commanded to bring the golden and silver vessels which his father Nebuchadnezzar had taken out of the temple which *was* in Jerusalem; that the king, and his princes, his wives, and his concubines, might drink therein. . . . They drank wine, and praised the gods of gold and of silver, of brass, of iron, of wood, and of stone.

Daniel **5** 1ff

. . . Cyrus the king brought forth the vessels of the house of the LORD, which Nebuchadnezzar had brought forth out of Jerusalem, and put them in the house of his gods . . . by the hand of Mithredath the treasurer, and numbered them unto Sheshbazzar, the prince of Judah . . . thirty chargers of gold, a thousand chargers of silver, nine and twenty knives, thirty basons of gold, silver basons of a second *sort* four hundred and ten, *and* other vessels a thousand. All the vessels of gold and of silver *were* five thousand and four hundred.

Ezra **1** 7ff

'Plate' means artefacts made of silver, silver-gilt, or rarely gold. Such are the symbols of nations, institutions, and families; from the Crown Jewels, St Stephen's Crown of Hungary, the civic plate of ancient corporations, regimental and naval plate, the wine-coolers of well-to-do families and the teaspoons of the not so well-to-do, down to the little silver wedding-presents of the poor. These special things are brought out from hiding to be displayed on special occasions and to honour distinguished guests. In this context belong the plate of colleges and universities, old and new.

The ancient Hebrews bound up their fortunes with the liturgical plate of the Temple. Two-and-a-half thousand years later, we still sense the ancient writers' veneration for the vessels and implements presented in the dim past by the hero-kings David and Solomon; their sorrow as the kingdom weakened and treasures were looted or used to pay ransom, culminating in the sack of Jerusalem by Nebuchadnezzar; their disgust when the king's cronies tippled out of the sacred vessels at a vulgar orgy; and their joy when a friendly emperor, against all expectation, made inventory of what was left – still a goodly hoard – and sent them back to Jerusalem to their rightful place in the rebuilt Temple.

East Anglia has probably the greatest wealth of early plate in Europe, mostly on view in the British Museum: the amazing Iron Age hoards at Snettisham; the Roman treasures of Mildenhall, Hoxne, and Water Newton; and the royal East Anglian silver and silver-gilt excavated from the barrows at Sutton Hoo.

King Harold's plate is depicted on the Bayeux Tapestry (p. 43). Captured and brought to Normandy, such things astonished the relatively barbarian Normans:

> Likewise the silver or gold vessels were admired, of whose number or beauty it could be incredible to tell truly. An immense throng drank only from these cups, or from aurochs horns decorated with the same metal around both ends.
>
> *Conquest feast of William the Conqueror at Fécamp, 1067*
> (*Guillaume de Poitiers* **44**)

The Emperors of Russia hoarded fine plate. Queen Mary I (the terrible) began cultivating *détente* with Ivan the Terrible in 1557, and many embassies followed, all bearing costly gifts. Little survives from before 1609, when the treasury was sacked by the Poles, but from then on almost everything has been kept, either at St Petersburg or the Kremlin, including many pieces like the College's.[1]

Plate could be a matter of mere conspicuous consumption. Did not King João V of Portugal commission Paul Crespin, London goldsmith,[2] *c.*1727, to make for his mistress, a nun, a king-sized silver-gilt bathtub on three dolphin feet, adorned with Neptune, Diana and Actæon, Perseus and Andromeda, and with three mermaids inside?[3] College plate was not like this. The objects are often of no great intrinsic value: their significance depends on their workmanship, antiquity, and associations. Mostly they were not bought by the college, but given through gratitude or obligation by members and friends. They indicated affection and status, not wealth or power.

As well as the 'great plate' for special occasions, and the communion plate of the chapel, colleges had 'buttery plate' for everyday use. These articles were more utilitarian, long-lasting and a good investment, like this College's twelve silver pint mugs acquired in 1723, of which five are still in constant use.

Making Plate

Silver, as every schoolboy used to know, is malleable and ductile: it can be worked cold by hammering or drawing into wire. It is good-natured, up to a point; but hammering or stretching work-hardens the metal and makes it brittle. From time to time it has to be *annealed*, cautiously heated and cooled, to restore the crystal structure.

The chief processes are these:

1. ***Raising:*** a flat plate (made by hammering or rolling) is drawn into a hollow vessel by hammering it on a shaped wooden anvil or an iron stake, annealing it at intervals.
2. ***Bending*** flat sheets of silver and soldering them at the edges into a box or cylinder. The seam is supposed to be invisible. Once the shape has been achieved, the surface is finished by grinding, hammering, and polishing.
3. ***Wire-drawing:*** pulling a silver rod through successively smaller holes in a steel plate. The holes may be shaped to create the profiles of mouldings.
4. ***Casting:*** pouring molten silver into a mould created from a positive model of what is to be made. A common method of doing this is the *lost-wax* process. From an original model of a mermaid, a copy is made in wax. This is embedded in some refractory material which will withstand the high temperature. Silver is poured into the mould, displacing the wax and making a silver mermaid. This ancient process lends itself to the mass-production of difficult shapes like mermaids.
5. ***Chasing,*** used to decorate surfaces in low relief. The silversmith strikes the surface from the front with punches to displace the metal, forming incised lines or an impression of what is moulded on the punch. A ghost of the marks appears on the back. On Jacobean cups the surface between the incisions stands up in low relief, probably because the metal was stricken against a backing of leather or other soft material.
6. ***Embossing*** or ***repoussé*** work, used to make high relief. A hard metal die, excavated into the inverse likenesses of monsters or fruit, is held rigidly against the front surface. The back surface is hit with a small hammer to force the silver to conform to the die, creating positive

1 Jones *Russia.*
2 Makers of plate are traditionally called goldsmiths, although mostly they work in silver.
3 God recalled the holy recipient to her duty by sending a tempest which blew down the convent chimneys. She put on sackcloth and refused the gift, which remained for thirty years in the palace at Lisbon and then was consumed by earthquake. Delaforce A 1997 'Paul Crespin's silver-gilt bath for the King of Portugal' *BM* **139** 38–40.

monsters or fruit. The struck surface needs smoothing down; it can be seen half-rough inside the Bateman Tankard (§10.1.8). Rarely *repoussé* is meant to be seen from both sides (Leckhampton Bowl, §21.2.6; punch-ladles, §18.5.5).

7. ***Engraving,*** somewhere between drawing and carving, in which burins and tiny chisels are used to remove metal, ploughing lines or digging cavities. This is the normal method of drawing coats-of-arms, abstract decorations, or lettering not in relief. Engraved lines do not show through. ***Pouncing*** is a variant in which a needle pricks out rows of dots, or an area of dots to form a textured background.

8. ***Enamelling,*** filling hollows in the metal with molten, coloured glassy materials. This was much used in the early middle ages and then became rare, but is still occasionally done (e.g. Parker-Beldam Cup, §7.9).

9. ***Soldering,*** used to join components of a piece. Molten silver solder fuses to the silver parts and bonds them together as it solidifies. This is not simple playing with a soldering iron. Silver solder melts at about 700°C, a rather high temperature for ancient technology, and uncomfortably close to the melting-point of silver itself (893° for sterling silver). Not the least of the silversmith's skills is the precise handling of tiny pieces of red-hot metal. Many soldered-on castings are hollow, detectable by fragments of metal rattling around inside, or by the *blow-hole* provided to let out hot air which might otherwise spit out red-hot silver solder all over the shop.

10. ***Drop-forging*** and ***swaging,*** used for striking coins against a die and making spoons, forks, and wine-labels.

11. ***Spinning:*** a mechanized form of raising a bowl on a lathe.

12. ***Electrotyping,*** used to copy a piece by taking a mould and building up a thick electroplated deposit inside.

Silversmithing is an Iron Age craft: these methods (except the last two) were perfected then. *Repoussé* work began in Central Europe about 700 BC. The finest examples of wire-drawing are in the Snettisham Treasure of the first century BC. About that time an inhabitant of Welwyn was buried with two cups, in a curiously Adamesque-like style, which Hester Bateman herself would not be ashamed to have produced.[4]

In the middle ages different techniques were combined with great virtuosity. Such a simple object as the Horn-finial (p. 37) consists of ten pieces of silver (one missing), soldered together. The head was cast and finished by chasing. Each band of pierced tracery was cast, probably as a long strip, and then bent into an ellipse and closed by soldering. The battlements were cut out with a saw from a cast moulding. The crown was formed as a strip, decorated by engraving, and bent into a circle and soldered. The Parker Cup (§7.2) probably originated as 58 pieces of metal: 18 in the lid, 13 in the cup, and 27 in the base.

Casting, spinning, embossing, wire-drawing, and drop-forging lend themselves to mass-production. The same master mould produced the three coy mistresses on the Parker Cup, and doubtless a legion of mistresses recycled long ago.[5] Any student of steeple-cups knows how often the same *repoussé* shells and melons (§8.4, 8.5) recur from similar or identical dies. These methods flourished in late Elizabethan and Jacobean times, and contributed to the low cost of fabrication then. The few surviving vessels were not originally the unique works of art which they seem to be now. Whether this was so for the middle ages is difficult to judge, as survivors are even fewer.

Silversmithing was an international art. Foreign artisans worked in England on a much larger scale than one would suspect from the relatively few whose names, like Mieux and de Lamerie, are recorded. Many of them were subcontractors who never used their own maker's mark.[6]

In the 18th century mass-production began to be mechanized. There were specialist silversmiths, such as the Cafe brothers, candlestick-makers, and the Chawners, spooners. Spooners – often women – also made forks. Manufacture, once dispersed in many towns including Cambridge, became concentrated in the handful of cities that had assay offices. Candlestick-makers, many of them (like the Cafes) from Somerset, migrated to London. Engraving was often done by anonymous independent subcontractors.[7] Some silversmithies were cottage industries, forever forming and dissolving partnerships; others were big businesses, forerunners of Walker & Hall or Mappin & Webb. The maker's mark on

4 BM: PRB 1911.12-8, 27–8.

5 The Amerbach Cabinet, Basel, has a collection of original lead and boxwood casting patterns: Glanville (1990) pp. 194f.

6 Glanville (1990) pp. 86–99.

7 C Oman 1978 *English Engraved Silver 1150–1900* Faber, London.

an article is little more than a guarantee of the quality of the metal. Not every object with Paul de Lamerie's or Hester Bateman's mark was hammered and scraped, still less embossed or engraved, by their own hands.

Sterling and Britannia silver

Pure silver is too soft to make long-lasting artefacts: it is always alloyed, usually with copper, to harden it. When silver was expensive it was important to know how much base metal had been added. From ancient times the proper and legal composition, both for coins and artefacts, has been 92.5% silver, 7.5% base metal by weight. This is *sterling silver.*

In the 17th century people took to melting down half-crowns, or clipping their edges, and making the metal into spoons. Hanging (for murdering the coinage) was an insufficient deterrent. In 1697 the authorities tried to make the operation more difficult by legislating that artefacts contain more silver than coins. The new legal minimum, 95.8% silver, was called *Britannia silver* or *New Sterling.* This has a slightly bluish lustre, rather than the yellowish of sterling; it is softer, and objects made of it have more rounded corners and get worn more easily. Silversmiths disliked it. After 1720 it was no longer compulsory, but occasional objects continued to be made of it.

Silver solder is a low-melting-point alloy (supposedly at least 92.5% silver) used for joining components. It is slightly greyer than sterling silver, so the joins are not quite invisible.

Gilding

The silver parts of our early pieces are gilded, sometimes all over, sometimes only on the visible parts, and sometimes forming a pattern (***parcel-gilding***). From the Ostrich Egg (1592) onward there are some ungilded pieces, and after 1700 gilding is rare. Gilding was not particularly expensive; although partly mere fashion, it reduced the need for cleaning.

Early gilding was by fire. A solution of gold in quicksilver was painted on to the parts to be gilded. The piece was heated, evaporating the mercury (giving the gilder mirror-maker's disease), and leaving a coating of gold bonded to the silver, which was polished with a hare's foot. Parcel-gilding was fully developed by Roman times. In the 19th century gilding was replaced by the less dangerous cyanide-electroplating process.

The density of gilding varies. Medieval pieces often have a delicate film of gold through which the silver can be seen (***single-gilt***). From Elizabethan times onwards some pieces (often specified in inventories) were ***double-gilt*** to look like solid gold. Restorers have often re-gilded ancient surfaces, especially after repairs which involved soldering; they have rarely resisted the temptation to double- or treble-gild.

Hallmarks

Makers' marks stamped on silver may be derived from similar stamps on Roman pottery. They are usually accompanied by marks to certify the quality of the metal. The earliest silver object in Britain bearing such a ***hallmark*** is the Sutton Hoo charger, punched with the assay marks of the Byzantine Emperor Anastasius (491–518).[8]

Hallmarking, reintroduced in medieval England, grew into a system with up to five marks:

1. The standard mark, certifying that the metal contains the sterling percentage of silver. In the middle ages this was a crowned leopard's face. After 1544 it was replaced by a lion *passant* (that is, out for a walk). When Britannia silver was introduced the new standard was signified by a figure of Britannia. Since 1720 either the lion or Britannia is used, depending on the quality of the metal. On some very recent pieces the lion has metamorphosed into the mystic number 925.
2. The mark of the assay office. From 1544 the crowned leopard's face meant that the piece was assayed in London. During the Britannia period (1696 to 1720) it was replaced by a lion's head *erased* (pulled off the lion), in addition to the local mark of places other than London. In 1821 the leopard lost his crown and became the pussy-like feline familiar today. Other offices have different marks: an anchor for Birmingham, a crown for Sheffield, a harp for Dublin, etc.

8 Bruce-Mitford 28–31.

3. A maker's mark: the initials, shop sign, etc. of the manufacturer. Marks were supposed to be formally 'entered' or enrolled, and where the rolls survive the maker may be identifiable. But there were thousands of silversmiths,[9] the regulations discouraged them from ensuring that their marks were unique, and only a few per cent of their output survives. As the punches wore out they were replaced by more or less inexact copies. Before 1690 most identifications are problematic, and many silversmiths are known by only one piece. After 1690 the London rolls survive, and silversmiths can be identified if their initials are not too common.
4. A date-letter, changed year by year through the alphabet on a 20- or 25-year cycle. Different cycles are distinguished (sometimes with difficulty) by changes in the type-face, the shape of the surround, or by changes in the accompanying Sovereign's head. The cycles differ between assay offices.
5. The head of the King or Queen to show that tax had been paid, as required between 1784 and 1890.[10]

Hallmarks were struck with steel punches. Before *c*.1780 punches were big clumsy tools. They were too large for objects like spoons, which were marked on the stem when unfinished, and then stretched or touched up, leaving an oddly elongated mark. Lids and other loose pieces are often given a partial set of marks, but components made separately and soldered together are never marked.

Large silver pieces were tested by quantitative chemical analysis called *cupellation*, using a sample (*diet*) scraped off by the official assayer. Diet scrapes are visible on most large pieces down to 1820. They were nearly always taken from the underside of a piece, so were not much of a protection against fraud. Early pieces, lids, and small pieces were analyzed by the *touchstone*. A streak was made by rubbing the artefact on an abrasive stone, and compared with the colour of the streak left by a standard needle of known composition.

Or were they analyzed? The law required silver articles to be marked with the leopard's face from 1300 onwards, with the maker's mark from 1363 onwards, and with a date-letter for 1478 onwards. The statutes were often repeated and thus probably ineffective, and surviving pieces are seldom hallmarked before 1510. Policing, the responsibility of the Worshipful Company of Goldsmiths, was patchy. Penalties up to pillory and forfeiture of one ear were sporadically incurred, but these were not enough, for silversmiths were shy of bureaucracy. The regulations may have been evaded on the plea that pieces were privately commissioned and were not for sale. No surviving Cambridge piece is known to have any marks at all before the Anathema Cup at Pembroke College of 1481. Our earliest surviving marked piece is the St Paul Spoon of 1516. However, the 1526 inventory mentions a salt-cellar, now lost, with

> on the outside . . . a silver-gilt letter F next to the touch (*ly towch*)[11] from the gift of master Thomas Cosyn.

This seems to refer to the date-letter for 1483, mentioned as a distinguishing feature at a time when hallmarks were not universal. Cosyn became Fellow in 1452 and was Master 1487–1514.

Another factor is recycling. Hallmarked pieces would have been tempting to melt down because the quality of the metal would be known. In an age from which little survives, non-hallmarked articles should survive more often because their silver content would be difficult to establish.

After 1510 marks become commoner, but many pieces lack them even into the 1570s.

Some other European countries have hallmarking systems: Crete established one in 1360.[12] An example of Dutch hallmarking is the Queen Mary II flagon (§9.2).

Dodgers

From 1719 onwards a statute imposed a tax on hallmarked plate of 6*d*. per ounce. For this and other reasons, many pieces were either not marked or had a rudimentary set of marks imposed on a small disk of metal which was then soldered into a bigger piece. To do this incurred successively a fine of £100, two years' hard labour, or (after 1757) death without benefit of clergy. However, the legal and moral aspects were both confused: the maker could get off if the article was not made for sale, and many articles were recycled from others that had already paid the duty. The most respected silversmiths indulged in the practice, which

9 Grimwade gives biographies of some 2600 silversmiths registered in London alone between 1697 and 1837.
10 Goldsmiths' Company 1978 *Touching Gold & Silver: 500 years of hallmarks* London.
11 Probably the place from which the diet had been scraped.
12 J Jegerlehner *Byzantinische Zeitschrift* **13** (1904) 435–79.

Table 2.1. *Pieces with hallmark dates before 1535 at Cambridge and Oxford*

Cambridge		Oxford[13]	
1481	Anathema Cup, Pembroke		
1483?	Corpus Christi salt, now lost		
		1493	Basin, Corpus Christi
		1498	Chalices, Brasenose
1507	Beaker, Christ's	1506	Spoons, Corpus Christi
1507	Salt, Christ's	1507	Chalice & paten, Corpus Christi
		1514	Basin, Corpus Christi
		1515	Cup & cover, Corpus Christi
1516	St Paul Spoon, Corpus Christi	1516	Spoons, Corpus Christi
1520	Cup & cover, Christ's		
1521	Rose Mazer, Corpus Christi		
		1527	Chalice & paten, Corpus Christi
		1529	Mazer, All Souls
1531	Parker lid, Corpus Christi	1533	Cup & cover, Corpus Christi

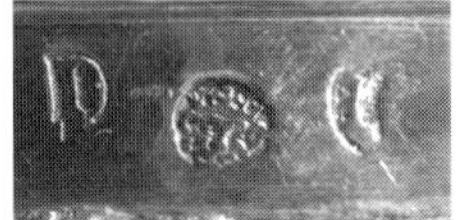
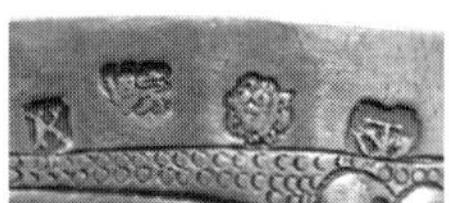
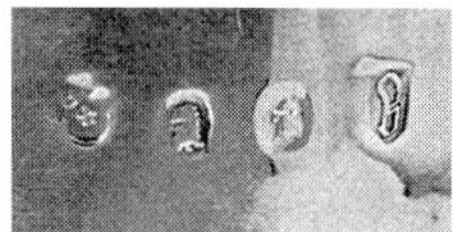
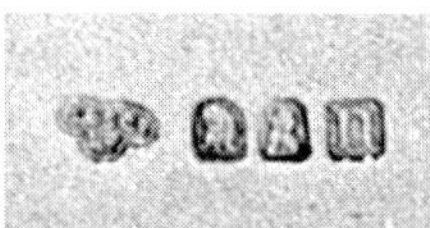
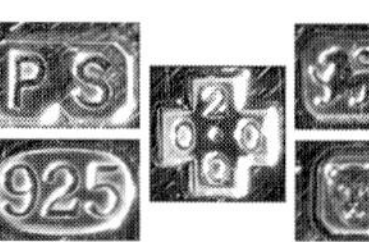

Some hallmarks on Corpus plate
1. *Rose Mazer (date 1521, the College's second earliest hallmark)* 2. *Ogle Cup (1607)* 3. *Lichfield Tankard (1715)* 4. *Page Bowl (1908)* 5. *Millennium hallmark 2000 (Tong-Walker Bowl)*

saved about 10% of the value of the metal, and were never hanged.[14]

Even small pieces such as casters are sometimes hallmarked on an insert or not hallmarked at all (p. 188). A possible motive might have been to use an alloy of lower silver content than the legal standard, which would have been stronger and more suitable for elaborate piercings.

Dating

Hallmarked pieces are easy to date, provided the date-letter is well struck – which it seldom is on early pieces – and the cycles distinctive. Discrepancies between the date-letter and a date inscribed on the piece can be instructive. If the inscription date is later than the hallmark date, the piece was not new when given to the College; if earlier, it was recycled from an earlier piece.

Pieces without inscription or hallmark are more fun. In principle it should be possible to get a radiocarbon date from a treasure like a horn or coconut which is partly organic. In practice this is seldom if ever done. Until recently it would involve sacrificing too much of the object to provide a sample. For the middle ages the calibration curve for radiocarbon is imprecise and sometimes

13 The Founder's Cup at Oriel is supposed to bear a Paris hallmark of 1463, but this is questionable: see Jones, *Oriel*.

14 'Duty dodgers in eighteenth-century plate' *in Silver at Partridge*, Partridge Fine Arts, London Oct. 1992, 20–3. Forbes J 2001 'Eighteenth century "duty dodgers"' *The Silver Society Journal* **13** 119–22.

ambiguous. And a single C14 date does not carry much weight: as anyone who has worked in this field knows, it is very common for one of a series of linked radiocarbon dates to be inexplicably out of sequence with the others. Although radiocarbon dating can now use much smaller samples, in my opinion the time has not yet come to use it on medieval composite plate.

There are two other sources of evidence: documents and typology. Documents, mainly inventories, tell us that an identifiable piece existed at a particular date, but seldom reveal when it was made.

Typology consists in grouping artefacts sharing some feature of structure, material, or decoration. If some of the objects can be dated independently by inscriptions, documents, radiocarbon, or by their relationship to some other datable object, they will establish the range of dates over which the feature was being made, and thus the possible dates of the other objects. Photographs, for example, can be roughly dated by the fashions in clothes or cars depicted, or by the construction or demolition date of a building shown or not shown, or by the kind of film used.

Constructing a typology of medieval plate is not easy, because comparative objects are few and themselves not directly dated. One often has to make do with comparisons with other media such as architecture or calligraphy. Nevertheless, some conclusions can be drawn. The Cup of the Three Kings, for example, has a distinctive style of silversmithing, especially the fringed edges that join the silver and wooden parts, and a distinctive style of inscription. These features are shared by a number of other cups, such as our Mazer without Print and the so-called 'Foundress's Cup' at Pembroke College. The Cup of the Three Kings is not in the inventory of Corpus cups in use up to *c*.1400, so probably is later. The Pembroke cup is recorded as the gift of a Fellow in the 1470s. From these and similar scraps of information we infer that this group of silver-mounted cups was fashionable in the mid-15th century, ending before date-lettered hallmarks became common.

Features created by mere fashion must be distinguished from functional points. Silver straps with a hinge at both ends, enclosing coconut-shells and ostrich eggs, run at least from the 14th century to the 17th (p. 50): they solve the problem of making a tight fit to a fragile material.

An aspect of typology now well developed is the analysis of the metal. There were variations with time in the proportions of elements accompanying silver, either deliberately added to harden it or accidental contaminants. Examples are shown in Appendix 2. Of the nine medieval to Jacobean pieces analyzed, eight – incuding six hallmarked pieces – contain less than the legal standard of silver. With the two earliest, the Swan Mazer and Cup of the Three Kings, this was due to deliberately adding more copper (itself contaminated with iron and nickel), rather than failing to get rid of the lead which was a natural contaminant in silver. Did silversmiths evade hallmarking because they knew their wares would fail the test?

Coats-of-Arms

From 1570 onwards the commonest addition to a piece is the donor's coat-of-arms, and often also the College's. Coats-of-arms, invented in the 12th century, are a symbol of an individual's family, an office such as a bishopric, or a college or corporate body. By the 18th century silversmiths would provide a blank cartouche on which to engrave the arms. Sometimes the original arms have been erased or cut out and a later owner's arms substituted.

The essential part of a coat-of-arms is the shield. The division of the shield, and the objects on it, are prescribed by the rules of heraldry, but the shape of the shield is a matter for artistic licence. The seven heraldic colours are usually represented by hatching with conventional patterns of lines or dots, as they would be in a black-and-white book illustration. I shall blazon the coats-of-arms (that is, describe them in heraldic form), giving the colours where they can be deciphered but not guessing where the hatching is missing.

Some coats-of-arms have *supporters* (e.g. lion and unicorn), and over the shield a *helmet* with a *wreath* around the top, and on the wreath a distinctive *crest*, whose original function was to identify the man inside the helmet. Supporters and crest are often omitted when the arms are engraved on silver. The crest (plus wreath) may be used by itself on pieces where the shield would be awkward. Alternatively, some feature from the shield may be isolated and used as a badge or logo.

Colleges rarely have supporters or crests (but the arms of Sidney Sussex are supported, with difficulty, by a bull and a porcupine). A feature of college arms is the *pseudo-crest*, a badge and wreath placed directly over the top of the shield without a helmet (p. 112).

A coat-of-arms was the mark of the upper class. Latin inscriptions describe many donors as *armiger*, possessor of coat-armour. However, the upper class was numerous, and someone who came down in the world did not forfeit the status.

Imitation Silver

Since the middle ages people – both coiners and honest artisans – have copied silver in cheaper materials. *Sheffield plate* was invented in 1742. An ingot of copper, with strips of silver welded to it top and bottom, is rolled, extruded, or drop-forged into various forms, retaining and stretching its silver coating. The copper shows through in engraving or when the piece gets worn.

In the 1840s this was largely superseded by *electroplating*, in which a thin layer of silver is deposited electrically on the surface of a copper or brass object. The silver layer tends to fill up small cavities and blunt sharp edges, resulting in coarser detail than real silver or Sheffield plate. Sheffield plate and electroplate often bear makers' marks looking vaguely like hallmarks.

Fashions in Silversmithing

Plate can be extremely conservative. Most of the College's hoard in Parker's time would not have been out of place on the Bayeux Tapestry or even at Sutton Hoo, nearly a thousand years before. However, silver as a decorative medium, especially at the upper end of the social scale, has its own branch of art history and lends itself to changes of fashion.

Some of the main shapes – salvers, two-handled cups, casters – have continued for thousands of years with varying functions and names. A rosewater basin can be re-designated a 'soup-dish' (Pembroke College); one generation's chamber-pot becomes another generation's loving-cup. Inkstands, ashtrays, and cruet-frames have been needed only in certain historical periods.

But, like all decorative arts, silversmithing has a typology of details and ornaments, by which a piece may often be dated to within twenty years or so. This is independent of technology: modern spinning and electrotyping were used as aids to mass-production rather than for devising new forms. One is seldom in doubt whether a salver is of *c.*1720 or *c.*1750.

Plate is most easily likened to architecture, and was often influenced by architectural models and pattern-books. However in England, and especially Cambridge, there is a marked discrepancy between architectural forms and the corresponding fashions in plate.

The dates in the following paragraphs are derived from examples in Corpus, and are often a little later than those in textbooks of silver which are based on upper-class examples.

In the middle ages the forms of silver were not particularly architectural. Cups look neither like cathedrals nor timber-framed houses, although they have battlements like towers and cresting like wooden rood-screens. Surviving objects are often composite, of silver set with enamel, or of wood, coconut, horn, etc. set in silver mounts. Calligraphy often forms part of the design.

With the Mannerist style, a brief period of fantasy and exuberance in the reign of Queen Elizabeth, silversmithing became a miniature of polite architecture. The Parker Cup (1571) is a miniature of a contemporary country mansion: both are replete with 'statuary and urnage', strapwork and oval windows, heroines and foliage and hidden surprises. The same forms recur in book illustration and bookbinding. Matthew Parker admired Mannerism in both silver and books. His pieces, although made in England, are very like others from Flanders and Germany.

In the 17th century, silver objects are dominated by shapes more than by decoration; they are related perhaps more to furniture than to other arts. Features such as

Table 2.2. *Stylistic periods in silver design, with Corpus examples*

High Medieval	1250–1400	Swan Mazer (§6.1)
Late Medieval	1400–1500	Cup of the Three Kings (§6.2)
Tudor	1500–1560	Parker Rosewater Bowl (§7.1, Plate 3)
Mannerist	1560–1580	Great Parker Cup (§7.2, Plate 4)
Late Elizabethan	1580–1605	Ostrich Cup (§7.7)
Jacobean	1605–1650	Jegon Cup (§8.4)
Baroque	1650–1739	Russell Coffee-pot (§11.1)
Rococo (Louis Quinze)	1739–1775	Walpole Coffee-pot (§11.5)
Adamesque (Directoire, Wedgwood, Neo-Classical)	1775–1795	Douglas Argyle (§11.8)
Regency	1795–1835	JBMH-Bateman Teapot (§11.12)
Victorian	1835–1890	Eyles Teapot (§11.14)
Art Nouveau (Arts-and-Crafts)	1890–1910	Espy Vase (§21.18.1)
Early 20th Century	1910–1950	Square Salts (§16.14)
Modernistic	1930–	Thomson Bowl (§22.6, Plate 7)

the steeple on the lids of cups seem to be peculiar to silver.

The baroque style reached England in the later 17th century. It is often attributed to Huguenot influence: several of the top silversmiths were refugees from France, Protestants expelled by Louis XIV in his tyrant mood. Baroque is a neo-Classical style, characterized by monumental symmetry, heavy mouldings, straight lines and quarter-circles, with little decoration except for inscriptions and coats-of-arms. As an architectural fashion it began several decades earlier, although baroque architecture did not become familiar in England until St Paul's Cathedral.

Fashion in silversmithing is well illustrated by the change from baroque to rococo, as shown by our series of coffee-pots, candlesticks, and salvers. Rococo objects have the appearance of informality and panache, all cusps and sinuosities; they have complex and asymmetric decoration applied by embossing, chasing, and engraving, often inspired by vegetation and sea-shells. If baroque is a miniature of stonemasons' architecture, rococo is of plasterers'.

The combination of ideas that constitute rococo, some of them so *outré* that later critics refused to accept them as genuine (§11.5), was taken up simultaneously by all the top silversmiths between 1737 and 1741. They stopped making baroque and switched to rococo, much as leading *couturiers* presumably assemble from time to time and vote on the forthcoming length of skirts. (For examples see parallels to the Walpole Coffee-pot, p. 144.)

A factor not to be underestimated is the tool-kit. To make rococo silver involved an investment in moulds, dies, chasing tools, etc. Resemblances in the details of cups etc. by different firms indicate that silversmiths such as Paul de Lamerie, George Wickes, and others collaborated in using each others' components.[15]

Baroque and rococo were Continental architectural styles. Only a few years separate the invention of rococo architecture in Munich and Dresden from the take-up of rococo silver in London. England took up rococo silver with enthusiasm, but disdained rococo architecture. (Had de Lamerie ever seen a rococo building?) English rococo, instead, is the art-form of cartography: maps, manuscript and printed, have details like those engraved on silver and doubtless derived from the same pattern-books.

Silversmiths suddenly stopped making rococo in *c.*1780, when clean lines again became fashionable. The new Adamesque style adapted to silverware the architectural and pottery details of Classical and Hellenistic Greece and southern Italy. These had become known through the studies of travellers such as Stuart and Revett, explorers of ancient Athens in 1751–4, and through finds of Classical Greek vases in Italy. (Ancient Greek *plate* was still unknown.) The silver version involved lightness and symmetrical curves, decorative flutes and reeds, horizontal patterned bands, and

15 'George II two handled cup and cover' *Silver at Partridge* (above) 26f.

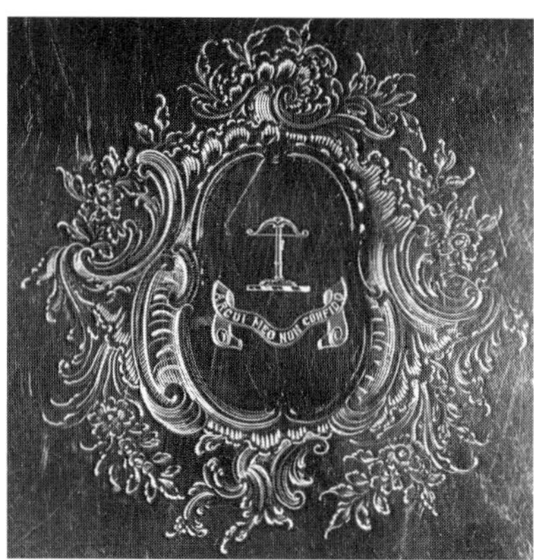

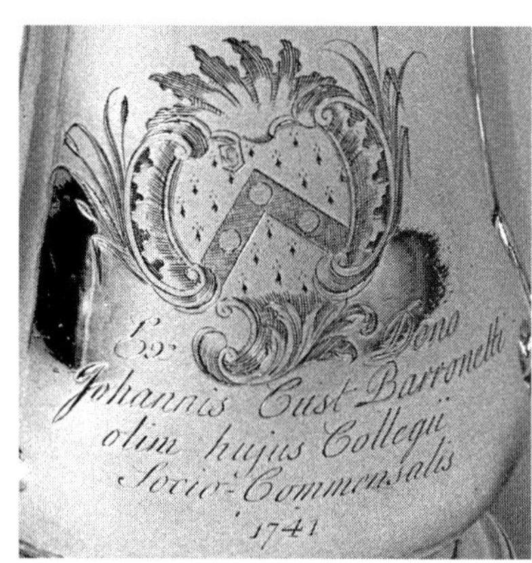

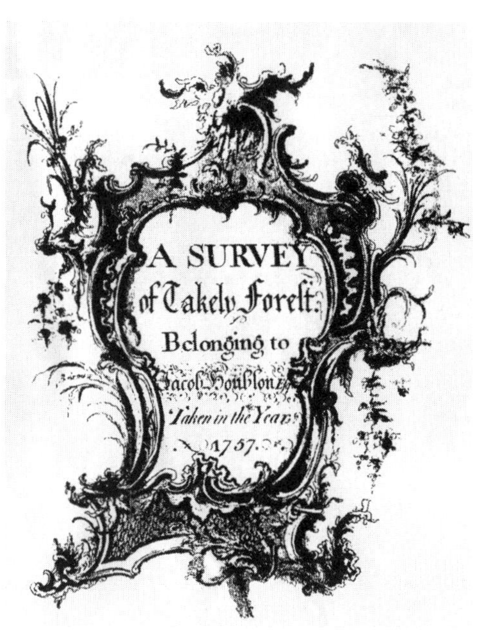

Cartouches:
(1) Baroque, from the Bateman Salver of 1728 (badge and motto later);
(2) Rococo, from the Cust Mug of 1741 (§10.2.4);
(3) Rococo, from the map of Hatfield Forest, Essex, made in 1757 for Jacob Houblon III. (He was son of the donor of something that the College recycled into the Houblon Candlesticks (§11.16), and patron of a rare example of rococo architecture in England, the Shell House still standing in the Forest.)[16]

engraved swags and ribbons. It too originated as miniature architecture: Robert and James Adam, although remembered as architects, had dabbled in silver design from 1758 onwards.[17]

The Adamesque style was followed, logically, by a Regency style adapted from certain Imperial Roman architectural forms; it was not closely related to 'Regency' architecture. Silversmiths had long been experimenting with neo-Roman forms – Pembroke College has pairs of such candlesticks dated 1757 and 1764 – but they did not catch on until the 1790s.

16 Hollingworth-Lander Map: Essex Record Office: D/DB P37.
17 Snodin M 1997 'Adam reassessed' *BM* **139** 17–25.

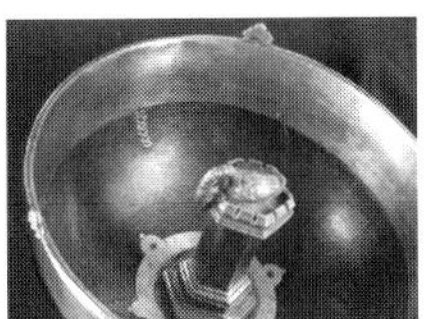

High Medieval
Swan Mazer

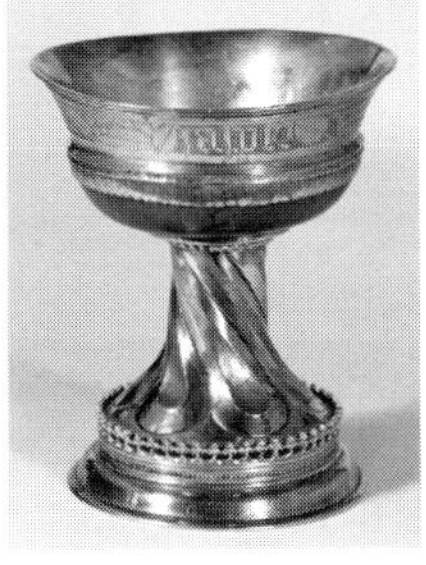

Late Medieval Cup
of the Three Kings

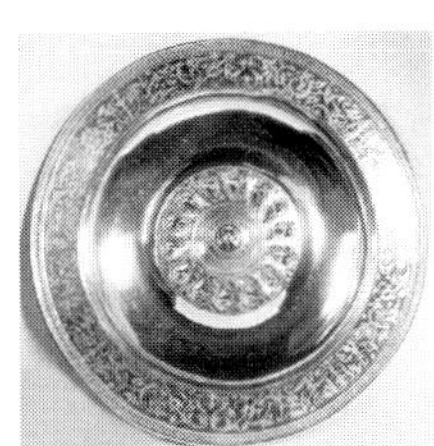

Tudor Parker
Rosewater Bowl

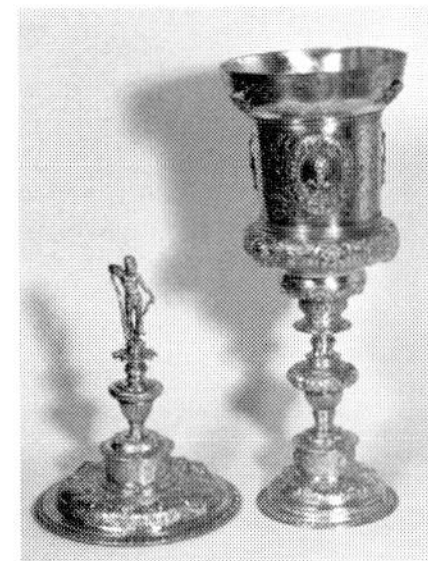

Mannerist
Great Parker Cup

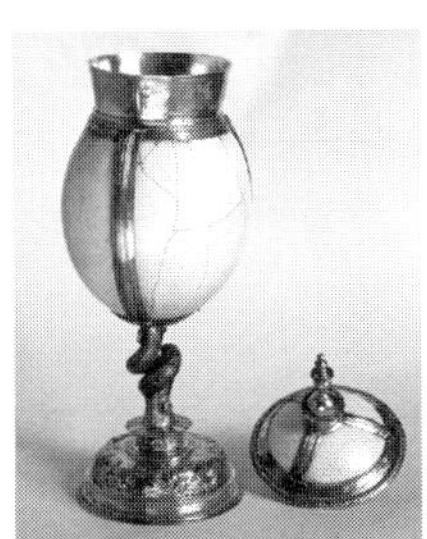

Late Elizabethan
Ostrich Cup

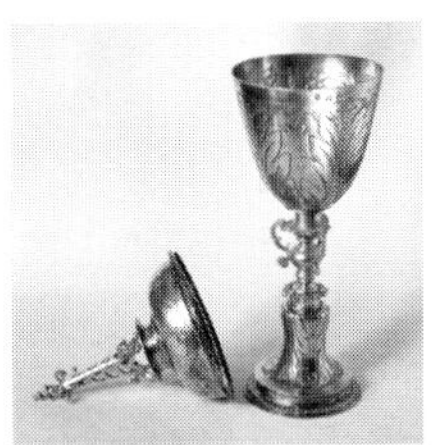

Jacobean
Jegon Cup

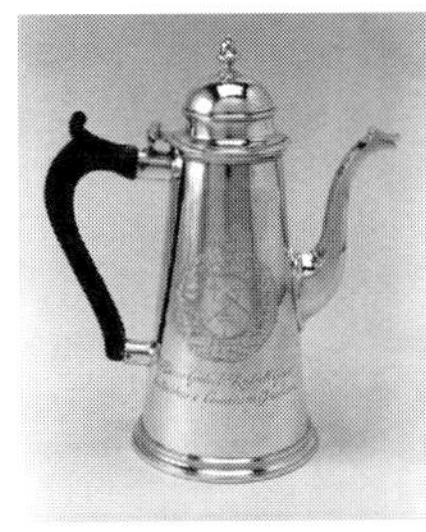

Baroque Russell
Coffee-pot

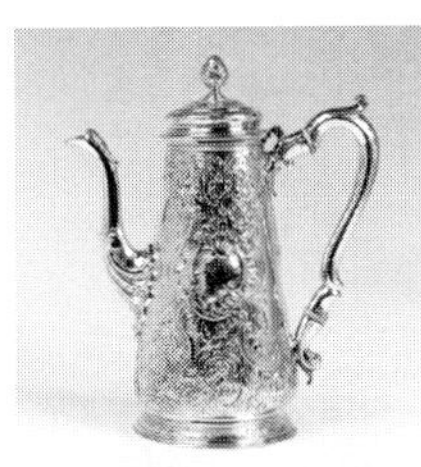

Rococo Walpole
Coffee-pot

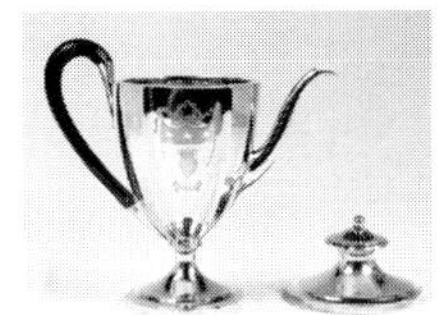

Adamesque
Douglas Argyle

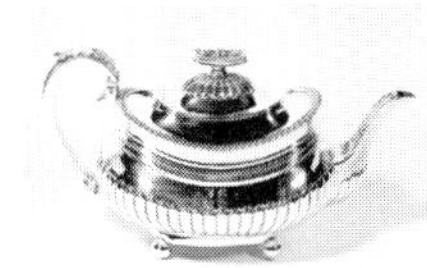

Regency
JBMH-Bateman
Teapot

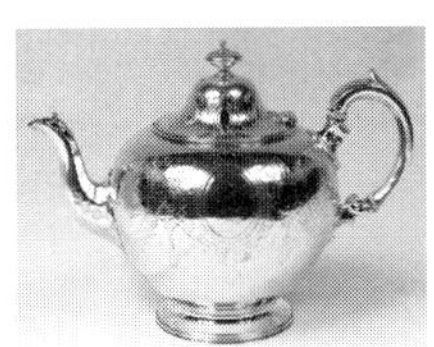

Victorian
Eyles Teapot

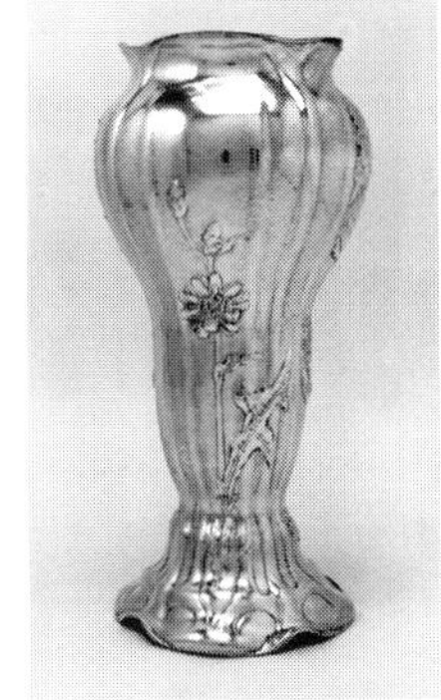

Art Nouveau
Espy Vase

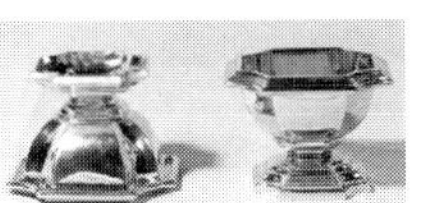

Early 20th
Square Salts

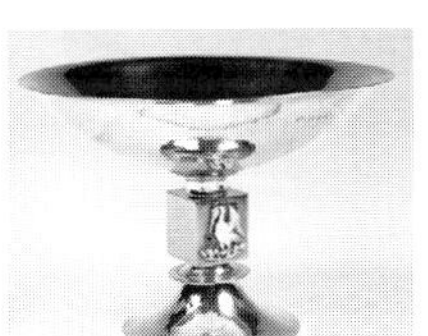

Modernistic
Thomson Bowl

In Victorian times the order becomes confused. Neo-Mannerist, neo-baroque, and neo-rococo can all be distinguished, but not in any particular time-sequence. Neo-Gothic imitates the forms of Gothic cathedrals rather than of Gothic plate. The Victorians excelled in giant, exuberant, super-rococo wine-cisterns, triple-gilt salvers, and other semi-vulgar upper-class works, not well represented in a college whose old members were chiefly country parsons (but see the Hankinson-Jennings Flagon, §9.7). At a lower social level, big firms of manufacturing silversmiths introduced new methods of mass-production, so that even quite poor people could own a few spoons or a christening cup.

The Art Nouveau fashion of the late 19th and early 20th century, so clearly defined in architecture and pottery, also applies to plate. The College has one characteristic piece, the Espy Vase (§21.18).

Silversmithing in the early to mid 20th century flourished chiefly in reproductions of Elizabethan and Jacobean forms. Original designs were formal, plain, and dull, baroque without its panache, for example the Butler Salver (§13.18).

After World War II silver manufacture collapsed: most of the big firms went out of business. It is said that the falling price of the metal was outweighed by an extortionate rate of purchase tax. However, silver as a craft material has had a revival; the ancient methods of fabrication are all still practised (Parker-Beldam Cup, §7.9). Silver has become a particularly happy medium for Modernistic art (Chapter 22).

3

Plate in the College

One shield of silver and azure for the master, and twelve shields of lesser size of very similar construction for the fellows, and they are of the same metal; and seven more shields of the same metal and azure for the lesser clerics, and on each shield are depicted the weapons of the Passion of Christ, and at the end the arms of good henry duke of lancaster our founder who gave these shields and very many other goods, to whose soul God be favourable, Amen.

Inventory by John Botener, 1376

[These objects are called 'stochynnys Enamelyd' in the inventory of 1526; the great ones weighed 16½ ounces, the small 11½ oz. Catherine Hall interprets them as ornaments for the staves of two canopies carried in the Corpus Christi procession; they were melted down when it was abolished at the Reformation.]

Colleges were not among the wealthier English institutions, and Corpus was not a rich college. However the plate inherited from the founder Gilds was augmented by gifts of early Fellows and well-wishers. By 1500 the hoard was roughly equivalent to that of a minor noble household (though colleges never developed the specifically noble habit of eating off silver plates). Following many disposals at the Reformation, the College received the illustrious gifts and bequests of Archbishop Matthew Parker. From the 1590s onwards hundreds of pieces came from Fellow-Commoners (p. 97f.), but few survive.

Donors' names were inscribed on each piece, and recorded in inventories. Almost anyone could give plate to the College. In 1746 we melted down a 'Large Tankard with L[or]d Sandwichs Arms'; I have failed to discover his connexion with Corpus. Pieces were given by Fellows and occasionally by undergraduates. Samuel Kerrich had been a Sizar (a poor student) and rose to be Fellow; on leaving in 1729 he gave a beautiful pair of miniature rococo candlesticks (p. 155).

Most College plate has always been gifts. However, in 1706 a plate fund was set up, financed from Fellows' subscriptions and from sales of plate. Items bought from it have no donor's name and no coat-of-arms appears.

Fellow-Commoners dwindled in the 19th century, but Fellows' gifts increased, including wedding fines after 1882. In 1955 the College received its single largest acquisition, the family hoard bequeathed by Aubrey Bateman. Benefactors in the late 20th century have been munificent with gifts of plate, large and small.

The great majority of the College's plate was hallmarked in London, and most of it, as far as one can tell, was made there. Cambridge goldsmiths did mainly repairs and inscriptions. Among our early plate, at most two alterations (see below) are known Cambridge work. Many donors of plate brought it from their home towns; it is surprising that no surviving piece has a Norwich hallmark, seeing how many members came from Norfolk.

On Feasts and the Uses of Plate

Down to the mid-18th century the College's daily diet was, as Tolkien's trolls in *The Hobbit* put it, 'Mutton yesterday, mutton today, and blimey, if it don't look like mutton again tomorrer', varied occasionally by pigeon

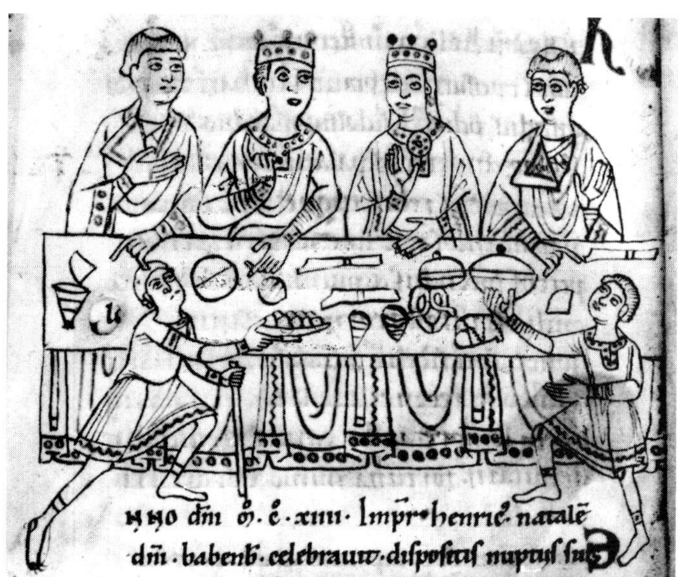

Wedding feast of the Empress Maud in 1114/15. Note the table-knives, mazers with lids, and a salver. From MS 373 f.95v. in the College library, drawn not long after the event.

and stockfish in Lent. It was eaten off pewter. After the Corpus Christi feast, 1496, we counted the 'pewtyr': 2 chargers (p. 169), 15 'patell', 50 'platers' (plus six from the Master), 62 dishes, 47 saucers, 6 salt-cellers. College accounts are full of buying, mending, and recycling pewter table-ware. In 1594 the Master and Fellows subscribed £7. 3*s*. 4*d*. for '2 garnishe of the best pewter . . . in waight 215' [pounds], which seems a lot for thirteen dons.[1] Pewter cost 8*d*. a pound, less than one-hundredth the price of silver, but it was heavier and softer and more was needed to make a vessel. The College had no respect for future archaeologists: not a scrap of pewter survives.

Plate was at first meant for feasts, which are not confined to the rich: many quite poor cultures concentrate their eating into special occasions. Feasts are an occasion of displaying special possessions, even at the humble level of 'bringing out the best china'.

Courtly feasts were feasts indeed: Henry III at Christmas would eat hundreds of deer and thousands of other beasts and birds. Books of etiquette and illustrations of feasts are concerned mainly with great banquets and the plate displayed at them. University and college feasts were scaled down from such mighty occasions.

Corpus Christi College had two original feasts. The Beadles' Feast was at Christmas, or on the Sunday after; it was probably taken over from the Gild of St Mary; it was so called because the University Beadles (whose survivor is the present Esquire Bedell) were the guests.[2] The Corpus Christi feast, held on Corpus Christi Day usually in early June, probably originated from the other Gild.

The earliest documented feast is Corpus Christi in 1388, a modest celebration involving 14*d*. worth of 'capons, pullets, rabbits & meat', and 8*d*. spent on actors. Live entertainment also happened at Christmas, with frequent payments to pipers (*fistulatores*) and actors. For Corpus Christi in 1446 we had mutton, capons, geese, etc., flavoured with ginger, cinnamon, saffron, cloves, pepper, and a little sugar; we drank 4*s*. 6*d*. worth of wine.[3]

The *Book of Beadles' and Corpus Christi Feasts* preserves fuller details from 1517 to 1562. At the Beadles' Feast wildfowl ('malards', 'pocards', 'tele', 'snype', buntings, and larks) and 'conys' (big rabbits) mounted the table, as well as solid fare such as a sheep, 'loyn of vele', and 'hinder partes of motton', maybe venison, finishing with 'wardens' (a kind of pear) and prunes. Drink comprised four sorts of beer (one with hops in it), gallons of 'clarett', and malmsey brought all the way from Crete. There were payments to 'a mynstrell luter' and 'y^e lord of mysrule'.

1 CC(A): *Registrum Accounts 1376–1484* f.228v.; *Audit Book 1598–1678*.
2 Information from Catherine Hall.
3 CC(A): *Registrum Accounts* f.111v., 188.

Corpus Christi was a serious feast lasting $1\frac{1}{2}$ days, devouring sheep and calves (sometimes killed on the spot), 'pyggys' (that is, piglets), 'Racke of moton', 'rabetts' (that is, baby rabbits), 'chekens', 'geysse', quails, pigeons, once a hapless bustard, with similar beer but less variety of wine, ending – then as now – with 'straweberies' or occasionally apples.[4]

After Parker's time the Beadles' Feast moved to Candlemas (the Purification of the Blessed Virgin Mary, 2 February) and became the Audit Feast. Christmas was marked instead by the ceremony of 'collaring the brawn', transforming two pigs (supplied by tenants) into brawn kept in a great tub and eaten over the ensuing weeks. The Corpus Christi Feast gave place to the Library Feast on 6 August, Parker's birthday, when representatives of Gonville & Caius College and Trinity Hall came to verify that Parker's books were still there (p. 68).

By 1610, as a list bound in the end of the Inventory Book shows, many College tenants, as part of their rent, contributed to the Audit Feast. These dues included 'Gammon of Bacon', mallards, '1 ffatt Pigg', gallons of claret wine and pottles of sack; but they were not just medieval survivals, for they included such exotica as oranges, pounds of sugar, and '1 fatt Turkey' (an American bird).

Feast accounts rarely mention plate, apart from occasional borrowings; a notable exception is the repair of the Horn after the Corpus Christi feast of 1558 (p. 41). Diners drank from 'stone' cups and from glasses. In the 17th century the Horn was used also at something called the Commencement (p. 41); maybe students drank from it before taking their degrees, as they do now.

Christmas, as in Cambridge colleges generally, faded away into a non-event after Fellows were allowed to marry and have families in 1882. In the 20th century the Corpus Christi Feast was re-established. The Candlemas feast has become the Queenborough Feast, named after Almeric Hugh Paget, Baron Queenborough, who endowed it.

Plate was used on ordinary occasions probably in the 16th century, as objects multiplied. By the 17th dons drank daily out of silver cups.

Most medieval drinking vessels had covers, though few survive. Halls then had no ceilings: diners would look up at the soot-blackened underside of the roof-tiles, and would not know what might fall into the drink. Lids become redundant with the spread of ceilings, *c*.1600.

Organization and Storage

College plate developed into the 'great plate' used on ceremonial occasions; the chapel vessels; the 'buttery plate' used at ordinary dinners; plate assigned to the Master; and plate which Fellows kept on loan in their rooms.

Ancient artefacts used at feasts, together with broken objects and those superfluous to daily use, were kept in a chest in the treasury. The small, vaulted, windowless chamber which still exists next to the former chapel under the 'gallery' built by Cosyn in *c*.1490 looks like a medieval strongroom; it was in St Bene't's churchyard, a public place, and would be difficult to break into without attracting attention. However, from at least the mid-17th century the plate was kept with Parker's manuscripts in the library over the Elizabethan chapel.[5]

The plate-cupboard in the Buttery was the domain of the *Promus*, or working butler. The office of *Pincerna*, or Butler, was given to undergraduates as a disguised scholarship. Most of the duties were performed by the *Promus*, a long-serving member of College staff.

The College was lackadaisical about keeping track of plate. For centuries there was never a complete inventory. Inventories were made for various categories of plate kept in different places; they often lasted for decades, new accessions being added and pieces disposed of being crossed out. One can never be sure that a piece not inventoried was not there.

Rarely is an article reported missing. At the beginning of the 1597/8 list is the note:

> *there is missing* A greate siluer pott *weighing* 16 oz. for which Robert Gill, Butler, payd three pounds . . . 1595 . . .
> [Italics indicate Latin words translated]

4 CC(A): *Liber Communorum Bedellorum & Corporis Christi.*
5 For arrangements in Oxford colleges see Hayward.

The butler's carelessness cost him something like two months' wages; however he was not charged the full value of the cup, which as scrap would have been worth £4. Another cup is annotated 'the cover was lost in Dr John Jegons time'.

The Pelican and the Lilies

Our founders and all the early Masters had their own coats-of-arms (or so Masters, the College historian, supposed), but they forgot to supply the College with any. When the College wanted armorial insignia it used the Instruments of the Passion of Christ, as on the shields carried in procession (see head of this chapter) and on the College seal (§6.6). In 1570 Parker arranged for a formal grant to the College of these arms: *Quarterly, 1 and 4: gules a pelican in piety argent. 2 and 3: azure three lilies of the second.*

This pelican is not the ornithological bird (*Pelecanus crispus*, from the Mediterranean) but the mythical pelican, represented as a swan with the head of an eagle. It nests in trees, and has the misfortune of quarrelling with its young when they hatch and inadvertently killing them. The mother pelican restores the chicks to life by pecking her own breast and wetting them with her blood. This story, out of the *Physiologus*, a late Roman pseudo-zoological treatise, was taken into Christian symbolism as a type of Christ redeeming humanity by his blood. The story thus far was familiar in the middle ages from the *Bestiary*, of which this College has a manuscript of *c.*1150 and one of *c.*1300.[6]

The mythical pelican then became linked, probably by St Thomas Aquinas, to the rising cult of Corpus Christi. It acquired a different symbolism, that of Christ continuing to feed the Church with his body and blood. This gave rise to the *heraldic* pelican, feeding the *living* chicks with its blood – often called a 'pelican in *his* piety', though the sexes are indistinguishable in this bird. This sort of pelican became the emblem of Corpus Christi gilds – though not, it seems, of the one at Cambridge, nor of the College before Parker's time. (Corpus Christi College, Oxford, acquired the pelican before Corpus Cambridge: it was already a badge of the founder, Bishop Fox.)

The white lilies on a blue background are an ancient symbol of the Virgin Mary. They were also the arms of the College of Stoke-by-Clare, Suffolk, Parker's country retreat in his youth, which he had tried to save from the rapacity of Henry VIII.[7]

Everyone knows an heraldic pelican when they meet one, but the Madonna Lily (*Lilium candidum*) is a Mediterranean herb which artists rarely saw. It is a mysterious plant, grown in gardens since Minoan Crete but probably unknown wild.[8] In medieval Cambridge it would have been imagined from whatever was on the sign of the Lilypot, an inn belonging to the College. The heraldic scrivener who illustrated Clarencieux King-of-Arms's grant had not the least idea what a lily was: how could he have had, on 23 December 1570? He would have scorned to draw a wyvern if asked for a bull, but instead of lilies he depicted something with upright flowers, four reflexed petals, and three stamens. (To be a lily a flower has to have six petals and six stamens and – a type of our Lady's humility – must bow its head; and three lilies should be conjoined, not separate.) From then until now artists depicting the College lilies have either copied him or substituted various herbs of their own, ranging in appearance from moss-campion to maize, none of them resembling the noble and immaculate original.

This College, having always kept its head down when there was trouble, has never had a helmet, and therefore has no crest. However, a third pelican is sometimes placed as a pseudo-crest (p. 14) on a wreath directly on top of the shield. This ramshackle arrangement is not a modern corruption of heraldry, but goes back at intervals as far as 1663 (Montacute Alms-Dish, §9.1). The pelican alone is often used as a badge on small objects.

6 CC(L): MS22 fo.166v, MS53 fo.201. The earlier MS says that there is a separate ornithological pelican. Another example is the pelican shown in Tibet on the 13th-century *Mappa Mundi* in Hereford Cathedral. I am grateful to Dr Christopher de Hamel for advice on pelicans.

7 Lamb p. 91.

8 I have found it on the cliffs of Mount Athos, but it seems to be an escape from hermits' gardens.

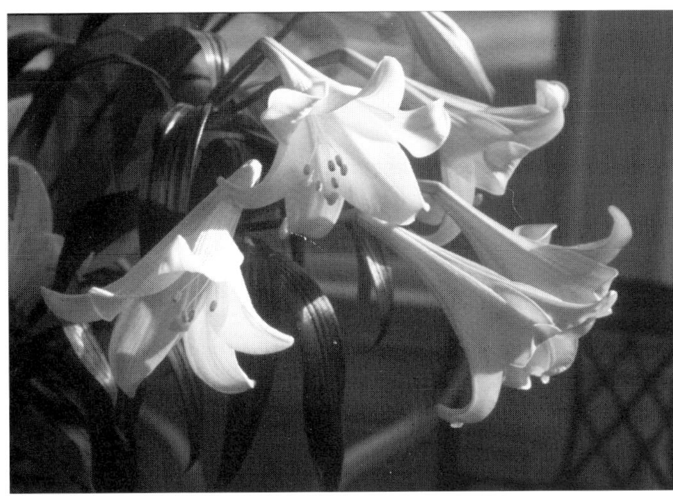

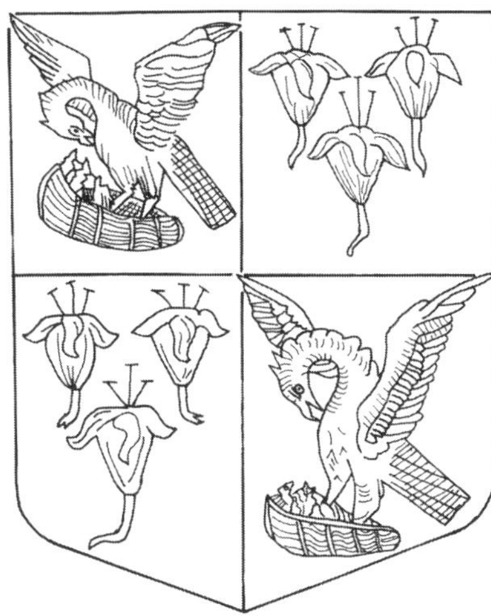

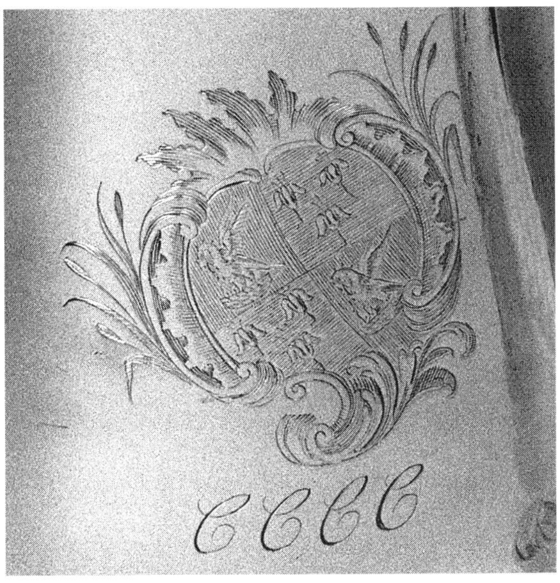

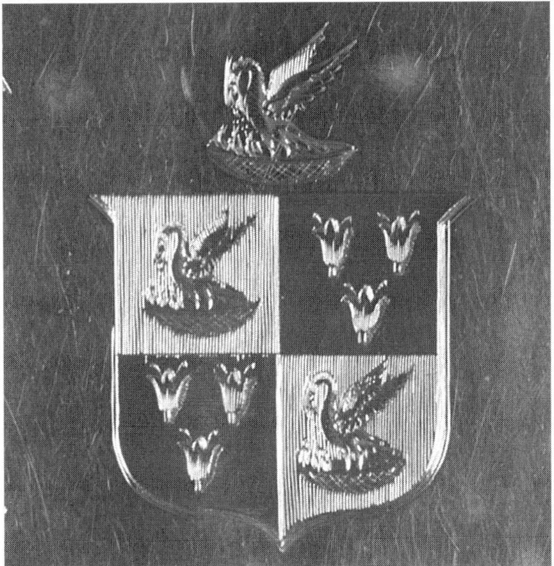

The College arms. Real lilies (Lilium candidum). Fierce pelicans and feeble 'lilies': from the original patent of arms of 1570. Rococo version: Cust Mug (p. 128). Victorian: Stephen Salver (p. 178).

Disposals

The subject of our Plate is a rather melancholy one. The explanation which has become traditional in most colleges, viz. that their silver was melted down for the King's service during the Civil Wars, is certainly inapplicable in our case. . . . The causes of our loss are of a more prosaic kind, consisting of indifference and theft. . . . Till very recent days, there does not seem to have been a vestige of what we call historic or antiquarian interest in the various college possessions. When a cup or spoon became much worn, or out of fashion, it was disposed of, and replaced by something new.

J. Venn, *Biographical History of Gonville and Caius College*, 1901

On the value of plate, and recycling

Early plate is much rarer than contemporary books, buildings, or woodland because it was recycled. Douglas Bennett says of Trinity College, Dublin 'The college plate, in the days when there were no banks, was the college money'. This would be an exaggeration for Corpus. Attitudes varied, and it takes only one dispersing Master, like Sowode, to undo centuries of conservation. However, the archives show that from the 15th to the 19th century it was normal to sell or melt down damaged or unfashionable articles, either to replace them with new plate or to raise funds to meet some College emergency. Occasionally the proceeds seem to have vanished into the petty cash.

To the modern mind this is absurd. Apart from artistic or antiquarian considerations (or the feelings of the donors), the value of scrap silver is trivial, little better than selling a picture for the value of the canvas. At present silver is exceptionally cheap, labour is expensive, and articles have antiquarian value. At the time of writing an ounce of silver was worth a little over £3, about one-eightieth the price of gold (itself depreciated). A craftsman works less than half an hour to earn an ounce of silver. A handmade piece costs typically about 100 times its melt-down value; an ancient piece can easily cost 100 times a modern copy.

Things were different then. In 1350 an ounce of silver was worth 2*s*. – indeed it *was* two shillings, since 24 silver pennies weighed one ounce – and it was a week's wage for a craftsman. Silver was about one-eleventh the price of gold. Relative to prices in general, silver was much more expensive than it is now, and labour was much cheaper.

The diagram shows the coinage value of silver (the number of pennies or shillings that an ounce would make) in relation to prices paid for unworked or scrap silver, and for articles of silver and silver-gilt. Prices of the metal follow fairly closely the coinage value. They never got far above, or folk would have melted down their pennies, death penalty notwithstanding. Lower prices may reflect difficulty in proving the quality of the metal.

During the middle ages the price of silver steadily rose in relation to the cost-of-living index. After a peak in 1550 it declined: the weight of a shilling remained steady (though the metal was of poorer quality) while the cost of living went up. Craftsmen's wages followed an intermediate course: as time went on men were paid more shillings but could buy less with them. By 1760 the craftsman, although his standard of living was well below that of 300 years earlier, had to work only three

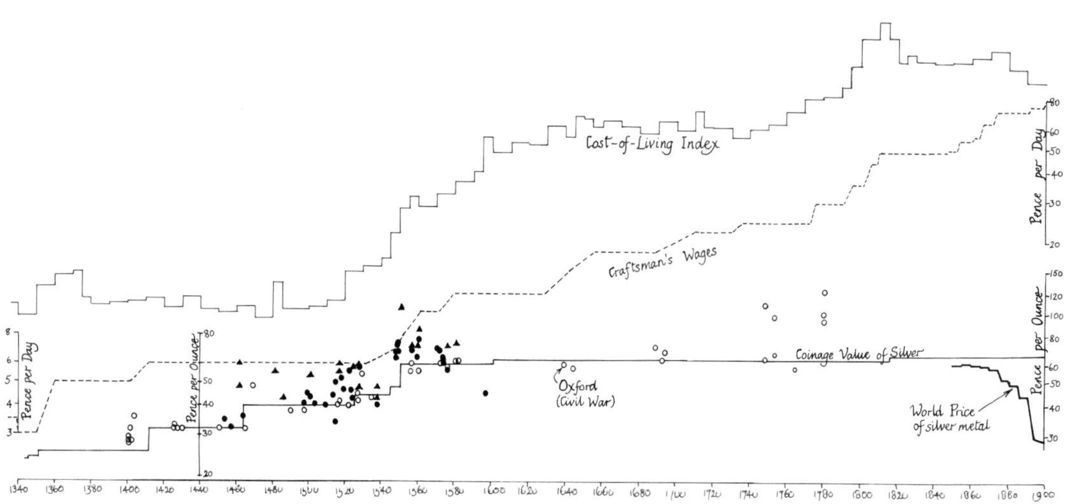

Price of silver in relation to wages and the cost of living (Brown-Hopkins index), 1340–1900. Black points: prices actually paid for silver objects (triangles indicate gilt). White points: prices paid for scrap silver. Note the logarithmic scale.

days to earn an ounce of silver. Thereafter the value of silver declined relative to both wages and prices.[9] In the late 19th century the price collapsed because world production had increased so greatly as to outweigh even the growing consumption of silver by photographers.

From at least 1460 to 1660 the value of the silver in an artefact was much greater than the cost of the workmanship. In 1493 Oriel College bought their Founder's Cup, a fine and elaborate piece weighing 33.35 ounces, for £4. 18*s.* 1*d.*, at 2*s.* 11*d.* an ounce, less than the value of the silver – but it has no hallmark, so the silver content would be difficult to prove. Silver articles seldom sold for more than 25% above their scrap value, or 50% above scrap value if gilt. Another factor seems to be the rise of mass-production (p. 9). By the 1590s the cost of 'changing' (recycling) artefacts was down to 8*d*. per ounce, representing something like half a day of silversmith's time; the new article would have cost 15% above the scrap value of the old.

Plate kept its value even if damaged. The sale of a 10-ounce cup in the 1590s would realize £2. 10*s*., worth two men's time for a month mending the roof. In the Civil War, Charles I stole about 25,000 ounces from fifteen of the seventeen Oxford colleges (p. 102), equivalent to £6300, which would pay 5000 troops for two weeks: a trifling fraction of the cost of the war, but attractive to an unscrupulous and penurious king.

Plate could be sold to meet emergency expenses, or 'changed' into a more useful or fashionable object. Less often it was bartered. In 1638 'Two olde salts and an olde beaker haueing noe name uppon y^{m}' were given to Francis Walsall, ex-Fellow, in return for a book.[10] It was not uncommon to melt plate less than twenty years old, even if the donor was still in residence.

At Corpus, recycling is first heard of in 1438 (p. 61). Many pieces melted down were in poor condition. Especially in the mid-17th century, much of the plate sold or melted after less than 20 years had been repaired, often several times. Occasionally a piece was melted almost as soon as it was received; maybe it was given to the College as scrap metal.

We frittered away much of the medieval plate in the 16th century. It is my horrid thought that the surviving ancient pieces escaped melting down mainly *because they lacked hallmarks* (p. 11); the value of the silver would have been reduced by the difficulty of proving it genuine.

Very few 17th-century artefacts survive: only six out of at least 219 secular objects acquired between 1590 and 1710. This, however, was a period of recurrent poverty, when the College was often kept going on a loan from the Bursar, and was plagued by major building repairs.

In 1648, when 45 cups were sold to pay for urgent repairs, the College ordered a book to be kept 'as a perpetual memory' of the donors. This record, later known as the Vellum Book, was entered on the back pages of an old library catalogue,[11] and after long oblivion was rediscovered by Catherine Hall. It is a beautiful transcript of the coats-of-arms, names, and dates of donors, and often of the weight of their gifts. Artists were paid to make additions, for example:

> P^{d} Brown for ye coats of Arms of ye Plates wch were sold, in ye vellum Book 5*s.*
>
> *Audit Book, 1694*

The Vellum Book continues down to 1743, but in later years is a catalogue of accessions; some of the pieces are still extant. It records 190 donors. It comprises most of the major disposals, but some pieces known from other sources are not in it: either the donors had no coat-armour, or the College forgot to enter them in the blank spaces which were left.

I have only once (p. 68) heard of a piece disposed of by the College coming to light again. Most were indelibly marked with the College's ownership. Although there was a second-hand trade in silver[12] it could be embarrassing, even dangerous, to be found with somebody else's plate. The silversmith who valued his neck would have converted it at once into an anonymous ingot. However, the College in *c*.1756 bought two huge tankards, on one of which the owner's name, clumsily erased, is still almost legible (§10.1.6). (See also the Bateman Salver of 1728, §13.4.)

Disposals declined in the 18th century, and are last heard of in 1852. A hard-and-fast distinction between gifts of plate and gifts of money had become established. The objects themselves lasted longer: they were more robust and seem to have been better treated. For example, in 1722 we melted down various objects, 60 to 90 years

9 EH Brown & SV Hopkins 1956 'Seven centuries of the prices of consumables, compared with builders' wage-rates' *Economica* **23** 296–313.

10 CC(A): Chapter-book II, 12 Jan. 1637/8.

11 CC(L): MS 490.

12 Glanville (1990) p. 75.

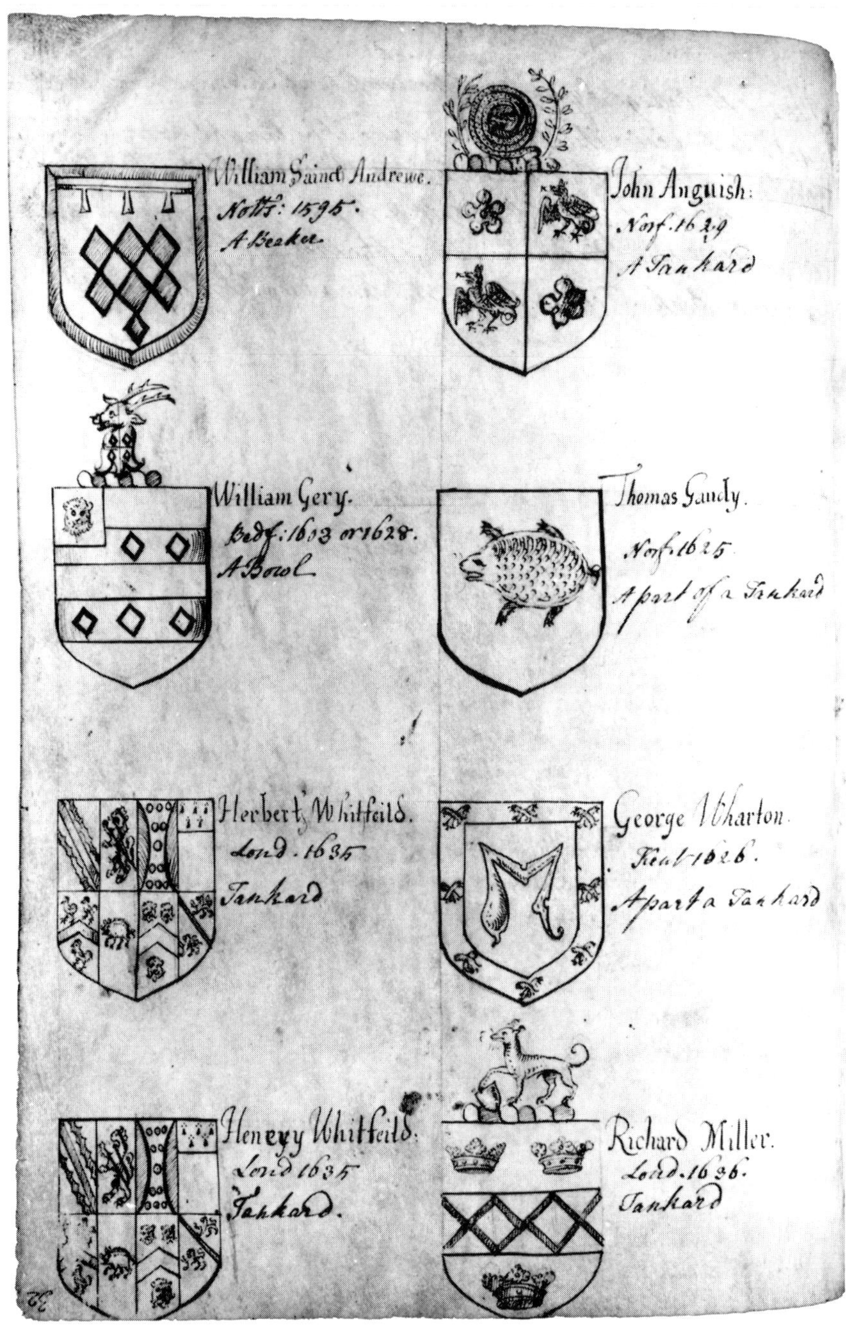

A page from the Vellum Book, recording the coats-of-arms on plate given by Fellow-Commoners and then melted down. The notes, added later by Robert Masters, College historian, are copied from contemporary records of the gifts. The beast at second right is the tortoise of the Gawdys, familiar to the writer in his childhood at Redenhall, Norfolk.

old, into twelve mugs. One of these lasted 3 years, one 51 years, four 57 years, one 110 years, and the remaining five are still in good condition after 279 years.

Plate as inalienable

The practice of melting plate becomes understandable as a combination of flimsy construction, rough treatment, the high value of the metal, and the difficulty of raising money on credit. The practice tailed off in the 18th and 19th centuries as these conditions ceased to operate. Much earlier, however, it did not apply to all plate.

The statutes of Bishop Fox, founder of Corpus Christi College, Oxford, in 1517 laid down that his and others' gifts of plate were not a mere asset but part of the College itself. He 'distinctly' forbade their ever leaving the college except to be repaired. His successors have faithfully carried out that charge; no ideology, hardship, or threat from the beleaguered Charles I moved them; and they still have his crozier, gold chalice and paten, rings, saltceller, etc. etc.

At Corpus, Cambridge, the greater effect of the Reformation tends to obscure the developing sense of the antiquarian value of plate. Matthew Parker (Chapter 7) emphasized that in giving us plate he was giving us the actual objects, not their value, and devised stringent conditions to prevent us from melting or pawning them. Shortly after his time the ancient Horn and Swan Mazer began to be respected as symbols of the College. The Horn was much used in the early 17th century, to judge by its frequent repair. The College treated Parker's gifts with respect, even those not protected by covenants (p. 70), and kept them out of the Civil War (p. 102).

There developed a separation between relatively short-lived everyday items and the 'great plate' as an integral and permanent part of the college. This was not confined to Corpus. In the Civil War colleges gave the King their broken cups and obsolete lids, and hid their greatest treasures. In the outside world there developed the idea of the *heirloom* – a treasure which a family was expected to preserve even if they fell on evil days and owned nothing else.[13]

Theft

Thefts from colleges are not new. In 1456 François Villon, four years after graduating as M.A. of the University of Paris, joined a gang who burgled the Collège de Navarre, picked the locks of two coffers (one inside the other), and extracted several hundred crowns in cash, leaving the plate. It was around Christmas, *morte saison*, when disasters happen to colleges. One of the gang, opening his mouth in a pub, let himself in for an unpleasant time helping the Bishop of Paris's police with their inquiries, but by then Villon was far, far away pursuing a third, last, brief career as a poet.[14]

Gonville & Caius College had buttery plate stolen in 1658. In 1800 there were two robberies of 2000 ounces, more than half the entire hoard. Two thieves were caught and sent down, one to Australia, one to the next world. More dramatic still was the theft of the chapel plate of Magdalen College, Oxford in 1786, and its sequel, ending in a handsome funeral for the robber.[15]

In Corpus some pewter was stolen in 1595–6; the pewterer and beadle were paid 2*s*. for recovering the swag and arresting the thieves.[16] The College's great theft was of the ancient Chapel plate; my researches date this to 1693 (p. 111), but the details remain hushed up.

Care of Plate

Cleaned Austin 1878 To 1928 50 Years

Graffito on one of the Fane Salvers

Misuse

Nearly all our plate is used, and most of it shows signs of wear, more from cleaning (see later) than from actual use. Some pieces, such as the Horn and Apostle Spoons,

13 Glanville (1990) p. 121, 57.
14 DB Wyndham Lewis 1928 *François Villon: a documented survey* Davies, London.
15 Venn **3** 133; Gunning **2** 128, 268; Jones, *Magdalen*, p. 3.
16 CC(A): Audit Book p. 73.

display identifiable signs of past misuse (pp. 33, 84). Another type of ill-treatment has left a multitude of little triangular pits all over the inside of many 15th- to 17th-century cups and bowls. Until some reader offers a better theory, I shall conjecture that this is the work of a young Fellow-Commoner chasing a small frog with the point of a dagger, and shall term it ***frog-poking.***

Repairs

The earliest recorded repair is in 1388, when the College spent 4*d*. on 'mending a basin and dish', probably among the vessels in Northwode's inventory.[17] The Horn was mended in 1558, the first recorded of many repairs, though probably not the earliest of those visible on the object itself (p. 36ff.).

College audit books record plate repairs from 1576 onwards, sometimes in general terms, but often specifically:

> [1599–1600] It to Peter Mienly for souldering Mr Courtneys pott 16d
> It for souldering & making cleane Mr Henrys pott 16d
> It for boyling colouring & making cleane 3 beakers Mr St Andrewes Bufkins Whiples 18d
> [1600–1] It to Peter Mieux for setting th'ear on a pot 18d
> for mending a crackt spoon, & a salt 6d

Four of the five objects mended in 1599 had been in the College's hands for only four years. The 'colouring' may mean re-gilding, evidently a routine operation.

Peter Muser, Mieux, Mienly – how *did* he spell his name? – was a Cambridge goldsmith who worked for the College from 1596 to 1627. His most elaborate commission was making the base of the Swan Mazer (p. 57); he probably made the plaque with the College arms on the Horn (p. 38).

Once (in 1614) is it explained why plate needed mending:

> Pd to Peter Muser for mending plate broken by y[e] fall of y[e] beame in M[r] pr[e]s[ident's] chamber 10*s*. 8*d*.[18]

We are not told whether the beam fell because the building was being repaired or because it had not been repaired.

In 1580–1 the College employed goldsmiths called George and Welles. One Erlin or Urlin worked for the College from 1713 to 1722,[19] and one York around 1750.

In the early and mid 17th century plate repairs were far commoner than now; in an average year they cost about 8*s*. My suspicion falls on the numbers and youth of Gentlemen Fellow-Commoners, high-spirited teenagers, careless when heated with ale (pp. 98f.). After 1650 repairs rapidly diminish and become more erratic, several years with none being followed by a big item: the Fellow-Commoners are known to have become more studious and the tankards heavier and more robust. For the last 150 years, as we have seen, plate has been stronger and more gently used, and has needed less repair.

One can seldom identify documented repairs, because the items were later melted down. Thomas Steward, Fellow-Commoner, gave in 1626 a delicate little tankard weighing only 11½ ounces, which was not up to the rough-and-tumble of Corpus High Table. It was repaired six times between 1635 and 1647, remained in use throughout the Civil War, and melted away in 1648.

Of the five surviving Jacobean objects, two have missing parts and one shows repair of unknown date. However, Peter Muser was paid to mark plate as well as mend it, and his hand can be recognized in inscriptions and coats-of-arms on all five (pp. 104–9).

Cleaning and abrasion

The Keeper of Plate is most often asked 'Where is it kept?' After giving a politely evasive answer, he is next asked 'How is it cleaned?'

Silver reacts with hydrogen sulphide to produce black silver sulphide. In the olden days, when eggs, things piled up outside the kitchen door, the College dunghills, 'ye ffellowes house of easement', and 'ye Schollers boggarts' contributed H_2S to the Cambridge atmosphere, the plate would inevitably have been black, unless it was gilded. Occasionally pieces were professionally cleaned by the goldsmith.

Cleaning silver – especially of the Britannia standard – is destructive and is best avoided. Traditional cleaners are gently abrasive, using whiting (calcium carbonate) or

17 CC(A): *Registrum Accounts 1376–1484* f.110.
18 CC(A): *Audits 1590–1678* p. 256.
19 Known as a manufacturer from 1698 onwards: Jackson p. 342.

rouge (one of the iron oxides) applied on a brush or soft cloth, and rubbed 'until it got hot', as a very conscientious former Butler is said to have remarked. Such vigorous treatment wears and distorts the metal, and clogs the pattern of engraving or *repoussé*.

Some cultures, particularly in Eastern Europe, never clean silver and regard black as its proper colour. This may have been so in medieval and Renaissance north-west Europe, where pictures often show silver in use as blackish. In the College cleaning may have been reserved for special occasions, as this item suggests:

> ffor scowringe ye plate at midsum' comencm^{t} 8*d*.
>
> *Audit Book 1575–6*

Our earliest non-gilded piece, the Ostrich Egg of 1592, shows no sign of having been cleaned, whereas the Berners Tankard of 1698 and most of its successors are badly abraded. Cleaning was particularly active in the 18th and 19th centuries. It was not normally done by the Butler. Many of those who worked at it, like Herman Austin, signed their names on salvers (pp. 172f.).

How do the original weights of articles compare with what they weigh now? Original weights may be inscribed on the piece by the maker, or added as graffiti, or recorded in archives. Comparison is possible with 65 articles, ranging in date from 1547 to 1926, but predominantly of the 18th century, omitting any with signs of mending or deliberate alteration. Forty-five have lost weight and only sixteen have apparently gained: on average a piece is now 2% lighter than when it was made.

Tankards, mugs, salvers, and spoons have typically lost 2–6% of their inscribed or graffito weight during the 200 years or so that they were cleaned. (The Butler Salver is an exception: its late date (1926) means that it can have had very little abrasive cleaning.) Occasionally a series of graffiti records a progressive loss of metal, as on the Bateman Salver of 1728 (§13.4), which has lost nearly 7%. The losses are not due to use: they are not concentrated on areas most exposed to wear, but are all over the visible surface. The disappearance of one-twentieth of a millimetre of metal from the surface of a salver or an inkstand is quite enough to lose crisp detail and reduce an inscription to a collection of dots and dashes. (Inscriptions on the underside, which was not cleaned, retain their sharp outlines.) The Burnet Salts (§16.2) have lost 15% of their original weight, and it shows.

Ceremonial cups, which were seldom used, show little systematic loss. Coffee-pots may even show gains, because deposits encrusting the inside outweigh the metal abraded from the outside. Ancient gilt plate shows no consistent loss of metal, for it too was not destructively cleaned; the variations may be due to rough-and-ready methods of weighing, or to heavy re-gilding.

Matters are different now, both with changes in the atmosphere and with the invention of liquid cleaners which dissolve silver sulphide without abrasion. (Items

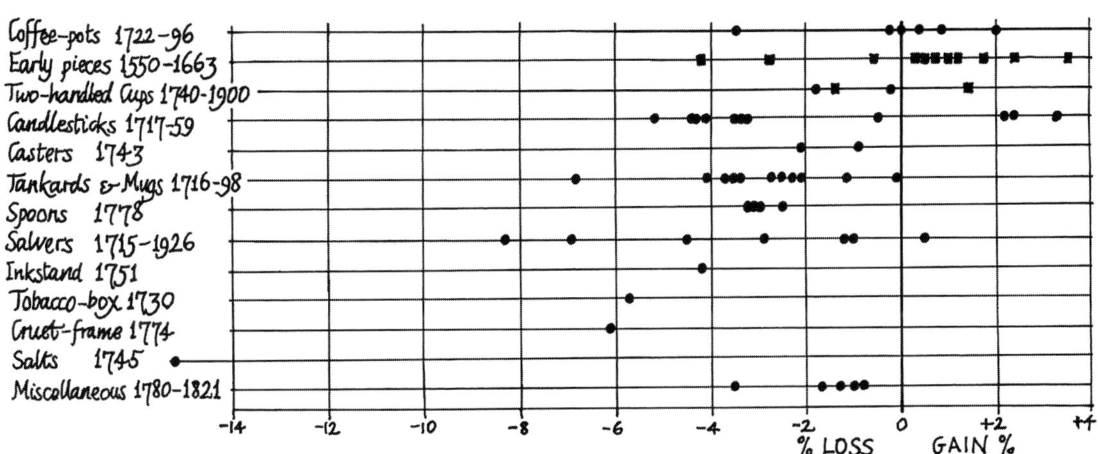

Loss or gain of metal (derived from comparing present weight with inscribed or archival weight) from different kinds of artefact, as a function of date of manufacture. Squares are for gilt pieces.

seldom used are stored in airtight polythene bags.) The 1930s inventory recorded all the inscriptions on spoons and forks which could then be read. Sixty years on, they are no worse: I can now read all those inscriptions and have deciphered a few then given up as unreadable.

Exhibitions

The first known public display was at the Archaeological Institute's meeting in Trinity College in 1854, when 'the gold plate of Caius, Corpus & Christs looked very beautiful'.[20] Another exhibition, with a notable catalogue by J.E. Foster and T.D. Atkinson, was held in the Fitzwilliam Museum in 1895.

Other exhibitions include:

Goodhart Rose-water Bowl and Beaker at the World's Fair in New York in 1940.

Swan Mazer at 'Treasures of Cambridge', Goldsmiths' Hall, 1959.

Burgess Coffee-pot at 'Hall-Mark RCA', exhibition of work by former students of the Royal College of Art, 1966.

Stanley Flagon and Paten at 'Haags silver uit vijf eeuwen', The Hague, 1967.

Ogle and Gough Cups and Serpent Candlesticks at the British Week in Tokyo, 1969: they came back damaged, but probably not by the Japanese.[21]

Several pieces among the 'Treasures of Cambridge' at the Fitzwilliam and the Victoria & Albert Museum in 1975.

Rose Mazer at 'Touching Gold & Silver: 500 years of hallmarks', Goldsmiths' Hall, 1978.

Swan Mazer at 'The Goldsmith & The Grape', Goldsmiths' Hall, 1983.

Heathcote Coffee-pot and Rigby Candlesticks at the Paul de Lamerie exhibition, 1990.

Horn and Swan Mazer at the 'Age of Chivalry' in the Royal Academy in 1987–8.

Goodhart Rose-water Bowl and Beaker in 'Metalmorphosis' (British Council exhibition of early modernistic metalwork), Prague and Berlin, 1999.

Electrotyping

The mid-19th century was a time of great technological advance, including the electrolytic method of reproducing finely detailed metal objects such as the copper plates from which maps were printed. This was patented in 1840 by George and Henry Elkington for mass-producing silver, usually in the form of a copper base plated with silver. After much publicity at the Great Exhibition of 1851, it was taken up in 1852 by the new Museum of Manufactures, precursor of the Victoria & Albert Museum, for reproducing ancient pieces. The object was educational: to enable students of design and of art history to see and handle artefacts otherwise visible, at best, only in the cases of distant museums. An international movement grew up, culminating in 1867 in a 'CONVENTION for promoting universally REPRODUCTIONS of WORKS of ART for the benefit of MUSEUMS of all COUNTRIES', signed by fifteen princes and archdukes. The Victoria & Albert Museum collaborated with the Elkingtons to build up a collection of silver and silver-gilt objects from all over Britain and Europe. They were of copper, electroplated with silver and gold, and bore a combined stamp of the Museum and Elkington's. Duplicates were distributed to other museums, and some were for sale.

The Museum began negotiations with Corpus and other colleges in 1873. In 1880 the Fellows resolved:

> A letter having been received from the Science and Art Department requesting the loan of certain pieces of antique College plate for the purpose of their being reproduced by the Electrotype process, it was agreed to accede to the request . . .[22]

The work was swift: the Rosewater Basin and Ewer were away from the College for only four days. Other pieces copied, according to the Museum's register list, were the Horn, Cup of the Three Kings, Great Parker Cup,

20 Romilly p. 182.

21 G. Bushnell's correspondence file 23 Dec. 1969.

22 Governing Body minutes, 27 Feb. 1880.

Parker Salt, four Apostle Spoons, and the Champernowne, Jegon, Ogle, and Johnson Cups. The Ostrich Egg was sent to the Victoria & Albert Museum for repair, apparently as a *quid pro quo*. Between 1882 and 1904 the College authorized duplicates of certain pieces to be made for the Metropolitan Museum of Art and for Salford, Preston, Plymouth, and Dundee Museums, but refused permission for Sheffield, Bradford, and Birmingham.[23] In 1914 a facsimile of the Parker Salt was presented to M.R. James in appreciation of his cataloguing the Parker Manuscripts.[24] Mr Roger F. Gardiner tells me of a copper-gilt replica of the Rosewater Basin in Ontario, Canada, so it looks as though one of the electrotypes got away. Some electrotypes are the earliest known representations of historic pieces, giving valuable evidence for the history of damage and alteration.

Interest in electrotypes did not last. It became unfashionable for design students to be inspired by Elizabethan plate; book illustrations gave a better impression of the real thing; and some originals became accessible through international exhibitions and easier foreign travel.

Electrotypes are not quite the exact copy of the original that they were claimed to be. The metal was electrolytically deposited in a mould in a cold version of the casting process.[25] The V&A's copy of the Parker Salt is thicker and heavier than the original. It reproduces the details, including the fine pin-pricked incription and the reverse of the *repoussé* work on the inside (though the hallmarks have been deleted, as was customary). However, they have been touched up with files and chisels, giving a very different appearance from the original. The component parts, compared with the original, are crudely soldered together; the holes of the pepper-pot have never been pierced. A thick clumsy layer of gold replaces the translucent gilding of the original.

Aubrey Bateman

By far the greatest modern donor of plate was Aubrey Bateman (1865–1954). A Herefordshire man, he was a Corpus undergraduate in the 1890s. He settled in Bath in 1923, and rose to be its eloquent and popular Mayor; indeed he was Mayor six times. He saw Bath through evil days in World War II, moved the Royal United Hospital to more spacious premises, and restored the Pump Room to its ancient glory.

Bateman was a remarkably generous benefactor to the College. His chief legacy was to the Chapel, out of which the present organ was built in 1968. He bequeathed also the magnificent furniture now in the Master's Lodge, and most of his plate to be used in the Master's Lodge or at High Table.

The Bateman plate is a family collection, hoarded from several branches of his ancestors going back to the early 18th century. Their heraldry is diverse: the commonest emblem is the badge or crest of a pheasant – or part of a pheasant – with the motto NEC PRECE NEC PRETIO (Not for love or money).

23 Registers and Correspondence of the Metalwork Department, Victoria & Albert Museum. S Bury 1971 *Victorian Electroplate* Country Life, London pp. 46ff. I am indebted to Ann Eatwell of the Metalwork Department for her most helpful assistance.

24 Bury p. 134.

25 Or it could be directly deposited on the original object, for example by a villain seeking to turn his girl-enemy into a silver sofa: see Dorothy L. Sayers, *The Abominable History of the Man with Copper Fingers*.

4

The Great Horn or Bugle

But mine horn shall be exalted like the horn of the wild-ox.

Psalm **92** 10

Save me from the lion's mouth: thou has heard me also from among the horns of the wild-oxen.

Psalm **22** 21
[The classic translations have 'unicorn', following a misunderstanding in the Septuagint.]

One great horn, in English *bugel*, with silver-gilt feet, and a silver-gilt head of an emperor on the tail, with a silver lid at the top of which are four gilt acorns.

John Northwode's inventory of College plate, c.1385
[*the words* anglice bugel *are added as an afterthought*]

Are there materials sufficient to fabricate an Essay on this Horn?

Letter of Michael Tyson, Fellow, to Richard Gough, 1772(Lamb p. 409)
[*Yes, there were: see p. 41*]

At the high table they drank ale out of the great horn & Blunt clumsily deluged his neighbour Mr Mould (who had to go out – so wet was he). Whewell made them all roar by saying that Blunt if he didn't moisten his clay yet had wetted the mould . . .

Quincentenary feast, 1852 (Romilly pp. 123–4)

The Corpus Horn (Plate 1) is the oldest and most romantic treasure of either Cambridge or Oxford. Founders and benefactors and most of the College's members have drunk from it; it is the horn of a majestic extinct animal; it was won with valour; it links us with the Gilds our predecessors, and farther back with Anglo-Saxon kings and with Iron Age tribes in the remote forests of Central Europe, who drank from such horns at their feasts – we are the only tribe that still does so.

The horn – a left horn – is golden brown in colour, blackish towards the tip, with minute streaks giving a beautiful silky sheen. It has four silver-gilt mounts: a *brim* round the mouth; a *plaque* with the College's arms; a *band* round the middle with two legs and feet, and with two rings on the band; and a *finial* in the shape of a bearded head wearing a curious pointed crown.[1] Mysterious dark patches are the ghosts of earlier silver mounts now lost, like the indents of missing brasses in the floor of a church. On the underside are about sixty curious pits, which Paula Hardwick, expert on horns and horning, identifies as gnawed by a particular weevil which attacks horn when set down on a damp surface.

It measures as follows:

	inches	cm
Whole object, measured round the outside of the curve from tip to mouth	28.5	72.3
Similar measurement of interior from end to mouth	21.4	54.5
Across the chord from tip to the front of the mouth	18.5	47
Height standing on table	11.1	28.4
Circumference at mouth	13.5	34
Horn only, measured round outside of curve	c.26.5	c.68
Inside diameter below mouth	3.9	9.8
Thickness of horn		0.4

The horn holds 3.26 English pints = 1.85 litres.

1 Its shape has been likened to 'an amphibian crawling out of the slime on to dry land': P Stone 1961 'Some famous drinking-horns in Britain' *Apollo* April 101–3, May 143–5.

Table 4.1. *Dimensions of subfossil aurochs horn-cores*

Locality	Length round outside of curve, cm	Length across chord, cm	Girth at base, cm	Diameter of base, cm	Museum of Zoology no.
Barrington, gravel	82	54	35	10 × 11½	H29038
Barrington, gravel	?	?	35	9½ × 11½	H29039
Quy Water, clay under peat	*c*.69	*c*.45	33½	8½ × 11½	H29050
'Fens'	*c*.73	?	32½	10 × 11	H29042
'Fens'	?	?	30	8 × 11	H29045
Wicken Fen skeleton	59	43	29½	8½ × 10	H29021
Corpus Horn (inside measurement)	54.5	46	31½	9.9 × 9.8	
Hertford Castle (biggest of 39 cores of *c*.1700)	>44	?	28½		

What Is It?

The Horn has been described variously as ox, aurochs, or buffalo. Water buffalo horns can be excluded, being single-curved and flattened along their length. Bison horns are single-curved and abruptly tapering. This leaves aurochs and domestic cattle.

The aurochs, *Bos primigenius*, was the wild-ox of most of Europe and beyond in Pleistocene times. After the last ice age it came back to England, where the Mesolithic people of Star Carr (east Yorkshire) ate it, but it died out by the Bronze Age. By Roman times it was confined to Germany and farther east. The last survivors were emparked at Jaktorów near Warsaw, where the very last aur-cow died in 1627.

How is the aurochs, *Bos primigenius*, different from the tame bull, *Bos taurus*? The answer will never be certain, because domestic cattle (and the mysterious 'wild' park cattle, like those of Chillingham) are descended from aurochs; they are not really a separate species. Up to a point they can be separated on size, shape, and possibly colour. Aurochsen had much larger horns than cattle; only a few breeds rival them in size, such as the South African ox (from which modern great horns come) and unusual horns of the Texas Longhorn.[2] All the apparent aurochs horns are brown or yellowish; big ox-horns often have black and white patterns.

A cow's or aurochs's horn is a layer of horn on the outside of a bony core, from which it can be pulled off after the animal is dead. The core is a fairly tight fit, at most a centimetre less in girth than the outside measurements of the horn. The horn, however, ends in a solid point: the last 5 inches or so of the Corpus horn are solid. Our horn is deeply scratched on the inside, probably when it was pulled off the rough horn-core.

Aurochsen once existed around Cambridge. In 1874 a complete skeleton was excavated from Wicken Fen, and can be seen in the Museum of Zoology.[3] It was a terrible animal, standing 6 feet 0 in. (1.83 m) high at the withers, much bigger than any modern bull or the Chillingham bull who stands nearby. The Museum has a number of other excavated horn-cores; those complete enough to be measured are given in Table 4.1.

These cores show the same three-dimensional curve as the Corpus horn, although it is less marked on the first 'Fens' horn. They repeat the one-sided expansion at the mouth which is characteristic of the Corpus horn. The two from Barrington and probably the one from Quy are likely to be Pleistocene in date (at least 100,000 years old). The others were found embedded in peat – they are stained black – and date from Holocene (post-glacial) times: between about 3500 BC, when peat began to form in the Fens, and 1500 BC when the animal

2 Dobie JF 1941 *The Longhorns* Little, Brown & Co, Boston (Mass.) ch. 12.

3 It is labelled 'Drainer's Ditch, Burwell'; there seems to be no Drainer's Ditch in Burwell, but there is a Drainers' Dyke in Wicken Fen adjacent.

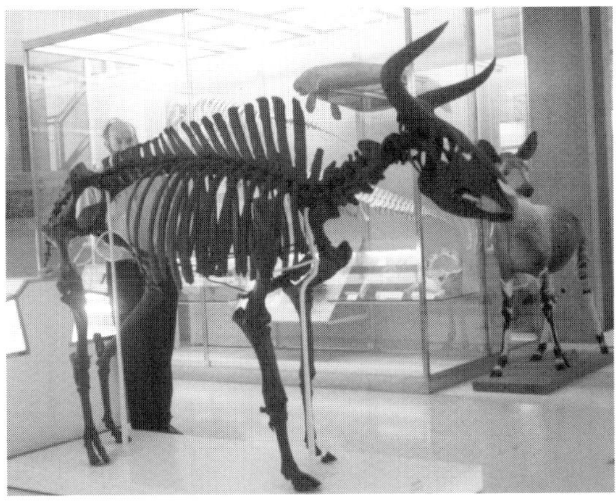

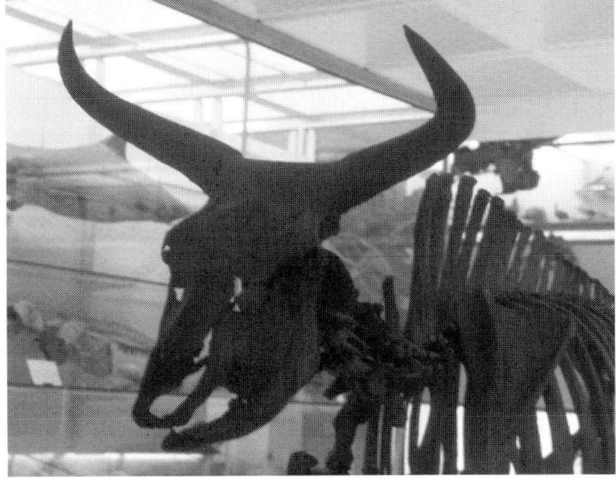

The Wicken Fen aurochs compared with a 6-foot man

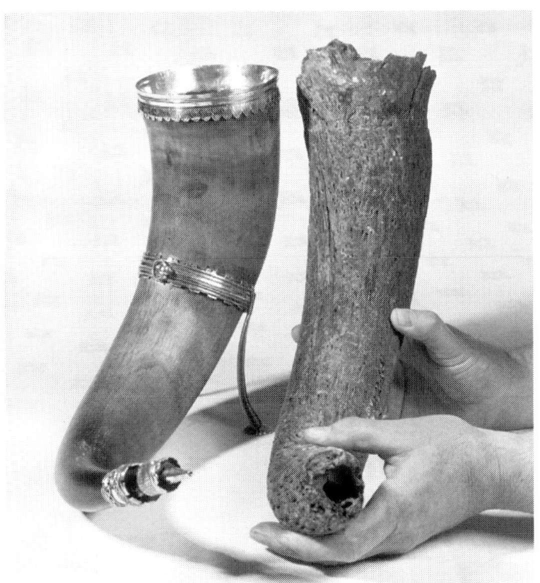

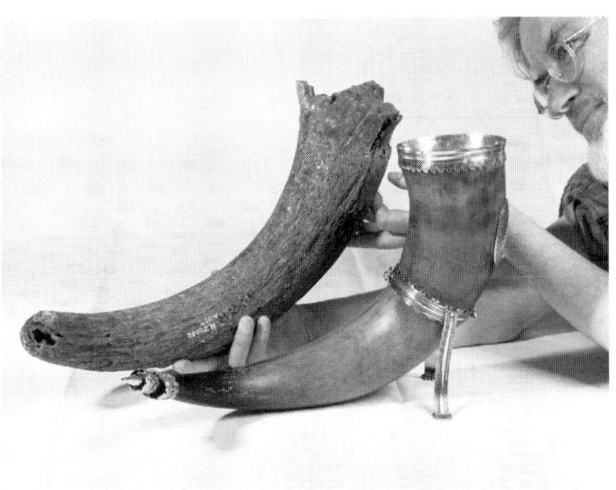

The Horn compared with a prehistoric (Holocene) aurochs horn-core

became extinct in England. The Wicken specimen has a radiocarbon date corresponding to Late Neolithic, 3000 BC.[4]

4 D Yalden 1999 *History of British Mammals* Poyser Natural History, London.
J Clutton-Brock 1986 'New dates for old animals: the reindeer, the aurochs, and the wild horse in prehistoric Britain' *Archaeozoologia, Mélanges* 111–17.

The Corpus horn is a remarkably good fit in size and shape to Holocene aurochs horn-cores from the Fens; it is a little smaller than the Wicken Fen aurochs's. Pleistocene horns from earlier interglacials were distinctly bigger.

A wider set of data was assembled when the drinking-horns from Sutton Hoo were identified. Horns from Holocene male aurochsen ranged from 25.7 to 39.5 cm circumference at the base, 43.3 to 84.5 cm long along the outer curve. Females were smaller.[5] On the criteria used at Sutton Hoo, therefore, the Corpus horn is definitely from an aur-bull, a little below average size.

Domestic cattle horns are rarely as big as the Corpus horn. A dump of hornworker's waste, dated *c*.1700, has been excavated at Hertford Castle. Out of 39 horn-cores the biggest is smaller than ours.[6] Big horns, most useful to horners, came from a proto-longhorn breed which is depicted with single-curved horns.

Prehistoric horn-cores are elliptical at the base, whereas our horn is round. This may not be significant: a horner could easily have bent the heated horn into a circular section.[7]

Medieval England knew little of the aurochs, which was called a *bugle:*

> The bugle . . . is yliche [like] to an oxe and is a fers [fierce] beste . . . in Germania beth wild oxen with so large hornes that the kynges bord is y-serued with drynke therof.
>
> *John Trevisa, translating (1398) Bartholomæus Anglicus's 13th-century Latin treatise* De Proprietatibus Rerum, XVIII. xv.

It became confused with water-buffalo and other bovines: 'A thousand bugles of Ynde [India]'.[8] Our horn was called a bugle into the 17th century.

The Silver Parts

The finial

This is the only silver mount universally regarded as original. A bearded, moustachio'd head, with slit eyes, sunken cheeks, and long lanky hair, wears a crown with a spiked top. He looks out of a tower, and has been interpreted as a watchman. He resembles, especially in hairstyle, Louis IX's statue at Manneville (Eure), *c*.1307.[9]

The finial was made of ten components joined with silver solder: spike, crown (2 parts), head, neck, tower (2 parts), stem, and base, plus a missing bobble on the very end. Tower and base have battlements and pierced quatrefoils. They are usually supposed to be all contemporary. All parts are single-gilt, with rather variable density of gilding. How the finial was originally attached is not clear, since there are few glues that work well with both silver and horn. At some time the joint at the base of the tower has been crudely mended with ordinary lead solder. For a time a screw was botched through one of the quatrefoils.

Bands of quatrefoils are a 13th-century architectural feature (e.g. west front of Salisbury Cathedral, *c*.1260), although they may be later on the Continent. The work shows none of the devices of late-medieval composite vessels: in particular it joins on to the horn by battlements, not by an engrailed fringe.

Paula Hardwick claims that the seven parts differ in style and in the quality of the silver, and interprets this as meaning that only the base is certainly original, all the other parts being possible later replacements.[10] But if this were true, the replacement parts ought to betray the period at which the alteration was done and to be inconsistent with the original – as are other silver mounts of the horn. Since this inconsistency is barely detectable, it would date the alteration very soon after the original was made. For some reason the finial would have been drastically and skilfully altered in the first few decades of its life, and then merely patched up during the next 650 years. I propose instead that it is all original, the slight inconsistencies representing different batches of metal and the varying skills of the workmen who made the different parts.

The brim

This, often supposed to be of Elizabethan date, is made from a strip of metal with a moulding. The lower half is split on either side of the horn, and has a distinctive

5 W Oddy & C Grigson in Bruce-Mitford pp. 406–8.
6 P Armitage 1978 'Hertfordshire cattle and London meat markets in the 17th and 18th centuries' *London Archaeologist* **3** 217–23.
7 For hornworking see P Hardwick 1981 *Discovering Horn* Lutterworth, Guildford.
8 *Kyng Alisaunder* (undated romance) line 5103.
9 MW Labarge 1968 *Saint Louis* Eyre & Spottiswoode, London.
10 Letter to O. Rackham, 7 Feb. 1982.

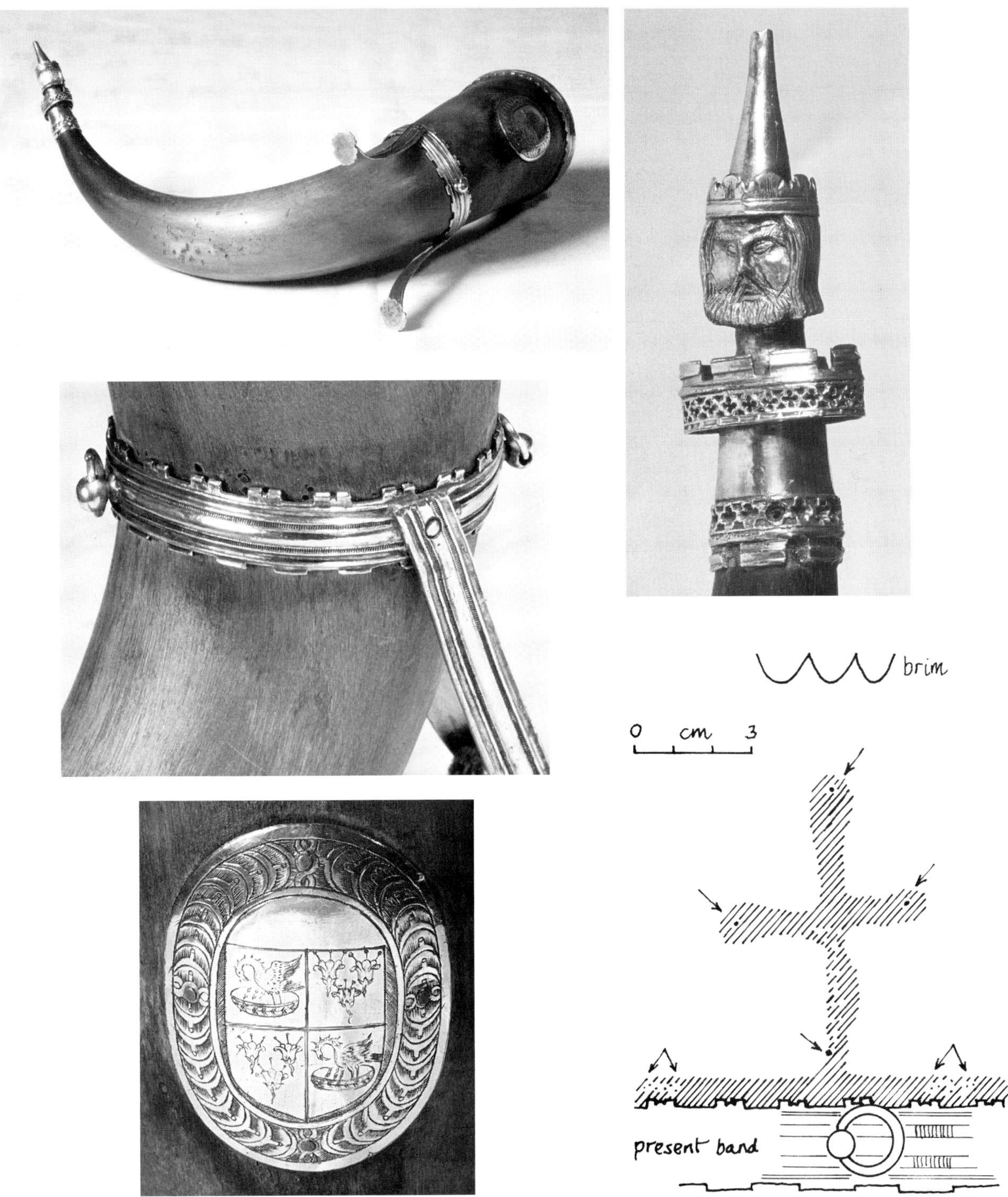

The Horn (note weevil-pits on the underside), its finial, band, and plaque.
The ghost of a former band and attachment is drawn as if flattened out. The arrows point to nail-holes.

fringe, a margin engrailed (cut into rounded lobes) and engraved (p. 56). Four rivets through lobes of the fringe pass through the horn and the interior part of the brim. Fringes are typically found, as here, where silver joins another material; they are a means of making a watertight join against a slightly irregular surface. They are typical of the period 1400 to 1550; they are absent, for example, from the Swan Mazer (earlier) and the Ostrich Cup (later).

The brim might thus be a late-medieval replacement. However, its fringe closely resembles (though at a larger scale) the crown of the finial. The details are similar, and are cut with similar tools and to a minute standard of craftsmanship. The fringes of the 15th- and 16th-century mazers are different: even the Cup of the Three Kings shows comparatively slovenly detail (p. 56). I am persuaded that the workshop that produced the crown also made the fringe. If the finial is late 13th century, as the features of the head and the tracery indicate, then so is the brim. (The triangles may even be a last echo of the mouthpiece triangles of the Taplow and Sutton Hoo horns, p. 42.) Over a century elapses before the next surviving datable fringe, but so few examples remain from this interval that this gap is not conclusive.

The brim is double-gilt; probably it has been re-gilded, since there is little wear on the gilding.

The band and feet

The band is silver single-gilt, with a moulding which looks mass-produced by extruding it through a rolling-mill, rather as lead cames (the H-section bars which hold the glass in a stained-glass window) are made. On either side are vestigial battlements, made by sawing notches in the metal. Two of the hollow mouldings are knurled inside with a series of little grooves, whose irregular spacing shows that they were cut by hand. On the band are two pierced knobs with silver rings. Riveted to the band are two legs, lengths of the same moulded strip but without the battlements; they end in two cast rosettelike feet. The rings are awkwardly placed either for attaching a lid or for a strap to hang the horn, as other horns have. However they have been much used, for the holes in the knobs which carry them are enlarged by wear (just as the holes in the strap-lugs of a camera get worn).[11]

Under the band, and projecting beyond it on one side, is the ghost – in the form of a brown discoloration – of an earlier band, probably a wide band such as other medieval horns have. In the part which is now visible are three groups of holes in the horn, evidently for tiny nails which attached the original band: one brass nail still remains. The nails (which do not go through the horn) are irregularly placed: it would seem that the band often worked loose and needed re-nailing. (Numerous nails are characteristic of pre-1350 mazers, p. 63.) The ghost projects upwards towards the mouth of the horn in the form of an asymmetrical three-lobed extension, with a tiny rivet (passing through the horn) in each lobe. This was presumably an ornamental or heraldic feature connected with whoever first commissioned the horn.

The present apparatus of band and legs looks like a clumsy repair reusing medieval material from some other object. The battlements are in the style of those on the Founder's Cup at Trinity Hall, said to be *c.*1350.

The 'two feete' are mentioned in the 1573/4 inventory. In 1609 Peter Muser, the College goldsmith, was paid 5*s*. 6*d*. 'for mendinge the foote of the horne'.[12]

The plaque

The double-gilt plaque, attached by four rivets through the horn, has the College arms in a decorative border. The arms prove it to be of Parker's time or later (p. 22). They are of the standard type – lively pelican and nondescript lilies – deriving from the original grant of arms. The shield is an ordinary Elizabethan to Jacobean shape. The most distinctive feature is the border motif, which I shall call a scale-chain. Scale-chains occur on several other pieces dated between 1562 and 1608 (pp. 78, 104, 106, 108). (They seem to be rare outside Corpus and are not well known to writers on plate.)

The plaque could well be the work of Peter Muser the Cambridge goldsmith, who did major repairs to the Horn in 1615 (p. 41).

11 The amount of wear tells against the theory that the rings were for attaching knick-knacks like those hung on the straps of other horns (Oman 1972, above).

12 CC(A): *Audit Book 1590–1608* p. 222.

History of the Corpus Horn

The Horn, as we shall see, was always a mysterious and mystic object. How did such a very rare artefact, the drinking-vessel of kings, come into the treasury of a society of poor scholars?

It is first mentioned in the earliest College inventory, in the part written by John Northwode in *c*.1385 (pp. 48, 276). The Horn was among those objects which had no remembered donors, and which therefore were presumably inherited from the Gild of St Mary.

Where did it come from?

If it is an aurochs horn, it would have come from Poland or perhaps Germany, where aurochsen still remained in the middle ages.

Dr Charles Oman, the great historian of silver, claimed that its provenance turns on whose head is represented on the little end. In the 14th century John Northwode thought it was an emperor; in modern times it has been conjectured to be Edward III, king when the College was founded. In 1971 Peter Hawker, keeper of the treasury of Lincoln Cathedral, identified the headgear – a crown with a tall conical finial – as a medieval form of Papal tiara, and the figure as the early pope Cornelius.[13] The many 'portraits' of Popes in the 15th-century Book of Benefactors of St Alban's Abbey, in the Parker Library, are shown wearing such a crown, but with a knob or bobble at the top. The point of the crown on the Horn has been broken off, but could easily have been such a bobble.[14]

If this is a Pope's head, then which Pope? The patron of horns was St Cornelius. He was a controversial figure, a colleague of St Cyprian, elected Pope in the dark days of AD 251, during a lull in Decius's persecution. After one year, in which he managed to excommunicate the hardliner Novatian, persecution resumed and he was sent down to Civitavecchia, where he died of natural causes. He acquired a miraculous

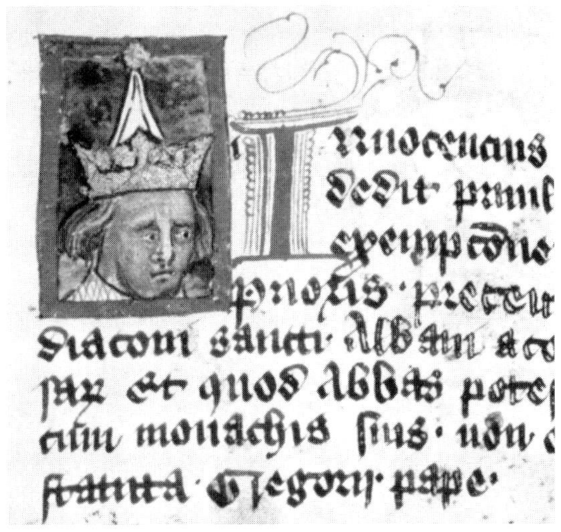

Pope Innocent IV, from the Benefactors' Book of St Alban's Abbey (CC(L): MS 7 f.210)

horn in this way:

> . . . S. Cornelius's horn is preserved in S. Cornelius's monastery [Cornelimünster]; the feverish are in the habit of drinking from it, and many of them are given health. From which it is the custom for the likeness of the Saint to be painted or sculpted with a horn inserted into his hand . . . In [his manuscript] Life a crude fable is told about a gryphon. . . . [In Civitavecchia] *a gryphon, a great bird, came to him suffering from something like the falling sickness, which the Saint cured, praying first. The gryphon, feeling himself healed, shook off one of his claws and left it with S. Cornelius by way of thanks; he then used it for a drinking-vessel, and is painted with it.*
>
> *Acta Sanctorum, 14 September, p. 186a,* §298

The falling sickess was epilepsy – a serious matter in ancient Rome, since (like foot-and-mouth disease in 2001) it prevented anyone else from doing public business. For the reward to be practical, a griffin or gryphon should have been about the size of the largest dinosaur. (For the natural history of griffins see the Ostrich Cup, p. 92).

Cornelius had been a perfectly good family name in ancient Rome, but later became associated with horns (Latin *cornu*). In the 8th century passing Franks translated the Pope's head and an arm beyond the Alps to be relics in Cornelimünster, six miles from their capital city

13 Oman C 1972 'Cambridge and Cornelimünster' *Aachener Kunstblätter* **43** 305–7.
Bushnell GHS 1973 'The Corpus Horn' *LCA* **52** 28–30.

14 The first Pope to wear three crowns was apparently Clement VI (1342–52).

of Aachen (Aix-la-Chapelle).[15] The rest of him ended a hundred miles away in Ronse, west of Brussels. He was the patron saint of epileptics (though not so good as the nearby Three Kings of Cologne), and his minster became a minor place of pilgrimage. Catherine Hall tells me that he is still venerated in Belgium and Luxemburg, and always shown with a horn. He was not well known in England, though there is said to be a St Cornely in Cornwall.

Griffins'-claw horns were widely known. Edward III had 'un corn de griffon pour boir' garnished with gilt copper. Charles VI of France had one with two bird feet, like the Queen's College and Christ's Hospital horns. A 16th-century cow-horn from Mainz proclaims **Ich bin ein Greiffen clo** ['I am a griffin's claw'] on the brim; it was, of course, made for the von Greiffenclau family.[16] In 1640 a griffin's claw 15 inches long and 12 inches in girth (smaller than ours) was among the chief treasures of St Cornelius's church, Compiègne.[17] Another, identified as a 'buffalo horn', presumably water-buffalo, lies in the treasury of Brunswick Cathedral, the gift of the hero Henry the Lion.[18] Two griffin's claws are used as vessels for holy oils in Györ Cathedral, Hungary.[19]

The Horn and the Gilds

The possibility is that our horn was originally a present from Cornelimünster or Aachen, which was noted for goldsmithing and not too far from the source of aurochsen. From stylistic comparisons I would settle for a date in the late 13th century.

Northwode did not know who gave the Horn, for the Gild had faded away by 1385. However John Josselyn, Matthew Parker's secretary, writing *c.*1569, thought he knew:

> John de Goldcorne, who in his time was Alderman of the said Gild [the united Gild of Corpus Christi and the Virgin Mary], gave a great drinking-horn adorned with a lid, with its appendages of silver-gilt, which the brethren of the same Gild made use of very liberally, especially at the feast of Corpus Christi.
>
> *Historiola* §9

Until recently everyone believed this account, assuming it to be based on contemporary documents which Josselyn had seen. When the Gilds were united and the College founded in 1352, Mr Goldcorne, a Cambridge citizen, supposedly gave the united Gilds a golden horn, relic of a family visit to Cornelimünster; he himself was probably named after it.

However the College has faithfully preserved the archives of the two gilds, and Catherine Hall has re-read them. Both kept full lists of their members, especially deceased members: these had to be remembered in the gilds' prayers, and the College remembers some of them to this day. The gilds should have remembered Goldcorne, and they did not. St Mary's had been headed by an Alderman, but no Alderman is known for Corpus Christi nor for the united Gild. Goldcorne is mentioned only in a deed of 1353, in which the infant College exchanged properties with the infant Gonville Hall, now Gonville & Caius College. One of the houses had formerly been occupied by a John Goldcorne. There is no other record of his existence. Mrs Hall concludes that he was a man of straw, probably a John Doe or Richard Roe, a mere name inserted to fill the place of a tenant whose name was forgotten. His connexion with the golden horn arose in the fertile imagination of Josselyn, writing at a time when puns of that kind were fashionable.[20]

Rare though great horns were, it was just possible for a modest town gild to own one. The Gild of the Blessed Virgin Mary at Boston had a 'drynkynge horne ornate with silv' and gilte' in 1534.[21]

Later history

These splendid relics of a forgotten institution were little regarded by the College, especially after the Reformation. The chalices, the griffin's eggs, the spiceplates, the Cup of our Lady, the Cup of the Three Bears, the Beryl have gone the way of the Gild's chasuble with gold dragons and cocks, Eltisley's bedspread embroidered with a woodwose and a woodwosess, the pillow with a fiend piping and a woman trumpeting, and the quilt with 'an ape looking in an urinal'.

In the 1526 inventory the horn appears as: 'Item one great drinking horn of bugle with appendages'. This is,

15 Oman pointed out that a pope is shown wearing a pointed crown, like the finial of our horn, on Charlemagne's reliquary at Aachen.
16 BM: Waddesdon Bequest.
17 Gay, *Glossaire archéologique* s. 'Grifon'.
18 Catalogue of 1995 Exhibition on Heinrich der Löwe, 3 119. (I owe this reference to Catherine Hall.)
19 Report from E.S. Higgs to G.H.S. Bushnell, after seeing our horn.
20 Hall. 21 Cripps p. 278.

however, written in the margin in a slightly later hand. In the *c*.1544 inventory it comes at the end: 'Item a great bugle set in silver gilt'. As Catherine Hall has pointed out, these entries imply that the horn was an unfashionable piece languishing at the bottom of the common chest, minus its lid.

But a revival was coming. In the Feast Book accounts Mrs Hall found:

To ye goldsmith for mindynge of the horne xijd.

Evidently it had been used and damaged at the Corpus Christi feast in 1558.[22]

By 1573 the horn was back in pride of place as symbol of the College, as it has been ever since. It appears at the top of the inventory of 1573/4, second only to the new gift of the Parker Cup:

> Item A bugle tipped wth silver wth two feete of the same gilt.

It is similarly described in inventories down to 1670 ('A Bugle Tip & feet gilt').

Its new status resulted in much use and frequent repairs:

[1580] Georg. Goldsmith for mending the great horne 2*s*. 6*d*.
[1593] For mendinge the Colldg Horne and foure Colldg potts 8*s*. 6*d*.
[1610] To Peter Muser the Goldsmithe for mendinge the foote of the horne 5*s*. 6*d*.
[1613] To Peter Muser for mending ye horne broken at Commencement last 6*d*.
[1615] To Peter Muser for souldering & adding silver to the Coll Horne 2*s*. 6*d*.
[1615] To Peter Muser fr to gild the Coll Horne Jacob 9 22*s*.
[1615] To Peter Muser for the siluer work about the Horne after 2*s* the ounce 28*s*., and for siluer added of his owne 18*d* 29*s*. 6*d*.[23]
[1752] mending Founder's Horn 1*s*.

There is an extraordinary story from this period. The late Anthony Dent (Corpus undergraduate, 1934–7) claimed that

> At some time in the reign of James I it was stolen from the hall but found again on a rubbish-heap, stripped of its silver mounting. The present one is therefore Jacobean only. It is said that on the parts once covered by the mounting – and immediately covered with new silver on recovery – were 'rude characters'.[24]

If true, this might account for the loss of the original band, but where did the story come from? I cannot find it in any of the College histories. The three expensive repairs of 1615 might underly it, but there is nothing in the Audit Book or Chapter Book to suggest that this was the reason for them. The first and third repairs came nine months apart. The second repair has a note 'Jacob 9', apparently meaning that the work was done in 1611–12, the ninth year of King James I. These repairs presumably resulted from three different accidents.

The earliest publication of 'the venerable Horn of the Gild' is by Michael Tyson, Fellow (1767–76) in 1773, after Robert Masters's history of the College had brought the Gilds back to notice. His drawing shows it exactly as now, with bands, feet, and finial; the lid and the knob on the very tip were already missing. The one difference is that the plaque with the College arms is not shown; the text, however, says 'On the front of the large end are the arms of the College'. Detailed lithographs of 1839 show the horn as it is now, including the plaque, the broken tip of the finial, and a crude peg fastening the finial to the horn.[25]

Horns of Story and Excavation

In the Old Testament the giant wild-ox, *re'em*, symbolized strength and untameability and formidable horns. He was nearly as dangerous as a lion; in the *Book of Job* God laughs at the notion of using him to plough and cart with.[26] I doubt whether many Hebrews had seen him. The Bible says nothing about his habitat, but other evidence puts him in fens and wetland forests. The Pharaohs had hunted him in the papyrus fens. For the Assyrians he was a kingly beast of chase, hunted in the Tigris fens; as bas-reliefs show, their kings liked to be shown in mortal

22 CC(A): *Liber Communorum Bedellorum & Corporis Christi* f.33v.
23 CC(A): *Audit Book 1598–1678* p. 43, 222, 2417[*sic*], 265, 267.
24 A Dent 1974 *Lost Beasts of Britain* Harrap, London pp. 34f.
25 Tyson 1773 'Account of the Horn belonging to *Corpus Christi College, Cambridge*' *Archaeologia* **3** 19.
JJ Smith (ed) 1840 *The Cambridge Portfolio* Parker, London **1** 297f.
26 *Numbers* **23** 22; *Deuteronomy* **33** 17; *Isaiah* **34** 7; *Job* **39** 9–12.

combat with him. An aurochs was as worthy of the royal spear as the lion himself.

A famous passage in Julius Cæsar's *Gallic War* tells of the beasts of the Hercynian Wood, that dread region around modern Bayreuth and Pilsen:

> There is a third kind, which are called *urus*. These are in size a little below elephants, in appearance and colour and shape like bulls. Great is their strength and great their speed; they spare neither man nor beast whom they notice. [The natives] eagerly catch and kill them in pits. Young men harden themselves in this task and practise this kind of hunting; and whoever has killed the most of them displays the horns in public, which are a witness, and they give him great praise . . . The size of the horns and colour and appearance are very different from the horns of our oxen. These, eagerly sought for, they surround with silver on the mouths and use as cups in the grandest feasts.[27]

Cæsar went to Germany in 55 BC. He kept well clear of the Hercynian Wood, but his account rings true and agrees with everything else we know about the beast. The Wicken Fen aurochs was indeed sub-elephantine, bigger than a rhinoceros and with twice the weaponry, with tremendous shoulder muscles and probably the speed of a racehorse: it would have been a beast worth hunting. Later writers tend to give the aurochs a wider distribution, owing to confusion with big domestic bulls: we can discount the notion that St Saturninus of Toulouse was martyred by means of an aurochs.[28]

Cæsar's word *urus* is a Latinization of the Germanic *Ur*, still the German word for the animal.[29] This makes a fleeting appearance in Old English in the Runic Poem, a set of verses illustrating the runic alphabet (F is for Fee, U is for Ur, Th is for Thorn, . . .).

> U – Ur is spirited and over-horned,
> beast of much fierceness fighteth with horns
> great fen-dweller it is a proud creature.

The Runic Poem probably was based on Continental predecessors: the writer is unlikely to have seen the animal.[30]

The Anglo-Saxons prized the semi-fabulous Ur's horns and were buried with them. Three horns found with other rich grave-goods in a great barrow at Taplow, Buckinghamshire, excavated in 1883, were ornamented with intricately embossed and gilded silver triangles around the mouth and with long silver finials.[31] In the Sutton Hoo ship burial, a king of East Anglia took two great horns to the grave. They had triangle-adorned brims like the Taplow horns and wonderful bird finials, all in silver-gilt. The largest Taplow horn is 10.0 cm diameter at the mouth; the Sutton Hoo horns are 10.4 and 9.6 cm diameter[32] (the Corpus horn is 9.8 cm). They are all on display at the British Museum.

Royal drinking-horns continued through the Anglo-Saxon period. Crowland Abbey had a great horn, and forged a charter to prove that Witlaf king of Mercia (827–840) had given them

> the horn of his table, that the elders of the monastery might drink thence on feasts of saints, and in their blessings might remember now and then the soul of Witlaf the donor.

The Bayeux Tapestry shows two great horns at Harold's feast at Bosham in 1064. They are depicted with broader metal brims than ours, with similar complicated finials, without feet, and with a spot on the side which probably represents one of a pair of rings for hanging up the horn. At Easter 1067 King William drank out of them at Fécamp. In contemporary Wales, too, horns were included with cups and rings among the royal treasure.[33]

Gervase of Tilbury, judicial murderer and short-story writer of the 1210s, has a tale about the rarity and romance of drinking from a great horn, especially an ancient horn out of a barrow. After his famous story of the demon knight of Wandlebury near Cambridge, he continues:

> In the county of Gloucester there is a hunting wood, replete with boars, harts, and all manner of venison . . . In this silvan wood-pasture there was a hillock, rising to a man-high summit. Knights and other hunters were in the habit of climbing it, when they were exhausted with heat and thirst . . . But if anyone who had been abandoned by his comrades in this place and situation

27 Cæsar, *De Bello Gallico* vi.28.
28 E Griffith 1827 *The Animal Kingdom arranged in conformity with its organization by the Baron Cuvier* Whittaker, London **4** 410ff.
29 Also *Auer*; 'aurochs' seems to be an English corruption.
30 RI Page 1973 *An Introduction to English Runes* Methuen, London.
31 *Victoria County History, Buckinghamshire* **1** (1905) 200.
32 Bruce-Mitford pp. 316–47. At Sutton Hoo little remained of the horns themselves, and they had to be reconstructed from the fragmentary silver parts. An earlier restoration made them 15 cm in diameter at the mouth, bigger even than Pleistocene horns. In the present restoration they seem to be too long.
33 M Williams 1915 'Life in Wales in medieval times' *Transactions of the Honourable Society of the Cymmrodorion* (1914–15) 136–94.

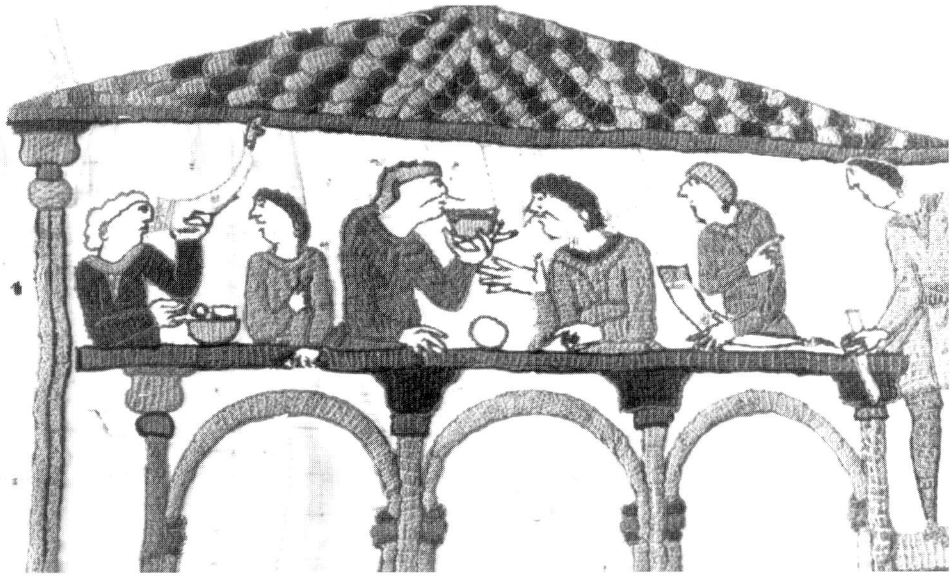

King Harold and his henchmen drinking from horns and mazers, from the Bayeux Tapestry. The lord on the left is about to get an unpleasant surprise (p. 45).

> were to say alone, as if speaking to someone else, 'I'm thirsty', immediately there would appear from the side a toastmaster of elegant appearance and humorous face. He would proffer a great horn, adorned with gold and gems, as was the custom among the most ancient English. The nectar offered was of an unknown but most delicious savour; on quaffing it all the fever and tiredness of the heated body fled away . . . But after the nectar had been drunk, the waiter would offer a napkin to dry the mouth; and having done his duty he would disappear, staying for no tip for his service nor talk for his curiosity.
>
> [After this had gone on for many years] one day a knight came hunting from that city; he asked for drink and took the horn; he did not return it to the butler as custom and politeness required, but kept it for his own use. But the illustrious lord and earl of Gloucester, discovering the truth of the matter, punished the robber, and gave the horn to . . . King Henry [I], lest he should be thought an abettor of the crime . . .[34]

Is this a real legend of the Forest of Dean, inspired by Anglo-Saxon funerary horns? One detail that gives it verisimilitude is the mention of wild swine: in the 13th century Dean was almost the only remaining haunt of them in England.

Surviving medieval horns

Medieval great horns, far rarer than mazers or even coconuts (Appendix 3), were a supreme status symbol. Roger Mortimer, murderer of King Edward II, possessed three horns of bugle. About the time the College was founded, Edward III gave John de Foxle a great gold-mounted bugle-horn, which he in turn bequeathed to Richard II. Apart from surviving examples, I have come across only ten mentioned in English wills, inventories, etc. – not counting lesser horns or those of elephant or unicorn ivory. (These include the 'great drinking-horn garnished with silver gilt' secured by Cardinal Wolsey for his short-lived St Frideswide's College, Oxford – what became of it?) There are a few others in Continental archives.[35]

Horns, like ours, became unfashionable at the end of the middle ages. Henry VIII had about 25 horns of various kinds, including three 'Antique hornes garnished with silver guilte' with baldrics. How many of these were aurochs will never be known, but by the end of this reign

34 *Otia Imperialia* lx.

35 CC Oman 1944 'English medieval drinking-horns' *The Connoisseur* **114** 20–4; Gay, s. 'Corne', 'Grifon'; Cripps pp. 277f.; Jones *Christ Church.*

they were languishing among the royal bric-à-brac in various palaces.[36]

Probably six English medieval aurochs drinking-horns survive above ground, as well as a blowing-horn, the Common Horn of Ripon. There are also a few horns which appear to be cattle's.

The closest to ours is the Wassail Horn of Queen's College, Oxford, an aurochs horn like ours in size, its mirror image in shape, but darker in colour. It has three broad silver-gilt bands, each joined to the horn by fringes, bearing the name of the horn, wacceyl. The horn stands on three bird-like feet fixed to the second and third bands. The finial is a lion's head. At some time, the horn was cut in three pieces underneath the bands and mounted on a silver-gilt liner; it was given a lid with an eagle as handle. The original is thought to have been given by Robert de Eglesfeld, founder of the college, between 1341 and 1349,[37] although the fringed mounts look 15th- rather than 14th-century. The Fareham Horn (at Hart House University, Toronto) is said to be similar.

The Pewsey Horn is smaller than ours, small enough to be doubtful whether it is of aurochs. It has a plain brim with two rings, and a broad band round the middle, standing on two legs ending in hounds'-feet. There are ghosts of a wider original brim and of a broad band near the little end. The hound's-head finial unscrews, from which it has been inferred that this was a musical as well as a drinking horn; however it would be difficult to play it without a mouthpiece. On the band is written:

> Kyng Knowd geve Wyllyam Pewse
> Thys horne to holde by thy lond.

This is a tenurial horn; it constituted the title-deed to a piece of land in Wiltshire, and once was produced in court to prove ownership. It claims to derive title from King Cnut (1016–35), but the language and calligraphy are 15th-century.[38] The Pewsey family had it into the 20th century; it now lies in the Victoria & Albert Museum.

The tenurial horn of Tutbury may be aurochs, but is a different shape; it has (or had) iron rings on the brim and middle band, with a black silk carrying-strap with metal buckles. The tenurial horn of Boarstall (Oxford) also has a carrying-strap with seal and ring; it appears to be cut out of some thick-walled horn, presumably not aurochs. Other 'horns', like the tenurial horn of Savernake Forest, are hollowed out of elephant ivory.

The latest aurochs horn may be that of Christ's Hospital. It is like ours in size and shape. On the brim, everted in the style of our later mazers, is the inscription **In God isal'**. Its fringed band has bird-like feet. The finial is a Tudor rose. It is first documented in 1557; the style strongly suggests a late 15th-century date.[39]

The Ribblesdale Horn, although of near-aurochs size, has light-coloured stripes suggestive of a big ox-horn. There are two bands with three legs in 15th-century armour.[40]

In Germany and Denmark small, strongly curved ox-horns are harnessed by lengthwise bands with a hinge at each end, in the manner of our Coconut Cup and other fragile objects (p. 50). Their styles range from mid-15th to late 16th centuries. There is one in the Victoria & Albert Museum.

The Horn in Use

> Lift not up your horn on high . . .
>
> *Psalm* **75** 6
>
> Nolite extollere cornu in altum
>
> *16th-cent.? inscription on the Ribblesdale Horn*

Anglo-Saxon horns, and perhaps ours in its earliest incarnation, had no feet. As in the Bayeux Tapestry, the drinker had to consume the entire three pints ('Down in One!', as we used to say when I was an undergraduate), or hand the horn to his neighbour.

Ceremonial cups are now used in a loving-cup ceremony. The drinker's two neighbours rise and

36 Starkey 1998 *passim.*
37 M Campbell 1987 'Wassail horn' *Age of Chivalry* §546.
38 Pegge 1773 'Of the Horn, as a Charter or Instrument of Conveyance. Some Observations on Mr. *Samuel Foxlowe's* Horn; as likewise on the Nature and Kinds of these Horns in general. . . . Of the *Pusey* Horn. . . . Of the *Borstal* Horn' *Archaeologia* **3** 1–17.
39 NM Penzer 1960 'Christ's Hospital plate' *Apollo* July 16–19.
40 Stone 1961 (p. 33).

watch over him while he drinks, lest an enemy slay him. This is a wise precaution, since in 978 the fifteen-year-old St Edward King and Martyr, whose church is the next but one to Corpus, was stabbed in the back while drinking by ruffians hired by his stepmother.

This formal ceremony, however, may not go back to the origin of the horn.[41] It looks like a development of the *grace-cup* custom, whereby after the closing grace diners would pass round a last drink before leaving the room. The College's earliest grace-cup, presented in the late 17th century, was melted down in 1746. Its successor, a 'Large Two-eared Cup', was the gift of William Wood, undergraduate in 1716; it weighed 32$\frac{3}{4}$ ounces, much the same as the Bateman Cup and Cover (p. 130). It lasted a century, and was melted in 1817.[42]

The horn is celebrated for being difficult to drink from.[43] When the level is getting low the sudden release of an air-lock causes the contents to jump out over the drinker's beard, or even into his neighbour's lap. To prevent this the little end should be held down. One of Harold's drinking companions is shown on the Bayeux Tapestry getting this wrong.

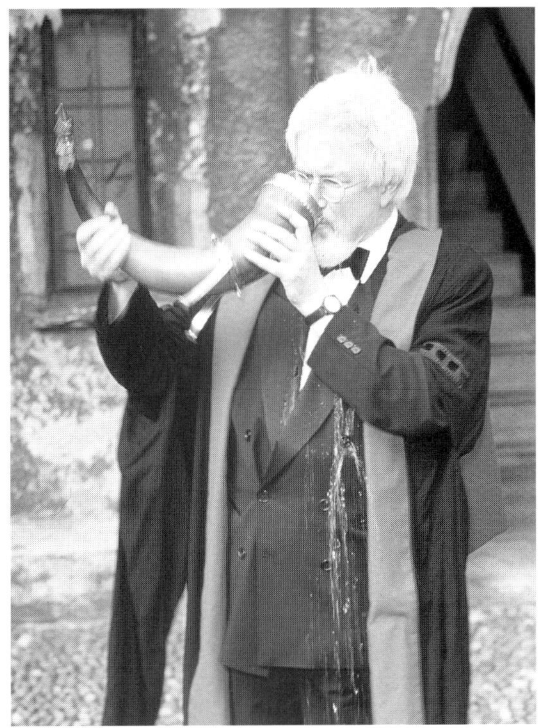

How not to drink from the Horn

41 The association with Edward appears to have been invented by Joseph Strutt, antiquary, in 1775. C Blair in *Goldsmith & Grape* p. 11.

42 CC(A): Inventories, 1670, 1706, 1752/3, and 1817.

43 For the taste of the contents see the Forest of Dean horn (pp. 42f.). There are three traditions as to what it is: (1) mead; (2) a secret formula passed down from Promus to Promus since 1352; (3) the contents of the half-empty bottles and glasses from the previous feast.

5

Plate of the Gilds: the Coconut Cup

First, one great black cup, in English Nut*, with a long foot of silver-gilt and a gilt lid.

** anglice note*, added later in same hand
Northwode's addition to the 1376 inventory

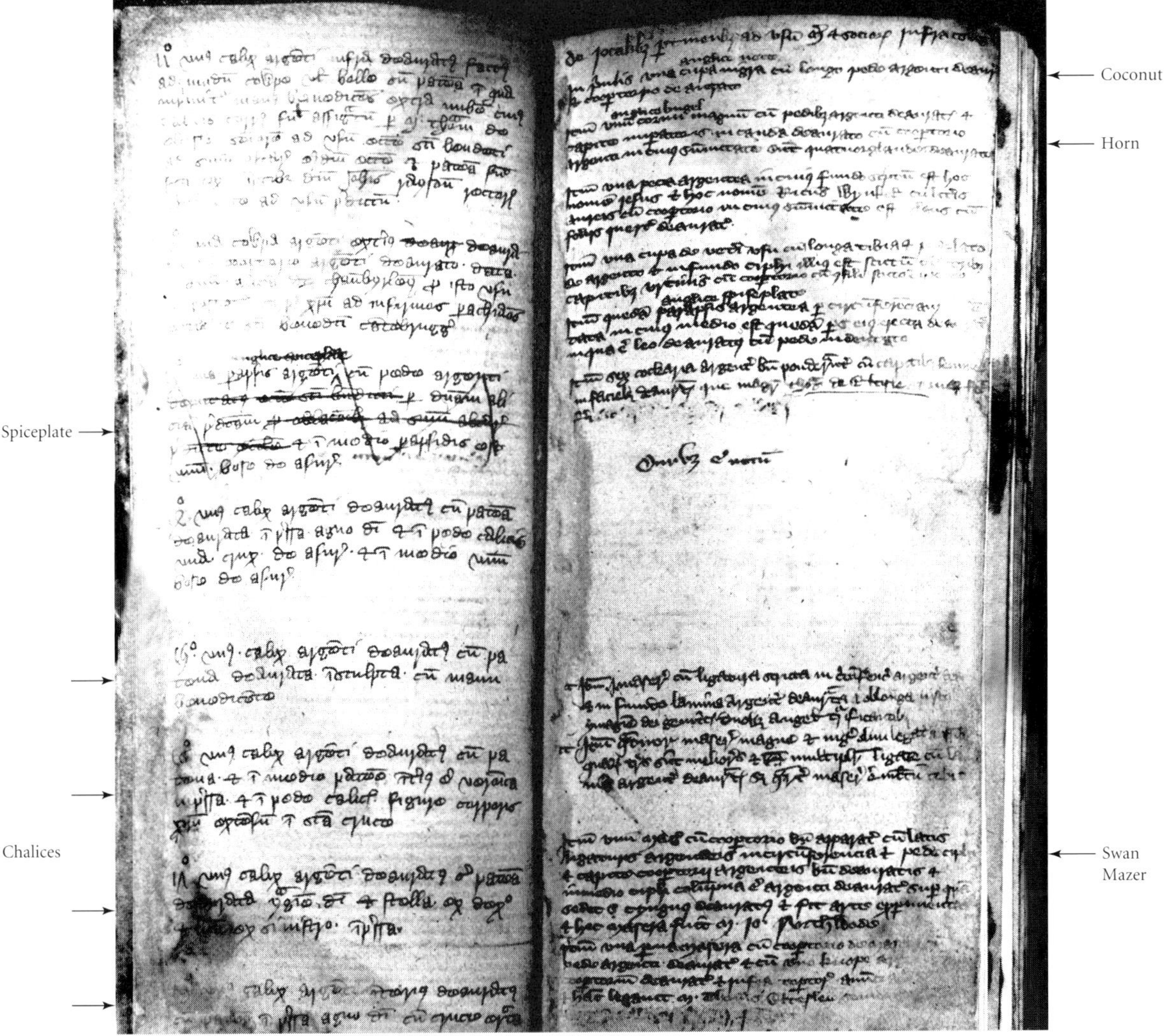

The 1376 inventory, with Botener's hand on the left and Northwode's additions on the right (see Appendix I).

The 1376 Inventory

The key to the College's earliest plate is a scruffy and tattered little notebook containing a Latin inventory of the College's possessions, begun in 1376 by John Botener and continued by John Northwode, both Fellows.

The Inventory begins with a catalogue of the 64 books in the College library. It next cites 'the vestments and textiles belonging to the use of [St Bene't's] church which are the college's and not the parishioners'', a long list which soon turns secular with a very jolly set of embroidered bedclothes and other non-ecclesiastical furnishings. Then comes an extensive hoard of plate, sacred and profane, this being mostly in Northwode's writing. A translation is given in Appendix 1, where I try to resolve the date of this complicated document. Like other inventories, it went on for several years, with new items being added and items disposed of being crossed out.

Many items in the Inventory have names of donors, including Thomas de Eltisle, first Master, early Fellows, and well-wishers like Alice de Chaumberleyn. Others have no names: their origin and significance were already lost in the mists of time. What can this mean but that the College had inherited them from the Gilds? They would mainly have come from the Gild of St Mary, since that of Corpus Christi had hardly had time to accumulate treasure. Of four of the mazers it is stated that the brethren had given them.

The Gild plate, as taken over by the College, comprised 23 items. There were five chalices with patens (each with beautiful decoration lovingly described), as befitted a society whose functions included saying masses. The paraphernalia of the Corpus Christi procession included a monstrous monstrance weighing 78 ounces (p. 95), twenty silver-enamelled shields or 'stockings', and something called a Beryl (*birle*)[1] weighing more than a pound. Other ecclesiastical plate included two cruets (p. 187), a pyx, and a reliquary with relics of six saints 'but it is not known of which'.

Secular plate comprised the Horn, two cups supposedly made of vulture's eggs (p. 92), a coconut, Richard Winkele's cup with its lid, an ancient cup with three bears in it, and a salver-like object called a spiceplate. Table silver comprised three knives, six spoons ending in maidens' heads with their hair in nets, and two basins (p. 73). There were five mazers, one of them dilapidated, by *c*.1385.

The College did not take good care of these venerable objects. The bowls, knives, and spoons were crossed out before the Inventory was finished: possibly the rioters of 1381 (p. 3) pocketed them. The reliquary and the five mazers are not heard of again, except that the accounts attached to the Inventory mention the sale of a *murra* (mazer) in 1407–8 for 6*s*. 8*d*.[2] The five chalices, monstrance, and *birles* remained until the Reformation, but then were frittered away. By Parker's time all that was left of the Gild plate were the Horn, Coconut, Vulture (by then reinterpreted as a Griffin) Cup, and possibly the lid of one of the other cups. The Griffin Cup disappeared about the time the College acquired the Ostrich Egg (p. 88); only the Horn and Coconut still survive.

The Black Nut or Coconut Cup

Item a black nutt with 1 foote guilt & cou[r] [cover] beside

Inventory of plate, 1604/5

8.8 in. high; 3.9 in. diameter at mouth; 4.2 in. maximum diameter.

Our coconut is a biggish one, sawn off at the end with the 'eyes', polished on the outside with three bands of incised grooves, and left rough on the inside. It is fitted with a silver brim, grooved with a rope moulding in the groove, incised with hatched triangles below the moulding. This is joined to the under-part by three silver straps, curved to fit the nut and hinged at both ends. The under-part has a scalloped edge and joins abruptly to the stem. The stem has a big hexagonal knop, below which is a plain hexagonal base. All the silver is single-gilt. The nut is nearly black, which seems to be its natural colour rather than due to paint (p. 61).

1 Not necessarily what the reader would call a beryl. The medieval word meant something used to make reliquaries, spoons, and even a ewer: e.g. Palgrave **2** 249.
2 CC(A): *Registrum Accounts 1376–1484* f.101.

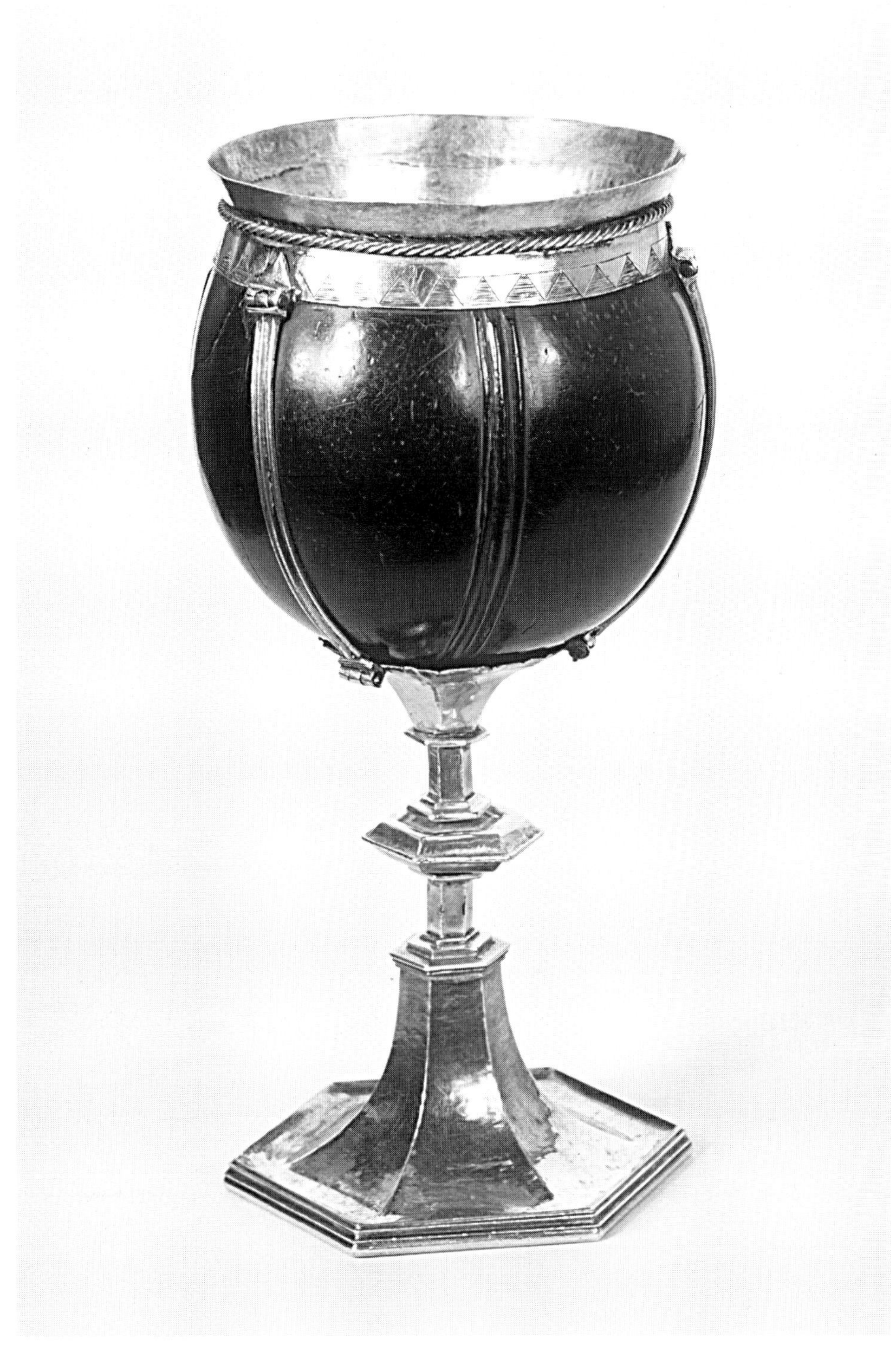

A big crack dates from before 1902. The lid has long gone, unless the Knob (p. 62) is its finial.

Silver straps (inventories call them *bars*), ending in hinge mounts, are used to harness a cup made of a fragile material that will not withstand hammering or the heat of soldering. They occur on coconut and ostrich cups of whatever date; on the 'Got-help-mir' drinking horn in the Victoria & Albert Museum; on a cup made out of a Chinese celadon bowl, supposed to be early 16th century, in New College, Oxford; on some late mazers (p. 62); and on the cheap tigerware pots which the Elizabethans, for some reason, liked to set in silver.[3]

The stem is an odd shape, like a chalice stem, unlike the trumpet bases of other coconut cups. It is assembled from a stack of knops and stems, and makes a rather awkward join (mended with solder) with the under-part of the cup. It might be a replacement put together from medieval oddments, although the workmanship is good.

The base was made in 1928 (London hallmark n), replacing an earlier modern base.

History of the Nut

A nut is the first item in Northwode's list of secular plate of *c*.1385, followed by the Horn. No donor is named, so probably it was inherited from the Gild of St Mary.

Later the College acquired a bigger and better coconut, as in the 1526 inventory:

> Item *ly Blacke Notte* with foot and lid gilt outside
>
> 12 oz.
>
> ....
>
> Item Cup with lid called *ly Notte* Price of each ounce 4s 8d and weigh together
>
> 30 oz.

The *c*.1544 inventory has only the first nut: 'Item a nut set in silver with a cover gilt', the weight of 12 oz. added in the margin. In 1573/4 it appears as 'Item the blacke nutt wth a foote, barrs & cov^r^ of silvr gilt'. It appears in all the later inventories: it still, if truth were told, had its lid in 1670.

Commentators, from Foster & Atkinson onwards, have regarded the present cup as 15th-century, without explaining why. There is no direct evidence that it was a replacement of the 14th-century nut. Of the two nuts present in 1526, ours is the smaller, as is clear from its weight (now about 11 oz. troy). The other nut, to have weighed 30 oz., must have been a much more elaborate piece heavily loaded with silver. Since Northwode is meticulous in describing elaborate articles, his brief mention of the nut indicates that it was the simple 12-oz. nut, not the 30-oz. one.

In 1980 Dr Rolf Fritz of Münster, specialist in coconut cups, examined ours, and wrote to me thus:

> Your cup is quite divergent from the typical English special forms that so predominate. There is no example in England that has a chalice-like knop. However, such forms occur in Germany, as far as the small corpus of material allows such a conclusion. Your cup . . . is perhaps an import from the Continent. The style of the knop and the triangular ornament definitely indicate the 14th century: we should cautiously say the 2nd half of the 14th century, perhaps Continental (south German?). . . . The inside left rough is remarkable; varnish is the rule.

The world of coconut cups

The medievals loved cups of rare and romantic materials. A coconut is the fruit of the palm *Cocos nucifera*, containing the world's biggest seed except the double coconut. The coconut palm, one of the most useful trees, is of mysterious origin probably somewhere in the Pacific. By the middle ages it had reached India, whence the nuts were brought to England and made into cups. They were usually called just Nut, sometimes 'nut of India'; the word *coconut* appears *c*.1600.

The inventories etc. analyzed by Cripps, historian of plate, mention about thirty nut cups between 1259 and 1596. If all these were made of coconut[4] they imply that coconut cups were much less common than mazers but three times as common as ostrich eggs (Appendix 3). This may seem surprising, seeing that to reach England coconuts had to travel through the land of ostriches. Coconuts could belong to ordinary people: Mary Mansell of St Clement's, Cambridge, in 1636 bequeathed

> my drinking nutt topped and ribbed with silver and standing upon a foote of an Eagles claw with the cover thereunto belonging.[5]

Dr Fritz knew about 25 surviving medieval coconut cups in England and 25 on the Continent. This implies

3 Glanville (1990) pp. 333–5.

4 A few other cups were tantalizingly said to be called nut but made of mazer.

5 Information kindly supplied by Dr Tom Faber.

a survival rate higher than for mazers or ostrich eggs. In England coconut cups were seldom made after 1540; on the Continent they continued to flourish because they neutralized poison. They were made of a half double-coconut (*Lodoicea maldivica*) when that began to be imported from the Seychelles, *c*.1580. A fine coconut cup in the Mannerist style is depicted in Hermann tom Ring's fresco of the Persian Sibyl, arch-poisoner, in Münster Cathedral. There is one hallmarked 1660 in the Gemeentemuseum, The Hague.[6]

Gonville Hall, now Gonville & Caius College, has two coconut cups. The larger, though smaller than ours, has its brim and hinged straps fringed with fleurs-de-lys, and a trumpet-shaped base resting on three lions. It is usually ascribed to the 15th century; I would put it early in that century. The other is a very small coconut with a fringed brim, pierced hinged straps, and a unique trumpet base with curved ribs; it is probably of the mid to late 15th century.

In Oxford there are six coconuts, belonging to New College (three), Exeter, Oriel, and Queen's. All are more elaborate than ours. Four appear to be of the 15th century; the Oriel cup has a high fluted stem and closely matches our Three Kings mazer. One of New College's has a unique mount in the likeness of a pollard hawthorn tree, standing in a park pale, whose boughs enclose the nut; its Gothic inscription indicates a 15th-century date. Another in New College, marked 1584, resembles our Ostrich Cup.[7]

Others ascribed to the 15th century belong to Eton College, Temple Newsam, and the Vintners', Armourers', and Ironmongers' Companies, London.[8] One of the last is the wonderful Mannerist coconut supposed to have been given by Queen Elizabeth to Sir Francis Drake, *c*.1580. Coconut cups, like other types, persisted longer in Scotland: a noble specimen, complete with hinged straps, is attributed to William Scott the Elder in Aberdeen *c*.1670.[9] There was something of a revival of the fashion in the 18th century.[10]

These cups have nothing in common with ours except the three hinged bars, a functional device resistant to changes of fashion. They generally have trumpet-shaped bases and fringes at the junction of silver and nut. Most are in the style, and belong to the age, of our mazer Cup of the Three Kings. Our big, plain, simple coconut cup, on stylistic as well as documentary grounds, belongs to an earlier age.

Conclusion

The Horn came back into favour in the sixteenth century; the Nut survived, forgotten and under-valued. Scholars, too, have neglected it as being a minor piece of the 15th century. This analysis tends to show that it is indeed the nut mentioned in Northwode's inventory, whose origin had been forgotten by 1385. It is thus a legacy from the Gild of St Mary before the College was founded, second in date only to the Horn, the third oldest piece of plate in a Cambridge college, and maybe the oldest coconut to survive above ground.

6 R Fritz 1977 'Der Kokosnußpokal der persischen Sibylle von Hermann tom Ring und seine Bedeutung' *Westfalen* **55** 93–7. *Haags silver uit vijf eeuwen* Haags Gemeentemuseum 1967, §47.
7 Moffatt plates XII, XIX, XXIV, XXXV–VI.
8 Cripps p.275; Glanville (1990) p.154.
9 Aberdeen Art Gallery & Museums (reported to me by the Rev. Mark Pryce).
10 EH Pinto 'Nut Treen Part I'. *Apollo* (Jan. 1950) 23–5.

6

Medieval College Plate: Mazers, Seals, and the Knob

To make and forge the harness of a cup of mazer (*hennap de mazre*) of which the foot is garnished with gold, with a border of raised *fleurs-de-lys*, and at the bottom of the bowl it has an enamel of [the coat-of-arms of] France, and on the lid a finial of a *fleur-de-lys* enamelled after the life, and it has a crown of gold around the same attached by a screw, sitting on a ledge enamelled in green; the whole weighs 1 mark 2 ounces* of gold at 22 carats; outlay and workmanship £45†.

* Probably about 10 modern ounces, 300 grams. † Presumably Paris pounds.

The best mazer of John the Good, spendthrift king of France, 1351[1]

Merchants and sellers in mazer-shops (*de magdelins*) shall pay for each sack of cups of mazer, of which the sack [contains] 80 cups, 2 *s*.

Mazers as throwaway drinking-vessels of the poor: city regulations of Paris, 1355

Item one maser with lid, well harnessed with broad silver bands on the circumference and foot of the cup and on the top of the lid, of silver well gilt, and in the middle of the cup is a column of silver-gilt, on which sits a gilt swan, and it is made by experimental art, and this maser was of Mr Jo[hn] Northwode.

The Swan Mazer of Corpus Christi College, as described by the donor, c.1385 *(p. 47)*

If the College's original treasures were inherited from the Gilds, benefactors soon gave more. At the very beginning Henry Duke of Lancaster gave twenty silver shields for the College to carry in the Corpus Christi procession. The Botener–Northwode inventory (Appendix 1) records the gift (among secular plate) of a 'vulture's-egg' cup, later supposed to be the one bequeathed by Henry de Tangmer, who died in 1361 (p. 91); six silver spoons from Robert de Eltisle (p. 84); and seven fine mazers, one (the Swan Mazer) from Northwode himself, and the others from other named benefactors. Early benefactors had given two chalices and patens to St Bene't's Church, and a collection-plate already crossed out from the inventory. By *c*.1400 these thirteen items had been added to the 23 inherited from the Gilds.

There came further accessions of secular plate. In 1410 the College bought three *maseras* for £1 each and sold one for 13*s*. 4*d*.,[2] and at least five others were given before 1510. Silver salt-cellers began late in the 15th century. Ornamental cups, some of more than 20 ounces, multiplied in the early 16th. By 1530 the College owned some 45 items (including sixteen mazers), weighing about 730 ounces.

As with Gild plate, the College's early plate was expendable. Parker added the following note to the 1526 inventory:

> Nearly all these were alienated and sold in the time of William Sowode, master, with the consent of the fellows, as they assert.

What wheeling and dealing lie behind this? Sowode was Parker's predecessor as Master (1523–44). Parker himself was in the College as a Fellow since *c*.1527, but in 1535 had withdrawn from Cambridge. Sowode, an enthusiastic reformer, would have approved scrapping the apparatus of the Corpus Christi procession, the Monstrance, Shields, and Beryl, after the procession was given up in 1535. But much secular plate also, such as the greater coconut cup and the Leopard Cup, had disappeared by the time of the *c*.1545 inventory. Some changes may have been due

1 This and the following: Gay **2** 6b.
2 CC(A): *Registrum Accounts 1376–1484* f.44., 44v.

to wear and tear: the thirteen apostle spoons given by Thomas Cosyn (Master 1487–1515) were replaced by a new set of 12 apostle spoons during the currency of the 1526 inventory.

The Mazers

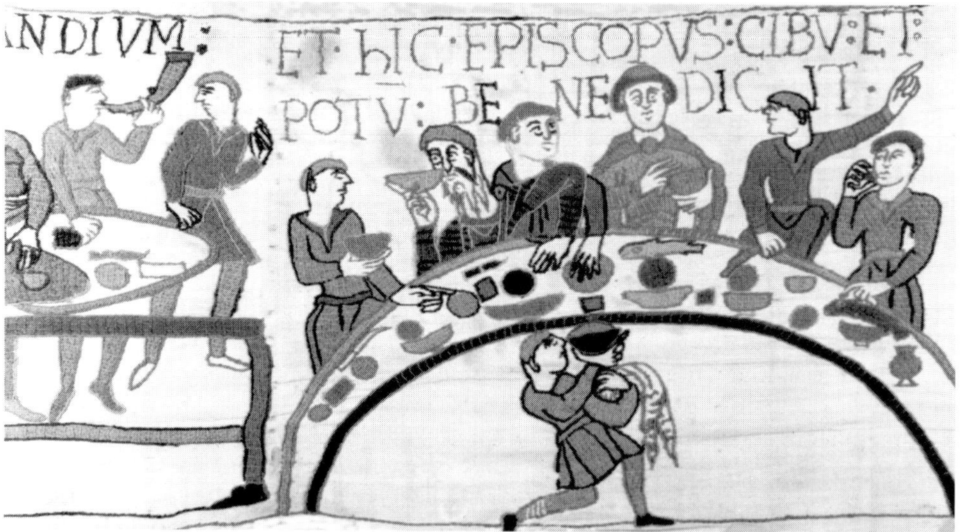

Mazers in the field: William the Conqueror's military picnic at Pevensey before the Battle of Hastings, from the Bayeux Tapestry

From this period are the College's four surviving mazers (out of at least 24 of which there are records). Mazers are wooden drinking-bowls, made out of the common maple tree, *Acer campestre.* Of the millions made in England, some eighty are now preserved above ground.[3] Almost all the survivors are rare 'fine' mazers, mounted in silver for special occasions, rather than the common run of everyday drinking-ware:[4] just as museums of costume have more wedding dresses than workmen's overalls.

Cups were commonly made of wood in Anglo-Saxon and medieval England. This is normally the despair of archaeologists, who would much rather have their subjects drink out of imperishable earthenware, but on occasion ancient cups are preserved in waterlogged deposits. The famous Coppergate, York, is the street not of policemen but of cuppers or cupmakers, and its excavators found great numbers of spoilt wooden cups and cup-cores of the tenth century AD.[5] Ordinary wooden cups were found in every medieval household. They were not always maple: as late as 1503, provisions for the Lord Mayor of London's feast included 800 'asshen cuppis'.[6]

Fine wooden drinking-vessels go back at least to Anglo-Saxon times. The Sutton Hoo ship-barrow contained six maple-wood bottles and six cups with silver-gilt mounts. The cups, deep and lopsided, were identified as burr walnut.[7]

The earliest written record is probably the *mæsen* cups in an inventory of *c.*1073.[8] On the Bayeux Tapestry King Harold is shown handing a fine mazer, shaped like our

3 Pinto (1969) pp. 42–6.

4 Two ordinary mazers survive at Canterbury (see later).

5 Hall RA 1982 '10th century woodworking in Coppergate, York' *Woodworking Techniques before A.D. 1500* ed S McGrail *British Archaeological Reports International Series* **129** 231–43.

6 *Babees Book* p. 379.

7 Bruce-Mitford pp. 347–74.

8 Thorpe B 1865 *Diplomatarium Anglicanum Ævi Saxonici* 429.

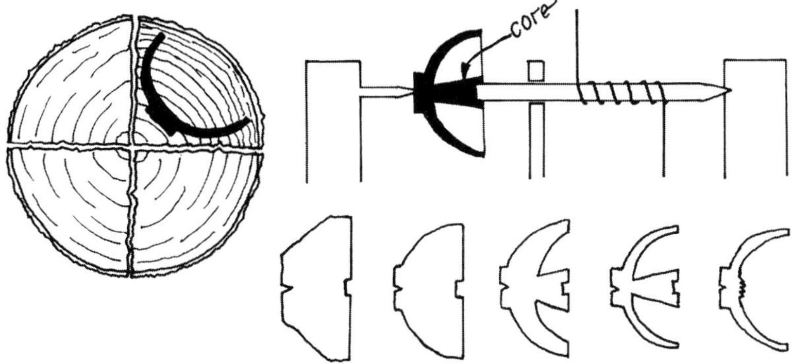

How an ordinary mazer sits in the original tree; diagram of a mazer lathe; stages in making a mazer. After Carole Morris.

Swan Mazer and with a similar broad metal brim, to a guest at his feast in Bosham (p. 43). William's picnic after landing at Pevensey included five mazers, one with a metal brim and the others ordinary. Those unused to mazers might think them an awkward shape for drinking out of, but those in the Tapestry are handleless bowls like ours, and seem to have been the usual drinking-vessels of the 11th century.

A cup, humble or grand, was turned on a lathe, like the pole-lathes, driven by the turner's feet, to be seen in demonstrations of woodland crafts today.[9] Their back-and-forth motion is difficult to get used to, but in skilled hands gives precise results. A blank, usually made by splitting a short log into four, was hewn to a roughly circular shape. This blank was mounted with its flat surface attached to the mandrel of the lathe, rotating against the spur of the lathe centre which pressed into a pit in the base of the cup. The cupper shaped first the outside of the cup. Next he cut out the inside, leaving a core to keep hold of the mandrel. Finally he cut or broke off the core – throwing it away for archaeologists, maybe, to find and misidentify as a 'bung' or 'child's top'. Often he did the preliminary shaping while the wood was newly felled, set it aside to dry and warp out of shape, and turned it to its final shape after the warping was finished.[10]

Wide bowls like our mazers are the commonest shape from Anglo-Saxon times onwards, and the easiest shape to make. A skilled cupper, by stopping a pole-lathe at slightly less than a whole revolution, can create an up-standing lug or handle, but this was rarely done.

What are mazers made of?

The obscure word 'mazer' appears to have two meanings: (1) the wood of maple; (2) something spotty, like measles. The link usually given is that mazers were made from the wood of the bosses or burrs which grow on the trunk of the common maple, with a spotty appearance like bird's-eye maple.[11] Both meanings have parallels in other languages: *masarnen* is Welsh for a maple-tree, and in German *Masern* are measles and *Maserholz* is burry wood. Maybe two different words of similar spelling have become confused.[12]

'Mazer' is often rendered in Latin as *murra* or *mirra*, the ancient Roman word for a very precious type of stone or glass cup.

All our cups are of the same wood, almost certainly maple, although it is not very distinctive and cannot be verified microscopically without cutting out a sample. Maple was a common tree in medieval as in modern England, and had few other specific uses except for musical instruments.[13] It warps and splits little,

9 The earliest picture of a pole-lathe, as far as I know, is from Delft in 1610: Pinto plate 1.

10 Morris C 1982 'Aspects of Anglo-Saxon and Anglo-Scandinavian lathe-turning' *Woodworking Techniques* (above) 245–61.

11 A will of 1365 mentions two cups of mazer, of which the better was *vocatum knopmazer* (Cripps p. 248); this suggests that only the better sort of mazer-wood came from burrs.

12 For a fuller discussion, with examples, see Cripps p. 235.

13 As investigated by Dr Graeme Lawson of this College.

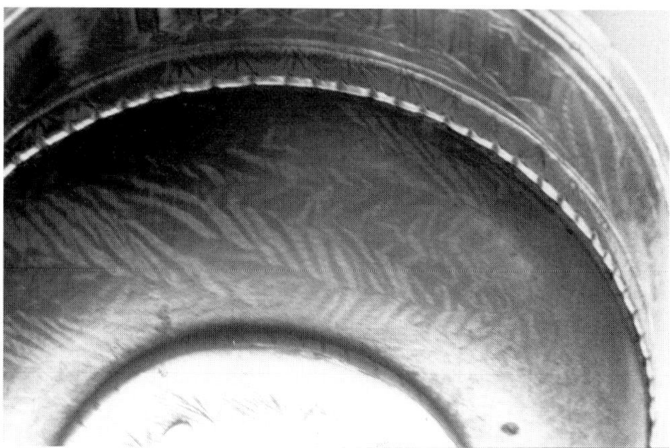

Feather grain in the Cup of the Three Kings.

and does not taint the drink. Maple is the commonest identification of archaeological cups, followed by alder, ash, and yew: rare finds of box and pine are reported.

Our cups are not made of the normal wood of the tree, but of a part selected for its contorted grain. This makes a beautiful feather-like figure, once a feature of all our cups, now barely visible beneath centuries of human grease. Having felled many maples, I am not sure exactly how this grew, but probably not in burrs. At least two cups – the Three Kings and Mazer Without Print – are made from a slice across the tree-trunk, with the pith passing vertically through the middle. This was very unusual: most cups were turned from slices round the circumference of the tree, as illustrated on p. 55. If the pith was included the cupper needed to take great care against splitting.

Feather-grain mazers seem to be rare. Most of those in the Canterbury hoards are made either from bird's-eye maple, probably from bosses, or from a variant with ripple grain. Coarse mazers are made from the ordinary wood.

A common metal fitting was the *print*, a boss in the middle of the inside (e.g. 'unum rose prynte' in one of 1454), where it hides the rough place left by detaching the core. Early prints, like many at Canterbury, are made by embossing (printing) a sheet of silver, and are attached by many nails or rivets. Ours are thicker and lack obvious fastenings.

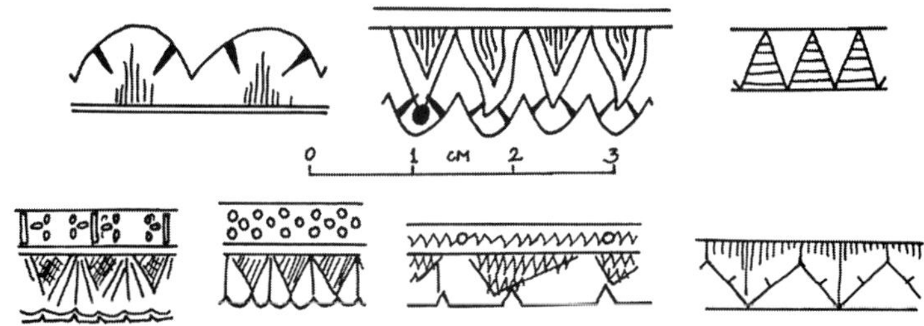

Fringes. Crown of Horn (13th cent.); brim of Horn (date uncertain); Coconut (14th cent.); Cup of Three Kings (15th); Mazer Without Print (15th); Rose Mazer (1521); Ostrich (1592)

Most surviving mazers have silver brims, attached by a tongue-and-groove joint, and often thinned out at the edge into a fringe.[14] Some have silver feet: sometimes the silver extends so far that little maple-wood is visible.

6.1 Swan Mazer

Plate 2. 5.1 in. diam. × 2.8 high.

This, our earliest, is the most complex mazer either surviving or known from descriptions. It was given by John Northwode, writer of the additions to our earliest inventory, which dates its arrival in the College to *c.*1380. It is still much as Northwode himself described it (see head of chapter), although the lid has vanished. The broad silver-gilt brim round the circumference has a milled edge and three strawberry-leaf lugs to hold the lid. It extends the cup upwards, like planks added to the sides of a dugout boat, being fitted to the edge of the wood with a tongue-and-groove joint. A crack in the wood has been neatly stitched with brass wire.[15] There are remains of varnish inside.

In the middle is a hexagonal column with battlements, on which sits a swan with folded wings. Brim, column, and swan have their delicate original single gilding. The column resembles the gold tower which stands instead of a print in one of the mazers at All Souls' College, Oxford.

The foot, with its fringe of tongues, has long been recognized as a replacement. A search of the College accounts reveals that it was made in 1606:

> To Peter Muser the goldsmyth for makeing a foote of silver for the Swan mazor, wth guildinge thereof and plate of sylver within syde of the same, and his worke thereof
> 19*s*.

This is the only certainly identifiable surviving piece by Muser, the College's plate-repairer (p. 28); indeed it is one of the very few College works by a Cambridge silversmith. He did an excellent job; the design is like that of the 1523 mazer.

The 'experimental art' referred to by Northwode (p. 53) is this. The column is hollow and contains a syphon; around the hexagonal base are 24 holes. If the cup is over-filled, so that the level of liquid reaches the swan's bill, the syphon takes over and deposits the entire contents through a hole in the base into the drinker's lap.

The Swan Mazer would remain a unique example of the experimental humour of the middle ages, but for the survival of the notebook of Villard de Honnecourt, the 13th-century French virtuoso.[16] He has a diagram of a vessel shaped like the Swan Mazer, of which he says:

> Here is a singweeper (*cantepleure*) which can be made in 1 *henap* in this manner: that in the middle the *henap* should have a turret, should have 1 tube (*behot*), which is held in the bottom of the *henap*; but that the tube should be as long as the *henap* is deep; & in the turret should have 3 cross-pieces against the bottom of the *henap*; such that the wine in the cup can get into the tube; and above the tower should have 1 bird which should hold its beak so low that when the *henap* is full it drinks; then the wine can run through the midst of the tube and through the midst of the foot of the *henap*, which is double; and – listen well – the bird must be hollow.

The word *henap* appears in English and French as a type of mazer or other drinking-vessel. The word refers to the shape, not the material. (Is not a *hamper*, Latin *hanaperium*, a special basket for carrying *henaps*?) This one was evidently made – if ever it was made, for as shown in the diagram it would not work[17] – of metal, with a hollow base. If over-filled, the bird seemed to drink the liquid, which disappeared into the hollow base.

By the 1850s the syphon was not working: 'The lower extremity of the tube has been long plugged up, and the mischievous trickery of the machine forgotten' (Willis). It is said to have been restored by Sir George Thomson in 1924 by way of a wedding fine. The writer can vouch that it still works.

14 There seems to be no technical word for the fringe. One might expect the term *frounce*, Latin *frontinella*, often used in medieval descriptions of mazers, to refer to the fringe, as a variant of a dressmaker's *flounce*. But it is sometimes stated that the frounce is what we now call the print: e.g. 'a mazer with an image of Saint Katheryne called Frounce in the bottom', 1433 (Cripps p. 249).

15 About one surviving mazer in six has ancient metal repairs. Similar repairs are common in archaeological wooden cups, even coarse ones: Morris (above) pp. 257ff.

16 Willis. Dr Christopher Norton drew my attention to this parallel. Foster & Atkinson p. 8.

17 The Bishop of Durham, however, owned a cup called Chanteplure in 1259: Cripps p. 271.

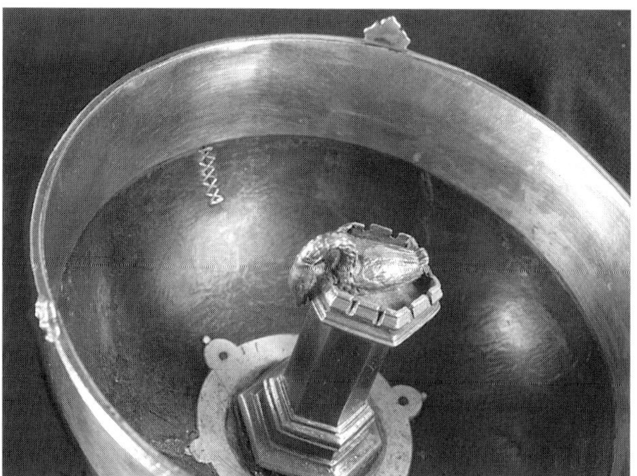

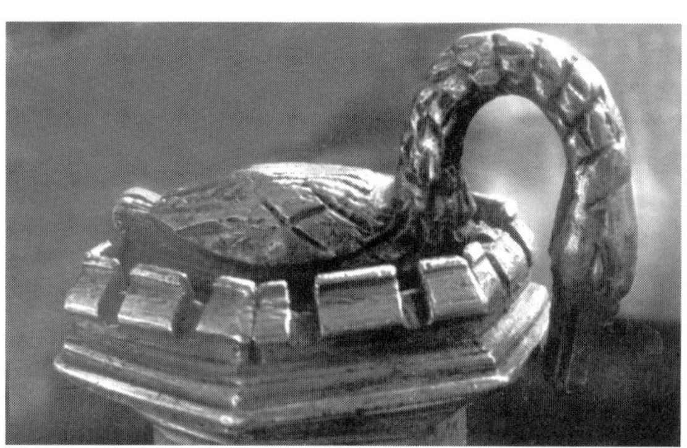

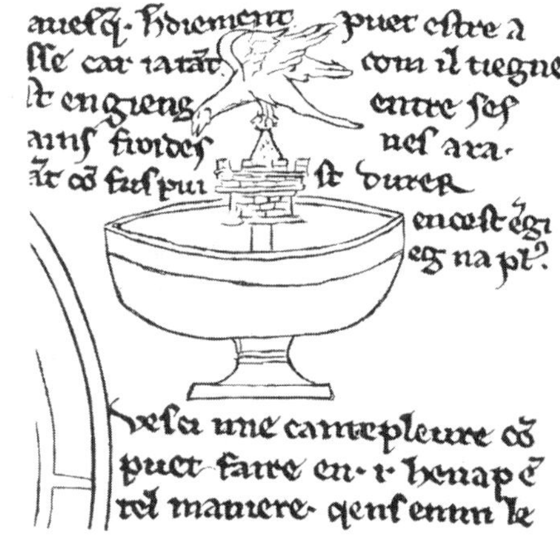

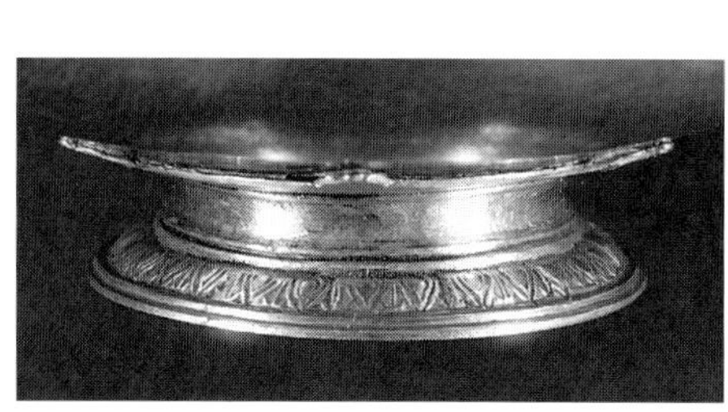

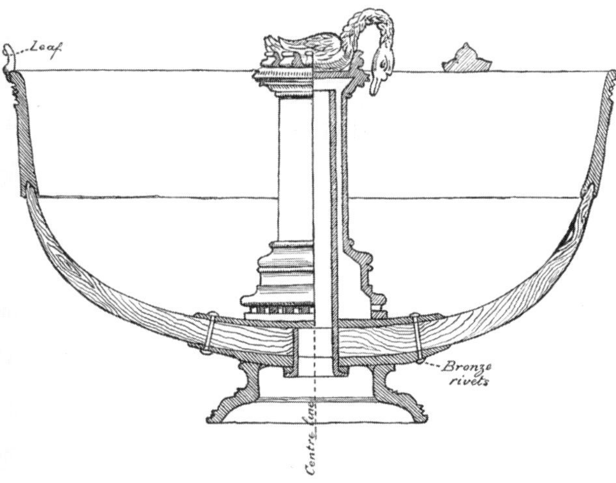

The Swan Mazer. (1) interior showing stitched crack; (2) detail of swan; (3)Villard de Honnecourt's singweeper cup, after Willis; (4) foot made by Peter Muser in 1606; (5) section of the Swan Mazer (after Foster & Atkinson).

The lid of the Swan Mazer, which was itself a mazer, suffered a curious fate. On 27 January 1578/9 the Master and Fellows signed a deed giving Sir Nicholas Bacon

> one mazer wth a foote & a lip of silver & gilt, wch was the Cover to another mazer called the Swan mazer, & nowe made vnto ye fashion of the sayd Swan mazer in all poynts.[18]

> Payd to a goldsmith in London at the south gate of [St] pouls for making a swan of silver to the old mazer which was gyven to the L. keper 15*s*.
>
> CC(A): XXIX A3

The motive, as Catherine Hall explains, was to stimulate his desultory benefactions to the College. The gift was ineffective: he gave nothing more, and died a year later. By 1895 his descendants had forgotten it. Maybe it will turn up one day.

6.2 Cup of the Three Kings

Plate 2. 4.7 in. diam. × 5.4 high.

This is a magnificent 'standing' mazer. The small wooden cup, with its ripple grain, is extended by a broad, fringed, double-gilt brim, engraved with three crowns, leaves, and the words **jasper melchior balthasar**. The single-gilt stem is ornamented with six spiralling lobes, and the top of the foot with a pierced cresting of leaves. Inside is a print with a fringed border, picked out in green enamel, depicting a squirrel eating a nut while being ferried by a fish.

The stem is detachable, coming apart with what seems to be the world's earliest bayonet joint.

The ornament on the brim is minute in detail but rather roughly executed. The fringe has an edge merely notched instead of engrailed; the triangular ornament is incised in outline and filled in with hatching. Above is a band covered with tiny raised decoration.

The words on the cup are the 'traditional' names of the Magi who honoured the birth of Christ:

> Now when Jesus was born in Bethlehem of Judæa in the days of Herod the king, behold, there came wise men from the east . . .
>
> *St Matthew* **2** 1

This original story gathered the successive accretions that the Wise Men were three (or twelve in the Eastern Church), that they were kings, that they were called Jasper, Melchior, and Balthasar, and that they are now in Cologne Cathedral, working miracles. Jasper ('Sir Jasper, do not touch me!') is the English form of German *Kaspar*. The identical names are on the Holy Trinity, Colchester mazer of similar style but lacking a high base.

The date of our mazer depends on that of the very similar 'Foundress's Cup' at Pembroke College. This is now all metal, but seems originally to have been a mazer, of which the wooden part has been replaced in silver-gilt. The stem lacks the lobed ornament, but the piece is otherwise almost identical, with two inscriptions in identical lettering to ours. It is recorded as given by Richard Sokeborn, Fellow 1470–8. Standing mazers are documented from 1442 onwards,[19] and the Pembroke one – and by implication ours – probably dates from the mid-15th century.

Pierced cresting, as on the base of our cup, occurs on several medieval mazers and coconut cups in Oxford and Cambridge: for example the Founder's Cup of Oriel College, apparently acquired in 1493. The Warden's Grace-cup of New College, Oxford, probably a little later than ours, has similar cresting, and another example of the foot detachable by a bayonet joint.[20] The Worshipful Company of Ironmongers has another very similar cup, probably later, made of a coconut.[21]

Spiral ornament on the stem, though rare, has a long currency. A parallel is the Hill Salt of New College, whose Gothic inscription refers to the Warden from 1475 to 1494. Christ Church, Oxford, has a cup with raised spiral ribs on the stem made as late as 1765.[22] We shall meet spiral lobes again on the Parker Rosewater Bowl.

Our cup, with its lid, was probably bequeathed by Richard Brocher, who endowed the first known scholarship in the College. A 'maser with a fote [foot] gylte' is linked with him by the 1510 and 1513 inventory entries. It had a cover with a silver-gilt knob (p. 62). He died in

18 CC(A): Misc. Docs §39. Printed in Masters p. 84. I am grateful to Mrs Hall for bringing this to my attention.
19 Cripps p. 249.
20 Jones *Oriel;* Moffatt Plate XXXI.
21 *Goldsmith & Grape* no. 16.
22 Moffatt Plates XXXII, LXXIV.

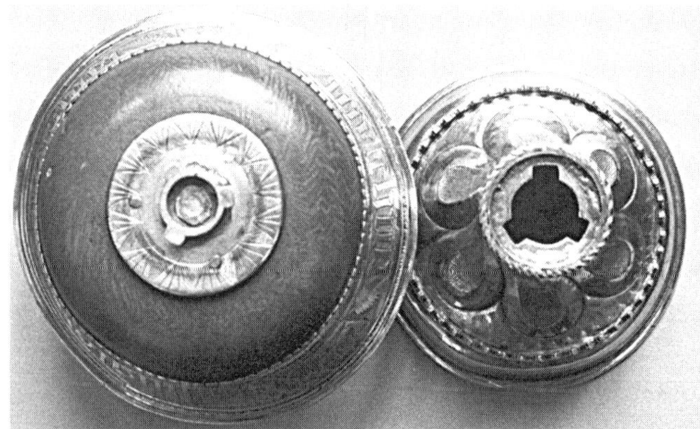
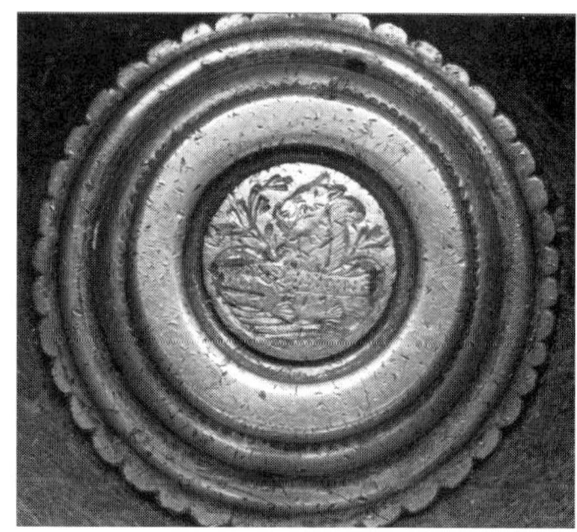

Cup of the Three Kings: bayonet joint dismantled; print of squirrel riding a fish.

1489, having been a Fellow for 37 years. This would agree with a stylistic mid-15th-century date.

The 1526 record of the cup mentions the names of the 'kings of Cologne'. The lid, last heard of in 1573/4, was of painted wood with a silver knob; it recalls the surviving wooden lid of one of the Harbledown mazers, though that is a century earlier (see below).

The small size of the cup suggests that perhaps it was made out of the core of a bigger cup, economizing the rare feather-grained wood. It is shown exactly as now in the earliest known illustration (Smith 1845).

The cup has been frog-poked inside with such vigour as to wreck the enamel.

6.3 Mazer Without Print

4.9 in. diam. × 2.1 high.

A simpler version of the Cup of the Three Kings, lacking the inscription, foot, and print. It is of the same shape and feather-grained wood, and very similar in details. It too is double-gilt. On the inside the core has been carefully cut off leaving a smooth surface. On the underside is a projecting wooden base, cut down to leave only a very small hole from the lathe centring.

The fringe of the brim is properly engrailed and of rather better workmanship than the Three Kings. Above it is a band of tiny raised bosses like those on the Three Kings. All the details point to the same mid-15th-century

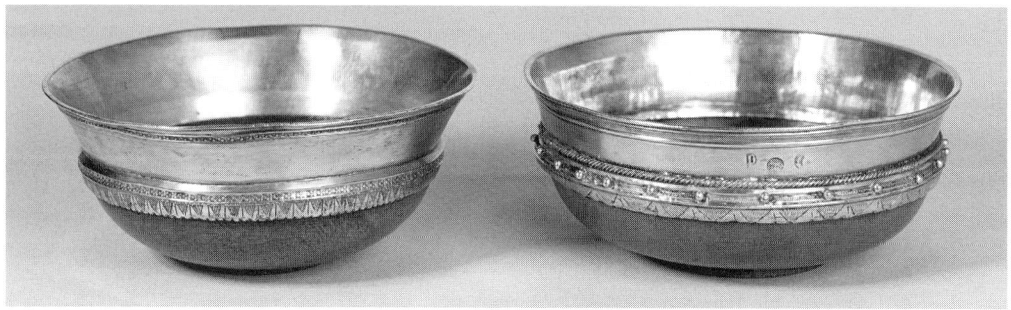

Mazer without Print (left); Rose Maser.

date. One of the mazers of Oriel College has most of the details of ours, and a Gothic-letter inscription like that on our Cup of the Three Kings.[23]

The 1510 inventory indicates that this was either given by Thomas Tyard (Fellow *c*.1478) or bequeathed by J. Swayne or Thomas Salysbury (otherwise unknown).

6.4 Rose Mazer (Mazer With Print)

4.9 in. diam. × 2.0 high.

This very late mazer differs in style from the others, but is also of feather-grained wood. It has a broad, nearly upright brim, double gilt, with a hollow moulding set with little balls and bordered with a fringe. Inside is a print with a five-petalled flower and sprigs (a 'rose' in contemporary documents), with purple and green enamel.

It is our second earliest piece to have a hallmark, consisting of the usual crowned leopard's face, the letter D which establishes the date as 1521, and the maker's mark (p. 12). Commentators read the last as a hand holding a ragged staff, but it is unique and the maker has not been identified. Flower-and-sprig prints occur also on the Oriel College mazer (*c*.1470) and on that of Whitgift's Hospital, Croydon, hallmarked 1508.[24]

The brim is of cruder workmanship still than the earlier mazers. The engrailed edge is reduced to a rough set of V-notches, the triangles roughly scratched and filled in by zigzag doodlings with a burin. The little balls are set at irregular intervals. The print has a similar fringe.

This too has a projecting wooden base, with a large pit where the centring spike entered.

It is probably the 'mazer with a rose in the bottom' among the five added by Parker to the 1526 inventory. No donor is known. It has been roughly frog-poked and most of the enamel lost.

Documentation of the College's Mazers

In its first fifty years the College hoarded twelve mazers, listed by John Northwode (Appendix 1). Five were inherited from the Gilds, one was the Swan Mazer given by Northwode himself, and the others by Thomas Eltisley (first Master), Richard de Billingford (fifth Master), John Deveros, Peter Fornham, and Thomas Trench (Fellows), and an illegible donor.

All these were fine mazers, worth keeping even if decrepit; whether the College also had ordinary mazers I do not know. Several had prints with images of the Virgin Mary or the Annunciation; only two had lids. Six mazers were 'black', probably made of ordinary wood painted black, like two surviving at Canterbury.

Mazers were not particularly permanent. They were often disposed of, as shown by this entry:

> Item, from Ric. Lumbard [recently admitted Fellow] for a tablecloth, towel, mazer (*murra*) and spoon, by dispensation of the Fellows
>
> 10*s*.
>
> *Accounts, 1437–8*

In 1429–30 sixpence was spent 'on making a mazer' (*in factura masere*): the College could hardly have commissioned a new fine mazer for so little, so probably a repair is meant. It could even be the medieval repair still visible on the Swan Mazer.[25]

By 1481 the College possessed at least eight *maserys* (none described in identifiable detail) and had disposed of one (p. 278). The partial inventories of 1510 and 1513 includes mazers given by Richard Brocher (identified with the Cup of the Three Kings, above), Thomas Brocher (Fellow 1478–92, died 1505), Thomas Salysbury (unknown), and bequeathed by John Swayne (unknown). Some of the fine mazers were kept in the pantry, presumably for everyday use. This would explain the fairly rapid turnover and the marks of misuse on the surviving specimens.

The 1526 inventory records 12 mazers, including the Swan, Three Kings, and Mazer without Print. Their weights are given but not their origins; some could still have been mazers from the Gilds. Parker's additions bring the total up to 17. The College may have acquired the other five soon after 1526, but since the original inventory seems to be incomplete it may be that Parker

23 Jones *Oriel*. 24 Hope.
25 CC(A): *Registrum Accounts 1376–1484* ff.155v, 121.

found and entered them soon after he became a Fellow in 1533. Two mazers, including the Three Kings, were of the rare 'standing' pattern with a high foot. Five of the late mazers had 'bars', a term used also of the Coconut Cup (p. 50), which may mean vertical silver straps hinged at both ends, a rare feature of mazers.[26]

By *c*.1545 eleven mazers survived (p. 282), including 'a olde broken maser' and one called 'newe'. Disaster struck them, and by 1573/4 there were only the present four, plus the wooden lids of the Three Kings and Swan. Successive inventories thereafter list the Swan Mazer, the standing mazer, and the two others.

Fine mazers were fashionable from before the foundation of the College. They were roughly treated, lasting on average 70 years. Their greatest numbers were in the 1520s, after which they suddenly went out of fashion. Forty years later they had become antiques, and the survivors were regarded as treasures.

6.5 The Knob

Plate 2. 1.0 in. diameter, 1.7 high.

Six cast leaves, clearly recognizable as common hawthorn (*Cratægus monogyna*), surround a central cone on a six-lobed knop. The whole is double-gilt. No marks. Mounted on a modern base.

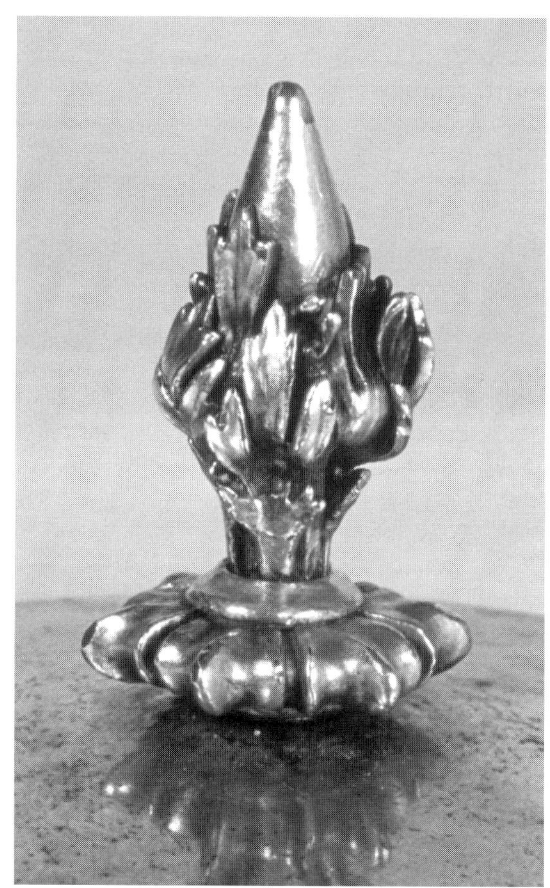

This mysterious little object is surely the world's most beautiful knob: even the veins of the hawthorns are moulded. But it appears in no inventory and no account of the College plate.

Hawthorn is one of the commonest plants in English medieval sculpture. This style of rendering it, strongly curved in three dimensions and with raised veins, is highly characteristic of the early 14th century.[27] A stone version forms one of the finials of the niches inside the chancel of Grantchester church, *c*.1340.

Two documents may throw a little light on it. The 1573/4 inventory mentions a lid to the Cup of the Three Kings. One can well imagine that the wooden lid might have disintegrated, leaving the knob to roll around unrecorded for centuries in a corner of the plate chest. However, the style of the knob is hard to reconcile with the Cup of the Three Kings, whose lid should have been a high cone or spire ending in a finial, like those of the Foundress's Cup at Christ's College, Cambridge, or the coconut cup at Oriel College. The 1630 inventory includes 'A cover, & some broken pieces' knocking about in the bottom of the Chest.

I conjecture that this knob is all that remains of the wooden lid of one of the mazers that the College inherited from the Gild of St Mary. When the original mazer disintegrated it served as the lid of the Cup of the Three Kings. If anyone has a better theory, let us hear it.

26 Hope describes a very late mazer hallmarked 1585–6, harnessed with such straps.

27 Examples: choir stalls of Winchester Cathedral; vault bosses, Ely Lady Chapel. K Basford 1978 *The Green Man* Brewer, Woodbridge (1998) plates 53, 57–60.

The World of Mazers[28]

Mazers were far commoner than horns or coconuts (Appendix 3). For a small college to have sixteen fine mazers would not have been particularly unusual, although only two other institutions have four or more surviving – All Souls' College, Oxford with nine (including lids) and Harbledown Hospital, Canterbury with eight.

King Henry II is said to have had a Keeper of the Mazers among his ministers.[29] Hope and Cripps listed, between them, about 600 mazers recorded in English documents from the 12th century to 1592, in the context of inventories, wills, and burglaries, and of thefts by Henry VIII from gilds and abbeys. Christ Church, Canterbury had a hoard of 182 mazers in 1328. Most recorded mazers were mounted in silver; some had warlike names like Spang and Crumpledud.[30] Decorations included images of God and the Saints, and secular motifs, but no coats-of-arms. One and the same mazer could have 'a prynt in the bothom' depicting the martyrdom of St Thomas (p. 83) and 'a plate of sylvr and gilte wt an Ape lokynge in an urynall'.

From records of 1454 and 1475, the cost of a fine mazer at Cambridge of similar size to ours was 4*s*. the ounce: the feather maple-wood of which ours are made may thus have been at least as costly, ounce for ounce, as silver.

Some mazers were huge. Of the 47 mentioned at York, 33 were 'usual' mazers, the other 14 being 'great and wide'. Henry IV possessed '1 large mazer containing 3 gallons'. A very few great mazers survive. The Scrope Mazer at York Minster, once belonging to the Gild of Corpus Christi there, has the virtue of remitting 40 days in Purgatory, provided the penitent drink its contents (some three-quarters of a gallon) 'soberly . . . with moderation and not excessively'.[31] Mazers reached Scotland: at James III's wedding-feast in 1449 four head of bishops and an abbot drank from 'ung grant hanap de bois'.

In France, 12th-century troubadours sang of heroes drinking from mazer bowls, *hanaps de mazre*. The word, referring to the burry wood, was later spelt *madre*. Fine *hanaps de madre* were set in silver, with lids, handles, octagonal bases, and occasionally a tower with an armed statue in the middle. When his mazers were broken the king of France sought out a *maderinier* to insert silver plates and stitch the cracks with silver wire, as in our Swan Mazer. Similar cups were of rare woods such as cypress (from Crete), tamarisk, lign-aloe, and plane, or of pearl-shell, jasper, or serpentine, or of the skull of a valiant enemy.[32]

Surviving mazers

There are two principal kinds. The first kind are deep vessels, with upright sides, walls almost paper-thin, and plain silver brims; the wood is often bird's-eye maple; the print is a thin plate of silver fastened by many tiny nails or rivets; there is rarely a foot; decoration is confined to the print. Indications of date, where any, point to the 14th century, although the Bayeux Tapestry shows that this form may be much older.

At Canterbury the medieval Hospitals of St Nicholas Harbledown and St John Northgate have between them a hoard of eleven mazers, counting one lid.[33] These include seven of the kind just described. The most elaborate is the great Guy of Warwick Mazer, with a print showing the tenth-century hero rescuing a lion from a dragon.[34] It has seven repairs by a master mazer-mender, each with rivets and fine wire, covered on both sides by silver plates riveted through the wood, which must have been done while it was still used for drinking. Another, of bird's-eye maple, has a print containing a jewel called Becket's Shoe-Buckle, presumably to warn if the drink is poisoned, like the one in the lid of the Poison Tankard, Clare College. Another has a print with the Virgin & Child, like our Cup of our Lady.

28 See Hope, or for the later phase of mazers see Glanville (1990) pp. 25–33.
29 Pinto (1996).
30 One was called ABELL, so may have been made of the white poplar or *abele*, that rare medieval tree.
31 Cripps pp. 239f. I cannot say whether this has recently been tested.
32 Gay s. *hanap, madre.*
Cuming HS 1895 'On Skull-Goblets' *Journal of the Archaeological Association* **NS 1** 234–41.
33 Displayed in Canterbury City Museum (Poor Priests' Hospital) and the Cathedral Treasury. I have been able to examine them through the kind offices of Kenneth Reedie, Curator of Museums & Galleries, Canon Ingram Hill, and Alexander Wheaten.
34 Guy was a popular figure of romance in the 14th century. Historical figures not infrequently slew dragons: Dieudonné de Gozon killed one in Rhodes shortly before he became Grand Master of the Knights Hospitallers in 1346; Wolfgang von Prack bagged another near Corvara in the Dolomites *c*.1500.

Most of the Harbledown and Northgate mazers belong to this first class, of 14th-century or earlier date, as do the '**Hold Yowre Tunge**' Mazer in the Victoria & Albert Museum and the Swan Mazer at Corpus.

The second class of surviving mazers are shallow, thickish-walled cups with broad brims, fringes, and Gothic-letter inscriptions in the manner of the Cup of the Three Kings. The wood is often feather-grain maple. The closest parallel to ours is the Shirley or '**Fille-the-kup**' Mazer, which must have come from the same workshop as the Three Kings.[35] Others in this style belong to the Ironmongers' Company and Oriel College. The Lowthorpe Mazer in York Minster is very like our Mazer Without Print. One at All Souls' College, Oxford has a tower-like print, like our Swan Mazer but without the hydraulics.[36] Indications of date, if any, point to between 1440 and 1470, with some Tudor examples like our Rose Mazer.

Lids very seldom survive. The four known to me are more dissimilar than the mazers themselves. Two mazers at All Souls' have lids which are themselves mazers. Two other lids have no metal fittings. The lid of a great mazer at Harbledown, *c*.1350, is probably beech, painted with lions and a dwarf oak-tree. Another lid at All Souls' is said to be pine, painted and gilded.

At Canterbury there are two coarse mazers, roughly turned and painted black; and a unique fine mazer without metal parts, with an exceptionally beautiful ripple grain.

The end of mazers

Fine mazers continued to be made into the 1530s, inscribed in Tudor capital letters like those on the screen of King's College Chapel. They had already fallen from fashion in France; now they were to do so in England. The vast post-mortem inventory of Henry VIII in 1547 mentions only 'Twoo Masers of woodde and garnyshed with silver gilt'.[37] In Scotland they went on to develop an elegant mid-16th-century style.

Mazers took on an after-life as antiques, cherished and mended[38] and misunderstood and occasionally modernized, but seldom made. They had a brief reincarnation in the 'James I' standing cups, of which Corpus has the earliest example (p. 94). By 1629, the Rev. Zachary Boyd could exhort the readers of his *Last Battell* to 'Take now the Cuppe of Saluation, the great Mazer of [God's] Mercie.'

George III shall have the last word. At his crowning in 1761, one Thomas Rider stepped forward and presented the king with three maple cups, his ancient obligation for holding the manor of Bilsington Inferior. The king turned to the Mayor of Oxford and gave him the wooden cups, taking in exchange a gold cup and cover.

6.6 The College Seal

Colleges and corporate bodies, including the Gild of St Mary, had seals to authenticate important documents. In a solemn ceremony the Master and two Fellows would unlock the ponderous hutch wherein the Common Seal resided; a Chaffwax would melt a red waxen blank onto a tag at the foot of the parchment; and a Spigurnel would stamp the metal seal on the hot wax.

'The Common Seal of the College weighing $2\frac{3}{4}$ ounces' appears in the 1526 plate inventory, together with the Master's seal, with silver chains, weighing $5\frac{1}{2}$ oz. The Common Seal went back to the College's first year: its impression appears on a document of 13 August 1353.[39] This fine specimen of 14th-century die-sinking depicted the Coronation of the Virgin, a shield with a diagram of the Holy Trinity, another shield with the instruments of Christ's Passion (cross, garland, nails, cane with sponge, spear, two scourges), and at the bottom seven benefactors holding a model of a lead-roofed church with a spire. Round the edge were the words: **S'. coe. domus. corporis. xpi. + be. marie. cantebriggie.** (Co[mmon] s[eal] of the house of Corpus Chr[ist]i & Bl[essed] Mary of Cambridge.) Impressions of it appear, for example, on Parker's covenants of 1574 regarding the plate (pp. 69f.). 'The weapons of the Passion of Christ' were apparently the earliest emblem of the College (p. 19).

35 Cripps p. 238. 36 Moffatt Plate XLVI. 37 Starkey §822.

38 The Smythe mazer at Harbledown has a replacement print dated 1603.

39 Hall p. 80.

The Little Seal, from Parker's time, first inventoried in 1591, had the coat-of-arms of the College, with regrettable lilies (p. 22).

Modern administrators hate the fun of sealing documents, and for many years the College has not done so: when a paper is ordered to be sealed, it is instead stamped with an embossing machine which produces a perfunctory imitation of the seal. (The documents are usually investment certificates of the greatest banality.) The seals themselves disappeared long ago.

The surviving seal

An office clear-out has brought a Common Seal back to light. It is a silver plaque engraved (in intaglio) as described above, and containing traces of wax. The handle has been cut off, and there is no hallmark. It is not the original but a copy made, for unknown reasons, at some date between 1574 and 1823. Here and there in the design are shallow pits: evidently the die-sinker's method, given a seal-matrix to copy, was to drill a set of holes down to the levels required by various features and to excavate the metal between them, leaving the bottoms of some of the holes exposed.

Dimensions: 6.4 by 4.1 by 0.6 cm.

It would be perfectly possible to use this Seal should the College have occasion to issue a ceremonial document under seal. There must be dons, like the writer, who cherish the ambition to be a Spigurnel or even a Chaffwax.

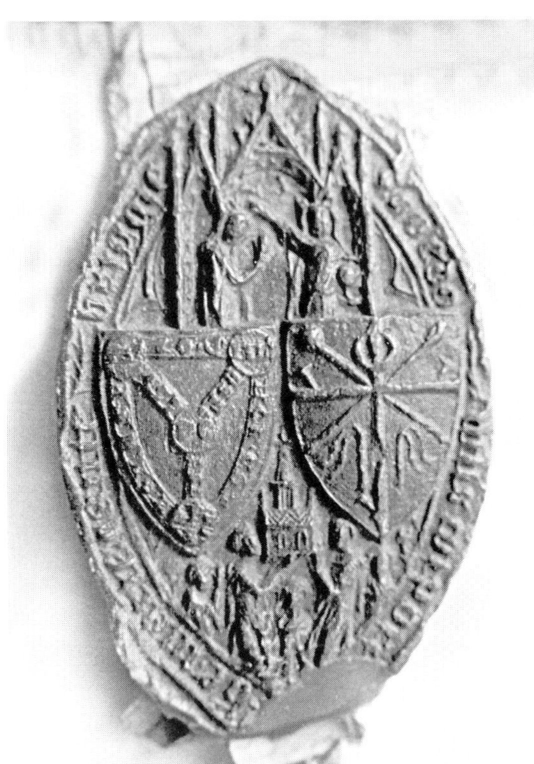

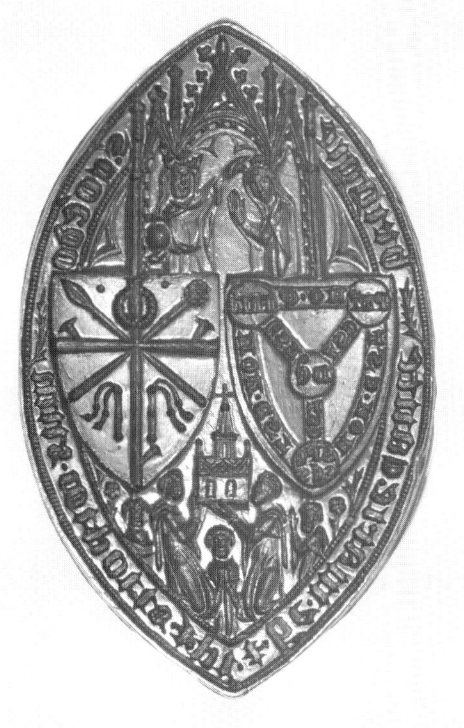

Impression of the original seal, from a Parker covenant; the surviving seal.

7

Parkeriana and Elizabethan Plate

Matthew Parker

by Catherine Hall and Oliver Rackham

Parkeri corpus peri. . ent vt et omnia Parca,
Menti at Parkeri Parca nocere nequat.

(The body of Parker, like everything [else, shall] perish by Fate;
but may Fate be unable to hurt the soul of Parker.)

Motto of Parker's son written on the Neame Cup (p. 93)

Matthew Parker (1504–75),[1] Archbishop of Canterbury, the College's greatest benefactor, was the son of a cloth manufacturer in Norwich. He came to the College as an undergraduate in 1520, under the old-fashioned Master, Peter Nobys. He took his degrees, and was elected Fellow in 1527, under William Sowode, a Master of the opposite persuasion, who would have introduced him to the 'White Horse' group of Norfolk reformers. Parker made a name for himself as a preacher, one of the more moderate of the Cambridge group of Protestant reformers. He earned the affection of Anne Boleyn, to whom he was a faithful friend from throne to block. Somehow he continued afterwards in the good graces of Henry VIII, who in 1544 leant on the College to elect him Master.

As Master, Parker was energetic and efficient, even though he had other jobs to do, such as being Dean of Stoke-by-Clare College (Suffolk) and Dean of Lincoln Cathedral. He conserved the College's endowments and founded scholarships. In 1547 he ventured to marry, which was his undoing, for when Queen Mary came to the throne six years later she sacked all the married clergy and married Masters.

Parker spent the next five years in retirement, allowing Mary to forget to burn him. Elizabeth, coming to the throne, needed a new Archbishop of Canterbury; she remembered Parker's devotion to her mother, and persuaded him to accept in 1559. He spent the remaining sixteen years of his life helping the Queen to re-settle the Church of England, picking up the pieces after thirty years of violent conflict.

Parker was a good Protestant but not a fanatic. He went less far than Cranmer, and had not shared Cranmer's fate. But his vestments had been spattered with a queen's life-blood; he had sniffed the martyr-fire of his Cambridge friend Thomas Bilney, and one of his first duties as Archbishop was to pay the long-overdue bill for the ton-and-a-half of faggots that had consumed his predecessor.[2] He was the literary executor of Cranmer and of the Continental reformer Martin Bucer. But he had a very strong sense of continuity, and for him the Church of Britain, *Britannica Ecclesia*, already had a thousand years of existence, albeit corrupted by the excesses of late-medieval Roman Catholicism. He had an impossible task: he could hardly have made the Church of England acceptable to everyone from devout Papists to Anabaptists; but he went a long way, and some corners of the Anglican Church still embody his ideals of toleration and continuity.

The search for evidence of continuity led Parker to try to reassemble what was left of the contents of the monastic libraries, broken up 25 years before. This left him with a uniquely huge library of manuscripts, plus his own voluminous papers and those relating to Bucer and Cranmer. As with ecologists in the 20th century, he then had to find an institution that could be relied upon

1 Not to be confused with Nosey Parker, the invention of a 20th-century cartoonist.

2 D McCulloch *Thomas Cranmer: a life* Yale University Press 1996 p. 584; CC(L) MS 128 p. 401.

to keep his data-base safely and not break it up again after his death.

But Parker was more than the relentless pursuer of a tendentious theory. He was immensely interested in historical records, especially marking passages that mentioned past archbishops and bishops and kings who supported the Church. He loved liturgical books. He was the earliest Anglo-Saxon scholar: owning as he did one-quarter of the surviving manuscripts in that language, he made it his business to read them (and to find out, for example, that in earlier times clergy, like himself, had married). Many of his manuscripts, such as the great illustrated Bibles or the Chronicles of Matthew Paris, are of little doctrinal significance and must have been valued as historical records or works of art.

Parker, indeed, was a lover of objects of beauty and continuity, especially large and colourful ones. As Master he had taken an interest in the plate, then (as he notes) sadly depleted by the loss of many items dating from the early years of the College, especially Sowode's disposal of those displayed in the Corpus Christi procession or thought to have Popish associations. As Archbishop he remembered his happier days as Master, and probably wished to restore the College treasure to its former magnificence. This time he was concerned to frustrate any attempt by his successors in the College to sell his gifts or use them as security for loans. The conditions he attached to them were not an idle precaution: within 15 years of his death the College pawned £47 worth of other plate to the University, and apparently never saw it again (p. 3).[3]

Parker's attitude to plate was complex. As Vice-Chancellor he had been involved in selling the University's giant silver crucifix, weighing 336 ounces, bigger than any piece Corpus has ever had. As Archbishop he pulled rank to help the College to recover two pieces: the historic Cosyn Salt, alienated in the Sowode disposal; and a basin and ewer newly made for the College at the order of Lawrence Moptyd, his successor as Master, and appropriated by Moptyd's nephew on his death. But Parker immediately purchased these from the College, presumably for his personal use, and what happened to them is unknown.[4]

As Master, Parker found the plate-chests emptier than they had been when his predecessor arrived. Sowode, to whom Parker felt himself much indebted, had carried out improvements (such as panelling the College hall and extending and modernizing the rectory house of Landbeach) not from careful husbanding of college resources, nor from the fruits of his own labours, nor from his own generosity, but from depredations upon the plate – depredations going well beyond the limits of removal of 'superstitious ornaments' or fair substitution of new for old.

This must not happen again. The elaborate and ingenious schemes by which Parker safeguarded the long-term custody of his library and plate have been widely admired.[5] They involved Gonville & Caius College and Trinity Hall as well as Corpus Christi. These were the three colleges with the closest links to Norwich and Norfolk, for Parker remained fiercely loyal to his native city, and (rightly) regarded Norfolk men as the salt of the earth. Even as an undergraduate he had selected his closest personal friends from among them, and to their connexions he had owed his recommendation to the royal court. As Archbishop he retained and strengthened these friendships by his support of John Caius, becoming perhaps the only man that eccentric doctor fully trusted. The ex-Corpus civil lawyer, Thomas Legge, then at Trinity Hall, was accepted by Caius, at Parker's suggestion, to be his successor in his college.

Parker recognized that the endowment of scholarships and fellowships, where possible with priority for Norfolk men or Canterbury men, was the soundest long-term investment for the future of the University, the church, and the nation. In Corpus he endowed five Norfolk scholarships,[6] five Canterbury scholarships, and four Norwich fellowships. In Caius, then as now the premier medical college, he founded a scholarship for a student of medicine, and in Trinity Hall for a law student.

Parker's plate and his schemes for protecting it

Parker's gifts, like his lifetime, cover the change from the middle ages to the Renaissance. The Rosewater Basin, Two Cups and One Lid, and Apostle Spoons are Gothic in

3 CC(A): *Audits 1590–1678*, account for 1590, p.[19].
4 Lamb p. 108; CC(L) MS 106 pp. 659, 686. 5 Clifford.
6 These continued on a reduced scale into the 1960s; the compiler of this book was nearly the last recipient of Parker's generosity.

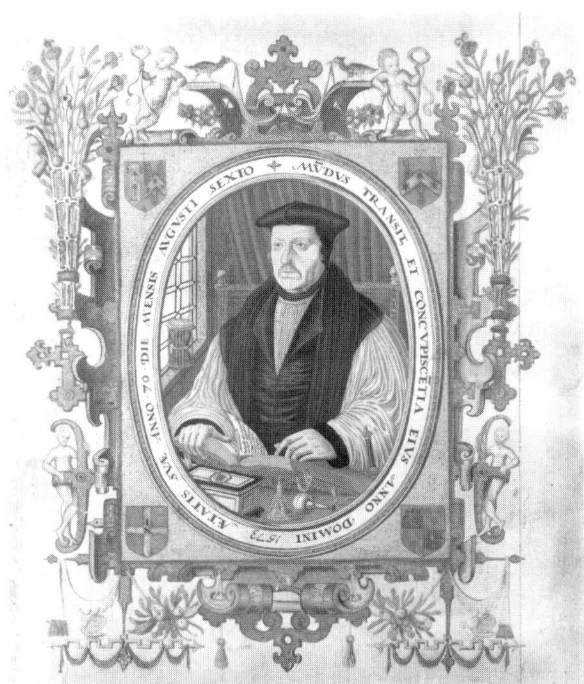

Matthew Parker. This portrait illustrates his Mannerist taste in book illustration, repeated also on his plate. The plants illustrated, however, are European, not American. The arms are those of himself as Archbishop, himself, Corpus Christi College, and his Cathedral. From CC(L): MS 582, inner cover.

style; the Standing Cup, Salt, Tankard, and Communion Cup are Mannerist.

His coat-of-arms, which appears on most of Parker's gifts, reads: *Gules, between three keys argent a chevron of the same charged with three estoiles.* (The three stars were a personal augmentation, rather like the letters OBE after one's name today.) It may be impaled by the arms of his Archbishopric: *Azure on a pallium proper with four crosses fitchy, in chief a cross patée of the second*; or by the arms of Canterbury Cathedral: *Azure, on a Latin cross argent the letters I X.* (A pallium is a Y-shaped vestment symbolizing the links between Canterbury and the Pope; Parker must have chosen to retain it.)

Parker, nurtured in the world of commerce, was used to negotiating intricate and fair deals. His gifts of plate to his three colleges were carefully planned to secure the proper administration of his endowments. He made similar but independent arrangements with the City of Norwich, the fourth recipient of his gifts of plate.[7]

In preparation for his great bequest of manuscripts and books, Parker experimented with arrangements surrounding some earlier gifts of plate. His three colleges were made participants with the Archbishop in a series of agreements between January 1569/70 and February 1571/2.

On 1 January 1569/70, to mark the tenth anniversary of his consecration as Archbishop, Parker gave each of the three colleges a great silver-gilt standing cup, specially commissioned to a design of his own choosing, crowded with ornament in the Mannerist style fashionable also in architecture, printing, and bookbinding. The lid of each cup culminated in a male, female, or infant figure – nude, armed, and heroic. Half-hidden on each is a Latin inscription recording the donor, recipient, date, and its weight. Corpus's cup is the most magnificent.

To guard against any one college casually disposing of its cup, Parker had a series of bonds drawn up. If the cup was lost a forfeit was to be paid to one of the other colleges, which kept the signed and sealed bond, with a precise drawing of the cup and its inscription on the back. Thus Gonville & Caius College was given, and still has,

> An Obligacion wherin the M^r^ & fellows of Corpus Christi College in Cambrige be bounde to the M^r^ & Fellowes of Gunwell & Caius College in Cambrige for y^e^

7 CC(A): XLA 33 (13 June 1572).

safe Keeping of the Plate wch Matthew Parker gave them 12° Eliz.[8]

It is dated 14 March 12 Elizabeth [1569/70], signed by the new Master Thomas Aldrich and four Fellows, and sealed with the Corpus seal; it has a penalty clause of £26 6*s* 8*d* for losing the cup (about twice the melt-down value), and a drawing of the cup (p. 76).

Corpus keeps similar bonds recording the cups given simultaneously to Gonville & Caius College and Trinity Hall, and also one for the basin and ewer given to the Corporation of Norwich.[9] Only the Caius bond was signed and sealed by the opposite parties, and their cup remains intact. The others appear never to have been sealed, enabling Trinity Hall with impunity to lose the heroine Judith from the finial of their cup, and Norwich Corporation to recycle their gift into sauce-boats (p. 73).

Parker celebrated his sixty-fifth birthday by giving Corpus a communion cup and cover, engraved 'on the inward boll' with the names of donor and recipient and the date 6 August 1569 'ÆTATIS SUE PRECISE COMPLETO .65.', the weight $43\frac{1}{4}$ ounces. A detailed drawing and description are on the dorse of a draft bond, intended to be signed and sealed by Trinity Hall, but never completed or sent there.[10] There is, however, a signed memorandum by John Caius witnessing to Parker's foundations in Corpus of Norwich scholars and Fellows and the gift of a certain silver cup to that college, with an indenture against alienation dated 6 August 1569.[11]

These bonds were redoubled. Two sets were drawn up in triplicate, to be jointly sealed, so that all three colleges were witnesses to the whole range of Parker's benefactions to date. The first, dated 6 August 1570, of which Corpus has all three copies, lists

> certaine Silver plate to be kepte and reserved within the said three Colledges for ever, without any manner of Alienacion impignoracion* or transportation of any parte of the same owte of the said Colledge.
>
> *pawning

The second set, dated 1 February 1571/2, is a more elaborate version entitled 'Letters Testimonial'. It brings up to date the Archbishop's munificence to each college, ending with the further gift

> at thensealing* of this present writing testimonyall one gylt pott with a cover weighing [in the case of Corpus] sixtene ounces and a half.[12]
>
> *the ensealing

These 'potts' are the Parker Tankards which each college still has (p. 87).

There is also a curious indenture with the College, dated 28 February 1569/70, signed and sealed by Parker, explaining that whereas the Archbishop 'of his mere benevolence' has given the College a cup and cover weighing 43 ounces, yet the Master and Fellows 'are contented to committ again into the handes of the said Matthew the said Communion Cuppe for his use during his life, if he so longe will use the same', and promising that within six days of the return of the cup the College will enter into a bond with Trinity Hall not to alienate. This may explain why the original bond drawn up for Trinity Hall was drafted but never executed.

Parker's economical habit of giving gifts but retaining life use of them makes sense of another document dated 26 June 'a thousande five hundreth threscore and fiftene', a month after his death. This is a receipt under the College seal from Robert Norgate, the Master, to John Baker of Cambridge, Parker's younger half-brother and executor, for 'one basene and ewer', 'a communion cup with a cover', 'one salte with a cover', and '13 spones'.[13] This explains why the College's 1573/4 inventory mentions Parker's three other gifts – the great cup, the tankard, and the lid and two cups – but not these four.

John Parker, the Archbishop's son and principal executor, got a similar receipt from the Mayor and Corporation of Norwich for their basin and ewer, given by the Archbishop in his lifetime 'yet redelyvered agayne by Indenture . . . to be occupyed by hym during his Naturall life'. Baker also had receipts from the Masters of Trinity Hall and of Gonville & Caius for three silver bowls each. These last, however, were bequests and not old gifts 'redelivered'; there were no penalties against alienation, and neither college still has them.[14]

8 G&C: Treasury Box III.10. 9 CC(A): XLA 64, 67, 65.
10 CC(A): XLA 66. 11 CC(A): XLA 69.
12 CC(A): XLA 26, 26a, 26b, 30, 31, 32. 13 CC(A): XLA 51, 49.
14 CC(A): XLA 50, 52.

7.1 Parker's Rosewater Basin & Ewer

So thyn ewery be arayed with basyns & ewers, & water hote & colde, and se ye have napkyns...

The Boke of Kervyng, 1515

Two-thirds of the way through a feast, when the hall gets hot and stuffy, a basin of rosewater is passed round the table for the diners to dip their napkins and wash their faces and behind their ears. Rosewater, a traditional product of Bulgaria, is water scented with an extract of the petals of special varieties of roses.[15]

This custom continues an ancient practice of washing at the dinner-table, shown on the Bayeux Tapestry (p. 54) and mentioned in all medieval books of etiquette.[16] Before forks were used, people's fingers got greasy, and they went through the motions of washing them – which can hardly have been effective, since none of the rule-books mentions soap. (However, Americans who still eat with their fingers somehow avoid the need for much washing.)

The basin and ewer (Plate 3)

Basin 17.8 in. in diameter, 1.7 high; jug 8.6 in. high.

This is the grandest piece that Matthew Parker gave the College. Indeed it is said to be the grandest object of its time to survive anywhere; the Kremlin, or St Petersburg, or the Imperial Treasury in Vienna, has not its match. It is not Elizabethan but Henrician: it bears the London date-letter H for 1545.

The basin is of an annular shape, with an island in the middle on which is a boss; the hollow base of the jug sits on the boss. The island is deeply embossed with spiral lobes; the outer flange and the top of the island are engraved in arabesque patterns (not showing on the underside). On the boss are Parker's enamelled arms, encircled by his motto MVNDVS TRANSIT ET CONCUPICENTIA EIVS (The world passeth away, and the lust thereof – *I John* **2** 17), with an Archbishop's cross behind.

Inscriptions (around the underside): MATTHÆVS . CANTVAR . DEDIT . COLLE° . CORPORIS . CHRI . CANTAB . 1° . SEPT . A° . 1570 . CONSECRIS . SVÆ . 11° . ET . ÆTATIS . SVÆ . 67. | VNCIÆ 122 : DI. (Matthew of Canterbury gave [me] to the College of Corpus Christi at Cambridge on 1 Sept. in the year 1570 in the 11th [year] of his consecration and the 67th of his age. 122½ ounces.)

The jug (or *ewer,* a vessel for water) is octagonal in plan, with a hinged lid whose flat top repeats the engraving and spiral lobes of the basin. Alternate panels are ornamented with arabesques matching those on the basin, but chased, so that they show on the inside. The spout has a heart-shaped orifice, and communicates with the jug by five holes to strain out cockroaches or other swimmers. On the boss are Parker's arms impaled by those of his cathedral, with an Archbishop's cross behind, surrounded by the motto given above. The date-inscription is 1 . 5 . 70.

The maker's mark is a queen's head, known otherwise on a cup of 1544; no silversmith's shop at the sign of the Queen's Head has yet been identified (Jackson 1989).

The inside of the basin and outside of jug and lid are treble-gilt, except for the arms; this was done after the 1570 additions, and may be a 19th-century tampering. The underside of the basin is single-gilt; the inside of the jug is plain silver.

History

This object was somewhat of an antique when Parker gave it. The coats-of-arms are additions connected with the gift, and must replace (or hide) earlier plaques. They are in the Mannerist style of 1570 rather than the late Gothic of 1545. On the basin, the arms surmount an upstanding boss with intricate raised, probably cast, detail resembling two of the bands on the Parker Cup. Similar detail is repeated on the lower band of the foot of the jug. Both these parts appear to be 1570 alterations. The addition of the boss to the basin would require enlarging the base of the jug to fit over it.

The present weight of basin and ewer is 123.4 ounces, less than an ounce heavier than the inscribed weight.

15 An inferior sort is said to be made from roseroot (*Sedum rosea*) in the Faeroes: *Botanical Journal of Scotland* **46** (1994) 615.

16 *Babees Book.*

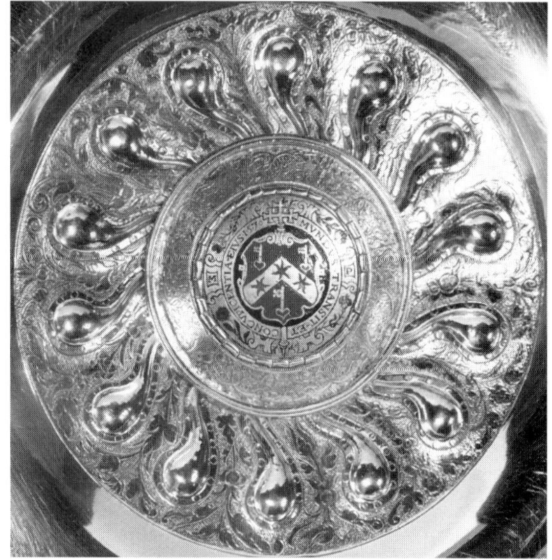

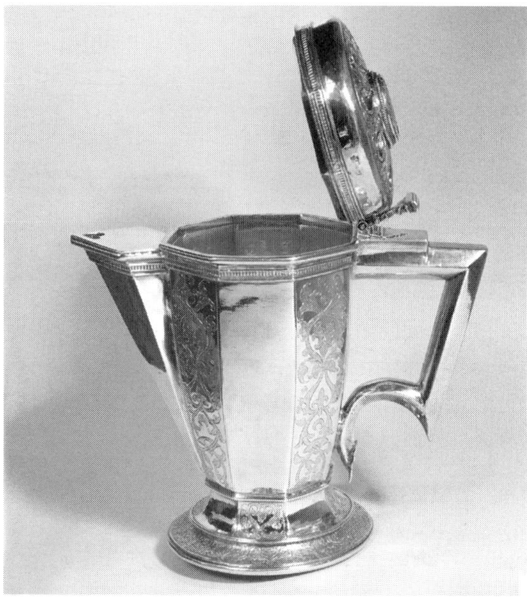

Parker's coats-of-arms and surrounding decoration on the basin (left) and lid of the ewer (right).
Below: the ewer, and the inconsistent decoration on the ring at its base, added in 1570.

This confirms that the inscription was added after the 1570 alterations. The difference may represent the weight of the added gilding.

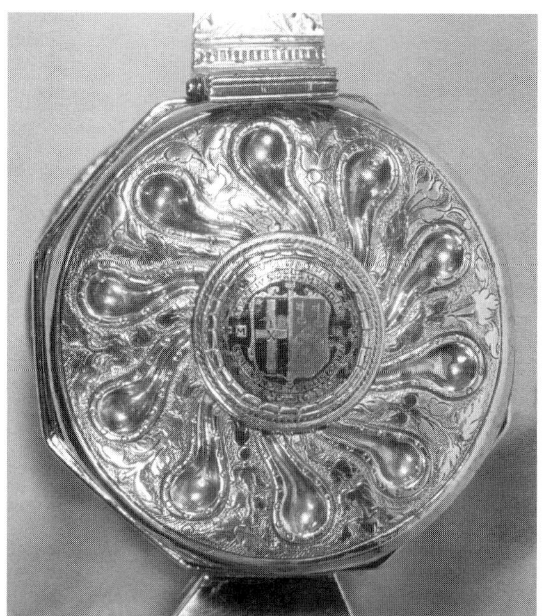

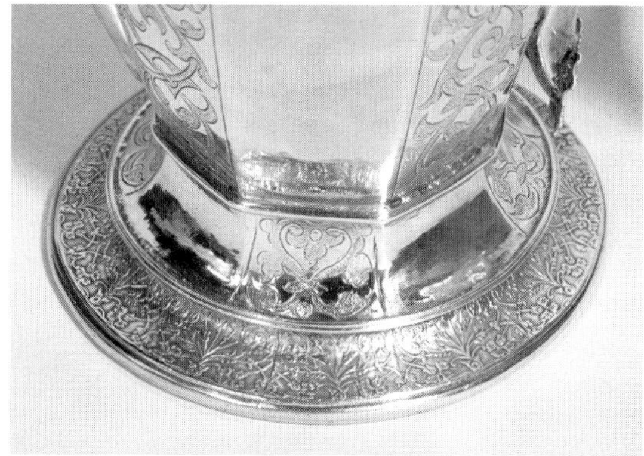

The piece was made when Parker was Master of the College, but probably not for him, since he was not a very rich man. Maybe one day someone will devise a means of reading the original device underneath Parker's arms.

Parker took back his gift during his lifetime, so it is absent from the 1573/4 inventory; it appears on the post-mortem receipt of 1575 (p. 70) and on subsequent inventories.

The world of basins and ewers

Many Roman examples of this type of basin are known; one found its way to East Anglia and was buried at Sutton

Hoo. This had straight fluting, but the spiral kind of fluting was also Roman.[17] Basins with a circle of spiral lobes and a central enamelled plaque were made in the mid-14th century, to judge by the Bermondsey Dish now in the Victoria & Albert Museum.[18] They were made in other countries and other materials: Kelvingrove Museum, Glasgow has a great faience dish, said to be Venetian, with two rows of such depressed spiral lobes.

The basin (*pelvis*) appears in inventories from the 1280s onwards, usually as a 'pair of basins' (*par pelvium*). Silver ewers seem not to be associated with basins until 1500.[19]

The Botener inventory of 1376 includes among the secular plate:

> one shallow bowl (*peluis plana*) and a shallow wash-basin, and the bowl is as big in circumference as a bushel (*modius*).

These may have been inherited from the Gild of St Mary. A bushel is an 8-gallon measure for corn; it would normally be about 15 inches in diameter, so the bowl would have been somewhat smaller than the Parker Rosewater-Basin. This entry was crossed out, indicating that we had disposed of the pieces (or had them looted in 1381), and replaced by 'one bowl . . . on a pedestal with a convex wash-basin (*lauacro gibboso*)', added in Northwode's hand. These perhaps were the *lavacrum & patella* repaired for 4*d*. in 1388, but do not appear in later inventories.

Lawrence Moptyd, Parker's successor as Master, commissioned a silver-gilt basin and ewer to be made by Christopher Ryngsted for the College. When he died in 1557 Parker as Archbishop extracted them from his executor, but never returned them to the College (p. 68). (They would be too late to be the present basin and ewer.)

Parker's basin and ewer are probably the earliest set to survive anywhere. The basin's obvious predecessors are the two 'ablution basins', hallmarked 1493 and 1514, presented to Corpus Christi College, Oxford, by Bishop Fox the founder. These too have central plaques with the donor's coat-of-arms in enamel, but sun's rays instead of spiral flutes. One has a little spout for draining the contents, showing that it is a sacred basin for the priest to wash his fingers after Mass.[20] Very few pre-Reformation liturgical basins survive, but their descendants are the big alms-dishes used at Protestant services (cf. the Montacute Dish, p. 112).

Another silver-gilt ewer and basin, said to have been made in Bruges *c*.1550, is the Mostyn set now in the National Museum of Wales, Cardiff.

Parker gave the City of Norwich, where his half-brother was Mayor, an even larger and more magnificent ewer and basin, weighing 175 ounces. These were new and in a Mannerist style similar to the Great Parker Cup. He left a stringent (but unratified) deed of gift backed up by drawings in the Norwich archives and in the College. Nevertheless, the Corporation in 1761, having a more recent set given by the Duke of Norfolk, recycled them, it is said, into four mighty sauce-boats.[21] In 1904 the Mayor had a replica made on the basis of the drawing.

The next rosewater set, in date and in grandeur, in Cambridge is the Harington basin and ewer, in late Elizabethan style of 1606, at Sidney Sussex College. Merton College, Oxford, has a rosewater 'dish' with similar chasing, dated 1605.[22] In the Victoria & Albert Museum are the huge basin and ewer, with arms obliterated, of the Goldsmiths' Company, made in 1611 and sold in 1637. After a lull in the 19th century, such vessels continued to be made down to the present.

In 1632 the College created a second 'Bas. Eure' by melting six Fellow-Commoners' gifts. It would have weighed about 70 ounces, a little over half the weight of the Parker set. It was apparently melted in turn in 1715 for £17. 18*s*. 7*d*. worth of metal, put towards a new 'Bason & Ewer' costing £43. 5*s*. 7*d*. The fate of this truly magnificent piece is unknown. For everyday use the College had several pewter basins and ewers, forever being melted down and recycled.[23]

17 Bruce-Mitford Fig. 53.
18 *Age of Chivalry* §156, Fig. 115.
19 Cripps pp. 269f.
20 Philippa Glanville, *Corpus Silver* chapter VI.
21 R. Emmerson 1984 *Norwich Regalia & Civic Plate* Norfolk Museums Service, Norwich.
22 Jones *Merton* Pl.2.
23 CC(A): Chapter Book II, 4 April 1632; Audit Book 1590–1685 *passim*.

7.2 Parker's Great Standing Cup (Plate 4)

> **Inpri[mi]s** a greate standinge cup of silver, wth a Cover of the same gilt, wayinge in toto liii [53] uncs of the gyft of Matthew archbysshope of Cant^{r}b
>
> *1573/4 Inventory* [*last 8 words in another hand*]

On 1 January 1569 (or, as we would say, 10 January 1570) Matthew Parker presented to the College 'one certaine cuppe with the couer whole gilte weyeng fiftie thre ownces . . . perpetuallye to remayne within the said college'. Gonville & Caius College and Trinity Hall were to make sure that we kept it. If it were 'lost or stollen' we had to have a replica made.

Our cup – the second grandest cup in Cambridge, after the Vice-Chancellor's Cup of 1592 – is a triumph of the technical virtuosity of the Mannerist style: of cherubs and of strapwork, of American fruits and lions' faces, of leafage and tropical citruses, of *décolletée* ladies leaning out of pomegranate-encrusted oval windows, of tiny delicate posies and secretary-birds and garlands, of devilish little masks, of Marcus Aurelius hidden inside the lid and a nude hero teetering wearily on the summit – these are architectural motifs, the romantic essence of Wollaton Hall (Nottingham) condensed to one-fiftieth scale.

The cup comes in three parts: the lid, bowl, and base. The bowl is a somewhat insecure push-fit into the base. The whole is double-gilt, except for the base of the lid which is single-gilt, and the underside and the parts of the bowl and base which fit together, which are plain silver.

Even such an elaborate piece as this was probably meant to be drunk out of. The inside of the detachable bowl is smooth, with no *repoussé* to complicate washing-up.

Summary of decorative features

The base and stem comprise the following tiers (from the bottom up), each tier usually with three or six features.

(1) Fringe of hearts-and-arrows.

(2) Lion; melancholy face with long ears; moustachio'd face; apples and pears between.

(3) Cherubs (separate castings); secretary-birds.

(4) Posies of apples and three different kinds of citruses.

(5), (6) Posies of apples, pears, melons.

(7) Man (or is he a bulldog?) with long ears and tongue hanging out; melancholy man; melancholy lion; three different citruses between them.

The bowl has:

(8) Three identical ladies, each in an oval of pomegranates.

(9) Three cherubs.

The lid has:

(10) Engraved Roman emperor on underside. (Dr Christopher Kelly identifies him tentatively as Marcus Aurelius.)

(11) Moustachio'd man showing his teeth; citrus (?shaddock, predecessor of grapefruit); face of lion chewing a ring; ?squash (a globular gourd, whose stalk bears a tendril, showing that it is not a citrus); cherub; 2-tiered orange.

(12) Secretary-birds.

(13) Apples, scaly pears, peeled oranges, grapes.

(14) Nude hero.

Dimensions: Cup 13.6 × 5.8 in. Lid 6.3 × 8.3. Total height 21.4.

Inscription and marks

Inscription underneath: + MATTHÆVS . CANTVAR . DEDIT . COLLEO . CORPORIS . CHRI . CANTAB . 1º . JAN . Aº . DNI . 1569 . CONSECIS . SVÆ . IIº . ET ÆTATIS . SVÆ 66 (Matthew of Canterbury gave [me] to the College of Corpus Christi, Cambridge, 1 January A.D. 1570, in the 11th year of his consecration and the 66th of his age.) Weight inscribed as 53 ounces: present weight 54.3 oz.

Maker's mark: a bunch of grapes. London date-letter 𝔪 for 1569.

Construction

Each section is made of many parts: the base consists of a dozen components held together on a central rod.

All the techniques of silversmithing are combined. The boldly modelled lions' faces and citrus fruits on

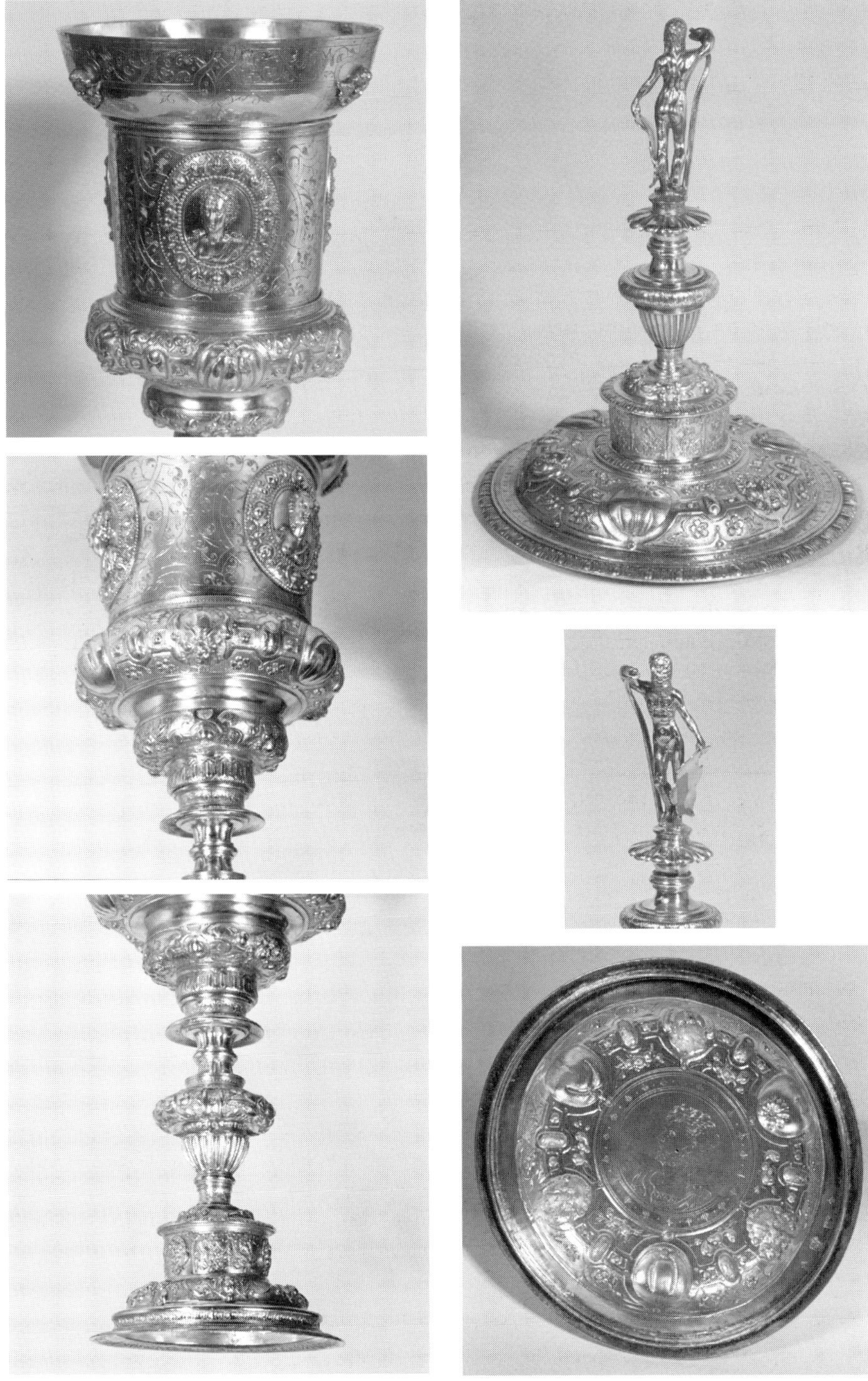

Parker Cup: details from top to bottom, and underside of the lid

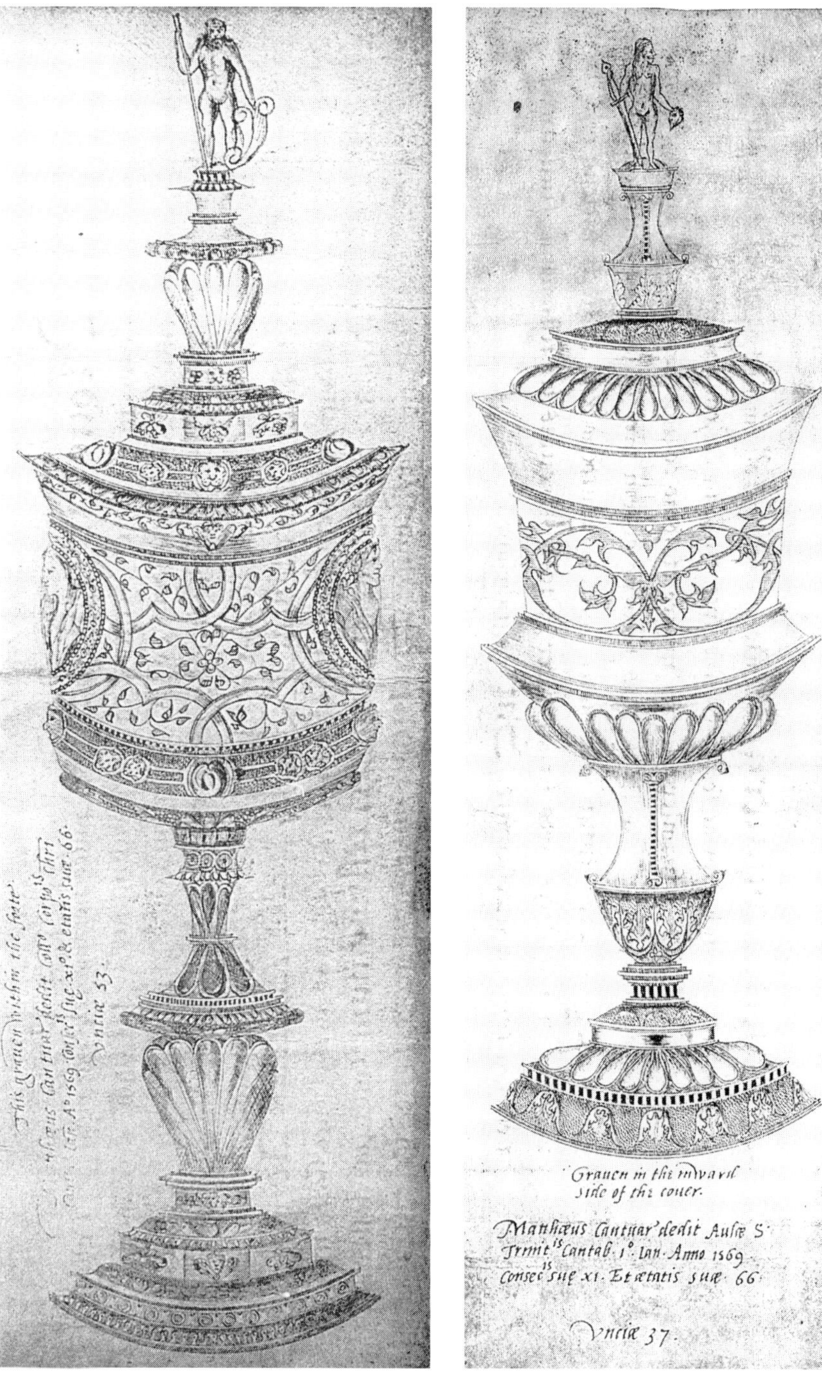

Left: contemporary drawing of the Parker Cup, from the bond in Gonville & Caius College archives
Right: drawing of the Judith Cup at Trinity Hall, from the bond in Corpus archives (CC(A): XLA 67)

lid and base are virtuoso examples of *repoussé* work, embossed from the inside against a mould. The ladies on the bowl are castings, made separately and soldered on, each with a blowhole under her left ear. Between them are engraved sketches of foliage. The cherubs and the ovals round the ladies are also separate castings, but the masks are *repoussé*. The tiny reliefs on the drums of lid and base also appear to be castings.

What does it all mean?

Nude statues are common finials on cups of the period: Hercules gesticulates on top of the great cup of St John's College (1617), and an armed heroine teeters over Bishop Barlow's Cup in Trinity Hall (1608). Our hero leans on a staff,[24] resting his shield. The companion cup at Gonville & Caius College (see below) is presided over by his little nephew, a childish naked warrior. The drawing of the Trinity Hall cup shows that he once had a niece, a nude heroine (Judith?) with a sword in one hand and a man's head in the other, but she, alas, has disappeared.

The semi-devils, common on Mannerist plate (as the Parker Tankard, p. 87), may have been meant for satyrs or the god Pan, rather than the Archbishop's spiritual foe. The *décolletée* ladies, identical triplets, may be Diana, although their hair-dos suggest the serpent-tressed Gorgon Medusa.

Amid these Classical allusions, which generations of schoolmasters were beating into their boys, modern discovery was well represented by tropical Asian and American fruits; these were to set a fashion in plate lasting into the next century (p. 108). One is certainly a pumpkin or squash, which must have been grown from seed borrowed from an American Indian garden. A sort of scaly pear may be some other exotic fruit, possibly an avocado pear from the West Indies. Others are different sorts of citrus from S.E. Asia. Oranges, though known since the middle ages, were still a romantic curiosity of mysterious Oriental colour and scent. Other kinds of citrus fruit, including some no longer known, had come to join them. The secretary-birds (if I identify them rightly) are a genus of serpent-eaters from the Old World tropics. It is surprising to find all these known so early in England, which had only begun to make direct contact with other continents, and was still far from beginning an overseas empire. The cup is too early to depict the four portentous results of American contact – tobacco, potato, maize, and tomato.

24 The drawing of our cup in Gonville & Caius archives shows that the staff is not a spear which has lost its tip. It has, however, been bent, together with the arm holding it, by someone dropping the lid.

Other great cups

On the same day Parker gave less elaborate cups to Gonville & Caius and Trinity Hall, with drawings in Corpus archives. These are almost identical to each other, pre-Mannerist in style, without the strapwork, *repoussé*, and little castings. They have no hallmarks and are undated.

These were a revival of the medieval custom of ceremonial standing cups as an alternative marvel to horns, mazers, griffins' eggs, etc. A rare Gothic survival, too spiky to drink from without a long straw, is the Leigh Cup of 1499 in Mercers' Hall, London.

Parker's gifts started a Cambridge fashion. Similar objects include the Founder's Cup of *c.*1575, given to Emmanuel College in 1584, the 1586 cup now among the chapel plate of Magdalene College, and the Vice-Chancellor's Cup of 1592. Outside Cambridge the fashion soon went off the rails, leading to cups in the likeness of cocks, royal oaks, women, peafowl, and other undrinkable shapes.

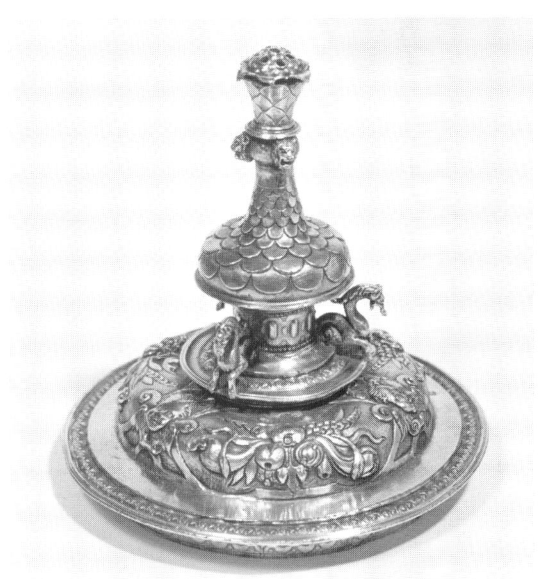

Pepper-pot lid of Parker's salt

7.3 Parker's Salt-Celler (Plate 5)

PRIMO . SEPTEMBRIS . ANNO . DNI . 1.5.70 . MATTHAEVS . ARCHIEPVS . CANT-VARIENSIS . DEDIT . COLLEGIO . CORPORIS . CHRISTI . CANTABRIGIÆ | SALINVM . HOC . CVM . PIXIDE . PRO . PIPERE . IN . OPERCVLO . CVM . 13 . COCLEARIBVS . DEAVRATIS . QVÆ . HENT . CHRVM . ET . APLOS . PONDERANT . OZ . 64
On the first of September, Anno Domini 1570, Matthew Archbishop of Canterbury gave to the College of Corpus Christi at Cambridge this celler, with a box for pepper in the lid, with 13 silver-gilt spoons which represent Christ and the Ap[ost]les. They weigh 64 ounces,

Inscription on the Parker Salt

Parker's salt-celler stands in front of the chief guest at a feast. A shallow cavity for not very much salt forms the top of a hollow cylindrical drum, which stands on three feet in the likeness of sea-rhinoceroses. Overlapping the salt-dish, and forming a push-fit with it, is the lid, of which the upper part is a pepper-box, the six holes for which form the finial.

The decoration is another Mannerist masterpiece. On the drum, three faces – an American chief, the Devil in one of his rare good moods, and a bearded man with long ears – glare out of strapwork roundels, between which hang swags of foliage with squashes, pomegranates, pears (or 'scaly pears', maybe avocados), figs, and an American squash. The base is ornamented with 'acanthus' leaves. The lid has three different cherub faces between clusters of grapes, pears, scaly pears, gourds, and pomegranates, as well as foliage and scale-chains. Three little cast sea-horses (of the heraldic, not the zoological kind) form brackets to the scaly pepper-box roof, ascending past three little lions' faces to the holes at the top.

It is made from thinnish sheet metal, single-gilt outside. The detail is beautifully crisp, less cast and engraved than on the Parker Cup and Parker Tankard; it has neither been obscured by heavy gilding nor destroyed by cleaning. As on most Mannerist pieces, the maker left little room for inscriptions or coats-of-arms. The fruit etc. continue the allusions to America, some years before Hawkins and Drake had voyaged there, that we noted on the Parker Cup.

It is unlikely to have been much used: there is no corrosion to suggest that anyone put salt in it. The pepper-box is attached by a crude nut and bolt, evidently not original. The weight inscription creates a puzzle. The present weight of the Salt and Spoons is 66.0 ounces, or 66.2 ounces if we add the missing haloes of three Apostles. The inscribed weight is 64 ounces: it is difficult to see where the extra two ounces (75 grams) of metal can be.

The maker's mark, RD (or BD) monogram, is attributed to Robert Danbe, a prolific silversmith of the 1550s and 1560s, with at least five apprentices.[25] Date-letter: 𝔢 for 1562.

This, too, was reclaimed by Parker and kept until his death. The earliest known illustration (Smith 1845) shows it as now. The Victoria & Albert electrotype copy (p. 30) shows that the monstrous feet were already bent by 1880.

Celler: 11.6 in. high (7.0 without lid); 6.5 greatest diameter. Lid: 5.2 in. high by 5.1.

The world of salt

As everyone is told, the middle ages were addicted to salt, and a ceremonial salt-celler in the likeness of a hare, woman, tower, man, dragon, morris-dance, olifant, etc. sat on every upper-class high table. Salts could be more varied in shape than anything else. A survivor is the huge salt, of silver double-gilt, crystal, pearl, and enamel, adorned with countless harts, hares, and pious pelicans entangled in filigree, presented by Bishop Fox to Corpus Christi College, Oxford: surely the most intricate article of plate to survive from the middle ages. This, like the almost as elaborate Hill Salt of *c.*1490 in New College, is

25 Clifford. Our example, badly struck, looks more like BD.

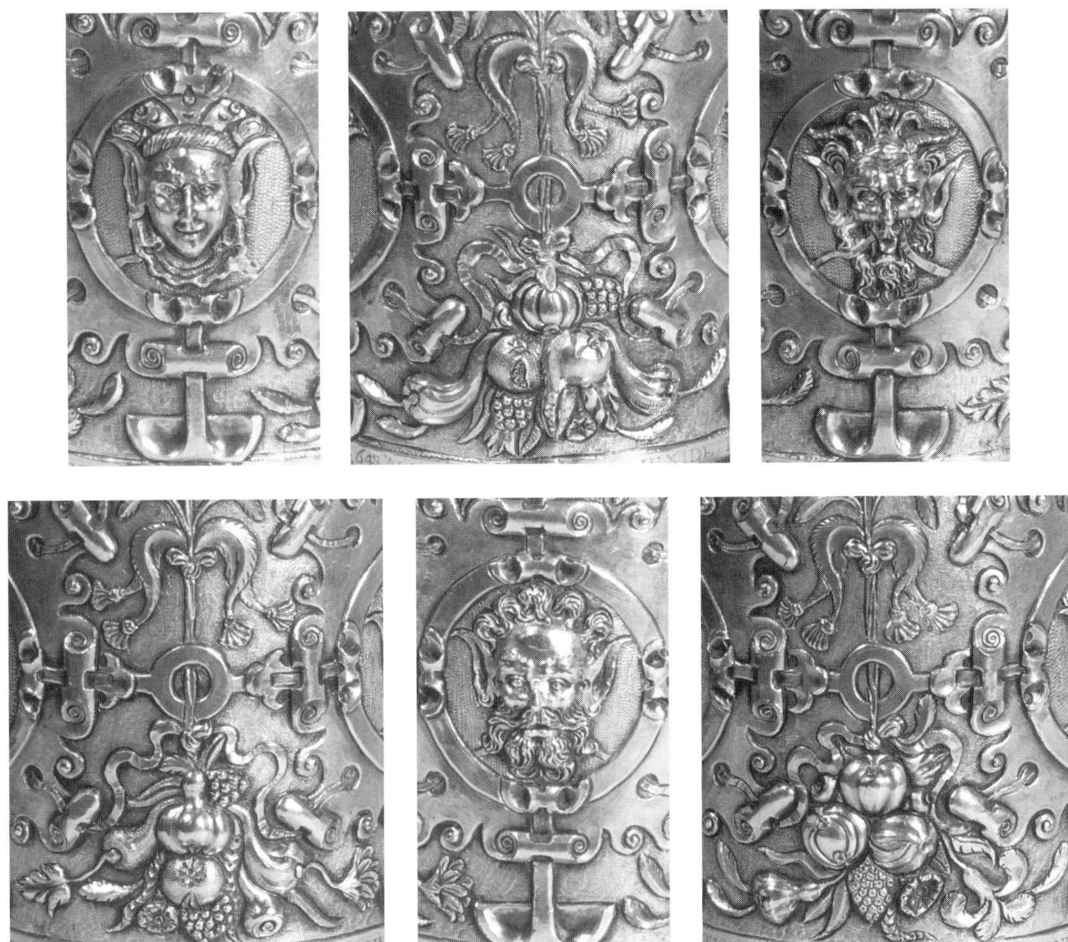

Warriors, the Devil, tropical and American fruit: details from the Parker Salt

of an hour-glass shape with a large central knop and a high lid.[26]

Corpus Christi Cambridge had no grand salt until 1483, when Thomas Cosyn gave one. This was alienated by Sowode but recovered, and then bought, by Parker (p. 68). We never saw it again, unless it was the 'longe olde salte wth a couer guilte', weighing 21 ounces, which appears in inventories down to 1670. We had three or four smaller silver or gilt salers, which are difficult to trace through successive inventories.

26 Marian Campbell in *Corpus Silver* chapter V.

Cylinder salts of the Parker type begin with an example at Corpus Oxford dated 1554. Norwich Corporation has one a little earlier than Parker's, and the Mostyn Salt is 24 years later. The Goldsmiths' Company has one of 1567, almost the same as ours (though by a different maker), standing on three lions, and with a warrior instead of a pepper-pot. The shape goes on through the 17th century, ending with a salt in the likeness of the Eddystone Lighthouse, made in 1698. (The lighthouse succumbed to the hurricane of 1703, leaving only the salt.) The Lighthouse seems to be the only other cylinder salt with a pepper-pot in the top, though this combination was frequent in the smaller 'bell' salts.

7.4 The Apostle Spoons

I'll be a Gossip. Bewford,
I have an odd apostle-spoon.

Beaumont & Fletcher, *Noble Gentleman*
[Fletcher, Corpus undergraduate, 1591–4, could have known of the odd Apostle Spoon]

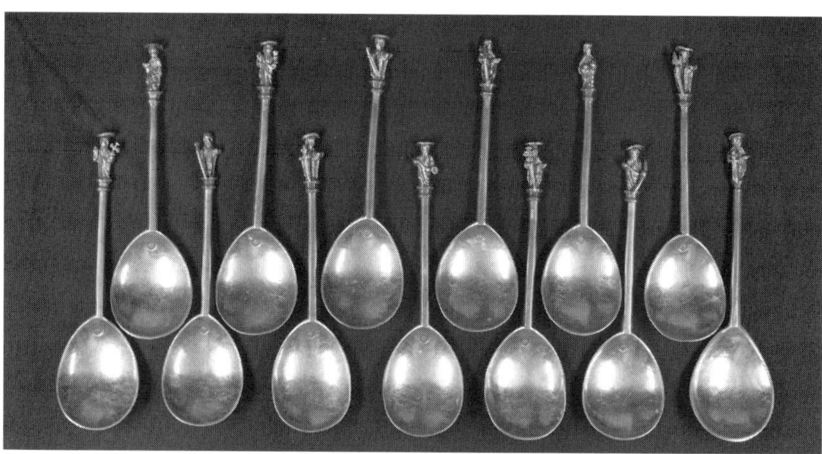

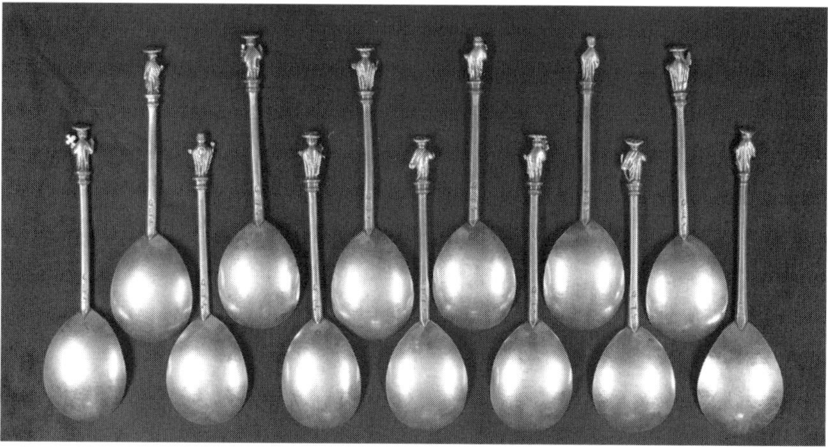

On 1 September 1570 Parker presented to the College '13 spoons of silver-gilt which have Christ and the Apostles', as he says on the Parker Salt-celler (p. 78). We have them still. Though meant for show, they have been in the wars. Three have lost their haloes; and all are scratched by use. They are comfortable to use and sit well in the hand. They are 7.0 in. long – those that still have haloes – 2.0 in. wide, except for St Paul who is bigger.

Parker's spoons are of a distinctively English shape, with a 'fig-shaped' bowl and slightly tapering stem of hexagonal section. This had a very long currency: the *Age of Chivalry* exhibition displayed seven from *c*.1300 to 1410, and the form was still fashionable until 1660. Only the shape of the base of the bowl and the angle between bowl and stem vary slightly but systematically over the decades (as shown by How & How in their classic book on Tudor and Stuart spoons). Political and religious upheaval had little effect on spoons, symbolic though they often were.

Early spoons of this type have knobs, acorns, or (as with the Founder's Spoon of Winchester College) a jewel as finials. They were made as separate bowl, stem, and finial, then soldered together. The finials were cast by the lost-wax process; with our spoons, the Apostles' haloes and some of their emblems are separate castings.[27] Figurines were often women's heads, sometimes Apostles, but could be lions, owls (as on one of the Corpus Oxford sets), heroes, woodwoses, or nude women. (How & How knew of one set in which the figurines were integral with the spoon.)

St Paul (7.3 by 2.1 in.) is the College's earliest hallmarked piece. The leopard's-face standard mark is at the top of the bowl. On the back of the stem are the letter **s** for 1515 and a human heart, the mark of an unidentified maker (who also made the 1516 spoons at Corpus Christi, Oxford). St Paul has a more tapering stem than his colleagues; his halo is a solid disk, not pierced; and his bowl has a slightly hammer-marked finish. He weighs 2.25 ounces (70 g); the others are constant at around 2.05 oz (64 g).

The other twelve bear the 1566 date-letter i. The maker's mark was too wide to strike on the narrow stem of a spoon, and always appears truncated. It appears to be a jackdaw's foot, the mark of Francis Jackson, a London spooner in a big way of business, who was often fined for making bad spoons (Kent). The twelve figurines were cast from only eight models: Philip, Bartholomew, and Matthias are the same apart from their added-on emblems; Matthew is the same as Simon; Thomas is the same as Jude.

Christ and the Apostles

The Apostles, 'The Twelve', were a particular group of the associates of Jesus. The New Testament gives four lists, which are not quite the same.[28] The traditional combined list is:

Peter *alias* Simon
James 'the Great'
John the brother of James
Andrew the brother of Peter
Philip
Bartholomew
Matthew
Thomas
James 'the Less'
Jude *alias* Thaddæus *alias* Lebbæus
Simon
Judas Iscariot the traitor

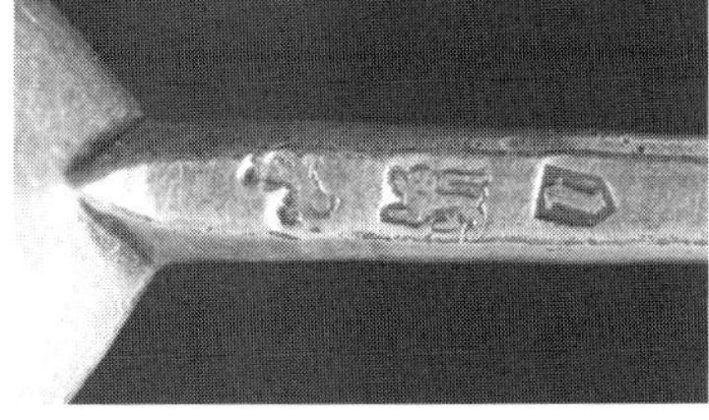
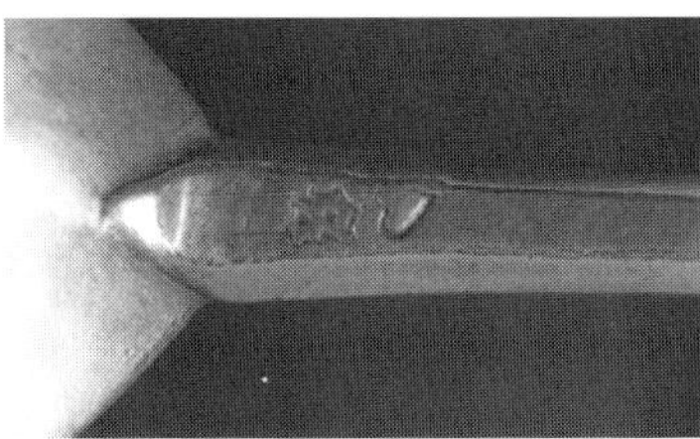
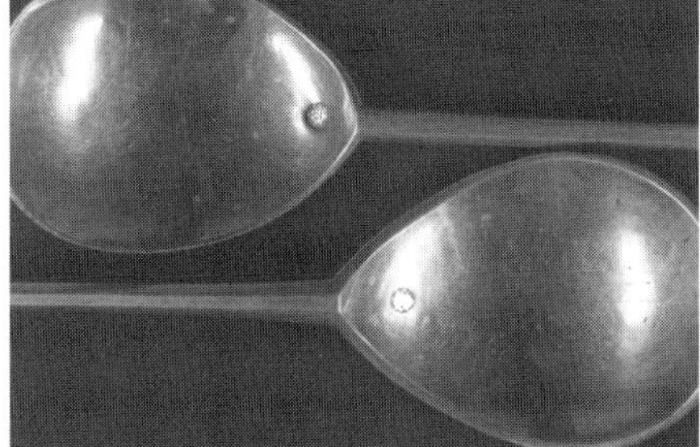
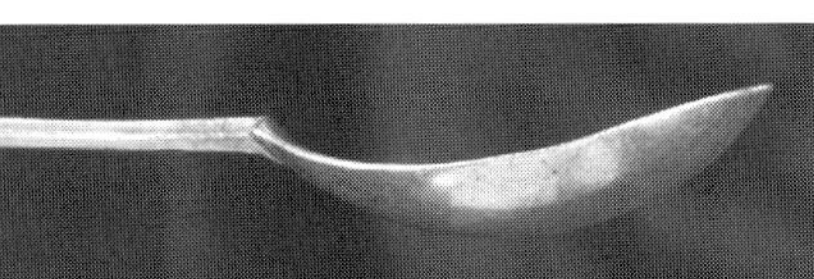
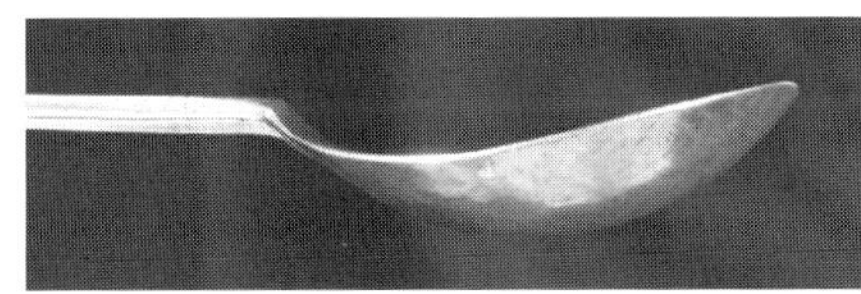
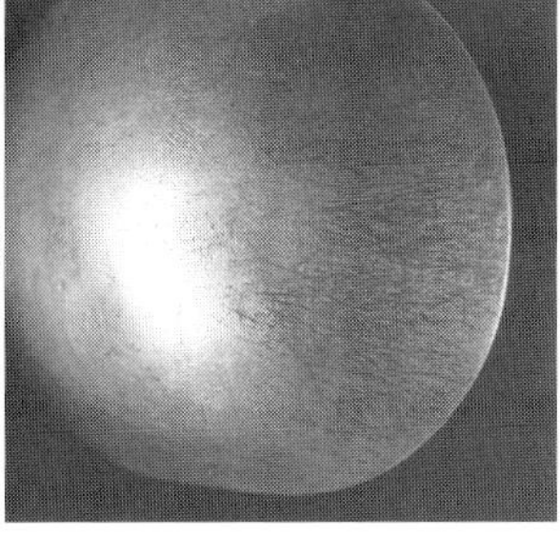

Details of the College spoons, St Paul being the lower one of each pair.
Hallmarks on stem; bowl and leopard mark; side view; scratches under bowl.

27 Marian Campbell in *Corpus Silver* chapter V.
28 *Matthew* **10** 2–4; *Mark* **3** 16–19; *Luke* **6** 14–16; *Acts of the Apostles* **1** 13.

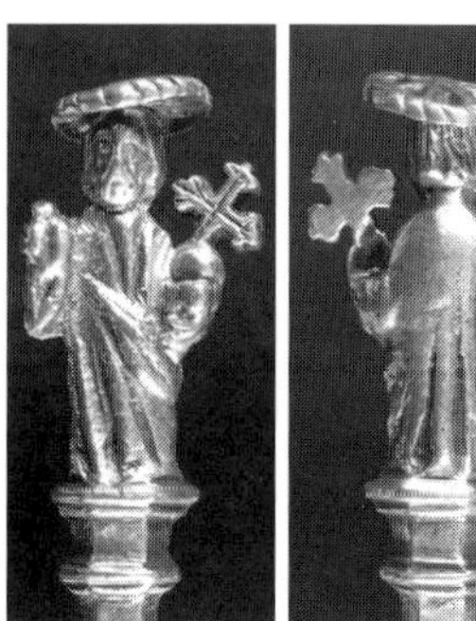
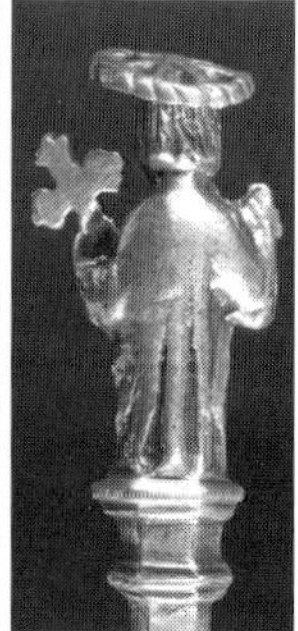

←The Master, Jesus Christ

Represented as Ruler of the World, Κοσμοκράτωρ. By medieval convention he carries a globe with a cross on it; his right hand is raised in blessing. He is no larger than the others.

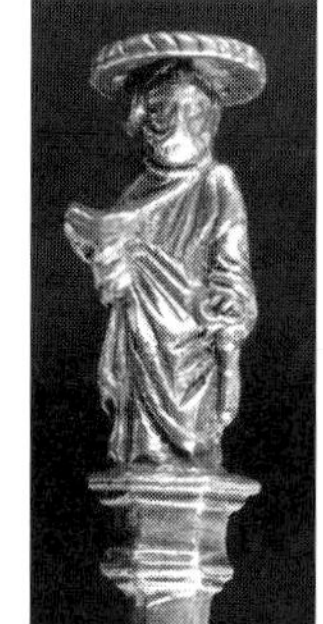
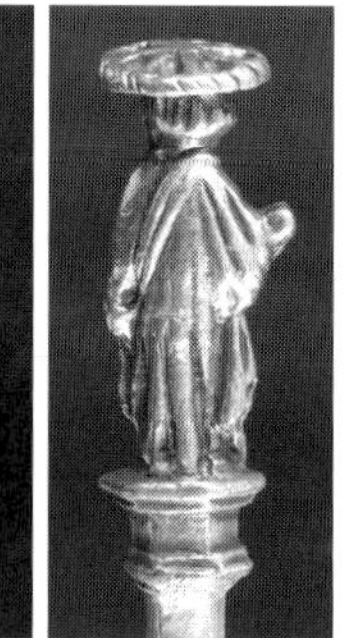

St Peter→

Chief of the Apostles and thought of as the first Pope; should carry 'the keys of the kingdom of heaven' (*Matthew* **16** 19). Here, as usually on Apostle spoons, he has only one key.

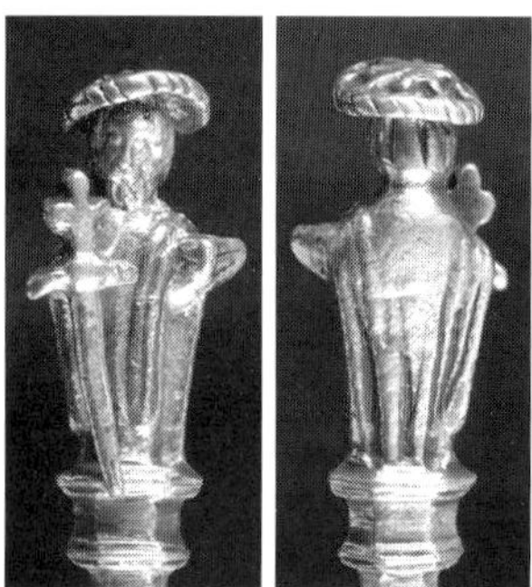

←St James 'the Great'

One of the chief Apostles, slain with the sword by Herod Agrippa I in *c*.43 AD (*Acts of the Apostles* **12** 2). He has a pilgrim's staff and hat, in anticipation of his relics becoming the focus of a great medieval pilgrimage to Compostella in NW Spain. His hat is on his back because originally he had a halo and it would have been improper to wear a hat over it, unless it was raining.

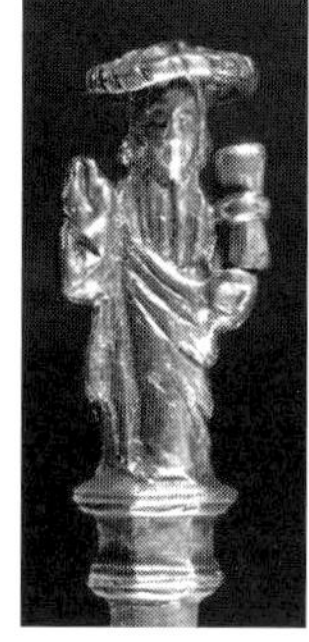
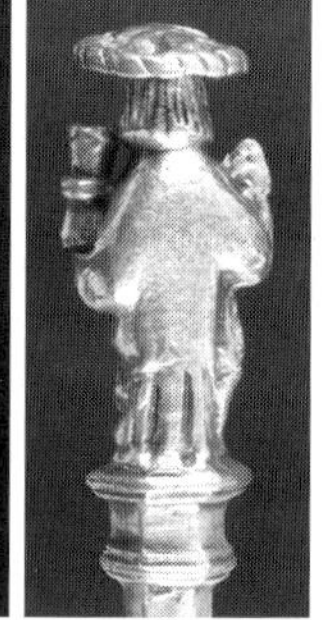

St John 'the Evangelist'→

Thought of as the author of the *Epistles of St John* and *Revelation* as well as the Gospel. Instead of holding a book his right hand pronounces a blessing. His attribute is a cup, said to be the 'cup of sorrow', the tribulations which Jesus foresaw for John and his brother in later life (*St Matthew* **21** 23 'Ye shall indeed drink of my cup'). The only Apostle who shaves.

St Andrew is missing; his very distinctive X-shaped cross would be unmistakeable.

←St Philip

Friend of Andrew (*St John* **12** 20–2) and the least imaginative of the Apostles; for some reason carries a double cross of Lorraine.

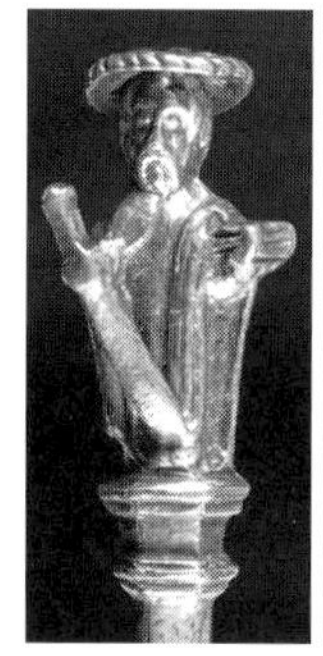
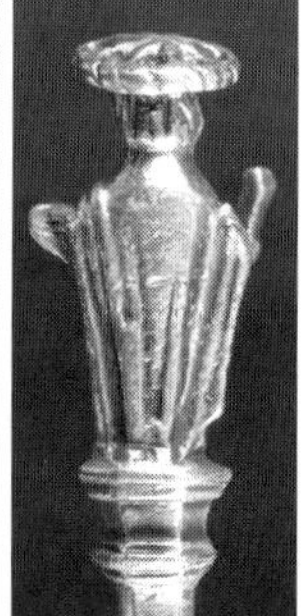

St Bartholomew→

Holds a stout butcher's knife wherewith he was supposed to have been flayed alive by the Armenians, whom he had tried to convert.

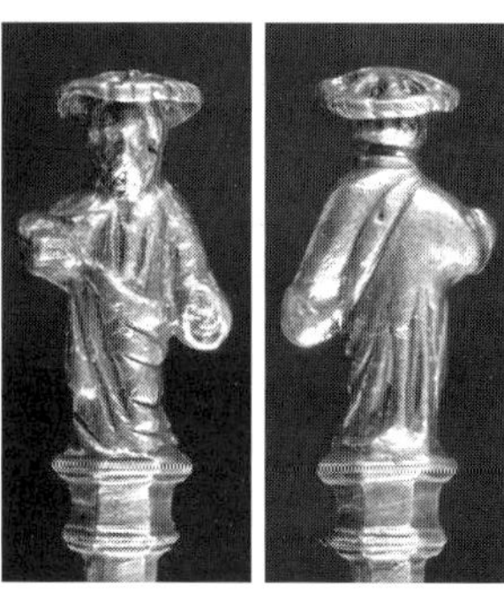

←St Matthew

Carries a satchel or portable filing system (part missing), in token of his duties as tax-collector (*St Matthew* **9** 9).

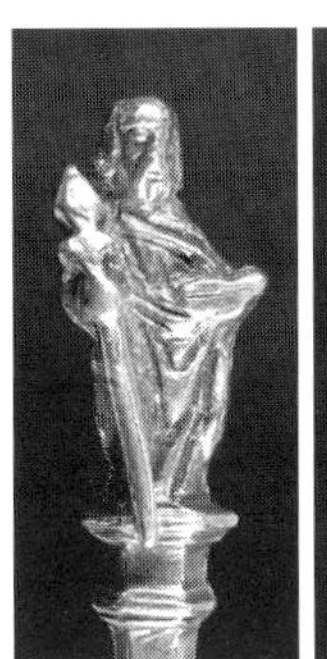
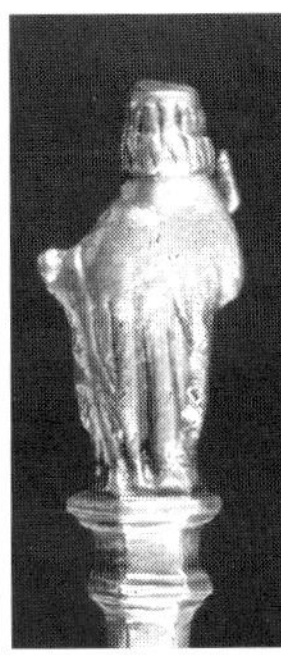

←St Thomas

Armed with the spear wherewith he was supposedly transfixed by the opposition near Madras. The weapon is a special boar-hunting spear with a crossbar; pigsticking is still a martial art in India.[29] He has lost his halo. His memory is still green among Christians in South India.

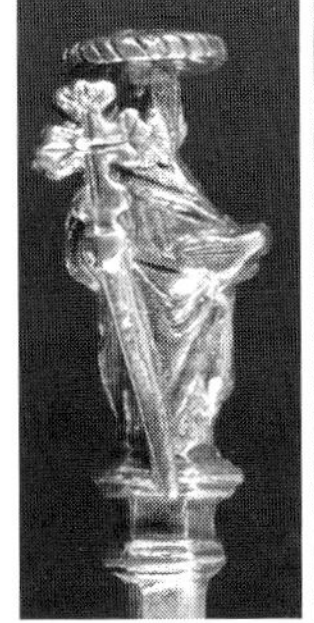
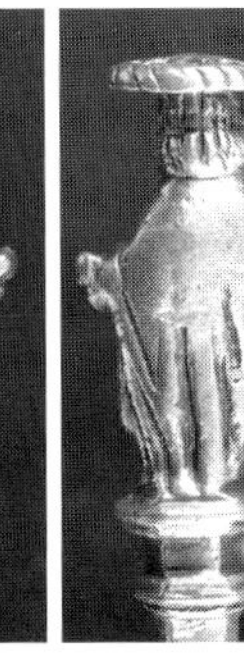

St Jude→

('Judas not Iscariot', *St John* **14** 22) carries a processional cross, for no known reason.

←St James 'the Less'

Carries three of the stones wherewith (according to Hegesippus) the Pharisees stoned him after casting him from a pinnacle of the Temple in Jerusalem. His halo has fallen off. He is not easily distinguished from two non-Apostles: St Stephen, who also carries stones, and St Nicholas, who carries three bags of money and sometimes terminates a spoon. St James is more often shown with the 'fuller's bat', an improvised weapon wherewith someone else spiflicated him.

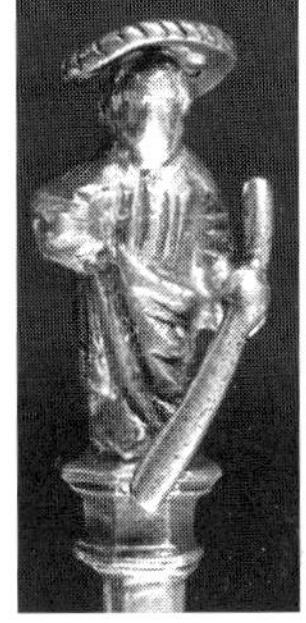
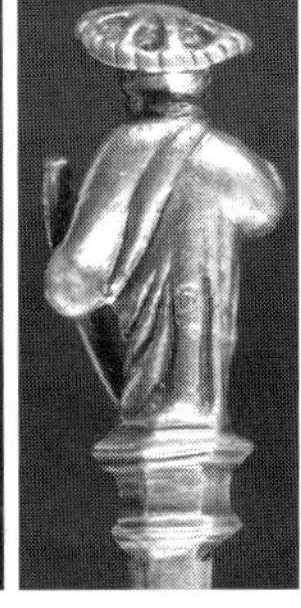

St Simon →

Holds an oar, perhaps because he owned a fishing-boat and lent it to Jesus (*St Luke* **5** 3). Or it could be a debased form of the crosscut saw wherewith the Persians were said to have divided him. Or could it be St James the Less's fuller's bat? but in that case who is the Apostle with the stones?

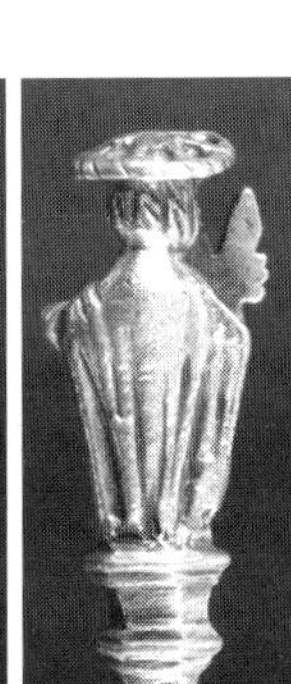

←St Matthias

Successor to Judas Iscariot; carries the axe wherewith he was said to have been subdivided, either by the men of Colchis (Abkhazia, a rough part of the Caucasus where such things could happen, indeed still can) or by the Cannibals, whom he was converting.

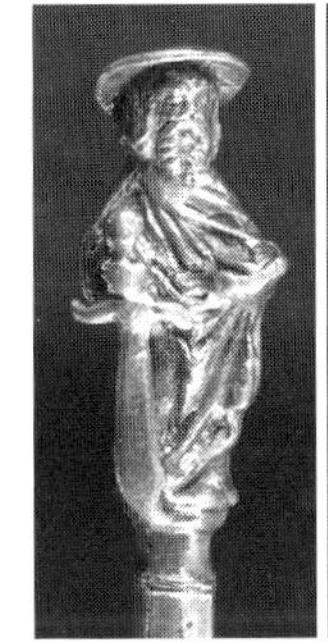
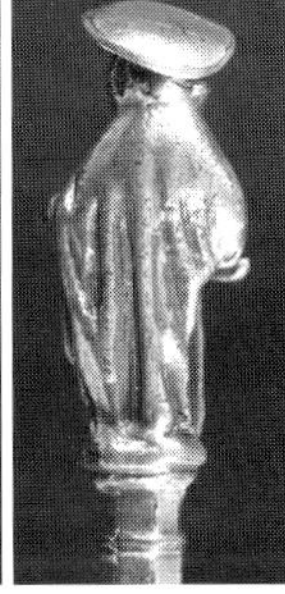

St Paul →

51 years older than his colleagues. Armed with the sword wherewith he was supposed to have been beheaded, as befitted his dignity as a Roman citizen (*Acts of Apostles* **22** 25).

29 Sir Alexander Wardrop *Modern Pig-Sticking* London 1914. For its continuation in the Republic of India, I am indebted to His Excellency K. Bhagwat-Singh (Corpus undergraduate 1947).

The place of Judas Iscariot is customarily filled either by Matthias, who was formally elected to fill the vacancy (*Acts of the Apostles* **1** 23), or by St Paul, who regarded himself as an extra apostle (*II Corinthians* **1** 1).

Apostles, like other Saints, were traditionally identified by some emblem, such as the weapons with which they were martyred. There is a surprising lack of agreement about the emblems. I have done my best to identify these, on the basis that they are all meant to be Apostles.[30] They all also carry books (except Christ and St John). All originally had haloes; the three missing haloes had already gone by 1845, the date of the earliest known picture.[31]

History of the Parker spoons

The spoons, like the salt, were retained by Parker during his lifetime, and do not appear in inventories until 1591/2. Parker's gifts were hoarded 'in the Treasurie Hutche' with other ceremonial plate, according to the 1573/4 inventory. However, the spoons have certainly been used. They all bear scratches on the back of the bowl, mainly on the left side of the far end, just where they would be worn by a right-handed person digging porridge from a coarse earthenware bowl. St Paul is equally scratched, showing that the wear occurred after he was co-opted.

The College's Spoons

Silver spoons go back to the foundation of the College, indeed before. The 1376 inventory records six spoons with maidens' heads with netted hair-dos, evidently from the Gilds. Robert de Eltisle, the first Master's nephew, gave six more, ending in gilt-faced women (p. 277). Down to Parker's time the College had owned (at various times) at least 94 silver spoons; mostly they had women's heads for handles, but there were a dozen leopards and a set of St Wulstan and the Eleven Acorns.

Spoons, though not readily traced from inventory to inventory, seem seldom to have lasted more than 50 years (unlike those in daily use now, some of which are more than 200 years old). The count reached 54 in 1526 and thereafter declined; by 1618 we had Parker's thirteen, plus 24 for ordinary use in the buttery, and a few wounded in the repair box. The 1526 inventory included thirteen Apostle spoons given by Thomas Cosyn some 40 years before, but they were crossed out and replaced by a set of twelve 'new' spoons.

One explanation for our odd St Paul is that we lost St Andrew and hastily replaced him with a singleton out of a junk-shop. However, he could also be the single Apostle remaining in 1573/4, possibly a survivor of Cosyn's thirteen, provided with twelve new companions when Parker died. Another explanation is suggested by a note in the Governing Body minutes in 1632: 'Item twelve spoons for the Master's uses in the servery. & another damaged spoon.' If this refers to the present set it would explain both the wear and the replacement of one spoon.[32]

Everyday spoons may have been of horn or wood and thus omitted from the inventories. Others, like knives (p. 205), may have been the property of the diners. Repairs to spoons are occasionally recorded in the 17th-century audit book. I fear that many others went to someone else's pigs (see below).

Spoons and spooning

People presumably have been using spoons ever since soup and porridge were invented. The Romans thought of them as derived from shells (Latin *cochlea*, giving rise to *coclear*). In the northern world spoons were supposed to originate from chips of wood (modern German *Span*, a chip). Makers of wooden or horn spoons were a regular trade in the middle ages, to judge by the surname *Spooner* or place-names such as *Spooner Row* on the Cambridge–Norwich railway.

Silver spoons, with a characteristic double bend where the bowl joins the stem, often appear in Roman hoards of plate. Some were for liturgical use at baptisms, administering Communion, and anointing the Sovereign

30 I am indebted to Mr S. B. P. Perceval for lengthy discussions of the identifications, especially the problem of St James the Less.

31 Smith. 32 CC(A): Chapter Book II, 8 Sept. 1632.

at coronations. In the middle ages silver spoons were common, even among middle-class people. Merton College's tenant farmer at Gamlingay in 1314–15 had four silver spoons, which sold for 3*s*. 2*d*., as well as two novels (*libri de Romance*).[33] At 9$\frac{1}{2}$d. a second-hand spoon was worth about three days' wages of a craftsman, six novels, or nearly three rabbits. Thorold Rogers has many examples of buying and selling silver spoons at Cambridge and elsewhere from the 1450s onwards.

Sets of thirteen need not be Christ and the Apostles. Dr Sokeborn, Fellow 1470–8, gave Pembroke College '13 silver spoons with stems summited in the manner of a tower' (St John Hope 1887).

Ancient spoons very rarely survive as complete sets. Individual spoons get thrown out accidentally with the rubbish. If the owner keeps his own pigs, as St John's College did from 1939 to 1954, the spoons go out in the swill, are rejected by the pigs, sink to the bottom of the trough, are recovered by the gardener and returned.[34] If not, they find their way, centuries later, into the collections of metal-detectorists.

How & How knew of about 20 surviving sets or fragments of sets. At most five sets of 13 can claim to be complete. The finest of all are the six large and six middle-sized figurines of Apostles which adorn the crozier of Bishop Fox, founder of Corpus Christi College, Oxford. These were evidently meant as spoon-finials, though the big ones would have been for larger spoons than any that survive. They were made early in the development of the form, from moulds that had not been worn with use, and are in mint condition, never having been fingered by horny-handed dons.[35]

Surviving figurine spoons are nearly all by different makers, which confirms the very low rate of survival. The originally crisp forms got rounded and debased as the moulds were worn and copied. The Parker spoons show signs of this decline, but it was to get much worse, to the point where – according to How & How – the Virgin Mary could be confused with Buddha.

The only close parallel to the Parker Spoons are the set of thirteen in the British Museum, hallmarked 1536. Only the figurines are gilt. They lack haloes. They are less used than ours, and the figurines are crisper. The set has the Virgin Mary instead of Christ, includes (like ours) both Paul and Matthias, and has a St Andrew but no Simon.

7.5 Parker's Lid and Two Cups

> Itm two pownced potts wth on cov^{r} of silv^{r} parcell gilt of the gift of ~~my L.~~ Matthewe Archbish of Canterburie wth his Armes on the botom of eche pot & on the top of the Cov^{r}.
>
> *1573/4 Inventory*

These curious little objects were among Matthew Parker's late gifts. There have only ever been two cups and one lid; the cups can hardly be drunk out of; one of the cups was new when it was given, the other was 15 years old, and the lid was 24 years earlier still. The second cup is the College's last object in Gothic style, with no trace of the Mannerist fashion of the Parker Salt made eight years earlier.

Each cup has a base, a bulbous body with hollow flutings, three-staged foot, and two cast dragon-handles. The neck and alternate flutes of the body are engraved with foliage. The foot has two stages of fluting. The torus between base and body is bent from a mass-produced tube of metal, ornamented with foliage and upside-down human heads. Cups and lid are single-gilt outside. They rattle when shaken owing to debris trapped inside the torus.

The later cup may have been copied from the first. The foliage is slightly different, and the engraving is different and shows through inside. The heads on the torus are faint, but are upside-down as on the older cup. The lid, with its flutings and big flat knob, is in the general style of the cups, but is not an obvious match.

Matthew Parker's personal arms are pounced on the underside of each pot, with his initials, M.C, for Matthæus Cantuariensis, and on the top of the lid.

The cups are similar in shape, though not in decoration, to one (with matching lid) given by Robert

33 Merton College: Record 5370. 34 Dr G.C. Evans, *pers. comm.*
35 Timothy Wilson, *Corpus Silver* chapter II.

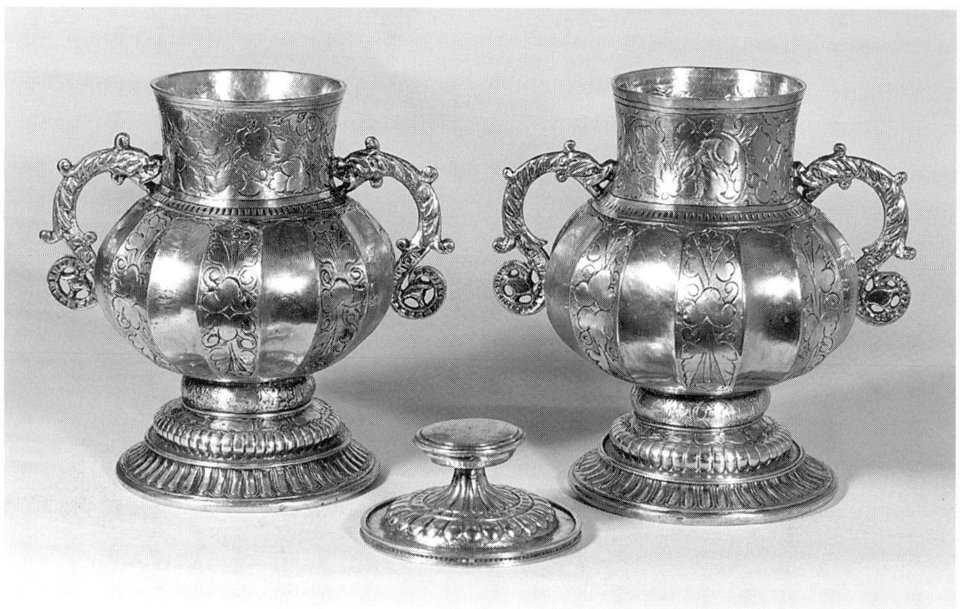

Morwent to Corpus Christi College, Oxford, in 1533. 'TL' may be the London goldsmith Lawrence Truechild; his work includes the Morwent Salt which, although two years earlier, had progressed to the Mannerist style.[36]

These cups are not entirely impractical: they are among the earliest surviving examples of posset cups. Posset was a horrid mixture of curdled milk and ale or sack; the narrow top is said to have been used to gather the floating curd, so that it could be removed leaving the clear fluid (Cripps p. 306). (The shape goes back to the Bayeux Tapestry, see p. 54). Similar cups, called ox-eyes, were fashionable in 17th-century Oxford. Posset itself continued well into the 19th century.

Table 7.1. *Particulars of the Lid and Two Cups*

	Lid	Cup	Other cup
Height, inches	1.3	5.0	5.1
Length across handles and diameter, inches	2.7 (diam.)	5.6 × 3.6	5.5 × 3.9
Gilding	double outside	double outside and base	double outside and base
Date-letter	London O for 1531	London S for 1555	London n for 1570
Maker's mark	IC with orb and cross between (+ inscribed N reversed)	TL monogram in shield	IP in 'baroque' shield
What is known of the maker	John Crathorn?, maker of cups and apostle spoons, 1527–31 (Jackson)	Maker of cups, and of a salt at Corpus Christi Oxford, 1553–6	Maker especially of communion cups, 1562–79 (Jackson)

36 Helen Clifford, *Corpus Silver* p. 273.

7.6 Parker's Tankard

Itm a Can wth a cover of silver dubble gilt & pounced, of the gifte of my L. Archbishope of Canterburie, wth his Armes on the botom vnc 16. et di. [16$\frac{1}{2}$ ounces]

1573/4 Inventory

Math: Parker Itm a Tankerd or can wth a cov^r^ guilte 16–1–0 [ounces]

1591/2 Inventory

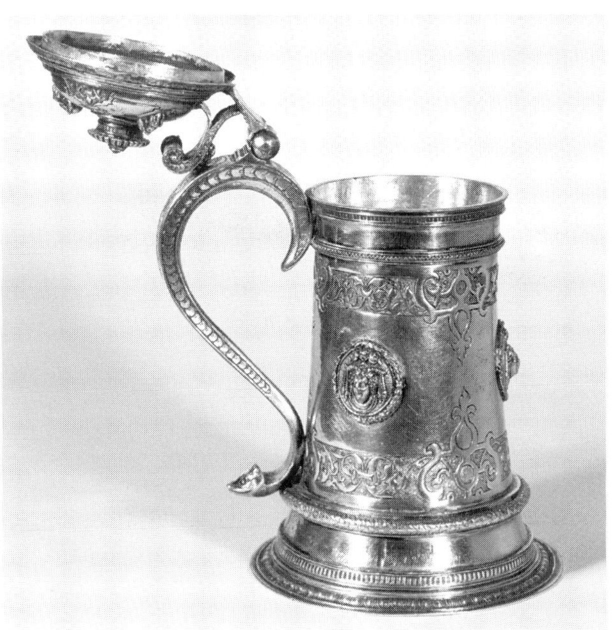

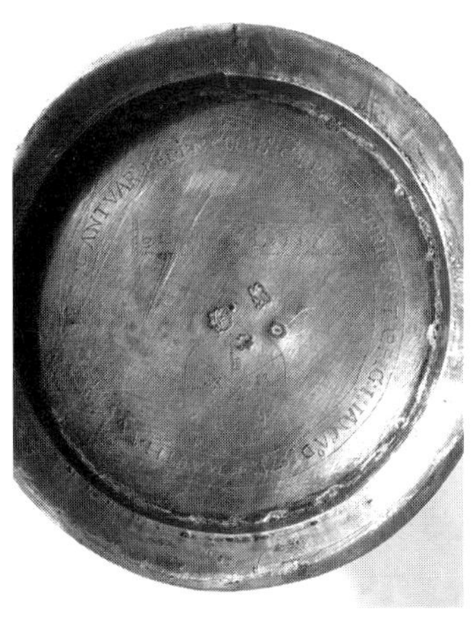

This was Parker's last gift to the College during his lifetime. The body is ornamented with embossed strapwork and foliage, and three cast medallions with the faces of she-devils, pouting out of laurel-moulded ovals. Each has a scarf draped over her horns, and is crowned with apples and grapes. Rings of hearts-and-darts encircle the top and foot. The lid has three aged men in caps, strapwork and foliage, ending in a reel surmounted by a rayed disc; the finial is lost. On the thumbpiece is a casting of an American chief. Scale-chains border the handle and thumbpiece. It is double-gilt, except underneath and inside.

6.4 (high) by 4.3 by 5.5 inches. It holds 0.38 litre = 0.66 English pint.

Underneath is pounced: + MATTHÆVS : ARCHIEPS : CANTVAR : DEDIT : COLLE^O^ : CORPORIS : CHRI : CANTABRIG : 1 : IAN : A^O^ D 1571 : (Matthew Archbish. Canter. gave [me] to the Coll. of Corpus Chri. at Cambridge, 1 Jan. 1572), and Parker's arms. Weight inscribed as 16$\frac{1}{2}$ ounces; present weight 16.4 oz.

London date-letter **o** for 1571. Maker's mark of a bird in a cruciform cartouche, attributed to Affabel Partridge, prolific maker of cups, plates, salts etc. 1555–77.[37] Prominent diet-scrape.

This piece, in high Mannerist style, is a miniature of the Great Parker Cup. Although awkward for serious drinking it has been used, to judge by the wear where the thumbpiece hits the handle. To modern English eyes it looks German, because the shape still continues in Germany as a standard type of beer-mug. In England

37 I. Pickford in Jackson.

these tall tankards continued in fashion only until the 1630s, but had a further lease of life in the form of church flagons (p. 113).

This is the 'gylt pott' given by Parker as a witness to the sealing of a triplicate indenture recording his other gifts (p. 70). As was his custom, on the same day Parker gave slightly less elaborate tankards to Gonville & Caius College and Trinity Hall. These are identical to each other, one year earlier than ours and by a different maker, and lack the *appliqué* heads.

The world of tankards

A tankard was originally a portable tank, a stave-built or leathern bucket. In 1276 an inquest was held on someone drowned in an accident with a certain tankard (Cripps p. 297). By the late 15th century tankards were common: the ship *Mary Howard* had 52 of them in 1482.[38] In 1459 the College spent 2*d*. on mending tankards (*em'da' tankardorum*), probably not of silver.[39] A 'tancard' appears in the *c*.1481 inventory among the kitchen equipment, so was probably not a drinking vessel.

Whatever such early tankards may have been, by the late 16th century we find the word transferred to the drinking-vessel previously called a *can:* a mug with handle, hinged lid, and flat base, and on the lid a thumbpiece for the skilled toper to hold the lid open. Parker's can, and its fellows at Gonville & Caius College and Trinity Hall, are among the earliest surviving.

By the mid-17th century tankards were the most popular of drinking vessels; the many in the College were constantly used and abused (p. 99).

7.7 The Wrest, Ostrich-Egg, or Gripe's Eye (Plate 6)

A silver wrest Or white estriche egg in a case

Note added at the end of the 1591/2 inventory of plate

The Fletcher Cup

This cup, the next surviving object after Parker, is a sawn-off ostrich egg with a silver base and brim, and an ostrich-egg lid. The egg is mounted between three silver straps joining the brim to the under-part; these have hinges at each end, like coconut cups (p. 50) and others of fragile materials. Similar straps, hinged only at the lower end, enclose the eggshell of the lid, joining the silver rim to a large knob riveted through the shell.

The silver parts (not gilded) are minutely decorated. The largest tier of the base is embossed and engraved with four sea-monsters and shells of cowries and bivalves. The stem is the likeness of a twisted and forked tree-trunk; one fork is sawn off, the other ends in the saucer-like rim under the cup, engraved almost invisibly with three faces (one Shakespeareish) and arabesques. The broad silver brim is delicately engraved with foliage, sea-monsters, bivalves, a short hairy marine worm, the initials RB, and the coat-of-arms of Bristol diocese (*three crowns in pale*) impaling Fletcher, the donor (*a cross paty pierced between four scallops*). The lower part of the brim is engraved with a last, vestigial, apology for a fringe. On the lid are engraved four mayflies, three butterflies, a 2-spot ladybird, a cockroach, a dragonfly, and a lacewing-fly. The edges of base and lid have tongue-like gadroons.

Cup: 11.6 in. high by 4.6 diameter. Lid: 3.7 high by 4.3 in.

London hallmarks on base and rim are P for 1592; RW with pellet above for the maker (unidentified, but could be the same as for the Johnson Cup of 1616, p. 109). On the underside is an inscription in an Elizabethan hand in mirror-image writing: Pee No XX.[40]

The cup, twenty years later than Parker's Mannerist pieces, shows a transition to the Jacobean style. It sparkles with fun. This was a fashion: the plate inventory of 1591/2 is decorated with whimsical sketches curiously like those on the cup, though there can be no direct connexion. Some details have parallels elsewhere. A twisted and forked tree-trunk, with one arm sawn off, supports

38 I Friel 1995 *The Good Ship* British Museum Press p. 119.

39 CC(A): *Liber Albus* part II f. 43.

40 One Anthony Pee gave the College a silver beaker about this time: CC(A) Misc. Docs 1480–1700 p. 4.

the Gourd-shaped Cup of Christ's Hospital, dated 1594, and two English gourd-shaped cups, dated 1589 and 1604, in the Kremlin. Two bottles in the Tsar's English hoard, of 1580 and 1606, repeat details of the Ostrich Cup.[41]

The ostrich-shell has been broken into 16 pieces and glued together; this happened before it was described by Cripps in *c*.1876. It was also repaired by the Victoria & Albert Museum in 1880 'in accordance with the Offer kindly made by Mr Wallis', probably as a recompense for letting them electrotype the other plate (pp. 30f.).[42]

The silver is in excellent condition and shows no sign of having been cleaned. Cleaning would show up as abrading of the metal and discolouration of the adjacent eggshell. Probably the egg was little used in the 18th and 19th centuries when excessive cleaning was customary.

In early inventories the cup is described as a Wrest, which seems to be a unique word for an ostrich cup. Possibly it alludes to the twisted base.

The case

This is a work of art, contemporary with the cup and an equally remarkable survival. Its construction is highly professional. The carcase is of oak, covered with hard (boiled?) leather on the outside and green baize inside. The circular base is in one piece, attached to one half of the foot. The two hinged halves have a half-lap joint to make a dust-tight fit.

The carcase is made of ten sections glued together. The base is two-ply, of thin boards glued at right angles. The five cylindrical sections are of thin boards, generally $\frac{1}{10}$ inch ($2\frac{1}{2}$ mm) thick. To bend them round into cylinders they are made flexible by saw-cuts at intervals part-way through the thickness (like the curved sides of a coffin). The body, with its barrel-shaped curve, is further cut into gores. The four near-horizontal sections are a little thicker, apparently turned on a lathe.

The leather outside is decorated with blind stamps and tooling in the style of an Elizabethan book-binding. Eleven plain bands and a number of vertical straps divide it into rectangular fields. Other toolings, including scallop shells, decorate the sloping upper surface of the foot.

The crude iron hinge is probably not original. It is covered by a clumsy patch of coarser leather, obliterating the stamped detail. A fragment of original tooling indicates that the original hinge was surrounded by a lozenge-shaped cartouche.

Joining the halves were six brass hooks and eyes, of which four survive. The hooks, handmade and slightly decorative, pivot on brass nails, originally clenched and driven back through the wood and leather to form a projecting stop against which the hook rests when open.

There was a handle, consisting of a leather strap fastened by brass nails to each half at the top of the body. A fragment of this remains on one side. At some stage the lower free part of this fragment was converted into a fringe by slitting it with a knife; three of the slits penetrated into the leather of the body underneath. On the opposite side the strap has disappeared, its site being marked by a patch of the same leather as that around the hinge, with three slits in the body leather. Cripps's drawing shows that the strap alterations had happened before 1895.

Cases very rarely survive. Parker's Standing Cup, Communion Cup, and Salt each had a case in the inventory of 1591/2. The 16th-century chalice of Great Gransden church (Huntingdonshire) has a surviving boiled-leather case.[43] The case for the Tyttenhanger chalice, made 1714, is in the Victoria & Albert Museum; it resembles ours in its half-lap join, tooled leather cover, and brass hooks. In the Waddesdon Collection (British Museum) is a Flemish 16th-century tabernacle in a shaped wood and leather case, liberated by British troops in the Peninsular War and restored within an inch of its life. Oriel College has a wood and leather case for a rococo two-handled cup of 1742.[44]

The Audit Book for 1708 has this item:

> Ostrich's Egg and mending ye Case for it
> £ 1. 0s. 6*d*.

This rather large sum suggests that this was when the egg got broken and maybe the hinge was replaced.

The case is shabby: how should we repair it, considering the very specialized crafts involved? The clumsy replacement of the hinge would be an unfortunate precedent. So far the writer has failed to find a professional mender of ostrich-egg cases.

41 Penzer; Jones *Russia*.
42 CC(A): draft Governing Body minutes 27 Feb. 1880; letter book 9 Mar. 1880.
43 Information from Professor William Horbury, former Vicar.
44 Jones *Oriel* Pl. 11. For other cases see Hayward.

The Ostrich-egg Case. Construction on left, ornamentation on right.

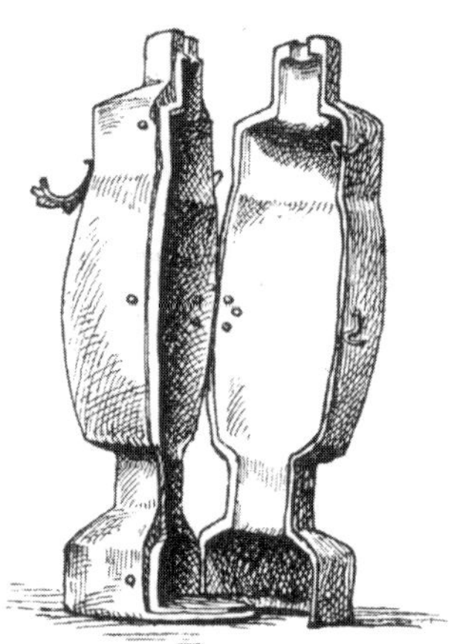

Ostrich-egg Case, after Foster & Atkinson (1985), showing closing flange and remains of strap.

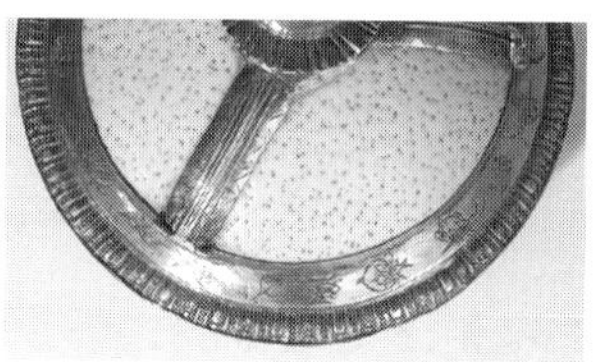

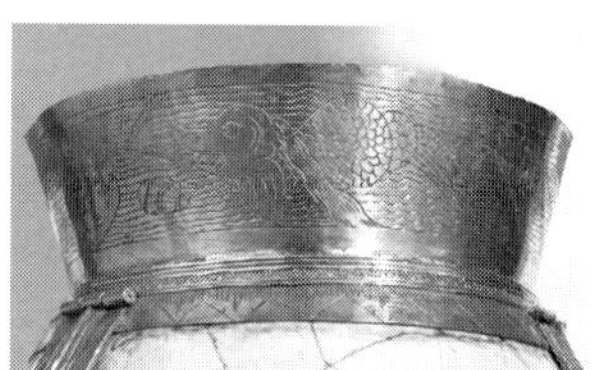

Engravings on the Ostrich Cup

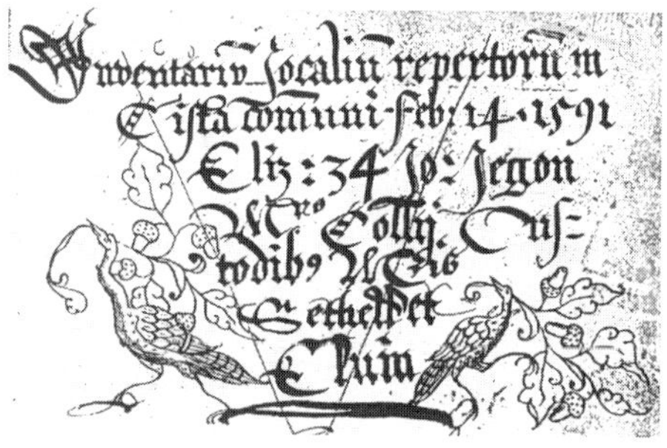

Decoration of the 1591/2 inventory

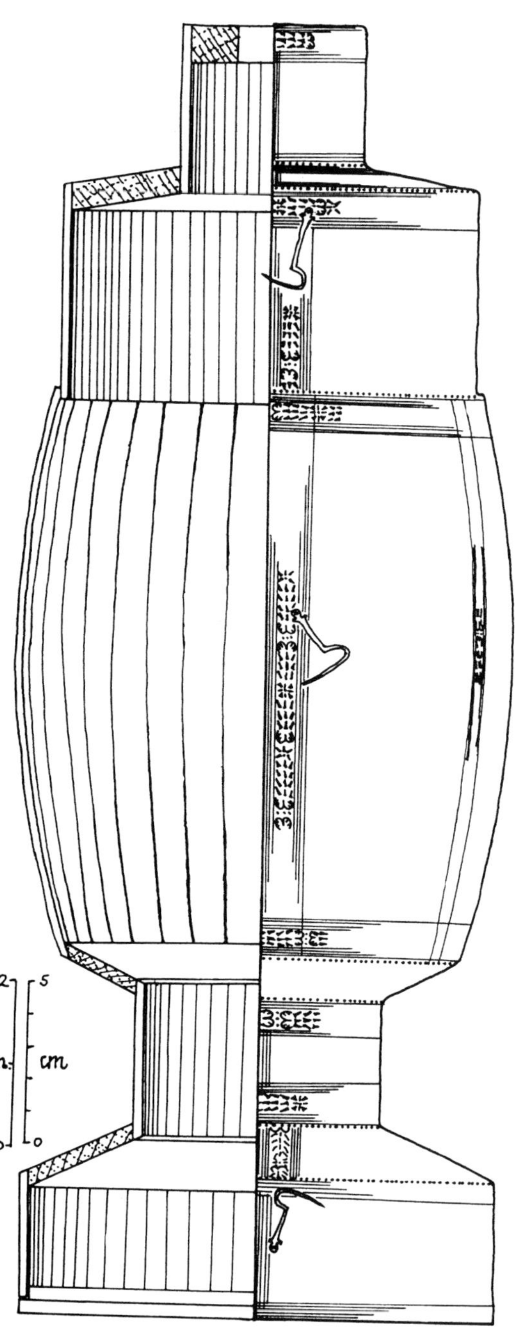

Ostriches

Ostriches are now confined to Africa south of the Sahara; until the 19th century they lived also in Arabia, North Africa, and Palestine. (It is a Biblical bird, described in *Job* **39** 13–18.) The lid is made from a different egg from the cup: the eggshell has a pattern of large pits widely spaced, in contrast to the finer pitting on the cup. There is a 'legend' that the lid comes from a south African ostrich and the body from a north African one.[45] There may be some basis for this, as there are four geographical subspecies of ostrich. The eggs in Cambridge University Museum of Zoology vary in pitting; the only one with a provenance, from South Africa, has the same pattern as the Corpus lid.

Richard Fletcher, first victim of smoking

Bishop Fletcher, the donor, is one of many old members whom the College remembers by the unusual manner of their deaths. On 15 June 1596, according to Camden's *Annals*, he 'immoderately consumed Nicotian draughts, and breathed out his life'.[46] As far as I can discover, he is the earliest known individual among the hundreds of millions of martyrs to tobacco (Chapter 19). He did not die in vain: eight years later tobacco was denounced by the King as an evil and addictive drug.

Fletcher, born *c*.1525, Trinity College man and proud Calvinist, 'of comely person and elegant manners', was brought to Corpus as a Fellow by Parker in 1569. He was not a kindly man like Parker. Four years later Queen Elizabeth made him her Chaplain and Dean of Peterborough. On him fell the task of persecuting the captive Mary Queen of Scots, upon whom he 'obtruded his unwelcome ministrations . . . with the insolence of unfeeling bigotry'.[47] At her execution in 1587 his sermon drew her attention to her 'past, present, and future condition'. In swift sequence he was promoted Bishop of Bristol, Worcester, and London, and was a successful persecutor of religious dissidents. But 'put not your trust in princes'. Being a widower, he made the mistake of marrying a second wife, which blasted his favour with Elizabeth – who did not exactly approve of people marrying, still less of bishops, less still of bishops for the second time. He fell into disgrace, banishment, debt, and drug-addiction, and as Fuller says, 'seeking to lose his sorrows in a *mist of smoak*, died of the immoderate taking thereof'.[48]

He remembered the College, where his son John Fletcher, the famous playwright, was an undergraduate from 1591. He bequeathed to the College his 'piece of plate of one estriges egg'. The hallmark shows that he had acquired it in earlier and happier years, just before he was translated to Worcester. Somehow the College got it before Fletcher's creditors did, and a note was duly scribbled after the end of the 1591/2 inventory. It apppears in subsequent inventories down to 1670 as 'a silver Wrest or white Estridg Cup, wth a case'.

Earlier eggs

Previously the College had owned two cups made from great eggs harnessed in silver. Both were listed by John Botener in 1376 (Appendix 1). One, with a boiled-leather case, was bequeathed by Henry de Tangmer, Cambridge goldsmith and banker, a generous founder of the College;[49] the other had no known donor and may have come from one of the Gilds. Both are described by Botener as 'made of a vulture's egg', but were called in Middle English *grypishey*, 'griffin's egg'.

Josselyn, College historian of the 1560s, writes, among Tangmer's gifts:

> Item, he gave that cup which is called *the Gripes eye* around 1342, formerly for that purpose, that it should be a pyx in which the Eucharist is carried around; when (as it is said) a certain other more suitable monstrance was afterwards given by Sir John de Cambridge, knight, it was converted into a common cup. This cup, made from an egg, was broken in the days of Lawrence Maptit [Master 1553–7], and was renewed from silver material in the time of John Porey [Master 1557–9].

He confuses the details: Sir John died in 1335, long before Tangmer died and bequeathed the egg.[50] But the story

45 Jones *Cambridge* p. 43.

46 *Nicosia immodice hausta obruit, vitam efflauit.* For Jean Nicot, father of nicotine and introducer of tobacco to Europe, see p. 231. Smoke was thought of as a kind of 'drie drink', as Henry Butts, another unfortunate member of Corpus, put it (*Diets drie Dinner*, 1599).

47 E Venables, *Dictionary of National Biography*.

48 Lamb pp. 323f.

49 Information from Catherine Hall.

50 Hall p. 68.

explains why 'vulture's eggs' were listed among ecclesiastical objects: they were thought to have been used, as a precious material, for carrying the Host in the Corpus Christi procession. (A huge silver-gilt tabernacle for that purpose, without a donor's name, precedes the eggs in the list.)

Both eggs survived into the 16th century. The 1526 inventory still had one *grypys Egg*, then a secular cup, and records that the College had just got rid of the other. The survivor appears in the list of 1573/4 as 'Itm the gripes egge, wth a Cover of silv^{r} parcell gilt'. By 1591/2 it had disappeared, displaced by Fletcher's gift.

Josselyn's last words imply that when the shell broke it was replaced with a silver egg, much as happened to the Pembroke College mazer (p. 59). However, Robert Masters and some other historians supposed this to be the origin of the present Ostrich Cup. But it is clear from the date-letter and arms that Fletcher's cup was made in his lifetime and did not come to the College until his death.

Of griffins, vultures, griffon-vultures, and ostriches

Griffins'-egg cups, such as ours, were rarer than coconuts, though not as rare as drinking-horns. The Empress Maud in 1167 bequeathed to Bec Abbey in France, among other treasure, two griffins' eggs, gripped by silver legs and claws.[51] Cripps lists ten, documented between 1251 and 1490. Henry VI possessed three 'Gripes eyes covered garnysshed wt silver and gilt', and Henry VIII had two, plus 'a Cuppe made of an Oistriche Egge' with two golden snakes as handle. A few other griffins' eggs are recorded in France, and one in Scotland.[52] Only in Corpus were they interpreted as vultures' eggs. Although the English language had known the word 'ostrich' since Wyclif's translation of the Bible in the 1380s, the earliest object listed as an ostrich egg was Henry VIII's in 1547.

Vulture, griffin, and ostrich have separate entries in the two medieval *Bestiary* manuscripts in the Parker Library. The vulture, it was said, is too big to fly far; it smells corpses from afar; it is always female and parthenogenetic; it lives 100 years; it follows armies sniffing for prey. The griffin, a winged quadruped, is much bigger; it lives in the Arctic; it has a lion's body and an eagle's wings and face; it devours beeves and tears horses and men.[53] The ostrich does not fly; it buries its eggs in the sand, forgets where it has put them, and never returns.[54]

There was, however, a confusion between griffin and vulture, beginning in the middle ages. It still continues in the name Griffon Vulture. This, *Gyps fulvus*, the biggest European bird, still haunts Crete and Spain; more than once it has sniffed out (or rather spied) the writer from afar and investigated his state of mortality in some waterless gorge. It used to be widespread, feeding on sheep that fell over cliffs, though never in Britain.

Griffon-vulture eggs, though the biggest among vultures, are not impressive. Those in Cambridge Zoology Museum vary around 9.4 cm long by 7.0 cm in diameter, not much bigger than a goose egg, and white. If made into a cup they would hold about one-third of a pint: a reasonable-sized wine-glass, but too small for a grand ceremonial cup. Griffin eggs – supposing the reproductive tract of a griffin to belong to the eagle part – should be very much larger, holding several gallons, but the Museum was unable to produce one. The weights given in 1526, $25\frac{1}{2}$ and 12 oz troy, would be much too great for silver-mounted vulture eggs and too little for griffin eggs, but are possible for ostrich eggs.

I infer that medieval gripe's-eye cups were really ostrich-eggs, but cannot say why they were not recognized as such but confused with griffins or vultures. None is known to survive. We would hardly know what they were, but for the chance that cups of ostrich continued to be made later than mazers.

The world of ostrich cups

Decorated ostrich-egg cups, or cups imitating ostrich eggs, were precious objects back to Bronze Age Crete and Mycenæ.

Individual cups were short-lived. There appear to be four other English survivors:

51 I thank Dr E.M.C. van Houts for this information.

52 Palgrave **2** 251; Starkey §734, 15801, 3676; Gay, s. *Griffon.*

53 Marco Polo met a man who had encountered another species of griffin in Madagascar. It was all bird, and lived on elephants, which it killed by flying up with them and dropping them. (Gay, s. *Griffon.*)

54 CC(L): MS 53 ff199, 190v, 200; MS 22 f168v.

1. The Ducie Cup of 1584, very like ours, but rather more elaborate and Mannerist in style, as befits its earlier date.

2. The Carter Cup of Queen's College, Oxford, dated 1588. It is made of a smooth egg, mounted in the same structure as ours, but very different in detail. The style is Mannerist but restrained, with straps in the likeness of bearded men, and none of the usual delicate engraving; the base looks forward to our Champernowne Cup of 1602. It was presented to the college about 60 years ago.

3. The Exeter College, Oxford, ostrich egg of 1610, shell deeply pitted like our lid, adorned with silver ostrich feet and feathers and crowned with an ostrich. The base is like that of our Jegon Cup of 1608.[55]

4. A fully-developed baroque piece, presented to the Rev. James Stopes in 1623 by a grateful congregation whom he had served for 46 years.[56]

The Waddesdon Collection (British Museum) has three ostrich vessels of the late 16th century, from Augsburg, Nuremberg, and Prague; the eggs show the same kind of variation in the pitting as ours.

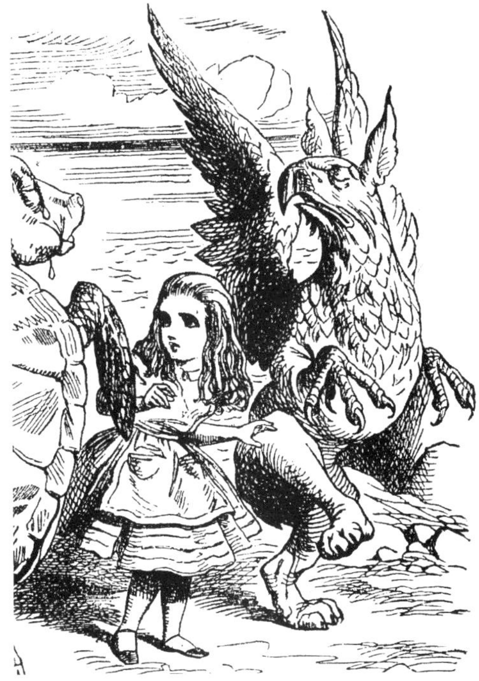

A Gryphon or Griffin, as accurately drawn by Tenniel. To preserve the scale Alice must be in her giantess phase.

7.8 The Neame Cup (Plate 5)

> The Master having reported that he had received from Mrs Mary Neame an offer to present to the College a wooden standing cup on the base of which were painted arms of Matthew Parker . . . and which the officials at the Victoria and Albert Museum believed to be of Elizabethan workmanship and to be the earliest English cup of its Type agreed that the offer be gratefully accepted and that the thanks of the College be expressed . . . and be sealed with the College seal.
>
> CC(A): *Minutes of the Executive Body, 5 Nov. 1935*

This is an unexpected addition to the Parkeriana: a great lathe-turned wooden standing cup – a super-mazer – with a painted underside. The outside is richly decorated in incised lines, cut through a dark original varnish.

The bowl is divided into four panels. One bears the royal arms of Queen Elizabeth, with a lion and unicorn and the somewhat garbled motto ER DEVET . MONDROIT (*E[lizabetha] R[egina] Dieu et mon droit*). In the next panel is a carthorse-like unicorn. The next has an ostrich eating a horseshoe, as ostriches traditionally do.[57] Then comes a hart semi-couchant (about to get up), gorged royally (with a crown as collar and a lead

55 Moffatt Plate XIII. 56 Cripps pp. 275ff; Jones *Queen's* Pl.15.

57 The ostrich eating a horseshoe is said to be a badge of the Earls of Leicester: FB Zincke 1887 *Some materials for the history of Wherstead* Ipswich.

with tassel attached to the crown). Blank spaces contain gear-wheels. The stem and base are ornamented with roundels.

Height 10.6 in. Outer diameter of bowl 7.0 in. Diameter of base 6.5 in.

The wood, obscured by varnish outside and dirt inside, is probably maple.[58] The bowl has no print, but a small boss marks where the core was cut off (p. 52). It has apparently been turned from a quarter-log. It has cracked along the radius; the cracks started from nail-holes. The stem and base are separate pieces tightly socketing into one another.

The underside is delicately painted (Plate 5). The background is dark green. In the middle are three shields-of-arms: a large one of the Parker family, between one of Parker's parents and one of Parker as Archbishop of Canterbury.[59] Lest there be any mistake, the outer ones are labelled in red: *Parentum* and *Archiep'i Parker.* They lie on a red-and-white mantling, with a gold-edged closed helmet bearing the crest of *an elephant's head proper, tusked or.* Over the top is the word DONA = TORI (To the Giver). Underneath is the motto printed on p. 67. Although the damaged third word is difficult to restore, the sense must be 'The body of Parker and everything [else] perish by Fate; but may Fate be unable to destroy the mind [that is, 'soul'] of Parker'. It is a typical Elizabethan motto, a pun on *Parca,* the Roman goddess of Fate, and *Parker.*

The cup was not made for a silver harness, but got one later. Silver straps enclosed the brim and bottom of the bowl, joined by four straps overlying the columns between panels. Others encircled the base. All these were later removed, except for one surviving round the stem; they have left discolorations where the silver reacted with the wood, and also the tiny silver nails which attached them.

The silver brim was added in 1933 by William Neal of Clerkenwell (London date-letter 𝔰, maker WN).

How we got the cup, and its significance[60]

According to legend, a Major Gore found the cup in a greengrocer's in Highgate, used as a measure for dried peas. (I estimate its contents at 3.7 pints or 2.1 litres, approximately $3\frac{2}{3}$ lb of dried peas, level measure.[61]) His daughter-in-law, Mrs Mary Neame, recognized its significance, had the silver brim added lest it fall apart at the cracks, and in 1935 gave it to the College.[62] The flaking paint was fixed by Arthur Shearsby in 1950.

This is what experts call a 'James I armorial standing cup': a large bowl decorated with incision, with a turned stem and base consisting of at least two additional pieces of wood. They are often dated, and are not normally silver-mounted. Pinto lists 28 examples, dated from 1603 (when James I came to the throne) to 1687.[63] Ours is Elizabethan and the earliest known. It is in the style of the Parker Communion Cup, and probably 20–30 years before 1603.

The painted arms and inscriptions show that it was given to someone by a child of Archbishop Parker, presumably his surviving son John. John Parker, born in 1548, was a Fellow-Commoner of Peterhouse; married the Bishop of Ely's daughter; entered the upper class; was honoured by the official grant of an elephant's-head crest in 1572; moved to Cambridge, but (being married) not to this College; took an M.A. in 1600; was knighted by James I (for being his father's son?); wasted his father's substance; fell into poverty; touched the College for £10 from our charity fund in 1618; and was buried a year later in Great St Mary's at the College's expense (£23, which would buy quite a lot of funeral).[64] Richard Parker, Fellow 1598–1601, was probably his son.

58 Later wooden objects are often called 'sycamore', which would be difficult to distinguish from maple. This cup is rather early for sycamore timber to exist in England, unless it was imported.

59 Parker family: *Gules a chevron between three keys argent.* (It lacks the three stars which were Matthew Parker's personal augmentation.)
Parker's parents: the above impaling *barry of three sable and or,* for Harlestone.
Archbishop: *vert a star or above a pallium sable* impaling Parker. (For the correct version of these arms see p. 69.)

60 Much of this is derived from notes by the late Professor Bruce Dickins in the plate archives.

61 I find the bulk density for dried peas to be 0.797 kg per litre.

62 *LCA* **19** (1936) 9.

63 Pinto p. 34.

64 Venn. The funeral, but not the charity payment, is recorded in CC(A) *Audits 1590–1678* p.301.

7.9 Epilogue – the Parker Communion Cup and Parker-Beldam Cup (Plate 8)

> *Matthœus Archieps Cantuar dedit Collegio Corporis christi Cantab. 6 Augusti A^{0} Dni 1569. œtatis sue precise completo. 65.*
> Matthew Archbish. of Canter. gave [me] to the College of Corpus Christi Cambr. 6 August A.D. 1569, on his age of 65 precisely completed.
>
> *Inscription on the original Parker Communion Cup*

> CALICEM PRISTINVM DEDIT COLL. CORP. CHR. MATTHÆVS PARKER ARCHIEPS CANTVAR A. D. 1569 HANC SIMILITVDINEM DEDIT ROBERTVS BELDAM A. D. 1999
> Matthew Parker Archbish. of Canter. gave the original chalice to the Coll. of Corp. Chr. A.D. 1569. Robert Beldam gave this replica A.D. 1999.
>
> *Inscription on the Parker-Beldam Cup*[65]

On his 65th birthday Matthew Parker gave the College an extraordinary object:

> Item one greate standinge Cup with the Cover of Silver and whole gilt Comonlye called Communion Cupp with the appurtenance weyinge xliii oz qur.*
>
> *List of plate attached to Parker's bond of 1569* [66]
>
> *43$\frac{1}{4}$ ounces.

It was a big cup with a hemispherical bowl on a baluster-like stem, with a domed lid on the acme of which stood a vertical disc bearing Parker's arms. Cup and lid were elaborately embossed with strapwork and grotesque figures.

This 'communion cup' would have been awkward for administering the Lord's Supper. It was utterly unlike the practical, unadorned, bell-shaped communion cups which Parker was recommending to Anglican parishes, and which were made in thousands during his lifetime (Clifford). It was unlike anything else. The rich detail was entirely secular. I can only conjecture that the disk atop the lid was inspired by a monstrance, a vertical disk with transparent sides in which was displayed a consecrated wafer. Parker would have known '*le monstraunt* of silver, wholly gilt, weighing 78$\frac{1}{2}$ ounces' (1526 inventory) which had once been the centrepiece of the Corpus Christi procession, the climax of the College's year. Was the finial of his cup meant as a reminder of earlier and happier, if somewhat 'superstitious', days when he was a young don?

Parker immediately borrowed the cup for his lifetime – evidently Lambeth Palace was short of chalices. Perhaps for that reason, the bond making Corpus, Gonville & Caius College, and Trinity Hall jointly responsible for its welfare was never signed. When the College got it back on his death, it apparently served as the Communion cup in Chapel until stolen in 1693 (p. 111).

Re-creating the cup

The Parker Communion Cup would have remained as one of the many objects sadly lost to the College, but for two happy events. A drawing of it remained in the Parker Library on the back of the bond. And in 1998 Mr Robert Beldam, the College's greatest benefactor since Parker, decided to give the College a piece of plate worthy to stand beside the great and ancient pieces. From this coincidence, and with the help of the Goldsmiths' Company, it was decided to make a replica – as far as possible – of Parker's cup.

This was a challenge. The last time anything of the sort had been attempted was in 1904, when the Mayor of Norwich made a replica of Parker's basin and ewer which the City had destroyed in 1761. The complexity of the piece meant that specialists in *repoussé* work, chasing, and enamel would have to be called in. The work was undertaken by the Clerkenwell partnership of H. 'Charlie' Fowler and Barry L. Worsfold.

The drawing was meant for identifying the cup rather than copying it. Fortunately, the Gonville & Caius drawing of the Great Parker Cup can be compared with

65 I acknowledge the help and advice of Professor Geoffrey Woodhead in drafting these words.
66 CC(A): XLA 66.

the cup itself to determine the type of discrepancy to be allowed for. For help with details, photographs and squeezes were taken of similar details on the Great Parker Cup and Parker Salt.

The cup – gilt except for the finial – is embossed and chased with three herms hugging themselves, lions with rings in their mouths, grotesque masks, foliage and swags, etc. It is remarkably profane for a communion cup, and lacks the American allusions typical of Parker's other gifts. One side of the finial is enamelled with Parker's coat-of-arms, his Archbishop's cross, and his initials MP. The other side (not shown in the drawing) now bears Mr Beldam's arms: *azure a chevron or between two stars rayant in chief and a lion rampant argent.* Crest: *a white lion rampant.* Motto: DAT DEUS INCREMENTUM (God giveth the increase – cf *1 Corinthians* 3 6, 7).

Cup 6.3 in. × 7.8 high. Lid 6.3 × 7.2. total height 14.1. Marks: London Z for 1999; 925; HCF for makers.

The cup was presented to the College by Mr Beldam on 6 November 1999, in the presence of Messrs Fowler and Worsfold. It is a magnificent reminder of Mr Beldam's generosity. It also shows that there are still workers in silver who can rival the great silversmiths of the past: there can be no more exacting test of craftsmanship than making a Mannerist cup.

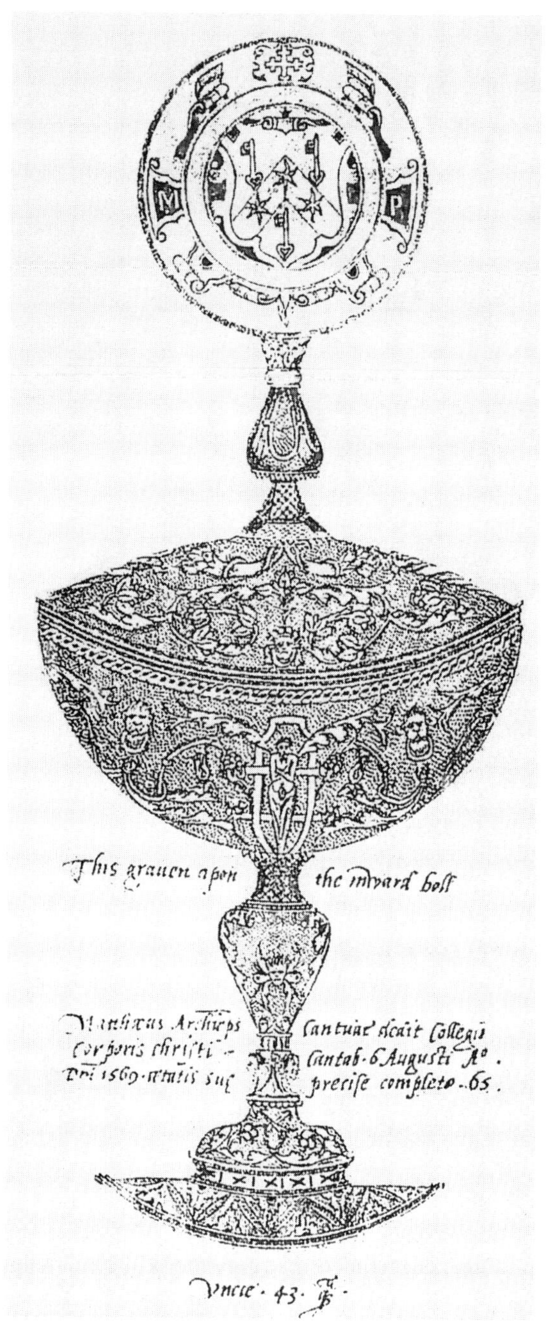

Contemporary drawing of the Parker Communion Cup

8

Fellow-Commoners and the Civil War:

Steeple-Cups, Bowls, and Sometime Tankards

Gladstone (Prime Minister): A wonderful collection! but surely the College ought to be ashamed of itself for possessing so many treasures.
Perowne (Master): Ashamed? And why ashamed?
Gladstone: Because they should have been sent to King Charles.
Perowne, with a smile: On the contrary, our collection would not have delayed the King's fate for a single instant, and, had it been sent, I should not now have had the pleasure of showing it to Mr. Gladstone.

Anecdote of Gladstone's visit in 1887, related by Catling

Matthew Parker died in 1575, having done his best to restore the College's plate hoard to its pre-1523 glory. He encouraged other donors: the inventory of 1573/4 includes, for example, nine cups not mentioned in earlier lists, several being opulent pieces weighing at least 30 ounces.

Disaster struck again when Sir Nicholas Bacon started the building of a new chapel without enough endowment. To keep the project going the College pawned and lost £46. 13*s*. 4*d*. worth of plate, about 180 ounces. There may have been other sales. We never saw again the 'pot with a Cover of silvr parcell gilt, a mayden hed on ye top', nor the 'standinge cup wth a covr silvr & dubble gilt . . . wth an olde groat [coin] in the top of the inward side of the Covr'. Even a 'standing pece wth a covr silver dubble gilt wth a rose in ye top', weighing 31 ounces, disappeared, although the College had covenanted with the donor, John Aldrich, Mayor of Norwich and father of a Master of the College, never to part with it. Little survived except Parker's gifts and pieces, like the Ostrich Egg, that were difficult to melt.

Fellow-Commoners and their Gifts

A momentous change intervened. In 1590 John Jegon came to Corpus from Queens' College as Master, and brought with him one of his students, Roger Manners II, aged 14, heir to the Earl of Rutland. The young nobleman was admitted to 'fellows' commons', presenting the College with 'one bowl (*unum le boule*) gilded with lid weighing 16$\frac{1}{2}$ ounces'.[1] His uncle, the third Earl, although not a Cambridge student, had presented a bowl, as well as helping out with the Chapel and founding scholarships (which are still awarded). The family's coat-of-arms, the second most complex in the College, is displayed in the Hall. Roger II was a normal if precocious student, taking his degree and going on to a conventional upper-class career, including a customary stretch in the Tower of London. His bowl is last heard of in the 1640s, but the Earl's was used in Chapel until it was stolen in 1693 (p. 111).

The corporate body of the College is 'the Master, Fellows, and Scholars',[2] but long ago it had acquired associated members. Some were Pensioners, who ate at the Scholars' table and came in the 16th century to comprise the majority of undergraduates. Others were senior members, graduates of the College, ex-Fellows living in Cambridge, prospective Fellows awaiting a vacancy, benefactors, etc., who ate 'superior commons' at the

1 CC(A): Chapter Book I p. 259.

2 Class distinction is most visible in archives relating to sanitation: the annual accounts record the separate repairs, provision of candles, and emptying of 'ye Masters house of office', 'ye ffellowes bocardo', and 'ye Schollers boggarts'.

Fellows' table. These were known as *Socio Commensalis*, 'Table-Companion to a Fellow', or in English as Fellow-Commoners. They correspond to modern High Table Members.[3]

The 'Gentleman' Fellow-Commoner, in the line of Roger Manners, was a bird of a very different feather. He was a boy from an upper-class or upper-middle-class family; he wore a silken gown; he often did not matriculate, and was technically never a member of the University; he sat no examination and took no degree unless the King commanded it; but he was addressed as Mr, as if he was already a Master of Arts; and he was called behind his back, at least in later years, an Empty Bottle.[4] Usually he stayed for only a year or two and moved on to one of the Inns of Court. One begins to think of him as a well-to-do student doing a gap year between school and law school.[5]

There had been occasional noble commoners for centuries,[6] but Manners began the regular line of 'Gentlemen'. Historians are reticent about them, but they were important members of the College. They were supposed to present a piece of plate worth at least £4, in return for being admitted to the High Table.[7] Graduate Fellow-Commoners of the old kind were normally excused from giving plate.

Over the 260 years of their existence, Gentlemen Fellow-Commoners contributed at least 270 items of plate, nearly as much as the entire College hoard today excluding the Bateman bequest.[8] But from the first hundred years only six items (including the Montacute Alms-Dish, §9.1) survive.

John Jegon's first task as Master was to rescue the College's finances from the chapel-building fiasco. Fellow-Commoners were people who could be charged extra. By 1596 the College saw a need 'to augment the number of Graduate superior Commoners in this College'.[9] Another function was to secure influential patrons. During the Civil War it doubtless helped to have the son of the Earl of Essex, Parliamentary commander.

Gentlemen Fellow-Commoners were seldom men of fame or learning: indeed, before the 18th century, presenting plate to the College almost guaranteed a lack of academic distinction. All that some of them did with their lives, as far as we know, was give a cup to their college, which the College melted down. Others were different. William Courtney, great-nephew of Roger Manners II, was an undergraduate in 1595; knighted in 1599, he was the earliest known College soldier. Robert Drury became Gentleman in 1588 at the tender (but not exceptional) age of 13; at sixteen he was knighted and gave us a 'siluer pott'; he achieved an MA in 1599, was elected to Parliament, and died aged 27. Daubridgecourt Belcher scraped fame as translator of the Dutch play *Hans Beer Pot, His Invisible Comedy*. Robert Bertie, son of Lord Willoughby de Eresby, rose to be a Royalist general and fell at Edgehill, the first known member of the College to be slain in battle.

Down to 1700, about one in four donors of plate came from Norfolk and one in seven from Kent, counties connected with Matthew Parker. Suffolk, Essex, and Lincolnshire were also strongly represented. Fellow-Commoners came from merchant families of Norwich such as Anguish and Pykerell, Norfolk gentry such as Gawdy and Paston, and Suffolk squires such as Tollemache and Cornwallis. In 1595 Peregrine and Robert Bertie, sons of Baron Willoughby of Grimsthorpe (Lincs),[10] were admitted Fellow-Commoner, together with the tutor they brought with them, Robert Johnston the Scot; all three contributed two silver cups.

John Jegon in his Mastership (1590–1602) admitted nearly forty Gentlemen Fellow-Commoners. They flourished also under Richard Love (1632–60), especially

3 The word *Commoner* in Cambridge means 'one entitled to commons', the daily rations of mutton etc. The term Fellow-Commoner is now used for school-teachers and other professional people who spend a sabbatical term at the College – a class of Fellow-Commoner whom our forebears would surely recognize.

4 Bury p. 22.

5 Professor John Baker, of St Catharine's College, kindly tells me that this was a usual pattern. He adds that the Inns of Court were themselves 'a kind of finishing school for the gentry, enabling them to sample the pleasures of the metropolis and get to know who was who. The vast majority of members had no intention of being called to the Bar and did not read any law.'

6 Cobban.

7 For example CC(A): Chapter Book II, 19 March 1632/3, 20 April 1633.

8 The Chapter Book contains lists of Gentlemen Commoners and their gifts down to 1640. The artefacts, as they arrived, were booked among external revenue in the Audit Book. They were listed at irregular intervals in the Inventory Books. Some of the disposals are recorded in Governing Body minutes in the College Order Book. None of these four sources is entirely complete or consistent, but together they are a record of some 320 objects and what became of them.

9 CC(A): Ordinance, 28 January 1595/6, Chapter Book I p. 102.

10 Their descendant still has the amazing house with its grandest of all parks.

Table 8.1. *Acquisitions of plate, 1590–1778*

Date	Master	Number of accessions: Total	Fellow Com-moners'	Fellow Commoners' per year	Predominant type	Typical weight, ounces	Aver-age life, years	No. still extant
1590–1602	John Jegon	43	39	3.3	beakers > 'bowls'	9	39	0
1602–18	Thomas Jegon	27	25	1.6	'bowls'	10	31	5
1618–26	Samuel Walsall	22	18	2.3	'pots', tankards	11	25	0
1626–32	Henry Butts	8	8	1.0	tankards	15	20	0
1632–42	Richard Love	29	28	2.9	tankards	14	32	0
1642–8 (Civil War)	Richard Love	21	19	3.2	tankards	14	50	0
1649–61 (Commonwealth)	Richard Love	20	19	1.5	quart tankards	20	46	0
1661–7	Francis Wilford	9	8	0.9	quart tankards	20?	33	0
1667–93	John Spencer	24	14	0.5	quart (or bigger) tankards	25	72	0
1693–8	William Stanley	3	3	0.6		33	50	1
1698–1716	Thomas Greene	15	9	0.5	tankards etc.	27	64	2
1716–24	Samuel Bradford	11	9	0.9	teapots, candlesticks &c.	27	40	2
1724–44	Matthias Mawson	42	31	1.5	candlesticks, coffee-pots, tools etc.	30	41	30
1744–50	Edmund Castle	14	10	1.7	candlesticks	35	6	8
1750–64	John Green	12	8	0.6	inkstands	40	14	5
1764–78	John Barnardiston	9	6	0.4	salvers	28	–	8

during the Civil War; six came in the one year 1647. These two very shrewd Masters, in hard times for the College, found it useful to take rich boys off their parents' hands for a year or two. The mind boggles at what these flighty teenagers – some of whom could hardly speak Latin – would have done to a society of ten Fellows; but Cambridge dons themselves were younger than now.

As time went on Fellow-Commoners became fewer, more of them had claims to learning, and the objects they gave were bigger and grander. Jegon's was the age of goblets: did not Falstaff in 1598 swear marriage to Mistress Quickly 'upon a parcel-gilt goblet'?[11] However, a more usual Fellow-Commoner's gift was a small standing 'bowl' weighing about 9 ounces, worth only about half of the £4 it was supposed to be. In the 1620s it became a pint tankard of about 14 ounces, and in Love's time a quart tankard of about 20 ounces. Later in the century thirst increased, and giant tankards weighing 30 ounces or more were presented. Although these gifts were well used, as the repair bills show, there was no systematic plan of acquisitions: some Gentlemen merely produced oddments from the family hoard.

From 1725 to 1750 Gentlemen Fellow-Commoners had a golden age. The Masters, Matthias Mawson and Edmund Castle, each admitted more than one a year, and searched hard for scholarly talent among the upper classes. Charles Chauncy, Francis Eyles, and the four Yorke brothers went on to be among the more distinguished members of the College in that century, as well as contributing fine artefacts to the plate.

Fellow-Commoners continued well into the 19th century but rarely gave plate, although six pint mugs of 1861 bear inscriptions from Fellow-Commoners of the 1840s. The title continued into the 1870s but I know nothing of what it meant: Donald Donaldson, benefactor to the College in 1913, had been a Fellow-Commoner and had given plate in 1877 (p. 218).

11 *Henry IV Part II* Act II scene i.

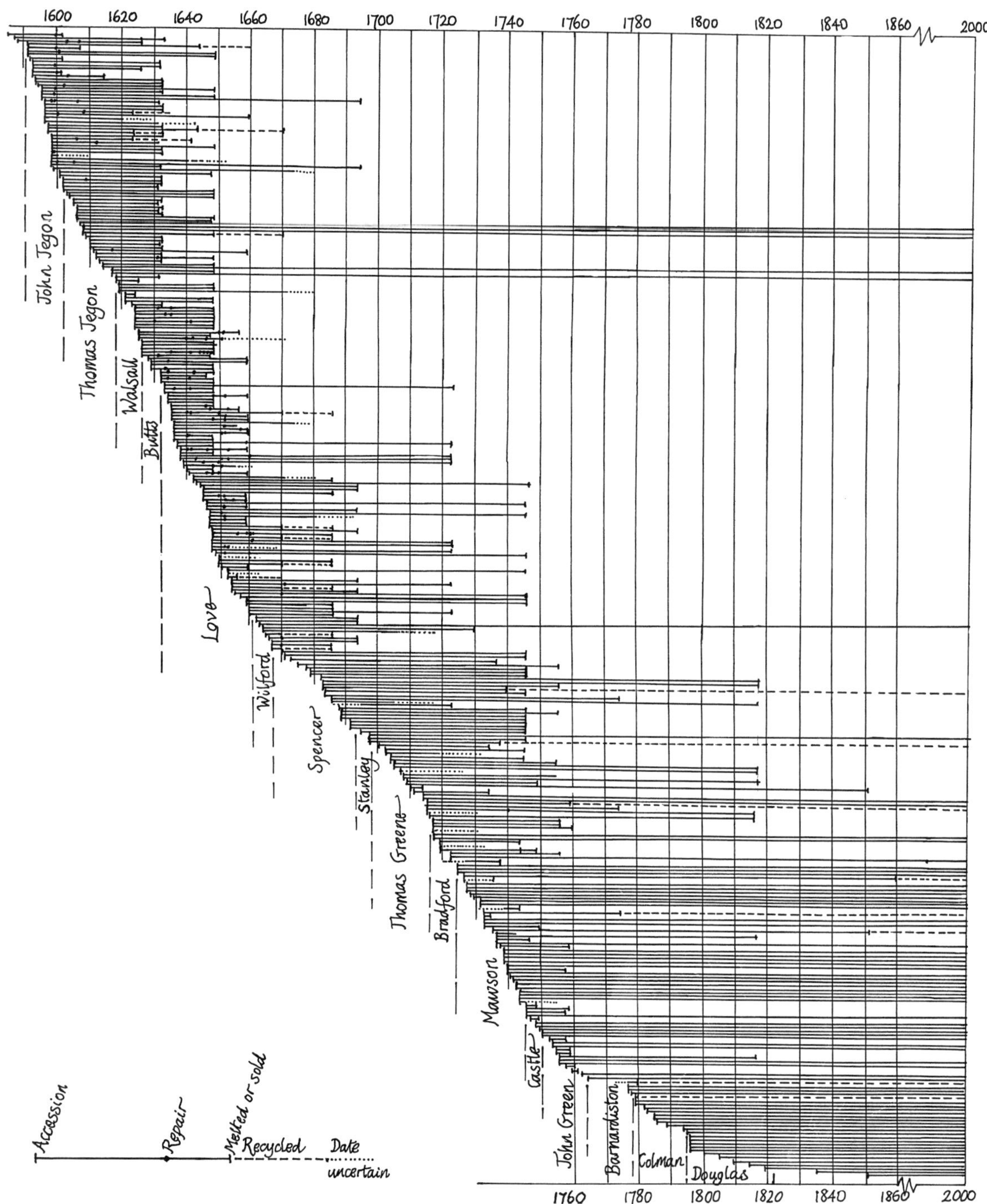

Gifts of plate by Fellow-Commoners and others, 1593–1851, and what happened to them. Each horizontal line represents the life of one piece (about 330 in all). The reigns of Masters are shown on the left.

The Civil War

A 'legend' of Cambridge has it that all the other Colleges either gave their plate to King Charles I or had it plundered by Cromwell. Corpus, uniquely, saved the whole collection by the ingenuity of Richard Love, Master, who shut down the College and divided the plate among the Fellows; when better times returned, they brought it all back, and it still survives. What is the reality?

Some Cambridge colleges supported the King; some (not necessarily different colleges) had links with Cromwell and other Parliamentarians. Corpus had little reason to think well of Charles: his indifference, among other factors, had driven the Master, Henry Butts, hero of the plague in 1630, to suicide. In 1632 Richard Love (1596–1660), Fellow of Clare, was appointed his successor by the interfering King.

Ten years later the clouds of civil war were gathering. In March 1642 the King's son, the future Charles II, visited the University, and Corpus contributed to his entertainment. But another cloud, blacker than war, had gathered. On 6 June the Vice-Chancellor shut down the University because of another plague, and the College followed the same day:

> In regard of y[e] plague in y[e] Towne it was agreed y[t]
> all fellowes and schollars w[ch] desired the same might
> be absent from ye Colledge till they might
> safely returne . . . [12]

The King, like all English kings and queens, needed money. He had left it too late to invent income-tax, and with his usual penurious ingenuity had devised unpleasant ways of fund-raising. On 29 June he wrote to the Vice-Chancellor inviting colleges and private individuals to lend him money, to be 'repaid by us with interest of eight pounds per cent . . . as soon as it shall please God to settle the distraction of this poor kingdom'. He proposed, moreover, that the colleges should deposit their plate with him 'for the better security and safety thereof', telling them that the opposition intended 'a sequestration upon the plate of our Universities . . . to employ the same against us'. He dispensed masters of colleges from obeying any college statute to the contrary. He 'faithfully' promised to return the plate 'when our propositions for the peace of this kingdom shall be hearkened to', a condition which (at the time I write this) has yet to be fulfilled.

The College's reaction to these events was to transfer to the library 36 tankards, beakers, etc. and a few oddments. A list of them, dated 7 July, says 'All these were brought into the Library upon the dispersion of the Colledge'.[13] This list is a fragment of an otherwise lost plate log-book, and it may record little more than a routine locking-up of the everyday plate at the start of the Long Vacation, brought forward this year because of the plague. Or it may be an extra precaution taken after receiving the King's letter a week before, to which the College declined to respond.

The King declared war on Parliament on 22 August. The Governing Body held a meeting three days later for routine business, and then none until normal activity was resumed on 17 January. The College did not shut down altogether, however, for the log-book fragment records plate being issued from the library to three resident Fellows on 17 October.

Other colleges were more responsive. On 8 August St John's College loaded 2065½ ounces 'grocer's weight' of plate (1883 oz. troy, 59 kg) into two fir boxes and sent them to the king's agent at Leicester. Cromwell was tipped off and ambushed the road at 'Loler Hedges' (the present elm-wood on the Huntingdon road at Lolworth), but the messengers supposedly evaded him 'through by-paths and secret ways'. Throwing away the plate had no result, save to bring down Cromwell's wrath on the college. Queens' and Jesus Colleges and Peterhouse sent their plate (or at least their damaged plate) to the King; Pembroke sent 'all that they could spare'; so did Magdalene, but it was intercepted on the way.[14]

At Oxford, on 6 January 1643 Charles made a proclamation calling on the Colleges to 'lend' him their plate at the rate of 5*s*. per ounce, 6*d*. more if it was gilt.

12 CC(A): Chapter Book 17 Jan. 1642/3, 6 June 1643.
13 CC(L): MS 624.
14 T Baker, Ejected Fellow *History of the College of St John the Evangelist, Cambridge*
J Heywood & T Wright 1854 *Cambridge University Transactions during the Puritan Controversies of the 16th and 17th Centuries* Bohn, London
J Twigg 1987 *A History of Queens' College, Cambridge*. Boydell, Woodbridge
Smith p. 5
Glanville (1990) p. 121.

The martyr King had a habit of casting into dungeons those who refused him loans; he was there on the spot, and so were the dungeons of Oxford Castle.[15] Fifteen of the seventeen Colleges lent him some 25,000 ounces – nearly three-quarters of a ton – of plate, and never saw it again.[16]

In these circumstances, on 9 March 1642/3, Richard Love called together his seven resident colleagues, who unanimously resolved[17]

> In consideration of the danger in these times . . . so much of the plate . . as ye said Master & Fellows shall thinke fitt' shall be removed out of the treasurie . . and every Fellow residing in ye Coll. shall have in his custody two or three pieces of plate for his peculiar use: As likewise that the said Master shall have in his custody for his use such pieces of plate as he shall thinke fitt: And in case any of the foresaid pieces . . . shall violently be taken away from any of them they shall not be responsible for ye same. For the rest of the said plate wch shall be taken out of the treasury it is agreed that the Master taking to him any one of ye Fellowes whome he shall thinke fitt and to be known only to himselfe shall dispose of ye same in the most convenient way he can for the safeguard therof and in case any casuall miscarriage of y^{e} said plate should happen it is not to be charged upon the Master or that Fellow assumed by him, but their best care and diligence is only requested, and the successe committed to Almighty God . . .

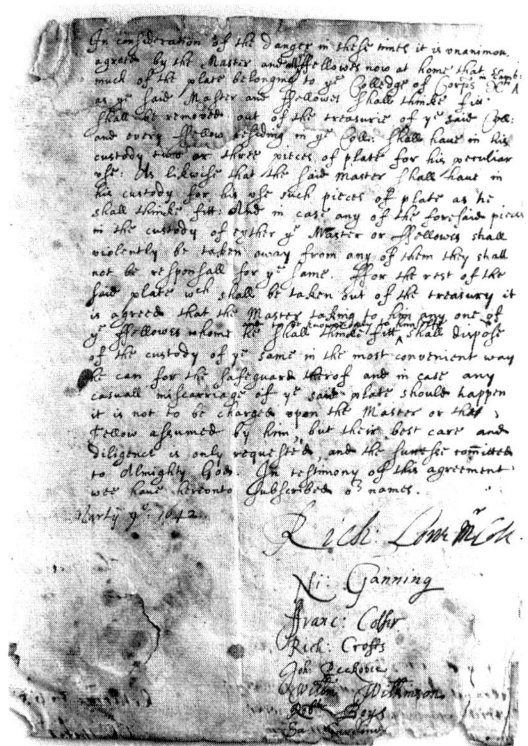

College Order dispersing the plate, 1642/3

The items remained dispersed for six years, until on 9 May 1648 they were 'return'd into the Colledge treasurie' in the presence of Love and eleven Fellows: they are listed on another fragment of the log-book.

Richard Love was studiously neutral in the Civil War. He had no intention of letting the plate fall into the hands of either side: he probably foresaw that the College would need money for repairs and must conserve its assets. The decision to disperse part of the plate was probably moved by events at Oxford, and by the prowling menace of nearby Parliamentary armies. Cromwell had punished those colleges, especially St John's, which had sent their plate to the King, but his troops were renowned for discipline and did not indulge in casual looting. But other commanders' soldiery got out of hand, and in April sacked Peterborough Cathedral. It was as well not to put temptation in their way. In 1648, with the King safely under lock and key, the plate could return to the light of day.

What were the objects dispersed among the dons in March 1642/3? They were not the entire hoard. The list of items dispersed is remarkable for what it leaves out. It comprises 58 items out of about 120 which the College can be shown to have owned at the time; only six out of the eighteen items that still survive are on the list. The dispersal included Parker's pieces – the 'gilt bason & Ewer wth 13 gilt spoones' – and a few other great treasures, such as the Seckford Cup and the Sugar-box; these were, I suppose, stashed in that hoard of which only Love and an undisclosed colleague had the secret. The others comprised some 48 tankards and drinking-vessels of the kind that had been secreted in the Library in the previous

15 O Rackham 1990 *The Last Forest: a History of Hatfield Forest* Dent, London.

16 Moffatt p. x. Magdalen College contributed some 3600 ounces, Exeter College 3000 ounces. Corpus Cambridge in 1622 (before some big disposals) had 630 ounces of plate; its entire hoard today weighs about 8000 ounces.

17 CC(L): MS 624.

Table 8.2. *Fate of College secular plate after the 1642/3 dispersal*

	Dispersed in 1642/3	Not dispersed in 1642/3	Total
Pre-Parker pieces (all still surviving)	–	6	6
Parker pieces (all still surviving)	6	–	6
Elizabethan and Jacobean pieces:			
melted in 1647	–	3	3
melted in 1648	33	15	48
melted in 1658/9	3	8	11
lost since 1659	16	10	26
still surviving	–	6	6
TOTAL	58	48	106

Long Vacation (though the lists differ). The idea probably was that individual Fellows could claim that their 'two or three pieces' each (in reality about four each) were their personal property if Parliament or King tried to requisition corporate plate.

What were the other 50-odd items which Love did not disperse? They included the Communion plate, to requisition which would have been a war crime. Also missing from the 1642/3 list are the Horn, mazers, coconut etc. These had not enough silver content to be plunderable: it is not easy to melt an ostrich egg. Unexplained absences from the dispersal list are four, if not all five, of the surviving Jacobean cups.

The 1642 plague over, the College returned to normal for the remainder of the Civil War and Commonwealth. Some Fellows were ejected by Parliamentary Commissioners (one of them, however, had already made himself a nuisance by not paying his bills). Richard Love remained Master. The College was heavily taxed and times were hard, but the Governing Body continued to meet, to elect scholars and Gentlemen, present candidates for degrees, appoint porters and butlers, lease College property, whip or send down undergraduates 'for bad morals', invite Gonville & Caius and Trinity Hall to inspect the library, feast them afterwards, repair buildings, and even institute clergy to College livings, almost as if nothing untoward was happening outside. They admitted Gentlemen Fellow-Commoners and received their cups and tankards more actively than ever. The most obvious sign that the times were out of joint was a decline in the consumption of Communion wine, from about 21*s.* worth a year around 1640 to one-third of that value in the 1650s.

The College's non-dispersed plate remained very much in use throughout the 1640s, to judge by the annual repair bills. None of the nine items known to have been mended between 1643 and 1648 appears on the list of pieces dispersed.

The first action of the Fellows, after the plate had been brought back from hiding, was to sell more than half the items.

> Memorandum y^{t} . . . ye Master of ye Coll: & all ye foresayd persons did survey y^{e} plate . . . & found nothing wanting. And in regard y^{t} y^{e} Colledge by reason of these times is wholely out of stocke . . . ther is evident necessity y^{t} y^{e} Colledge bee repaired forth with as well in y^{e} slateing as otherwise, y^{e} Master & y^{e} Chest=Keepers wer requested to consider what plate might best be parted with for y^{e} defraying of y^{e} charges of y^{e} sayde repaires . . .
>
> *Governing Body minutes, 22 May 1648*

Two days later it was resolved 'y^{t} a Goldsmith bee procured to weigh such plate'. An undated list, lying loose in the plate-book, of 'Potts', 'Beakers', 'Bowles', and 'Tankards', can be shown (by comparison with other inventories) to comprise the plate then sold. Forty-eight items added up to 582$\frac{1}{4}$ ounces, the scrap value of which, at 4*s.* 10*d.* the ounce, came to £140. 14*s.* (equivalent to about £14,000 in the money of 2000).[18] The repairs, including the collapsed Master's gallery, cost £182.

It now becomes possible to understand Love's dispersal. He wanted to protect Parker's treasures, and also those minor pieces, given by Fellow-Commoners over

18 Had we kept them, 48 Jacobean cups would now be worth some £2$\frac{1}{2}$ million.

the previous 50 years, which were regarded as disposable capital. The fact that two-thirds of the pieces sold in 1648 came from the dispersed hoard suggests that he had already decided that some plate would have to go for emergency repairs, and had made a preliminary selection: the theft or requisitioning of those items would be a serious matter for the College. He did not hide cups, salts, basins, etc. needed for the normal functioning of the College, nor the Communion plate, nor medieval pieces that were not worth stealing. A few items among those not dispersed in 1642 were recycled in 1647.

What happened at other Colleges? Among the six colleges that had thrown their plate at the King, the only surviving pre-1642 items, apart from later accessions, are the Hercules Cup at St John's, the chapel plate at Peterhouse, the 'Foundress's' and Anathema Cups at Pembroke, and one cup at Queens' given by an important Royalist. At Caius, which (despite Venn's lament) has a goodly hoard, Batchcroft, the Master, refused to send any plate to the King.[19] At Emmanuel the plate was divided among the Fellows, with less happy results than at Corpus. Holdsworth, the Master, wrote in despair:

> The college plate for which I stand engaged must be supply'd whatever else miscarry; if other fellows have not restored theirs, it is no example for me nor credit for them.[20]

This college, although founded only in 1584, has several pre-1642 articles. Despite Love's fears it seems that Cambridge colleges that lost their plate had only themselves to blame: Parliament did not steal any.

At Oxford the King did not steal the entire plate of the 15 colleges, but surviving pre-1640 pieces tend to be composite objects like coconuts, without much silver content. New College apparently fobbed him off with a few lids, and still has a big collection. Corpus Christi College kept the King quiet by giving him £700, and may have hidden the plate, which remains the finest pre-Civil-War hoard in Oxford.[21]

Surviving 'Jacobean' Cups

These are the sorry survivors of a sorely stricken field. Inventories record about 150 cups given to the College between 1577 and 1647, of which six (excluding the Ostrich) remain. The others had all perished by 1750.

Why did the Grim Reaper spare these particular five? We do not know; but there was something special about them as early as 1630. The inventory of plate then 'Left in ye Chest' includes the Horn, Coconut, mazers, Parker's gifts, ostrich egg, and also 'Dr Jegons gild cup with Cover', 'The Brothers gilt cup covered', 'Champernouns gilt cup covered', 'A gilt wine bowle with foote', and 'William Johnsons Cupp', and twelve other items which have not survived. These were evidently regarded as the College's chief treasures.

Some of these cups have lids, others (according to the inventories) never had them. These mark the coming of the Age of Ceilings, when people were losing their fear of Things that Fall Into the Drink.

8.1 Champernowne Cup and Cover (Plate 6)

1602 (London date-letter interpreted as E). 3.3 × 7.5 in.

The plain, inverted-bell bowl is jointed to a stem of many tiered parts, with three scroll brackets (one missing since before 1902). The lid, of two superimposed domes, has a reel finial on which stands a warrior in tunic, kilt, and baldric, with moustachios and a morion on his head, carrying a shield and staff. Stamped tongue mouldings ring the base and lid; shells adorn the knop of the stem; scale-chain on base; moresque foliage engraved on the top of the base and brim of the cup. Cup and lid are single gilt outside, double inside; underside of base not gilt.

Mr Champernowne was prodigiously armigerous. His nineteen quarterings (outdoing Roger Manners's sixteen) are pricked on the bowl;[22] his crest (*a swan sitting in a crown, with a horseshoe in its bill*) is on

19 J Walker 1862 *The Sufferings of the Clergy during the Great Rebellion* ii.145.

20 S Bendall, C Brooke, P Collinson 1999 *A History of Emmanuel College, Cambridge*. Boydell, Woodbridge

21 *Corpus Silver* pp. 203, 274.

22 *Quarterly of twenty: (1) and (18) a saltire vair between twelve billets [Champernowne]; (2) three bendlets [Okeston]; two chevrons, in a canton a mullet [Rohant]; (4) two lions passant [Gouldington of Bedford]; (5) a chevron between three cockatrices [Boys]; (6) a chevron between three eagles' heads erased, as many acorns on the chevron [Childerlegh]; (7) a chevron engrailed between three*

the warrior's shield. Mortality is represented by three naïvely engraved skulls. The cup is inscribed in the hand of Peter Muser, College goldsmith (p. 28) *Ex dono Johannis Champernowne, Collegiu Corporis Christi.*, and 11 *once*. (Present weight 11.2 ounces.)

Maker's mark: monogram AB (unidentified: found on cups and beakers down to 1617).

The reel is attached by six rivets of different sizes, evidently repairs (although no repair is recorded). The top of the staff is probably broken. The bottom of the cup is scratched and frog-poked.

John Champernowne, from Modbury in Devon, became Fellow Commoner in 1606; he stayed three years, matriculating in 1608, and disappeared into the Inner Temple in 1609. He had had the cup as a boy. The 1622 inventory describes it as

> Mr *John Champernoon* a gilt bowle wth cover

Such a deep vessel, then called a 'bowl', would now be called a 'wine cup', a common type at the time. The embossed, tiered foot, domed lid with a reel, and figurine are relics of the Mannerist period (cf Parker Cup). The three little brackets, each a separate casting, had a short fashion from *c*.1600–20.

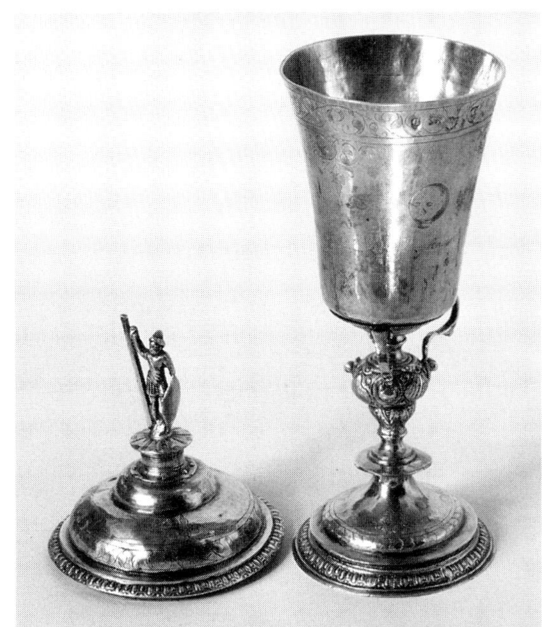

8.2 Harrington Tazza (Plate 6)

1606 (London I). 6.0 × 4.6 in.

This elegant, fruity, single-gilt piece has a shallow bowl, arousing thoughts of ice-cream sundaes in viewers of a certain age. The base, heavily embossed with little oranges and other fruit, ends in a large knop, from which three serpentlets stand on their tails to hold a tier of fruit on which rests the bottom of the cup. The bowl is engraved outside and inside with bands of foliage and fruit; in the middle inside is engraved the bust of an unshaven ruffian in a hair-net, with a tunic knotted over his shoulder.

Inscription (in Peter Muser's hand): *Coll. Corpo. Christi* and 8^on^ 1^d^ [$8\frac{1}{2}$ ounces; present weight 8.30 oz]. The hallmarks were struck after the piece was engraved. The maker's monogram, CB, occurs on many cups between 1596 and 1633.

This piece too is scratched and frog-poked on the decorated interior.

The donor has hitherto not been identified, but the inventories point to one possible person, Edmund Harrington, admitted Fellow-Commoner in 1606.[23] His gift, 'Harrington a gilt goblett', weighing $8\frac{1}{4}$ ounces, was registered at the audit in 1607. As early as 1630 the donor's name disappears from the inventory, although the cup can still be identified. 'Harrington' was added in the margin of the 1640 inventory, and appears intermittently in inventories down to 1670. The name then disappears, probably because it was not written on the cup and people's memories had failed. Harrington had a Fellow-Commoner's brief career and vanished into the night of history; all we know of him is that he came from Essex and gave this cup.

Tazza, Italian for 'cup', is the technical term for this shape, which occurs rather rarely from the 1580s

martlets [Bickley]; (8) three hones [De la Hone]; (9) a chevron between three shovelers [Compton]; (10) three ravens' heads erased [Norris]; (11) barry nebuly [Blount]; (12) two wolves passant, on a bordure eight saltires [Ayala]; (13) a castle [Mountjoy or Sanchat]; (14) vairy [Gresley]; (15) three fleurs-de-lys [Holt]; (16) a fess, three covered cups in chief [Westcot]; (17) fretty [unknown]; (19) a bend with three horseshoes thereon [Ferrers of Bere Ferrers]; (20) an eagle [Bigberie].* From Jones (1910).

* *Spatula clypeata*, a kind of duck.

23 Another Harrington came up as Sizar in 1610, but Sizars, poor students, seldom gave treasure.

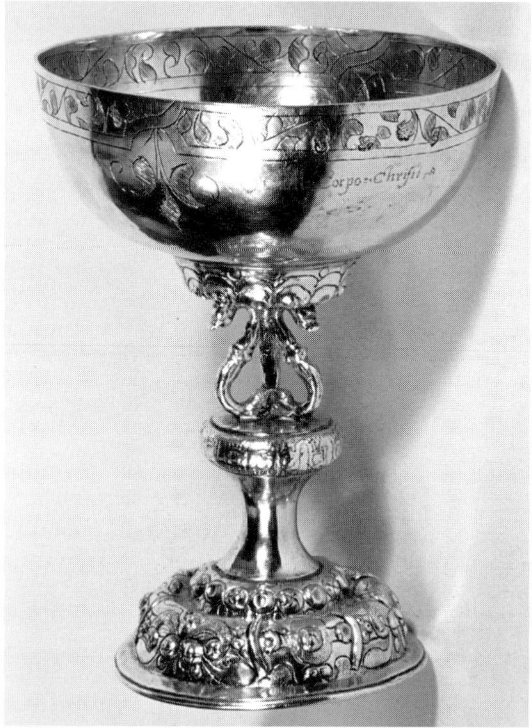

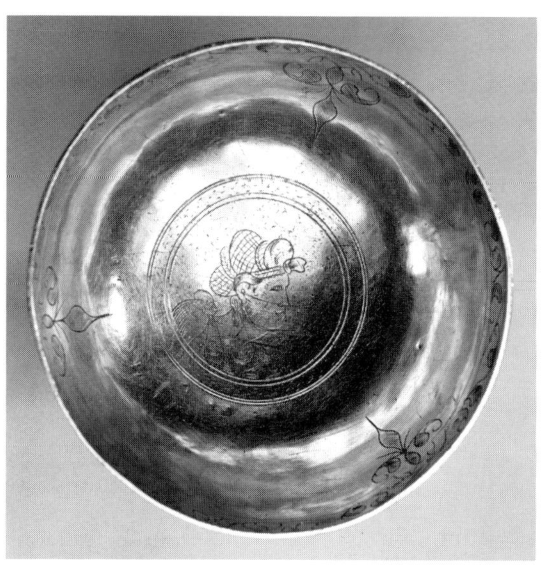

onwards. The ornament is weakly Mannerist, like the Champernowne. The same maker made another *tazza* for the Armourers' Company.[24]

8.3 Cup of the Two Brothers (Ogle Cup)

1607 (London K). Cup 8.8 × 4.2 in.; lid 6.2 × 4.5.

This is a steeple-cup, the modern name given to those with a spire-like finial. The cup, double-gilt except underneath,[25] has a domed lid, with three little dragons supporting a three-sided steeple ending in a knob. The entire surface is decorated with *repoussé* and deep chasing, including tongue-moulding, scale-chains, scallop-shells on the knop, jolly sea-monsters (all different) on bowl and lid, and chevrons on the steeple imitating the shape of the lead sheets on a real spire.

The pounced inscription, in Peter Muser's hand, reads: *Munusculu' duoru' fratru' RO et TO in 9ber 1607 + Collegiu' Corporis Christi* (A little gift from two brothers R.O. and T.O. in November 1607). Weight 15 *unc* [present weight 15.2 ounces]. Maker's monogram, TW, is found on a few other cups from 1603 to 1608. Slightly frog-poked inside.

Thomas and Robert Ogle, probably sons of Sir Richard Ogle of Pinchbeck in the Lincolnshire Fens, came up as Fellow Commoners in 1607. Nothing more is heard of Thomas; Robert Ogle went off to the Inner Temple in 1609. Their cup is mentioned in the 1622 inventory as:

> Mr $_{\text{gilt}}$ *Robert & Thomas Ogles* silver bowle wth cover 15–0–0 [ounces]

Steeple-cups are known from the 1560s onwards, and were fashionable from 1599 to *c*.1640. This fine example, with all the silversmithing techniques displayed in a smallish piece, still has some old-fashioned details such as the marine-style decoration recalling the Ostrich Cup, and the strapwork so typical of Elizabethan detail. It could have been preserved as a work of art and for its

24 Cripps p. 351.

25 Foster & Atkinson (1896) say 'recently regilt', which could be right.

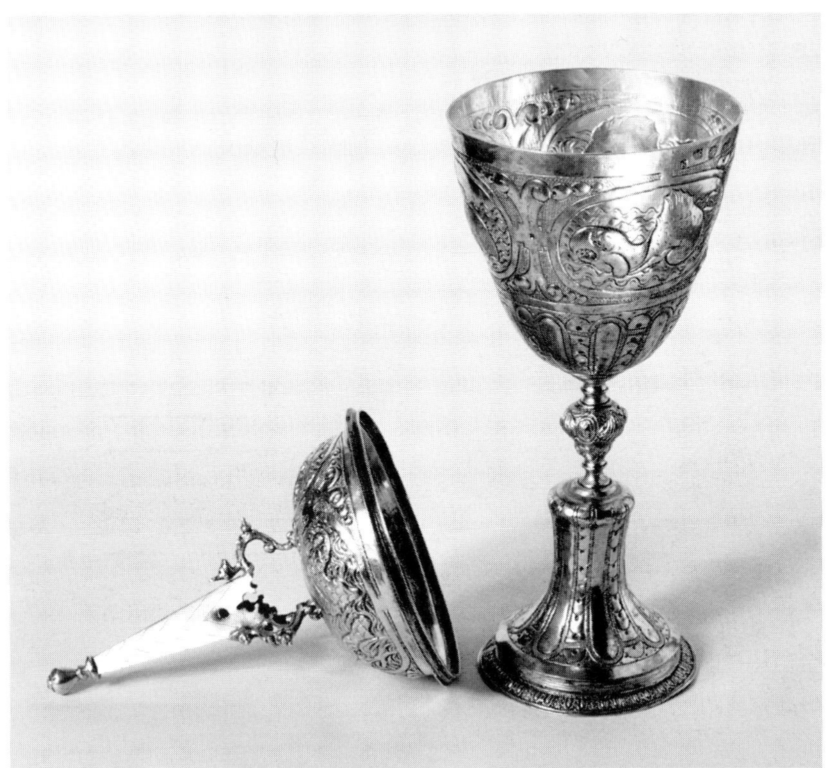

fine lid. We likewise kept the smaller 'Standing Cup wth a Cover gilt', given by the otherwise unknown brothers Thomas and Henry Seckford in *c*.1590; it survived the dangerous years, but we melted it in 1694.

8.4 Jegon Cup

1608 (London L). Cup 11.2 × 5.0 in.; lid 6.6 × 5.3.

This is a larger version of the Ogle Cup, almost identical in shape save for three knobbly brackets surmounting the knop, and for a reel on top of the lid. The steeple is pierced, with little cast curlicues at the top. The griffin brackets have been rudely sawn off and fixed to a crude gilt disk riveted to the reel; this botch was perpetrated before 1902. Foot, bowl, and lid are each deeply chased with three 'acanthus' leaves with decorated midribs. Between each of the leaves on the lid is an orange. In the same position on the bowl and foot is some kind of elongated melon or squash. Six tiny oranges appear on the lower knop.

Inscribed: EX DONO JOH'. JEGON'. EPI': NOR': MARTII X AN': DOM': 1614 [Of the gift of John Jegon, Bishop of Norwich, 10 March A.D. 1614/5]. Weight inscribed as XXI^{on} [21 ounces] on base, X^{on} [10 ounces] on lid [present weight of cup 21.0, of lid 10.5 ounces]. Maker's mark: IS with three pellets over a horn; similar marks occur on cups and an almsdish, 1606–9.

The Audit Book records for 1615 'To Peter Muser for marking my Lord of Norwich his Cup'. This positively identifies the inscription, like that on the other Jacobean cups, as Muser's hand.

The donor of this cup was very different from the others. John Jegon (1550–1617), of Coggeshall in Essex, had been a Fellow of Queens' College. In 1590 Queen Elizabeth and Lord Burghley, the Prime Minister, leant on Corpus Christi College to elect him Master, 'notwithstanding that we had in our own House . . . a man very fit for that place'. After this inauspicious beginning, he proved an able businessman, getting the College out of debt and recruiting benefactors; he was also a successful

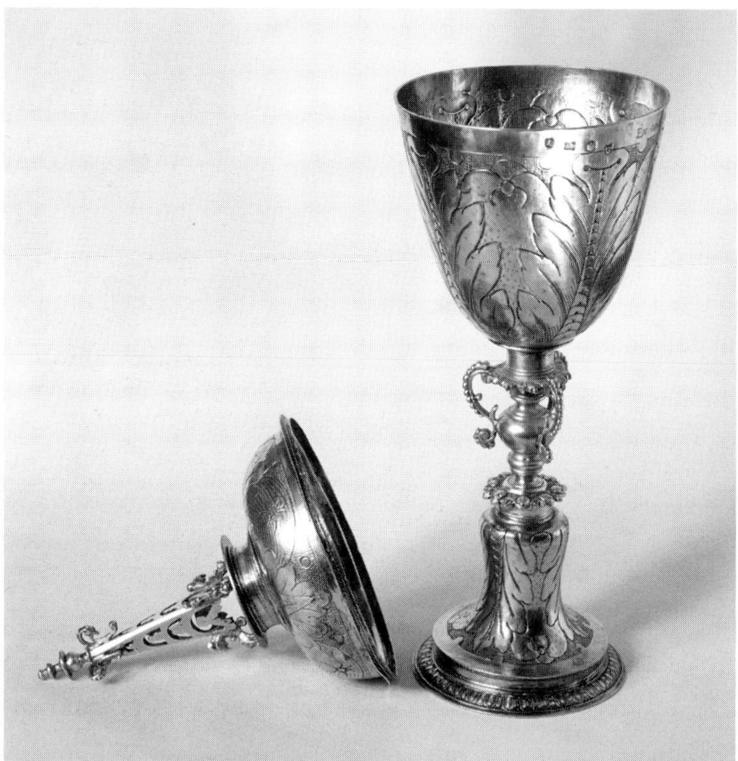

Vice-Chancellor of the University. His signature ends the 1591/2 plate inventory. His carved wooden arms were in the Chapel and are now in the Hall; his grim and austere portrait until recently glared down the Hall.

In 1602 he became Bishop of Norwich, being succeeded as Master by his brother Thomas. Norwich loved him not, 'being thought of a covetous disposition, and not so liberal to the poor as was expected from a bishop';[26] indeed a scurrilous rhymester sang of 'Bad Bishop Jeggon'.[27] He was accused of fraudulently burning his own palace; he wanted to burn William Sayer, the heretic, but was overruled by the Archbishop of Canterbury.[28] He gave us the cup (his only recorded act of generosity) after his retirement from Norwich.

The motif of acanthus leaves and oranges or orange-like objects is the commonest design for the bowls of standing cups in the 1610s, a fashion showing very little variation from maker to maker (like the repetitive mannerisms in the design of 'mountain' bicycles or 'trainer' shoes in the 1990s). Oranges had appeared on silver since the Parker Cup (p. 74); by this time they were no longer a great rarity. The elongated object is interpreted as a melon or a squash,[29] the latter being derived from the colonies in Virginia.

8.5 Johnson Cup

1616 (London T). 8.4 × 3.2 in.

The single-gilt bowl is embossed with three melons or squashes, three acanthus leaves, and shells at the base of the melons. The same motif, debased, is chased on the foot. The rim has a double chased line with three pendants.

Pounced inscriptions (Muser's hand again) read *William Johnson 1616, Coll. Corp. Christi*, and 9^{on} [weight;

26 Lamb p. 150.

27 AS Harvey 1936 *Ballads, Songs and Rhymes of East Anglia* Jarrold (I am indebted to the late Colin Ranson for this reference.)

28 WK Jordan 1936 *The development of religious tolerance in England . . . 1603–1640* Allen & Unwin, London pp. 33f.
PA Welsby 1962 *George Abbot, the unwanted Archbishop* SPCK, London p. 47.

29 Penzer.

present weight 8.7 ounces]. Donor's arms (*Quarterly: 1st & 4th, a canton charged with a bird; 2nd and 3rd, a chevron between three crescents*) are pounced on the bowl. The maker's mark, R between two pellets over W, occurs on other standing cups between 1617 and 1622. The leopard mark occurs on the base as well as the bowl.

William Johnson, from Canterbury, was an undergraduate in 1608 and B.A. in 1612. This cup could commemorate his taking his M.A. in 1615. Our earliest record of it, surprisingly, is in 1670: 'Mr William Johnsons Cup gilt. 1616'.

This is what Penzer, the authority on steeple-cups, calls the 'Standard' design of wine-cup, with 'acanthus' leaves, melons, and shells. It never had a lid. One in the Victoria & Albert Museum, of the same year, is almost identical but lacks the brackets.

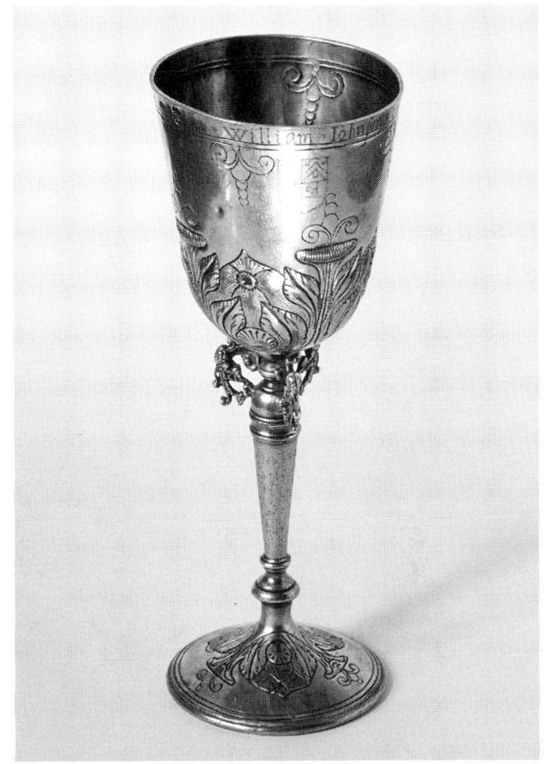

Comparisons with other cups

Steeple-cups and wine-cups are typical of their period, and the College doubtless had many more. The Tsar appreciated them, and his successors have kept his entire hoard. In the Kremlin are six cups with steeple lids, marked between 1604 and 1611, and twelve lidless cups of the Johnson type between 1612 and 1619 (plus one of 1639). A very constant feature are the three (occasionally four) reptilian or abstract brackets, of which the earliest example is 1589. Many of these cups are embossed with the type of 'acanthus' leaf on our Jegon Cup.[30]

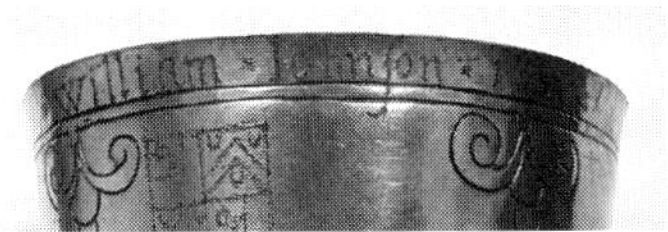
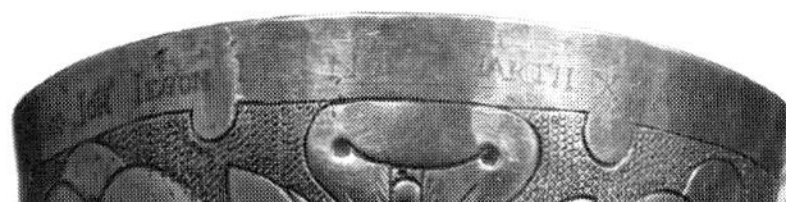
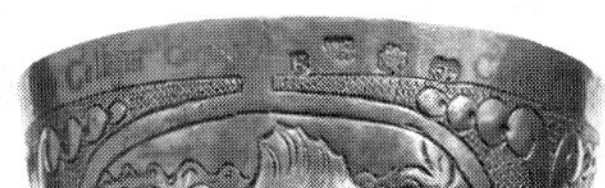

Muser's inscriptions on the Johnson, Jegon, and Ogle cups

30 Jones *Russia*.

9

Chapel Plate

... the Deacons, Church-wardens, ... shall receive the Alms for the Poor ... in a decent bason to be provided by the Parish for that purpose...

[a] *Here the Priest is to take the Paten into his hands:*
[b] *And here to break the Bread:*
[c] *And here to lay his hand upon all the Bread.*
[d] *Here he is to take the Cup into his hand:*
[e] *And here to lay his hand upon every vessel (be it Chalice or Flagon) in which there is any Wine to be consecrated.*

Rubrics for the Communion, Book of Common Prayer, 1662

The medieval College had magnificent sacred plate, inherited from the Gilds or given by early Masters and Fellows (p. 48). There was even more than the inventories mention: in 1461 Thomas Goldsmyth of Cambridge was paid 2*s*. for repairing 'the silver pyx of the Sacrament', not otherwise recorded.[1] As late as 1526 each Fellow was issued with his own chalice and paten. These treasures were frittered away: two chalices and patens were sold to build a dovehouse (not entirely trivial for a college that lived on mutton, dried cod, and pigeons). Little if anything survived when Matthew Parker presented the College with his extraordinary chalice (p. 95). This and other gifts (plus a base-metal flagon, bought in 1619 for 7*s*. 6*d*.[2]) brought us a rather miscellaneous set of Chapel plate by the 17th century.

This assemblage survived the Commonwealth only to meet with a new disaster:

> Stolen out of the Chappel of Corpus Christi College in Cambridge, on Easter-day, two large silver Flagons, with the Arms of the said College upon them ... Three silver and gilt Cups, two of them weighing together 43 Ounces, whereof one of them is chas'd, and hath the Arms of the Archbishop of Canterbury, and is mark'd M.P. and the other with a Cover, and has the Earl of Rutland's Arms upon it, together with the College Arms ... [there follows a description of the two robbers, one of whom 'pretends to be disorder'd in his mind']. Whoever gives notice of the said persons and Plate, so as they be secur'd, to the Butler of the said College ... shall have 3 Guinea's.
>
> *London Gazette*, 20 April 1693

The College audit book for 1693 records £3. 18*s*. spent on gazetting the theft; the reward of only £3. 3*s*. suggests lack of enthusiasm for recovering the plate. The description of the Parker Cup is difficult to reconcile with the drawing: perhaps it had already been recycled into a shape more suitable for liturgical use. The Earl of Rutland's cup was more than a century old (p. 97), and had been converted from secular use.

William Stanley, the new Master, replaced the stolen plate by a set suited to the usage of the time. The flagons and cup are of usual shapes for the period, resembling, for example, those dated 1707 at Hyattsville, Maryland (Cripps p. 208). These continued in regular use until the late 19th century, when they, in turn, had become unsuitable, and others were acquired. They are still used on Corpus Christi Day and other great feasts.

1 CC(A): *Liber Albus* part 2 f. 60.
2 CC(A): *Audits 1590–1678* p. 301.

9.1 Montacute Alms-Dish of 1663

By the entry of Gentlemen. . . . Mr Edward Mountagu and Henry [his] Brother Sons of the Earl of Mancast[er] one gilt basin for the use of the Chapel . . .

Audit-book, 1663

This grand object (Plate 7) is the sole survivor of the burglary. The great silver-gilt dish is 20.5 inches in diameter, superbly plain and decorated only with engraving.

In the middle is the Jesus monogram IHS under a cross, surrounded by rays of glory. On the rim are the donors' shield-of-arms,[3] the College's arms, and their two badges treated as crests on top of the shields, each enmantled by bunches of plumes (a common device for surrounding coats-of-arms on Restoration plate). The donors' badge is *the front half of a griffin couped, collared with an indented fesse* with an Earl's coronet hovering above. For the College, a pelican in his piety stands on a wreath. These are the earliest examples in the College of pseudo-crests (p. 14).

The inscription reads: *D D D Deo & Sacris Eduvardus et Henricus Montacutius filij Edvardi Comitis Mancestriæ et Regis Camerarij Domestici &c.* (Edward and Henry Montacute, sons of Edward Earl of Manchester and members of the Household to the King, gave this to God and the Holies.) There are three proof-corrections in this short text.

Date-letter: 𝔉 for 1663. Maker's mark: HG with three pellets above, and a star between two pellets below, in a pentagonal shield; unidentified.

The Montacutes or Montagus were among the then few learned members of the upper class. Their father the Earl had done the thankless job of Chancellor of the University during the Commonwealth: he had had to throw overtly Royalist dons out of Cambridge under Cromwell and to rehabilitate them under Charles II. Four sons were undergraduates at Corpus, and one became a Fellow. These two came up in 1662, becoming Masters of Arts in the same year [!]. Henry went on to the Inner Temple.

This was far above the usual standard of Gentlemen Fellow-Commoners' gifts. It was given just after the College had celebrated completing the Elizabethan Chapel in 1662, adorned at last with gold and crimson, with heraldry and stained glass and an organ – a celebration too of release from the grey poverty of the republican regime.

Medieval alms-dishes never survive, and are difficult to imagine: did not Henry VI have a golden 'almesdissh' called the Tiger, mounted upon a bear of gold with 19 rubies and 26 pearls?[4] From the mid-16th century onwards alms-dishes began to be made in the pattern of (or adapted from) redundant ablution basins and rose-water basins (p. 73). Ours is a magnificent example of this relatively common type.

3 *Quarterly: 1 & 4, a fesse indented of three points and a border (Montagu); 2 & 3, an eagle (Monthermer); the whole surmounted by an Earl's coronet.*

4 Palgrave 1836 **1** 370.

9.2–9.6 Replacement Chapel Plate

9.2, 9.3 Stanley Flagon and Paten of 1678

Flagon: 8.3 in. × 6.4 × 10.2 high. Paten: 8.7 in. × 2.5 high.
Flagon (container for Communion wine): a fine simple object, double-gilt inside and out, with a hinged lid with thumb-piece and a curved handle. Base embossed with 'acanthus' leaves; back of handle beaded. Faintly hammer-marked.
Paten: a small charger or standing plate with moulded rim, double-gilt. It is deeply scratched by cutting up Communion bread with a knife, the common Protestant practice before wafers became customary in the 19th century.

Both have the impaled arms of William III and Mary II as Prince of Orange and Princess of England, before they became King and Queen of England.[5]

Both have Dutch hallmarks: crowned lion, crowned stork (for the assay office of the Hague), date-letter D for 1678, and maker's mark of 'a rose in a crowned shield'.[6] They have large diet-scrapes.

Having no inscription, these would be a mystery, but for Masters's *History*, which reveals that they were given by William Stanley (1647–1731).[7] He came from Hinkley (Leicestershire) to St John's College as an undergraduate. At Corpus he became a Fellow as replacement for Daniel Scargill, ejected for atheism in 1669. Among various church preferments in more or less distant places, he became chaplain to Mary Stuart, who had married the Dutch Prince in 1677. When she became Queen of England and Scotland in 1688 she made him Clerk of her Closet and dispenser of her charities. He returned to the College as Master with great reluctance from 1693 to 1698; he catalogued the Parker manuscripts. After the robbery he gave the College these pieces. He was famous for charity and learning, a friend of the Huygens scientists, and is buried in St Paul's Cathedral.

Maybe these were really the gift of Queen Mary II herself; they had been hers when she was a princess in Holland. She and her successors often bestowed Communion sets on churches which lacked them, especially in America (Cripps pp. 207ff).

A cup came with the flagon and paten. It was somehow unsatisfactory and was replaced by the Swinerton Dyer cup, but the College kept 'The Old Gilt Communion Cup of Dr Stanley' until it perished in the melt-down of 1746; its lid was melted a year later.

The vessels are generous, big enough for a parish church. The flagon – bigger than the similar ones at St Bene't's – holds nearly three pints, equivalent to two modern bottles of wine, and the cup is to match.

5 His: *Quarterly: 1, billety and a lion (Nassau); 2, a lion rampant and a crown (Katzenellenbogen); 3, a fesse counterembattled (Vianden); 4, two lions (Dietz). Over all, three escutcheons: A, a fesse (Veere); B, quarterly: 1 & 4 a bend (Chalons); 2 & 3 a hunting-horn banded with strings (Orange); over all an escutcheon checky (Geneva); C, a fesse (Buren).* Hers: *the royal arms of England (twice), quartered with Scotland and Ireland, over all a label signifying the eldest child.* Supporters: *two lions rampant collared with labels.*

6 *Haags silver uit vijf eeuwen* Haags Gemeentemuseum 1967, §65.

7 Masters's source was probably the 1706 inventory, which mentions '1 Flaggon by Wm Stanley' and the other given by Samwell.

8 The ingenious reader will notice that New Year's Day for general purposes was 25 March, and for the London Assay Office 29 May (p. xii); therefore a piece ordered in early March 1704/5 and marked before the end of May would bear the 1704 letter.

9.4 Samwell Flagon

1704 (the curious London j). 8.3 in. × 6.4 × 10.2 high.

An English-made, very slightly larger copy of the Stanley flagon. Not hammer-marked. College arms and the inscription *Collegium Corporis Christi & B Virginis Mariæ in Universitate Cantabrigiensi 1704.* On the lid are the donor's arms (*Argent, two squirrels gules sitting back to back, with a Red Hand* [for a Baronet of Ulster]) and the text *Ex dono Thomæ Samwell Baronetti ex agro Northamptoniensi* (Of the gift of Thomas Samwell, Bart., from the land of Northampton).

Maker's mark: DI beneath what is interpreted as a cherub, with three objects below, for the obscure silversmith Isaac Dighton.

Thomas Samwell of Upton (Northants) entered the College in 1704, apparently as a Fellow-Commoner. He became MP for Coventry.

The Chapter Book records for March 1, 1704/5:[8]

> Agreed y^t ye Flagon used upon Communion days be sent up to London, by one of ye Carryers, to have another made by it, intended to be given by Sr Thomas Samuel, & y^t y^e old one be new washt over,* to make it answerable to y^e new one.

*This phrase probably means 're-gilded'; it was used of coiners silver-plating bad coin.

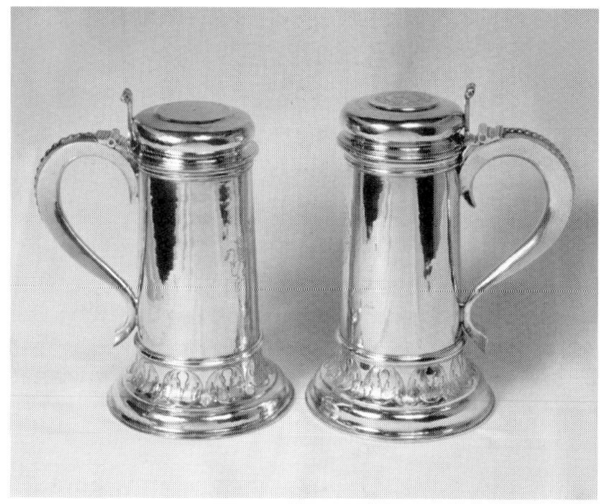

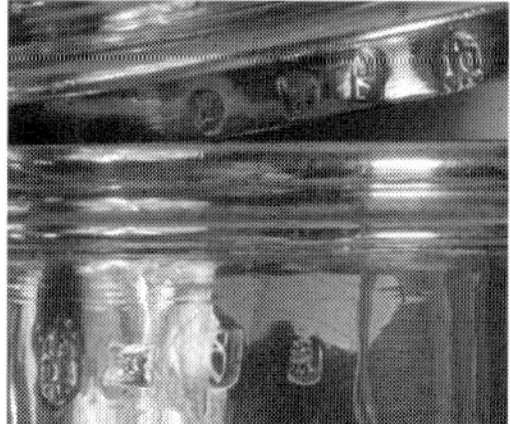

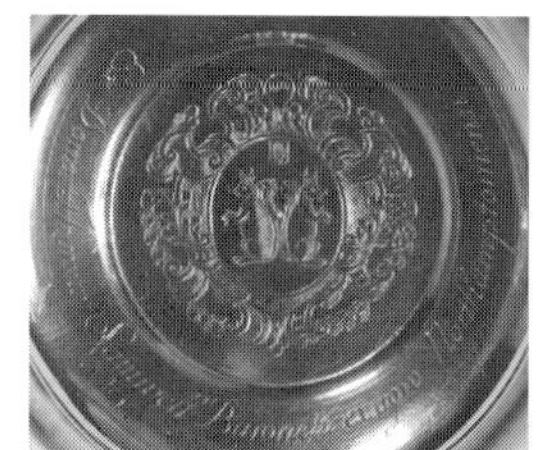

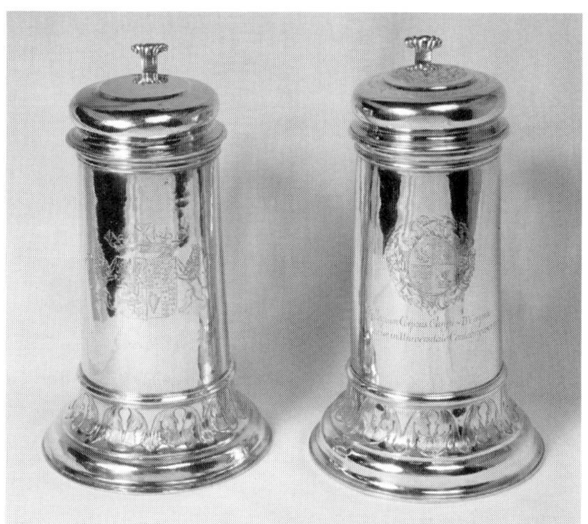

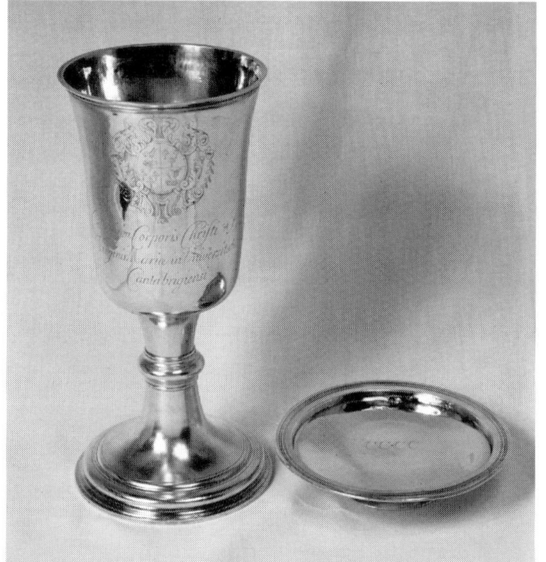

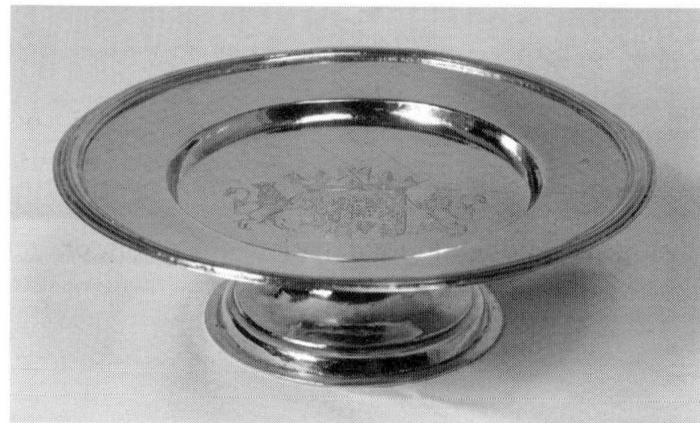

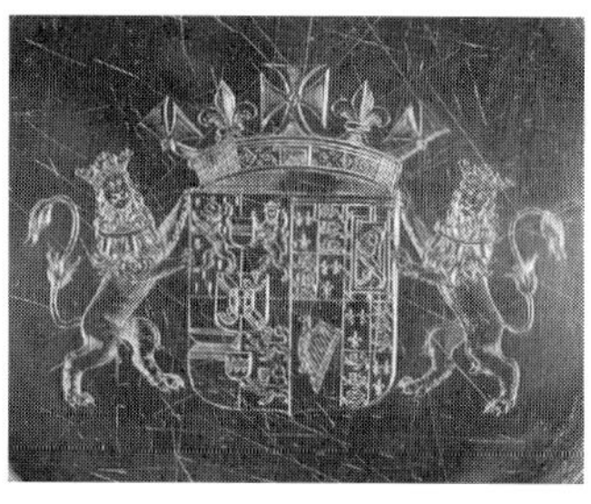

Top: Stanley (left) and Samwell Flagons, with Dutch hallmarks on the Stanley and Samwell's arms on lid.
Middle: Stanley and Samwell Flagons; Swinerton Dyer Cup and Paten
Bottom: Stanley Paten and its scratched Dutch coat-of-arms

A pair of flagons would be used: one for wine, the other for water. Liturgical practice at the time evidently made it possible to celebrate with only one, but inconvenient.

9.5, 9.6 Swinerton Dyer Cup and Paten of 1708

Cup: 5.2 in. (base), 5.0 (mouth), 10.6 high. Paten: 6.1 in. by 1.3 high. Britannia silver, double-gilt. *Cup:* deep bell-shaped bowl, on a stem with a moulding in the middle. Stem and base have a rough 'scoured' texture and thinner gilding than the bowl, and are a modern replacement; Jones's photograph of 1910 shows the base damaged as though by use as a cosh.

Arms: College's arms and donor's: *Quarterly, 1 & 4: Or a chief indented gules* [Dyer]; *2: Argent a cross paty sable* [Swinerton]; *3: Argent a cross paty sable and a border engrailed gules* [Swinerton]; *augmented with a Red Hand* [Baronet of Ulster]. Inscribed: *Collegium Corporis Christi & B Virginis Mariæ in Universitate Cantabrigiensi* and *Deo & Sacris DDD Swinerton Dyer Baronettus ex agro Essexiensi.* (Swinerton Dyer, Baronet, from the land of Essex, gave [me] to God and the Sacred).

Paten: a smaller version of the Dutch paten. It forms a lid for the cup, following Elizabethan precedent. Instead of arms is the donor's crest, *a goat's head in a crown.* Inscription CCCC. This paten has not been used for cutting bread.

Both bear the bizarre and poorly struck letter n for 1708. Maker's mark, PY under a crown, is for Benjamin Pyne, who had a long career as a maker of civic maces (including two for Oxford University).

The cup is a standard shape for the period, but the College's clergy now find it an awkward shape to administer. Evidently the communicant took the cup from the priest and drank a draught, not a sip.

Sir Swinerton Dyer, of Newton Hall, Great Dunmow (Essex), entered the College in 1705. He is said to be an ancestor of a well-known recent Master of St Catharine's.

9.7–9.19 Modern Chapel Plate

For most 18th-century parishes Holy Communion was a rare, solemn, corporate event, which everyone attended once a quarter. In the College, the Plate and Library log-book shows that the Communion plate was used five times a year: at Christmas, Easter, and one celebration each term. The vessels were signed out from the treasury and signed in again, sometimes months later. The earliest surviving entry is in 1706, when they were signed in by Stephen Hales, father of plant physiology, and John Ellis, undergraduate.[9] This was still going on in the 1800s.

In the 19th century the College was a stronghold of the Evangelical wing of the Church of England, having 'the character of a seminary full of Low Church ordinands' (Bury p. 126). Corpus was certainly devout: undergraduates had to attend Sunday and weekday services on pain of a fine. But devotion centred more on the Word than the Sacrament, which was probably not celebrated every Sunday.

As Patrick Bury relates, Evangelicalism declined in the late 19th century. Corpus took up Anglo-Catholicism, with which at least two Masters, E.C. Pearce (1914–27) and Sir Will Spens (1927–52), were in sympathy. Although the College was never very High Church, it favoured celebrating frequent Communion, calling for new, smaller sets of plate. High-Church priests celebrated the Eucharist with wafers instead of ordinary bread, and needed a wafer-box from which to count out the number needed. They tilted the cup to the lips of the kneeling communicant instead of handing it to him; this was awkward with the big deep cups of the 17th century. From 1883 onwards donors began to give new Chapel plate more suited to these practices.

9.7 Hankinson-Jennings Flagon

*c.*1860. Mostly silvered base metal. 11.3 by 8.5 by 18.3 high.

Cylindrical body with spout, foliated handle, hinged lid. Body has arcading and four figurines of standing Evangelists, bolted to their symbols of a lion, ox, man, and eagle. Many decorated bands. Lid in likeness of a fish-scale-tiled roof[10] with 4 crocketted ridges. Finial in form of a pelican in his piety, with 6 chicks.

Inscriptions: [1] I.M.D.G. [*In Majorem Dei Gloriam,* to the greater glory of God] & To The Fruitful Memory of Thomas Edwards Hankinson (C.C.C.C.). (Junior OP. & 1ST.

9 CC(L): MS 624A *verso:* a surviving leaf from the previous plate-book, preserved for the inventory on the other side.

10 St Botolph's Church has such tiles, dated 1842.

Class Classic) Priest, M.A. Nine Times Seatonian Prizeman Between 1831–42. IST. Minister of S^{T}. Matthews, Denmark Hill, Camberwell, Obit 1843. [2] To the Honoured Society of the Beloved, "Ancient & Religious House", C.C.C.C. H.E. Jennings, Chapel Clerk (1870–71). d.d. 1933.

Marks: Sheffield crown 𝔍ℜ & $ EP6.

There must be a story behind this extraordinary object. The two men concerned were parsons of south London churches a mile apart, but can never have met. Thomas Edwards Hankinson (1805–43) was admitted in 1824; he took the equivalent of a II-2 (*Junior Optime*) in the then compulsory Mathematics Tripos, but was more successful in Classics. Thomas Seaton, who died in 1741, endowed the prize which was offered (and still is) annually for an English poem by any Cambridge M.A. 'on a subject conducive to the honour of the Supreme Being and the recommendation of virtue'. Hankinson was not rich: the £40 fee for his M.A. made it impossible for him to 'live in love and honour . . . I must take my choice between starvation and imprisonment'. Prizes like the Seatonian kept such poor but able scholars alive.

The donor, Harnett Ellison Jennings, zoologist, undergraduate from 1868, was Vicar of St Clement's, East Dulwich 1885–1936, and then Prebendary of the curious church of St Endellion, Cornwall. He was noted for reminiscences of the College in its pious Evangelical period.

This huge vessel was presumably intended for liturgical use, if a sufficiently stalwart server could be found to lift it. Flagons usually come in pairs: was only one a sign of Evangelical practice?

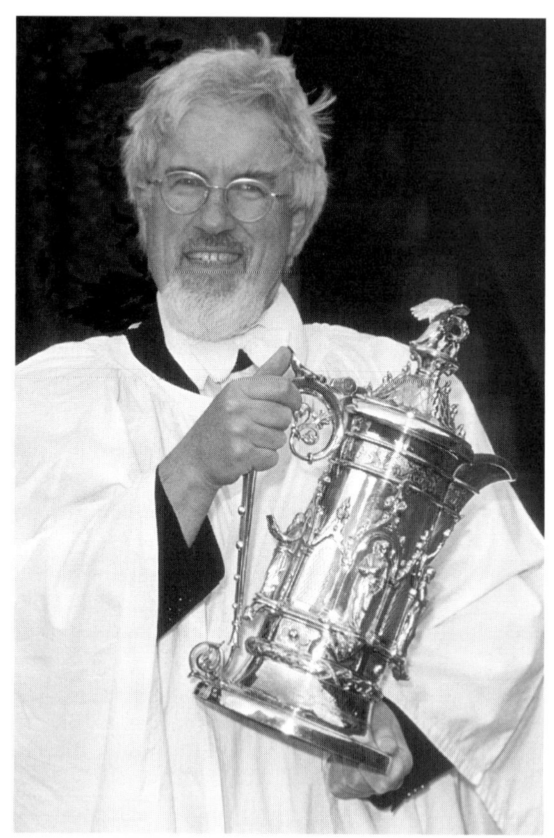

9.8 Perowne Chalice

1883 (London H). 9.8 in. high; base 7.8 in. extreme diameter; mouth 4.7 in. Double-gilt; treble-gilt inside. In velvet-lined oak case with brass corners.

The cup stands on a foot in the shape of a six-pointed star. Elaborate foliation and beading on and below knop; demi-angels on points of base.

College arms. Inscriptions: Deo et Sacris D.D.D. in vsvm Collegii Magister A.S. MDCCCLXXXIII [The Master gave [this] to God and the Sacred, for the use of the College, A.D. 1883]; Collegium Corporis Christi et Beatæ Mariæ Virginis Cantabrigiæ [College of

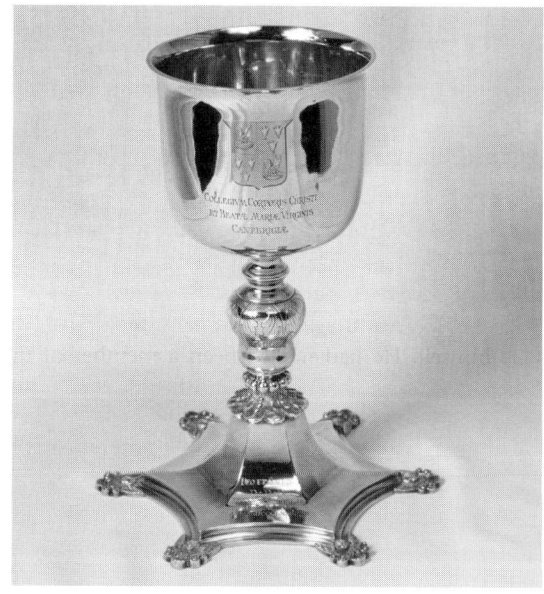

Corpus Christi and the Blessed Virgin Mary at Cambridge].

Maker's mark: S.S in ellipse.

Described by the donor as 'an exact replica of a Chalice in use in Her Majesty's Chapel Royal, Whitehall'.

For the career of Edward Henry 'The Sinner' Perowne (1826–1906), see under his two Bishop Green Cups of Eloquence (§10.4.4). He was Master of the College 1879–1906, and famed for his conservative views; but this gift shows that liturgical reform could influence even such a Master as he. There is no paten: presumably those of 1678 and 1708 were still used.

9.9 Perowne Alms-Dishes

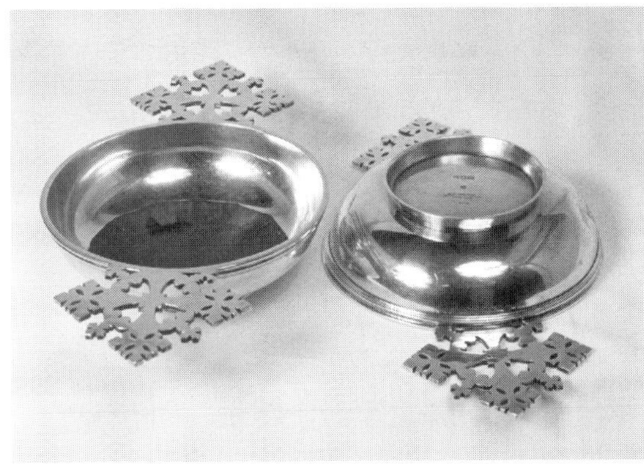

1896 (London a). 12.0 in. × 6.3 × 2.0 high.

Pair, double-gilt, with velvet liners, in velvet-lined oaken box.

Inscription: DEO ET SACRIS D.D.D. PER L ANNOS DISCIPULUS SCHOLARIS SOCIUS MAGISTER (A student, Scholar, Fellow, and Master for 50 years gave [this] to God and the Sacred).

Maker: W.C J.L. in shield. The marks, exceptionally, are repeated under the handles. Inscription: GOLDSMITHS & SILVERSMITHS COMPANY 112 REGENT S$^{\underline{T}}$. W.

Said by Catling to be designed by Edward Henry Perowne himself. He had indeed been a member of the College since 1846.

Big dent in one.

9.10 Wafer-Box (see next page)

1907 (London m). 3.7 by 2.2 by 1.9 in. high.

Rectangular base with rounded corners, four globular feet; subdivided for holding Communion wafers and counting the number required. Lid incised with a foliate cross.

Maker's mark: A R M & C^{O} L^{D} in rectangle.

Presumably acquired at the instigation of Will Spens (p. 115), elected Fellow early in 1907; a prominent lay High-Churchman, soon to become Tutor and later Master.

Used several times a week and dented with hard service.

9.11, 9.12 Sunday (Knight) Chalice and Paten

1911 (London q).

Chalice: 4.2 in. (diam. of cup), 5.4 (diam. at base), 7.5 in. high. Single-gilt, cup double-gilt inside. Octagonal stem; hollow base extending into stem and knop. Cup with two rectangles and two lozenges of incised foliation. Stem with moulded bands; incised lines along angles. Knop heavily foliated. Base with raised octafoil, foliated spandrels, foliated pattern round rim.

Paten: circular, 5.8 in. diam. Single-gilt. Hexafoil, with foliated spandrels.

Inscription (on both): *Deo et Sacris in usum Collegii C.C.C. et B.V.M. d.d. Henry Jos. Corbett Knight, D.D. Socius eps Gibraltar: MCMXI* (H.J.C. Knight, Fellow, Bishop of Gibraltar, gave [us] to God and the Sacred for the use of the College . . . . 1911).

On cup: apud te fons vitae (with thee is the well of life [*Psalm* **36** 9])

On both: LAMBERT COVENTRY ST LONDON

Maker's mark: HL in rectangle.

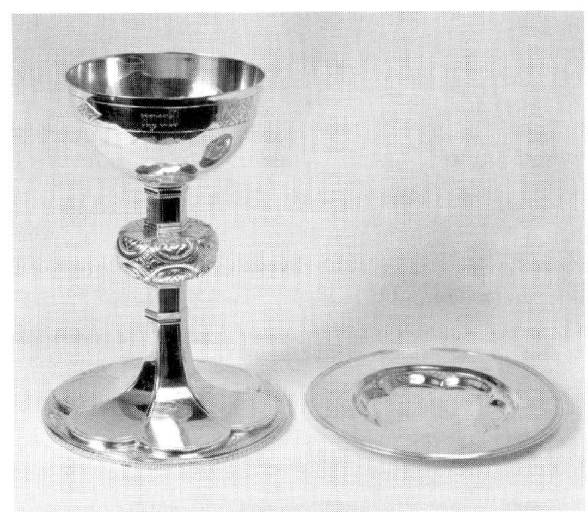

Case: oak box; hinged lid; velvet lining; brass handle, lock, and plate with CORPUS CHRISTI COLLEGE CAMBRIDGE 1911.

Donor: Henry Joseph Corbett 'Lazarus' Knight (1853–1920); of India; son of a poor parson; theologian, cyclist, cricketer (but could not afford to play), ascetic; poverty-stricken undergraduate at St Catharine's College 1878; Firsts in Classics and Theology; DD 1907; Rector of Marnhull (north Dorset, next to the Corpus living of Stalbridge) 1895–1901; Principal of what is now Westcott House 1901; Fellow of Corpus 1901–11; Prælector 1911; Bishop of Gibraltar 1911–20; founder of the Knight Exhibitions in Natural Science. His widow gave the Knight Cup (p. 133). This chalice is for use 'when the number of communicants is but small' (Bury pp. 237f).

Edge badly dented. Gilding very worn, especially on paten.

9.13, 9.14 Everyday Chalice and Paten

1953 (London T).

Chalice: 4.1 in. (diam. of cup), 4.0 (diam. of base), 5.3 in. high. Cup slightly hammer-textured inside and out; knop pierced and chased with vaguely Celtic strapwork and flowers; beaded band above knop, band of fleurs-de-lys below; zigzag incisions round base. Inscribed C C C C.

Paten: 5.7 in. diam. Flat with flat rim.

Maker's mark on both: C C^{O} L^{D} in trefoil.

Dented with active service.

9.15 Ciborium

1956 (London *a*). 3.7 in. (diam. of cup), 3.6 (diam. of base), 5.7 in. total height.

Like a chalice, but with tight-fitting lid, surmounted by Celtic-ish cross.

Maker's mark: A. R. M & C^{O} L^{D} in rectangle.

A somewhat High-Church piece, used for the priest's wafer and for extra wafers. This and the preceding would have been introduced by Roland Charles Walls (1917–), Chaplain and then Dean of Chapel 1953–61, whose profound spirituality is still a legend in the College.

9.16 McCrum Paten

1994 (Sheffield [rose] *u*). 6.7 in. diam., 1.4 high.

Deep dish with small convex bottom. Pelican on bottom, three lilies on sides. Green leather-covered case with green velvet lining.

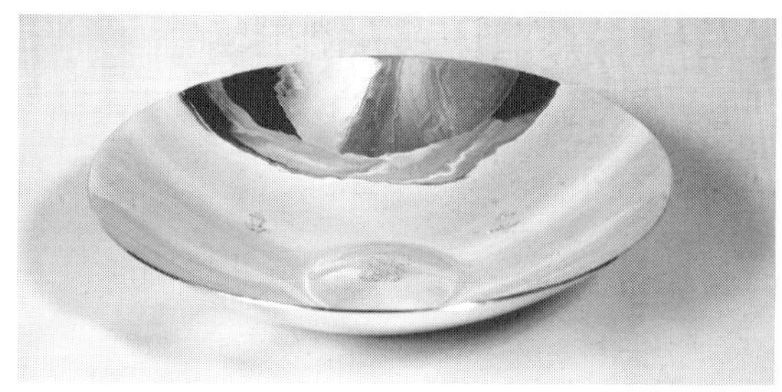

Inscription: C.C.C. et B.M.V. d.d. M.W. et C.M.K. M^{C}CRUM 1980–1994.

Maker's mark: AAB in rectangle with two indented corners.

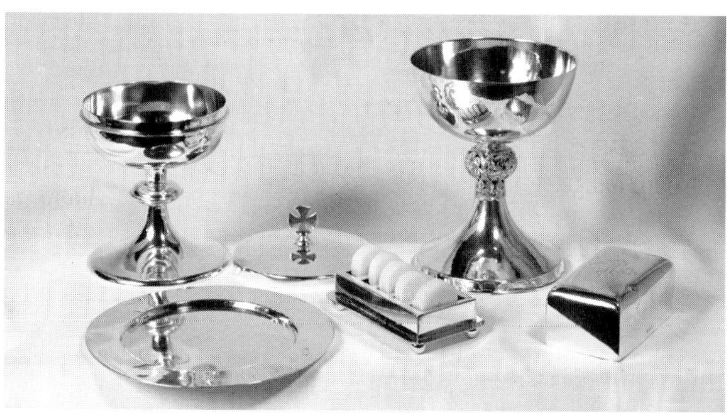

Ciborium with lid; Everyday Chalice and Paten; Wafer-box with lid

Given by Michael William McCrum (1924–) and his wife Christine to celebrate his Mastership. From Gosport; served in Royal Navy; admitted Scholar 1946; Classicist; Fellow 1949–80; Tutor 1951–62; chief designer and inspirer of Leckhampton, the College's campus for graduate students; Headmaster of Tonbridge School 1962–70 and Eton College 1970–80; returned as Master 1980–1994; Honorary Fellow 1994– .

A large paten like this is needed to celebrate the Eucharist with ordinary bread. It thus has the opposite significance to the Wafer-box, although the use of wafers is no longer particularly High-Church.

9.17 Tong-Walker Alms-dish

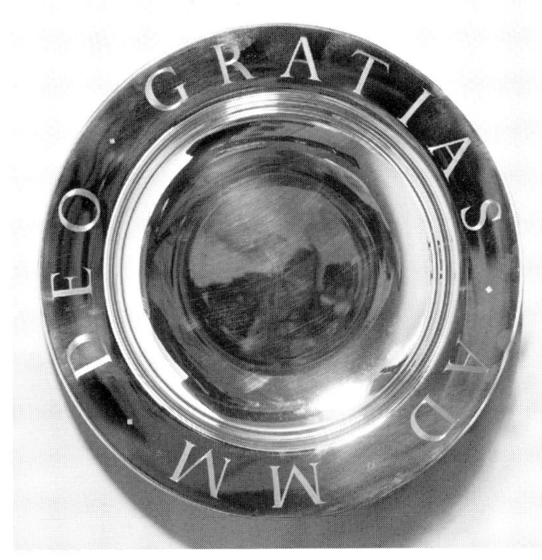

2000 (London a). 12.4 in. diam., 2.0 in. high. Shallow dish with flange.

Inscriptions: DEO. GRATIAS. AD. MM (Thanks to God. AD 2000) [underside] Collegio C.C. et B.V.M. Cantab. d.d. Paulus Tong Collegii A.M. item Collegii S. Ioan. apud Hong Kong Magister mm Collegium suum recordatus nec non memor Petri Knight Walker hon. c. D.D. olim Decani Cappellæ et postea per annos mcmlxxvii – lxxxix Episcopi Eliensis et hon. c. Socii Collegii. (Paul Tong, M.A. of the College, afterwards Master of the College of St John at Hong Kong, gave [me] in 2000 to the College of Corpus Christi and the Blessed Virgin Mary at Cambridge, remembering his College, and not unmindful of Peter Knight Walker, Honorary Doctor of Divinity, sometime Dean of Chapel, and later Bishop of Ely in the years 1977–89, and Honorary Fellow of the College.)

Marks: JAC in triangle; Millennium hallmark 2000 in cross; mystic number 925.

Paul Hin Sum Tong (1938–), lawyer and priest, came to Corpus in 1985; ordained and called to the Bar in Hong Kong; is now Master of St John's College, University of Hong Kong.

Peter Knight Walker (1919–), of Leeds, graduated from Queen's College, Oxford; served in the Navy; came to Corpus in 1958 as Dean of Chapel; later Principal of Westcott House; Bishop of Dorchester and then Ely; Honorary Fellow of Corpus 1978– and of three other Colleges. The writer remembers with affection the time when he and the Dean were freshmen together.

9.18 Tong-Walker Lavabo Bowl

2000 (London a). 8.1 in. diam., 1.7 in. high. Plain shallow dish shaped like a concave mirror, with small foot. To wash the priest's fingers before celebrating.

Inscription: Coll. C.C. et B.V.M. Cantab. d.d. P.T. mm (P[aul] T[ong] gave [me] to the College ... in 2000). *Adoro te devote, latens Deitas, Qui sub his figuris vere latitas. Pie Pelicane, Jesu Domine, Me immundum munda tuo sanguine.*[11] (I do adore thee devoutly, hidden Deity, who verily dost hide beneath these symbols. O pious Pelican, Lord Jesus, cleanse me, the unclean, by thy blood.)

Marks: P.S., otherwise as above.

11 Words of St Thomas Aquinas, written in the early years of devotion to Corpus Christi (p. 1).

9.19 Two Cruets

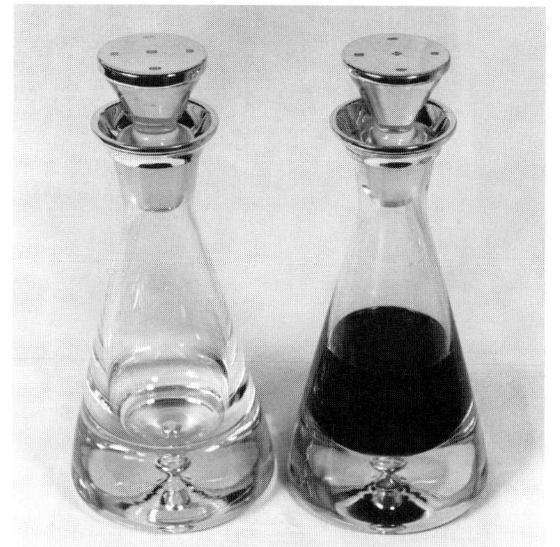

2001 (Birmingham b on one, Millennium hallmark on the other). 9.7 in. high.

Very heavy glass bottles with plain silver mouths and silver tops to the stoppers. Maker's mark B & C°. in ellipse.

10

Post-1690 Drinking Vessels

Come, Landlord, fill the flowing bowl
  Until it doth run over.
For tonight we'll merry merry be,
  For tonight we'll merry merry be.
    For tonight we'll merry merry be,
Tomorrow we'll be sober.

Origin unknown

[Inventories describe even a deep cup as a 'bowle']

10.1 Tankards

Hath his tankard touched your brain?

Ben Jonson, quoted in Dr Johnson's Dictionary

Tankards – mugs with one handle and a hinged lid – go back to Parker's time or before (p. 87). From 1620 to 1720 they were much the commonest Fellow-Commoner's gift: we had about 120 of them at one time or another, besides others belonging to Fellows.

Early tankards were smallish, weighing about 14 ounces. Probably they were of the squat Stuart shape with a flat lid and three ball feet. Our earliest survivor, of 1698, continues that shape. Later tankards are in a baroque style with high domed lid. They got mysteriously bigger, culminating in the giants of the 1730s. There must have been some practical reason for this, for the College, not having enough giant tankards, bought two second-hand: 'Two Tankards, bought at y[e] Mitre, Mark'd C.C.C.', as the 1757 buttery inventory says (see Great C.C.C.C. and Great Defaced below). We never quite rivalled Queen's College, Oxford, whose Lion Tankard of 1678 holds nearly $1\frac{1}{2}$ gallons and would take Samson and Hercules to drink out of it. St John's College, Cambridge has a noble series; Dr G.C. Evans tells me that they were probably used as decanters, since they pour well from every point on the rim. Tankards continued into the rococo period and beyond, providing an instructive series of styles.

10.1.1 Berners Tankard (*top of next page*)

1698 (London letter C). 8.2 in. × 5.5 × 7.7 high. 2.89 pints (1.64 l).

Flat-topped lid with forked-scroll thumbpiece; scroll handle ending in blank shield. College arms engraved in foliated and scrolled cartouche on lid. Donor's arms on body in similar cartouche: *Quarterly [or] and [vert].*

Inscription: *Ex Dono Guilelmij Berners Commensalis 1698.* (Of the gift of William Berners, [Fellow] Commoner 1698).

Maker's mark, RO between a fleur-de-lys and a pellet, for Alexander Roode.

William Berners, of Hertfordshire, came to the College in 1698.

A fine early baroque piece.

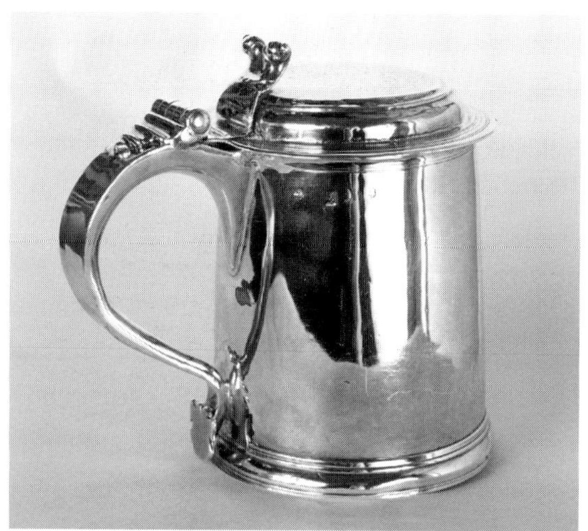

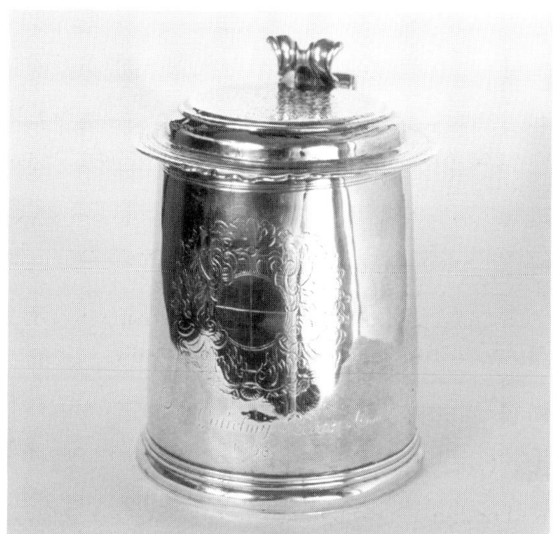

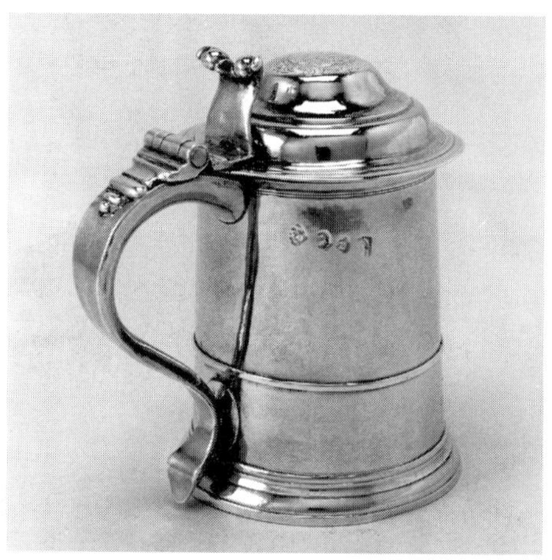

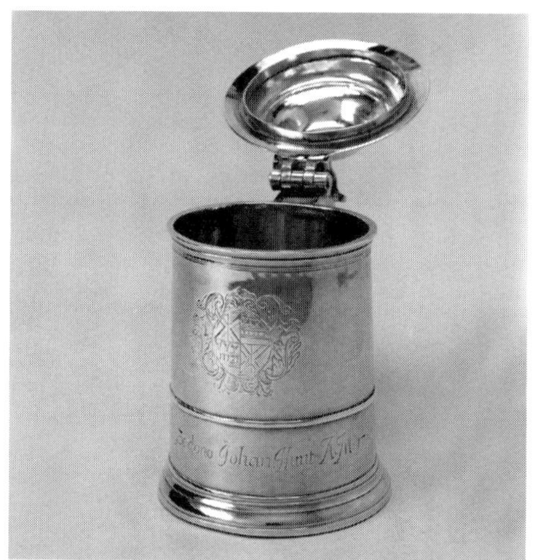

10.1.2 Hunt Tankard (*above*)

1715 (London 𝔲). Britannia silver. 5.1 × 3.9 × 5.5 in. high. 15.8 oz = 0.49 kg. 0.95 pint (0.54 l).

Domed lid; moulded thumbpiece; scroll handle with narrow tail; domed floor. Numerous mouldings. College arms on lid, donor's (*Quarterly: 1 & 4: per pale, argent and vert, a saltire counterchanged; 2 & 3: azure a fess ermine between two barrulets, three harts' heads in chief*) on body, on round foliated shields.

Inscription: *Ex Dono Johan: Hunt A.M. 1715* (Gift of John Hunt MA 1715)

Made by Alice Sheene, active 1700–*c.*1715 (mark SH in lozenge).

John Hunt of Suffolk (? – 1736) was admitted 1703; MA 1710; became Vicar of Mildenhall (Suffolk).

Fully developed baroque, with the characteristic thumbpiece of the period.

10.1.3 Lichfield Tankard (*opposite*)

1715 (London 𝔲). Britannia silver. 4.1 × 5.8 × 5.8 in. high. 1.11 pints (0.63 l).

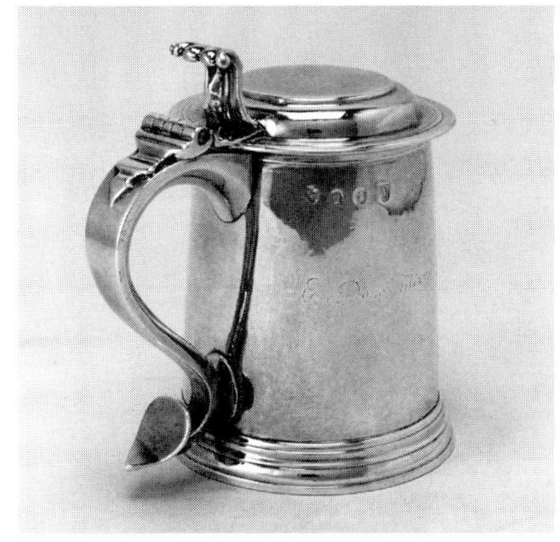

Flat-topped lid; moulded thumbpiece; scroll handle with Norman-shield-shaped tail. College arms with vestigial foliation.

Inscribed: ***Ex Dono Magistri Johannis Lichfield MB Nottinghamiensis*** (Of the gift of Mr J. Lichfield, M.B., of Nottingham).

Made by John Bache (*BA* in quatrefoil) from Shropshire, active 1680–*c.*1730, maker also of our early pint mugs and the de Lancey salver (§13.2).

John Lichfield was undergraduate in 1704; MB 1711.

A noble baroque piece, but sadly cleaned.

10.1.4 Great C.C.C.C Tankard

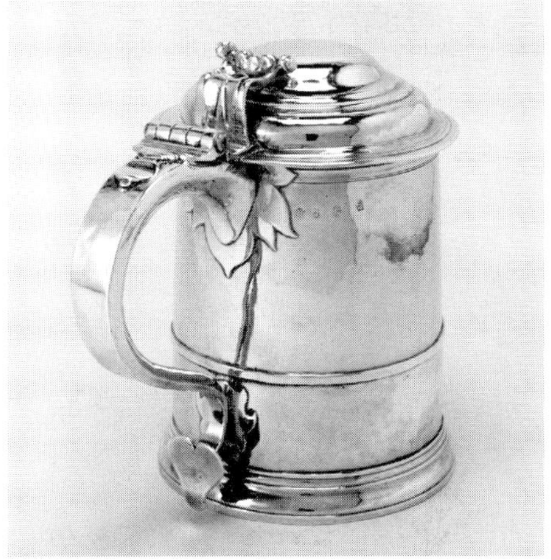

1716 (London A). Britannia silver. 7.8 × 5.7 × 8.6 in. high. 3.24 pints (1.84 l).

Domed lid with elaborate thumbpiece (bent right over); scroll handle. Plaque at top of handle shaped like an irregularly dentate leaf, at bottom heart-shaped. Foliated strapwork round College arms.

Inscription: ***C.C.C.C.*** Weight: ***S W A 38 = 7*** (present weight 36:15 ounces).

Made by William Penstone (P*E in quatrefoil).

Despite its heroic and apparently impractical size, this piece was useful enough for the College to buy it in 1757, rather than waiting for a Fellow-Commoner to give it.

10.1.5 Great Tilson Tankard

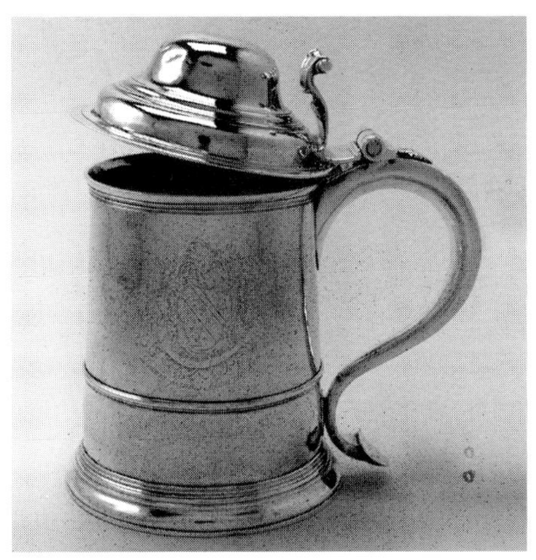

1731 (London Q). 8.4 × 6.0 × 8.6 in. high. 3.0 pints (1.70 l).

High-domed lid; elaborate thumbpiece with tongue; scroll handle with shield-like end.

College and donor's arms (*Or on a bend cotised between two garbs azure a mitre gules*) on asymmetric shields surrounded by cherubs' heads, scrolls, elaborate foliage and flowers. Inscription in a scroll.

Inscriptions: *Collegium Corporis Christi BVirginis Mariæ in Universitate Cantabrigiensi* \ *Donum Joannis Tilson Soc. Com:* (The College of Corpus Christi B. Virgin Mary in the University of Cambridge. Gift of John Tilson, Fellow Commoner.)

Maker's mark: crown and C.M, for Charles Martin, active 1720s–40s.

John Tilson of Westmorland was admitted Fellow Commoner in 1738. The College paid 8*d*. for transporting 'Mr Tilson's 3 p[in]t Tankard'.

The shape is typically late baroque, somewhat elaborated from the earlier plain form. The engraving, added 13 years later, is equally typical rococo.

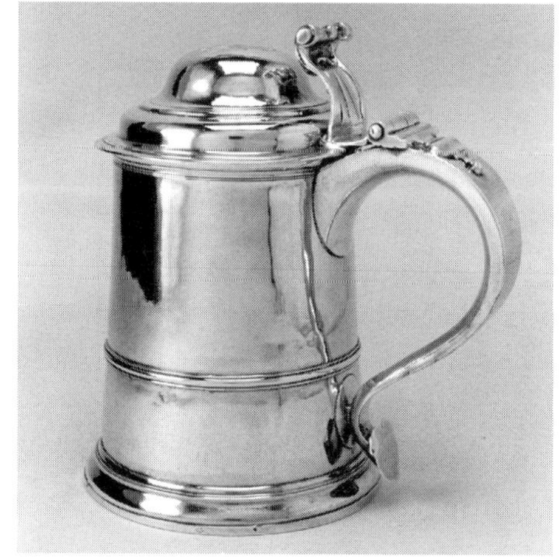

10.1.6 Great Defaced Tankard (*right*)

1743 (London h). 9.0 × 6.1 × 8.7 in. high. 3.43 pints (1.95 l).

High-domed lid; handle with end-plaque shaped like a Cape buffalo's head in silhouette.

College arms on fiddle-shaped shield with elaborate foliation. Traces of previous arms erased.

Inscribed **C.C.C.C.** Previous inscription erased: . *EO*. *W. GEORGE*. . Graffiti: 1864 | 42^{oz} 19^{dwt}| 42^{oz} 19^{dwt} [now weighs 42: 9 oz]

Maker's mark, *TF* in double shield, for Thomas Farren, active 1707–*c*.1742; Subordinate Goldsmith to the King 1723–42.

Another late baroque pot, the College's biggest, with rococo engraving added after it was bought in 1757. It weighs 3.3 kg (6½ lb) full.

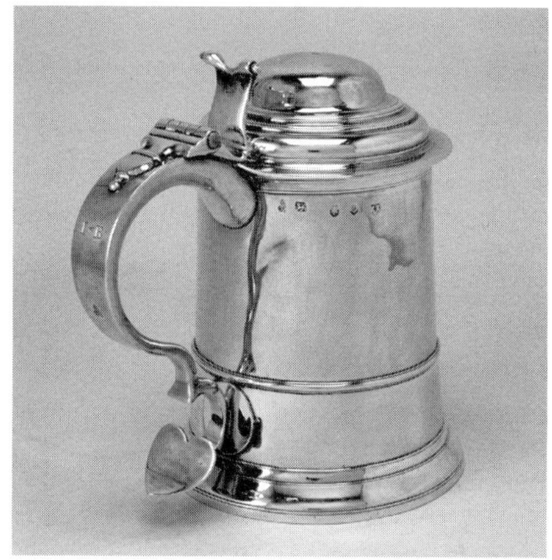

10.1.7 'IB' Tankard (*right*)

1753 (Newcastle O) 7.0 × 5.2 × 6.7 in. high. 1.87 pints (1.06 l).

Low-domed lid; thumbpiece with two scrolls; scroll handle with heart-shaped tail-plaque.

Anonymous, but for inscription I*B on handle. Graffito Z529 on base. Deeply scratched inside, as though by somebody frog-poking.

Maker's mark *O J:C* in trefoil, unidentified.

How it came to the College is not known.

10.1.8 [Bateman] Tankard (*next page*)

1773 (London 𝔖). 7.8 × 4.4 × 6.7 in. high. 1.85 pints (1.05 l).

Bulbous shape, everted foot; domed lid; pierced thumbpiece with tongue: handle with heart-shaped tail-plaque. *Repoussé* asymmetric cartouche intended for a coat-of-arms, roughly sandpapered inside and never finished.

No arms or inscription. Weight graffito: 24.3 [present weight 24.2 ounces].

Maker: WT in rectangle, for William Turton of Southwark, active 1757–95.

This is how silversmiths achieved the rococo style within the narrow limits of formal tankard design. Very like the Edmunds Tankard in New College, Oxford of 1792.

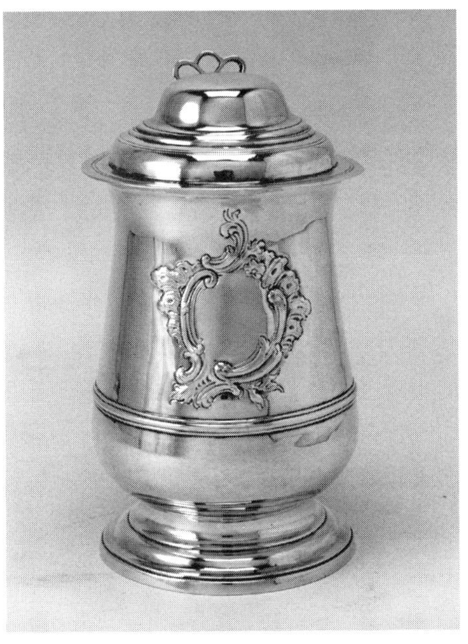

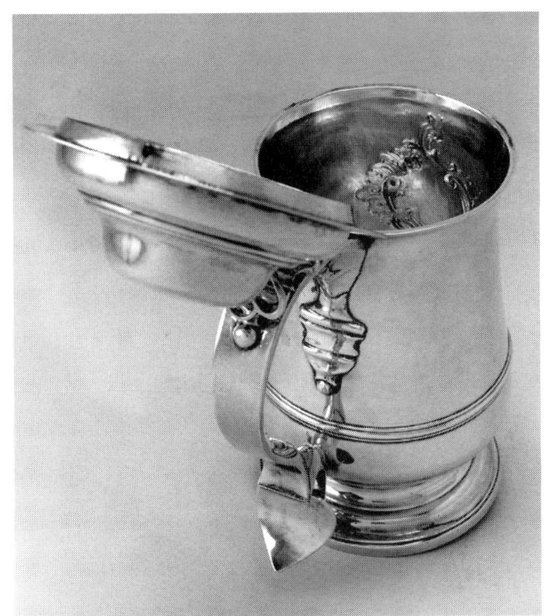

10.1.9 Lyon Tankard (*right*)

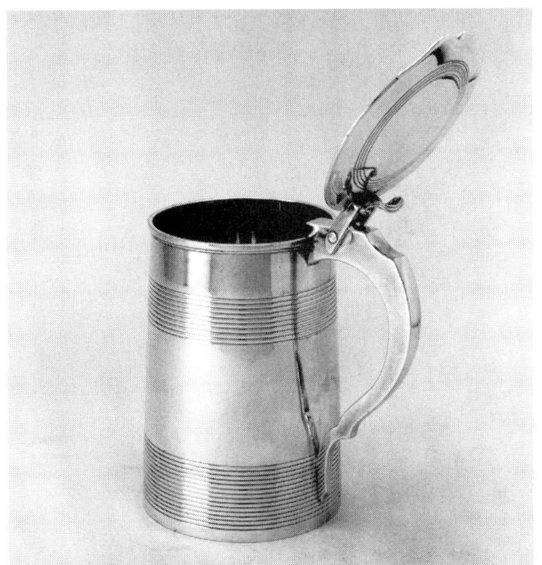

1798 (London C). 6.1 × 4.3 × 6.6 in. high. 1.97 pints (1.12 l).

Nearly flat lid with loop for thumb; 3-part hinge (instead of earlier 5-part); handle of square section. Plain except for incised reeds. College arms.

Inscription: *Thomaso Henrico Lyon per annos XIX commensali gratiae amicitiaegue pignus c.c. Mag. et Socc. Coll. Corp. Chr. et B.M.V. A.D. MCMXXXVIII* [Pledge of thanks and friendship, given to T.H. Lyon, Fellow-Commoner for 19 years, by the Master and Fellows of the College of Corpus Christi and Blessed Mary Virgin, AD 1938.]

Numerous graffiti, including: 28^{oz} || 2^{dw} and 28 || 9 [Weight is now 27:9 oz.]

Maker's mark, I·R in rectangle with corners cut off, unidentified (there being many with those initials).

Thomas Henry Lyon, architect, was admitted 1890. As College architect from 1913 onwards, he was responsible for the redecoration and present oak floor of the Hall; for de-ivying and rendering the Old Court and halting stone decay for 60 years; for adding garrets to the New Court; and for the decoration and fireplace of the Old Combination Room. He was brother-in-law of Edmund Courtenay Pearce, Master 1914–27. This cup was presented to him and bequeathed back to the College. [Information from Bury and from G.H.S. Bushnell.]

The Adamesque version of a tankard.

10.1.10 Great Butler Tankard

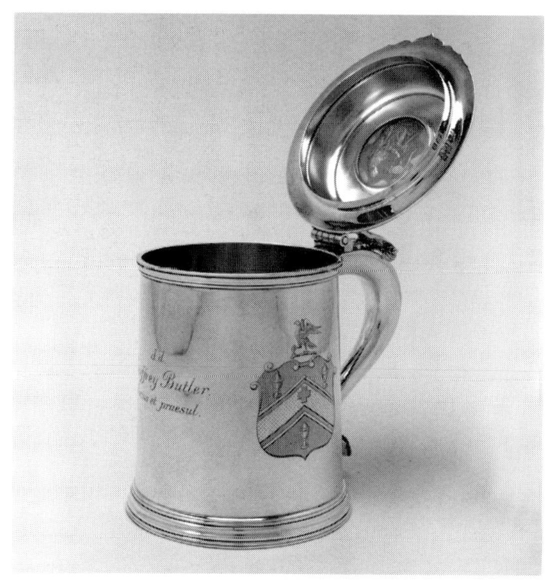

1929 (London **o**). Silver, with glass capsule in lid enclosing a Chancellor's Medal, a distinction awarded by the University for English verse. 7.5 × 5.4 × 7.9 in. high. 2.4 pints (1.36 l).

Flat-topped lid; elaborately foliated thumb-piece; scroll handle with heart-shaped plaque. College arms and donor's: *Gules three covered cups* [rendered as egg-cups with egg-cosies] *on a chevron between two chevronels or a cross azure.* Crest: *a pigeon bearing a covered cup in her foot.*

Maker: H.H.P in incised trefoil, for Henry Hodson Plante, active 1907–*c.*1980.

Chancellor's Medal: yellow metal. On obverse (top): Queen Victoria's head. VICTORIA D: G: BRITANNIARUM REGINA. W. WYON R.A. On reverse: a young man in a chair, reading a book, before a statue of Athena. G.G. BUTLER. TRINITY COLLEGE 1909[?] H.H.PLANTE 12 BURY ST ST JAMES'S S.W.

Given by the widow of Sir George Geoffrey Gilbert Butler (1887–1929), KBE, of London; modern historian, jester, promoter of Anglo-American relations; admitted to Trinity 1906; President of Cambridge Union Society; Fellow of Corpus 1910–29; Parker Librarian 1919–25; Burgess [Member of Parliament] for the University. The Butler Library (the College's student library) commemorates this man of many interests.

10.2 Thirty-Six Pint Mugs

> Receivd from London for the Plate sent up to be changed . . . 12 Pint Mugs wth the College Arms on the side & at the bottom marked wth the Number 1, 2, 3 &c the date of the Year 1723 & the Weight . . .
>
> *Inventory, 10 April 1723*

A mug is a drinking-can with one handle and no lid. It came into its own after the invention of ceilings made it safe to drink from an open vessel without fear of what might fall in. Mugs are the vessels least affected by fashion. The size and shape established in the early 18th century – a cylinder, 3.7 inches in diameter by 5.4 high, slightly tapering upwards, with moulded foot and scroll handle with thumb-projection – has remained constant for nearly 300 years, with only slight nods towards rococo or Victoriana.

The College has 36 almost identical mugs, which the writer remembers being kept in the Buttery and used for quaffing pints of ale. When this pleasant custom died out, the mugs languished for many years in a dungeon unused. In 1999, however, the Whitbread family presented two magnificent silver water-jugs (p. 274) for High Table, which gave occasion to bring back the mugs.

Drinking-vessels, even grand ones, should be made in definite sizes. Ours tend to come in multiples of half an English pint. But in handworking silver this is more easily said than done; even the routine problem of turning out mugs of an exact pint was never fully solved by silversmiths. These mugs vary from 0.99 to 1.22 pints; on average they contain 4% more than a pint.

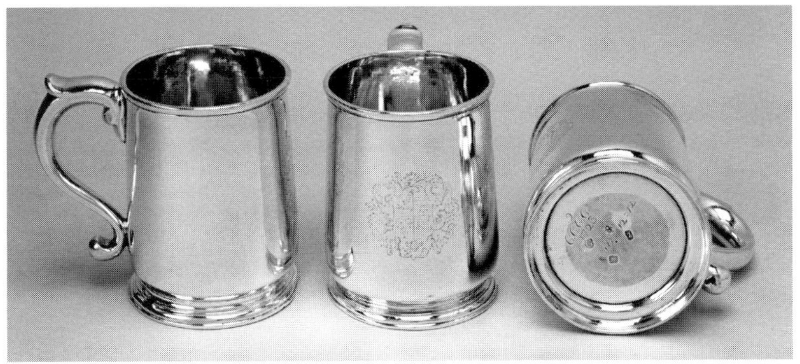

10.2.1 Five of the original twelve, dated 1723

1722 (London G). 4.6 × 3.7 × 5.3 in. high.

College arms, set in a shell amid baroque foliated strapwork. Maker's mark *I.B* in quatrefoil, for John Bache (see Lichfield Tankard, which has his earlier mark).

Numbered, with weight inscriptions thus:

				Present weight
1	*C.C.C.C.*	*1723*	***16 : 18 : 12***	[16: 8: 0]
5	*C.C.C.C.*	*1723*	***16 : 18***	[16: 6: 9]
6	*C.C.C.C.*	*1723*	***17 : 6 *: 12***	[16: 4: 18]
9	*C.C.C.C.*	*1723*	***16 : 12 *: 12***	[16: 4: 18]
10	*C.C.C.C.*	*1723*	***16 : 3 : 12***	[15: 15: 0]

*over erasure

In 1722/3 the College sent up to London fourteen pint and quart tankards, mostly given by Fellow Commoners between 1633 and 1659, but including – alas! – two great tankards with the College arms dated 1662, and twelve silver forks. These weighed 275 ounces in all, for which we received twelve mugs, a list of whose weights (agreeing with the inscriptions above) appears in the inventory. They added up to $202\frac{1}{2}$ oz: the difference of 70-odd ounces presumably paid for the workmanship. (*Book of Inventories, 1706–1811.*)

The mugs gradually diminished. No. 12 was evidently a casualty within three years (see below). An embarrassing moment is recorded on 22 March 1765:

> Two Pint Mugs wanted at the last Review: Found upon a 2[d]. Search in the MS. Library.

Mug No. 8 was condemned in 1775 and Nos 3, 4, 7, and 11 in 1779, presumably because they were broken. No. 2 disappeared after 1828. The others survive, though one-thirtieth of their metal has been cleaned away.

10.2.2 Addington Mug (*right below*)

1724 (London I). 4.6 × 3.6 × 5.4 in. high.

Slightly waisted. Vestigial thumb-knob on handle. College arms in strapwork and foliation on hatched background.

Inscription (on banner): *Coll: Corp: Christi Cantab Dono Caroli Addington A.M. 1725*. (Corpus Christi College Cambridge, by gift of Charles Addington, M.A. 1725.)

Maker's mark: • T.L • in a circle, for Timothy Lee.

Charles Addington of London was admitted 1716; MA 1723; ordained deacon 1725 (when he gave this mug), priest 1726.

Although made for presentation to the College, this differs markedly from the 1723 set.

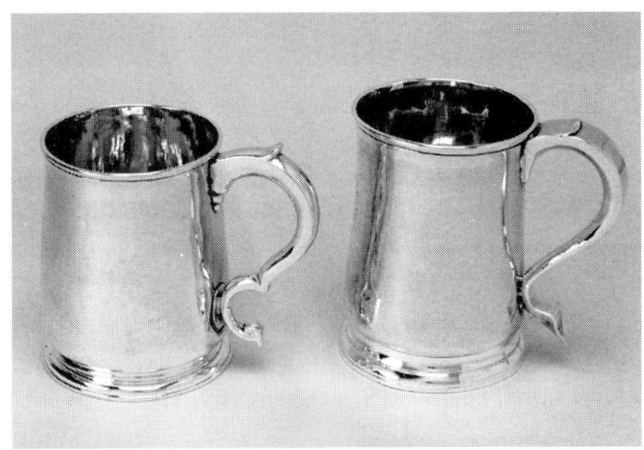

10.2.3 Mug No. 12 (*left above*)

1726 (London L)

Closely resembles its elder brethren, but one-third lighter. It has a more slender, S-shaped handle with roundel at base, and is battered and dented.

Inscribed: ***12 C.C.C.C. 1723 11 = 6*** [present weight 11: 1: 9] ***L ~~SS~~***

Mark: WoT in irregular trefoil: ?William Toone, entered 1725.

Cunningly substituted for the original No. 12, and not entered in the plate-book.

10.2.4 Two Cust Pint Mugs

1740–1 (London e, f). 5.1 × 3.7 × 5.4 in. high. 14.0 oz = 436 g.

Bulbous shape, curly rococo handle, moulded foot. College and donor's arms askew, on skew asymmetric rococo shields, magnificently surrounded by bulrushes (*Typha*) and other foliage. Donor's arms: *Ermine on a chevron sable three fountains with a Baronet's badge.*

> Heraldic fountains should be roundels (i.e. discs) barry wavy of six argent and azure. These are represented as roundels azure, which turns them into heraldic bilberries, called hurts.

Inscription: *CCCC \Ex Dono Johannis Cust Barronetti olim hujus Collegii Socio-Commensalis 1741* [Gift of J. Cust, Baronet, sometime Fellow Commoner of this College 1741] .

Maker's mark (on both): **AV•* in quatrefoil, for Aymé Videau, active *c.*1725–73; noted for 'particularly graceful flat chasing' (Grimwade), as on these mugs.

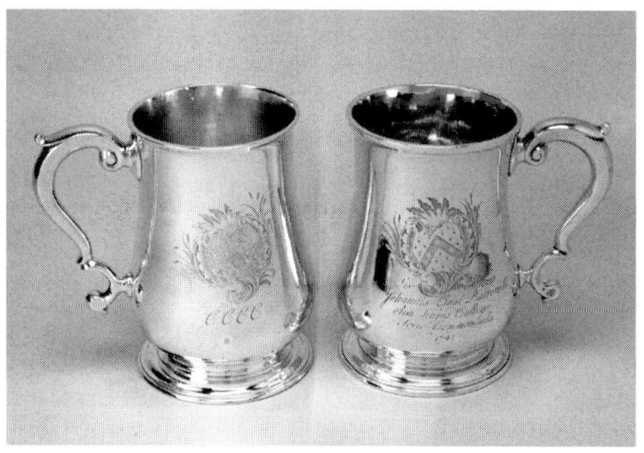

The two mugs are not identical: the 1740 is hammer-marked inside, the 1741 has a matt finish inside and looks newer, although the hallmarks are genuine. On the latter *Baronetti* is spelt with one *r*; graffito 15 = *//*

Added to the inventory in 1742: 'Two Pint Muggs by S[r] John Cust Bar[t].'

Sir John Cust, Baronet (1718–70) of Lincolnshire was admitted 1735; MA 1739; MP for Grantham five times; opponent of Wilkes; Speaker of the House of Commons 1761 and 1768–70; supposedly the least dignified or energetic of 18th-cent. Speakers; died of a filibuster. The College has a magnificent portrait of him. His family contributed several stained-glass windows to the Hall and Master's Lodge.

These are the only mugs that make a concession to rococo fashion in their shape. There is one of the same shape by Gairdner of Edinburgh, as late as 1786, in Kelvingrove Museum, Glasgow.

10.2.5 John Thomas, Holloway, Weston, Wilson, Richard Thomas, D'Orsey Pint Mugs

1861 (London f). 4.7 × 3.6 × 5.3 in. high.
Six mugs identical except for inscriptions. College arms on elliptical shield with rope border, around which is the inscription. The lilies are represented as a sort of inverted bell.

Inscriptions: *D.D. IOANNES THOMAS, HUJUS COLLEGII COMMENSALIS.* [John Thomas, Fellow-Commoner of this College, gave [me]]. *C. C. C. C. 1850.*

D.D. GEORGIUS HOLLOWAY, HUJUS COLLEGII COMMENSALIS. C. C. C. C. 1852.

D.D. MILES BRANTHWAYT WESTON, HUJUS COLLEGII COMMENSALIS. C. C. C. C. 1852.

D.D. FRANCISCUS GARRATT WILSON, HUJUS COLLEGII COMMENSALIS. C. C. C. C. 1853.

D.D. RICARDUS JACOBUS HARRIES THOMAS, HUJUS COLLEGII COMMENSALIS. C. C. C. C. 1859.

D.D. ALEXANDER JACOBUS DONALD D'ORSEY, HUJUS COLLEGII COMMENSALIS. C. C. C. C. 1860.

Maker's mark: GR EB in quatrefoil, for George John Richards (active 1844–67) & Edward Charles Brown (active *c.*1857–82).

Donors: John Thomas, admitted 1845; George Holloway, admitted 1843; Miles Branthwayt Weston, admitted 1842; the Rev. Francis Garratt Wilson, admitted 1844; the Rev. Richard James Harries Thomas, admitted 1848.

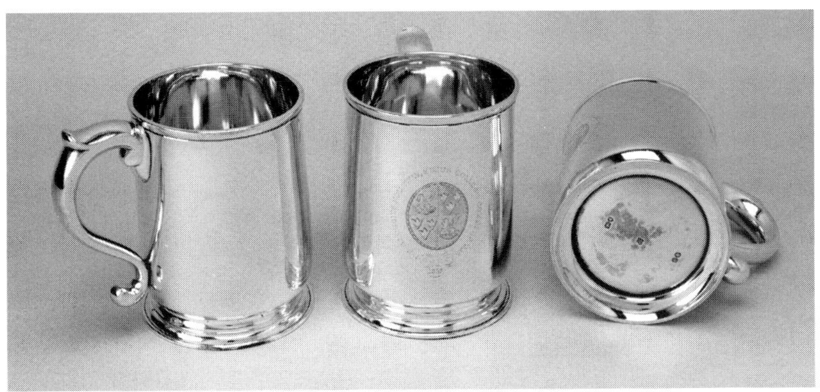

The Rev. Alexander James Donald D'Orsey, admitted 1846, became Professor of Public Reading & Speaking, King's College, London 1884–90.

10.2.6 Sixteen Mugs

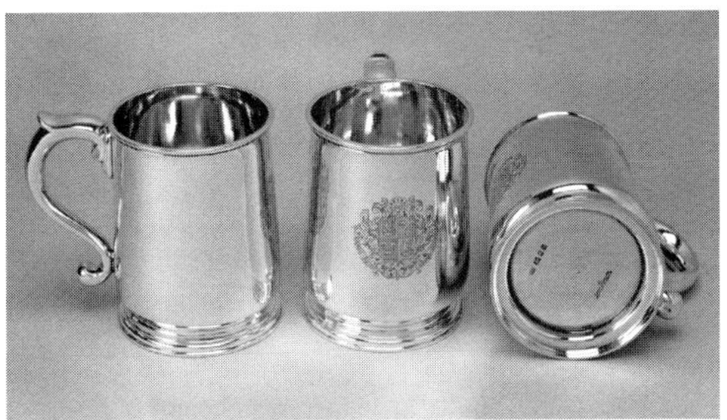

1928 (London 𝔫). 4.7 × 3.7 × 5.4 in. high.

Close copies of the 1723 set, including Baroque engraving around College arms.

Maker's inscription: crown + GARRARD & C^{O}. L^{TD} ALBEMARLE ST LONDON.W.1.

Maker's mark: SG, for Sebastian Garrard, 1818–.

Graffiti: M or N on one, N on another.

10.2.7 Carter, Goodhart, Sanders, Smyth, McCurdy Mugs

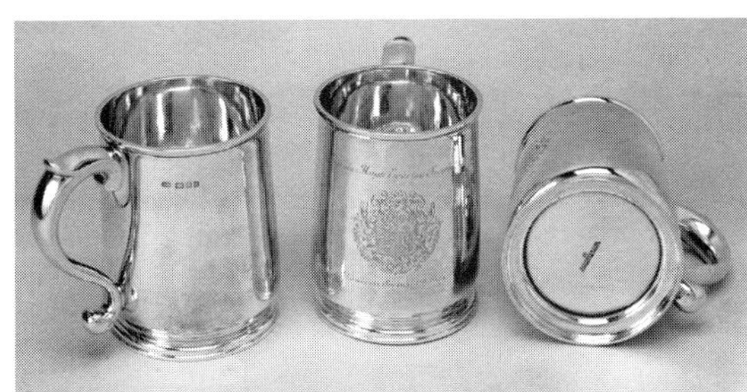

1929, 1930 (London 𝔬,𝔭). 4.7 × 3.7 × 5.4 in. high.

Identical to above save inscriptions; Carter's is one year older than the others.

Inscription: *Georgius Stuart Carter, Ph.D., Admissus Socius A.D. 1924* [George Stuart Carter, Ph.D., admitted Fellow A.D. 1924]

Arturus Lehman Goodhart, A.M. Admissus Socius A.D. 1924

Terentius Robertus Beaumont Sanders, A.M. Admissus Socius A.D. 1924

Carolus Hugh Egerton Smyth A.M. Admissus Socius A.D. 1925, 1937, 1946

Johannes Thomson MacCurdy, Sc.D., Admissus Socius A.D. 1924

Maker's mark as above, for Sebastian Garrard.

George Stuart Carter (1893–1969) was a tropical zoologist. His head was patted by Alfred Russell Wallace, discoverer of evolution. Came to Gonville & Caius College in 1913; elected Fellow of Corpus 1930; served as Prælector and Senior Tutor; directed the studies of the writer. He gave also the Carter Matchboxes (§19.4.9).

For Arthur Lehman Goodhart see Goodhart Rosewater Bowl (§22.3).

Terence Robert Beaumont Sanders, CB, (1901–85) of Charleville, Co. Cork, oarsman and specialist in engineering standards, came to Trinity College 1919. He was a Fellow of Corpus from 1924; Prælector and Dean of College.

Charles Hugh Egerton Smyth (1903–87) of China, historian and divine, was a Scholar of Corpus 1921, and three times Fellow (1925–32, 1937–46, 1946–). In the intervals he served as parish priest, being a Canon of Westminster 1946–. We have also his Bishop Green Cup (§10.4.9).

John Thomson MacCurdy (1886–1947) of Toronto, psychiatrist, specializing in wars and examinations; MD of Johns Hopkins University; came to Corpus as a High Table Member in 1922; elected Fellow in 1926; took Sc.D. in 1928. He was a great benefactor to the College, the MacCurdy Feast being endowed out of his estate.

10.3 Two-Handled Cups

Drinking from a big tankard requires force of arms when full and dexterity when nearly empty. One solution is a second handle. Pottery two-handled cups go back far into prehistory, and silver ones occur in Iron Age and Roman hoards. The form lapsed in the middle ages, being revived in the 1530s and going through many later stages. The characteristic big, heavy, ornate vessel, usually with a domed lid and finial, is characteristic of the Baroque period from 1700 onwards. These might be thought merely ceremonial vessels, with occasional use as loving-cups (see p. 45); however the repairs to some of ours indicate active service and actual combat.

With the growth of horse-racing, two-handled cups developed a double life as a favourite sporting trophy: they can easily be accepted from the saddle.

10.3.1 Gough Cup and Cover

*c.*1730 (no date-letter). 9.8 × 6.1 × 11.0 in. high; height without lid 6.75 in. 3.0 pints (1.70 l).

Straight, raised straps cast on body and lid. Handles with similar straps and with leaf-tongues on their tops. Hammered finish inside. College arms and donor's in strapwork cartouches with satyrs' faces.

Donor's arms: *Gules on a fesse argent between three boars' heads couped or a lion passant azure.* Possible trace of badge on lid.

Inscription: *C.C.C.C. \ D. Hen: Gough Baronett: de Edgbaston in Com: Waruic.* [Gift of Henry Gough, Baronet, of Edgbaston in the County of Warwick.] Graffito: 2/246

Marks: SP under a peacock, struck twice on the cup. Made by Simon Pantin II, of Rouen descent, active 1727–33; this mark was entered 1729. His very short career fixes the date.

Sir Henry Gough of London became Fellow-Commoner in 1728;[1] created Baronet of Edgbaston (near Birmingham) in the same year; barrister, MP for Hindon, Wiltshire.

The strapwork and satyrical faces are of the sub-phase of Baroque fashion, a revival of Mannerist, represented also by the Yorke Salver of 1715. The alternate long and short raised straps (cast, not *repoussé*), and the leaflike tops to the handles, are also characteristic. Parallels include the Metcalfe Cup of Queen's College, Oxford (D. Willaume 1712); Treby Cup (Paul de Lamerie, 1723); Empress Elizabeth's Cup, St Petersburg (1726); and Bligh Cup, Merton College (John Swift 1741).[2] The shape and raised straps had a long currency, for instance on a silver-gilt horse-racing cup, made by Robert Gray of Glasgow in 1821, in Kelvingrove Museum, Glasgow.

The maker was shy of getting the piece tested or of paying the tax on plate, but not of putting his own mark on it. Possibly he avoided the tax on the plea that the article was made to order and was not for sale.

Somebody dropped a clanger with the lid: a large hole has been clumsily repaired.

10.3.2 [Bateman] Cup and Cover

1740 (London e). 10.25 × 5.6 × 11.4 in. high; height without lid 7.6 in. 2.99 pints (1.70 l).

Scroll handles; domed lid with knob. Prominent moulding let in halfway down cup. Handles with rudimentary foliage. No arms or inscription.

Maker's mark, 𝕲𝖂 under Prince of Wales's feathers, for George Wickes, active 1722–47. He was goldsmith to

1 Audit Book, admission date. Lamb says 1725.

2 BM; Jones *Queen's* Pl.7; Jones *Russia*; Jones *Merton* Pl.5.

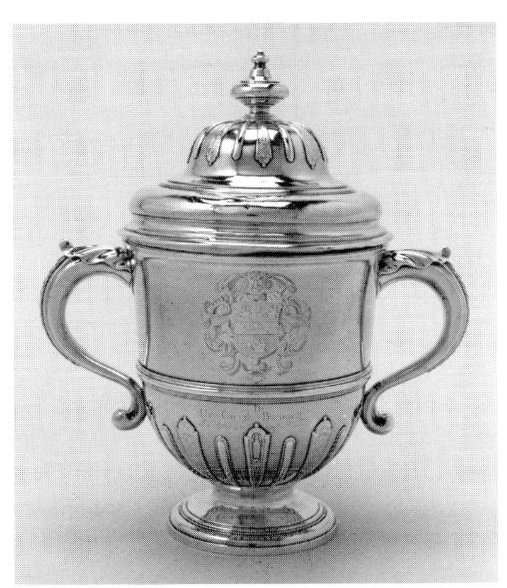
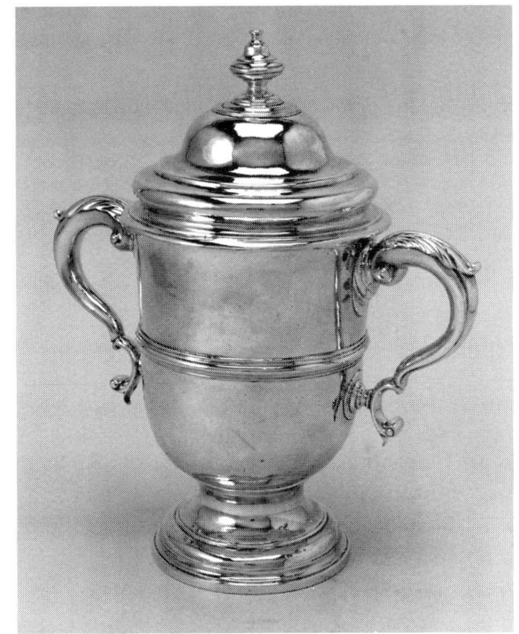
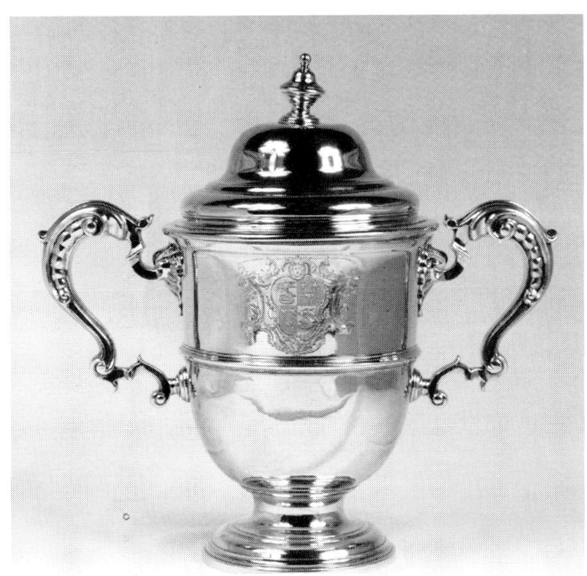
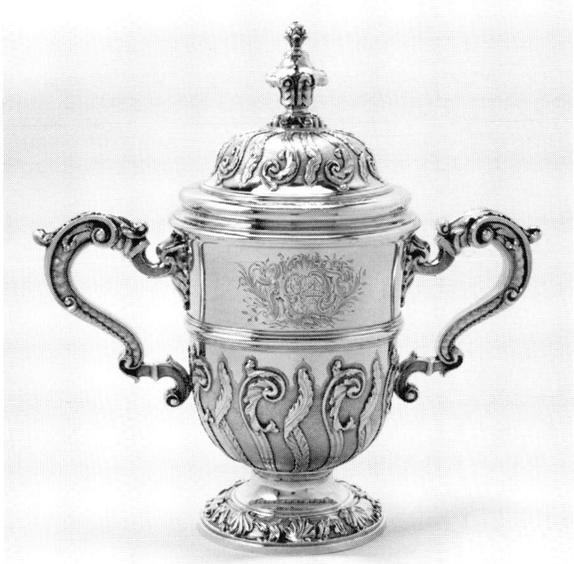

Two-Handled Cups: above, Gough (c.1730), Bateman (1740); below, Yorke (1740), Mawson (1740)

Frederick, the extravagant Prince of Wales; he hired out plate for functions including 'ye Oxford & Cambridge Entertainment'.

Numerous graffiti, including: 47.12 | 47.6 [present weight 46: 15 ounces].

Bequeathed by Aubrey Bateman.

This cup shows baroque style at its plainest: the purchaser was meant to do his own engraving.

Lid dented, with a minor split in the knob.

10.3.3 Yorke Cup and Cover

1740 (London e). 12.3 × 6.3 × 11.7 in. high; height without lid 7.7 in. 3.6 pints (2.07 l). Double-gilt.

Scrolled handles. Two different chased scrollwork cartouches, one with human face above College arms, the other with satyr's face above donor's arms. Domed lid with moulded finial. College arms and donor's: *Argent on a saltire azure a bezant, differenced with an annulet* [for a fifth son]. Crest (on lid): *dog's [?] head erased, with collar azure bearing a bezant.*

Inscriptions: *The Honourable James Yorke |C.C.C.C.* [on lid]. Weight: 75 = 16 [present weight of cup and lid 74: 18 oz].

Maker's mark, 𝔍𝔓 in quatrefoil with crown? and flower, is of the rare silversmith John Pero, ?of Dutch descent, active 1720–*c.*1740.

The Hon. James Yorke (*c.*1732–1808) was admitted 1748; D.D. 1770; Bishop successively of St David's, Gloucester, and Ely; youngest of the learned sons of the Earl of Hardwicke who gave us the Great Yorke Salver, Yorke Standish, Yorke Candlesticks, Yorke Mustard-Pot (recycled), and Yorke Dredgers.

The lid is dented.

10.3.4 Mawson Cup and Cover

1740 (London e). 11.9 in. × 5.65 × 11.3 high; height without lid 6.9 in. 2.5 pints (1.42 l). Single-gilt.

Body with moulded belt, below which are foliated scrolls between long narrow undulate leaves, all cast in high relief on a matted ground, and repeated on lid. Similar foliage and narrow leaves on foot. Handles with high-relief cast scrollwork, partly matted. Shell cartouche around arms, elaborately chased with foliage, flowers, and rye-grass. Finial of lid foliated and ending in a bulbous flower.

Donor's arms only: *Ermine a lion rampant*, impaled by: *a fesse ermine between two chevrons ermine, a covered cup in chief.* The first half is a simplified version of the Mawson arms, in which the background should be diagonally divided between ermine and ermines. The second half is mysterious: it is not the arms of Mawson's wife, for he had none, nor of any of his dioceses.

Weight inscription: *62 = 17* [present weight of cup and lid 63: 17]. Diet-scrape on the base.

Maker: mark **DW**, for David Williaume II (1693–1761), of French descent, son of the celebrated silversmith David Williaume I, but not thought of as a worthy successor. He beat silver from 1728 to 1746; he was also a banker and High Sheriff of Bedfordshire; he 'had little to do with the plate bearing his name, which scarcely shows Huguenot influence, probably being largely executed by native English journeymen' (Grimwade 1990). His mark appears also on the Walpole Coffee-pot (p. 143).

Matthias Mawson (1687–1770), of Chiswick, was Scholar 1701; B.A. 1704; Fellow 1707; Master 1724–44; Bishop of Llandaff 1738, of Chichester 1740, of Ely 1754 (how he combined these duties history does not relate); founder of the Mawson Studentships. As Vice-Chancellor he restored order to the Lent Term, and forbade medical students to dig up subjects for anatomy in the churchyards. The College has his portrait.

Of the three cups of 1740, in the brief transition between baroque and rococo fashion, this is the only one to be definitely rococo. Its fine workmanship belies the maker's poor reputation. It resembles the Gowran Cup,

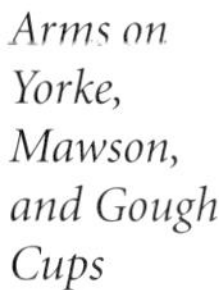

Arms on Yorke, Mawson, and Gough Cups

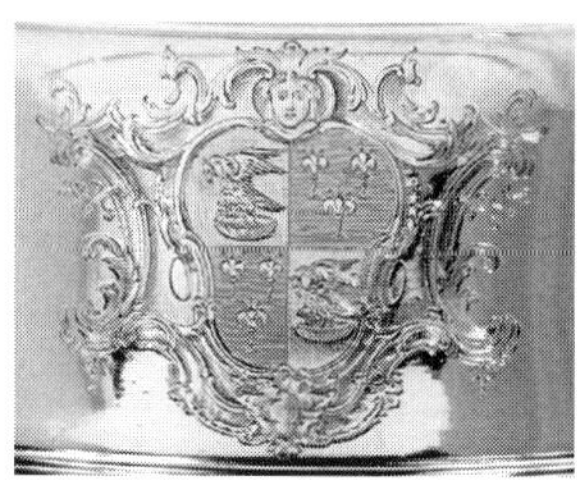

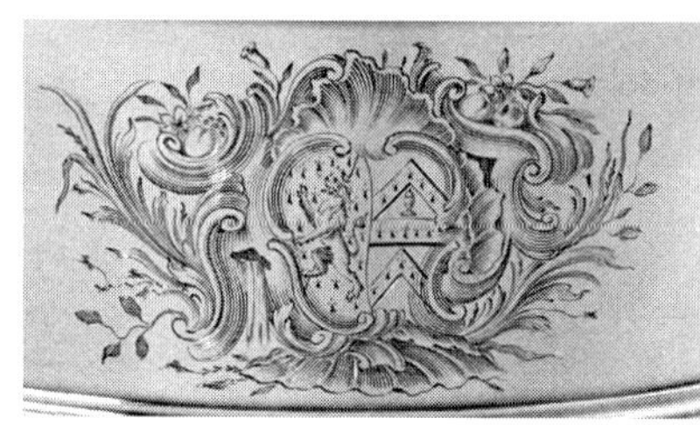

Queen's College, Oxford. The Goldsmiths' Company have an even grander rococo piece of 1739 by Paul de Lamerie. (Jones *Queen's* Pl. 7.; Cripps p. 295.)

The rim of the lid is badly dented.

10.3.5 Burnand Cup

1805 (Newcastle P). 9.8 × 5.2 × 9.5 in. high. 2.74 pints (1.56 l). Single-gilt inside.

Slightly elliptical in plan (? because squashed), trumpet base. Loop handles fluted in section, attached above by foliated scutcheons. No lid.

College arms. Inscription: *AMICITIÆ ERGO, SOCIIS ET SOCIO COMMENSALIBUS C.C.C. ET BEATOS* [*sic*] *MARIÆ VIRGINIS *DONO DEDIT* LUDOVICUS BURNAND, A.M. OLIM SOCIO COMMENSALIS* [For the sake of friendship, given to the Fellows and Fellow-Commoners of the College of Corpus Christi and Blessed Mary Virgin by L. Burnand MA, sometime Fellow-Commoner].

Mark T.W for Thomas Watson, entered 1793.

Lewis Whitmore Burnand (1840–1923), of London, was admitted undergraduate in 1861; MA 1869; one of the first stockbrokers in the College; director of Gresham House Estate Company. He seems to have returned as a Fellow-Commoner late in life, and to have given us an antique piece engraved with the wordy style of inscription characteristic of the 20th century.

A very late example of Adamesque style.

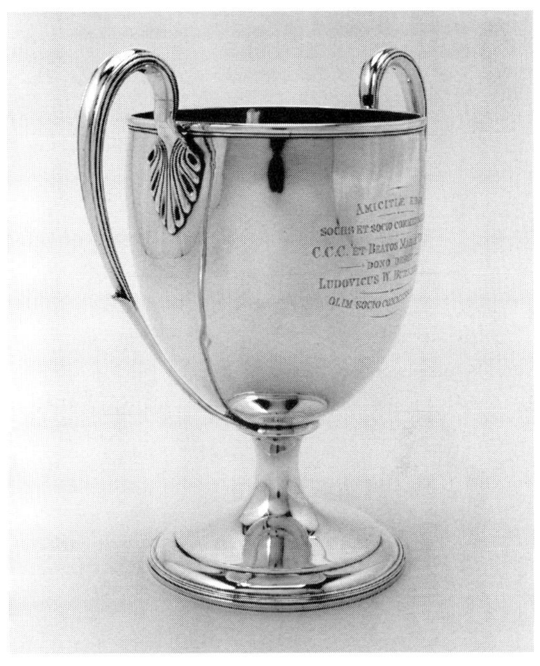

10.3.6 Knight Cup

1900 (London e). 12.8 × 7.7 × 9.6 in. high. 6.62 pints (3.76 l).

Plain, so-called 'Irish' pattern, with scroll handles. Wooden base. No lid.

Inscription: *PRESENTED TO THE REV. H.J.C. KNIGHT M.A. AND M^RS^ KNIGHT . FROM THEIR FRIENDS IN . MARNHULL AUGUST 1901* . Graffito weight 60.35 (present weight 60.25 oz).

Made by the Goldsmiths' and Silversmiths' Company Ltd (p. 180).

This mighty cup, holding more than three-quarters of a gallon, was given by M.B. Knight, widow of Henry Joseph Corbett 'Lazarus' Knight, Fellow and Bishop of Gibraltar (p. 117).

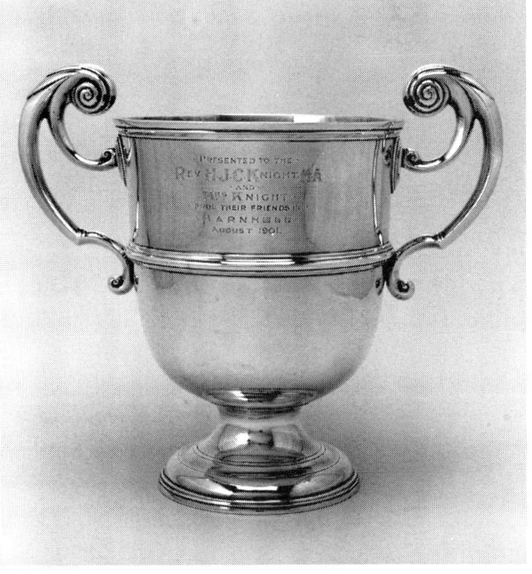

Dalby Cup and Medal *see Sporting Plate,* §*20.5.*

10.3.7 Hiley Cup and Cover

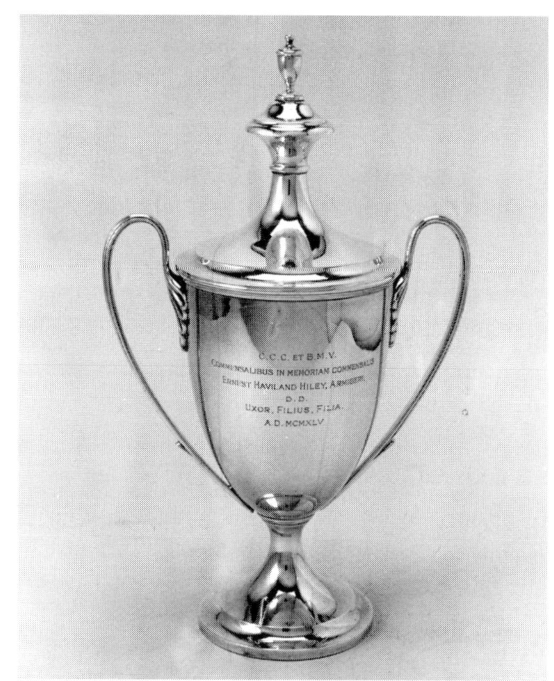

1939 (London D). 7.3 × 4.55 × 12.1 in. high; height without lid 8.7 in. 1.48 pints (0.81 l).

Rudimentary foliage on handles. Lid with finial in the likeness of a tiny handleless cup and cover.

Inscription: *C.C.C. ET B.M.V. COMMENSALIBVS IN MEMORIAM COMMENSALIS ERNEST HAVILAND HILEY. D.D. UXOR, FILIUS, FILIA. A.D. MCMXLV.* (His wife, son, and daughter gave this to the dining members of the College... in memory of Sir Ernest H. Hiley, dining member. A.D. 1945). Graffito: 5360 bz 155 λM

Maker: RC in baroque shield, for R. Comyns.

Sir Ernest Edward Hiley was a railwayman; KBE 1928; Chairman of Traffic Commissioners (Eastern Area) 1931–; died 1943.

Morris Cup and Cover see Modernistic Plate.

10.4 Bishop Green and other Cups without Handles

> . . . to purchase annually a piece of plate of the value of five pounds to the scholar who shall take the degree of B.A. with the greatest credit; likewise a piece of plate of the same value for the undergraduate or bachelor of arts, who shall make and speak the best declamation according to the judgment of the master and fellows; likewise a piece of plate of the same value to be given to that undergraduate who shall pass the best public examination in College.
>
> *Benefaction of Bishop Green, 1779*

Most of these cups are prizes awarded to undergraduates from the benefaction of John Green, Bishop of Ely, and bequeathed to the College on the death of the recipient.

John Green (1724–79), from Beverley, was Sizar and Fellow of St John's College. He taught Dr Samuel Johnson at Lichfield School and then became Dean of Lincoln. He was elected Master of Corpus in 1750; this election, supposedly by mistake for Thomas Greene, was held to 'prostitute the honour of the College'. He proved a generous and successful Master. He was Vice-Chancellor 1757–8, active in University politics and intrigue. In 1761 he was made Bishop of Lincoln, a preferment which nearly went by mistake to Thomas Greene. Among other benefactions to the College he left an estate to award cups as prizes in the three categories set out above. The writer of these notes was honoured with Bishop Green Cups under the third and first heads in 1960 and 1961, but makes no claim to a Cup of Eloquence.

The Adamesque shape of Bishop Green Cups was remarkably resistant to changes of fashion from at least the 1780s to the 1920s. More recent ones, such as the writer's, are beakers.

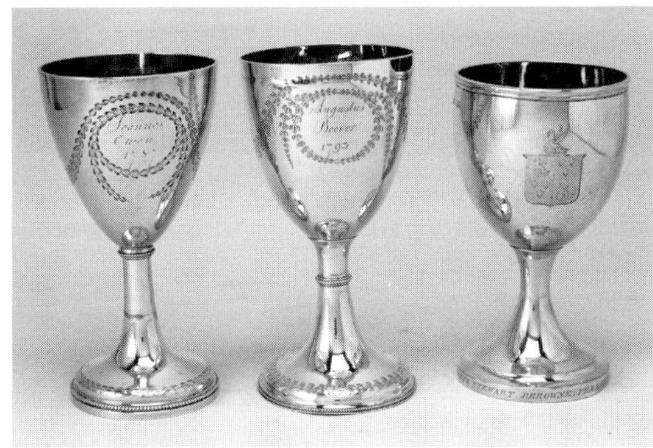

Owen, Beevor, E.H. Perowne Cups

10.4.1 Owen (Bishop Green) Cup

1786 (London l). 3.7 × 6.95 in. 8.7 oz (270 g), which is evidently what £5 would purchase then.

Double-gilt inside. Egg-shaped, trumpet-shaped foot. Beading round foot and top of stem; band of foliage round foot; swags of foliage on bowl.

Inscription: *C.C.C.C. Literarum Præmium* [Prize for Letters]\ *Joannes Owen 1787.*

Maker's mark: RG for Richard Gardiner.

John Owen (*c.*1765–1822), of London, was admitted 1784; MA 1791; Fellow 1789–94; famous traveller and divine; founder of the British & Foreign Bible Society.[3] The College has his portrait.

10.4.2 Beevor (Bishop Green) Cup

1793 (London s). 3.6 × 6.95 in. 7.1 oz (220 g).

Gilt inside. Almost identical to Owen Cup, but by a different maker, and a little lighter (due to inflation?).

Inscription: *C.C.C.C. Literarum Præmium.* [Prize for Letters]\ *Augustus Beevor 1793.*

Maker: HC for Henry Chawner (1764–1851) from a well-known family of silversmiths; became squire of Newton Valence, Hants.

Augustus Beevor of Norwich was admitted 1789; MA 1798.

10.4.3 J.J.S. Perowne (Bishop Green) Cup of Eloquence

1843 (London 𝔥). 3.75 × 6.55 in. 7.1 oz (220 g) (weight unaltered after 50 years and a world war).

3 JPC Roach 1993 'John Owen' *LCA* **72** 14–224.

Gilt inside. Egg-shaped, narrowed at mouth, trumpet-shaped foot.

Inscription: *JOHANNES JACOBUS STEWART PEROWNE, PRÆMIUM ELOQUENTIÆ,* [Prize for Eloquence] 1843. College arms, pelican pseudo-crest.

Maker's mark: crowned RG for Robert Garrard II (1793–1881), of the celebrated Garrard family of silversmiths.

John James Stuart Perowne (1823–1901), Old Testament scholar, was one of three Norwich brothers, Fellows of the College. He came from Bengal to the College in 1841; Mawson Scholar; he could not take an honours degree because he was no mathematician. Fellow 1850–62 and assistant Tutor; forfeited Fellowship on marriage; Hulsean Professor of Divinity 1875–8; Dean of Peterborough and rebuilder of the crossing-tower there, 1878–89; Honorary Fellow 1886–; declined Welsh bishopric in 1889 because he spoke no Welsh; Bishop of Worcester 1890–1901. The College has a magnificent portrait of him.

10.4.4 Two E.H. Perowne (Bishop Green) Cups of Eloquence

1847 and 1848 (London 𝔐 and 𝔑). 3.75 × 6.55 in. Average 8.2 oz (255 g).

Same pattern and maker as above.

Inscription: *EDVARDUS HENRICUS PEROWNE, ELOQUENTIÆ PRÆMIUM, C.C.C.C. 1847* [or 1848]. College arms with pelican pseudo-crest.

Edward Henry 'The Sinner' Perowne (1826–1906), brother of the above, was admitted 1846. A classicist and Evangelical divine, he was BD 1860, DD 1873; Fellow from 1850; Tutor in 1858; Master 1879–1906. As Vice-Chancellor (1879–81) he was an eloquent opponent of the revolutionary change of statute allowing Fellows of Colleges to marry. In his time the College ebbed low in numbers and academic distinction. He gave the Perowne Chalice and Alms-dishes, and the bust of Belvederean Apollo which towers above the Old Combination Room. His portrait hangs in Hall.

10.4.5 Burgess Vodka-Cup

Late 19th century. 1.9 × 2.4 in. high. A note describes it as 'Russian Drinking Cup Presented By Dr. Burgess'.

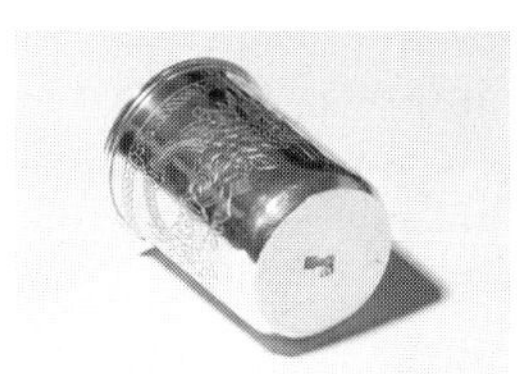

Tiny cylindrical beaker, gilt inside. Decorated in vaguely Art-Nouveau style with band of slanting rectangles and bow joining two posies.

Marked with three joined rectangles containing (1) A·A 1899; (2) 84; (3) horse with two riders trampling a human body. Maker's mark: K·K in rectangle.

Given by Malcolm Arthur Sheridan Burgess (1926–78), donor of the Burgess Coasters (§21.4.7).

10.4.6 Three Pearce (Bishop Green) Cups

1890, 1891, 1893 (London N, Q, S). 3.6 × 6.95 in. Average 8.6 oz (270 g).

Egg-shaped, trumpet foot, 3 grooves round top of stem, 1 groove round base.

Inscriptions: *Edmundus Courtenay Pearce Literarum Praemium 1890*
Edmundus Courtenay Pearce Litterarum Præmium 1891
Ds Edmundus Courtenay Pearce A.B. Philosophiæ Præmium 1893. College arms (with pelican pseudo-crest in 1891 and 1893).

Marked: CSH in trefoil | MUNSEY, SILVERSMITH, CAMBRIDGE. Made by Charles Stuart Harris of London, active 1852–*c.*1900, mainly a spooner.

E.C. Pearce (1870–1935), of London, was admitted 1889; Scholar; classicist, divine, and administrator; elected Fellow 1895; Dean of College; Master 1914–1927, D.D. and Mayor of Cambridge 1917; Vice-Chancellor 1921–4. After an ambitious and successful Mastership he became first Bishop of Derby in 1927. His portrait hangs in Hall.

10.4.7 Two Husbands (Bishop Green) Cups

1899 and 1900 (London d and e). 3.6 × 6.95 in. Average 8.7 oz (270 g).

As above, except for three flutes round top of stem.

Inscriptions: *Johannes Edwin Husbands, Literarum Præmium 1899*

Johannes Edwin Husbands Literarum Præmium 1900.

Left by J.E. Husbands, admitted 1898, to be used at undergraduate club dinners.

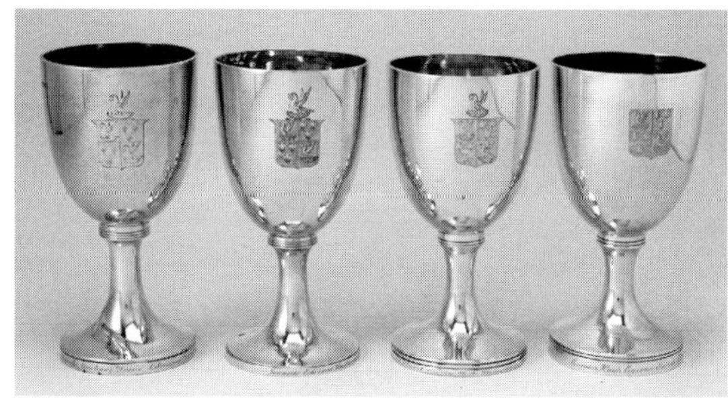

Pearce, Pearce, Savory, Smyth Cups

10.4.8 Savory (Bishop Green) Cup

1907 (London n). 3.6 × 6.95 in. 9.7 oz (300 g).

Egg-shaped, trumpet foot, 2 grooves round top of stem, 2 grooves round base.

Inscription: *Donald Stuart Savory B.A.*
Philosophiæ Præmium 1907. College arms, pelican pseudo-crest.

Maker's mark: DM in bifoil | MUNSEY, SILVERSMITH, CAMBRIDGE. David Munsey, one of the few Cambridge silversmiths, was active 1871–1914.

Donald Stuart Savory, admitted 1904, founded the Savory Studentships in 1929.

10.4.9 Smyth (Bishop Green) Cup

1923 (London h). 3.7 × 6.9 in.

Same pattern as above.

Inscription: *Carolus Hugh Egerton Smyth, Litterarum Præmium, 1923*. College arms.

Maker's mark: M & Co | MUNSEY, SILVERSMITH, CAMBRIDGE, for David Munsey's successors.

For Charles Hugh Egerton Smyth (1903–87) see his mug (§10.2.7).

10.4.10 Stewart Henry Perowne Standing Cup

1887 (London M). 4.75 × 9.55 in. 1.7 pints (0.97 l).

Single-gilt inside. Matt bands on bowl and foot; beading on 3 knops and foliage on 2; wreath round College arms.

Inscription: *Cor Cordium Cantabrigiensium A.S. MCMXLVI Sempiterna Honoret Pietas.* (May everlasting veneration honour . . . the heart of hearts of Cambridge men – an acrostic on the initials C[orpus] C[hristi] C[ollege] S[tewart] H[enry] P[erowne])

Made by Hunt & Roskell, successors to Paul Storr, active 1843–.

Stewart Henry Perowne, OBE (1901–89), archaeologist and Orientalist, was admitted 1920, BA 1923, Colonial Secretary in Barbados, 1947–51. He wrote many books on the history and archaeology of Palestine and the east Mediterranean.

Inspired by a type of standing cup without lid, common in the mid to late 17th century, of which the Compton Cup at Queens' College (1637) is one of the earliest.

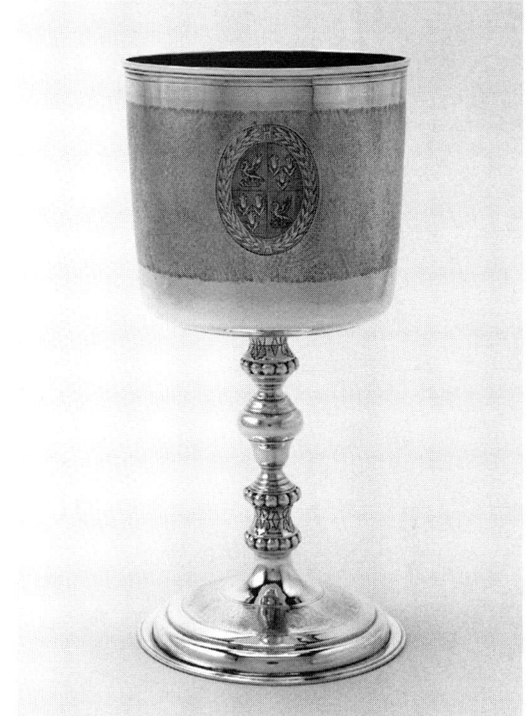

11

Coffee-Pots

also Argyles, Teapots and associated vessels

NATHANIEL CONOPIUS, a Cretan born, trained up in the Greek church, and became primate* to Cyrill patriarch of Constantinople† . . . When the said Cyrill was strangled by the visier (the grand signior of the Turks§ being not then returned from the siege of Babylon) Conopius to avoid the like barbarity fled thence and went into England . . . Dr Laud archbishop of Canterbury, that worthy person, sent him to Baliol college and allowed him a comfortable subsistence . . . Afterwards he became one of the chaplains or petty canons of Christ Church . . . In the beginning of November 1648 he was expelled the university by the barbarians, I mean the parliamentarian visitors . . . he returned into his own country among the barbarians, and was made bishop of Smyrna . . . while he continued in Baliol college he made the drink for his own use called coffee, and usually drank it every morning, being the first, as the antients of that house have informed me, that was ever drank in Oxon.

* A kind of chaplain.

† Kyrillos Loukaris (1572–1638) who had studied in Geneva and introduced Calvinist ideas to the Orthodox church, for which the ambassadors of the Roman Catholic powers suborned the Grand Vizir to have him liquidated.

§ Murad IV, the Smoker-slayer (p. 231).

Anthony à Wood, Athenæ Oxonienses, *3rd edn (1820)* **4** 808
(I am grateful to Professor William Horbury for this reference)

The Growth of a Vice

Coffee is the seed of *Coffea arabica*, a small tree (family Rubiaceæ) which grows in the understorey of tropical forest in Ethiopia, and other species of the genus in different parts of Africa. It contains the soft drug caffein, a weakly addictive, nearly harmless alkaloid; as with other mind-bending herbs its effect depends partly on other, less well known, substances that go with it.

Coffee was introduced to Turkey in the 16th century, being a liquor which did not offend Muslims. From there it was apparently introduced to Oxford (and to western Europe) by Konopios the Cretan in 1639. Soon after he was sent down, the first public coffee-house was opened in Oxford. There, and later in London, coffee became the lubricant of business lunches. By 1663 it was popular enough in Cambridge for the Vice-Chancellor to forbid undergraduates to drink it.[1]

Caffein occurs in other, unrelated plants, such as tea (*Camellia sinensis*), introduced to London a little later than coffee. Other caffein herbs that the writer has experienced include maté (*Ilex paraguensis*) and the notorious Black Drink of the Indians of the south-east United States (*I. vomitoria*).

English coffee-pots are much bigger than the *ibrik* in which coffee is made in the Ægean, and may be derived from teapots; both begin *c.*1670. Teapots can usually be recognized by the hard dark incrustation inside. The convention that coffee-pots are tall and teapots are squat is not reliable. Both are commoner in pottery.

The College's coffee-pot of 1719 appears to be the earliest surviving in Cambridge, except for a very similar one in St John's College. Our series of successively

1 University Archives: VC Ct 1/13 f.135. (reference from Dr M. Spufford).

bigger coffee-pots illustrates the Europe-wide growth of a vice satirized by Bach in his *Coffee Cantata*, *c.*1732.

Tea came to the College at almost the same time as coffee. 'A Tea Pott given by Mr Collins' was given *c.*1717, and two others by 1726. All our early coffee-pots survive, but none of the early teapots: we sold the Collins in 1756. Whether this is because the Fellows drank tea more often than coffee, or grew more lively under its influence, I leave the reader to judge. In fashionable circles there developed a tea-ceremony requiring a *caddy*, of which Pembroke College has a magnificent rococo example, comprising two containers, nippers for breaking up sugar (pp. 187f.), and twelve shell spoons, each in its compartment in a sharkskin case.

Silver, the world's best conductor of heat, is unsuitable for the handles or knobs of vessels for hot liquid. Either the handle is made of wood or an insulating false-tenon of ivory etc. is inserted between the silver handle and the pot.

Baroque Coffee-Pots (1719–1732)

11.1 Russell Coffee-Pot

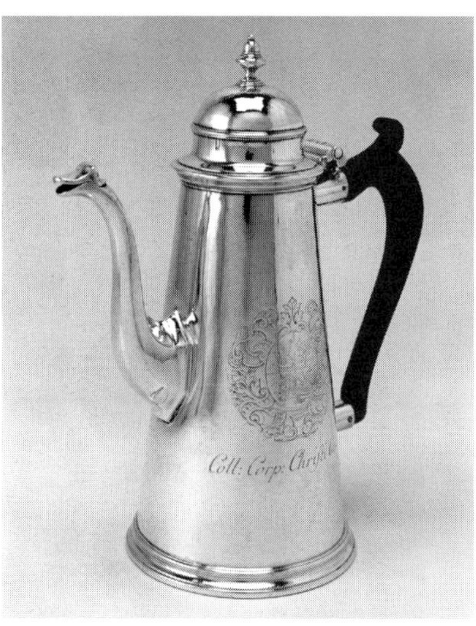

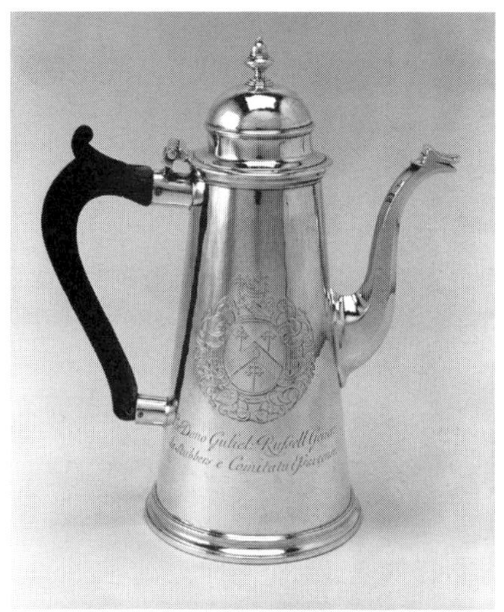

1719 (London D). 8.3 in. × 4.3 × 9.0 high.

Body chased with scrolled and foliated cartouches around arms. High domed lid with acorn-shaped knob. Double-curved spout of heptagonal section, ending in a sort of vestigial duck's head. Handle of slightly ring-porous wood (walnut?), attached by tenon above and below; top end renewed, tail lost.

College's arms and donor's: *A chevron with a scallop thereon, between three crosses crosslet fitchée* and crest: *a demi-lion rampant collared, charged on the body with a scallop on a chevron, holding between his paws a cross crosslet fitchée.* Inscribed: *Coll: Corp: Christi Cant:* and *Ex Dono Guliel: Russell Gener: de Stubbers e Comitatu Essexiensi.* (The gift of William Russell, Gentleman, of Stubbers from the County of Essex.)

Maker's mark: FO over a mullet, for Thomas Folkingham (active *c.*1690–1729).[2]

William Russell (*c.*1700–1754), admitted 1717, presumably a Fellow-Commoner; took no degree; retired to the life of a country squire. His home, Stubbers in North Ockendon, Essex, had once a famous botanical garden, where the first yucca in England is said to have bloomed in 1604,[3] now a rubbish-filled gravel-pit on the way to the Dartford Tunnel.

2 Incorrectly described by Jones, *Cambridge*.
3 *Victoria County History, Essex* 7 112ff.

This is the typical shape and rather plain style of a baroque coffee-pot. The Jenison Coffee-pot at Merton College, Oxford, made by H. Arnett & E. Pocock in 1727, is almost identical. St John's College, Cambridge has a similar one of *c*.1715.[4] Kelvingrove Museum, Glasgow, has another from London, 1710.

Specialists sometimes claim that these small early coffee-pots were really chocolate-pots, with a hole in the lid for a stirring-stick that has later been blocked. However, this would be difficult to do without leaving a trace.

11.2 Heathcote Coffee-Pot

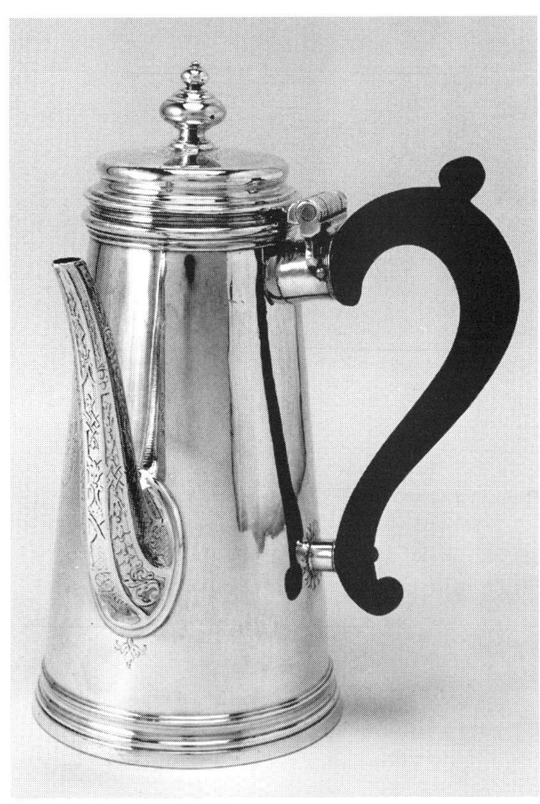

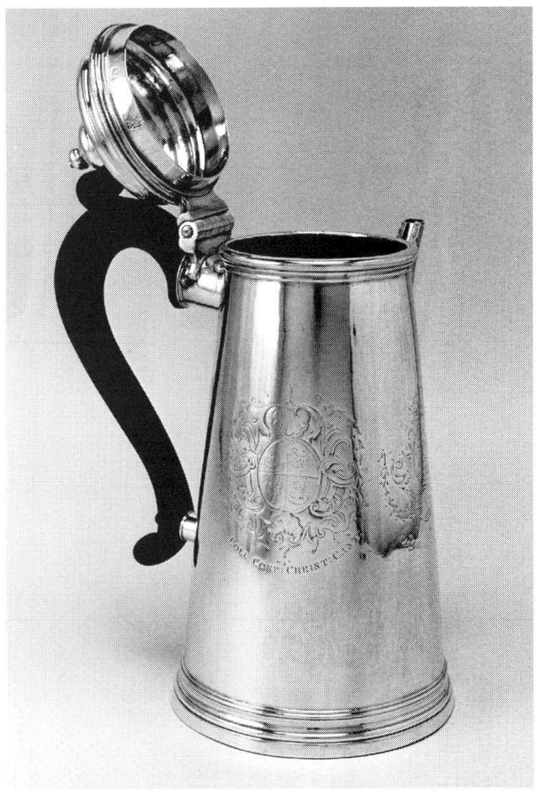

1722 (London G). 4.8 in. diam. × 9.4 high.

Tapering body, flat lid and bulbous finial, double-curved spout of octagonal section at right angles to handle. Handle of dense dark hard tropical wood, probably painted black, attached by tenon above and screw below. Spout deeply engraved in panels with strapwork, rosettes, foliage, and a rather Red Indian mask. Sunflower rosette round lower handle socket. Engraved octafoil round knob on lid.

College arms surrounded by shells and scrolls. Swags and a human face surround donor's: *Ermine three roundels, a cross or upon each.* Inscribed *COLL: CORP: CHRIST: CANT:* and *SAMUEL HEATHCOTE.* Weight inscribed: oz 34 = 11 [present weight 35:18].

Maker: probably Paul de Lamerie (1688–1751), greatest of silversmiths (see Rigby Candlesticks, §12.2). The mark, L A and two stars under a crown, closely resembles one of his three known marks.

Samuel Heathcote of Bere Alston (Devon) was admitted (Fellow-Commoner?) to this College in 1740, and simultaneously to Lincoln's Inn (like John Yorke, p. 157). He gave this old and magnificent piece in 1744, when the College paid 8*d*. for transporting it. We know nothing else about him.

4 Jones, *Merton* p. 12. Jones, *Cambridge* p.80.

This pot, with its rich but unobtrusive ornament, has a right-angled spout; a feature in coffee- and teapots about this time, although the earliest of all coffee-pots, that of 1670, has it. (Were any made for left-handed users?) The engraving is in the style of that on the Great Yorke Salver of 1715, by a different maker (p. 170).

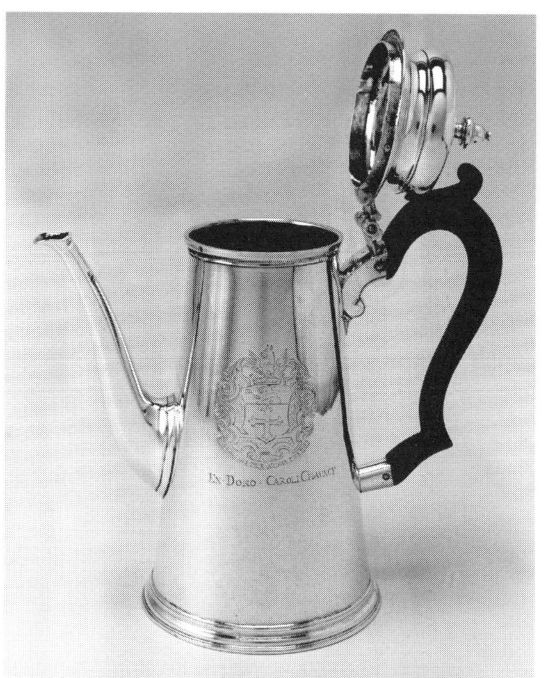

11.3 Chauncy Coffee-Pot

1728 (London N). 7.3 in. × 4.0 × 8.1 high.

Tapering body; octagonal spout; flat-topped lid with integral knob; handle of ?boxwood tenoned into two sockets. College and donor's arms engraved in foliated and scrolled cartouches with symmetrical rococo shields.

Donor's arms: *Gules a cross patonce* [i.e. with grapnel-like ends], *on a chief azure a lion passant or with a three-point label for difference.* Crest: *out of a Duke's coronet a demi-griffin charged with a three-point label.* Motto: SUBLIMIS · PER · ARDUA · TENDO [I crash on sublimely through difficulties – words meant to inspire generations of undergraduates].

Inscribed: *E. DONO CAROLI CHAVNCY \ Collegium Corporis Christi & B. Virginis Mariæ in Universitate Cantabrigiensi 1730* Weight: 19 = 3 [ounces; present weight 19:4]. Maker's mark fragmentary and unidentifiable.

The learned Charles Chauncy (?–1777) of London, doctor, antiquary, and collector, was promoted a Fellow-Commoner in 1729; M.D. 1738; Fellow both of the Royal Society and of the Society of Antiquaries.

The shape is still baroque but the decoration strays towards rococo, then just appearing in France.

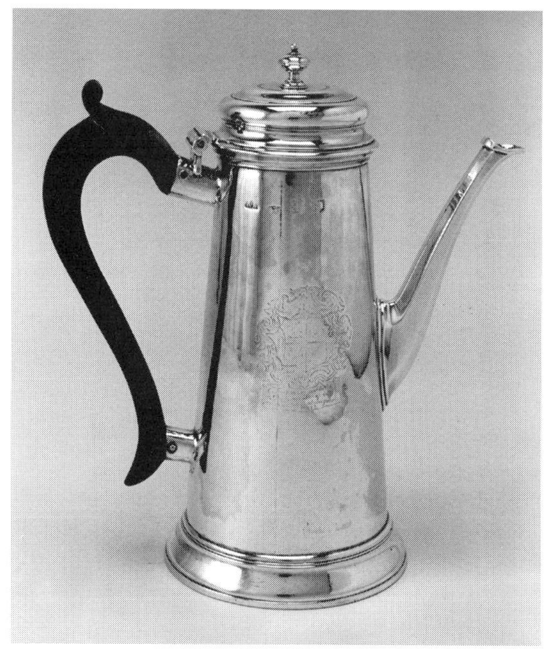

11.4 Jermy Coffee-Pot

1732 (London R). 8.1 in. × 4.3 × 8.9 high.

Tapering cylinder body (with visible seam); flattish hinged lid with small knob; octagonal spout. Handle of close-grained yellow wood (?maple or box), attached by tenons above and below; attachments reinforced by silver plates inside. Foliated cartouches with hatched backgrounds around College arms and donor's: *Quarterly, 1 & 4: a lion rampant guardant; 2 & 3: a goose. Crest on lid:* a griffin. Motto: *SPLENDIDUM . INSIGNE . VIRTUS* [Virtue, distinguished and shining].

Inscribed: *DONO DEDIT GULI^{E}LMUS JERMY ARM^{r}: DE BAYFIELD IN COM: NORF: SOCIO: COMMENSALI. MAR: 12°: 1732:3* [William Jermy, armiger, of Bayfield in the county of Norfolk, Fellow Commoner, gave this gift 12 March 1732/3.] *Collegium Corporis Christi & B: Virginis Maria* [sic] *in Universitate Cantabrigiensi 1732–3* Weight: 23 : 3 [ounces; present weight 23: 14].

Maker's mark: ? RB in rectangle, for Richard Bayley, active 1720–48, 'maker of good plain hollow-ware' (Grimshaw).

William Jermy was squire of the then deserted village of Bayfield near Holt, Norfolk. He became a Fellow Commoner in 1731, having previously (very unusually) been for six years at the Inner Temple.

This pot has poured much coffee, judging from the wear.

Rococo Coffee-pots (1743–1749)

11.5 Walpole Coffee-Pot

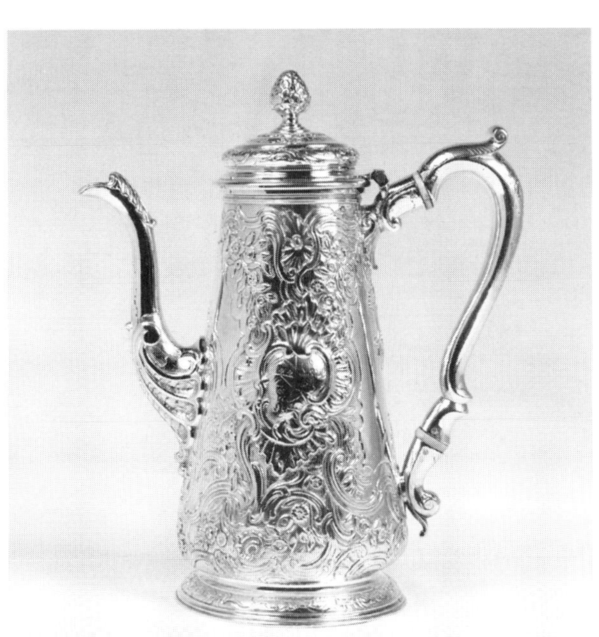

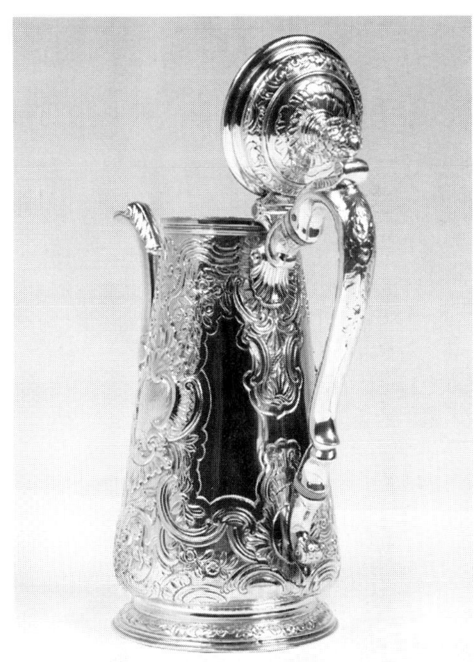

1743 (London h). 9.6 in. × 5.1 × 11.4 high.

Tapering body; double-curved spout; flattish hinged lid with ovoid scaly knob. The silver handle, attached through ivory plugs, is Victorian.

Cast leaf-tongue decorations surround the sockets of the handle and base of the spout. Body and lid are clothed in *repoussé* scrolls, shells, and *Camellia*-like flowers on a stippled background. Elaborate rococo cartouches surround the College's arms and donor's: *Quarterly, 1 & 4: on a fess between two chevrons three cross-crosslets* [for Walpole]; *2 & 3: vert a lion rampant.*

Inscribed: *Ex Dono Hor: Walpole Armigeri Honoratissimi Hor: Walpole Armigeri Filii natu maximi & hujus Collegii Socii Commensali.* [Gift of Horace Walpole, armiger, eldest son of the Right Honourable Horace Walpole, armiger, and Fellow-Commoner of this College.] Graffito: BX 2/57

Maker: mark *D W* and two stars in quatrefoil, for David Williaume II, maker also of the Mawson Cup (10.3.4).

The handle, which must replace an earlier silver handle, is decorated incongruously with cast leaf-tongue, stippled lines, and engraved flowers. It is marked with Victoria's head but no date-letter. The ivory plugs have mouldings which do not continue on to the handle.

Donor: Horace Walpole (1723–1809), nephew of Robert Walpole the Prime Minister, and cousin of *the* Horace Walpole of Strawberry Hill. He was admitted as Fellow Commoner 1741; MP for King's Lynn; became second Baron Walpole 1757; created Earl of Orford 1806.

This early rococo piece has characteristic asymmetrical, rich and not unobtrusive, ornament. It is too magnificent for modernistic critics: the authenticity of the *repoussé* decoration has been questioned in the belief that such an excess of ornament must have been added in Victorian times. But the marks have been struck through the *repoussé* work, which was distorted in the striking and has been touched up afterwards with stippled lines. The decoration therefore precedes the hallmarking.

It is possible, though risky, to improve a vessel by adding embossed decoration: see Bateman Sugar-bowl (p. 246) and Moule Cream-Jug (p. 257). The late Sir Desmond Lee had a cup to which embossing had undoubtedly been added later, resulting in cracks and holes in the metal. However, elaborately embossed ornament was, indeed, characteristic of rococo, as shown by these examples:

Shrubsole, London: coffee-pot made by James Gould in London, 1742, rococo decoration by same combination of methods as this.

Shrubsole Corp., New York: coffee-pot, 1743, by de Lamerie in his later years, almost identical decoration to Corpus's.

Garrard, London: coffee-pot by George Wickes, 1743, similar but gilt and with all-ivory handle. (Advertised in *Apollo*, June 1983 p.124; *Apollo*, May 1998; *The Times*, 18 June 1984.)

St Catharine's College: very similar coffee-pot, made in 1748, with the same mixture of cast and *repoussé* decoration.

Kelvingrove Museum, Glasgow: cream-jug marked in London, 1755, with very similar details.

Victoria & Albert Museum: elaborate rococo *repoussé*, 1769.

Kelvingrove: coffee-pot by Kerr & Dempster, Edinburgh, 1771, *repoussé* just like Corpus's, original silver handle attached by ivory plugs.

Trinity College, Dublin: Britannia silver, bulbous shape, richly *repoussé* with figure of heron, marked Dublin 1771.

Trinity College, Dublin: Britannia silver, bulbous shape, richly *repoussé* in *chinoiserie* style with mill, marked Dublin 1771. (Bennett §96, 97.)

11.6 Boscawen Coffee-Pot

1749 (poorly preserved London o). 6.8 in. × 3.7 × 8.4 high.

Body constricted to base; spout of round section; high domed lid with integral knob; handle of ?boxwood tenoned into two sockets. Leaf-tongue cast on spout. Bottom socket is vaguely batrachian. College and donor's (*Ermine a rose*) arms engraved in asymmetric rococo cartouches with foliated surrounds and wheat-plants.

Inscribed: *D.D. Hon. Nic. Boscawen A.M. C.C.C.C. 1750* [on base] C. Graffito: 17·7 *DL m* 9/193.

Maker unidentifiable (mark fragmentary).

This piece commemorates the graduation as M.A. of the learned nobleman Nicholas Boscawen (*c*.1735–1793), younger son of Viscount Falmouth; admitted 1743; D.D 1753; Prebendary of Westminster 1777–93. Tregothnan, the family seat in Cornwall, was later rebuilt by William Wilkins, architect of Corpus New Court.

To judge by the wear, this is the hardest-worked of our coffee-pots. Its weight is unaltered from when it was given; a deposit of coffee scale inside has balanced loss of silver from cleaning.

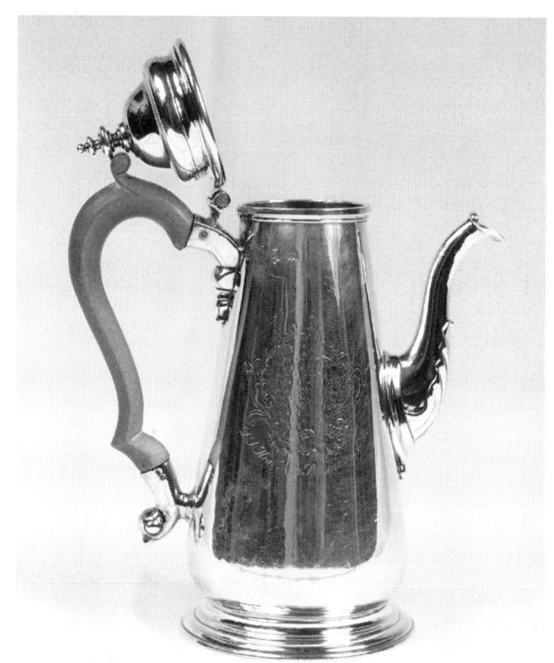

Adamesque Pots (1783–1797)

11.7 Gadsby Teapot

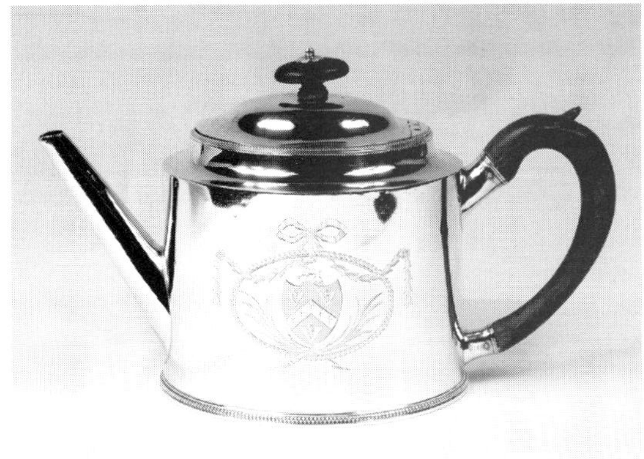

1783 (London h). 11.5 in. × 6.8 × 4.7 high.

Elliptical cylinder, slightly tapered upwards, with constricted mouth; domed lid with a little steam-hole; tripartite hinge cunningly set flush into lid; plain conical spout; C-shaped handle of hard greyish wood, tenoned and pinned into two sockets; knob on lid elliptical, of darker wood with bigger vessels, attached by bolt with square nut. Beading round base and mouth of pot.

Engraved with elliptical cartouches hanging from ribbons, with swags and two crossed branches of a *Cordyline*-like tree, contain arms of College (hatched for *sable* where there should be *gules*) and donor: *Sable a chevron ermine between three pheons argent.* Donor's crest: *a hart passant argent.*

Inscribed underneath: *Thomas Gadsby Socio Commensalis DD CCCC.*

Maker's mark, *HB* in a cottage loaf, is that of the celebrated Hester Bateman (1708–94), active 1761–90. This plain and simple shape is typical of the Adamesque fashion. As often, the hinge is a weak point and has been reinforced by a silver bar.

The Fellow-Commoner's gift of Thomas Gadsby of Bedfordshire (1759–1840), admitted 1777, M.A. 1784, Vicar of Wootton (Beds.) for 55 years.

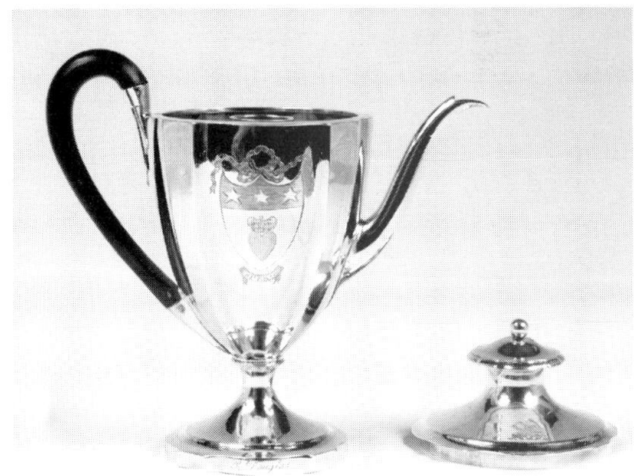

11.8 Douglas Argyle (*two illustrations*)

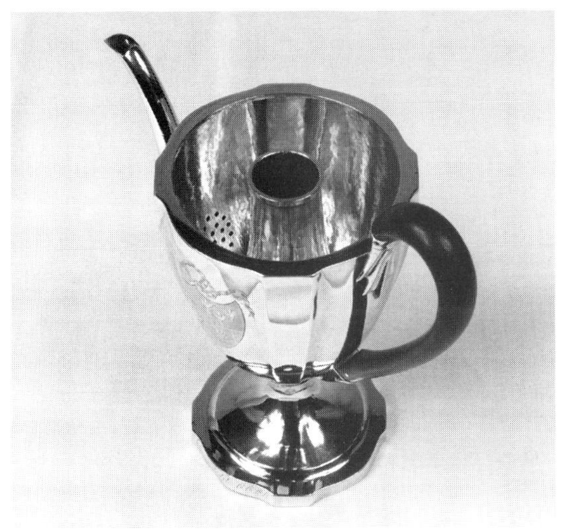

1789 (London O and King's head). 7.7 in. × 4.0 × 8.0 high.

Body shaped like a funerary urn, with four raised ribs; plain spout with long pouring-lip, communicating with body through 18 holes. Handle of ?boxwood tenoned into upper socket with pin, false-tenoned into lower socket; lower socket shaped like duck's foot. Hammered finish inside.

The detachable lid rises to a finial (echoing the section of the body) and small knob. It fits very closely inside the flanged top of the body; a lug on the lid registers with a notch on the body. Inside is a tapering inner compartment, not communicating with the body.

Engraved with College arms and donor's: *Argent a human heart imperially crowned gules, on a chief azure three estoiles of the first.* Pseudo-crest: *a heart gules.*

Maker: A·P P·P in square with cut corners, for A. Peterson & P. Podio, a rather obscure London partnership known 1783–90.

Given by Robert Douglas of Essex (1765–1806), admitted Fellow Commoner 1787; Bachelor of Law 1794; rose to be Rector of Hampton Lovett and also of Salwarpe (Worcs) 1799–1806; may have been a relative of Philip Douglas, Master (see Douglas Tureen §21.17.1). Presumably he claimed descent from the royal Scots Douglas family, with their badge of a bloody heart. He gave the Douglas Coasters (§21.4.3) in the same year.

This looks like a little chocolate-pot, fully Adamesque in style. What makes it an argyle is the inner compartment. What is it for?

> **Argyll.** A vessel of silver or metal, like a small coffee-pot, in which to serve up gravy, so as to keep it hot.
>
> *Oxford English Dictionary*, quoting an example of 1822.

Ours would be suitable for only the thinnest gravy, because the small holes (1.5 mm) would easily get clogged. The central compartment suggests the use of hot water or some other heating material, which would work no better than the same volume of extra gravy. Was it used to pour in boiling water to rescue congealed gravy?

Kelvingrove Museum, Glasgow, has an argyle working on the same principle, but dated 1780 and shaped like a little baroque coffee-pot. The Ormonde Argyle in the Victoria & Albert Museum is a squat-cylinder shape.

11.9 Bury Coffee-Pot (*below*)

1796 (London A). 9.25 in. × 4.9 × 10.85 high.

Ovoid body with keeled top; octagonal spout with bifid end; trumpet-shaped lid recessed into top of body, with hidden 5-part hinge. Handle of yellowish hardwood (?boxwood), thumbpiece broken, pegged into two sockets.

Body is ornamented below the equator with 4 × 3 *repoussé* ribs, engraved with delicate dotted lines. Moulded band surrounds equator. Vine-trail chased round top of body. Fishy flipper adjoins upper socket of handle. Bands of delicate engraving on top surface of body, at junction of foot, and on foot itself. Junction of foot and body has wavy decoration with dotted line outside it. Lid tapers into a finial with a gadrooned knob (with steam-hole beside it) surrounded by a rosette of 12 lanceolate, reflexed bracts.

Inscription: Patricio Bury Collegii C.C.C. et B.M.V. Socio et annalium eiusdem iam D.C. annos completis / enarratori disertissimo / Magister ceterique Socii d.d. A. D. MCMLII. (The Master and the other Fellows gave [me] to Patrick Bury, Fellow of the College of Corpus Christi and the Blessed Virgin Mary, most learned

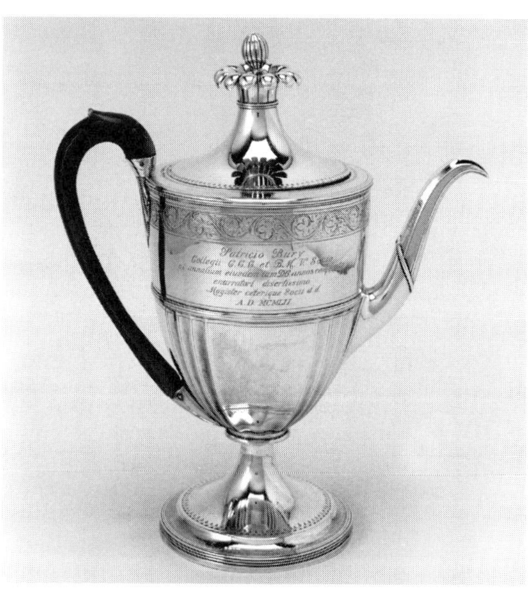

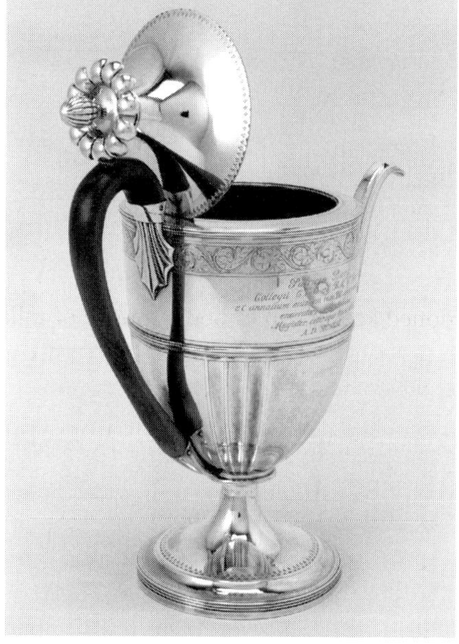

narrator, on completing 150 years of annals of the same [College], A.D. 1952.) Numerous graffiti of letters and numbers.

Maker's mark P.P in rectangle, for Peter Podio (§11.9), mark known 1790.

Given to John Patrick Tuer Bury (1933–87), of Trumpington; admitted 1927; Mawson Scholar and Foundation Scholar; Fellow 1933–87; Dean, Librarian, President; Warden of Leckhampton 1969–75; distinguished historian of France. It commemorates the publication of *The College of Corpus Christi and of the Blessed Virgin Mary: a history from 1822 to 1952*. It came to the College on his death.

One of the College's most ambitious examples of the Adamesque style.

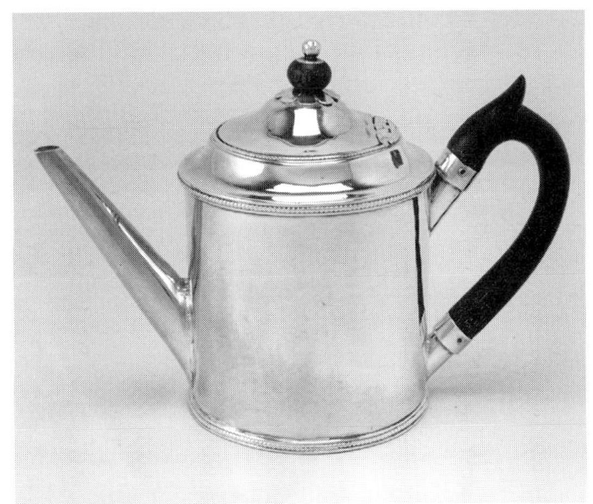

11.10 [Bateman] Coffee-like Pot

1797 (London B). 8.3 in. × 3.95 × 5.8 high.

Squat cylinder, with domed lid smaller in diameter than pot. Hinge set in thickness of lid. Handle of dark tropical hardwood, tenoned into silver sockets. Bands of beading around top and bottom of cylinder and mouth of pot. Lid ends in a disk cut into eight petals, capped by a wooden ball, on which is a silver ball finial (attached by a silver bolt with square nut). Entrance to spout pierced with about 62 holes.

Maker's mark, PB AB in square rectangle, of Peter (1740–1825) and Ann (1748–*c*.1810) Bateman. He was Hester Bateman's son and successor; from 1790 onwards they were pioneers in the machine-made plate that came to dominate middle- and lower-class silverware in the 19th century.

Bequeathed by Aubrey Bateman. Battered with hard service before the College had it.

Regency Pots

11.11 Guelder-Rose Jug

1817 (London b). 8.1 in. × 8.1 × 7.9 high.

Upright shape; bulbous base; short attached spout; handle of rectangular section, attached by ivory false-tenons. Lid with rosette (attached by silver wingnut) beneath cast knob. Bold *repoussé* fluting on body, spout, lid; gadrooned keel at top of body; tongue of foliage at base of spout. Knob in the shape of bracts opening to reveal an inflorescence like a young guelder-rose (*Viburnum opulus*).

The detail resembles the following piece, although there is no apparent connexion.

Maker's mark: JA in rectangle, for Joseph Angell I, active in London 1811–*c*.1840.

Weight inscription: 23-15 [present weight 23:8].

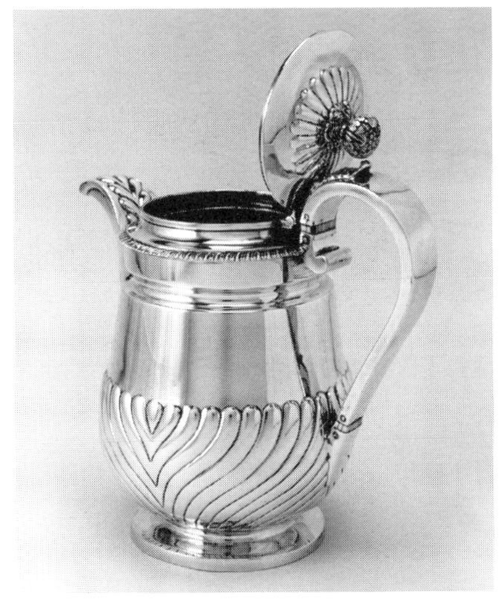

11.12 JBMH [Bateman] Teapot

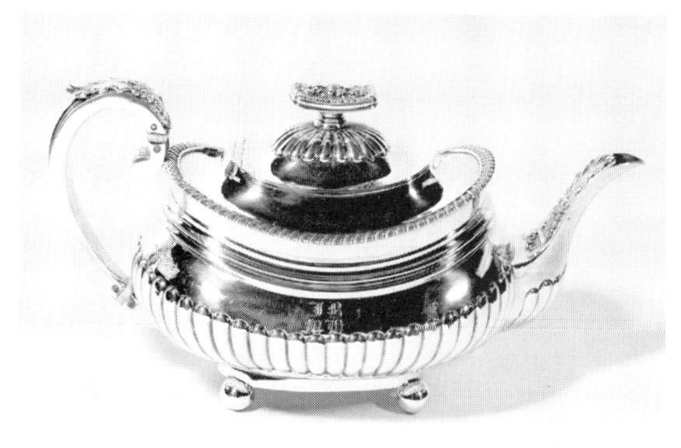

1820 (London e). 11.2 in. × 5.0 × 5.9 high.

Squat oblong with rounded corners, keeled saddle-shaped top, small lid. Spout of half-elliptical section, its entrance pierced with many holes. Handle of round section, held by ivory false-tenons. Oblong flat knob on lid, held by looped silver wing-nut. *Repoussé* flutings on body, lid, base of spout; keel elaborately gadrooned. Cast leaf-tongues on spout and handle. Knob *repoussé* with acorns, pears, grapes, etc. and with border of shells. Hinge set in thickness of lid.

Inscription: 𝕵𝕭 𝕸𝕳 27 inscribed on bottom. Graffito: 9|212.

Maker's mark M·S in ellipse, for Michael Starkey, active in London 1809–34.

Bequeathed by Aubrey Bateman.

Victoriana

11.13 Pooley Teapot and Pinnock Jug and Basin

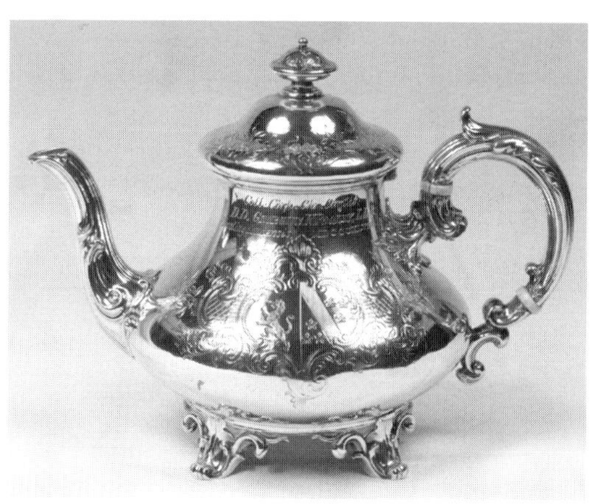

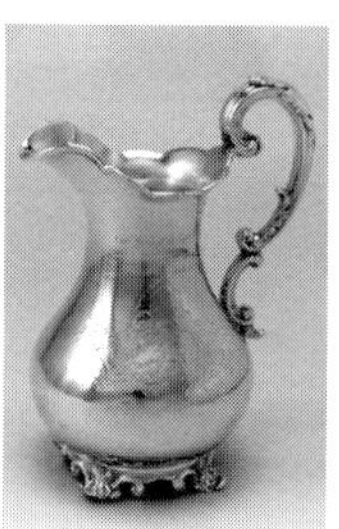

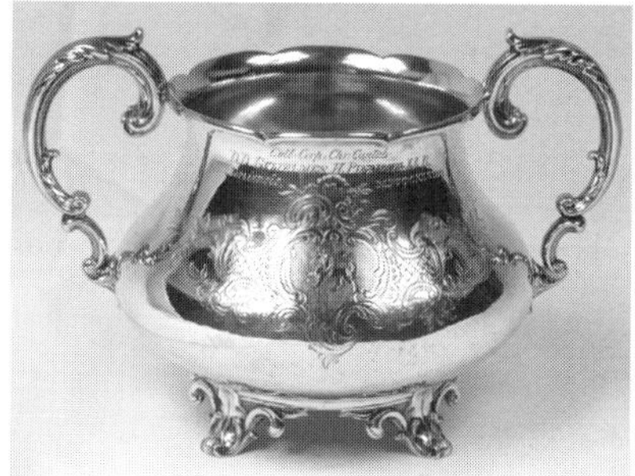

1849 (London 𝕺).

These three form a set, for pouring tea and adding cream and sugar, as was then the custom. (Alternatively, the third vessel could have been a *slop-basin*, for discarding the debris of tea-drinking.)

Teapot: 10.2 in. × 6.4 × 7.5 high.

Depressed-pear-shaped body on cast ring base with four feet; domed lid with knob attached by wing-nut; handle with thumbpiece, attached by ivory false-tenons to sockets. Foliated surround to upper handle-socket. Engraved flowers (some *Camellia*- and some daffodil-like) on lid and knob. Big cartouches for arms, engraved with olive and other foliage and mythical flowers. Weak hinge mended with silver insert.

Elaborate rococo shields for College's arms and donor's: *Argent a lion rampant sable, impaling argent a bend gules between six cinquefoils vert.*

Inscribed: *Coll: Corp: Chr: Cantab: D. D. GEORGIUS F. POOLEY, LL.B. Huntingdoniensis MDCCCXLVIIII.* (George F. Pooley Ll.B., of Huntingdon, gave [me] to the College of Corpus Christi, Cambridge.) Peters & Son, Cambridge. Graffito: 20 16

Jug: 6.5 in. × 3.5 × 4.9 high.

Globular, tapering into neck. Cast base with four foliated feet; two engraved cartouches with scrolls and foliage; elaborate scrolled handle.

College arms and donor's: *A lion passant.*

Inscription: *Coll: Corp: Chr: Cantab: D.D. GULIELMUS H. PINNOCK, LL.B. Hantoniensis, MDCCCXLVIII.* (William H. Pinnock, Ll.B., of [Sout]hampton, gave . . .) Peters & Son, Cambridge.

Two-handled Bowl: 8.0 in. × 5.7 × 5.3 high.

Thinly gilt inside. Depressed-pear-shaped body with contracted mouth; cast ring base with four feet; two C-shaped handles. Thickened cut-card margin at mouth. Engraving as on Pooley Teapot. Arms and inscription as on jug.

All three items bear the mark (E J B & W in quatrefoil) of Edward, John & William Barnard, a stage in the development of the great London firm of Edward Barnard & Sons, 1808–.

George Frederick Pooley (1808–1874) was admitted 1841 and took his Ll.B. in 1848, his teapot marking the occasion. Deserting the law (as many did), he became Rector of Cransford and Vicar of Bruisyard (Suffolk) 1846–84. William Henry Pinnock (1813–1885) was admitted 1843, took his Ll.B in 1850, deserted the law, became Anglican chaplain at Chantilly (France – home of lime-trees and horse-racing) 1870–6 and Vicar of Pinner (Middlesex) 1879–85.

The jug is much more worn and dented than the other pieces.

11.14 Eyles Teapot, with Jug and Basin

Teapot: 1858 (London c and Victoria's head). 10.0 in. × 5.7 × 7.2 high.

Nearly spherical, with foot; octagonal-section spout; round handle attached by ivory false-tenons; lid with high dome and finial attached by silver wing-nut. Plain foot with beaded edge. Six foliated cartouches chased on body: one contains arms, another the inscription, the others have drawings of cabbage-roses; two blank cartouches on lid and handle. Entrance to spout pierced with many holes.

College arms. Inscribed *Ex Dono Franc. Eyles Armigeri 1730*

Jug: 1860 (London e). 4.3 in. × 3.1 × 5.1 high.

Bulbous with foot; rococo spout. Six elaborately foliated cartouches, four containing posies, one for College arms, one blank. Small cartouche on handle.

Bowl: 1860 (London e). 8.3 in. × 5.5 × 4.2 high. 11.6 oz = 362 g.

Depressed-globose with foot; two cast handles. Beading round foot and mouth. Six foliated cartouches engraved on body (one contains arms, another blank, the others with cabbage-roses). Similar chasing on handles.

All three bear the mark EB JB in a quatrefoil, for Edward & John Barnard; this is the next stage in the history of the Barnard firm.

Sir Francis Eyles *alias* Sir Francis E. Haskin-Styles (*c*.1710–1762) was another of the learned Fellow-Commoners; admitted 1727 (College audit book 1728); Fellow of the Royal Society 1742; in 1745 succeeded as

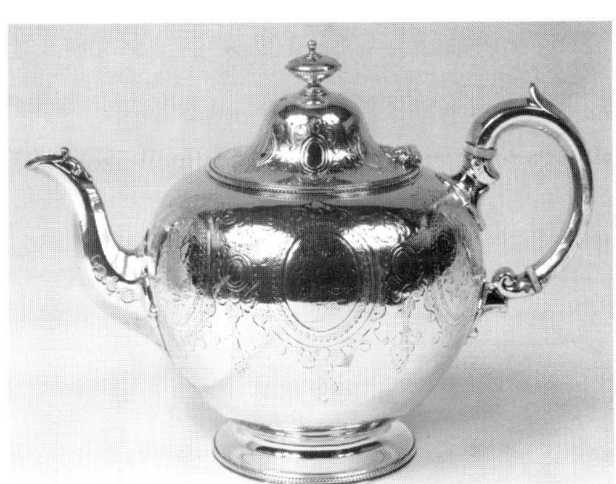

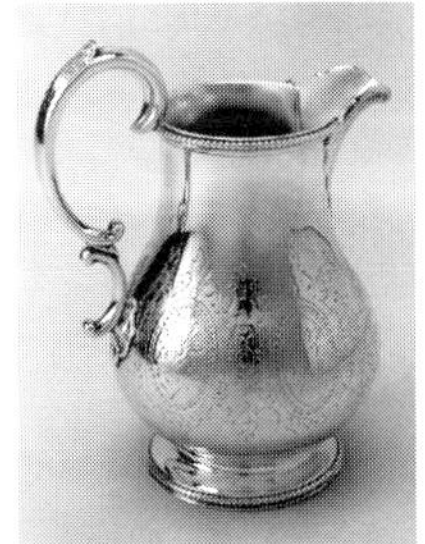

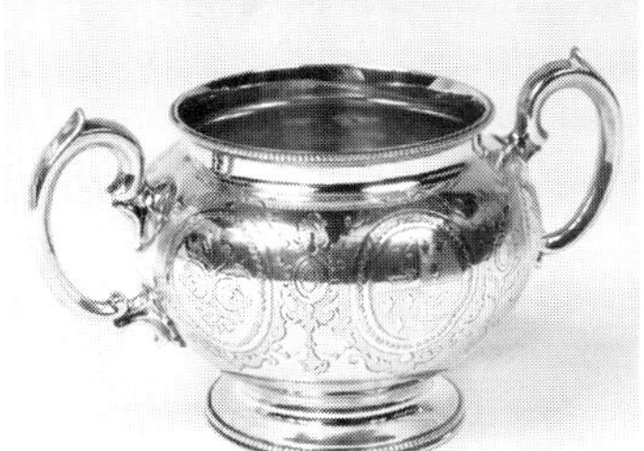

Baronet; squire of More Park (Herts.) and Gidea Hall, Essex (now Gidea Park golf-course, Romford). He gave us a great cup and cover weighing 54 ounces, which had it survived would have been a fitting companion to the Gough, Mawson, and Yorke Cups – but we recycled it into these humbler vessels, weighing 38 ounces.

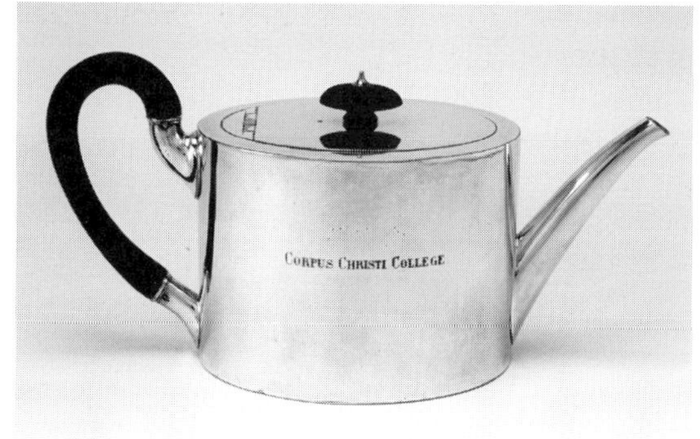

11.15 'Corpus Christi Collcgc' Victorian Tcapot

Silver-plated base metal, undated but *c.*1880. 10.8 × 4.4 in.

Elliptical cylinder, lid and hinge cunningly set flush with top surface. Curved cylindrical spout from near base, with multiple holes from body into spout. Handle of ebony-like wood, tenoned into sockets. Elliptical knob on lid of similar wood, attached by silver bolt with wingnut. Plain except for mouldings on sockets.

Inscribed: CORPUS CHRISTI COLLEGE 𝔊ℭ𝔓𝔖 4+

Maker's mark: Martin, Hall & Co., Sheffield firm (1854–1936).

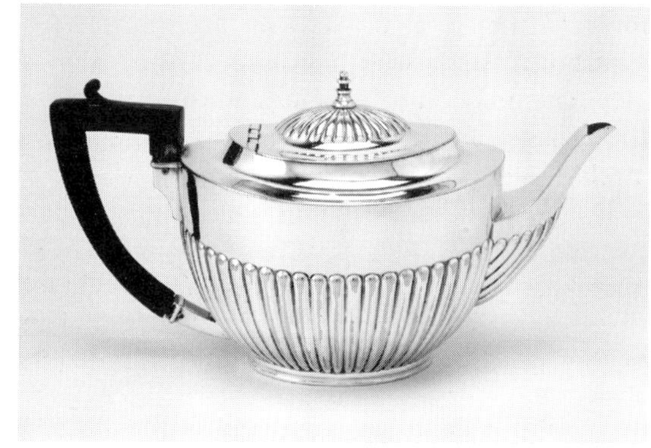

11.16 Anonymous Teapot

Probably electroplated base metal, undated but *c.*1900. 10.9in. × 5.1 × 5.6 high.

Squat elliptical plan. Saddle-shaped upper surface with flush-set lid and hinge. Domed middle of lid, with small knob attached by round-headed bolt. Half-round spout. Handle square in section, of a black substance, tenoned to two sockets. Bold *repoussé* fluting on lower half of body (including part of spout) and dome of lid.

Marks: eight arrows intersecting latticewise WH & SEP MP Δ in T-shaped outline 3690 4. Made by William Hutton of Sheffield.

Repeats a rococo fashion. In Kelvingrove Museum, Glasgow, is a similar silver teapot made by Hester Bateman in 1778.

Twentieth Century

11.17 Anonymous Coffee-Pot *c.*1920

Apparently silver, but no visible hallmarks. 6.7 in. × 4.1 × 9.0 high.

Pot-bellied with short spout; domed lid with small knob (missing a wood or ivory ring) attached by wingnut. Double-C handle of ebony-like black wood, tenoned into two silver sockets. Body boldly decorated (like the Regency pots) with *repoussé* panels of alternating flowers and fluting; *repoussé* flowers on spout. Lid with four floral panels; tongue-&-dart round edge.

Marks: CE N in 3-cusped triangle; 2328 BROOK & SON 87. GEORGE. ST EDINBURGH.

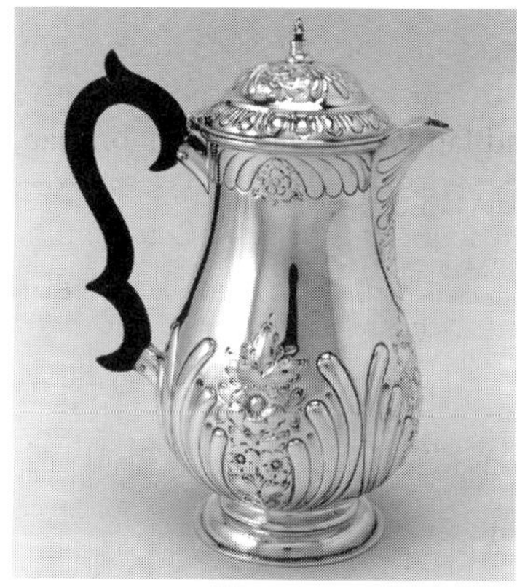

11.18 Two Langdon-Brown Milk-Jugs and Two Sugar-Bowls with Lids

1935 (London u).

Jugs: 4.6 in. × 2.5 × 5.3 high. Helmet profile with low foot, big spout, square-profile handle. Body unequal-sided octagonal. Moulded bands on rim, around upper part of body, and on foot; mouldings with 'capitals' on the eight angles. Foot touches table in eight places.

Bowls: 4.0 in. × 4.0 × 3.0 high. Octagonal, deep with low foot, decorated as jugs.

Lids to bowls: 4.3 in. × 4.3 × 2.1 high. Octagonal, low profile. Ivory knob attached by silver wingnut. Incised decoration at eight corners.

Jugs and bowls all have donor's arms: *Party per pale: dexter, azure 3 lozenges or, between them a bar erminois?, on a chief gules a leopard or; sinister, on a bend three eagles displayed sable, in dexter chief a mullet.* Pseudo-crest: *a mullet.* Inscription: WALTER LANGDON-BROWN EQ. AUR. R.P.P. ET SOC. d.d. COLL. CORP. CHR. ET B.M.V. MCMXXXV (Walter Langdon-Brown, Gilded Knight, Regius Professor of Physic and Fellow, gave [me] to the College . . . 1935).

George V's Jubilee hallmark as well as 1935 date-letter.

Maker's mark: ·HS· in quatrefoil, for Harold Stabler; also STABLER GOLDSMITHS & SILVERSMITHS C°. L. 112, REGENT ST W.1.

Sir Walter Langdon-Brown (1870–1946), of Bedford, learned physician and *raconteur,* had been a Scholar of St John's College. After a long professional life at St Bartholomew's Hospital he came to this College as Fellow in 1932 on becoming Regius Professor of Physic. This piece probably commemorates his knighting. Donor also of a chandelier and a lead in the Master's Lodge.

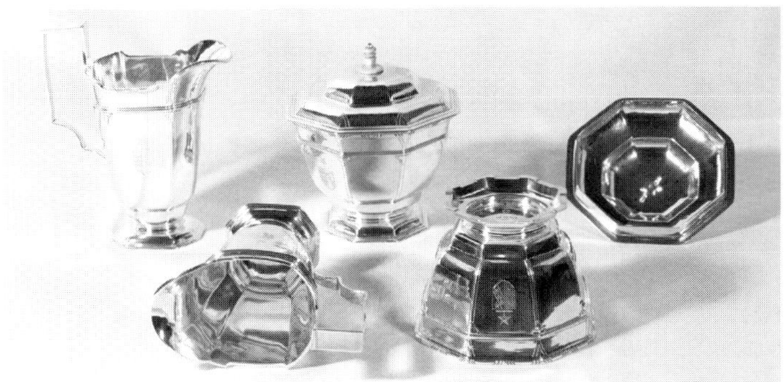

George Burgess Coffee-Pot *see* Modernistic Plate, p. 270.

Alexander Page Coffee- and Tea-Set

Given to Leckhampton in 1983 in memory of Alexander Page (1961–82), prospective member of the College, son of Raymond Ian Page, Fellow and Librarian, Elrington & Bosworth Professor of Anglo-Saxon (1984–91).

Although only two pieces were made for each other, the five items form a harmonious group in the same branch of 20th-century style.

11.19 Page Bowl and Lid

1908 (London n). Britannia silver. Bowl 4.0 in. × 2.8 high; lid 4.5 × 1.1 in.

Deep bowl with moulded foot and rim. Lid low, convex, with knob which acts as foot if the lid is inverted and used as a separate vessel, as in the picture; moulded rim and edge of foot; two ribs near margin;

Inscription: *A.H.T.P. 1982.*

Makers: Goldsmiths' & Silversmiths' Company Ltd (p. 180).

Graffiti: ~~96/3~~ 9070 11096

11.20 Page Jug

1913 (London s). 4.1 × 2.8 × 4.5 in. high.

Short acute spout, scroll handle with rudimentary thumbpiece. Large beads at base of spout; V-shaped foliation high on spout.

Inscription: *A.H.T.P. 1982*

Makers: Charles Stuart Harris & Sons, active 1897–1933.

11.21 Page Coffee-Pot

1928 (London n). 7.2 × 4.8 × 11.4 in. high.

Neo-baroque. Ovoid body, large waisted foot; short bridge-spout with acute end; handle of very dense wood ?painted red, scrolled and cusped with thumbpiece, pinned into two sockets; high domed lid, ending in acorn-knob, hinged from upper handle-socket.

Base moulded with heavy *repoussé* gadroons. Lower handle-socket attached sideways, with scroll on tail. Upper handle-socket with foliated attachment. Spout with three ribs each side, ribbed bottom finial. Gadrooned flange to lid. Acorn with four vertical beaded bands, arising from foliated cup.

Inscription: *ALEXANDER 1982 PAGE*

Makers: Goldsmiths' & Silversmiths' Company Ltd.

11.22 Page Teapot

1929 (London o). 8.5 in. × 4.8 × 11.4 high.

Sister to the Coffee-Pot, and repeats most of its decoration. Ovoid body, large waisted foot; spout arising from halfway up body; handle of greenish box-like wood, scrolled and cusped with thumbpiece, pinned into two sockets; high domed lid, ending in acorn-knob, hinged from upper handle-socket.

Spout has foliated and scrolled base and bifurcated end.

Inscription: *ALEXANDER 1982 PAGE*

Makers: Goldsmiths' & Silvermiths' Company Ltd.

11.23 Page Tray (not shown)

Undated. 24.4 × 14.3 × 1.65 in. high. Plated.

Elliptical; four squab feet; vertical parapet round sides pierced in rectangles to form a plain balustrade; integral loop handles. Floor delicately engraved with a broad band of foliated petals: two spirals alternating with eight curvilinear lozenges of vegetable-abstract patterns; interlace pattern inside.

Inscription: *In memory of 1982 Alexander Page.*

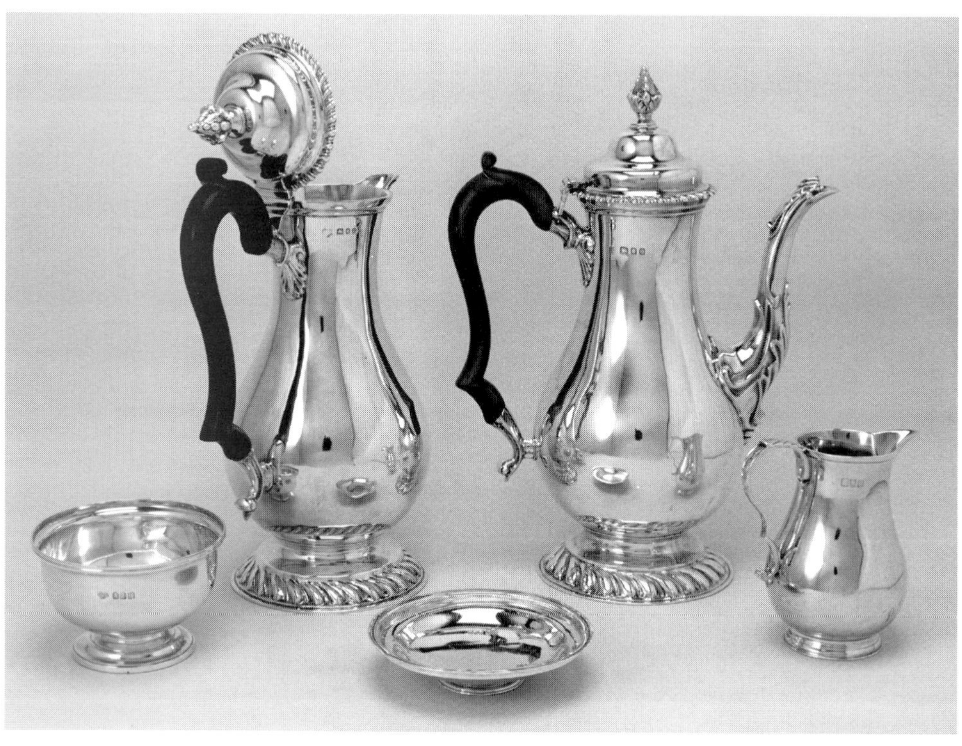

12

Candlesticks

Remember therefore from whence thou art fallen, and repent . . . or else I will come to thee quickly, and remove thy candlestick out of his place . . .

Revelation **2** 5

(The Greek word λυχνία, however, probably meant a stand for holding one of the Roman oil-lamps whose sherds still strew the landscape in Greek islands)

These are the treasures that bishop Æthelwold presented to the minster that is called Medehamstede, for the love of God and saint Peter [and] his soul's redemption: that is, then, one book of Christ beset with silver, and 3 crucifixes also beset with silver; 2 silver candlesticks and 2 silver-gilt (*.11. syluere candelsticcan and .11. ouergylde*). . .

Charter of Peterborough, c.*970*

(*Codex Diplomaticus* **5.** 101)

Cambridge lies in latitude 51° North, so that the day shrinks in midwinter to less than eight hours. Although the day's timetable was at least two hours earlier in the middle ages than it is now, artificial light was essential to scholarship and conviviality. Lighting fuel was beef or mutton fat, or beeswax for the rich and for church use. A humble form of light was the rushlight, a rush dipped in melted fat; if the flame inadvertently touched a beam it made the elliptical charred mark familiar on medieval timbers.

Candles, apparently of late Roman origin, were at first ecclesiastical. Secular ones were expensive and were more for communal use. Metal candlesticks are mentioned from late Anglo-Saxon times onwards. The College inventory of 1510 includes 'A candell styll of wyte plate', meaning ungilded silver. Audit Books from 1590 to 1685 show that Corpus was often buying or repairing iron, brass, or pewter candlesticks for the chapel, hall, etc. The 1678–9 audit mentions 'a nozzell for a candelstick in ye Chappell', which at 4*s*. must have been of silver.

Early silver candlesticks do not survive (because of a secondary use as weapons?). The earliest in a Cambridge college are the Pembroke pair of 1664, made for the chapel, with prickets or spikes whereon to impale candles. Clare College has a pair of secular candlesticks, with sockets, dated 1686; from 1710 onwards they become common.

Table candlesticks were among the commonest articles of plate in the 18th century. They usually come in pairs and are cast. The sockets ('nozzles') are often detachable. Many are Fellow-Commoners' gifts; the bases afford small surfaces on which to engrave tiny coats-of-arms and inscriptions. Nozzles are seldom inscribed or fully marked, and there can be doubt as to which candlesticks they belong to.

Baroque Candlesticks (1705–1737)

12.1 Two Jennings Candlesticks

1705 (London 𝕶). Britannia silver. 4.3 in. × 6.55 high.

Square base with cut corners and depressed top. Cartouches for arms with elaborate foliage, surmounted by a shell. College arms and donor's: *Argent* [?] *a chevron sable* [error for *gules*] *between three plummets* [which look like hexagonal lanterns].

Nozzles unmarked, but a good fit; square with concave corners, ribbed collar; both have had the tapered part renewed.

Inscription: *Dedit Georgius Jennings Armiger 1738.* (George Jennings, armiger, gave [me]).

Maker's mark, 𝕷𝖓 in shield, of the rare candlestick-maker William Lukin, from Oxfordshire, active 1699–1755.

Given by George Jennings of London (?–1790); admitted 1737; no known degree; MP successively for Whitchurch, St German's, Thetford; Comptroller-General of the Army. In presenting this second-hand pair he gave us our oldest candlesticks. Note the difference of style between the candlesticks and the engraving.

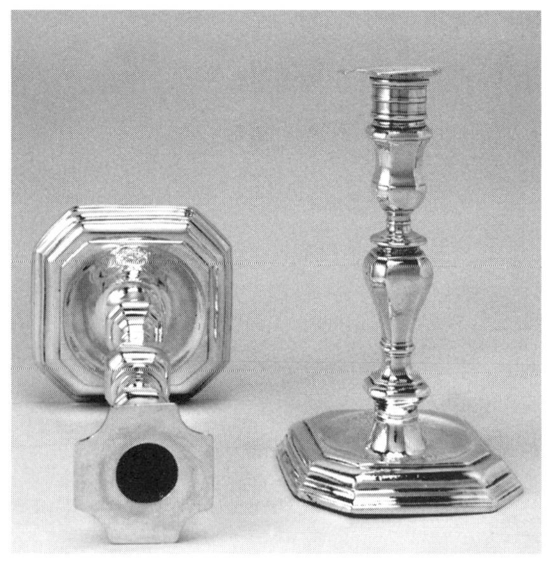

12.2 Two Rigby Candlesticks

1717 (London B). Britannia silver. 4.1 in. × 6.8 high.

Base square with concave corners and slightly depressed top, octagonal stem. Integral nozzles. College arms and those of the Rigbys of Lancashire: *Bendy of six argent & azure; on a chief sable three cinquefoils.*

Inscription: *Ex Dono Ricardi Rigby Armigeri* (From the gift of Richard Rigby, armiger.) Graffiti: *Cleaned by Herman Austin 50 Years* [on one] *H Austin 50 Years 1928* [on the other].

Made by Paul de Lamerie, greatest of silversmiths (1688–1751). A Dutchman from 's Hertogenbosch, he began work in London in 1705. He made also the Heathcote Coffee-Pot (§11.2). This piece bears his earliest maker's mark, LA under a crown and mullet, over a fleur-de-lys, registered in 1712.

This noble example of baroque design was given by Richard Rigby (1723–88) of Mistley (Essex), Fellow Commoner in 1738, 'defective in education', and a fine judge of candlesticks. He was a rake and politician, fond of women, 'drank fair', blushed purple (*lumen purpureum*), duellist and orgiast; MP for the rotten boroughs of Castle Rising, Sudbury (a constituency later famous as Dickens's 'Eatanswill'), and Tavistock; Lord of Trade; henchman of the Duke of Bedford, whom he saved from lynching at Lichfield races (1752); Master of the Rolls and Vice-Treasurer for Ireland; 'brazen boatswain of the Bloomsbury crew'; opponent of Wilkes and the Bribery Act; Paymaster of the Forces 1768–82, and famous for jovial office parties at the Pay Office; never married; d. of gout, leaving 'near half a million of public money' – which then was a lot of money – to his children. (*Dictionary of National Biography.*)

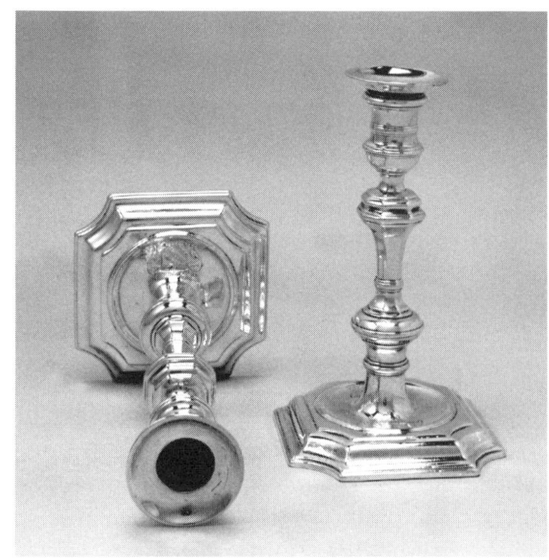

12.3 Two Thornbury Candlesticks

1718 (London C). Britannia silver. 4.25 in. × 7.5 high.

Hexagonal, base tapering into stem. College arms. *Lion-rampant* crest of the Thornburys of Kent. Nozzles unmarked (save for leopard's face on one), but a good fit; hexagonal, squat ribbed collar.

Inscribed: *The Gift of M^r. Thos. Thornbury*

Maker: M·C in rectangle, for Matthew Cooper I, from Newport Pagnell, London candlestick-maker from 1702.

Given by Thomas Thornbury of London, admitted 1717, otherwise unknown.

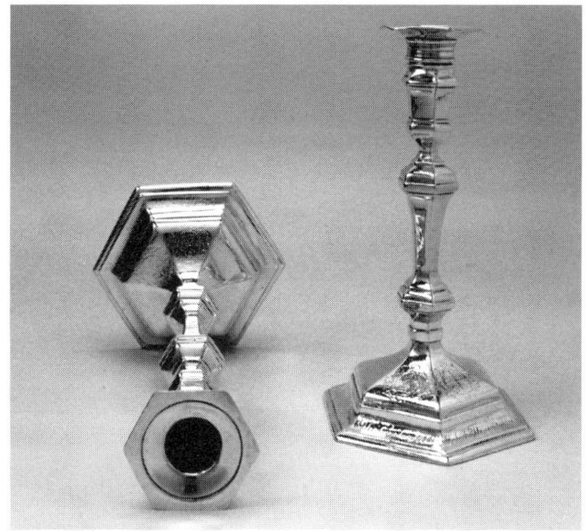

12.4 Two Hoste Candlesticks

1724 (London I). 4.15 in. × 7.9 high.

Hexagonal, base with depressed top. Much-worn College arms and donor's: *Azure a bull's head affronté couped at the neck, between two wings.* Nozzles unmarked (save for leopard's face on one), but a good fit; hexagonal, tall ribbed collar.

Inscribed: *Ex Dono Jacobi Hoste Norfolciensis Armigeri 1725* (From the gift of James Hoste of Norfolk, armiger) *Coll: Corp: Christi Cantab.*

No maker's mark.

James Hoste, squire of Sandringham (Norfolk), was admitted 1722. He presented Samuel Kerrich (donor of the following candlesticks) to the Vicarage of the next parish of Dersingham.

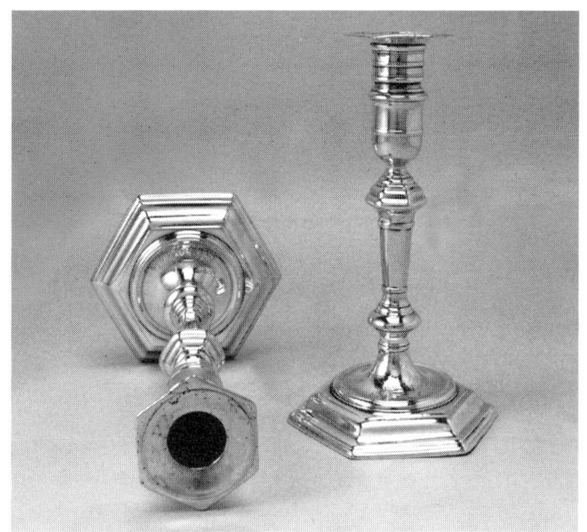

12.5 Two Kerrich Mini-Candlesticks

1729 (London O). 2.6 in. × 4.3 high.

Square with concave corners; base with slightly depressed top. Nozzles unmarked, square with concave corners, moulded rim.

Inscribed: ***COLL: CORP: CHRISTI: CANTAB: D. D. SAMUEL KERRICH A.M. EIUSDEM SOCIUS 1729*** (Given to Corpus Christi College, Cambridge by S. Kerrich, MA, Fellow of the same, 1729).

Monogram, IG in vertical ellipse, one of the many maker's marks of James Gould from Somerset; one of two brothers, prolific London candlestick-makers; active 1722–46.

Samuel Kerrich (?–1784) of Norfolk, was admitted Sizar 1714; Fellow 1719–29; Vicar of Dersingham, Norfolk 1729; DD 1735. He preached a University sermon on the suppression of the 1745 rebellion; his epitaph on Sarah Newton, his betrothed, can be read in St Bene't's

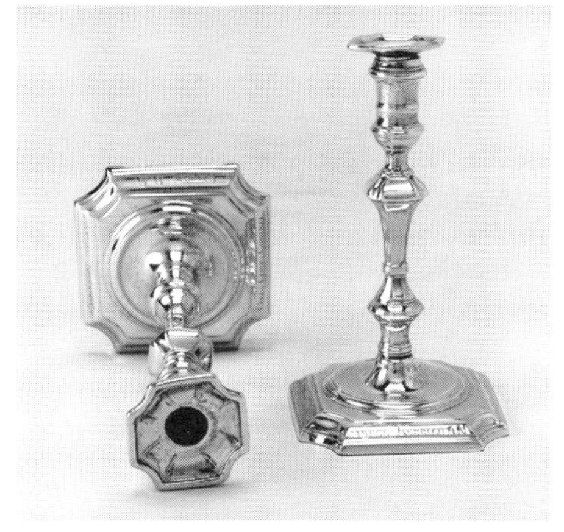

churchyard. Even a Sizar could give plate, although they seldom did.

12.6 Two Rychardson Candlesticks

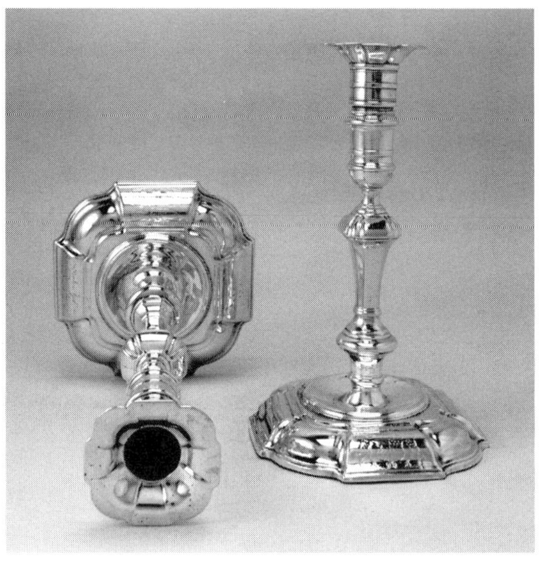

1733 (London S). 5.25 in. × 7.25 high.

Square base with convex corners and depressed top. Foliated cartouches containing College arms and donor's: *Quarterly, 1 & 4: or, on a chief sable three lions' heads erased; 2 & 3: ermine a canton charged with a St Andrew's cross; the whole surmounted with a Baron's coronet.* Supporters: *two steeds ermine.*

Maker's mark mis-struck, variously read as Thomas Parr, active 1733–63, or John Penfold, or TC.

Nozzles square with convex corners, eight flutes, tall ribbed collar. Marked with leopard passant and fragmentary maker's mark of ?John Cafe (see §17.10), but too big to fit any other candlestick.

Inscribed: *D.D. Præhon. Gul: Don: Rychardson Baro de Cramond in Regno Scotia* (Gift of the Right Honorable Will. Don. Richardson, Baron Cramond in the Realm of Scotland).

Given by the hapless William Donald Richardson (1715–35) of Norfolk; admitted to the College as nobleman 1731; last Baron Cramond; left us, fell into a consumption, and died at the age of 20.

12.7 Two Powlett Candlesticks

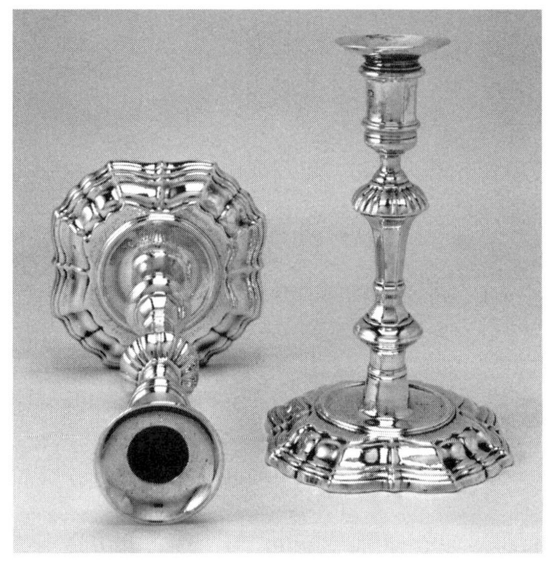

1737 (London b). 4.3 in. diagonal × 6.8 high.

Square base with cut corners and depressed top. Integral nozzle. Scrolled cartouches for College arms and donor's: *Azure* [should be *sable*] *three swords in pile argent, points in base.*

Inscribed *Ex Dono Honorabilis Caroli Powlett Socii Commensalis Collegii Corporis Christij.* (Gift of the Honourable C. Powlett, Fellow Commoner of Corpus Christi College.)

Monogram IG in square, another maker's mark of James Gould, see §12.5.

Charles Powlett (*c.*1718–1765) of Middlesex, Whig and soldier, was admitted Fellow Commoner 1735; he achieved an MA in 1737. He was MP for Lymington and then Hampshire; Lieutenant-Colonel 1745; Knight of the Bath 1753; Lieutenant of the Tower 1754–60; Lord-Lieutenant of Hampshire 1758–63; succeeded as 5th Duke of Bolton in 1759; bore the Queen's crown at the Coronation in 1761; shot himself.

Rococo Candlesticks (1742–1777)

12.8 Two Tufnell Candlesticks

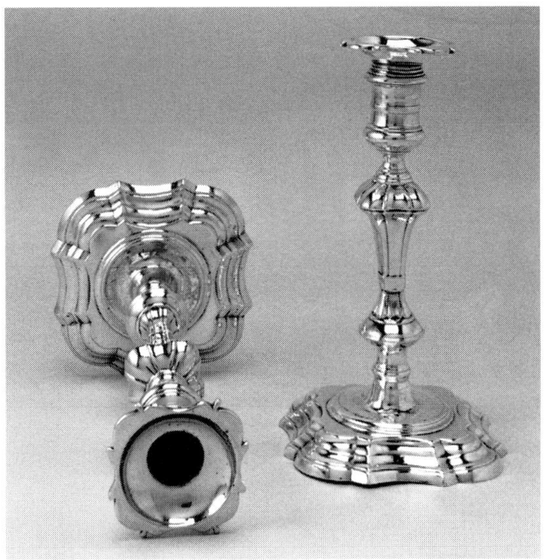

1742; nozzles 1841 (London g, 𝔉). 4.95 in. diagonal × 7.2–7.3 high.

Square base with concave sides, rounded corners, depressed top. Asymmetric shields, surrounded by grasses and herbs, for College arms and donor's: *On a fess between three ostrich feathers as many martlets.* Nozzles circular, moulded rim, fully marked.

Inscribed: *Donum Johannis Jolliffe Tufnell Armigeri Collegii Corporis Christi Commensalis Anno Domini : 1740 :* (Gift of John Jolliffe Tufnell, armiger, [Fellow-] Commoner of Corpus College).

Maker's mark, 𝔚 𝔊 in rectangle, for William Gould from Somerset, brother of James Gould who made §12.5 and §12.7: London candlestick-maker, active 1722–1763; made the famous chandelier of the Fishmongers' Company, but attributed it to another silversmith, and got into trouble for putting too much copper into the silver. Nozzles (replacing original ones) marked CTF GF in shield, for Charles Thomas Fox & George Fox, firm active 1841–1921.

Given by John Jolliffe Tufnell of London, admitted 1738; lawyer; MP for Beverley; founder of the Tufnell family of Langleys, Essex. The College audit records 8*d*. paid for transporting them.

One of the pair has had the middle of the base sawn out and replaced, leaving the base less depressed than the original; inscription undisturbed; arms (on the missing part) renewed.

The engraving of these candlesticks is more strongly rococo than the shape.

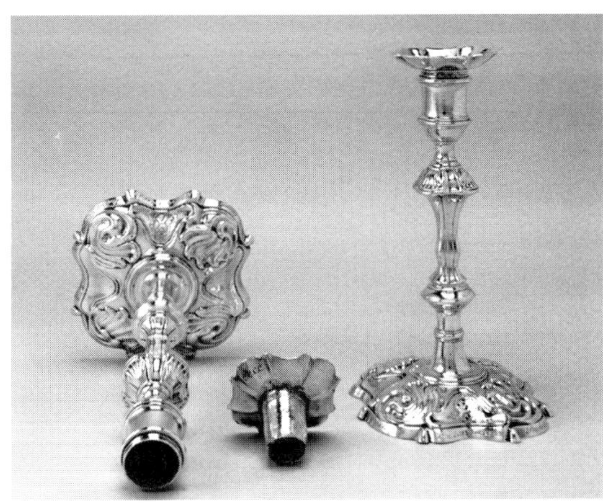

12.9 Two Yorke Candlesticks

1743 (London h). 4.8 in. diagonal × 7.35 high.

Shape fully rococo: square with concave sides and convex corners, base with convex profile. Scrolled shells in corners; stem partly fluted; shelly ornaments to knops. College arms and donor's: *Argent on a saltire azure a bezant.*

Inscription: *Donum Hon. JOAN. YORKE, A.M. Baron: de Hardwick Filii natu quarto: <1749* (Gift of the Hon. John Yorke, M.A., fourth-born son of Baron Hardwick, 1749) Weight: *37 = 16* p^r. [on both, evidently including nozzles] Graffito: p^r 37 = 7. [Present weight 36: 4 ounces including nozzles.]

Nozzles square with concave sides and rounded, cusped, corners; no marks. Inscribed **C.C.C.C.** Bottom of both badly battered.

Marked for William Gould, like the preceding pair.

Given by John Yorke (*c*.1728–1801) of London, second of the four Yorke brothers of Wimpole and Corpus; educated simultaneously at Corpus and Lincoln's Inn 1746–; MA 1749; called to the Bar 1754; MP.

12.10 Two Humfrey Candlesticks

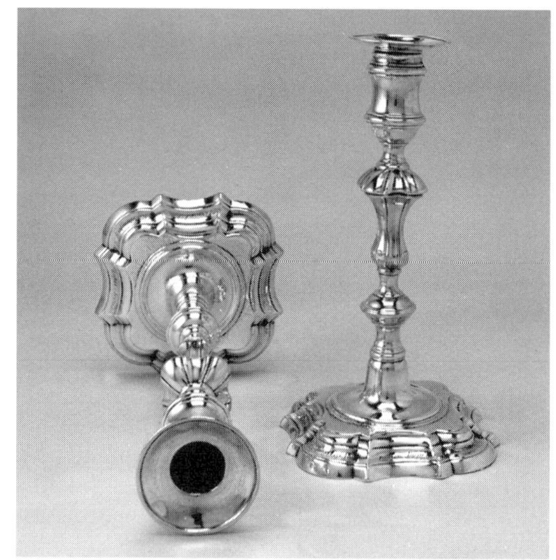

1749 (London o). 4.8 in. diagonal × 7.7 high.

Square with concave sides and rounded corners, base with depressed top, fluted stem. Foliated cartouches with College arms and donor's: *a lion rampant ducally crowned.*

Inscribed: *Dono dedit Ric: Humfrey M.A. nuper Socius* (Richard Humfrey MA, lately Fellow, gave the gift). Weight inscriptions *16:6* [present weight 16: 17 ounces including nozzle] *16.16* [present weight 17: 3 ounces], Graffito: *Cleaned by Herman Austin 50 Years* [on both].

Maker's mark, J:C under a 'flower', in a trefoil, for John Cafe, of the Cafe brothers from Somerset, prolific London candlestick-maker, active from *c.*1740, died 1757.

Nozzles unmarked. One inscribed *C: C: C: C N°1.*The other has a longer stem and no inscription, but the graffito *Cleaned by Herman Austin⁵⁰⁰ Years.* (The inventory records that the College bought 'a pair of Noscles for Candlesticks' between 1747 and 1750.)

Given by Richard Humfrey the elder (1722–1813) of Norwich; admitted 1739; Fellow 1745–9; MA 1746; Rector of Thorpe-next-Norwich (once the writer's home parish) for his last sixty years.

> The long life of this revered and excellent man was devoted to the active and zealous discharge of his pastoral duties, till rendered incapable by the afflictions of extreme age. Piety and Benevolence strongly marked his character.
>
> *Lamb p. 397*

12.11 Two Johnes Candlesticks

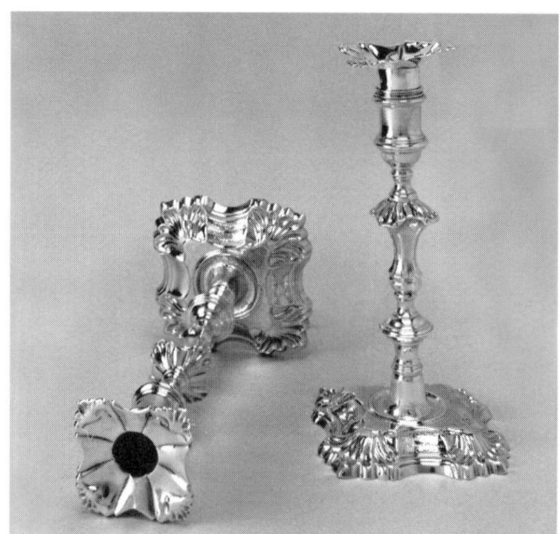

1750 (London p). 5.1 in. diagonal × 7.5 high.

Square base with concave sides, shell-moulded corners (not visible on underside), small depressed top. Knop on stem with shelly moulding. Engraved rococo cartouches, surrounded by plants, for College arms and donor's: *?Argent a chevron azure between three ravens sable.*

Inscription: *Thomas Johnes ex Agro Cereticano Arm. nuper Socio Com'ensali hujus Coll. D.D.* (Thomas Johnes of Cardiganshire [Welsh *Ceredigion*], armiger, lately Fellow Commoner of this College, gave the gift). Weight: *No 1 27:2 No 2 27:2* [present weight of the two is 25:17, including nozzles].

Mark: I·P in rococo cartouche, for John Preist [*sic*], London candlestick-maker.

Nozzles unmarked. Square, concave sides, convex corners, 8 flutes. Inscribed (in a different hand from that on candlesticks): *C.C.C.C. 1:13* or *1:11.*

Given by Thomas Johnes of Cardigan, admitted 1737, whom (like so many Fellow-Commoners) we remember only as a giver of plate, probably long after he had left the College. He was probably the father of Thomas Johnes (1748–1816), the famous landscaper of Hafod.

The College in 1751 paid 1*s*. for 'Cariage of Mr Johne's Candlesticks'.

12.12 Two De Lancey Candlesticks

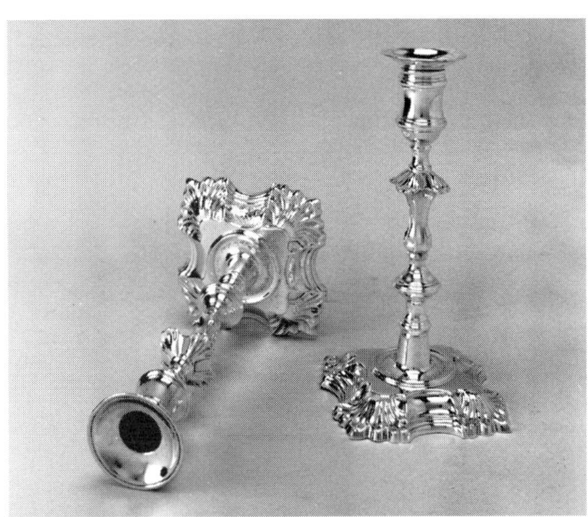

1752 (London r). 5.4 in. diagonal × 7.75 in. high.

Square with concave sides and shell-moulded corners (visible also on underside), base with small depressed top. Elaborately foliated symmetrical cartouche to College arms – the engraving cost 7*s*. in 1754 (Audit Book).

Inscription: *Ex dono Jacobi Delancey C.C.C.C. Socii Commensalis.* (Gift of J. DeLancey, Fellow Commoner of C.C.C.C.) Weight:*17 : 3 | 17* [present weight including nozzles is 33: 0 oz].

Nozzles unmarked, but in similar style and a good fit. Square, concave sides, pointed foliage at corners, 8 flutes. Inscribed *C.C.C.C.*

Marked for John Cafe, see §12.10.

Given by James De Lancey (1732–1800), admitted 1750, son of the Lieutenant-Governor of New York who had given the De Lancey Salver (p. 170). He became a wealthy American; after serving in the Seven Years' War, he imported racehorses and became 'Father of the New York Turf'. As a politician he backed a loser, and was reluctant to support the American revolutionaries; his nephew fought for the Crown in the War of Independence, becoming the Outlaw of the Bronx. De Lancey returned to England, lost his property in America, and died in Bath.

12.13 Two Miller Candlesticks

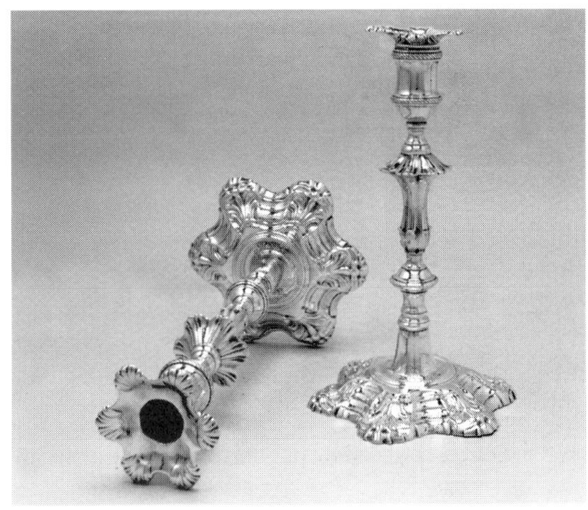

1755 (London u). 5.2 in. diagonal × 8.5 high.

Hexagonal flat-topped base with six sinuous lobes. Four bands of rope-moulding. Small foliated cartouches containing College arms and donor's: *Argent a fesse wavy ?azure between three [wolves'] heads erased.*

Inscribed: DONUM THO: *MILLER Arm*: 1756\C. C. C. C. Graffito: *H* on one base.

Nozzles unmarked; hexagonal, concave sides, shell corners, inscribed CCCC on top.

Marked for John Cafe, see §12.10. A classic 1750s rococo design.

Given by Thomas Miller of Sussex, admitted 1753. The College spent 1*s*. on transporting his gift.

12.14 Two Anonymous Candlesticks

1756 (London 𝔄). 5.3 in. diagonal × 8.5 high.

Identical to the above, but without donor's name or arms.

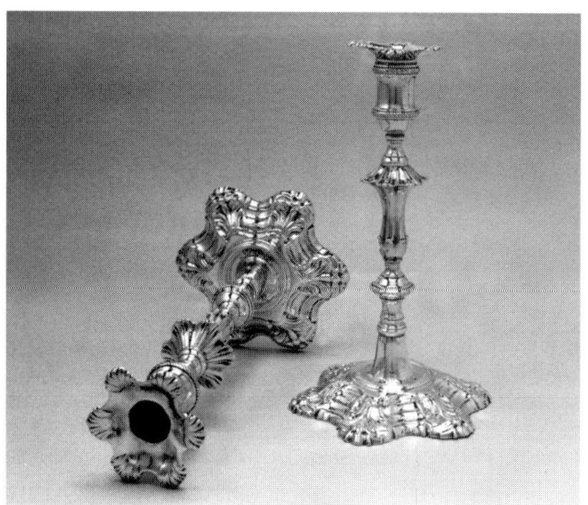

The anonymous inventory entry follows that for the Miller candlesticks. Probably recycled from some earlier piece whose donor had been forgotten.

12.15 Two Barrett Candlesticks

1759 (London 𝕯). 5.45 in. diagonal × 9.25 high.

Six-lobed base tapering into stem. Stylized apples at corners. Small foliated cartouches for College arms and donor's: *Quarterly, 1 & 4: on a chevron between three mullets as many [lions passant guardant]; 2 & 3: gules three harts.*

Inscription: *Bo*[t]. [bought] *with M*[r] *Barrett's Plate C. C. C. C.* Weight: 41.1 on both [present total weight including nozzles is 39: 13 ounces]. Graffito: *F* on one base.

Nozzles: hexagonal, concave sides, shells at corners. Inscribed *CCCC* on tube. Maker's mark as on candlesticks.

Maker's mark, 𝔚:ℭ under a small flower in a trefoil, indicates William Cafe, brother of John Cafe above, prolific candlestick-maker, active from 1747, bankrupt 1772, died 1802.

Donor: Thomas Barrett of Kent, admitted 1716, otherwise unknown. The inventory records that the College exchanged his punch-bowl for this fifteenth pair of silver candlesticks.

12.16 Two Houblon Candlesticks

1759 (London 𝕯). 5.45 in. diagonal × 9.2 high.

Identical to Barrett Candlesticks, save for donor's arms: *A ridged field, three hop-stems issuant therefrom, ascendant as many poles* (a pun on the name Houblon and French *houblon*, 'hop', i.e. *Humulus lupulus*). Same nozzles and maker.

Inscribed: *Bo*[t]. [Bought] *with M*[r] *Houblon's Plate C. C. C. C.* Weight: 41.17 on both [present total weight including nozzles is 40: 5 ounces] Graffiti: *F* on one, ?*G* on the other base.

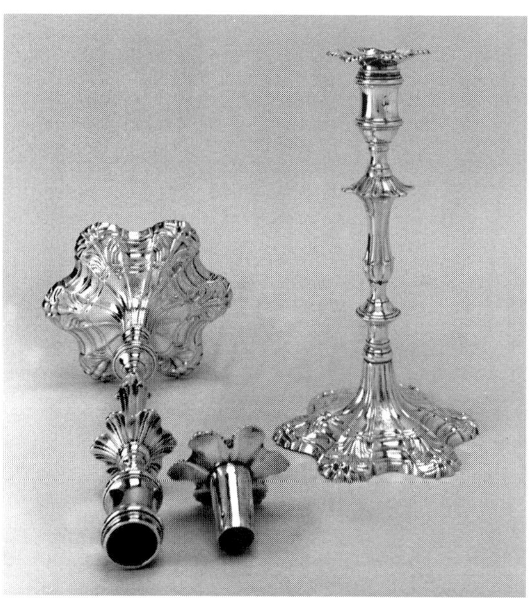

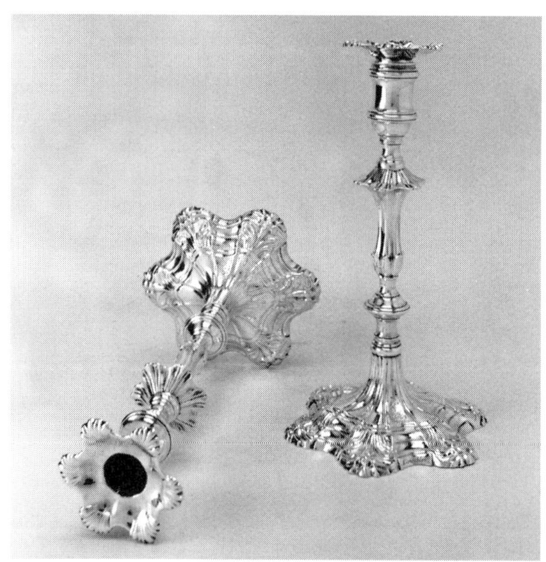

Jacob Houblon II (pronounced Hubblan) of London was admitted 1683, MA 1691; son of the first Governor of the Bank of England; descendant of the Houblons of Lille; ancestor of the Houblons who preserved Hatfield Forest, Essex. He gave a 'branch' – presumably an earlier sort of candlestick – which the College recycled into its sixteenth pair of silver candlesticks.

For more about the family see: O. Rackham (1989) *The Last Forest: the story of Hatfield Forest* Dent, London.

12.17 Two Wodehouse–Calvert–Cust Candlesticks

1759 (London 𝕯). 5.5 in. diagonal × 8.8 high.

Very like previous four. Elaborate ribs, moulding, stylized foliage at corners (these repeated on knop). Small foliated cartouche for College arms. Made by William Cafe, as above.

Inscription: *Mr. Wodehous. Mr. Calvert. Mr. Cust.* Weight: 38 : 4 [present total weight is 36: 4, including nozzles].

Nozzles: related to these candlesticks by the particular version of the maker's mark, and a good fit. Hexagonal, concave sides, shells at corners. Marked with leopard + maker's mark.

Philip Wodehouse of Kimberley (Norfolk), admitted 1686, gave a quart tankard. Felix Calvert of Hertfordshire, admitted 1708, gave candlesticks, snuffers, and a snuff-dish. Saville Cust of Lincs, admitted 1717, gave a salver. The College melted these gifts into its seventeenth pair of candlesticks and sold the surplus metal.

12.18 Two Malden Candlesticks

1777 (London b). 5.7 in. diagonal × 9.4 high.

Square base tapering into stem. Cast with scrolled shells at corners (visible underneath); foliated knop; four rows of beading. Shields between monocotyledonous plants for College arms and donor's: *Gules a lion rampant between two* [should be three] *crosses crosslet fitchy.*

Inscription: *Ex dono Nobilis Vicecomitis de Malden Praenobilis Comitis Essexiae Filii natu maximi C.C.C.C. 1777.* (Gift of the Noble Viscount Malden, eldest-born son of the Most Noble Earl of Essex, to C.C.C.C. 1777.)

Maker's mark, RI IS in square, for partners Robert Jones I (active *c*.1774–*c*.1780) & John Scofield (active 1776–*c*.1800), known for 'elegant design ... impeccable craftsmanship' (Grimwade 1990).

Nozzles uninscribed; square with convex sides and rounded corners with inward-turned shells. Leopard and maker's mark same as candlestick.

Given by George Capell, admitted 1752; MA 1777; became 25th Earl of Essex 1799.

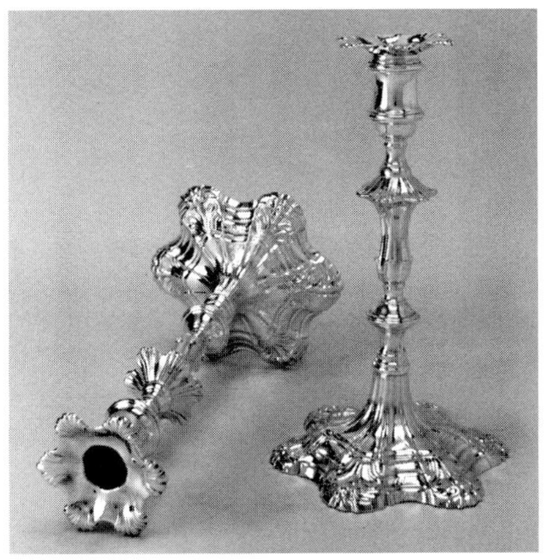

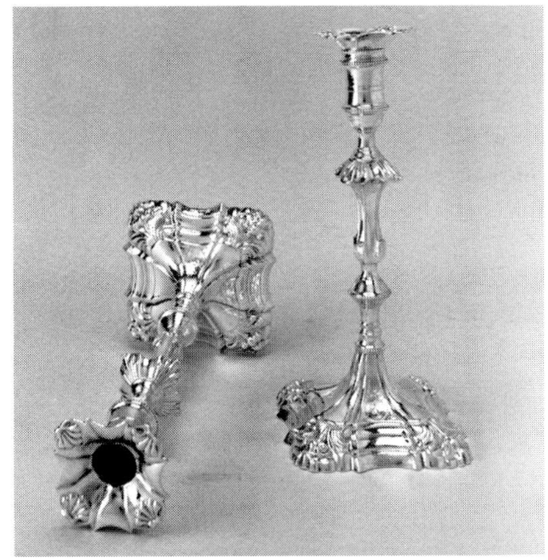

Adamesque Candlesticks (1785–1794)

12.19 Two Stannard Candlesticks

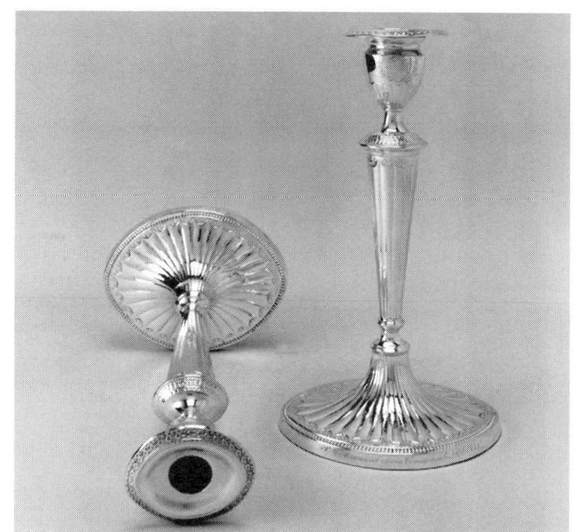

1785 (Sheffield y). 6.05 in. × 4.8 × 10.5 high.

Almond section throughout. Base with wooden infill. Urn-shaped top containing nozzle. Three zones of shallow flutes; beading and garlands of beads round edge of base; beading, billets, and string-of-beads on top of stem. 2 myrtle-branches round College coat-of-arms.

Inscription: *PH Stannard Socio Commensalis D.D. C.C.C.C.* \ *g* inside each socket

Maker's mark, I P & C° in rectangle, for John Parsons & Co., active 1783–.

Nozzles uninscribed, but same style and a good fit. Almond-shaped top, *repoussé* with billets and string-of-beads. One bears maker's mark.

Given by Philip Hob. Stannard, of a celebrated Norwich family; admitted 1780; BA 1786.

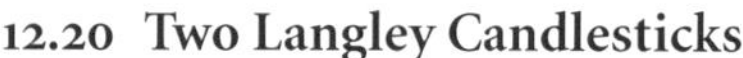

12.20 Two Langley Candlesticks

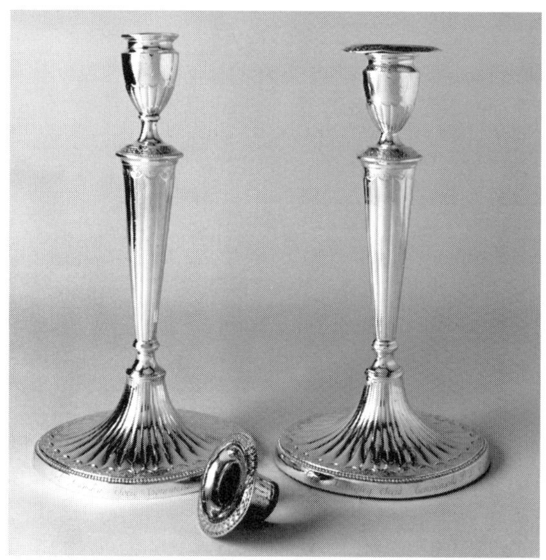

1785 (Sheffield y). 6.2 in. ×4.9 × 11.8 high.

Identical to the above, but a little bigger, and with College arms and donor's crest: *a griffin statant.* Both nozzles marked. Same maker. Wooden infill of one partly missing, revealing inside of *repoussé* fluting.

> This is not the medieval griffin (pp. 92f.), but a fowl with bird-of-prey's head and legs, bird's wings, dragon's tail.

Inscriptions: *Gul: Langley Socid* [*sic*] *Commensalis D.D. C.C.C.C.* \ *o* inside each socket.

Given probably by William Langley of Norfolk; admitted 1782; BA 1786. (Another William Langley of Norfolk was admitted 1780.)

12.21 Nelson–Oakes Mini-Candlestick and Box

1791 (London q).

Candlestick: 4.0 in. diameter × 2.8 high. A sconce, made to be carried around, with a saucer-shaped base to catch drips. Plain base with ribbed margin; moulded stem; vase-shaped socket; ribbed handle having oval thumbpiece with ribbed edge. Plain nozzle with ribbed edge.

Inscription on saucer: *Presented by VICE ADMIRAL HORATIO VISCOUNT NELSON, K.B. Duke of Bronti* [*sic*] *TO JULIA OAKES. 1804.*

Maker: HC in ellipse, for Henry Chawner 1764–1851; first entered 1786; from well-known family of silversmiths; became squire of Newton Valence, Hants.

Extinguisher: conical, ending in knob, ribbed margin, having hook to engage in square hole in thumbpiece. Formerly connected by a chain (one link remains) to a ring in the edge of the socket.

Box: 5.9 × 6.15 × 5.25 in. Oak, in the likeness of a ship's brass-bound chronometer box. Dovetail-jointed sides;

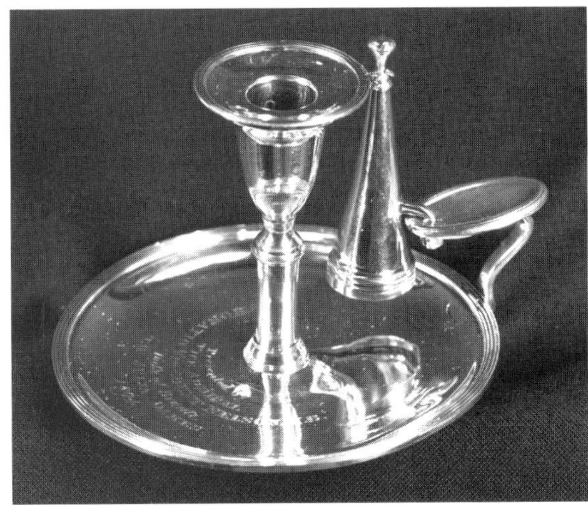

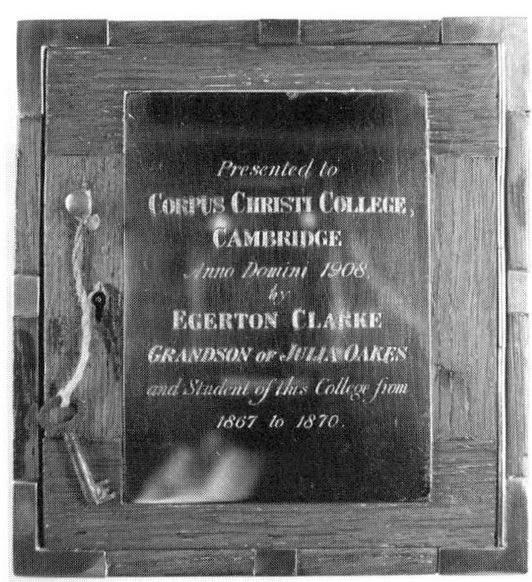

door of one plank recessed between the sides; base nailed on. Door has silver knob and silver plate, and mortice-lock with silver lock-plate and silver end to bolt. Silver bindings to corners and mid-sides, which are glued on. Four of the 18 silver bindings have dropped off and been replaced in wood. Replacements are cunningly made to hide the existence of the missing silver parts; where appropriate they have counterfeit dovetails and carpenter's setting-out lines. Inside lined with velvet, with velvet pad to receive bottom of candlestick. No marks.

Inscription on silver plate on door: *Presented to CORPUS CHRISTI COLLEGE CAMBRIDGE Anno Domini 1908, by EGERTON CLARKE GRANDSON OF JULIA OAKES and Student of this College from 1867 to 1870.*

Julia Oakes, born *c*.1791, was the daughter of Horatio Nelson's colleague Captain George Oakes. He was not a successful captain, but Nelson thought highly of him, and wrote in extenuation when he was court-martialled in 1794. Oakes then commanded the *Seahorse*, later to be Nelson's flagship at the attack on Santa Cruz in the Canary Islands in 1797. Oakes apparently retired sick in 1794, and died in 1797. His daughter married a Clarke *c*.1816.

For this I am indebted to Mary Le Forestier of Toronto, great-great-granddaughter of Julia Oakes and granddaughter of Egerton Clarke's brother, who still has George Oakes's sword. See: M Le Forestier 'In search of Julia' *The Nelson Dispatch* **4** (1993) 226–8.

The gift is a mysterious one. Admiral Nelson was at sea with the Mediterranean Fleet for the whole of 1804, never set foot on land, and was hardly in a position to present candlesticks to ladies. Nor is there any obvious reason for such a gift to the 13-year-old daughter of a dead friend. I conjecture that the candlestick is a christening present, made in 1791 and given in that or the following year, and that the date 1804 was added in error long after.

12.22 Four Bateman Octagonal Candlesticks

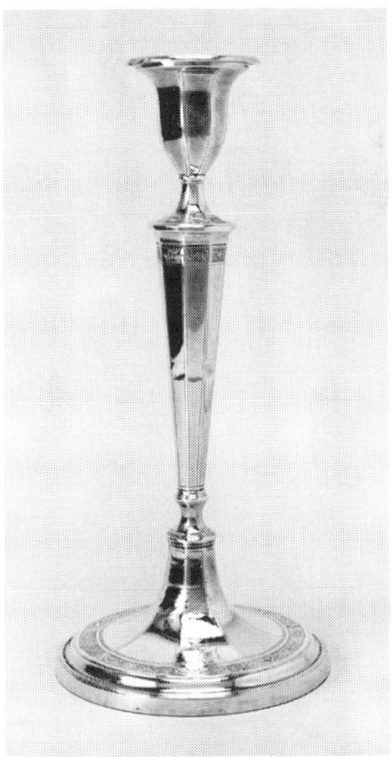

1793 (Sheffield **o**) and ?1794. 5.6 in. × 11.8 high.

Generally octagonal section on circular base. Ribbed band around foot. Three engraved bands of foliage and flowers; between these bands the sides are divided into panels by dotted lines. Base filled by a shaped disk of reddish wood.

Crest: *a hart.* Graffiti: [on one] 10/8 [on two] 11.

Three candlesticks are hallmarked with Sheffield o and King's head facing right for 1793; one has probably m for 1794 (the mark is dubious and the Sheffield cycle muddled).

Nozzles (only two): concave, rib-moulded edge. Fully marked except that one lacks the date-letter.

Maker: John Parsons & Co., like the Stannard candlesticks.

Aubrey Bateman's bequest.

Battered on the angles, as though by prolonged service as rolling-pins or weapons, erasing part of the decoration.

12.22a **Two Triple Tops** for the above

1793 (Sheffield o). 15.5 in. extreme width, 8.2 in. extreme height.

Campanulate sockets with reeded rims, fluted outside, each with 9 lanceolate, 1-veined leaves. The two outer sockets are on curved stems of octagonal section, each with 3 lanceolate, undulate leaves at its base. Beneath each outer socket is a drip tray with reeded margins, over 2 whorls of bracts, the outer whorl being reflexed. The sockets unscrew.

Inscription: *M* inside each socket. Maker illegible.

Nozzles: four, reeded margins, with the John Parsons & Co. mark.

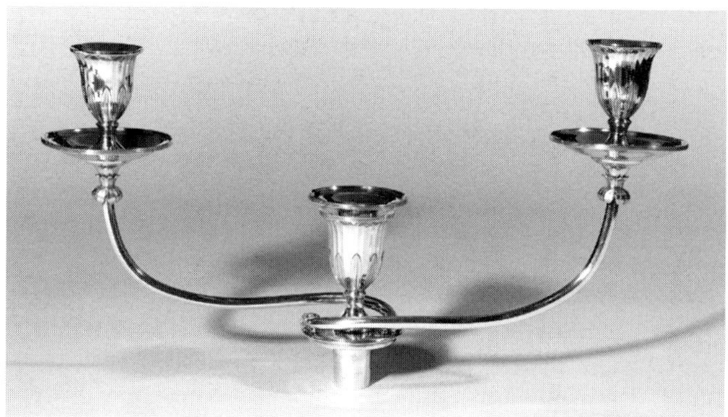

Regency Candlesticks (1797–1829)

12.23 Two Great Quadruple Serpent Candlesticks [Bateman-Martin]

1797 and 1798 (London B and C). Britannia silver and other metals. Base 6.9 × 13.2 in. high. Greatest span of top 14.5 in. Total height when assembled 23.0 in. Total weight 193 oz = 6.0 kg.

The convex base is ornamented with a band of alternate arrows and broad tonguelike leaves. It tapers into the stem through successive bands of opposite-leaved foliage, tonguelike leaves, beading, and undulate leaf-tongues. These motifs are repeated at the top of the stem. The surface is slightly pitted in the casting.

At the top the stem gives off three double-curved branches (not quite at 120° to each other). Non-venomous serpents with looped bodies act as brackets to support each branch; they are duly represented with dorsal scales, ventral scutes, and multiple teeth in their jaws. The stem and side-branches are adorned with undulate leaf-tongues. The terminal branch has rosettes and beading as well; its socket has convex petals and one row of beading.

The top as a whole is detachable from the stem; it ends in an iron rod passing through the hollow stem and secured underneath by a brass wingnut. The three sockets on the branches are detachable, each with an inner part, which screws into the end of the branch, and an outer part attached by a bayonet joint.

The detachable sockets have petaloid gadrooning and rows of beading. Marks as on base. They are not interchangeable, having scratched assembly-numbers *I II III* which correspond to numbers on the arms.

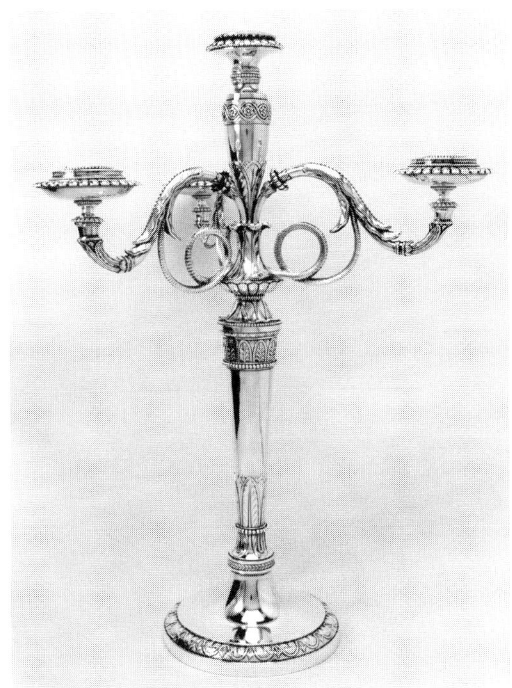

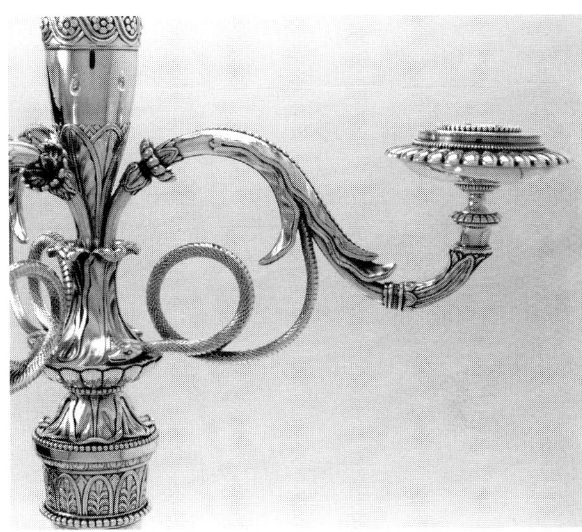

The 1797 candlestick is marked with Britannia and the London B for 1797. The maker's mark, *FM* in rectangle, may be for Francis Maguire, a very obscure London silversmith, who entered such a mark in 1798.

The 1798 candlestick is an accurate copy, identical in detail except that the base is not pitted. One half-socket is missing. Marked with Britannia and the London C for 1798. The maker's mark, PS in bifoil, is one of those used by the celebrated Paul Storr (1771–1844), of Soho (London), active 1793–1839. Was he in partnership with the little-known Maguire?

Serpents were a long-standing motif (for example on Henry VIII's ostrich cup, p. 92) which had been re-popularized by Paul de Lamerie.

These are our best examples of the grand and imposing Regency style. They were bequeathed by Aubrey Bateman 'in special memory' of his brother-in-law Eustace Meredyth Martin. Alas, when they were given Storr was unfashionable and the College forgot to honour the gift. Geoffrey Bushnell and the writer found them languishing in a cupboard, jet black from years of disuse. Their return to use brought incredulous gasps from some of our colleagues.

12.24 Two [Bateman] Triple Candlesticks

1822 (Sheffield Z). Bases 4.3 in. × 7.95 high. Triple tops 15.2 and 16.4 in. greatest width.

Silver bases with tropical hardwood infill, tapering into stem; plain moulded socket to receive triple top. Bands of ?*repoussé* foliage, shells, etc. around base, at junction of base and stem, and at top of stem. Inscribed *T* on socket.

Triple tops (said to be Sheffield-plate) are heavily cast to resemble stems, leaves and flowers of some climber

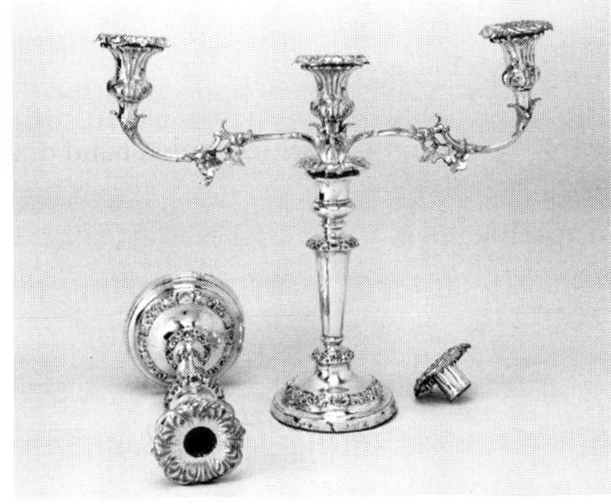

like morning-glory (*Ipomœa*); fluted sockets with foliage at their bases. No marks. Nozzles are thinly plated brass.

Six nozzles, very stylized foliage, unmarked.

Maker: I & TS in rectangle, for John & Thomas Settle of Sheffield, 1817–.

Bequeathed by Aubrey Bateman.

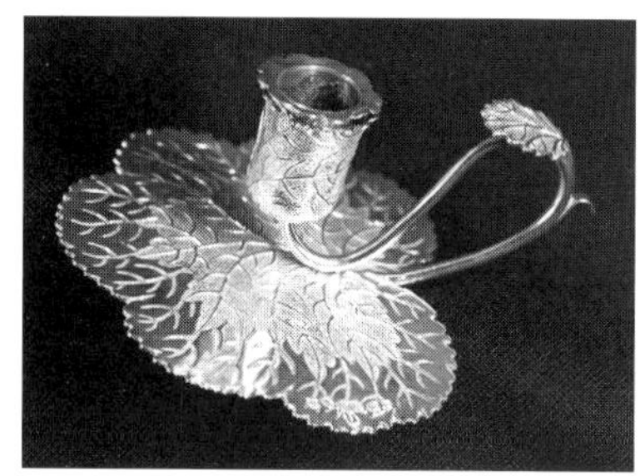

12.25 [Bateman] Micro-Candlestick

1829 (Birmingham 𝔣). 2.6 in. diameter × 1.2 high (depicted nearly actual size).

In the likeness of a shallowly 7-lobed, variegated leaf (e.g. geranium or *Alchemilla*), whose curved stalk forms the handle. Palmate veins delicately rendered. In middle of leaf is a cylindrical socket (veined like a leaf) and a tiny nozzle in a crenate surround. The leaf-stalk bears an ovate, veined stipule.

Maker: JW in ellipse, for Joseph Willimore, active 1818–29.

This dainty and unique object, unsuitable for college use, was bequeathed by Aubrey Bateman.

Victorian Candlesticks

12.26 Two Sheffield-plate Triple Candelabra

Date unknown. 18.6 in. ×6.6 × 22.4 high. Branches separate; three nozzles.

Octafoil base; fluted stem and tops; heavily foliated and flowered. Separate top with three nozzles. College arms. No marks.

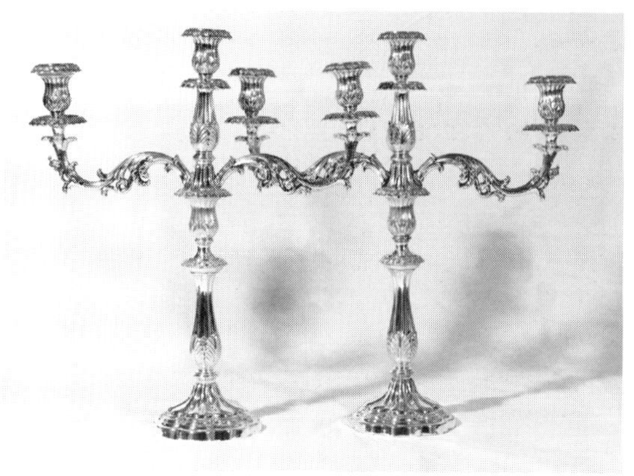

12.26a Two Sheffield-plate Triple Candelabra (*with the above: one of each*)

Date unknown. 20.0 in. ×6.4 × 21.9 high. Branches separate; three nozzles.

Forming a set with the previous, but not identical. Slender, less elaborate, less stoutly plated – copper shows through.

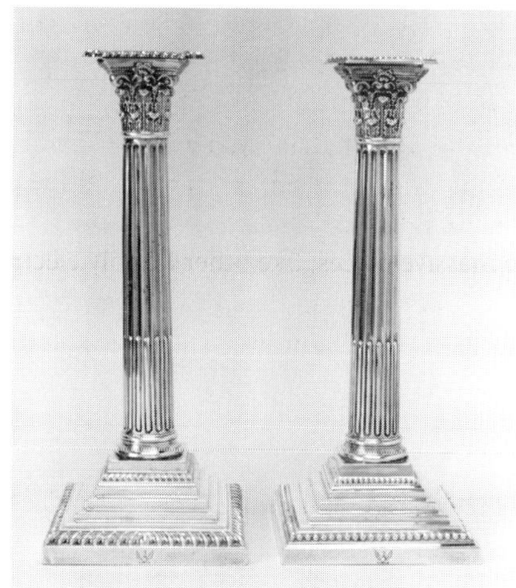

12.27 Two Bateman Corinthian Candlesticks

1896 and 1898 (London a and c). Identical except for detail of decoration. 4.8 in. square × 11.3 high.

On a base of ten steps stands a fluted Corinthian column with its base and capital. Heavy cast beading (or gadrooning) on 2nd and 9th step. Capital rather crudely cast. Top surface recessed. Nozzle square with circular cut-out corners; beaded & moulded edge.

Badge: *pheasant's head and wings*, for the family of Aubrey Bateman.

Maker's marks: CSH in rectangle and in trefoil, both for Charles Stuart Harris, active 1852–*c*.1900 (mainly a spooner).

Filling a hole in one base is a non-removable circular plate, 4.1 in. diameter, marked with Sheffield crown and maker's mark HA; added later for unknown reason.

Corinthian candlesticks had been made sporadically since the baroque period. The square base began in the rococo period – Pembroke College has six pairs dated between 1757 and 1781 – but these are its only representatives here.

Twentieth-Century Candlesticks

12.28 Four Neo-Adamesque Candlesticks

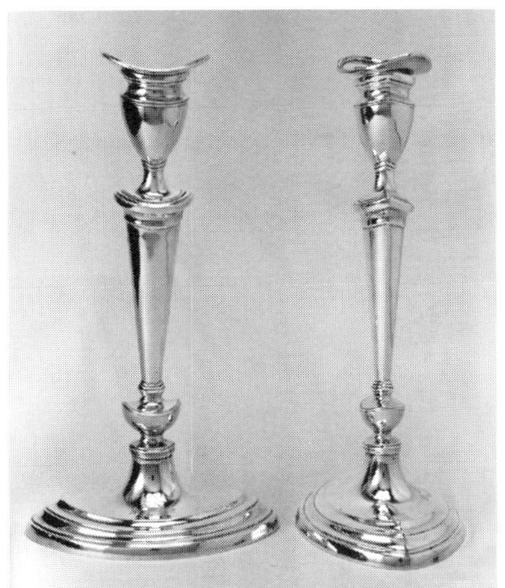

1902 (London g). 6.8 in. ×4.6 × 11.75 high.

Almond-section throughout; most parts are saddle-shaped (ends higher than middle). Stem with four knops, ending in vase-shaped socket with keel below top. Mouldings on top of base, knops, keel of socket.

Nozzles: almond-shaped, saddle top with ribbed moulding; fully marked.

Makers: Mappin & Webb, big manufacturing silversmiths.

12.29 Two Vincent Candlesticks

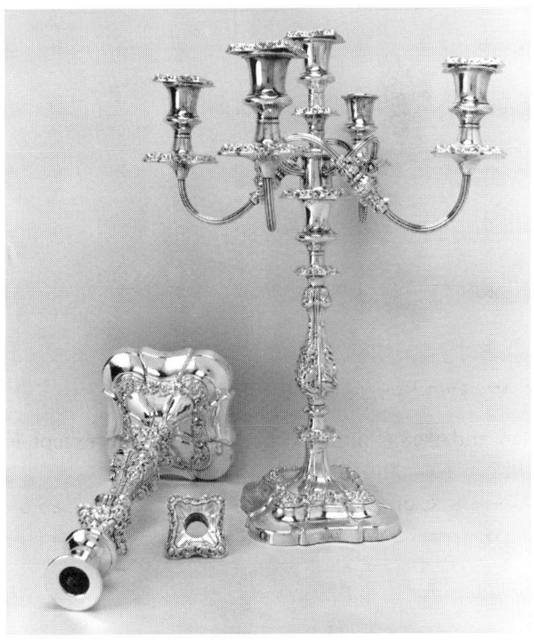

Undatable. Silvered copper. Base 7.4 in. diagonal × 12.6 high; spread of arms 14.6; total height 23.2.

Base and stem resemble a single candlestick, into the socket of which fits a top with four branches and five sockets with nozzles. The terminal nozzle is fitted with a separate finial which can take the place of the fifth candle. Base, knops, stem, drip-trays, and finial are adorned with foliage and *Camellia*-like flowers.

Inscription: E R V AD VITAM SOCIUS C.C.C DONO DEDIT ANN MCMLXII [E.R.V., Life Fellow of C.C.C., gave this gift in the year 1962].

Given by Eric Reginald Pearce 'Vinca' Vincent (1894–1978), German and Italian scholar at Oxford; Fellow of Corpus 1935–; Professor of Italian 1935–72; President of the College; CBE; numerous Italian honours.

These massive pieces, like other heavily electroplated objects, lack the sharp detail of silver or Sheffield plate.

Adrian Candlestick – *see* Modernistic Plate (p. 270).

13

Salvers or Waiters

And [Herodias's daughter] came in straightway with haste unto the king, and asked, saying, I will that thou give me by and by in a charger the head of John the Baptist.

St Mark **6** 25

Salver . . . is a new fashioned peece of wrought plate, broad and flat, with a foot underneath, and is used in giving Beer, or other liquid thing, to save the Carpit or Cloathes from drops.

Blount 1661

Gather the Droppings and leavings, out of the several Cups and Glasses and Salvers, into one.

Swift 1729

Salvers are mysterious objects with little evident use. They were a prolific vehicle for displaying Byzantine, baroque, rococo, or Adamesque fashion, and afforded flat surfaces for engraving fancy coats-of-arms. They might be put under bottles and glasses to catch the drips, but many of the grander ones have raised designs which would make this use impractical. Some say they are developed from the chargers or standing plates used for displaying heads of important persons (like Ali Pasha, p. 252), etc.

Salvers are of at least Roman antiquity. There are three in the Mildenhall Treasure, one being bigger than all but one of ours. Another giant, made in Constantinople *c.*500, was deposited, 2000 miles away and two centuries later, in the royal ship burial at Sutton Hoo. These have central feet: most later big salvers, instead, have three or more feet at the edges.

Our earliest salver-like object is described in the *c.*1376 inventory:

> One *perapsis* of silver [*added:* in English a spiceplate] with a silver foot, given to St Bene't's church by Lady Alice [de Chaumberleyn] for the offerings at the high altar of the said church, and in the middle of the *perapsis* is a boss of azure.

The entry is crossed out, showing that the College did not long retain it. Botener's addition to the list includes a more elaborate 'spiceplate' with a pillar in the middle bearing a gilt lion. The kitchen inventory of *c.*1481 lists three 'charjorys' [chargers] among the pewter. Various 'flat pieces' appear in later inventories.

Often salvers came in pairs. Some were made with matching two-handled cups, like the magnificent Houghton Cups & Salvers in the Victoria & Albert Museum. In the Victorian period they grew to size and elaboration beyond any possibity of use: the V & A has examples nearly 3 feet in diameter.

The College's present salvers seem to be the earliest surviving under that name in Cambridge, but there were several previous ones, the first being given by John Avery in *c.*1690. I do not understand why the College had so many. For putting under bottles they should have been rendered obsolete by the acquisition of coasters in 1770 and 1789. However the graffiti, some of which are themselves worn, show that salvers remained in general use until *c.*1870.

Baroque Salvers (1715–1732)

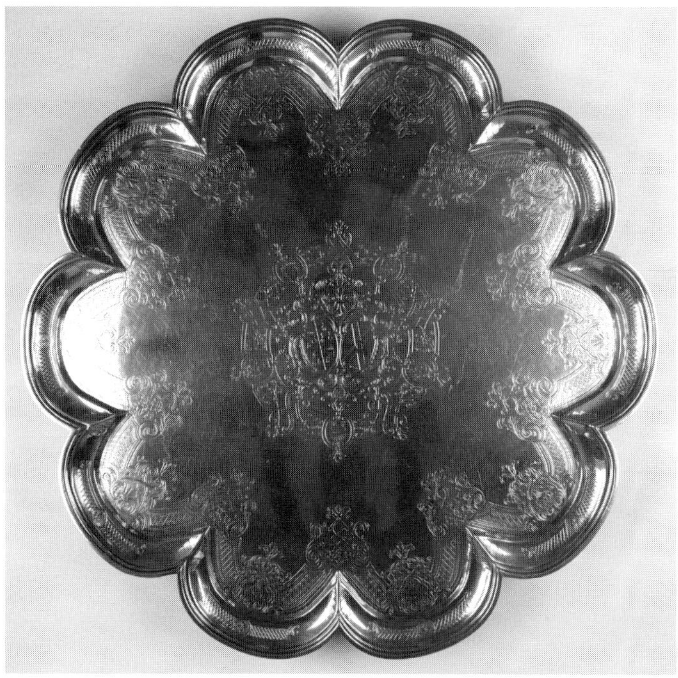

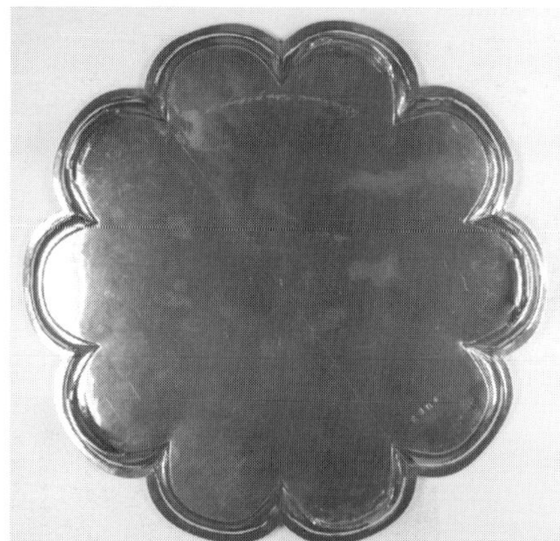

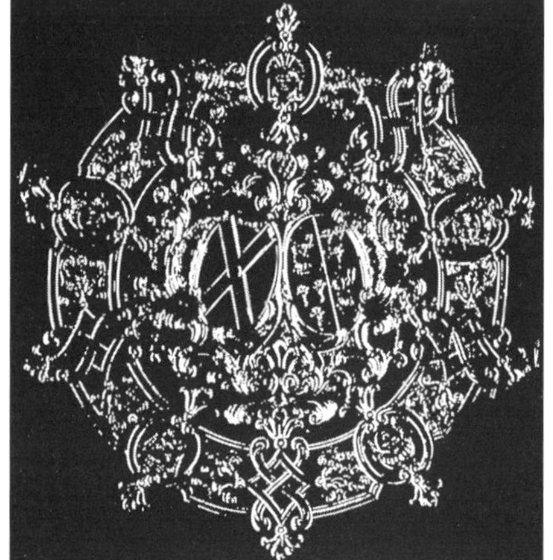

13.1 Great Yorke Salver (*front, back, detail above*)

1715 (London 𝕯). Britannia silver. 18.9 in. × 1.4 high.

Decafoil shape; border chased in Mannerist-baroque style with lozenge panels, scroll-foliage, shells, flower-vases, etc.; in the middle a large engraved panel of strapwork and foliage with four different grotesque human faces in 'Aztec' headdress and one satyr's face (the latter like those on the Yorke Cup, p. 132); five plain moulded feet. Setting-out lines on underside.

College arms and donor's: *Argent on a saltire azure a bezant; label of three points.*

Inscription: *Ex Dono Honorabilis Phillippi Yorke Armigeri 1740.*

Maker's mark (L.I under three conjoined flowers) is of Isaac Liger from Saumur, active in London 1704–28; made 'relatively small pieces of high quality with particularly outstanding engraving' (Grimwade 1990).

This splendid piece, weighing 107 ounces (3.34 kg), was given by the noble and learned Philip Yorke (1720–90), who much later gave the Yorke Inkstand (p. 183). The College paid 1*s*. 4*d*. for its transport, and (three years later) 10*s*. 6*d*. for engraving the arms (CC(A): *Audit Book*).

13.2 De Lancey Salver

1725 (London K). 9.0 in. × 2.5 in. high.

Charger with central pedestal; decoration confined to engraving.

College arms, baroque shield in elaborate baroque wreathing.

Inscription: *Donum Jacobi De Lancey e Provincia' Eboracen', apud Americanos Generosi; C.C.C. Socijs Commensal.* (Gift of James de Lancey, gentleman, from the province of [New] York among the Americans; Fellow-Commoner of C.C.C.)

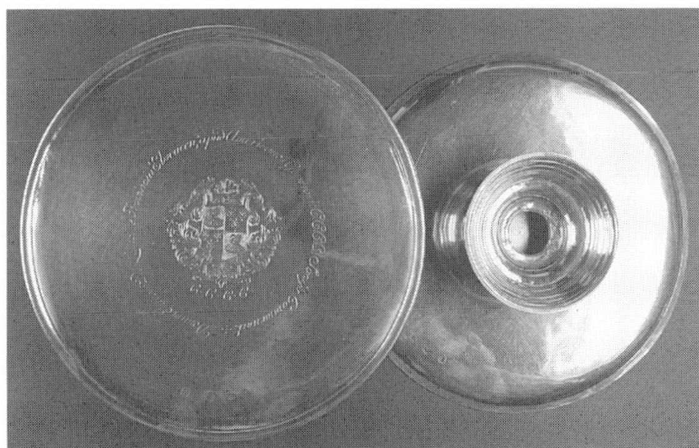

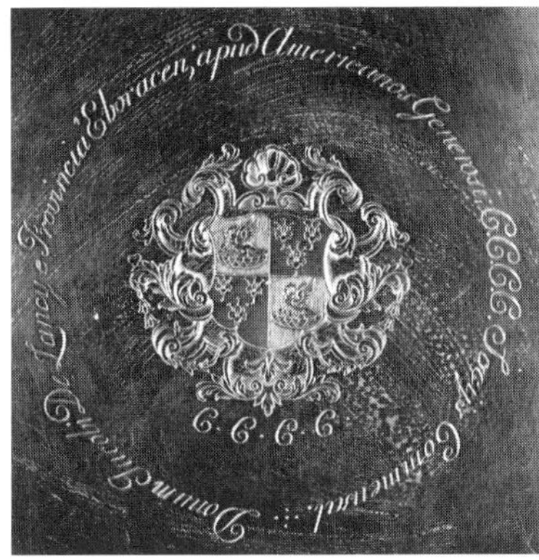

Maker's mark: IB and two stars in (incomplete) quatrefoil, for John Bache, maker also of the Lichfield Tankard and early mugs (§10.1.3, 10.2.1).

James de Lancey (1703–60) was the son of a Huguenot refugee from France who had established himself as a New York businessman. He went to Cambridge as a Fellow-Commoner in 1721, moving on (like many of his predecessors) to the Inner Temple without a Cambridge degree. This piece commemorates his return to America. He became Chief Justice of the Supreme Court of New York, and then Lieutenant-Governor of New York Province. He started the colonial administration along the path down to the American War of Independence, in which his son (donor of De Lancey Candlesticks) was to play a delicate part (p. 159) (*Dictionary of American Biography*).

13.3 Pelham Salver (*detail only*)

1725 (London K). 9.0 in. × 2.5 in. high.

Twin of the De Lancey Salver. The only difference, apart from a large dent, is the inscription: *Donum Thomæ Pelham Armig. Sussexien: C.C.C. Socijs Commensal'* (Gift of Thomas Pelham of Sussex).

Thomas Pelham, presumably a relative of the Pelhams, Earls of Chichester, and of Henry Pelham (donor of the Pelham Inkstand, §14.1), was admitted Fellow-Commoner in 1722.

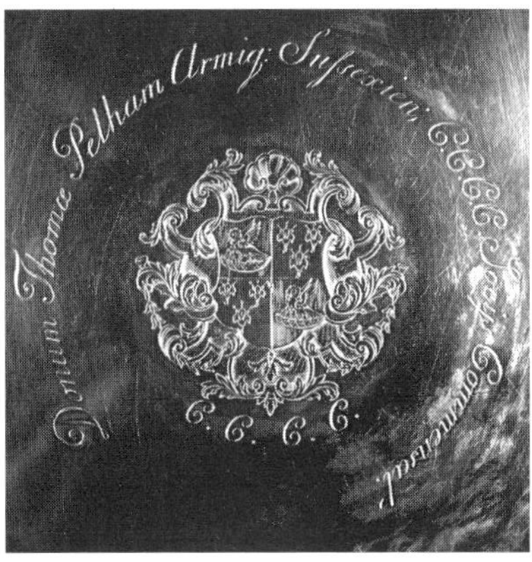

13.4 Bateman Salver of 1728

London N. 14.1 in. diameter, 1.6 in. high.

Round, with 'Chippendale' or 'pie-crust' border (eight pairs of rounded notches); on four feet with cast spirals.

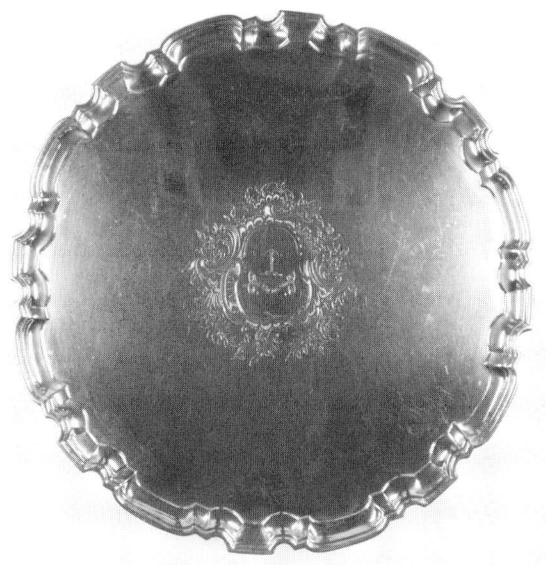

Original coat-of-arms erased and replaced by Victorian crest of a crossbow and the motto *ARCUI MEO NON CONFIDO* [I trust not in my bow]. Rococo cartouche elaborately foliated.

Inscription on back, largely erased: *Ex Dono [J]oannis H[o]oper . . Aug*^{t} *. . . . . Æt*^{t}*77.* Traces of original stippled coat-of-arms. Weight scratched out: *60*^{oz} = *2*^{pwts}. Graffiti: *56*^{ozs} *58 – 6 59 – 2 48.18* [Present weight 55: 7 oz].

Maker's mark, *J T* and jug in squarish surround, of John Tuite, active in Dublin 1710–20 and in London 1721–*c*.1740.

This recycled piece was inherited by Aubrey Bateman and from him by the College.

The border is characteristic of the period. A similar, hexagonal piece, of *c*.1728, by the Scots silversmith J.G. Bilsinds, is in Kelvingrove Museum, Glasgow.

13.5 Perry Salver or Waiter (*right*)

1732 (London R). 11.1 in. × 1.25 high.

Round, with 'Chippendale' border of eight (as above), on four feet. College arms and donor's on oval shields in an elaborate Mannerist-like strapwork surround; below them a head with palm-like 'Indian' headdress. Donor's arms: *Quarterly, 1 & 4: azure a fess embattled between three pears or; 2: vert a bend sinister or, in chief an estoile of eight points rayant or; 3: sable a cross between four roses argent.* Crest: *out of a mural crown a dexter arm armed and gauntleted brandishing a sword.*

Inscription: *Ex Dono Gulielmi Perry Armigeri de Turville in Comitatu Buckinghamiensi.* Weight, on reverse: *27 = 8 1732 I.* [Present weight 25: 14 oz.]

Graffiti: *E.R. GIRTON H. Austin 78 Jun 2*nd *1944* On rim: *W Dobbs Carless Shrubbs* (James Careless became 'Combination man' in 1846. William Dobbs, 'The Little Duke', was his successor from 1864 to 1900 and butler to the Master; he lived at Middleton Cottage and had a famous garden.)

Mark: GH in rectangle with cut corners; early work of George Hindmarsh, London salver-maker, active 1731–50.

Donor: William Perry, said to be of Middlesex, admitted 1730.

To judge by its worn condition, this middle-sized salver was one of the most used; it has lost 6% of its weight.

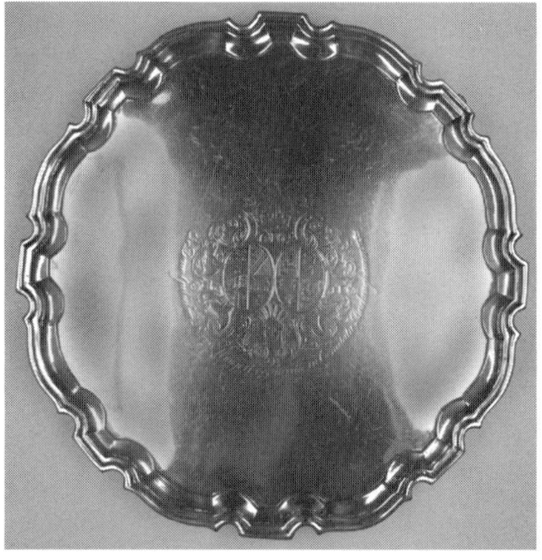

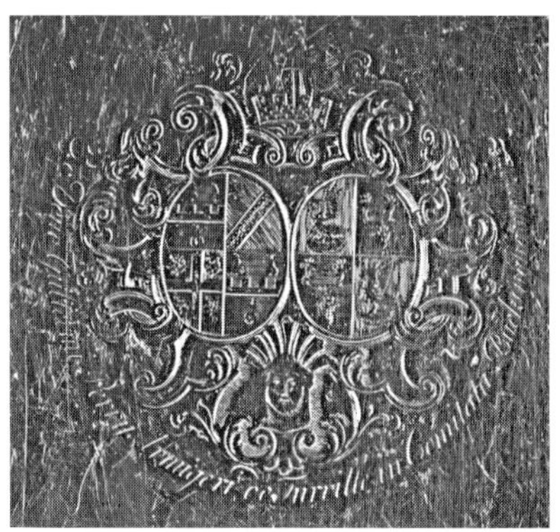

Rococo Salvers (1766–1779)

13.6 Small Bateman Salver of 1766

London 𝕷. 5.9 in. × 0.95 in. high.

Hexagon with internal cusps, gadrooned border, three feet. No arms or inscription.

Maker: RR for Robert Rew, entered 1754. (Richard Rugg's mark is smaller.)

Bequeathed by Aubrey Bateman.

The cusped hexagon is not a distinctively rococo shape: there is a London example of 1733 in Kelvingrove Museum, Glasgow.

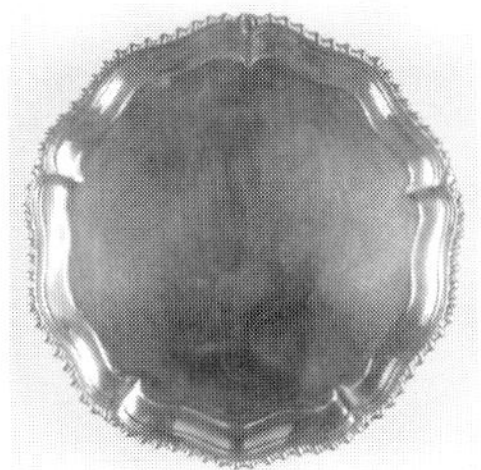

13.7 Three Fane Salvers

1777 (London Q). One middle-sized (11.9 in. × 1.5 high), two small (9.9 in. × 1.2 high). Differ only in graffiti.

Dodecagonal, gadrooned edge, three feet. College arms impaling donors' (*Azure three dexter gauntlets or*) on shields hanging by ribbon from swag. Oak foliage and acorns surround the inscription; they are represented as a hybrid between the two species of oak, *Quercus robur* and *Q. petræa,* the difference between which was not recognized at this time.

Inscribed: *C.C.C. Ex Dono Joannis & Francisci Fane Armig 1777.* (Corpus Christi College, of the gift of John and Francis Fane, armigers, 1777.)

Maker's mark: I·C in rectangle, for John Carter II, of London, active 1769–73.

Graffiti, large salver: *X* 14 near hallmark.

Small salver: *DB*)) [on base] X *W Dobbs John Fynn 1801* [on rim] *Herman Austin 1878 To 1928 Herman Austin 1887 Carless*

Second small salver: *ERN* [on base] X *Cleaned by H Austin 1884 50 Years W Dobbs Cleaned Austin 1878 To 1928 50 Years* [The two Austins are the same signature. The first '50 years' is an addition to the 1884 graffito.] For Dobbs see above.

John and Francis Fane of London were admitted 1768, probably as Fellow-Commoners.

These three 'waiters' were withdrawn in May 1777 'to have their Arm's engraved'.

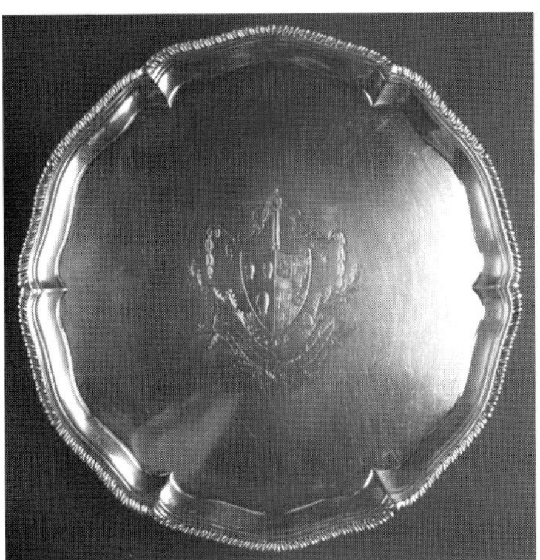

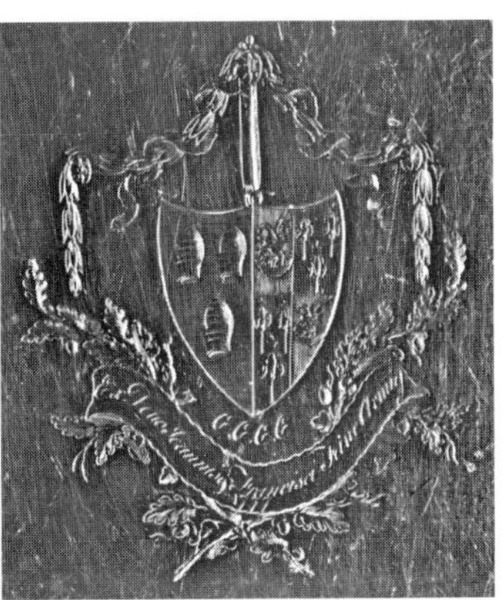

13.8 Great Irish (Tillotson) Salver

1779 (Dublin G). 18.0 in. × 2.3 high.

Octagonal; cusped rococo border; heavily chased with shellwork, roses, apples, pears, grapes, peaches etc. and three parrots. Four vaguely dolphinish legs, cockle-shell feet. Rococo cartouche with flowers and foliage, containing a formidable unidentified coat-of-arms, as follows:

> *Quarterly, 1st and 4th: Or, a barrulet dancetté sable between a crescent and a lion rampant; 2nd and 3rd: argent, a chevron sable between three boars'-heads couped.*

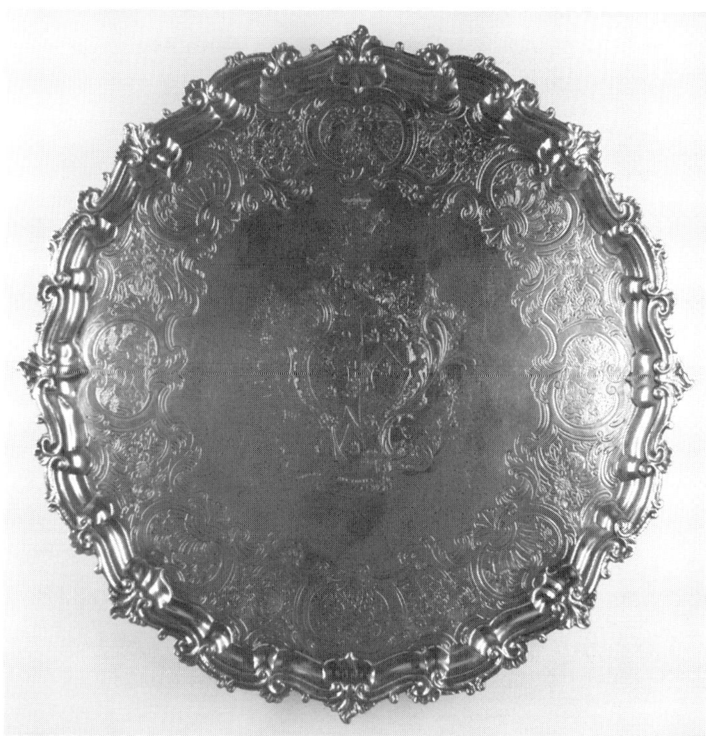

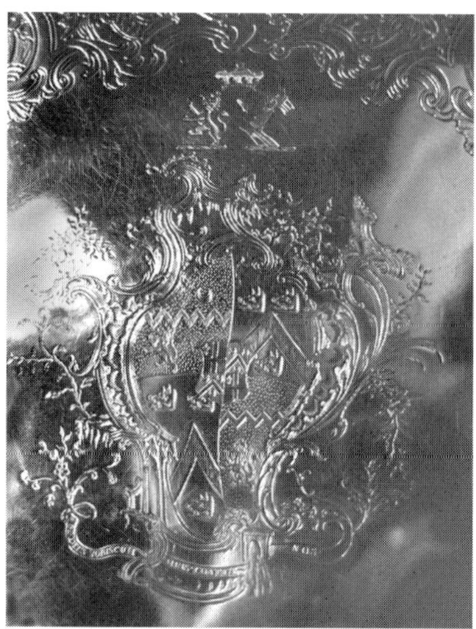

In pretence, quarterly, 1st and 4th: azure a cross argent, in the dexter chief one fleur-de-lys; 2nd and 3rd: gules a chevron argent between three crescents. Crests: dexter, *a beast* [a doggish lion] *rampant;* sinister, *a dexter arm armed, grasping a human leg armed couped.* Motto: *SI DEUS NOBISCUM QUIS CONTRA NOS* (If God [be] for us, who [can be] against us? *Romans* **8** 31).

The most readily recognized part is the arm-and-a-leg crest borne by branches of the Armstrong family with seats in Ireland (*Fairbairn's Crests*), but there is nothing else in the arms or motto to indicate these.

Weight 88.9 inscribed on back [present weight 85: 17 oz].

Marked with the Dublin G for 1779, Hibernia, and GB in oval for the Dublin maker George Beere.

This imposing piece was bequeathed by John Tillotson, dining member, 1985.

Adamesque Salvers (1779–1793)

13.9 Two Trotter Salvers (*facing page*)

1779 (London c). 8.25 in. diameter × 1.15 in. high.

Raised border with two rows of beading and one of 'acanthus-husks'; three cast palmette feet with vestigial claws; rather rough chasing around College arms.

Inscription: *Ex Dono Jacobi Trotter, Arm: 1779.* (Gift of James Trotter, armiger – but his arms are not shown.)

Mark: I·C T·H in square, for John Crouch I & Thomas Hannam, prolific salvermakers *c.*1770–90.

James Trotter of Westmorland was admitted undergraduate 1772; M.A. 1780.

These have been much used.

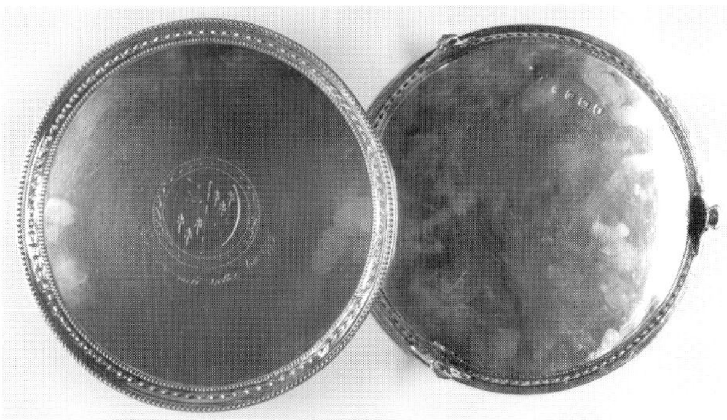

13.10 Two Adkin Salvers

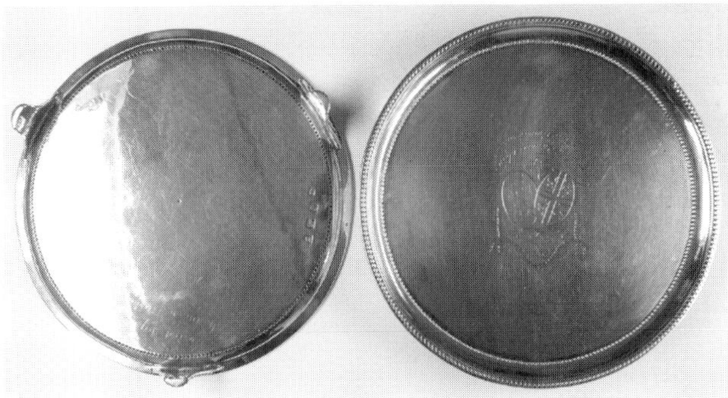

1782 (London f). 8.1 in. × 1.1 in. high.

Double-beaded edge, three beaded feet. College arms, overlapped by donor's (*A cross between four mullets*), on oval shields.

Inscription (weak but certain): *Dono dedit Thomas Adkin CCC Socio Commensalis.* (Thomas Adkin, Fellow Commoner, gave [me] as a gift to C.C.C.)

Graffiti: (on one) *Cleaned by Herman Austin 50 Years* [scratched out] *W Dobbs W Dobbs.* (On the other) *P Fynn F Strange 1876 H Austin 1878 C Stearn 1801 Fynn 1861 W Dobbs* [on rim] *Carless*

Mark: R·I in rectangle, for Robert Jones of London, active 1774–.

Given by Thomas Adkin of Norfolk, admitted 1777, B.A. 1782.

Rather worn, including the graffiti, showing that these salvers found a use throughout the 19th century.

13.11 Two Bateman Salvers of 1788 (*next page*)

London n. 9.5 in. × 1.2 high.

Hexagonal, very elaborate rococo cusped and foliated borders. Interior with chased work of flowers and foliage (mostly a ?*Geum* species); this chasing is secondary, being done after the arms were replaced.

A hexagonal piece has been cut out of the middle of each, doubtless to remove an original coat-of-arms. It has been replaced by soldering in a patch which bears the Bateman crest, *a demi-pheasant with wings erect.* Motto: *NEC PRECE NEC PRETIO.*

Maker's mark RH in rectangle, for Robert Hennell, otherwise known to the College as maker of salt-cellers.

Bequeathed by Aubrey Bateman. Much less worn than salvers made for the College.

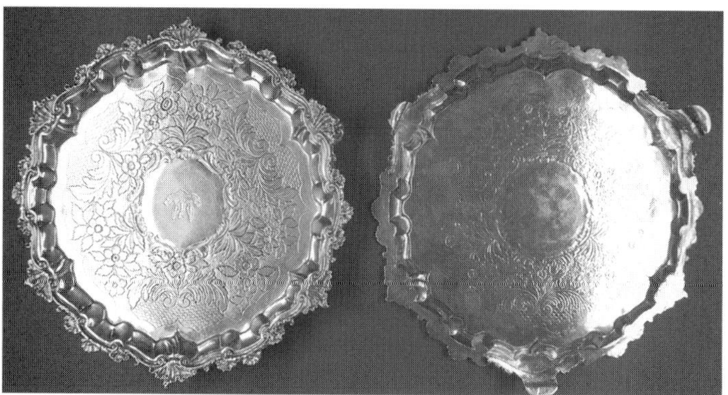

13.12 Bateman Oval Salver or Meat-Dish of 1793

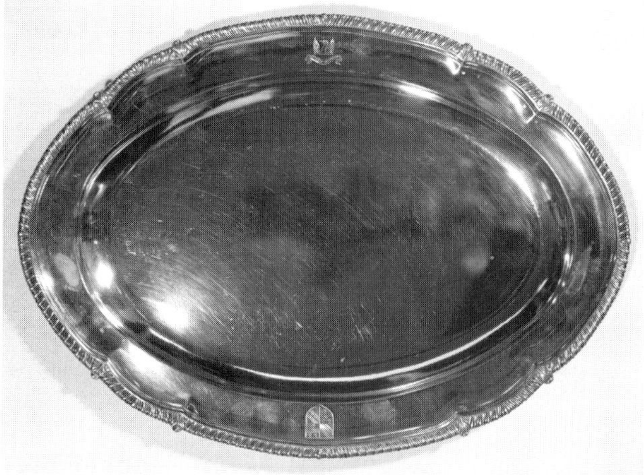

London S. 16.2 in. × 11.5 × 1.2 in. high.

Eight internal cusps, gadrooned edge, no feet. Blocked-up hole in raised margin at one end. Arms of Hanbury quartering Bateman: *Quarterly. 1 & 4: Or a rose on a fess sable between three ducks* [or similar fowl]. *2 & 3: Or a bend azure between two bendlets sable.* Crest: *a demi-pheasant with wings erect.* Motto: ***NEC PRECE NEC PRETIO.***

Marks: London S for 1793 (not 1813). P·S in bifoil.

An early work of the celebrated Paul Storr (1771–1844). A few old knife-scratches show that it has occasionally been put to the indignity of a meat-dish.

Bequeathed by Aubrey Bateman. According to the catalogue of Bateman plate, these arms were borne by Baron Bateman, 1837.

Victorian Salvers (*c.*1850–1901)

13.13 Giant Bateman Salver

Mid-19th century. 24.7 in. × 2.7 high. Rim and feet are 'Sheffield plate' (or more likely elecroplate) on copper core; the flat engraved base is probably silver.

Massive cast pierced margin with Victorian-rococo scrollwork; chased with scrollwork and foliage; three cast scrolled feet. A separate piece of silver let in bears the arms of Martin: *Parted per pale, two coats.* Dexter, *azure, sun and moon argent over a cross on a three-stepped plinth or.* Sinister, *quarterly, 1 & 4: argent fretty gules, a chief azure; 2 & 3: azure, a chevron or between three egg-cupped eggs of the same.* Helm: *closed steel in profile.* Crest: *an estoile rayant.* Motto: *SIC ITUR AD ASTRA* [Thus you get to the stars].

Marked with only the maker's mark, a setting (or rising) sun.

Family piece bequeathed by Aubrey Bateman; the arms are those of an ancestor of Eustace Martin of the serpent candlesticks (§11.23). The College's heaviest piece (197 oz, 6.13 kg), although most of it is not silver.

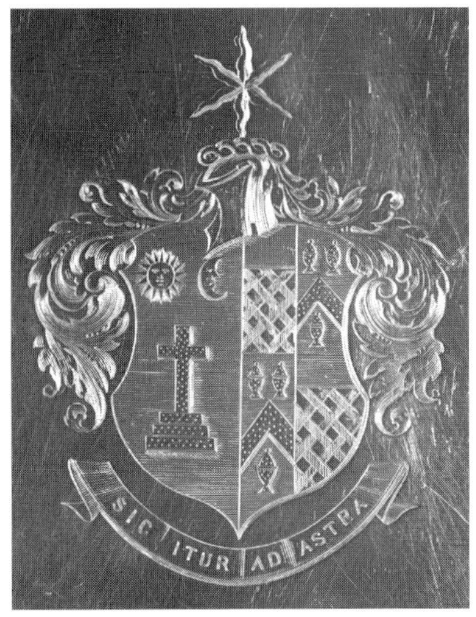

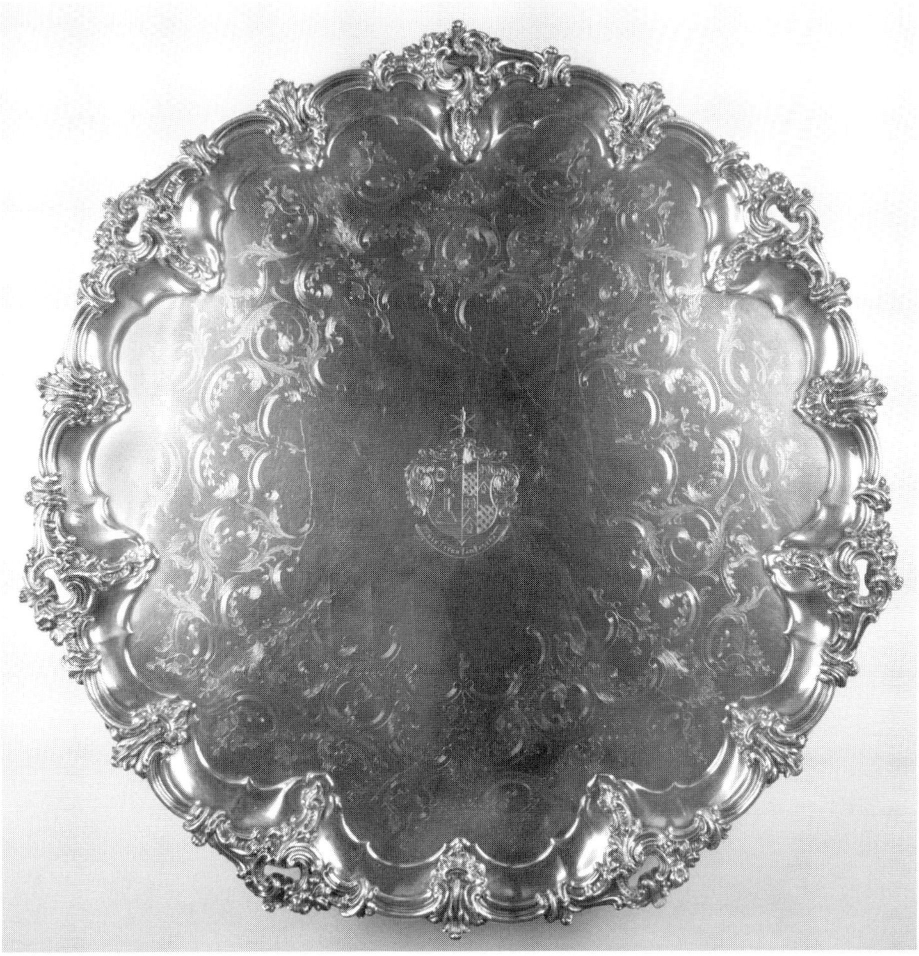

Giant Bateman Salver

13.14 Stephen Salver

1873 (London 𝔖). 8.4 in. × 0.95 high.

Plain round, chased with Victorian-Tudor strapwork and foliage. College arms with pelican pseudo-crest.

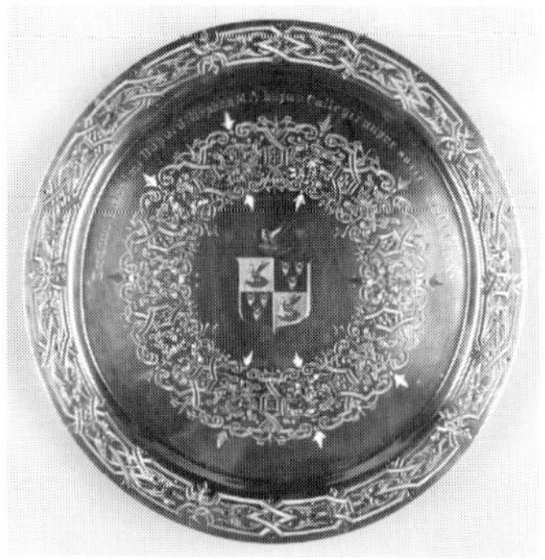

Inscribed: *Ex dono Gulielmi Duguid Stephen M.A. hujus Collegii nuper socii MDCCCLXXV* [Of the gift of William Duguid Stephen, M.A., lately Fellow of this College, 1875]. Graffito (on rim): *Herman Austin.*

Maker's mark: RMEH in quatrefoil, for Richard Martin & Ebenezer Hall (1820–1911); firm active 1854–1936. Supplier's mark: T. REED & C^{O}. CAMBRIDGE.

William Duguid Stephen (1842–1910), mathematician and priest, from Glass, Aberdeenshire, came from King's College, Aberdeen, to Corpus in 1866, and was Fellow 1871–4. After marrying – he was one of the last so to forfeit his Fellowship – he was Rector of Little Wilbraham and then of Landbeach, where he was 'a truly patriarchal figure' (Bury 1952).

This piece, still almost as new, was evidently given after salvers had become redundant.

13.15 Bateman Salver of 1897

Sheffield 𝔢. 9.9 in. × 1.3 high.

Pentagonal, very elaborate rococo cusped and foliated border, three feet.

Bateman crest (*demi-pheasant with wings erect*) and motto: NEC PRECE NEC PRETIO.

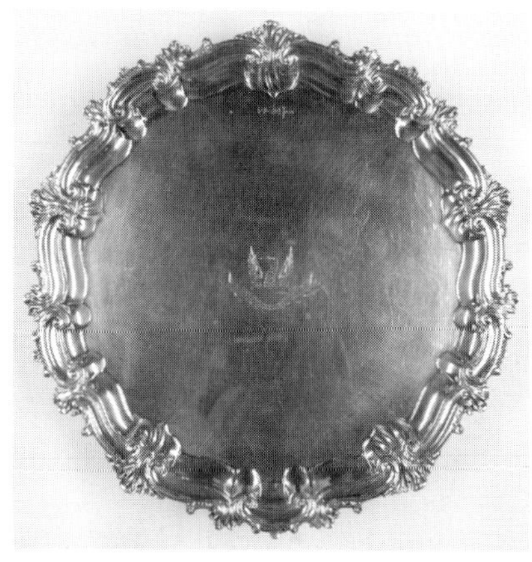

Made by Walker & Hall, 1853–.
Bequeathed by Aubrey Bateman.

13.16 Bateman Salver of 1899

Sheffield 𝔤. 14.0 in. × 1.3 high.

Hexagonal, elaborate cusped and foliated border, three feet.

Arms of Hanbury quartering Bateman, as on the Bateman 1793 salver (§13.12).

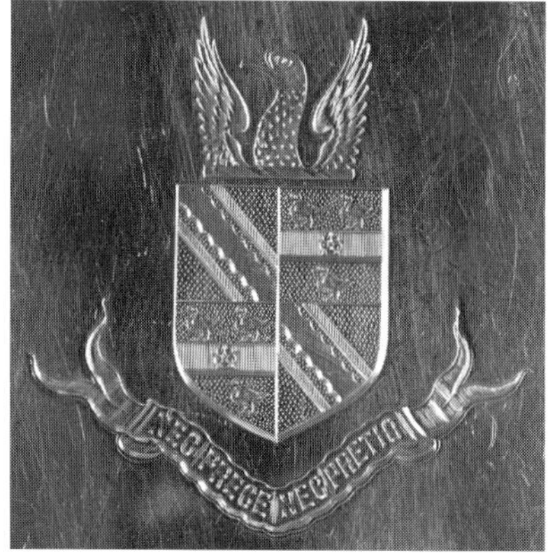

Made by Walker & Hall.
Bequeathed by Aubrey Bateman.

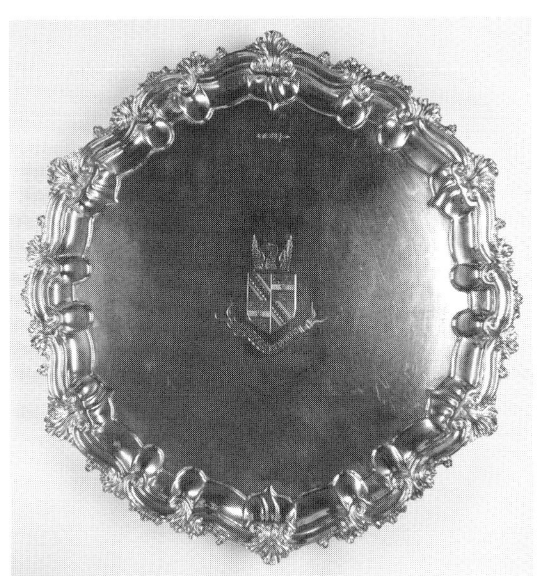

Crest: *a crossbow* (for the Jolliffe family, relatives of Bateman). Graffiti: *Jolliffe Crest 63.14 1/1/0 1/1/- crest cost 1 gn.\ 387/9.70 Na/- Joff L2442*

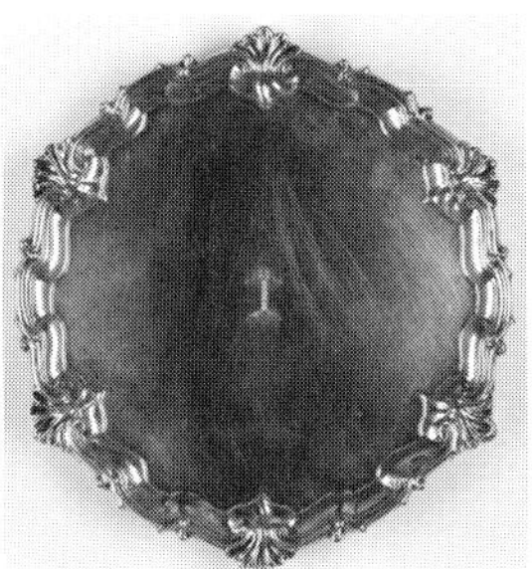

13.17 Small Bateman Salver of 1901

London f. 7.0 in. × 0.8 high.

Hexagonal, elaborate cusped and foliated border, three feet.

Maker's mark: WM B JS RD in shield, for Walter, John, Michael, & Stanley Barnard and Robert Dabock, a stage in the family firm of Barnard & Sons 1808–.

Bequeathed by Aubrey Bateman.

Twentieth-Century Salver

13.18 Butler Square Salver

1926 (London k). 13.95 in. square, 1.65 high.

Square, plain moulded margins, scalloped corners; four feet.

Inscribed: *Ricardo Austen Butler A.M.* |*Collegae Collegae suo* |*Omnia fausta et felicia ominati* |*d.d.*|*Magister et Socii* |*Collegii Corporis Christi* |*et Beatae Mariae Virginis* |*xx Apl. A.S. MCMXXVI.* (The Master and Fellows of the College of Corpus Christi and the Blessed Virgin Mary, comrades, presaging all that is happy and auspicious, gave this gift to their comrade Richard Austen Butler, M.A., 20 Apr. 1926.)

Graffiti: 44.90 | 197 ' 9 | 380.90 [Present weight 44.7 oz]

Maker's mark: G & L C^{O}. L^{TD} in double-outlined trefoil, for Gibson & Langman. Distributor's mark: GOLDSMITHS & SILVERSMITHS COMPANY 112 REGENT STREET W. William Gibson (1839–1913) was active 1865–1913. Sir John Lawrence Langman (1846–1928) was active 1882–1913. They founded the

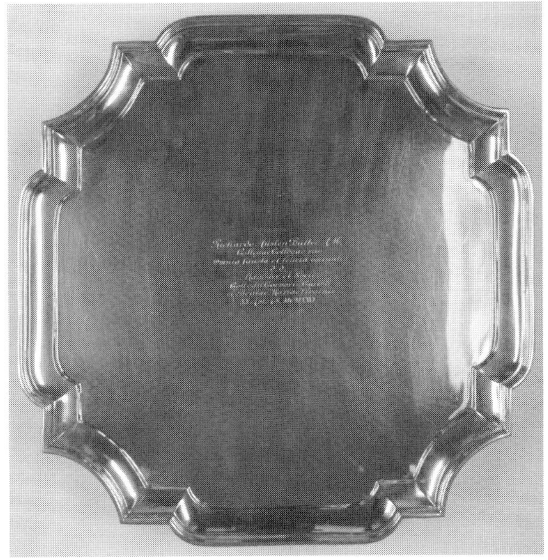

Goldsmiths' & Silversmiths' Company (not to be confused with the Worshipful Company of Goldsmiths). This version of the mark, with the directors' initials, seems not to be well known; their usual mark (see Knight Cup, p. 133) is the same shape but contains the Company's initials.

Richard Austen 'Rab' Butler (1902–82), linguist, statesman, 'a great public servant', came from India. He was an undergraduate at Pembroke College; Fellow of Corpus Christi 1925–9, Honorary Fellow after 1952, Master of Trinity 1965–77, Chancellor of Sheffield and Essex Universities; Conservative M.P., Cabinet Minister many times, Privy Councillor, declined an hereditary earldom, created Lord Butler of Saffron Walden.

This heavy piece, from the worst period of English silversmithing, was evidently a wedding present from the College.

14

Inkstands or Standishes

> ... Both the ink and the pen have given the writer trouble. The pen has spluttered twice in a single word, and has run dry three times in a short address ... Now, a private pen or ink-bottle is seldom allowed to be in such a state ... But you know the hotel ink and the hotel pen, where it is rare to get anything else.
>
> *A. Conan Doyle*, The Hound of the Baskervilles *(1902)*

A standish is a tray fitted for three containers, or two containers and a bell. Originally the containers were for ink, either pounce or sand, sometimes wafers, and sometimes lead shot.

Ink: an unstable, brown or black liquid, a solution of tannin (from oak marble-galls, imported from the east Mediterranean) with ferrous sulphate, used as a writing medium.

Pounce: a kind of size in powder form, used to fill the pores of absorbent paper to make it easier to write on.

Sand is said to have been sprinkled on the writing to absorb excess ink. (Does this work?) Alternatively it is said to have been not sand but powdered gum sandarach, an alternative to pounce. (This would explain why writers needed either pounce or 'sand', but not both.)

Lead shot were for rattling against the end of a quill or steel pen to dislodge dried ink and pounce.

Wafers: tiny red biscuits which the writer licked and used as adhesive to seal a letter.

Bell: used instead of wafers to summon a lackey bearing sealing-wax and a taper.

Standishes are depicted at least as far back as the early 17th century. It might be thought that a college would be replete with large and elegant ones, the tools of the inmates' trade. In practice most Fellows and students probably used humble or makeshift inkpots. The writer remembers the inkwells (sunk into school desks) of his childhood, the two-gallon stone jars of ink kept in the College undergraduate library, and the inky seeps and efflorescences and incrustations and fingerprints which embellished places of learning.

When pre-sized paper came into general use in the late 18th century, the pounce-dredger or sandbox became redundant and was often replaced by a second inkpot. Although fashionably symmetrical. this would have been impractical, for two inkpots would mean that the ink was used half as fast and had twice the opportunity to go bad.

The Pelham and Kenrick Standishes retain their original containers. The Yorke has been converted to a later pattern, showing that its use was more than merely ceremonial. The Bueno de Mesquita was made in the likeness of a converted inkstand after the reason for the alteration had been forgotten.

14.1 Pelham Inkstand

1751 (London q). Flat tray; sandbox; inkpot with lid; shot-box with lid.

Tray: 10.3 in. × 7.35 × 1.5 high,.

Flat-bottomed, with two long depressions for pens and three round depressions for vessels. Gadrooned edge with a shell at each corner; four scrolled feet each with a leaf-tongue. Rococo foliated cartouches, with what look like enlarged flowers of plantain (*Plantago*), surround College arms and donor's: *Quarterly: 1,4: three pelicans in their pieties. 2,3: two belt-ends in pale, buckled.* Motto: VIRTUE IS HONOUR.

Inscription (on elaborate foliated ribbon): *HENRICUS PELHAM ARM. EX AGRO SVSSEX DEDIT COLL: CORP: X.*[T1] (Henry Pelham, arm[iger], from the land of Sussex, gave [me] to the Coll. of Corpus Christi.)

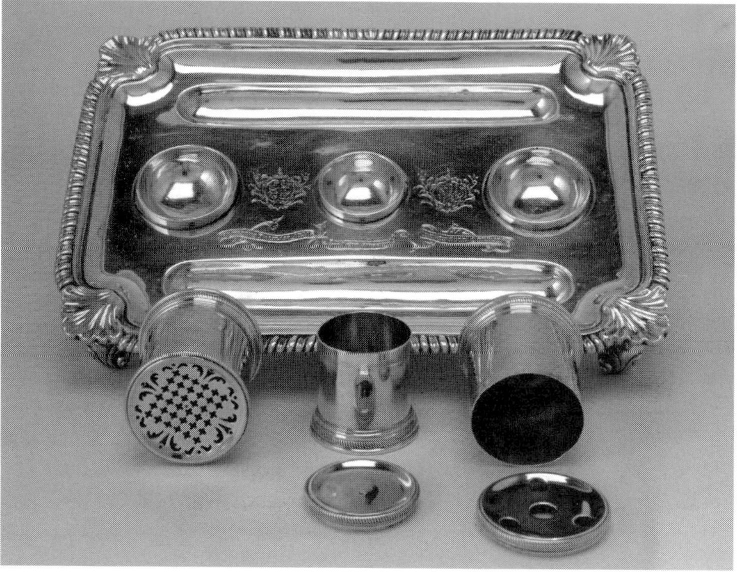

Graffito: *Cleaned by Herman Austin 50 Years / Cleaned by Herman Austin 30 Years*
Sandbox: 2.1 in. × 1.9 high. Cylinder with concave integral top; top pierced with 36 crosses and outer ring of foliated holes; top and bottom with plain and rope mouldings. Inscribed C.C.C.C.
Inkpot: 1.7 in. × 1.65 high (including lid)
Same shape but smaller; detachable unpierced lid. Graffito (inside lid): *MF* and curly tail.
Shot-box: 2.1 in. by 1.9 high (including lid)
As sandbox, but detachable lid is pierced with four bigger holes for pens. Inscribed C.C.C.C.

All four bear the same marks. Maker's mark, *GM* on rococo-shaped punch, for George Methuen, London, active 1741–61.

Henry Pelham of Sussex was Fellow Commoner 1746; became Fellow of Peterhouse 1751; probably a relative of the Pelhams, Earls of Chichester, and of Thomas Pelham (donor of the Pelham Salver, p. 171).

A rather restrained rococo piece. This pattern was probably invented by Paul de Lamerie: the Victoria & Albert Museum has one by him dated 1729.

The first container must be a box for fine sand, because the only way to fill it is through the holes. The sand (less any inky lumps) would be poured back into the box for reuse. The concave top is to make pouring easier. The Audit Book for 1752 records 2*s*. paid 'For Glass &c. for Mr Pelhams Ink Stand': an unexpected entry since all the gadgets are original and have no glass.

14.2 Kenrick Inkstand

1763 (London 𝕳). Tray with railing; three nearly identical glass jars with silver bases and silver caps with lids; three silver circles bolted to tray form sockets for jars.
Tray: 10.0 in. × 7.2 × 2.35 high.
One depression for pens; three pairs of holes for bolting on circles; four feet foliated and pierced; foliated openwork railing with gadrooned edge. Elaborately foliated engraved rococo cartouches for College arms and donor's: *Ermine a lion rampant.* Crest: *a sparrowhawk perched on two arrows.*

Inscription: *Matthaeus Kenrick L.L.B. Dono Dedit C,C,C,C.*
Jars: cut glass, 3.2 in. high (including top).
Jar-bases: 2 in. diam. Fringed edges fitting mouldings; garlands of foliage and stylized flowers. Decoration matches that on bottles round base of jar, secured

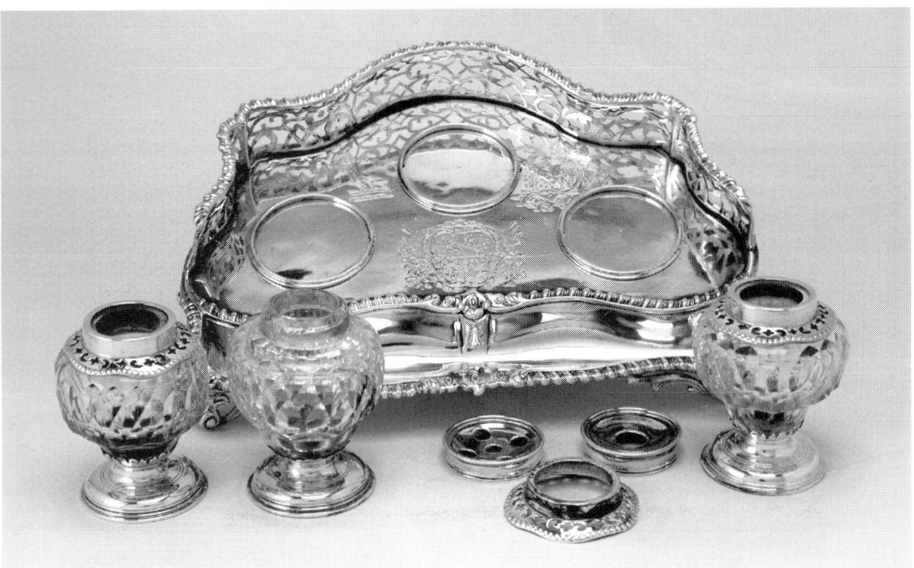

by silver bolt with wingnut passing through bottom of jar.

Jar-caps: 2.1 in. diam. Hexagonal skirt fits top of jar, with edge pierced with lozenges, crosses, commas. Lid fits into hole in top of cap.

Jar-lids: 1.6 in. diam. Depressed tops, moulded sides, beading round edges. One of the three is pierced with a central hole (for ink); one with five holes (for pens and shot); one with pierced and engraved foliation (for sand).

Circles: 2.2 in. diam., two integral bolts and silver nuts.

Maker's mark H SH B in square with engrailed corners, for S. Herbert, active 1750–, and an unidentified partner. Jar-lids marked only with a leopard.

Matthew Kenrick of London, one of three Corpus brothers, was admitted 1754; D.C.L. (= Doctor of Law) 1776. The gift was probably for his Ll.B.

A more flamboyantly rococo piece than the preceding, although the three nearly identical jars are unimaginative and impractical. Two nuts are missing.

14.3 Yorke Inkstand

1765 (London 𝕽) and later. Flat tray; two square glass inkpots with silver lids; silver plugs for holes in lids; silver bell; two silver squares and a silver circle, bolted to tray to form sockets for inkpots and bell.

Tray: 13.35 in. × 8.6 × 1.3 high.

Rococo shape; two recesses for pens; six feet (four at corners, two in middle). Raised border with two rows of scale-like mouldings; asymmetric cartouches with foliage and flowers; four shell-ornaments in middle of long sides; corner feet cast as pierced scrolls.

College arms and donor's: *Argent on a saltire azure a bezant.* Motto: *NEC CUPIAS NEC METUAS* (Don't be greedy or frightened). Inscription: *Ex dono Philippi Yorke A.M. de Erddig in Comitatu Denbighensi* (Gift of Philip Yorke, M.A., of Erddig in the county of Denbigh), *Scribimus indocti doctique.* Weight inscription: oz 34 [presumably including original accessories]. The second inscription, which is all but cleaned away, has been deciphered thanks to the palæographical skill and limitless memory of Professor A.G. Woodhead, who recognizes in it Horace's hexameter *Scribimus indocti doctique poemata passim*, 'Educated or uneducated, we are writing poems everywhere' (*Epistles* II.i.117). Horace was commenting on how the polite arts flourished in Augustus Cæsar's Rome, as Yorke evidently thought they did in Georgian Cambridge.

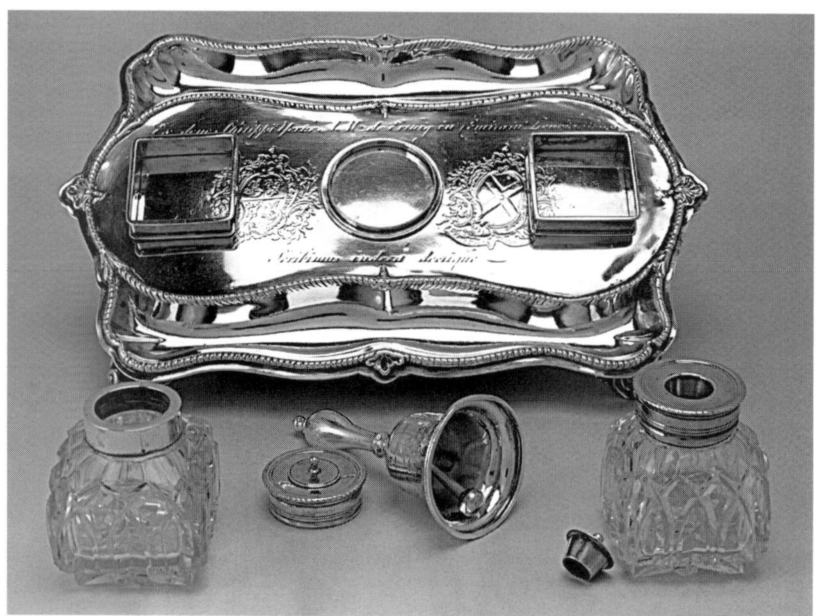

Maker's mark: W.P for William Plummer, silver basketmaker, active 1755–93.

Bottles: 2.4 in. square, 3.2 high with lid. Two identical, square, cut-glass. Mouth has silver collar and lid; in middle of lid is a funnel-shaped hole closed by a removable silver plug with a knob. Lid has reeded and rope-moulded edge. Unmarked.

Bell: 2.35 in. diam. by 4.8 long. Handbell with baluster handle and silver clapper; rope-mouldings; garlands of foliage and stylized flowers. Decoration matches that on bottles rather than tray. No marks.

Bottle-squares: 2.15 in. square, each attached by two built-in bolts with square nuts (one of the nuts is iron). No marks.

Bell-circle: 2.5 in. diameter, attached by three similar bolts. No marks.

A splendid rococo piece, marred by clumsy conversion at an unknown date. The tray is original, and so may be the bell and its ring, but the inkpots and squares (and the two middle feet) are certainly later. Originally there were three fittings, each attached by three bolts. One was in the middle, where the bell and its ring go now, and one at each end (for ink and pounce); the cartouches and arms came between them. On conversion the three bolt-holes at each end were plugged with silver, and replaced by four holes nearer the middle for attaching the silver squares. This makeshift arrangement partly hides the fine decoration of the cartouches. The new holes are surrounded by concentric scores underneath, where a clumsy mechanic has taken a spanner to the nuts.

Given by Philip Yorke (1720–90), Lord Royston, of London; eldest and most learned of the four Corpus sons of Lord Chancellor Hardwicke; admitted Nobleman 1737; Classicist, historian, University politician; Teller of the Exchequer 1736; Ll.D. 1749; second Earl of Hardwicke 1764; elected High Steward of the University 1764; Lord Lieutenant of Cambridgeshire. He began publication of the State Papers, a familiar tool of historical research. He had given the Great Yorke Salver, a much earlier piece. As lord of Wimpole Hall, he built the Eating Room and hired Capability Brown to redesign the north part of the park and build the Folly, 1764–90. He is buried in Wimpole church under a petrified lady garlanding a marble urn.

> Applied with a degree of assiduity and perseverance, not common in persons of his exalted rank, to those branches of science and literature, which are chiefly pursued in this University ... [his undergraduate work was] a proof of the learning and taste of the Society to which he belonged.
>
> *Masters*

Somewhat of a recluse and deficient in charm of manner.
Winstanley

Well versed in classical and general Learning; peculiarly distinguished by an extensive and accurate knowledge of History; ready and elegant in composition; fond of the Arts, and of the Objects of his youthful Studies, he promoted the first, by his Countenance and Liberality, the last by his example.
Epitaph

14.4 Bueno de Mesquita Inkstand

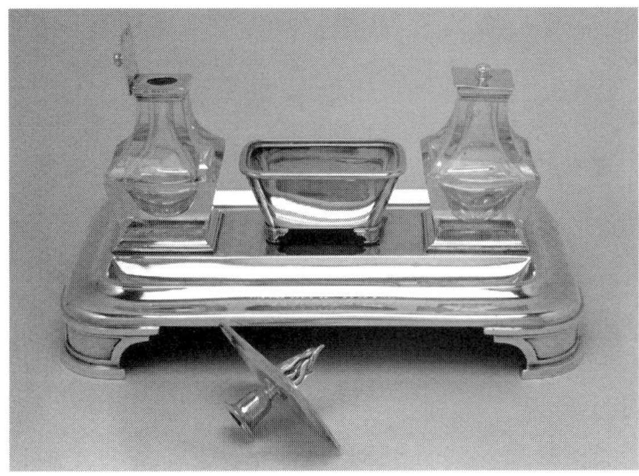

1843 (London 𝔥). Flat tray; central receptacle (? for wafers) bolted to tray, with lid; two square ink-bottles with hinged silver lids; two silver squares bolted to tray to form sockets for bottles.
Tray: 11.4 in. × 7.5 × 1.8 high. Rectangular with rounded corners; two recesses for pens; four cast feet with plain panels; pierced with 2 + 4 + 2 holes for fittings; concave mouldings at edges.

Inscription: *MAGISTRO SOCIIS COLL. C.C. ET B.V.M. D.D. D. M. BUENO DE MESQUITA SOCIUS A.D. MCMXLIII* (D.M. Bueno de Mesquita, Fellow, gave [me] to the Master [&] Fellows of the College of Corpus Christi and the Blessed Virgin Mary, A.D. 1943).
Wafer-box: 3.75 × 2.4 in. Rectangular, tapering below, with four feet like those of tray, ending in integral bolts with silver nuts (one missing). Lid has flame-like knob on one side and clapperless bell on the other.
Bottles: 3.9 in. high including lid. Heavy cut-glass; lids flat, with knobs.
Bottle-squares: each with two integral bolts with silver nuts.

Maker's mark on tray and bottles: EE B JW in quatrefoil, for Edward II and III, John I and William Barnard of Barnard & Sons 1808–.

Daniel Meredith Bueno de Mesquita (1913–89), historian, son of a London clergyman, was admitted Scholar 1931. He became Fellow 1939–48, and thereafter worked at Newcastle University and Christ Church, Oxford 1948. This piece is probably his wedding fine.

A rather plain Early Victorian piece, from the declining years of inkstands.

14.5 Bateman Inkpot

1914 (Birmingham p). 6.5 in. diam. by 3.2 high. Lined inside with leather; glass container for ink.

Crest (Bateman): *pheasant*, motto *NEC PRECE NEC PRETIO.*

Marks: Z, unidentified

A typical free-standing inkpot, shaped to be difficult to spill the contents.

Bequeathed by Aubrey Bateman.

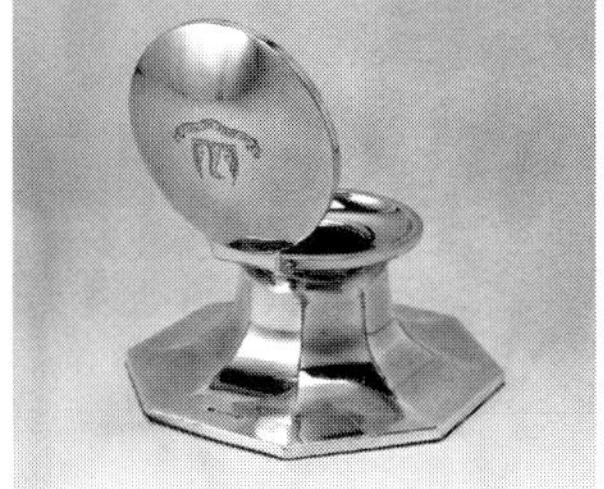

15

Casters or Dredgers, Cruet-Frames, Grinders, and the Administration of Sugar

> My carpet-bag–my cruet-stand, that holds my sauce and soy,–
> My roast potatoes!–all are gone!–and so's that vulgar Boy!
>
> R.H. Barham, *Misadventures at Margate (Ingoldsby Legends)*, 1840

A caster[1] or muffineer, known in the kitchen as a *dredger*, is a pierced container for sprinkling or casting powder or liquid. Our small ones are probably meant for ground pepper or powdered mustard, the bigger ones for crushed sugar: it is easy to confuse them. Other kinds are made for casting pounce, sand (p. 181), aspersions (in church), baby-powder, or ammonia (over fainting ladies). Henry VIII's inventory contains a 'castynge botell of gold'.

Our earliest caster (and perhaps the earliest in existence) is the pepper-pot in the lid of the Parker Salt (p. 78). Similar pepper-pots formed the lids of the bell-shaped salt-cellers fashionable in Jacobean times, of which none seems to survive in Cambridge.

The oldest separate casters are said to be the pair of *c.*1670 at Queen's College, Oxford. This College's earliest were given by William Allen in 1696; like other early casters they were a set of three.

Casters were among the first pieces to express rococo style. In the 20th century they have been joined by salt-sprinklers and by little handmills for grinding salt and pepper at the table.

On cruet-frames

A cruet is a small bottle to hold unconsecrated wine at Mass, or to contain soy sauce or other liquid condiment at meals. In 1376 the College had, presumably inherited from the Gild,

> two silver cruets (*cruetis argenti*) with silver caps, but the cap of one is gilt, the other not.

From about 1710 to 1910 it was the custom to place on the table a *cruet-frame* or *cruet-stand*, somewhat like an inkstand, holding sets of cruets and matching casters or pots for salt, sugar, mustard, etc. Although difficult to clean, these strange objects were not disdained by comparatively fashionable households. They are now usually derelict.

To judge by ours, cruet-frames were particularly in vogue in the 1770s and 1780s, and did hard service. Our four principal ones exemplify the abrupt changes between rococo, Adamesque, and Regency fashions. The Clayton frame is almost identical to the Knowle of 21 years earlier, but very unlike the Parson twelve years later.

On sugar and sugar-casters

Sugar (sucrose) has been consumed in ever-increasing quantities as an oriental spice, a condiment, a means of disguising bad wine and other acid flavours, a preservative, a recreational drug, and a food-processing chemical. As a simple carbohydrate it is common in plants, but few plants make it concentrated enough to be easily extracted.

The middle ages knew sucrose chiefly in the form of onions and honey, but cane sugar could be had for pepping up feasts; our provisions for Christmas 1457 included a few pence worth of 'sugar, cloves, & mace'.[2] In 1540 the College, pushing the boat out a little for the Corpus Christi feast, bought 3 pounds of sugar at 6*d*. a pound, equivalent to more than a goose.[3] A list, dated 1610, of the College tenants expected to provide edibles for the Audit feast includes two each rendering '1 Pound of Sugar', roughly equivalent to a 'fatt Turkey' or a brace of cocks.[4] In 1632 the College recycled three silver beakers, gifts of Elizabethan Fellow-Commoners, into a 'sugar

1 The variant spelling *castor*, which goes back intermittently in College inventories to 1706, appears to be a simple mistake, and has nothing to do with beavers.
2 CC (A): *Liber Albus* f. 76v.
3 CC(A): *Book of Beadles' Feasts*.
4 CC(A): stuck into the back cover of the second inventory book.

box'. This substantial piece – the beakers had weighed 24 ounces – graced High Table for over 100 years.

Next, in the 1690s, sugar became a condiment dispensed in casters. In 1746, having been given two new sets of casters, the College melted the Cholmley-Lambert-Bufkin sugar-box and the 1696 set of casters.

By the 1780s English people were spiking their drinks with sugar in larger quantities, and were becoming addicted. They needed bowls (p. 245), tongs (p. 229), and special spoons: the inventory for 1750 records the recent purchase by the College of $1\frac{1}{2}$ dozen 'Coffee Spoons'. Costly and bloody wars were fought over the West Indian islands which produced it. Many people, however, refused sugar because it was made with slave labour. As a drug it has proved injurious to health, though far less deadly than tobacco or alcohol. Some people still spoiled their tea and coffee with it at the time of writing.

Rococo (1733–1774)

15.1 Large and Small Hoadly Casters

1733 (inscription). Large one 3.2 × 7.8 in., small 2.4 × 6.2 in. Almost identical except in size.

Push-on lid pierced with alternate panels of foliated and X-shaped holes (and additional tiny holes in the small caster); foliated rococo cartouche for arms.

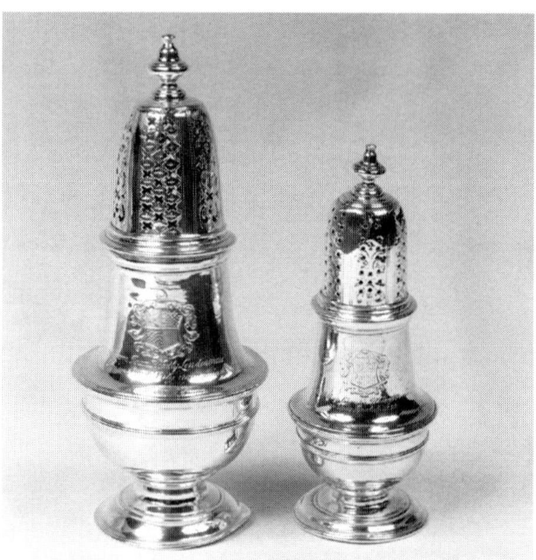

College arms and donor's: *Quarterly azure and or, in the first quarter a bird volant.* Pseudo-crest: *a bird over a crescent* [indicating a second son]. Inscription: *Donum Joan: Hoadly Londinensis Episc: Sarisb: Filij natu min.: Coll: Corp: Christi e: B. Virg: Mariæ in Univ. Cantab. 1733* (Gift of John Hoadly of London, younger son of the Bishop of Salisbury, to the College of Corpus Christi and the Blessed Virgin Mary in Cambridge University, 1733).

Marks on added piece in base, leopard's head + leopard passant guardant. No date-letter or maker's mark.

John Hoadly, son of Benjamin Hoadly, Bishop of Salisbury (later Winchester), was admitted 1730, B.C.L. 1736.

These are dodgers (p. 11), but why? Evading the plate tax of sixpence an ounce would hardly have been worthwhile for such small pieces. Possibly the object was to use a stronger alloy of lower silver content than the law allowed, which would have helped with the elaborate piercings.

Our earliest pieces to show the beginnings of rococo fashion. A third caster disappeared from the inventory after 1879.

15.2 Large and Small Yorke Casters

1743 (inscription). Large one: 3.2 × 8.45 in. Small one: 2.85 × 6.9 in. Almost identical except in size.

Push-on lid pierced with alternate panels of foliated and X-shaped holes; foliated rococo cartouche for donor's arms: *Argent on a saltire azure a [bezant].*

Inscription: *Donum Hon^lis Car. Yorke Præhon^lis Baron de Hardwicke Filii natu Sedi. 1743.* (Gift of the Honourable Charles Yorke, second son of the Right Honourable Baron Hardwicke.) Weight inscription: 43:15 17:4 (large); 43 = 15 12 = 17 (small). [Present weights 16:13 ounces (large), 12:9 (small)].

Among the last pieces made by Joseph Allen & Mordecai Fox, active 1729–43; marked IA MF.

Charles Yorke of London (1722–70) was admitted in 1739; MA 1749 or 1759; barrister; made Lord Chancellor and created Baron Morden and thereupon died of 'chagrin and despair'; magnificently buried in Wimpole church.

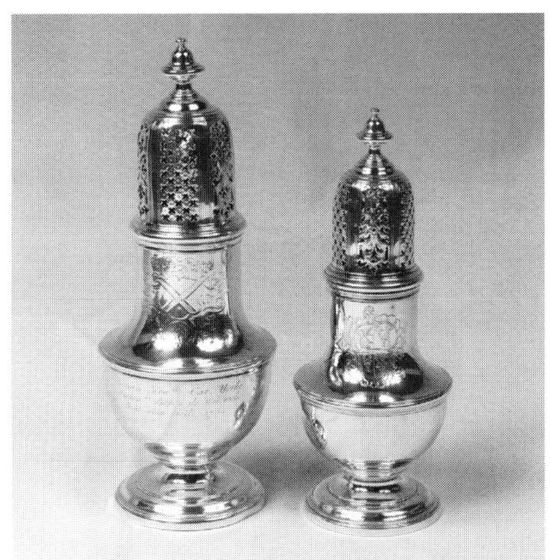

He possessed uncommon Endowments natural and acquired; was a complete Master of his own Profession . . . had an extensive knowledge of Polite Literature . . . His Stile in Composition and Speaking was nervous, elegant, and clear; and his Invention and Learning often furnished him with arguments, which had escaped the attention of Others. . . . both in his public and private station he always acted upon Principles of Virtue and Honor.

Epitaph

His brothers gave the Great Yorke Cup, Yorke Candlesticks, Great Yorke Salver and Yorke Standish.

A fine rococo pair. Instead of being dodgers, these are not hallmarked at all, but the makers did not hide their identity – perhaps on the plea that the articles were made to the client's order and were not for sale.

The 'sugar' caster has been much more cleaned, and thus probably more used, than the 'pepper' caster. A third caster was recycled in 1852 into a mustard-pot (p. 203).

15.3 Knowle Cruet-Frame and five vessels

1753 (London r). Silver stand in fivefold symmetry. Two glass cruets; three casters of different sizes.

Base 8.3 in. greatest diameter, 8.8 in. high with handle.

On a flat cinquefoil base (on five shell-feet) stand four double-curved piers, holding up seven circles, the five larger of which contain vessels. Instead of a fifth pier there is a plate bearing the College arms in a foliated and scrolled, very asymmetric rococo cartouche. A centre pillar, independent of the circles, screws into a hole (reinforced with a silver plate) in the base. Looped handle with rococo shells and foliation.

Maker's mark: *S·W* in rococo outline, for Samuel Wood (*c*.1704–94), prolific cruet-frame- and dredger-maker; he entered this mark 1739.

Two cruets: hexagonal cut-glass, with ground-glass stoppers, not exactly alike.

Two small casters: 1.9 × 5.3 in. high; pot-bellied, cylindrical top; cap chased and pierced in alternate pattern of lozenges and foliage, ending in acorn knob.

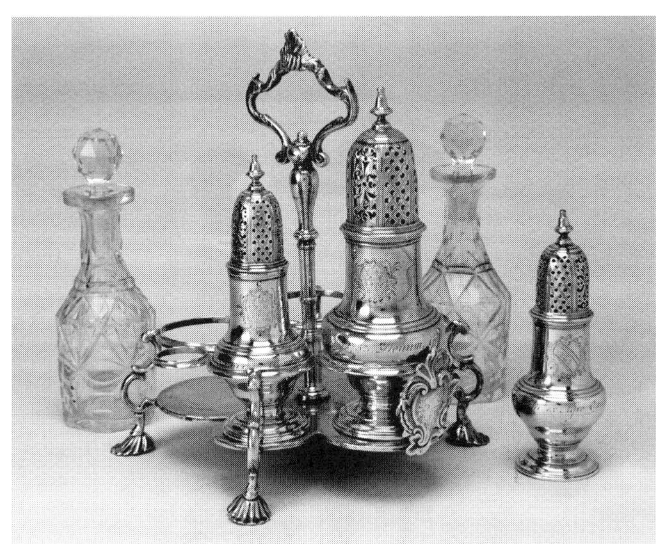

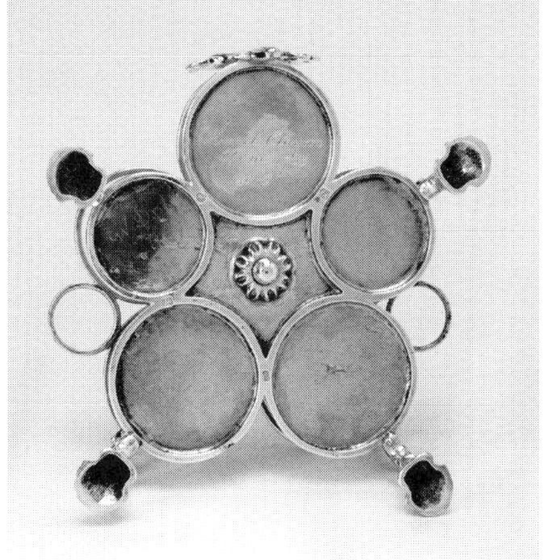

Large caster: 2.3 × 6.6 in.; identical but pierced with bigger holes.

All three casters bear arms of College and donor in chased foliated, shelled, very asymmetric cartouches. Inscribed *Donum Gilberti Knowle ex Agro Cantiano Armigeri. 1753* (Gift of Gilbert Knowle, armiger, from the land of Kent). One has letter *C* above College arms. Marks and maker as stand.

Donor's arms: *Argent, on a bend between two cotises sable a lion passant guardant argent crowned or.*

Given by Gilbert Knowle, admitted 1748; the Audit Book for 1754 records 1*s*. spent on bringing it.

15.4 Clayton Cruet-Frame and five vessels

1774 (London 𝕿). Silver stand in fivefold symmetry. Two glass cruets with silver caps; two casters of different sizes; one container like a caster but not pierced (mustard-pot?).

Base 8.3 in. greatest diameter; 8.5 high with handle.

Constructed like the preceding frame, except that the central pillar, with four moulded bands and a basal rosette at its base, ends in two knobs from which a flat looped handle arises. College arms in foliated rococo cartouche.

Inscription: *Kenrick Clayton Arm. 1733* |40..8| *C.C.C.C.* [Present weight of silver parts 40:20 ounces.]

Graffiti: *Herman Austin 1878 to 1928\Carless Dobbs\ 25 : 1*

Maker's mark: R·P, probably for Robert Piercy, cruet-frame- and caster-maker, active 1757–*c*.1777.

Two cruets: fine cut-glass, not alike.

Cruet-caps: cylindrical, ending in ovoid twisted knobs; inscribed C.C.C.C.; no marks; slightly too large for cruets.

Small caster: 1.9 × 5.7 in.; cap chased with bands of foliage and diagonal lines, pierced with small round holes, ending in twisted ovoid knob matching cruet-tops. Arms of College between sprays of foliage and flowers. Inscribed C.C.C.C. Marks and maker as stand.

Blind caster: identical but not pierced.

Large caster: 2.5 × 7.1 in. Identical to small caster but pierced with bigger holes shaped like flowers and foliage. Arms, inscription, marks, maker as before.

Replaced 'Two Boats for Sauce' given 41 years earlier by Kenrick Clayton of Marden, Surrey, who entered College 1737; later M.P. for Bletchingley and Baronet.

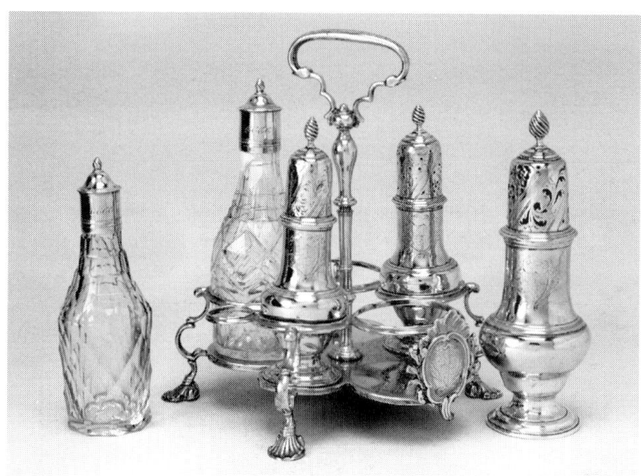

Adamesque (1784–1786)

15.5 Bateman-Jolliffe Caster

1784 (London i – before the introduction of the King's head in that year). 5.8 in. high.

Lid pierced in latticework all round; twisted finial.

Inscribed: *Virtue alone is happiness below Ino Jolliffe 1785*

Maker: SA in rectangle, probably for Stephen Adams I, lorimer and spooner, active *c.*1758–90.

Bequeathed by Aubrey Bateman, descendant of the happy and virtuous John Jolliffe (cf Bateman–Jolliffe Cigar-Box, p. 236).

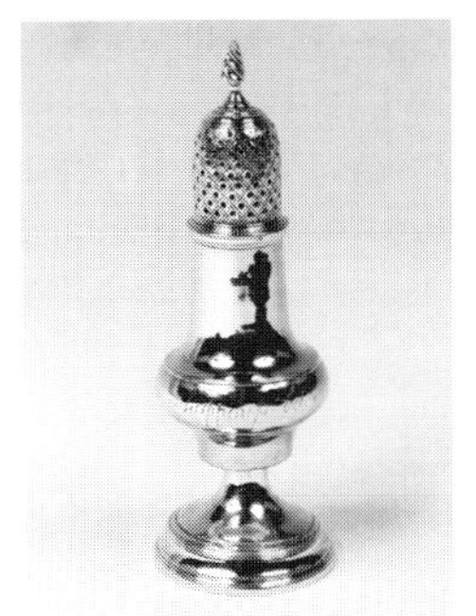

15.6 Parson Cruet-Frame and four cruets

1786 (London L) and later. Silver stand, varnished wooden floor. Four all-glass cruets, one with a tiny silver spoon attached to the stopper.

Base 7.2 in. × 4.3 wide; total height 9.5 in.

The barge-like stand on four legs has a flat floor covered with a silver plate. The central pillar, attached by a silver wing-nut and (later) washer, has a spacer for the bottles. Sides, pierced and engraved in a lozenge pattern at top, have an engraved blank cartouche with ribbons, foliage, and flowers. Stylized ryegrass is engraved round the inscription; legs end in stylized ball-&-claw feet; stylized wheat plants are engraved on openwork spacer.

The College arms are not placed in the cartouche, but represented as if suspended from a bow of ribbon.

Inscription: *Sam. Parson LLB Socis* [*sic*]
Commen: Salis [*sic*] DD CCCC 1787
Maker's mark illegible.
Cruets: four, fluted, with ground-glass stoppers.
Spoon projecting out of stopper: silver part 4.1 in. long, ending in long narrow bowl, truncated where handle enters. Marked 𝔓 for 1850 (if London). Maker's mark: G·R in rectangle, for George John Richards of London, active *c.*1845–67.

Given by Samuel P. Tregeare Parson of London; admitted 1781 or 1785; D.C.L. 1792.

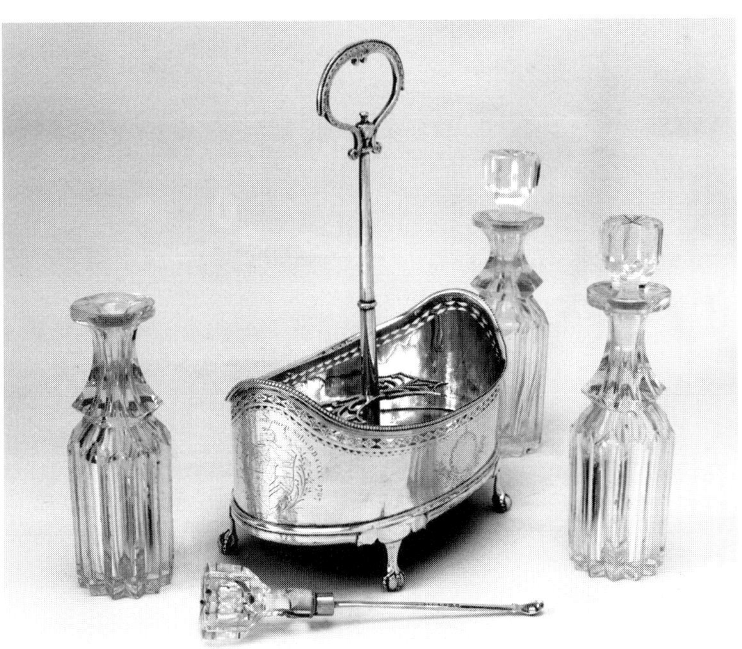

Regency (1816)

15.7 Glossop Cruet-Frame and four cruets

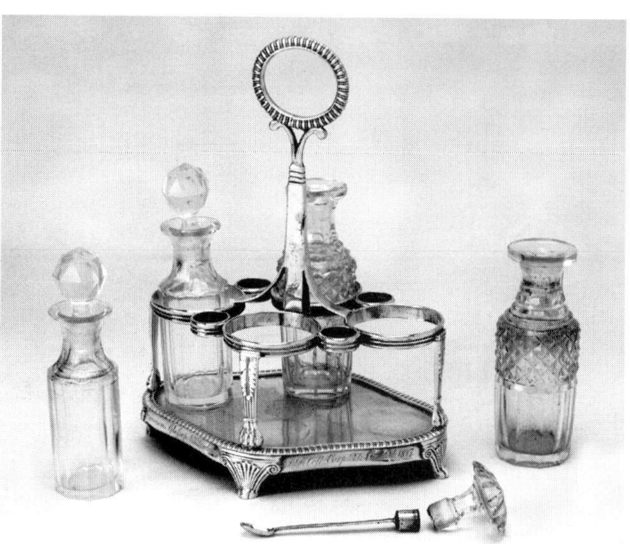

1816 (London a) and later. Silver stand with wooden floor. Four all-glass cruets, two with tiny silver spoons attached to the stopper.

Base 6.2 in. × 4.4 wide; total height 8.0 in.

Lozenge-shaped stand, floor covered with a silver plate. Four flat piers support a superstructure of eight circles, the four bigger containing bottles. Hollow rectangular central pillar. Base with gadrooned border; piers with ribs and leaf-tongues, ending in ball-&-claw feet; circles of superstructure ribbed; handle gadrooned.

College arms in rococo cartouche. No maker's mark.

Inscription: *Franciscus Glossop A.B Londinas* [*sic*] *d.D. Coll. Corp. Xti Cantab 1817.* (Francis Glossop, B.A., of London, gave [us] to the College . . .)

Cruets: 2 cut-glass, one with stopper and spoon, the other with spoon minus stopper; 2 decagonal with ground-glass stoppers, too small for stand.

Spoon attached to stopper: parcel-gilt; silver part 3.1 in. long; round bowl. Marked 𝔎 for 1845 (if London); no maker.

Spoon broken from stopper: single-gilt; tiny oblong spoon (3.0 in. long) mounted on long silver strip ending in socket for handle; tiny illegible Victorian hallmark.

Given by Francis Glossop of London, admitted 1812. This gift evidently marks his B.A. in 1812.

Victorian (1877–1899)

15.8 Nine Undergraduates' Cruet-Frames for three vessels each (not illustrated)

Two of 1877 (London B), three of 1878 (C), four of 1894 (T).

Silver stand for: (1) a glass cruet with silver collar and cap; (2) a cruet-like pepper-caster; (3) a glass mustard-cruet with silver lid.

7.8 to 8.2 in. high. Frames weigh 12.6 to 15.3 oz (391–476 g). Silver base-plate; four piers bearing three rings for vessels and a central handle, joined to base by four nuts. Undecorated.

Inscribed *Mens. Pens.* meaning that they were for the undergraduates' table.

Marks: (1877–8) C·E in ellipse, for Charles Edwards of London, active 1877–1903. (1894) C·B in ellipse + Roman lamp, for Charles Boyton II, active *c.*1873, died 1899, one of the many generations of Boyton & Son.

Cruets: nine survive, plus an elegant cut-glass 12-sided bottle. Eight have surviving silver collars: two marked for Charles Boyton II; three with Sheffield b for 1919 and mark M. & C° L in a quatrefoil, for Martin, Hall & Co. (1854–1936). The eight surviving caps are partly by Charles Edwards and partly bear Sheffield u for 1894 and I·C in rectangle for an unidentified maker.

Pepper-caster: one survives; 9-sided glass jar with silver collar, push-fit cap with six sets of comma-shaped piercings and moulded finial.

Mustard-pots: five survive; 9-sided glass jar with silver lid hinged to silver collar, with moulded finial. 4.75 to 4.9 in. high. All by Charles Boyton II.

15.9 Large Bateman Caster

1895 (London U). 3.2 × 7.7 in. high.

Octagonal throughout; lid with eight pairs of panels of foliated piercing, stepped top ending in octagonal knob.

Crest: *pheasant* with motto *NEC PRECE NEC PRETIO.*

Maker's mark, on body and lid: T • M in quatrefoil, is for Thomas Munday, active 1848–*c.*1896. Numerous graffiti.

This baroque revival piece was bequeathed by Aubrey Bateman.

15.10 Two Small Bateman Pepper-Casters (*not illustrated*)

1899 (Birmingham ʒ). 1.9 × 4.5 in. high.

Octagonal, keel below middle, high domed top pierced with dots, vase-like finial. Crest: *demi-pheasant.*

Made by Walker & Hall, 1853–.

Bequeathed by Aubrey Bateman.

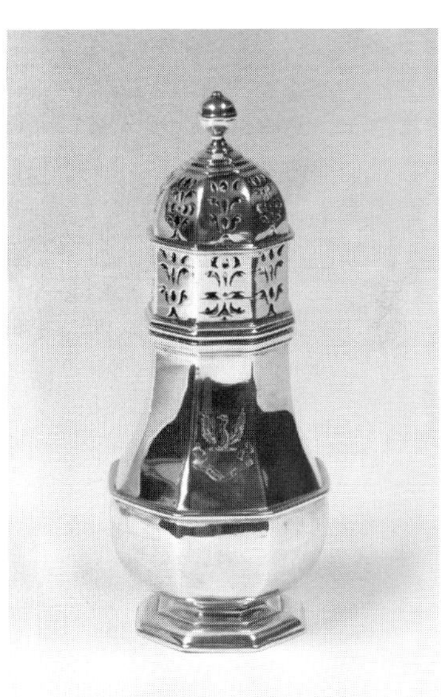

Twentieth Century

15.11 Du Plooy Sugar-Caster

1904 (Chester *D*). 3.4 × 8.0 in high.

High-domed top with sparse dot-and-comma piercings. Pointed twisted finial. 3 bands of deeply *repoussé* flowers and foliage on body. Maker illegible.

Given by Mrs M. Du Plooy, Schoolteacher Fellow Commoner 1996.

15.12 Four Bateman Casters

1928 (London n). 2.2 × 6.6 in. high.

Bulbous base and pedestal with two bands of gadrooning. Lid with 5 spiral bands of latticework with pierced holes, gadrooned at bottom, twisted finial.

Maker: RC • in baroque shield, for R. Comyns.

Bequeathed by Aubrey Bateman.

15.13 Two Faber Pepper-Grinders (*not illustrated*)

1958 (c). 1.6 × 2.8 in. Ebony and silver, steel works.

Two silver bands, silvered brass knob.

Inscription: **d.d. T.E.F. 1959** between badges of pelican and *a sleeved arm bearing a rose.*

Maker: C&A.

Thomas Erle Faber (1927–), physicist and publisher, from Oxford, came to Corpus from Trinity College as Fellow in 1953; he served as Prælector and Treasurer, and the writer remembers his teaching with affection. This is his wedding fine.

15.14 Two Chilver Pepper-Grinders (*not illustrated*)

1959 (*d*). 1.6 × 2.8 in. Elephant ivory (then legal), steel works.

Two silvered bands; one has silver knob, the other ivory.

Inscription: SOCIIS d.d. SOCIUS A.H.C. MCMLIX. (A.H.C., a Fellow, gave [me] to the Fellows, 1959.)

Maker: C&A.

Amos Henry, Baron Chilver of Cranfield (1926–), from Essex, engineer, came to Cambridge from Bristol in 1954; Fellow of Corpus 1958–61; Steward of the College; Honorary Fellow 1981–; Chadwick Professor, University College, London; Vice-Chancellor of the Institute of Technology, Cranfield, 1970–89; made a Lord 1987. This is his wedding fine.

15.15 Walters Salt-Grinder (*not illustrated*)

1978 (*D*). 1.7 × 2.8 in. All silver, polythene works.

Knurled knob with letter S.

Inscription: **d.d. P.M.W. MCMLXXIX.**

Maker: JAC in triangle.

Philip Max Walters (1949–), linguist, son of Max Walters the Cambridge botanist, came as an undergraduate in 1968; Research Fellow 1976–9; a director of Keston College (now Keston Institute) for research on religion in Communist and ex-Communist countries. This is his wedding fine.

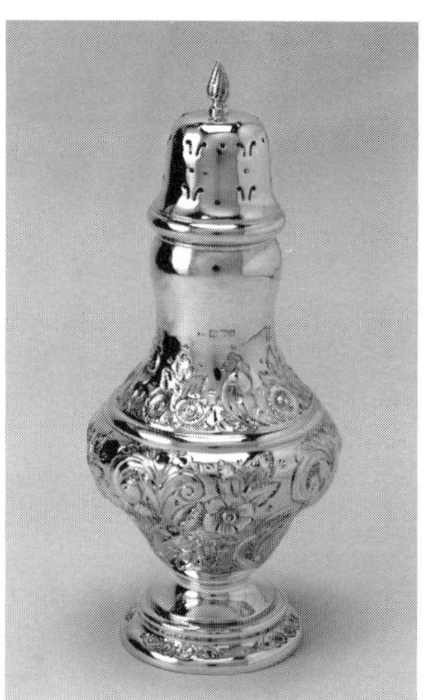

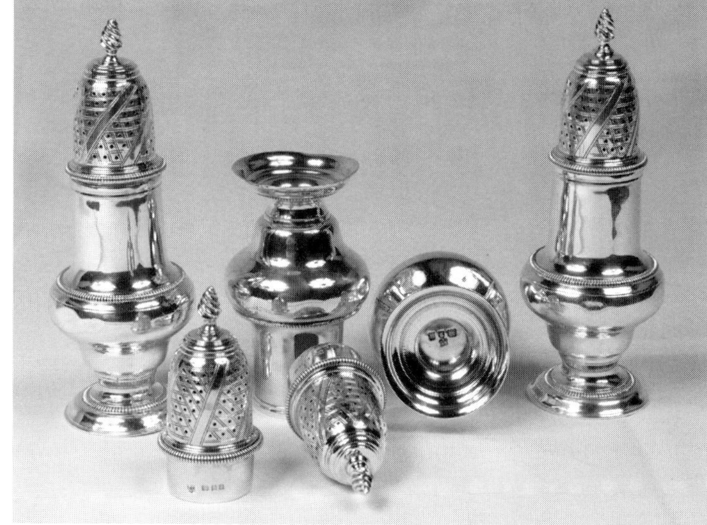

Du Plooy (left) and Bateman (1928) Casters.

16

Salts & Saltspoons

𝔖alts 3

	onz
In primis a double bell salt wth Cover silver	$13\frac{1}{2}$
Item a silver bell salt mri Sonds	$9\frac{3}{4}$
Item mri Swalman a low salt wthout Covr	$8\frac{1}{2}$
[added] Item mr Thomas Rivet a silver bell salt	10

so found Feb. 6. 1618 & Feb. 13. 1621

Inventory of buttery plate, 1604/5

[William Sonde of Kent gave a tankard in 1596, recycled into this salt. Geoffrey Swalman of Kent gave a salt in 1597. Thomas Revett of Suffolk gave a salt in 1608. All three were Fellow-Commoners. The first two salts were melted in the 1620s, the last in the mid-17th century.]

A *saler* or *celler*, miscalled a *salt-cellar*, is the everyday equivalent to the great ceremonial salt such as Parker's. A common type in the 17th century, no longer surviving at Cambridge, was the bell salt, with three superimposed compartments for salt, pepper, and something else. Another was the low 'trencher' salt.

With the invention of ceilings, and thus less need for lids to keep debris out of the salt, there appear the three-legged baroque and rococo salts. Salts are often gilded or have glass liners to protect the silver from the corrosive contents. The salt-caster and salt-grinder (§15.15) are 20th-century fashions.

To judge by children's etiquette books, the practice of dipping one's food in the salt was disapproved of, and therefore was presumably common, in the middle ages. Polite people scooped salt out with the point of a knife. The fastidious 19th century invented the salt-spoon, a tiny ladle. (The writer was taught to put a little heap of salt on the side of his plate. It was, he knows not why, bad manners to sprinkle salt on the food.) Saltspoons tend to be associated with particular cellers, although they were usually made separately by spooners.

Baroque Salts (1733)

16.1 Two Mynors Salts

1733 (London S). 2.8 in. × 1.8 high.

Round bowl narrowed at mouth, three cabriole legs.

Inscription: *MAGISTRO ET SOCIIS COLLEGII CORPORIS CHRISTI ET B.M.V. D.D. H.C.B. MYNORS. XXV DEC: A.S. MCMXXVIII.* (H.C.B. Mynors gave these to the Master and Fellows of the College of Corpus Christi and the Blessed Virgin Mary, 25 Dec. A.D.1928.)

Crest: *a Baron's coronet surmounted by an arm in plate-armour, grasping a luce* [pike] *or other fish.*

Maker: EW and broad arrow for Edward Wood (*c.*1700–1752), salt-celler-maker of Puddledock Hill, London.

Sir Humphrey Charles Baskerville Mynors (1903–89) of Wiltshire, son of a parson, mathematician, came as Scholar 1922. He was Fellow 1926–33, Tutor and Prælector; Honorary Fellow 1953–. Deputy Governor of the Bank of England 1954–64; Baronet 1964.

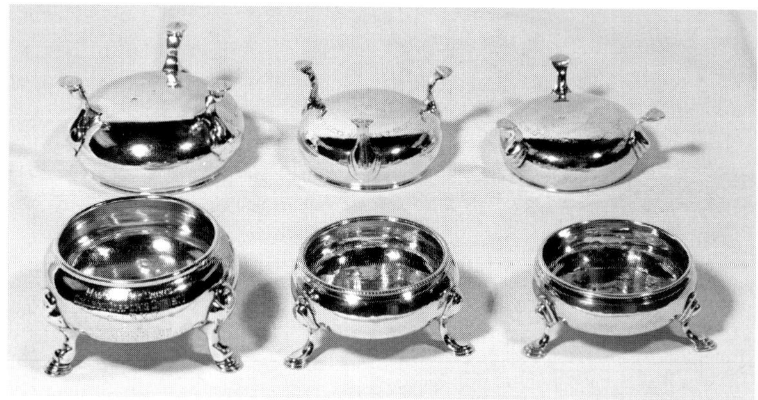

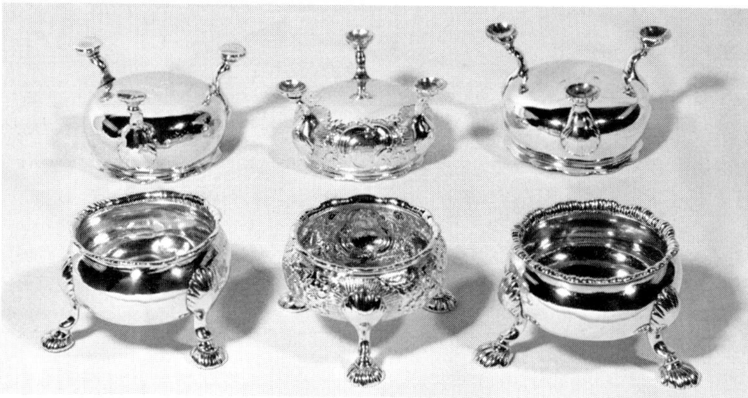

Eighteenth-century Salts. Above: Mynors (§16.1), Strachan (16.5), Dykes Bower (§16.7). Below: CCC (16.4), Burnet (§16.2), JMJ (16.6), Bateman (§16.3).

Rococo Salts (1745–1795)

16.2 Four Burnet Salts

1745 (London k). 3.0 in. × 2.0 high.

Round bowl with constricted mouth, three cabriole legs, feet flat underneath. Gadrooning on rim (less on one piece). Oblong cartouche. Grass-like cast ribs on lower legs.

Inscription: *GVL^{MS} BURNET ARM. DEDIT CCCC* (very faint) (Willm Burnet, armiger, gave [us] to C.C.C.C.) Arms lost.

Maker's mark: mullet and C M or G M (very worn).

William Burnet, son of the Governor of New York, was admitted 1741, presumably as a Fellow-Commoner; left for the Middle Temple 1742.

The most worn and battered articles still in general use. When given to the College their weight, entered in the Vellum Book, was 20 oz. 5 dwt. They now weigh 17 oz. 3 dwt: 15% of the metal has been lost through cleaning and a little corrosion. The arms on all four and the inscriptions on three are reduced to indecipherable pinpricks.

16.3 Six [Bateman] Salts

1754 (London t) 2.95 in. × 2.0 high. Gilt inside.

Almost identical to the above, but much less worn.

Maker's mark: DRHH in cross, for David Hennell I from Newport Pagnell (1712–85) and his son Robert Hennell I (1741–1811), partners in London 1763–.

Bequeathed by Aubrey Bateman.

16.4 Four 'C.C.C.C.' Salts

1756 (London 𝔄). 2.8 in. × 2.05 high.

Almost identical to the Bateman Salts and apparently by the same maker, but not gilt, very battered and worn and slightly corroded. Arms worn away, maker's mark indecipherable.

Inscribed ***C. C. C. C.*** (discernible only on one salt).

16.5 Two Charles Strachan Salts

1762 and 1775 (London 𝔊, 𝔘). 2.4 in. × 1.3 high.

Almost a pair. Shallow round bowl, three legs. The earlier one has rope-moulding round mouth, the later has beading.

Inscription: *D.D. C. STRACHAN SOCIUS MAGISTRO ET SOCIIS COLLEGII CORPORIS CHRISTI ET B.V.M. A.S. MCMXXXVII.* (Gift of C. Strachan to the Master and Fellows of the College . . . A.D. 1937.)

Makers' marks illegible. The 1775 salt is very similar to the Dykes Bower (below) and may be by the same maker.

Charles Strachan (1907–93) of Aberdeen; mathematician; came as Affiliated Student 1929; Scholar; Fellow 1934–7. He was Reader in Natural Philosophy, Aberdeen University 1964–77.

The earlier one is much corroded.

16.6 Six Bateman-Jolliffe 'JMJ' Salts (five survive)

1760s and 1795? Three not quite identical pairs, evidently with different histories (and various graffiti) before they were inscribed. 2.85 in. × 2.0 high. Four gilt inside.

Round bowl with constricted mouth, three legs. Bowl elaborately *repoussé* and chased with various stylized flowers and foliage; rococo cartouche. Gadrooning on rim. Grass-like cast ribs on lower legs.

Monogram *JMJ*.

Pair A: not gilt; date illegible. Maker's mark fragmentary for the Hennells (see §16.3). Very tarnished inside, cracked and badly mended.

Pair B: thinly gilt inside; margin less gadrooned than A; London date-letter ?L for 1766. Maker's mark fragmentary, probably also Hennell.

Pair C: traces of gilding inside; London date-letter u for 1795 (1835 would be possible). Maker's mark fragmentary GL [?] in rectangle. Good condition.

Given by Aubrey Bateman, from one of his Jolliffe relatives (cf §19.4.4).

Typically rococo, but one pair is late for that style. The *repoussé* and chased work have been suspected of being later additions, but there is no internal evidence of this, and such an alteration would be surprising on all six, since they are not a set. Salts are a conservative type of object in which the sequence of fashions is subdued.

16.7 Two Dykes Bower Salts

1776 (London a; 1736 would be possible). 2.4 in. × 1.15 high.

Shallow round bowl, three legs. Straight beading round mouth. Almost identical to Strachan Salt of 1775.

Inscription: *MAGISTRO ET SOCIIS COLLEGII CORPORIS CHRISTI ET B.V.M. D.D. J. DYKES BOWER SOCIUS A.S. MCMXXXVII.*

Maker: T.S in rectangle, for Thomas Shepherd from Wiltshire, active in London 1769–89.

John Dykes Bower (1905–81) of Gloucester, famous organist, was Organ Scholar 1922; Fellow 1934–7; honorary D.Mus., Oxford, 1944; Honorary Fellow of Corpus 1980–; co-designer of the Chapel organ.

Slightly pitted.

Adamesque Salts (1803)

16.8 Four Lee Salt-Boats

1803 (London H). 4.0 in. × 2.45 × 1.9 high. Blue glass liners.

Boat-shaped, elliptical pedestal. Moulding of 3 ribs round rim of bowl and of foot.

Inscription (round pedestals) .:. *MAG ET SOC COLL CORP CHR ET B.V.M. d.d. H.D.P. LEE SOCIUS XXIII*

MAR MCMXXXV (H.D.P. Lee, Fellow, gave [us] to the Master and Fellows . . .).

Makers' mark: R·H S·H in rectangle, for Robert Hennell I (1741–1811) and Samuel Hennell (1778–1837). This partnership began 1802.

Sir Henry Desmond Pritchard Lee (1908–93) of Nottingham, Classical scholar, came as Scholar 1927. He was Fellow 1933–68 and 1978–93; Tutor 1935–48; Headmaster of Clifton College 1948–54 and of Winchester College 1954–68; knighted 1961; President of Hughes Hall 1974–8. These are presumably his wedding fine.

All four scratched underneath.

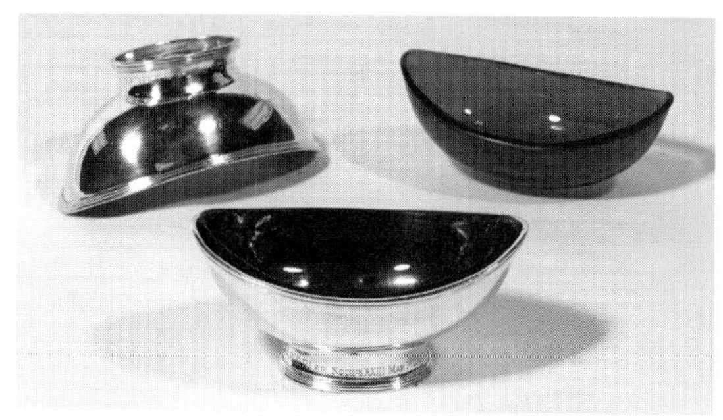

Regency Salts (1810–1821)

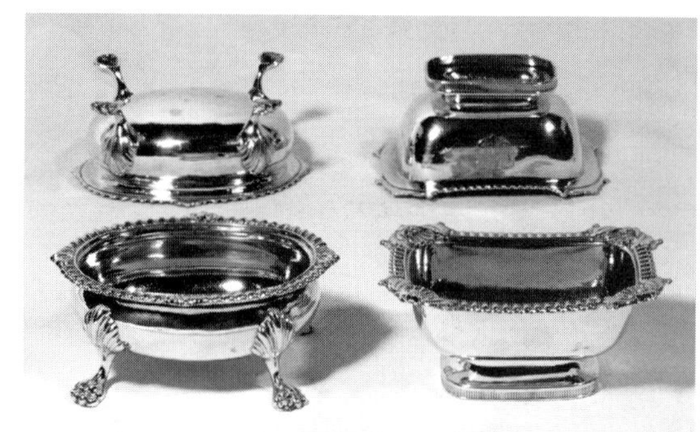

Oval and Rectangular Salts (§16.10, 16.9)

16.9 Six Rectangular Salts

1810–3 (London P (two), R (two), S (two)). 4.0 in. × 2.9 × 1.8 high.

Shells and foliage (separately cast) in corners; gadrooned border; rectangular pedestal with milled edge.

College arms, on baroque shield.

Makers' mark: RE EB, for the very big firm of Rebecca Emes & Edward Barnard I, 1808–.

Given by John David Gathorne-Hardy (1900–78), fourth Earl of Cranbrook; Deputy Regional Commissioner for East Anglia in World War II, and thus second-in-command to Sir Will Spens (see §21.19); CBE 1955; a much-appreciated member of Corpus's High Table; father of the present Lord Cranbrook, a graduate of the College.

Much corroded inside; some of the ears at the corners missing.

16.10 Two Oval Salts

1816 (Edinburgh k) 4.2 in. × 3.1 × 1.7 high. Gilt inside.

Oval; mouth constricted with broad everted rim bearing four shell-features or foliated cusps; four vaguely lionish feet. Legs with grass-mouldings.

Maker's mark: JH in rectangle, unidentified (many Edinburgh silversmiths had these initials).

Reputedly given by A.L. Goodhart (see Goodhart Bowl).

Victorian Salts (1821–1859)

16.11 Two Ogilvie Salts (*not illustrated*)

1821 (London f). 2.65 in. × 1.6 high. Traces of gilding inside.

Same pattern as Burnet, Bateman, and C.C.C.C. Salts, but later and little worn.

Inscription: *EX DONO CAROLI MACIVOR GRANT OGILVIE SOC COMM MCMXXXIII*

Maker: E·F in quatrefoil, for Edward Farrell of London, first entered 1819.

Donor: Sir Charles MacIvor Grant Ogilvie, Fellow Commoner 1931, later CSI, CBE.

One of our earliest pieces to be a deliberate copy of an earlier style. Farrell is known for his 'revival rococo style' (Grimwade 1990).

16.12 Four Matthews Salts

1859 (London 𝔡 for 1859). 3.55 in. × 2.2 high. Single-gilt inside.

Round bowl with markedly constricted mouth, three feet. Bowl deeply *repoussé* with *Cistus*-like flowers and with empty cartouche on one side. Gadrooned rim. Feet cast, with lions' paws and lions' faces.

Inscription: *C.C.C. ET B.M.V. D.D. GEORGIUS MATTHEWS QUI PER XXXV FERE ANNOS CELLERIUS FUIT MANET AMICUS* (Gift to the College . . . of George Matthews, who was Cellarer for nearly 35 years and remains a friend.)

Maker: R.H in bifoil, for Robert Harper of London, active *c*.1859–*c*.1890.

Given by George Matthews, College Butler until 1946.

Slightly pitted.

Another anachronistic rococo item.

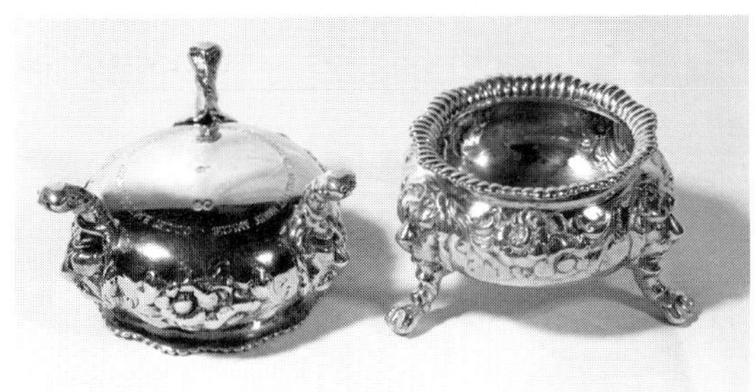

Twentieth-Century Salts

16.13 Bateman Salt

?1922 (London ?𝔤 in 3-tailed shield). 3.6 in. × 2.1 × 2.1 high. Blue glass liner.

Elliptical on 4 clawed feet, no floor. Heavy moulding round rim. Pierced with rectangles and arches.

Badge: *demi-pheasant.* Motto: NEC PRECE NEC PRETIO.

Maker: AJH in butterfly outline, for Alfred James How, active 1897–*c*.1925.

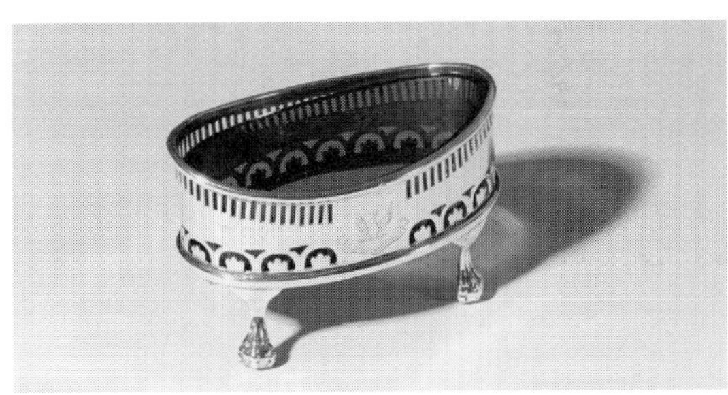

16.14 Four Square 'Comyns' Salts

1933 (London 𝔖). 3.8 in. square × 2.85 high.

Square with inverted-rounded corners, central pedestal. Moulded rim and pedestal.

Maker: RC in baroque cartouche, for R. Comyns.

Reputedly given by one Drury.

Coarse pieces, typical of the period, with plenty of silver (which was getting cheap) and not much craftsmanship. Much pitted with use.

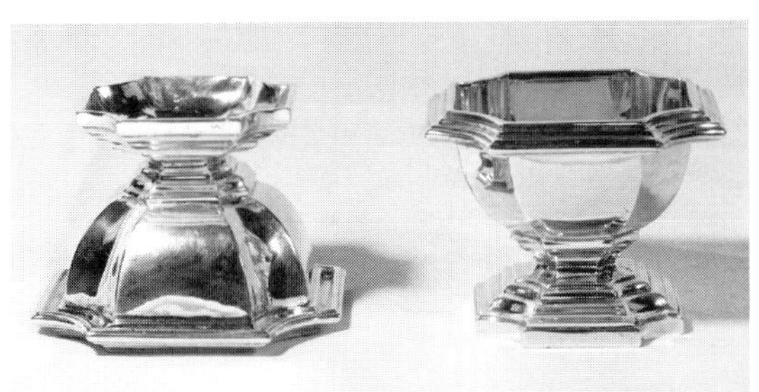

11.17a Salt-Spoons (see also Bateman Mini-Ladles, §18.4.8)

Name	Date	Length, in.	Handle	Bowl	Inscription or Arms	Maker's mark	Notes
1	1806 (Lond. L + Geo. III)	4.1	Old English	circular, drop	*SC*	illegible	goes with following
1	1813 (Lond. S + Geo. III)	4.1	Old English	circular, drop	*SC*	RT in rectangle (unid.)	made for Six Rectangular Salts?
Mynors 2	1808 (Lond. N)	3.8	Old English	transverse, drop	*H. C. B. MYNORS*	PB WT in square (not certain)	go with Mynors Salts, but not made for them
College Arms 4	1813 (Lond. S + Geo. III)	4.2	fiddle	transverse, drop	Coll. arms on baroque shield	. E . . in square, ? for Rebecca Emes & Edward Barnard I	probably made for 6 Rectangular Salts
Lee 4	1786–1821 (Geo. III, no letter)	4.2	Old English, pointed	transverse, pointed	*H.D.P.L.* [for Lee] *W T.S*	R.B in rectangle, unid.	go with Lee Salt-boats, but not made for them
Jackson 6	1814 (Dublin S)	4.5	King's pattern (elaborately foliated with shells)	transverse			Britannia silver. Labelled 'from Mr Jackson' in hand of Alan Wilson, Butler; not known which Jackson
Ogilvie 2	1825 (Lond. k)	3.9	Old English	transverse	*CMGO* [for Ogilvie]	J.M in rectangle, unid.	go with Ogilvie Salts, but not made for them
JMJ 2	1830 (Lond. p)	4.1	fiddle	transverse; lightly gilt	*JMJ*	R·H in rectangle, incuse X: ?for Robert Hennell II	not made for JMJ salts; formerly 4
Bateman 3	1835 (Lond. u)	4.7	hybrid shape with strapwork & shells	circular	demi-pheasant crest	WT LB in square, for Theobalds & Lockington	added to six Bateman salts; one with trace of gilding inside
Bateman 1	1839 (Lond. 𝔇)	4.7	ditto	circular	ditto	WT RA in square, for Theobalds & Atkinson	added to six Bateman salts
Bateman 2	1865 (Lond. 𝔨) – not 1845	4.7	ditto	circular	ditto	ISH under arch, for Samuel Hunt	ditto; one lightly gilt inside & out
1	1836 (Lond. 𝔄)	4.2	fiddle	transverse	none	. L . L CL in rectangle + mullet, unid.	battered
Dykes Bower 2	1854 (Lond. 𝔗)	4.0	Old English	transverse, drop	*JDB* for Dykes Bower	CB in oval, ?for Charles Boyton I (§18.1.18)	not made for Dykes Bower salts
4 With Shells	1869 (Lond. 𝔬)	4.5	King's pattern	transverse, shell + foliage	none	triangle + GA in bifoil, for G.W. Adams	go with Matthews Salts?
4 Shovels	1873 (Lond. 𝔰)	4.1	flattish, reeded	fan-shaped shovel	none	R.C in baroque shield, unid.	go with square 'Comyns' salts of 1933?
Under-graduate 15	1876 (Lond. A)	3.75	Old English	circular + drop	*Mens Pens Coll. Corp. Chr.* + pelican	GA in bifoil + 6 in square for G.W. Adams	undergraduate salts were presumably not silver
1	1883 (Lond. H)	3.5	fiddle	transverse	none	PKD in rectangle (uncertain)	corroded
1	1912 (Lond. r)	3.7	Hanoverian	circular, rat-tail	lion rampant in crown	S^B W&H L^D for Walker & Hall?	
Shell-shaped CCCC 4	illegible	3.5	Hanoverian	elongated scallop shell	*C.C.C.C.*	none	not identical; 2 partly gilt; repairs
Shell-shaped PJD 1	illegible	3.4	Hanoverian	elongated scallop shell	*PJD*	none	
Loopy CCCC 4	no marks	3.2–3.4	long thin shaft looped to form handle	circular	*C.C.C.C.*	none	gilt inside; 2 mended + 1 cannibalized

Notes:
For William Theobalds, spooner, see §18.4.8.
For John Samuel Hunt, of Hunt & Roskell, see §21.4.4.
For George William Adams (1808–95), famous London spooner, see 18.2.14.
PJD: a Philip John Durrant was admitted 1919; later Tutor of Selwyn.

17

Mustards and Mustard-Spoons

We feed [Carlo] only once a day and not too much then, so that he is always as keen as mustard.

C. Doyle, *The Copper Beeches*

Mustard, the ground seeds of *Brassica nigra* and *Sinapis arvensis*, is an ancient and widespread spice, used for flavouring and medicine, and one of the few indigenous to Britain; it traditionally went with brawn (p. 21). Mustard-pots are tiny tankard-like or basket-like silver containers for mustard flour made into a mud or paste. We have no known example of a dredger for sprinkling dry mustard.

The College bought a mustard-pot in 1678 for 2*s*. 6*d*., which for that money could not have been of silver.[1] Silver mustards are rare before 1750. Mustard is a corrosive herb: silver pots usually have blue glass liners or are gilt inside. A notch for the spoon is usually cut out of the lid.

A little spoon is assigned by tradition to each of the College's mustard pots, although many of them are of different provenance.

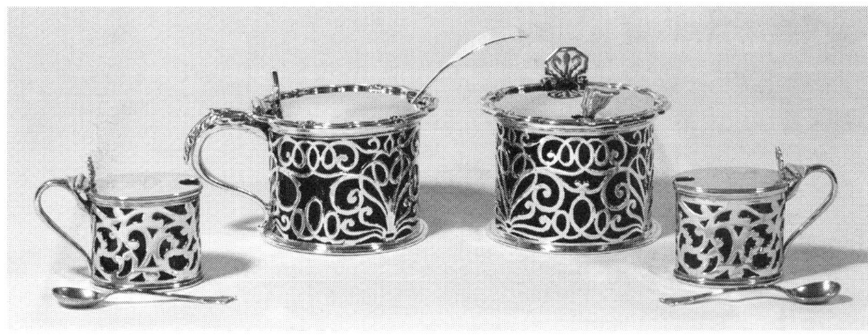

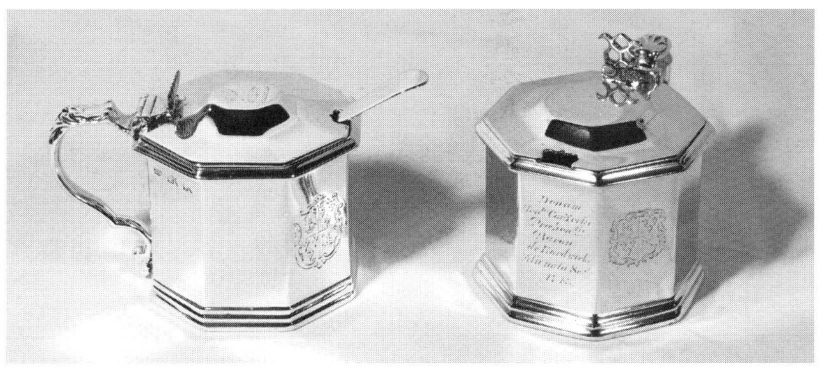

Above: Bateman Mustards of 1898, 1836, 1912, 1898. Below: Harpur and Yorke Mustards.

1 CC(A): *Audit Book 1590–1685*.

17.1 Fisher Mustard-Pot

1800 (London E). Silver, gilt inside hinged lid. 3.9 in. × 2.9 × 2.7 high.

Cylindrical mini-tankard, solid floor, very flat lid with two horns by way of thumbpiece, S-handle. Four reeds on rim and base. Vestigial foliation on handle. Spoon-notch cut out of body (and out of very thick blue glass liner). College arms on lid in foliated surround.

Inscription: *E dono Edmundi Fisher hujus Collegii Commensalis* (Of the gift of Edmund Fisher, [Fellow-] Commoner of this College.) Graffito: *H. Austin 1878 to 1928*

Maker's mark: *WA* in ellipse, for the obscure William Allen III.

Associated spoon: 4.2 in. long. 1813 (London S). Transverse bowl, thinly gilt inside. Fiddle-pattern with drop. College arms. Maker's mark illegible.

Edmund Fisher, of Cambridge, was admitted 1792, MA 1800.

Pot and spoon have seen long service and conscientious cleaning at the hands of Austin and his colleagues, judging by the worn state of the College arms.

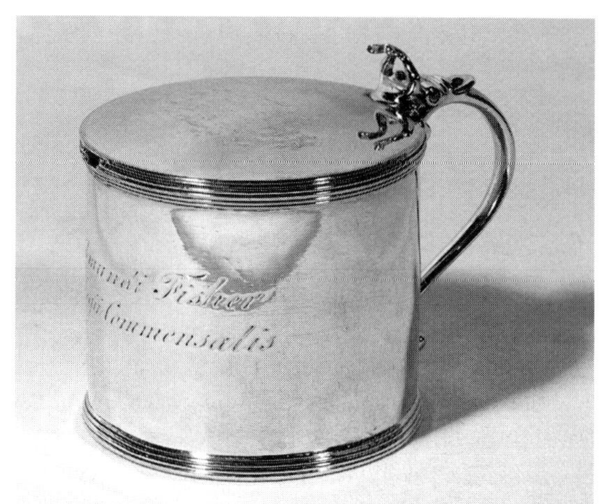

17.2 Society of Medicine Mustard-Barrel

1804 (London I). 3.6 in. × 2.5 × 2.9 high. 3

Barrel-shaped, open floor, low domed hinged lid, strap handle. Body decorated with ribbed bands; shell thumbpiece to lid. Cylindrical blue glass liner.

Inscription: *DONO DEDERVNT E SOCIETATE BRITANNICA MEDICINA PLERIQVE DOCTISSIMI MENS: IVN: A.D. MCMXL VIII* (The majority of the most learned of the British Society of Medicine gave [me] in the month of June A.D. 1948)

Maker's mark: F in square with cut corners, for Charles Fox.

Associated spoon inscribed ELKINGTON PLATE ENGLAND.

Battered, especially lid. Spoon very corroded.

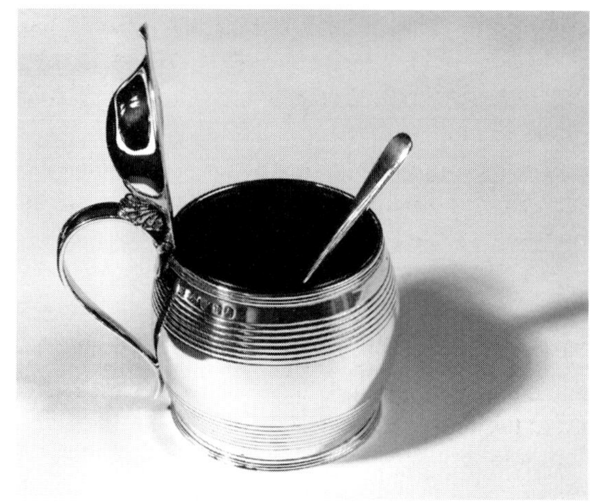

17.3 [Bateman] Mustard-Basket and Spoon of 1836 *Illustrated on* p. 201

London letter 𝔄. Silver, gilt inside lid. 4.3 in. × 3.2 × 3.0 high.

Sides pierced to leave interlace of curving bars; open floor; plain round nearly flat lid resting on rebate; pierced thumbpiece, S-shaped handle. Rim cusped in hexafoil pattern, with vestigial palmettes. Foliated handle. Blue glass liner.

Maker's mark: CR GS in square, for Charles Reily & George Storer, London snuff-box-makers, active 1829–.

Spoon: 4.6 in. long. Miniature ladle, fiddle-pattern, with round bowl and long, very curved handle. Handle bordered with single groove in front, double groove in back. Hallmarks and maker's mark as on pot.

Bequeathed by Aubrey Bateman. Forms a pair with his 1912 one.

17.4 Harpur Mustard-Pot *Illustrated on* p. 201

1852 (London 𝕽). 3.9 in. × 2.8 × 3.2 high.

Plain octagon, lid with flat top, C-handle. Foliated cartouches for arms; foliated handle with shell on top; shell thumbpiece to lid. Blue glass liner.

College arms (with pelican pseudo-crest, repeated on lid) and donor's: *A lion rampant within a bordure engrailed.*

Inscribed: *Dedit Edvardus Harpur Armiger Derbiensis Soc: Comm: 1733.* (Edward Harpur of Derby, Fellow Commoner, gave [me] 1733.) Graffiti: 36290 HA 1878.

Mark GR in rectangle, for George John Richards (active 1845–*c*.1857) of Richards & Brown, London. On base: PETERS & SON CAMBRIDGE.

Associated spoon: 5.0 in. long. Miniature ladle, fiddle-pattern, with round bowl and long, very curved handle. Pelican pseudo-crest. Inscribed: *CCCC.* Date-letter London 𝕻 for 1850. Mark: triangle + EE, probably for Elizabeth Eaton (see §18.1.18).

All we know of Edward Harpur is that he joined the College in 1733 and gave us a quart tankard, which shrank into this pot 120 years later.

17.5 Yorke Mustard-Pot (*Illustrated on* p. 201)

1852 (London 𝕽). 4.0 in. × 2.8 × 3.2 high. Almost identical to the above.

Donor's arms: *Argent on a saltire azure a [bezant].*

Inscription: *Donum Hon^lis Car. Yorke Praehon^lis Baron de Hardwicke Filii natu Se^di 1743.* (Gift of the Honourable Charles Yorke, second son of the Right Honourable Baron Hardwicke 1743.)

Recycled from one of the three casters given by Charles Yorke (§15.2).

Disused; glass liner missing.

17.6 Eight Undergraduates' Mustard-Spoons (*not illustrated*)

1877 (two; London B) and 1895 (six: London U). 5.8 in.

Narrow bowl, 'Old English' tapered handle. Plain, with drop at root of handle and 'Hanoverian' cusp at its tip. Pelican badge.

Inscription: *Mens: Pens: Coll: Corp. Chr.*

Makers' marks: 1877, GA in bifoil + heart, for George William Adams (see §18.1.26). 1895, GMJ in rectangle (George Maudsley Jackson II of Bristol, active 1877–*c*.1915)

17.7 Ahmed Mustard-Basket

1894 (Birmingham u). 3.9 in. × 2.5 × 3.9 high.

Almond-shaped in plan, saddle-shaped in profile; floor open; lid hinged on long side, with knob; C handle. Ribs on feet. Sides pierced with four bands of slits. Blue glass liner.

Inscription: *The gift of* HAROON AHMED *Fellow, married 1969.*

Maker's mark: B & T in ellipse, unidentified.

Haroon Ahmed (1936–), of Calcutta and Karachi, the present Master, came via Imperial College, London and King's College, Cambridge to become a Fellow of Corpus 1966. Professor of Microelectronics; Head of the Microelectronics Research Centre; elected Master in 2000. He gave this piece on marrying Anne Goodrich.

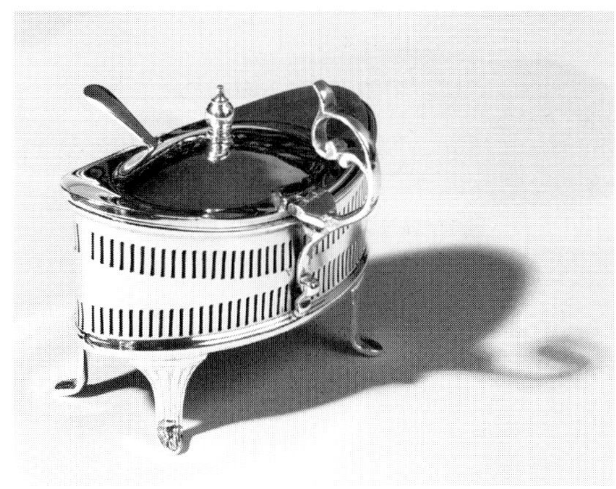

17.8 Two Bateman Small Mustard-Baskets and Mustard-Spoons (*Illustrated on* p. 201)

1898 (London c). 2.7 in. × 1.4 × 2.0 high.

Oval cylinder with loop handle; large hole in base. Rather coarse foliated piercing. Shell-shaped thumb-piece. Blue glass liner.

Bateman crest, *a pheasant*, with motto *NEC PRECE NEC PRETIO*.

Maker's mark: fragmentary for Charles Stuart Harris & Sons (see below).

Spoons: 2.9 in. long; elongated bowl, trifid handle (a characteristic feature of 17th-century spoons, of which this is the only surviving example in the College's entire hoard); ribbing on distal part of handle; same marks.

17.9 Beck Mustard-Pot

1911 (Sheffield t). 3.0 in. × 2.3 × 2.4 high.

Mini-tankard with rounded edge to bottom, three sideways-projecting feet, S-handle. Flat hat-shaped lid with rim, thumb-piece, and hinge. Blue glass liner. Inscribed 10 on lid.

Maker's mark: GB & S in baroque shield, unidentified.

Associated spoon: London a + King's head for 1816. 3.9 in. long. Old English with transverse bowl. Mark, WS in oval, for one of the William Sumner spooners.

Given in 1997 on the eightieth birthday of Arnold Hugh William Beck (1916–97), of Norfolk; graduate and Fellow of University College, London; Fellow of Corpus 1962–; Professor of Electrical Engineering 1966–83.

17.10 [Bateman] Mustard-Basket of 1912 (*Illustrated on* p. 201)

London r for 1912 (no king's head). Gilt inside lid, traces of gilding inside body. 4.3 in. × 3.2 × 3.0 high.

A close copy of the 1836 mustard-pot. Marks were struck on one of the bars after piercing.

Maker's mark: C S & H S in shield, for Charles Stuart Harris & Sons, active 1897–1933.

Possible associated spoon: 1800 (London E). 4.6 in. long. Miniature ladle, fiddle-pattern, with round bowl and long, very curved handle; double reed surrounds both sides. Maker's mark WE WF in square for William Eley I and William Fearn, partners 1797–.

17.11 Hawkes Mustard-Pot

1931 (London q). Britannia silver. 3.5 in. × 2.3 × 2.6 high.

Rectangular with cut-off corners; sides concavely tapering; flat lid; S-handle; round-bottomed cavity inside. Rim and base heavily moulded; plain handle and lid; thumbpiece on lid with twisted ears. No liner. College arms.

Inscribed: *DONO DEDIT T.O. HAWKES A.S. MCMLXVI* TESSIERS L^{TD} LONDON

Mark: AP FP in shield, for Arthur Martin Parsons and Frank Herbert Parsons, of Tessiers Ltd, founded *c*.1841.

Associated spoon: 1890 (Sheffield X). 2.5 in. long. Tiny spoon of Hanoverian pattern, long bowl passing gradually into handle. Marked WB, unidentified.

Trevor Ongley Hawkes (1936–), Scholar of Trinity College, was Fellow of Corpus 1965–7; Reader in Mathematics, Warwick University 1977–. This is his fine for marrying in 1966.

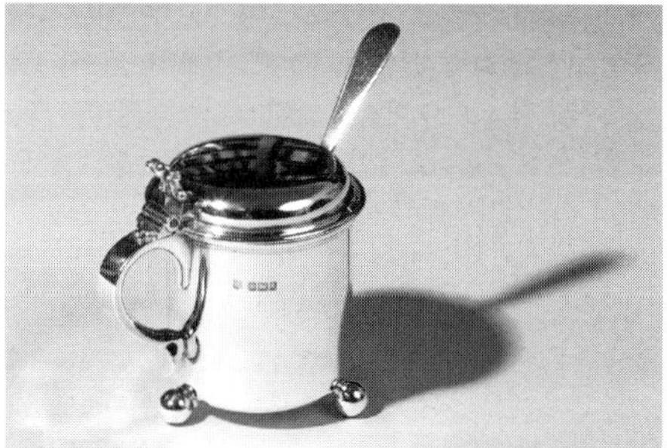

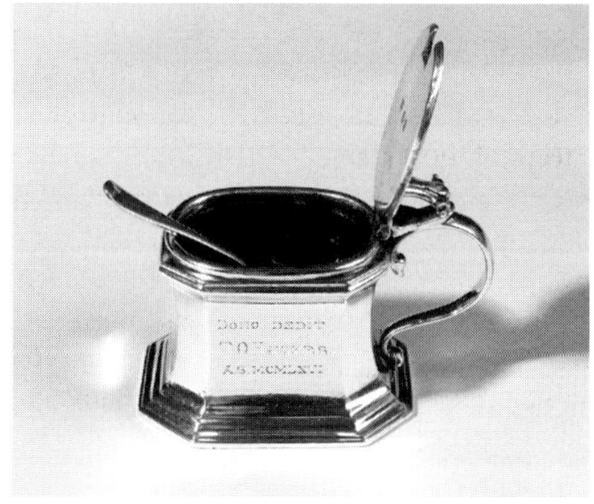

18

Tools or Flatware

I could not see my table-spoons – I look'd, but could not see
The little fiddle-pattern 'd ones I use when I'm at tea;
– I could not see my sugar-tongs – my silver watch – oh, dear!
I know 'twas on the mantel-piece when I went out for beer.

R.H. Barham, *Misadventures at Margate (Ingoldsby Legends)*

Tools for eating have become stepwise more complex. Spoons, knives, and forks were known in the middle ages, but knives were usually brought by the diner, and forks were rare.

Eating implements were late to become Fellow-Commoners' gifts. The earliest donor was Michael Stanhope, whose spoons still survive from 1738. Some were presented by Fellow-Commoners long after leaving Cambridge. Others were bought out of the plate fund (p. 19) or recycled from earlier gifts.

From the early 18th century to the 1850s there was a lively turnover in spoons, forever getting broken, worn, replaced, and recycled. Forks and dessert-spoons came into constant use immediately on their introduction, to judge by the condition of ours. They were recruited in dozens and half-dozens; their ranks were attenuated with time and casualties; they were much used and cleaned, and many inscriptions have been cleaned away (pp. 28f.). The College also gained odd spoons from unknown sources, as well as losing them. Teaspoons were less used.

Undergraduates were supplied with silver forks and spoons from 1837 onwards. These are inscribed *Mens: Pens: Coll Corp Chr.*, meaning that they are for the table (*mensa*) of Pensioners, ordinary undergraduates, although by then Scholars and Sizars ate at the same table. Those made down to 1875 bear the letter 𝔉 in a garter, the ownership mark of John Fynn, Head Porter 1804–48, and his successors on the College staff, who hired them to students at so much a term. The College later acquired them and added more. They remained in use by undergraduates until the 1950s.

In the 20th century spoons and forks had a much quieter life. The last big acquisition was in 1928; occasional ones have gone to the pigs (p. 85); there have been repairs but no replacements.

18.1 Spoons

The early history of spoons is dealt with under the Apostle Spoons (Chapter 7). Our everyday spoons begin in the baroque period: Stuart ones were probably rather lightly built and did not survive the rough hands and sharp teeth of those days.

Even such an apparently functional object as a spoon affords scope for fashion and typology. The bowl can be elliptical, oval (bigger at one end), or pointed; a spoon with a transverse bowl becomes a *ladle* (§18.4). Most of our early (rococo) spoons have the shape of handle called ***Hanoverian,*** a tapering handle with the end turning upward away from the belly. Down to 1780 they were inscribed on the underside, since – it seems – butlers were in the sensible habit of laying spoons on the table belly-upward. An alternative shape, commoner in the 19th century, is ***Old English*** (known in the College as ***round***), with a downward curve, towards the belly, at the end. In the 1810s (but see §18.4.3) there came the ***fiddle-pattern,*** with a down-curved handle having prominent shoulders at its base. To strengthen the junction of bowl and handle there can be a ***rat-tail,*** running under the bowl, or a rounded fillet called a ***drop.*** (The rat-tail is a Roman invention: there was one at Sutton Hoo.)

Spoons descend from the *giant* 'serving' spoon, a foot long or more and weighing 5–6 ounces, through the *large* 'table' spoon, the commonest size (8–9 in., 2–2½ ounces, though some early ones are lighter), the *small* 'dessert' spoon (6½–7½ in., 1–1½ ounces), to the *very small* teaspoon or coffee-spoon, 6 in. long or less and weighing an ounce or so. The last two sizes begin *c*.1790. Later spoons tend to be heavier for their size. (For smaller spoons still see under Mustards and Salts, and the spoonlets attached to cruets and the Snuff-Horn.)

18.1.1 Giant [Bateman] Spoon

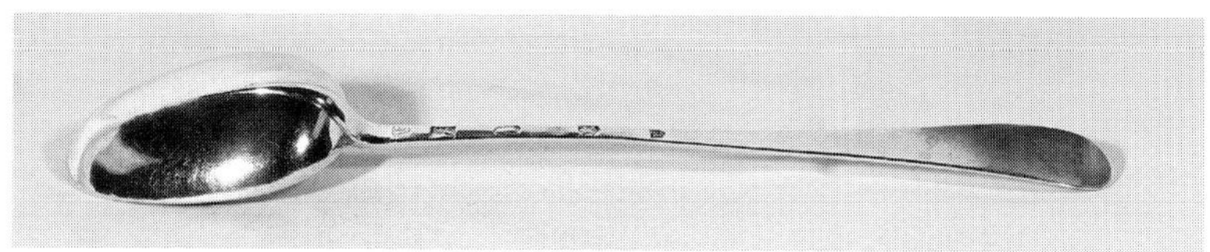

1715 (Exeter P + Britannia + griffin). 13.1 in. Britannia silver.

Old English pattern; oblong bowl with rat-tail; handle parallel to, but lower than, plane of rim of bowl; end of handle with bold obtuse cusp.

Maker's mark: illegible, could be John Elston Jr.

Inscription: TDWP 1715 [+curlicue]

This noble implement, bequeathed by Aubrey Bateman, is our only Exeter object.

18.1.2 Ten Stanhope Large Spoons

1738 (London c). Britannia silver. 8.3 in.

Oval bowl, ribbed Hanoverian handle, rat-tail.

Donor's arms in round shield: *Quarterly gules and ermine.*

Inscription: *Ex Dono Mich: Stanhope S.T.P.* [From the gift of Michael Stanhope D.D.]

Maker's mark: WI in rectangle, for one of the two James Wilks, active 1722–*c*.1740.

Michael Stanhope, of Nottinghamshire, admitted 1698; S.T.P. 1717; Canon of Windsor 1730; 'author of several sermons'. He later gave fish-knives (§18.3.1).

These survive from an original dozen: one disappeared between 1795 and 1817, and one after 1833. Still in normal use, despite being made of a weak alloy. Most of the stems have been mended; marks poorly preserved.

18.1.3 Ten William Northey Large Spoons

1739 (London d). 8.0 in.

Narrowly oval bowl, Hanoverian handle, drop at its root.

Badges: *cockatrice* (for donor) and *pelican*

Inscriptions: *W. Northey : Arm : de Compt · Bass:* \ *C.C.C.C.*

Maker: TPye in cut-away rectangle, for Thomas Pye, active in London 1739–.

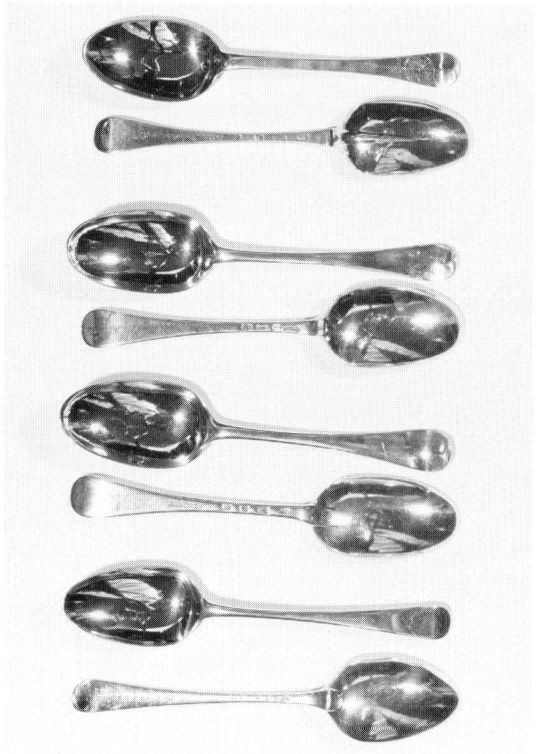

Stanhope, Northey, C.C.C.C., and C.C.C. et B.V.M. large spoons

Given by William Northey of Compton Bassett (Wilts), admitted 1739; gave also fish-knives.

18.1.4 Six 'C.C.C.C.' Numbered Large Spoons

1756 (London 𝔄). 8.1 in. Evidently survivors of original 12.

Narrowly oval bowl, Hanoverian handle, rat-tail. College arms.

18.1.6 Four 'Pelican' Giant Spoons

?1778 (London c; could be C for 1798). 12.1 in.

Tapering bowl, massive Old English handle with drop. Pelican pseudo-crest.

Weight inscriptions: *6"11 1* \ *6"11 2* \ *6"7 3* \ *6"5 4* [Present weights 6: 9, 6: 8, 6: 4, 6: 2.]

Marks badly stretched, abraded by cleaning, and largely illegible.

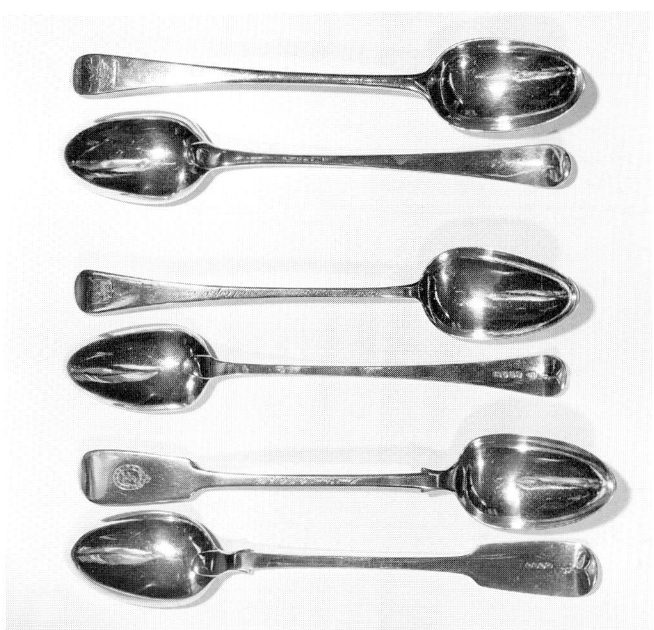

Pelican, Trafford-Milner, Undergraduate (1837) Giant Spoons

Inscriptions: *C.C.C.C.* \ *N°. 1 N°. 5 N°. 8 N°. 9 N°. 11 N°. 12*

Maker: *IC* in oval, for ??Isaac Colland, who entered a different *IC* mark in 1747.

18.1.5 Ten 'C.C.C. et B.V.M.' Large Spoons

1770 (London 𝔓). 8.1 in.

Narrowly oval bowl, Hanoverian handle, drop at its root. Rococo cartouche and shields of College arms and donor's: *Argent a bend between cotises engrailed sable.*

Inscription: *C · C · C· et B · V · M· in U · C ·* 1770. Maker illegible.

Unusually, the donor is indicated only by his arms, which are unidentified.

18.1.7 Two Nasmith Large Spoons (*illustrated on next page*)

1794 (London t). 8.5 in.

Narrowly oval bowl with Old English handle.

Inscription: *The Gift of the Rev^d. M^r. Nasmith.*

Inscription: *JSA* delicately foliated; mysterious, for the spoons can hardly have had a previous owner.

Marks: GC in rectangle, for George Cowles of Gloucester, active London 1777–, died 1811.

James Nasmith (1740–1808) of Norwich, son of Dissenters, was admitted 1760 and was Fellow 1765–76; medievalist, magistrate, farmer, and country parson. He catalogued the Parker manuscripts in 1775. He declined

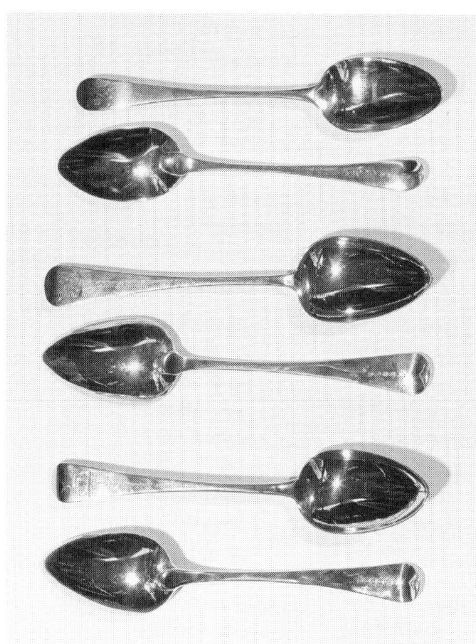

Nasmith, Denne, Robinson Large Spoons

to be Master of the College; he was rector of Leverington (Isle of Ely) and D.D. 1797.

18.1.8 Two Trafford and Two Milner Giant Spoons (*see previous page*)

1796 (London A). 11.8 in. Light weight.

Old English, taper bowl with drop. College arms.

Inscriptions: *Clement Trafford Eq. aur. D.D. Coll. Corp. Xti Cantab.* (Clement Trafford, Knight, gave [me] to the College of Corpus Christi, Cambridge). Partly legible, lacunæ supplied from next item.

Carolus Milner A.B. Eboracensis D.D. Coll. Corp. Xti Cantab. (Charles Milner, B.A., of York[shire], gave [me] to the College of Corpus Christi, Cambridge).

Maker's mark: RC in rectangle (not quite identical in the two pairs), probably for Richard Crossley, spooner, active 1775–1815.

Donors: Clement Trafford of Lincolnshire, later Sir Clement, was admitted 1756; no degree recorded, presumably a Gentleman Fellow-Commoner. The audit of 1776 records that he gave 10*s*. for plate; these spoons are presumably from a later gift. Charles Cottam Milner of Yorkshire was admitted 1783; B.A. 1788.

18.1.9 Twelve Trafford and Two Milner Small Spoons (*not illustrated*)

1796 (London A). 6.7 in.

Small version of the above, with same arms, inscriptions, marks, donors.

The other ten Milner spoons had bit the dust by 1852 and were recycled (see below).

18.1.10 Two 'Gothic HG' Giant Spoons (*not illustrated*)

1797 (London B + George III). 11.8 in.

Tapering bowl, Old English handle with drop.

Inscription: 𝔥𝔊 | E on back

Maker's mark: PB AB in rectangle, for Peter & Ann Bateman (§11.10).

Donor unidentified.

18.1.11 Twelve Denne Large Spoons

Four ?1798 (London ?C). Six 1812 (London R). Two ?1818 (London ?c). 8.9 in.

Pointed bowl (especially in the 1818 version), Old English handle with drop.

College arms.

Inscription: *Ex dono Johannis Denne. Coll: Soc: 1743* [From the gift of John Denne, Fellow of the College 1743]

Makers' marks: (1798) RC in rectangle with cut-off corners, for Richard Crossley, spooner, active 1775–, died 1815.

(1812): SG EW IR in rectangle, for Samuel Godbehere (active 1784–*c*.1820), Edward Wigan (active 1786–1818), James Boult (active 1781–*c*.1830, later tried his hand at banking).

(1818): GS in rectangle nicked at top, for Samuel Godbehere.

Two John Dennes from Kent were Fellows. The senior (*c*.1690–1767) was admitted 1708, Fellow 1716–21, Tutor; became Archdeacon of Rochester; one of the Corpus group of historians and antiquaries of that period. His son (1726–1800) was admitted 1743; Fellow 1749–53; became Chaplain to Maidstone Gaol; died of an occupational disease, 'an intermitting fever of the mind', brought on 35 years previously when he was involved in a desperate jail-break by two of his flock.

Presumably these spoons were recycled at different times from an earlier set given by the Dennes when the son became an undergraduate.

18.1.12 Six Robinson Large Spoons

1810 (London P). 8.8 in.

Pointed bowl, Old English handle with drop.

Crest: *hart gorged with a collar or wreath.*

Inscription: *Ex Dono Sirmor Robinson, Soc. Com. C.C.C.C.*

Maker's mark: MS ES, for Mary Sumner, active 1807–, and ?daughter Eliza, active 1809–, spooners.

Donor: ?S.W.K. Robinson of Durham, admitted 1809.

18.1.13 Six [Robinson] Very Small Spoons

1810 (London P + King's head). 5.3 in.

Subtriangular bowl, Old English handle with drop.

Inscription: C.C.C.C. Crest: *a hart.*

Maker's mark: WS in oval, for one of the William Sumner spooners.

Went with the above, and with Sirmor Robinson's Spring-Tongs (§18.10.2). Very little used.

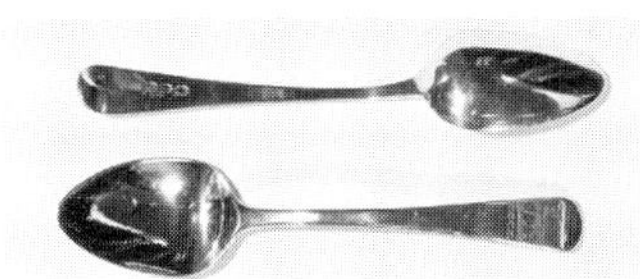

18.1.14 Six Bateman Small Spoons (*not illustrated*)

1814 (Dublin S – could be 1863). 6.3 in.

Rather pointed bowl; fiddle-pattern handle with rat-tail.

Inscription: LAW. Pheasant crest.

Maker's mark: M in square, unidentified.

Bequeathed by Aubrey Bateman: was L.A.W. an ancestor?

18.1.15 Four Day, Three Law, Four Forster Large Spoons (*not illustrated*)

1816 (London a). 8.7 in.

Oval bowl, fiddle-pattern handle. College arms.

Inscriptions: *Georgius Dayi A.B. N.deriensis D.D. Coll. Corp. Xti Cantab.*

Ricardus Matchet Law A.B. Feyeliensis [?] *D.D. Coll. Corp. Xti Cantab.*

Thomas Forster Middlesexiensis D.D. Coll. Corp. Xti Cantab.

Maker's mark: JB in rectangle, for James Beebe, spooner, active 1811–*c*.1840.

Donors: George Day of Norwich and Richard Matchett Law of Norfolk were admitted 1811 and became M.A. in 1819. The spoons (probably survivors of 18) celebrate their B.A.s. Thomas Forster of Middlesex, admitted 1812, took the rare degree of Bachelor of Music in 1818. Day, Law, and possibly Forster (see p. 213) joined in giving 18 small forks at the same time. The engraver was ignorant of the Latin for Norwich or Norfolk.

18.1.16 Ten Roope Ilbert Small Spoons (*not illustrated*)

1828 (London n). 6.7 in.

Elliptical bowl, Old English handle with drop. College arms.

Inscription: *Gul. Roope Ilbert. Devoniensis D.D. Coll. Corp. Xti Cantab.* (William Roope Ilbert, of Devon, gave [me] to the College of Corpus Christi, Cambridge)

Maker's mark: WC in rectangle, for William Chawner II (active 1804–34).

Donor: William Roope Ilbert of Devon was admitted 1826. His degree is inscribed on his forks (p. 213).

Originally twelve, the others recycled in 1879 (§18.2.6).

18.1.17 Twelve 'Coll. Corp. Chr.' Large Spoons (*not illustrated*)

1830 (London p). 8.7 in.

Same as §18.1.15. College arms.

Inscription: *Coll. Corp. Chr. Cantabrigiae*

Maker's mark: W:B in rectangle, for ?William Barber, spooner, active 1828–.

18.1.18 Eighteen Undergraduate Giant Spoons (*illustrated on p. 207*)

Nine of 1837 (London 𝔅 and William IV's head), six of 1851 (London 𝔔), three of 1866 (London 𝔩). 12.2 in.

Oval bowl, fiddle-pattern handle with drop.

Inscription: *Mens: Pens: Coll Corp Chr:* large 𝔉 inside garter

Marks: (1837): WE in bifoil, for William Eaton, spooner, entered 1840, died 1845, incuse *M.*

(1851): CB in ellipse, probably for Charles Boyton I, spooner, active 1825–94.

(1866): EE in bifoil + incuse ?fleur-de-lys, for Elizabeth Eaton, spooner, active *c*.1845–*c*.1866.

18.1.19 Forty-six Undergraduate Small Spoons

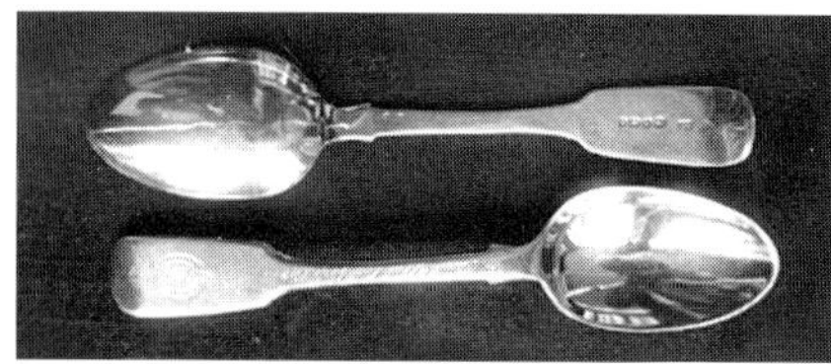

Sixteen of 1837 (London 𝕭 and William IV's head), two of 1852 (London 𝕽), six of 1854 (London 𝕿), thirteen of 1863 (London 𝔥), nine of 1866 (London 𝔩). 7.2 in.

Shape and inscriptions as above.

Makers' marks: (1837) William Eaton, as above.

(1852): ?FE in rectangle, for Frederick Edwards, spooner, active 1840–*c*.1851. (These are not of the identical shape; one lacks inscription, on the other it is very faint).

(1854): CB in ellipse, probably for Charles Boyton I, as above.

(1863 and 1866): SW in rectangle, for Susan Whitaker, spooner, active 1852–*c*.1895).

18.1.20 Very Small Shovel-shaped Spoon (*not illustrated*)

1837 (London 𝕭). 5.6 in.

Bowl in shape of rectangle with two rounded corners.

College arms + pelican pseudo-crest.

Maker: James Beebe (§8.1.15).

18.1.21 Thirty-two Undergraduate Large Spoons

Three of 1848 (London 𝕹), twelve of 1854 (London 𝕿), twelve of 1858 (London 𝔠), five of 1866 (London 𝔩). 8.9 in.

Oval bowl, fiddle-pattern handle with drop.

Inscription: *Mens: Pens: Coll Corp Chr.* large 𝕱 inside garter.

Makers' marks: (1848 and 1854): CB in rectangle, for Charles Boyton I (see above).

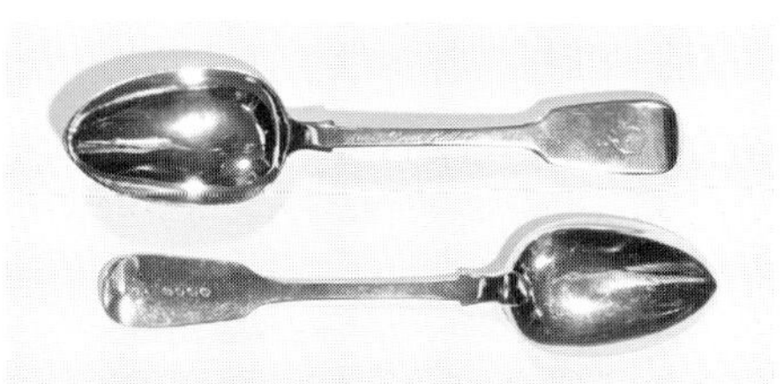

(1858): EE JE in ellipse, for ?Elizabeth Eaton and her son John Eaton.

(1866): CB in ellipse, for Charles Boyton I.

18.1.22 Six 'Gothic Q' Small Spoons (*not illustrated*)

1851 (London 𝕼). 7.2 in.

Same as undergraduate small spoons (§18.1.19), but very vigorously cleaned. Remains of College arms.

Inscription: *Ex dono G . . . . Comm:*

Maker's mark: EE in rectangle, ?for Elizabeth Edwards, active 1851–.

18.1.23 Six 'Gothic R' Small Spoons

1852 (London 𝕽). Same as above.

Inscription: *Ex dono G . . . . Soc.: Comm:*

Maker's mark: EE in bifoil, for Elizabeth Eaton (§18.1.18).

This and the previous item went with the forks commemorating various illegible Fellow-Commoners (§18.2.10–12).

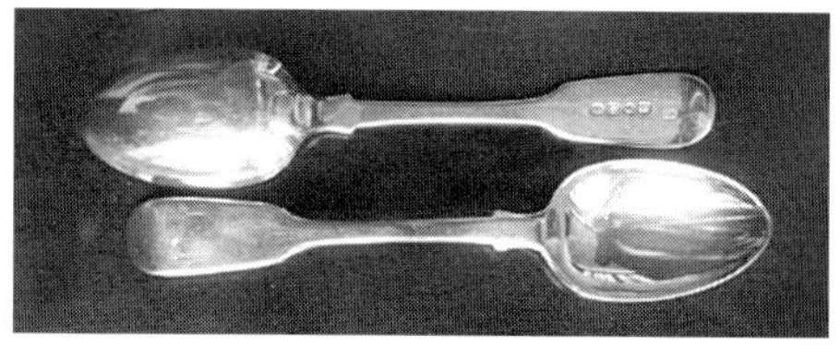

18.1.24 Ten Recycled Milner Small Spoons (*not illustrated*)

1852 (London 𝕽). 6.7 in.

Copies of the two surviving Milner spoons of 1796 (§18.1.8). No maker's mark.

18.1.25 Forty-Six Undergraduate Very Small Spoons

Fifteen of 1852 (London 𝕽), nine of 1863 (London 𝔥), eleven of 1868, (London 𝔲) eleven of 1874 (London 𝔱). 5.8 in.

Oval bowl, fiddle-pattern handle with drop.

Inscription: large 𝕱 inside garter.

Maker's mark: all by Susan Whitaker (§18.1.19).

18.1.26 Six Bateman Very Small Spoons

1863 (Dublin S + Hibernia). 6.2 in.

Pointed bowl, fiddle-pattern handle, rat-tail.

Crest: *demi-pheasant.*

Bequeathed by Aubrey Bateman.

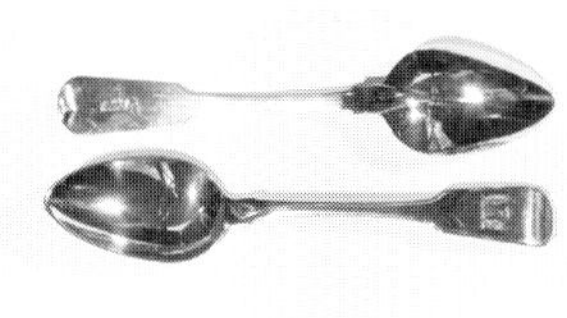

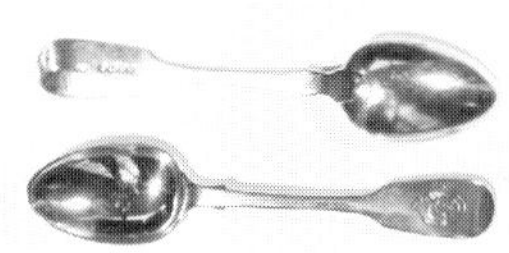

Bateman and Undergraduate Very Small Spoons

18.1.27 Seventy Undergraduate Small Spoons

28 of 1876 (London A), 17 of 1877 (London B), 26 of 1883 (London). 7.0 in.

Oval bowl, Old English handle with drop.

Inscription: *Mens. Pens. Coll Corp Chr.* Pelican badge.

Makers' marks: (1876 and 1877): GA in bifoil, for George William Adams (1808–95), famous London spooner.

(1883): CS H in trefoil, for Charles Stuart Harris of London.

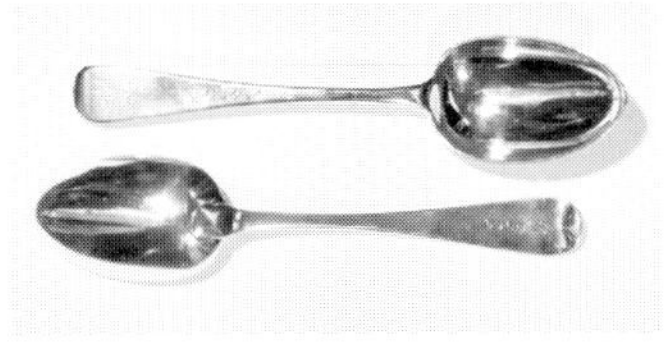

18.1.28 Two Recycled Roope Ilbert Small Spoons (*not illustrated*)

1879 (London D). 6.7 in.

Like original (§18.1.16) but oval bowl, same inscription and donor. College arms.

Maker: Susan Whitaker (§18.1.19).

18.1.29 Twelve Undergraduate Large Spoons

1894 (London T). 8.5 in.

Oval pointed bowl Old English handle with drop.

Inscription: *Mens: Pens: Coll: Corp. Chr.* Pelican badge.

Maker's mark: C·S·H in rectangle, for Charles Stuart Harris of London.

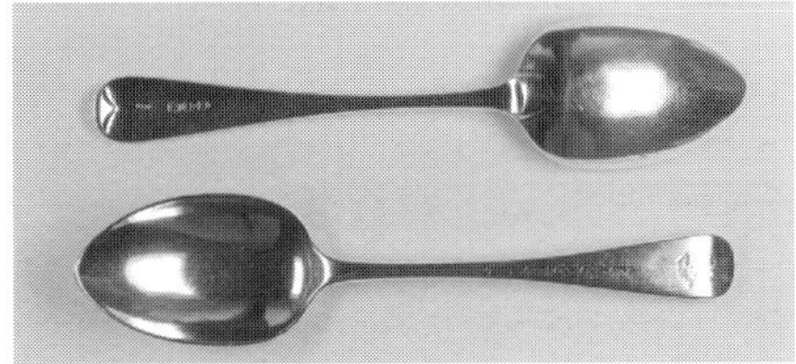

18.1.30 Four [Bateman] Statuesque Spoons

1896 (London a). 9.4 in.

Repoussé bowl; twisted, foliated stem, ending in figurine of (1) nun with book; (2) woman in sari with pot; (3) man in doublet & hose; (4) monk with tankard & drinking-horn.

Maker's mark: J . N . M on very broad shield, for John Newton Mappin, mark used 1886–98, of the firm Mappin & Webb 1863–.

Bequeathed by Aubrey Bateman.

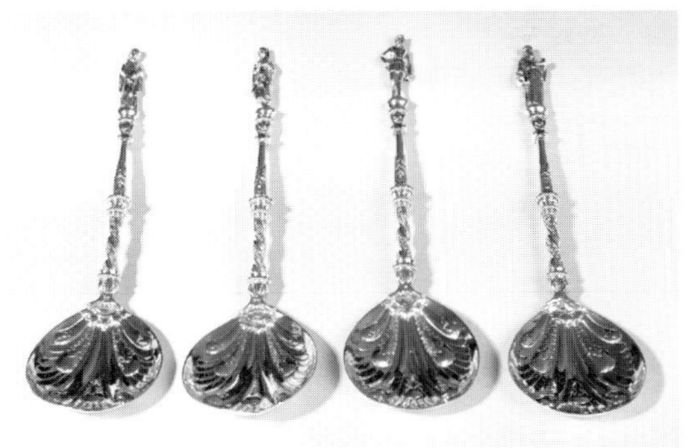

18.1.31 Twelve Bateman Very Small Spoons (*not illustrated*)

1899 (Sheffield 𝔤). 5.4 in.

Rather pointed bowl; Hanoverian handle with long drop at its root.

Pheasant crest.

Maker's mark: W&H on flag, for Walker & Hall.

18.1.32 **Strays** from someone else's flock:

8.2 in. 1758 (London 𝕮); Hanoverian; very long drop; inscribed (later) *JIR* monogram; maker illegible.

8.1 in., 1763 (London 𝕳); Hanoverian; flowing rococo foliation on back of bowl; inscribed W I ∴ R letters forming a triangle; C.H in rectangle, unidentified.

8.7 in., 1799 (London D); Old English; inscribed (later) *JFJ* monogram; PB AB WB for relatives of Hester Bateman.

8.2 in., 19th cent. (date-letter illegible); Old English; maker SA.

8.8 in., 1813 (?London S); Old English; inscribed *WAN* monogram; maker SB IB.

6.7 in., *c*.1830 (Newcastle, no date-letter); fiddle-pattern; CR in oval, ?for Charles Rawlings, active 1817–*c*.1850.

6.7 in., *c*.1850 (Newcastle, no date-letter); weakly fiddle-pattern; inscribed *MFC* monogram; SB IB, ? for Samuel Bailey and another.

8.4 in, 1891 (London Q); narrowly oval, Old English handle with rat-tail; AB HHW for Benson & Webb, active 1889–94, owners of Hunt & Roskell, successors to Paul Storr.

8.1 in., 1915 (Sheffield x); Hanoverian; crest *a demi-lion rampant emerging from a mural crown* (unidentified); W H & S[S] · L[D]., for William Hutton & Sons Ltd, manufacturing silversmiths 1864–1930.

18.2 Forks

SLEDGE. Forks! what be they?
MEER. The laudable use of forks,
Brought into custom here, as they are in Italy,
To the sparing of napkins.

Ben Jonson, The Divell is an Asse (1616), V.iii.

The use of forks at meals is rather a conventional matter than a test by which to measure the advance of civilization.

W.J. Cripps, 1891.

A fork for pitching hay into the orifice of a hayloft is as old as haymaking. The mini-fork, doing the same office for the human body, is younger than eating. Occasional *furchetti* go back in inventories to *c*.1300, but mostly for the purpose of eating green ginger, whatever that was. Fastidious people might bring their own fork to dinner, but the rest of humanity – even those who had been to the East and tried chopsticks – managed with only knives and spoons. The rival art of eating with fingers and licking away the grease still lingers in America, where the author's friends have been known to congratulate him on his mastery of the fork.

Table forks became familiar in England *c*.1610, between the time of Shakespeare (who does not mention them) and Ben Jonson (who does). However, down to the 18th century, if the College possessed forks they were not of silver. The earliest to appear in inventories were a dozen that we had in 1706 and melted in 1723.

Our forks resemble contemporary spoons (but are a little heavier), and were often made by spooners. They are all four-tined. The fiddle-pattern handle is predominant.

There are two sizes: 'small' or 'dessert' forks about 7 inches long (weight $1\frac{1}{2}$–2 ounces), and 'large', 'table', or 'meat' forks about 8 inches long ($2\frac{1}{2}$–3 ounces).

18.2.1 Twelve Spiller and Twelve May Large Forks

1810 (London P – maker's mark proves it is not p for 1830). 8.0 in.

Fiddle-pattern. College arms.

Inscriptions: *Thomas Spiller A.B. Essexensis D.D. Coll. Corp. Xti Cantab.* (Thomas Spiller, B.A., of Essex gave [me] to the College of Corpus Christi Cambridge.)

Arthurus Stert May A.B. Londinens. D.D. Coll. Corp. Xti Cantab. (but one, very worn, inscription appears to read *Arthur H. . . . . . . A.B. Londinens. D.D. Coll. Corp. Xti Cantab.*)

Maker's mark: WE WF WC in rectangle, for William Eley II (active 1805–41), William Fearn (§18.2.18), and William Chawner II (§18.1.16). This partnership in spooning began in 1808.

Arthur Stert May, of London, was admitted 1806, B.A. 1808. Spiller is not otherwise recorded.

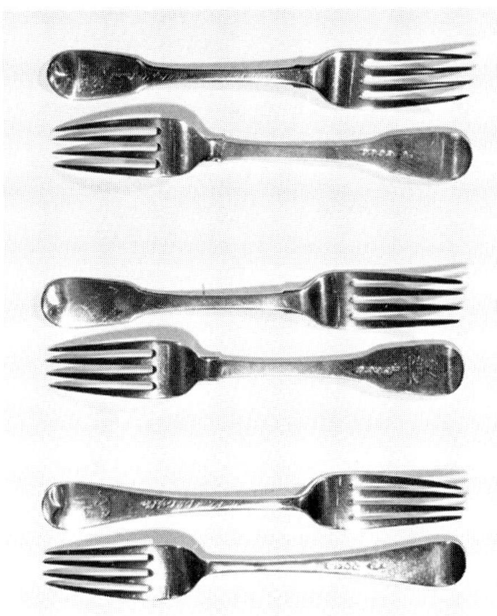

Spiller-May, Pelican, Undergraduate (1876) Large Forks

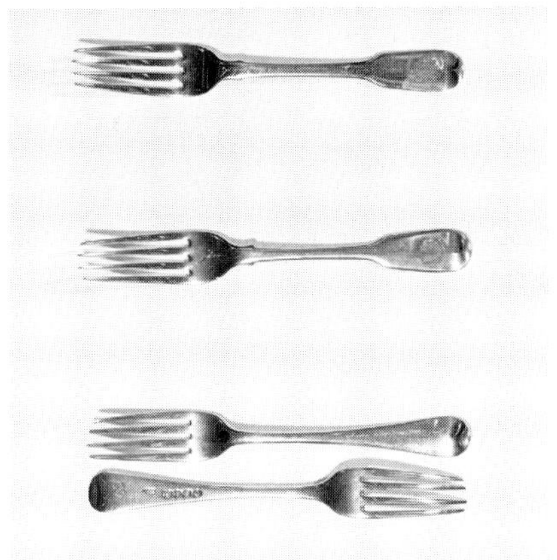

Day, Rashdall, Roope Ilbert Forks

18.2.2 Six Day, Six Law, Six Forster [?] Small Forks

1816 (London a). 6.8 in.

Fiddle-pattern. College arms. Maker's mark illegible.

Inscriptions: *Georgius Day A.B. Nord. . . . DD Coll Corp Chr Cantab* (George Day, B.A., of Nor[wich] gave [me] to the College of Corpus Christi Cambridge.)

Ricardus Matchet Law A.B. Norfolciensis D.D. Col Corp. Xti Cantab (the name is identified from the better-preserved spoons given by the same donor).

Franciscus Terston Middlesexensis D.D. Coll Corp Chr Cantab

For Day and Law see their spoons (§18.1.15). Francis Terston is otherwise unknown: I suspect a mistake for Thomas Forster of Middlesex, who joined with Day and Law, and Forster joined in giving spoons; the inscriptions on the spoons are notably ill-spelt.

18.2.3 Twenty-Four 'Pelican' Large Forks

1822 (London g). 7.8 in.

Fiddle-pattern. Pelican pseudo-crest.

Maker's mark: WC in rectangle under incuse pellet, for William Chawner II (see §18.2.1).

18.2.4 Two 'C.C.C.' + Pelican Large Forks of 1825 (*not illustrated*)

1825 (London k). 7.8 in.

Fiddle-pattern handle.

Inscription: *In usum Commensalium* (For the use of [Fellow-] Commoners) + **C.C.C.** + pelican.

Maker's mark illegible.

18.2.5 Two Small Forks of 1826, stolen from an unknown bishop? (*not illustrated*)

1826 (London l). 7.9 in.

Fiddle-pattern handle. Badge: ?mitre (defaced).

Numbered 12 and 18. No maker's mark.

18.2.6 Six Roope Ilbert Large Forks (*not illustrated*)

1828 (London n). 7.7 in.

Old English handle. College arms.

Inscription: *Gul. Roope Ilbert M.A. Devoniensis D.D. Coll. Corp. Xti Cantab.* (William Roope Ilbert, M.A., of

Devon, gave [me] to the College of Corpus Christi, Cambridge)

Maker: William Chawner II ((see §18.2.1).

William Roope Ilbert of Devon was admitted 1826. This is apparently the only record of his taking a degree. He also gave spoons (§18.1.16).

18.2.7 Six Roope Ilbert Small Forks (*illustrated on previous page*)

1828 (London n). 6.5 in. Small version of above.

18.2.8 Six Kirwan and Six Rashdall Small Forks (*illustrated on previous page*)

1835 (London u). 6.8 in.

Fiddle-pattern. College arms.

Inscriptions: *C.L. Fitzjohn M [?] Kirwan A.B. Eliensis [?] D.D. Coll. Corp. Chr. Cantab. | Johannes Rashdall A.B. . . . . Chr. Cantab.*

Maker's mark: JS AS R in pentagon, for Joseph I & Albert I Savory, part of A.B. Savory & Sons 1833–66. Their mark with an R is not otherwise recorded.

Donors: C. Lionel Fitzjohn Kirwan, of County Mayo, Ireland, was admitted 1828. The clan country of Kirwan (O Ciardhubháin) is in Co. Galway, just over the border from Mayo.

John Rashdall of Lincolnshire, admitted 1826, was B.A. 1832 and Vicar of Dawlish, Devon 1864–*c*.1869; he also gave a fish-knife (§18.3.7).

18.2.9 116 Undergraduate Large Forks

Ninety-eight of 1837 (London 𝕭 and William IV's head). Five of 1854 (London 𝕿). Seven of 1865 (London 𝔨). Nine of 1866 (London 𝔩) 8.2 in.

Fiddle-pattern. Inscription: *Mens: Pens: Coll Corp Chr:* large 𝕱 inside garter | 𝕸 (the last only on original 98).

Maker's marks: (1837) WE in bifoil, for William Eaton, spooner, active 1840–5.

(1854 and 1865–6) . CB in ellipse, probably for Charles Boyton I (see §18.1.18).

18.2.10 Twenty-three 'Gothic O' Large Forks (*not illustrated*)

1850 (London 𝕺). 8.3 in.

Fiddle-pattern. Remains of College arms.

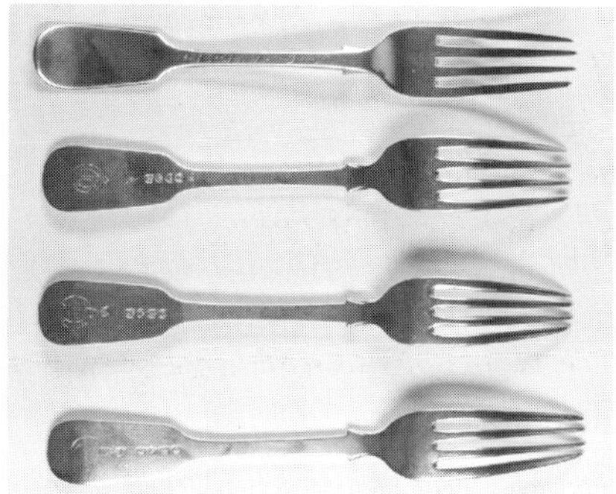

Undergraduate Large Forks of 1837, 1837, 1865, 1866

Inscriptions: on twelve *Ex dono F. Wentworth D. . . y [?] Soc: Comm:.* On eleven *Ex dono Johannis . eede [?] Soc: Comm:*

EE, ? for Elizabeth Edwards, active 1851–.

Gift of two Fellow-Commoners, now untraceable.

Other (worn-out) Fellow-Commoners gave the three following items, identical except in size, and also probably made by Elizabeth Edwards.

18.2.11 Six 'Gothic Q' Small Forks (*not illustrated*)

1851 (London 𝕼). 6.8 in.

As above. Inscription: *Ex dono R . . . . omm:*

18.2.12 Eighteen Ashurst ('Gothic R') Large Forks (*not illustrated*)

1852 (London 𝕽). 8.3 in.

As above. Inscription: *Ex dono Eduar . . . . Soc: Comm:*

The 1852 inventory shows that these were acquired in exchange for '1 Large Dish (Ashurst)'. Edward Ashurst, of London, was Fellow-Commoner in 1717.

18.2.13 Six Thoroton ('Gothic R') Small Forks (*not illustrated*)

1852 (London 𝕽). 6.8 in.

As above. Inscription: *Ex dono P . . . . Comm:*

In 1852 twelve small forks were acquired in exchange for Thoroton's mug. Robert Thoroton, of Nottinghamshire, was Fellow-Commoner in 1710, MA 1718; the 1760 inventory mentions his 'Pint Pot'.

18.2.14 Two 'C.C.C.' + Pelican Large Forks (*not illustrated*)

1865 and 1875 (London k, u). 8.0 in.
Hanoverian handle.
C.C.C. + pelican (cf §18.2.6).
GA in bifoil, for G.W. Adams (§18.1.26).

18.2.15 Sixty-nine Undergraduate Large Forks (*illustrated on p. 213*)

1876 (London A). 8.0 in.
Hanoverian handle. Pelican badge. Inscription: *Mens: Pens: Coll: Corp: Chr:*
Made by George William Adams, above.

18.2.16 Sixty-seven Undergraduate Small Forks (*not illustrated*)

Forty-nine of 1876 (London A), twenty-two of 1911 (London q). 6.9 in.
Hanoverian handle. Pelican badge. Inscription: *Mens. Pens. Coll Corp Chr*
Maker: (1876) George William Adams, above.
(1911) HA & C° in hexagon, for Holland, Aldwinckle & Co, active 1883–*c.*1922 (this mark not otherwise recorded).

18.2.17 Two Pelican Large Forks (*not illustrated*)

1887 (London M). 7.9 in.
Hanoverian handle with drop. Pelican badge.
CB in bifoil, prob. Charles Boyton I (§18.1.18).

18.2.18 Strays (*not illustrated*)

7.7 in.; 1798 (London C + King's head); Hanoverian; crest a *griffin;* W.S in rectangle for one of the William Sumner spooners.

7.9 in.; 1809 (London o); Hanoverian; crest *griffin swallowing handkerchief;* mark GS W[F] in square with rounded corners, for George Smith III and William Fearn, very prolific London spooners 1774–90.

6.5 in.; 1836 (Sheffield r); Hanoverian; mark R & E in pentagon, unidentified.

18.3 Fish-Eaters, Butter-Tools, and Trowels

Take the dish-cover up!
  Ah, *that* is so hard that I fear I'm unable!
For it holds it like glue –
  Holds the lid to the dish, while it lies in the middle:
Which is easiest to do,
  Un-dish-cover the fish, or dishcover the riddle?

Lewis Carroll, Through the Looking-Glass

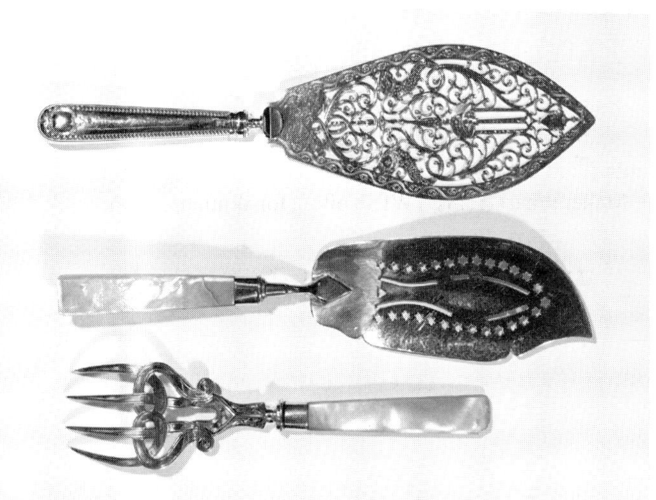

Bateman Fish-Trowel (or is it a Cake-Lifter?) of 1777
Pearly Fish-Trowel and Fork

The writer belongs to the last generation to be brought up on table-knives of rusty steel, needing to be scoured (in polite households) in a mysterious apparatus called a knife-machine. The *soupçon* of long-eaten fish mingles so indissolubly with that of steel that a fastidious age introduced non-ferrous knives for eating fish. Silver fish-knives are said to have been invented by Paul de Lamerie *c*.1740. Our early specimens cannot be proved authentic since the blades, worn by battle with tough and bony fishes, have been replaced: they all bear the mark of Goldsmiths' and Silversmiths' Co. Ltd and the London date-letter l for 1926.

There developed also fish-trowels or fish-slices for lifting fish stuck to the dish, hard work which sooner or later breaks these large delicate tools. Later came miniature fish-knives for eating butter. The College does not have specialized fish-forks.

18.3.1 Three Stanhope and Three Anonymous Pistoliform Fish-Knives

c.1746?, blades 1926. Total length 8.9 in., of which blade 4.7 in.

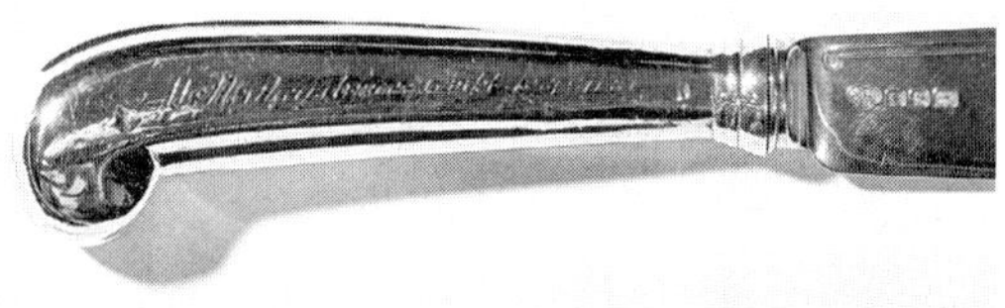

Pistol-shaped handle; blade with swept tip and notch; collar at junction; double reed on both sides of back.

Three handles inscribed: *Ex Dono: Mich: Stanhope S.T.P.* [of the gift of Michael Stanhope, Doctor of Divinity], with an illegible coat-of-arms. Maker's mark IT, uncertain; no date-letter.

For Michael Stanhope see his spoons (§18.1.2).

18.3.2 Eighteen William Northey Pistoliform Fish-Knives (*not illustrated*)

Identical to above, save for inscription: *W. Northey: Arm*[r] *: de Compt · Bass: A.M.* (W. Northey, armiger [arms not shown], of Compton Bassett, M.A.). No maker's mark on handle. See William Northey Spoons (§18.1.3).

18.3.3 Bateman Dolphin Fish-Trowel of 1777 (*illustrated on previous page*)

London date-letter b. 12.3 in.

Blade flat, acute, elaborately pierced in likeness of two dolphins, fountain and urn, chased both sides. Solid handle with beading and two blank cartouches.

Maker's mark: WA in rectangle, repeated on handle, for William Abdy I, active 1763, died 1790.

Bequeathed by Aubrey Bateman.

18.3.4 Pitcairn Fish-Trowel

1795 (London u). 11.6 in.

Blade symmetrical (like an assegai), slightly concave, pierced with a quadrilateral of bars. Fiddle-pattern handle. Two engraved leafy boughs surround the College arms and donor's: *Three lozenges gules in a bordure ermine.*

Inscription: *David Pitcairn M.D. Fifensis D.D. Coll. Corp. Xti Cantab.* (David Pitcairn of Fife, Doctor of Medicine, gave [me] to the College . . .)

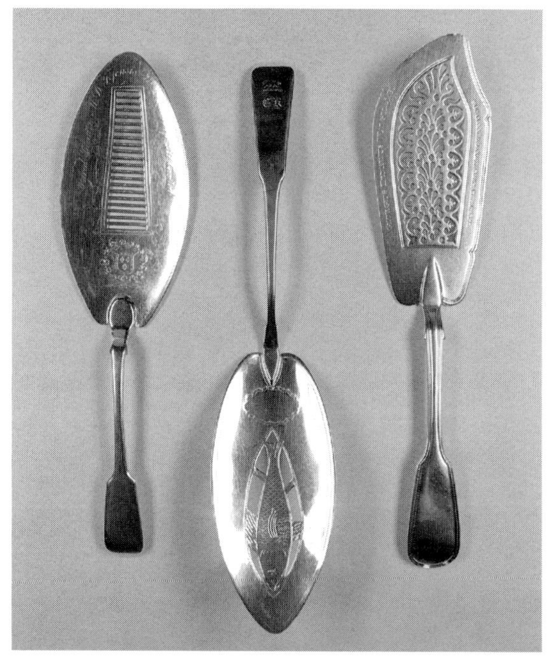

Pitcairn, Irish, Walsh Fish-Trowels

Maker's mark, HC in ellipse, for Henry Chawner, 1764–1851.

David Pitcairn of Fife was admitted 1773, M.D. 1784.

18.3.5 Bringhurst, Edward Northey, Doctor's Fish-Knives (one of each)

1796 (London A), blade 1926. Total length 8.7–9.0 in., of which blade 4.8 in.

Straight handle with rounded end and three reeds; blade as §18.3.1.

Inscriptions on handle: (1) . . . *Johannes Bringhurst Socio Commensalis Lincolniensis D.D. Coll: Corp: Xti Cantab.* (John Bringhurst, Fellow-Commoner of Lincoln, gave [me]).

(2) *Eduardus Northey A.M. Willemiensis D.D. Coll: Corp: Xti Cantab.*

(3) . . . *M.D. Tilensis D.D. Coll: Corp: Xti Cantab.*

Maker: MB in rectangle, uncertain.

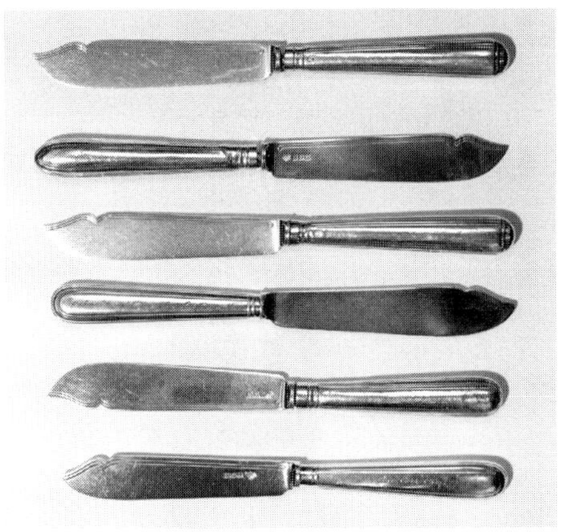

Fish-knives: Edward Northey, Three Crosses, Doctor's, Rashdall, Donaldson, Coll. Corp. Chr.

John Bringhurst of Lincolnshire was admitted 1779. Edward Northey of Wiltshire, admitted 1773, took M.A. 1780. They gave plate to the College long after they left. The third donor was an unidentified Doctor of Medicine.

18.3.6 Irish Fishy Fish-Trowel

1808 (Dublin M + Hibernia). 12.6 in.

Blade symmetrical like an assegai, concave, engraved with a large fish and pierced to emphasize its outline. Vestigial-fiddle-pattern handle. Blank cartouche with wavy outline.

Initials 𝔊𝔎 and crest of *a swine*, significance unknown. Inscription on the back is defaced and illegible.

Maker's mark GN in ellipse, unidentified (there was a George Nangle in London).

18.3.7 Rashdall Fish-Knife

1829 (London o, uncertain), blades 1926. Length 8.7 in., of which blade 4.8 in.

Straight, reeded handle with rounded end.

Handles inscribed: *Johannes Rashdall A.B. Lincolniensis D.D. Coll. Corp. Chri: Cantab*

Maker's marks on handle illegible.

For John Rashdall see his forks (§18.2.10).

18.3.8 Two 'Three Crosses' Fish-knives

c.1830 (marks illegible), blades 1926. Length 9.0 in., of which blade 4.8 in.

Donor's arms (*Argent a closet* [i.e a narrow bar] *dancetty gules between three cross-crosslets*) in oval shield with vertical feature behind. No inscription; donor unidentified.

18.3.9 Walsh Fish-Trowel (*illustrated on previous page*)

1835 (London u). 12.3 in.

Blade shaped like a fish-knife, with swept tip and two notches on back, pierced with foliated holes, marginal reeding on one side. Reeded fiddle-pattern handle.

Inscription: *GEORGIUS HENRICUS WALSH A. B. SOC. COMM. D. D. COLL. CORP. CHR. CANT.* (George Henry Walsh, B.A., Fellow-Commoner, gave [me] to the College of Corpus Christi at Cambridge)

Maker's mark: MC + incuse ×, unidentified.

George Henry Walsh was admitted 1826.

18.3.10 Three Falconer Butter-Knives

1844, 1860, 1879 (London 𝔍, 𝔢, D). 7.8–7.9 in.

Blade with swept tip and two notches, double-reeded on back. Fiddle-pattern handle.

Inscription: *d.d. K · J · F MCMLXXVIII*

Makers' marks: (1844) JS AS in rectangle, for Joseph & Albert Savory, spooners (AB Savory & Sons 1833–66).

(1860) WS (unidentified, there being many with these initials).

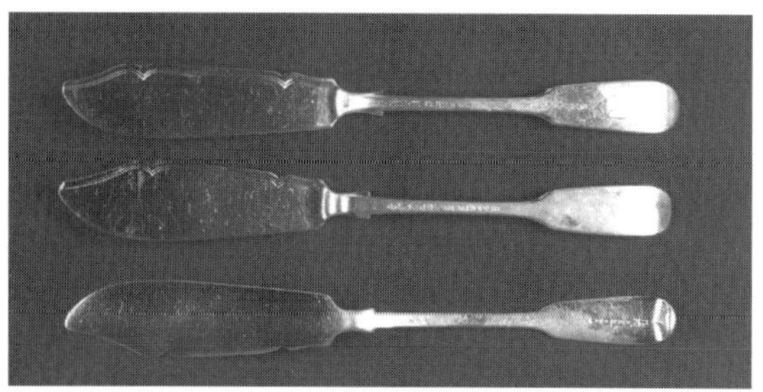

Wallis and two Falconer Butter-knives

(1879) HH in bifoil (maker Henry Holland & Son *c*.1850–*c*.1878).

Kenneth John Falconer (1952–), distinguished mathematician and authority on the wooden spoons awarded to undistinguished mathematicians (Appendix 4), was admitted Scholar 1971; Foundation Scholar 1973; Caldwell Student 1974–7; Fellow 1977–80; Professor of Pure Mathematics, St Andrew's 1993–. These are his wedding fine.

18.3.11 Two Undergraduate Fish-Trowels

1877 (London B). 12.1 in.

Blade shaped like a fish-knife, with swept tip and two notches, pierced in pattern, marginal reeding on one side. Fiddle-pattern handle.

Inscription: *Mens: Pens: Coll: Corp Chr* + pelican

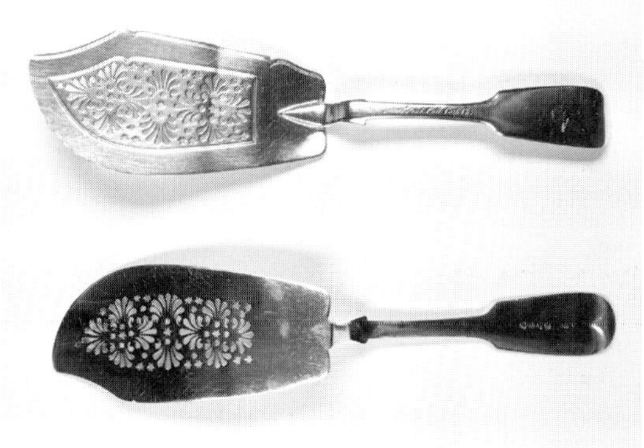

Maker's mark: GA in bifoil, for George William Adams (§18.1.26).

18.3.12 Six Crispin, Five Carpenter, Six Howorth, Six Donaldson Fish-Knives
(*illustrated on previous page*)

1877 (Birmingham c). Total length 8.7 in., of which blade 4.8 in.

Blade with curved edge, swept tip, notch; double reed on both sides of handle and one side of back. Straight handle. College arms.

Inscriptions:

(1) *Ex dono Henrici Shuter Crispin Soc: Comm: 1873 Coll: Corp: Chr:*
(2) *Ex dono Johannis Carpenter Soc: Comm: 1876 Coll: Corp: Chr:*
(3) *Ex dono Henrici Haworth Soc: Comm: 1876 Coll: Corp: Chr:*
(4) *Ex dono Donald Donaldson Soc: Comm: 1877 Coll: Corp: Chr:*

Maker's mark: J.G in rectangle with cut-off corners, for John Gammage, active *c*.1864–*c*.1902.

Four Fellow-Commoners' gifts. Henry Shuter Crispin was admitted 1871, Henry Howorth in 1872, John Carpenter in 1876.

Donald Donaldson, admitted 1867, died 1913, endowed the Donaldson Studentship.

18.3.13 Wallis Butter-Knife

1883 (London H). 7.8 in.

Blade with swept tip and two notches, doubly-reeded on back on one side. Fiddle-pattern handle. College arms with pelican pseudo-crest.

Inscription: *COLL: CORP. CHRISTI CANT: E DON: A . . . . JOS. WALLIS. SOC. 1883* [. . . from the gift of A– Jos. Wallis, Fellow, 1883]

Maker's mark, F.H in heart, for Francis Higgins & Sons, manufacturing spooners 1868–1940.

Arnold Joseph Wallis (1856–1913), distinguished mathematician, Scholar of Trinity College, came to Corpus as Fellow in 1879. He served as Bursar 1899–; Senior Proctor 1900–1; Town Councillor 1902–5. He founded the Gravediggers' Society and Amalgamation

Club, and abolished fines for non-attendance at Chapel. He gave the Wallis Stilton-Spade (§18.8.3).

18.3.14 Pearly Fish-Trowel & Fork (*illustrated on p. 215*)

Late Victorian? Plated brass, mother-of-pearl handles. Trowel 11.6 in. long; fork 9.5

Fish-trowel pierced with rude outline of fish bordered by stars. Fork pierced with interlace.

This elaborate, seemingly impractical piece has in fact been wrecked by much use.

18.3.15 Griffin Butter-Fork

1912 (Sheffield 𝔲, less probable reading 𝔫 for 1905). 6.5 in.

Flat 3-pronged fork engraved on one side; mother-of-pearl handle; embossed silver ferrule bearing tiny hallmark.

Wedding fine presented by Dr Miranda H. Griffin, linguist and Research Fellow, in 2000.

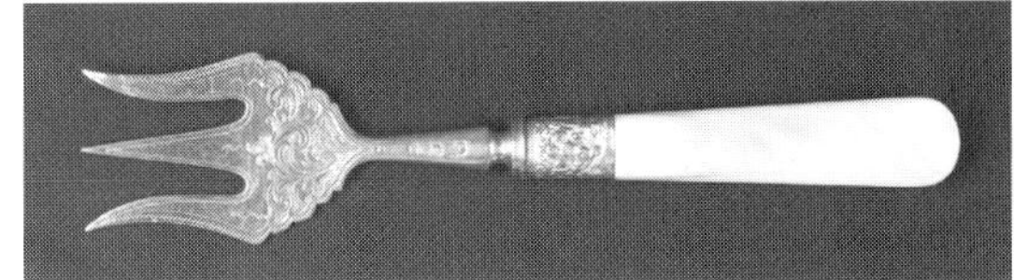

18.3.16 139 'Coll. Corp. Chr.' Fish-Knives (*illustrated on p. 217*)

1928 (Sheffield l). Total length 8.5 in., of which blade 4.6 in.

Straight handle; blade with swept tip and notch; double reed on both sides of handle and one side of back.

Inscription (on handle): *Coll: Corp: Chr.*

Makers' mark: G & S C° L^TD in double trefoil, for Goldsmiths' and Silversmiths' Co. Ltd (see §13.18).

Presumably the remnant of one gross or great hundred of 12 dozen.

18.3.17 Schlarb Cake-Slice

Given 2001. 8.6 in. long. Blade with foliar handle.

German hallmarks: WMF (maker), crescent moon, crown, and the Euro-mystic number 925.

Given by Beatrix Schlarb, Fellow and biochemist, on her marriage.

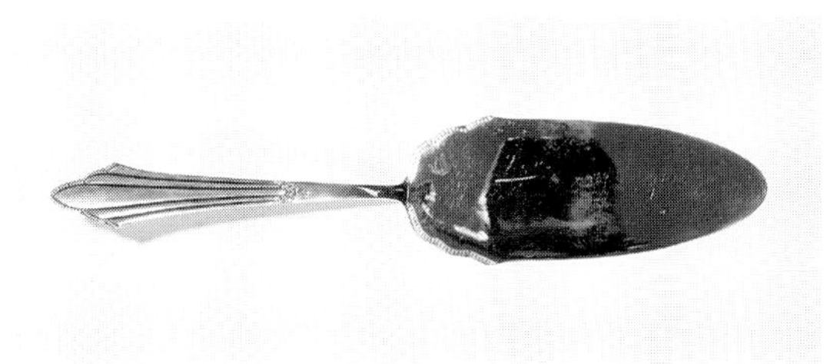

18.4 Ladles

A ladle is a tool for conveying liquid, such as molten lead, from one vessel to another. It differs from a spoon in its circular or transversely elongated bowl. If the handle is not in one piece with the bowl it is a ***punch-ladle,*** which see. The handle is strongly curved and usually of the Old English shape.

Originally ladles were kitchen tools; for example the College bought a brass one (*vno ladil de laton*) in 1459 (*Liber Albus* part II f.43).

Most of our bigger ladles look as if they have been in the wars: they would make handy life-preservers or coshes.

For ladles with holes see ***Strainers.***

18.4.1 Two Great 'CCCC' Ladles (*see next page*)

1774 (London 𝔗). 13.3 in. One disused.

Old English tapered handle with drop at its root.

Inscription: *CCCC* 8 » 6 on drop.

Maker's mark: TC; unidentified (many small firms had these initials).

18.4.2 Five Middle-sized 'Coll: Corp: Christi' Ladles (*bottom of next page*)

1776 and 1779. 7.6 in. One badly damaged.

Round bowl at an angle to Old English handle.with drop. Inscribed *Coll: Corp: Christi*

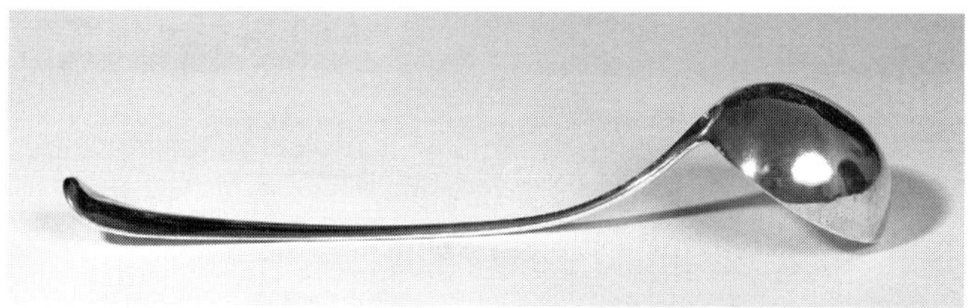

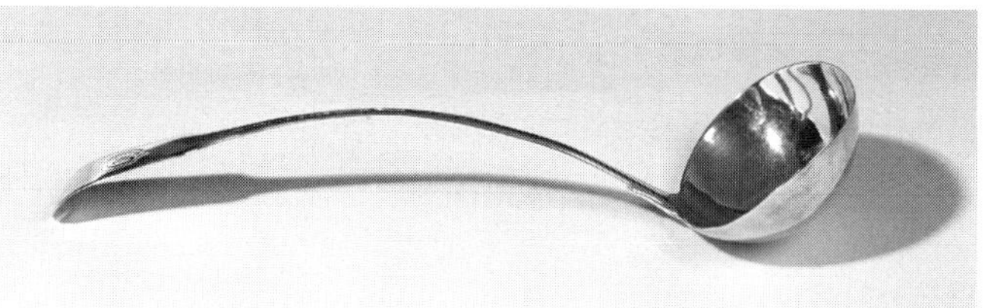

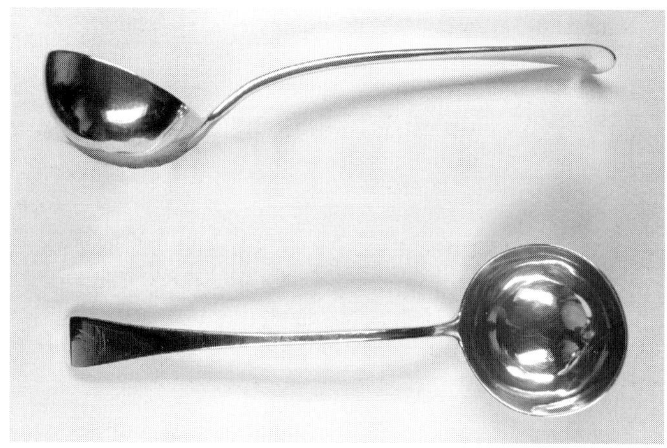

Great ladles:
CCCC of 1774
Undergraduate of 1789
Undergraduate of 1876
Undergraduate of 1876

Marks: Two bear London a for 1776. Two have London d for 1779, and maker's mark WS CC in square, for William Sumner I (spooner, active 1770–80) and Richard Crossley (spooner, active 1775–1815). Other marks illegible.

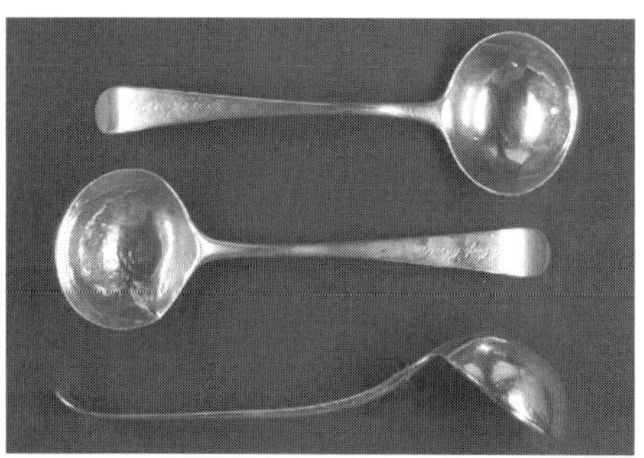

18.4.3 Undergraduate Great Ladle (*above*)

1789 (London o). 12.8 in.

Very curved fiddle-pattern handle with drop at its root.

Inscription: *Mens: Pens: Coll: Cor . . . hr* with 𝔍𝔉 in garter.

Maker's mark: *JW*, for John Wren, spooner, entered 1777, active to *c.*1800.

Handle mended, with loss of part of inscription.

An anomalous piece, 48 years older than any other article for undergraduate use, and 21 years older than our next oldest fiddle-handled article. The date-mark, however, is very clear. Probably it came second-hand.

18.4.4 Two Hart and Two Lister Small Ladles

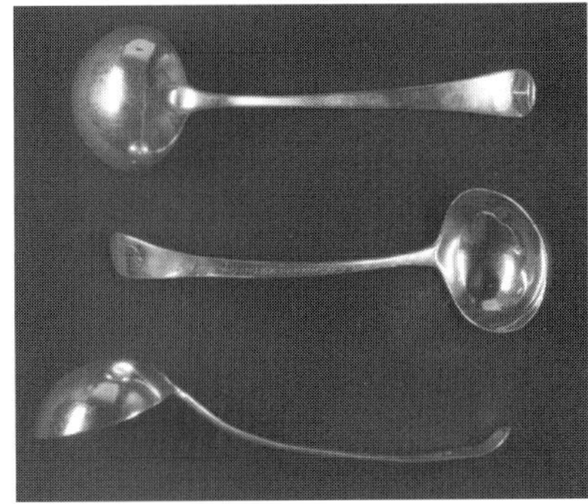

1796 (London A). 6.9 in.

Round bowl at an angle to curving Old English handle with drop. College arms.

Inscriptions: *B. Hart A.B. Middlesexiensis D.D. Coll. Corp. Xti Cantab.* (B. Hart, B.A., of Middlesex, gave [me] to the College . . .).

Georgius Lister LL.B. Lincolniensis D.D. Coll. Corp. Xti Cantab. (George Lister, Ll.B., of Lincoln[shire] . . .).

Maker's mark: RC, for Richard Crossley, spooner, active 1775–1815.

Donors: Benjamin Hart of Middlesex, admitted 1793, B.A. 1797; George Lister of Lincolnshire, admitted 1787; Ll.B. 1793.

Three have had their stems replaced, losing marks or part of the inscription; the fourth is barely legible.

18.4.5 Anonymous Small Ladle (*not illustrated*)

*c.*1810. 7.0 in. Fiddle-pattern, drop bowl. Inscribed 𝕮.

Marks: Newcastle Assay Office; no date-letter; GM in ellipse, ? for George Murray.

18.4.6 Undergraduate Ladle (*not illustrated*)

1811 (q + King's head). Battered, disused.

Fiddle-pattern, drop at root of handle.

Inscribed: *Mens: Pens: Coll: Corp: Chr:* 𝕱 in garter

Maker: *CM JW* in oval-ish punch, not known.

18.4.7 Two Small Bateman Ladles

1815 and 1831 (London U, q). 7.2 in.

Round bowl at an angle to fiddle-pattern handle with double drop. Pheasant crest.

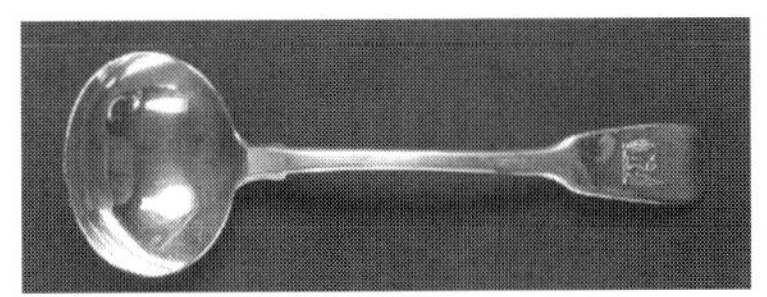

Makers' marks: (1815) WE WF in square (William Eley II and William Fearn).

(1831) WC (William Chawner II, see 18.2.3).

18.4.8 Six Bateman Strapwork Mini-Ladles

Three of 1835, one of 1839, two of 1865 (London u, 𝕯, 𝔨). 4.7 in.

Transverse bowl; tapered handle with dognose end, joined to bowl by triple foliation.

Latticed strapwork on both sides of handle; shells on both sides of finial. Crest: *pheasant.*

Maker's marks: WT LB for William Theobalds and Lockington Bunn, partnership 1835–; WT RA for William Theobalds & Robert Metcalf Atkinson 1838–; John Samuel Hunt 1855–.

Meant as saltspoons? The three sets are indistinguishable except by the marks.

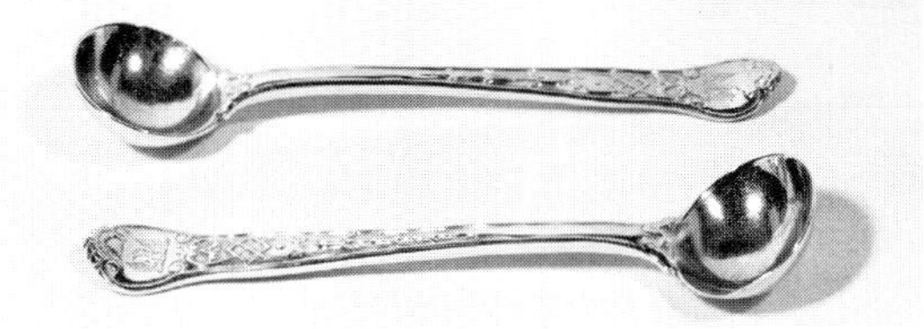

18.4.9 Three 'Mens. Pens.' Great Ladles (*illustrated on previous page*)

1876 (London A). 13.3 in.

'Old English' tapered handle with cusp; drop at its root. Pelican badge.

Inscription: *Mens: Pens: Coll: Corp: Chr:*

Maker's marks: GA in bifoil, C in circle, for George William Adams (§18.1.26).

18.4.10 Statuesque Ladle (*not illustrated*)

1900 (London a). 9.25 in. by 2.5 in.

Bowl *repoussé* with shell-like pattern. Stem cast with vine-trails, acanthus leaves etc., ending in a woman in a sari-like robe.

Maker's mark: J.N.M in broad shield, for John Newton Mappin (§18.1.30).

18.5 Punch-Ladles

I accompanied the Duke to an East India vessell that lay at Blackwall. . . Amongst other spirituous drinks, as punch, etc. they gave us. . .

Evelyn's Diary 16 Jan. 1662

Punch. Take one quart of Claret Wine, half a pint of Brandy, and a little Nutmeg grated, a little Sugar, and the Juice of a Lemon, and so drink it.

Hannah Wolley, The Queen-like Closet 1670

Punch is a mixed liquor containing spirit, lemon, spice, and sugar. It is apparently of 17th-century Anglo-Indian origin, and acquired something of the status of the later cocktails (which never caught on in Cambridge). It was usually ladled hot in small quantities out of a *punch-bowl* (§21.2.6–7; a silver chamber-pot would do). On later punch-ladles a lip was provided for pouring into a glass, rather than drinking out of the ladle.

The ladle should have a handle of some organic material, silver being too good a conductor of heat. Usually there are these parts: the *bowl,* which may have a *coin* inset in the bottom; the silver *stem,* ending in a *socket*; the organic *handle*; and the silver *finial.* Punch-ladles are often marked on the stem as well as the bowl, but the marks are lightly struck and often illegible.

Punch-ladles are delicate tools and do not survive being used as weapons late in the evening. To judge by the number and condition of ours, punch was a favourite drink from 1770 to 1830. However, the College had drunk similar drinks long before. In 1705 Stephen Hales and four others, with matching funds from the College itself, purchased a *monteith,* a huge bowl weighing 82 ounces. Thomas Barret, otherwise unknown, added a punch-bowl *c.*1716. The first mention of a punch-ladle is in the College audit for 1735; since it cost only 9*d*. it was not silver.

The Beacon punch-ladles, our earliest of silver, were added to the inventory in 1742. We melted the monteith in 1756, and recycled the bowl into candlesticks in 1760 (p. 160).

Handles are sometimes made of wood: holly is said to be traditional, but I am not sure of distinguishing it from boxwood without cutting a section. An alternative is whalebone, which is not bone but the horny black mouth-skin of plankton-feeding whales, used as the plastic of the 18th and 19th centuries.

18.5.1 Beacon No. 1 Punch-Ladle

1715 (Britannia + 𝔟) 12.9 × 2.6 in. Britannia silver and ?boxwood.

Circular flattish-bottomed bowl, everted rim.

Turned wooden handle ending in knob, pegged into long socket with reeded top.

Inscription: *Corp. Xti Coll. D.D. Edv. Beacon A.M. ejusd. Coll. nuper Soc. №. 1* (Edward Beacon, M.A., lately Fellow, gave [me] to the College of Corpus Christi).

Maker's mark: crown and GO in cottage loaf, for John Goode or John Corporon.

Edward Beacon (?–1767) of Norwich was admitted 1722; Fellow 1729–34; later became Rector of Wattisfield (Suffolk) and Calbourne (Isle of Wight).

There is no assay office mark, but only London used 𝔟 at any possible date.

18.5.2 Beacon No. 2 Punch-Ladle

1739 (London d). 12.6 × 2.4 in. Silver and ?boxwood.

Circular round-bottomed bowl, everted rim. Long socket. Turned wooden handle ending in knob. Inscription as above, except for *№. 2.*

Maker's mark *JK* with a pear between the letters, unidentified.

Donor as above. Bowl cracked.

18.5.3 Florin Punch-Ladle

*c.*1760. 14.8 × 3.5 in. Handle of ?whalebone.

Circular bowl, flattish bottom, everted margin; round stem with socket and pin, squarish finial. *Repoussé* flowers and foliage on bowl, struck from inside. Inset in bottom is a new florin (two-shilling piece) of George II, 1758.

No marks. Handle broken and warped.

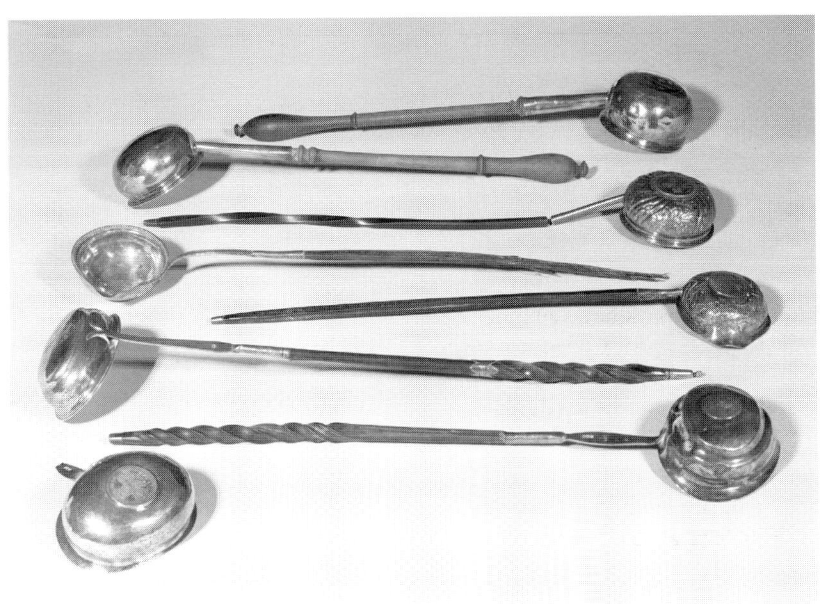

Punch-Ladles:
Beacon No. 1 1715
Beacon No. 2 1739
Florin c.1760
One-sided 1778
One-sided Florin 1785
Kennedy-Craufurd-Stuart 1803
Shilling 1820
Florin c.1820

18.5.4 One-Sided Punch-Ladle

1778 (London c, no King's head, thus not 1818). Now 14.7 in. long; 2.8 × 2.4 in. bowl. Whalebone handle.

Circular bowl, everted margin, one lip. Flat stem merging into socket. Beading round rim; gadroon-like engraving on stem; 3 lines round socket. Square handle, not twisted.

Maker's mark: GS in rectangle.

Handle badly frayed, end missing.

18.5.5 [Bateman] Punch-Ladle (*illustrated on next page*)

Late 18th century: no date-letter. 14.7 in. Whalebone handle.

Transverse elliptical bowl with undulate margin, one spout, *repoussé* decoration in bottom (struck from outside); stem slightly forked at attachment to bowl; socket with rivet. Twisted handle with blunt cylindrical silver finial.

Makers's mark AV in rectangle, unidentified.

Previously mended at attachment of bowl and in lower part of whalebone.

Bateman bequest.

18.5.6 One-sided Florin Punch-Ladle

1785 (London k). 13.6 in. long, bowl 2.3 × 2.6 in. Whalebone handle.

Flattish bowl with everted rim, one pronounced lip; round stem ending in socket with pin; square untwisted handle; small finial. Bowl *repoussé* with flowers and beading round coin. Inset in bottom is a gilded florin of Queen Anne, 1711.

Maker's mark: GG or GC, for George Giles

Graffito: *Fynn* [mid-19th-cent. College porter or keeper of buttery, §13.10].

Coin is crudely soldered in with ordinary solder, perhaps replacing an original shilling. Stem broken and mended by telescoping.

18.5.7 Kennedy-Craufurd-Stuart Punch-Ladle

1803 (London H). 15.0 in. long; bowl 3.3 × 2.2 in. Whalebone handle.

Transverse elliptical bowl with flattish bottom, 2 constrictions, everted rim with 3 reeds. Flattish stem of silver with 3 reeds, attached to bowl by 2 tails. Handle with reeded silver band halfway up, twisted above band. Octagonal finial ending in acorn-like knob.

Inscriptions: *R* [earlier owner?] D.D. CAROLUS KENNEDY-CRAUFURD-STUART. A.S. MCMXXXI.

Donor's arms: *Quarterly: 1st and 3rd: or on a bend gules two crossed swords between two 5-petalled flowers, overlying a bar checky argent and azure. 2nd: gules a millrind* on a fess ermine between three 5-pointed stars. 4th: argent a chevron gules between three crosses ?fitchy.* Closed helm; *?hawk* as crest.

*The cruciform iron fitting at the centre of a millstone, securing it to the shaft.

Maker's mark: fragmentary,? for E. Morley.

Presumably a Fellow Commoner's gift. Acquired in 1931, long after the College had given up drinking punch, and so in good condition.

18.5.8 Shilling Punch-Ladle (*illustrated on previous page*)

1820 (London e). $14\frac{1}{2}$ in. long; 3.0 × 2.5 bowl. Whalebone handle.

Bowl originally transversely elliptical with vestigial lips; bottom with inset coin; two constrictions, everted rim. Flattish stem with two tails. Handle twisted in upper part. Plain octagonal silver finial.

Set with a shilling of George III, 1787.

Maker's mark I·B in rectangle, for John Baxter, active *c*.1808–*c*.1840.

Has been much used: stem wobbly; weak joint to handle has been mended.

18.5.9 Florin Punch-Ladle (*illustrated on previous page*)

c.1820? Bowl 3.0 × 2.35 in. Whalebone handle. Very similar to above.

Deep bowl, everted rim, two vestigial lips. Flat stem attached by two vestigial tails. Slightly twisted handle; no finial. Set with George II florin of 1745.

Broken stem.

18.5.10 [Bateman] Punch-Ladle

1830? (London p, faint). 12.9 in. ?Whalebone handle.

Transverse elliptical bowl with undulate margin, spout at each end; forked attachment of stem. Twisted handle of ?whalebone. Sharp-pointed finial.

Maker's mark: F·W in rectangle, unidentified.

Bateman bequest.

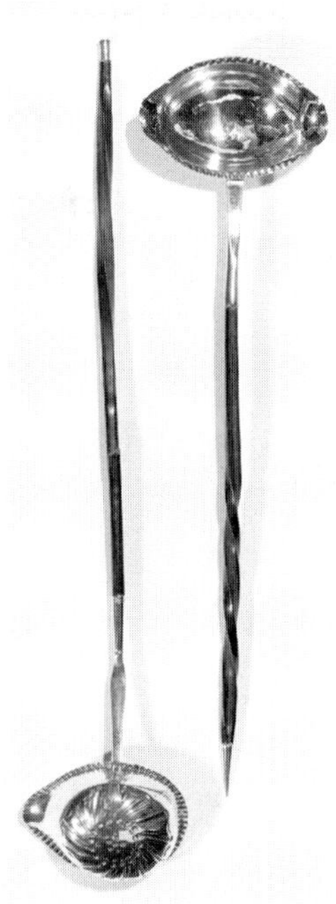

Bateman Punch-ladles of late 18th century (left) and of 1830

18.6 Knife-and-Fork Set

One pair of knives with handles of silver enamelled, with one forklet of Crystal.

Edward I's Wardrobe Accounts, 1300 (Cripps (1891) p. 314)

(The earliest mention of an eating-fork in England)

18.6 Case of Twelve Cowell [Fruit-] Knives and Twelve Forks

1881 (Sheffield O and young Victoria's head). Knives 8.3 in.; forks 7.0 in.; case 14.5 by 10.0 by 2.7 in. high.

Knives: pistoline handle, ribbed socket; blade with swept, enlarged, rounded end.

Forks: pistoline handle; blade with long bulbous stem and 3 tapering sharp tines.

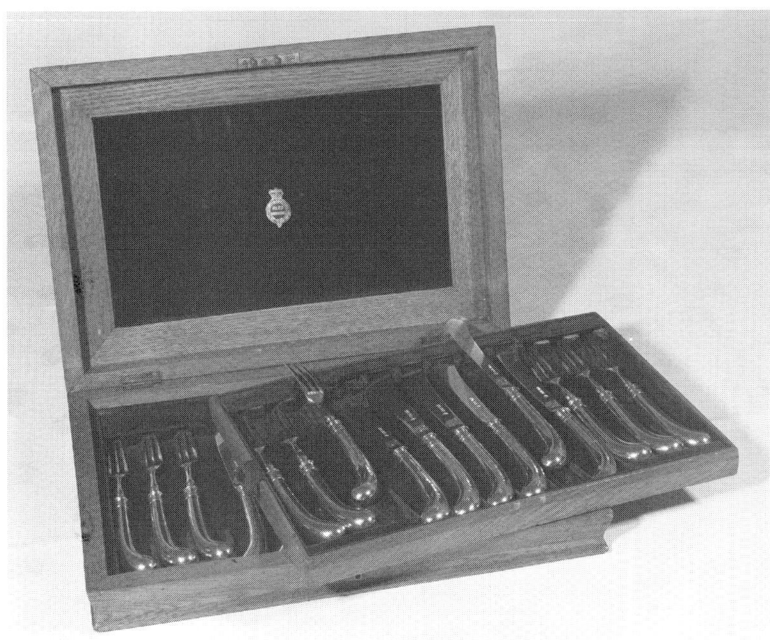

Case: two-decker, velvet-lined, in oak box with brass lock. Brass plate on lid with College arms, inscribed CORP: CHR: COLL: CANT

Marks (on handles and blades of knives and forks): RM EH in lozenge, for Richard Martin & Ebenezer Hall, manufacturing silversmiths, 1863–1936.

(on lock): crown VR *REED & SON CAMBRIDGE* SECURE PATENT.

(on velvet lining): REED CAMBRIDGE TO THE QUEEN AND H.R.H. PRINCE CONSORT.

Inscriptions: (on every handle): *Ex dono E.B. Cowell Socii et linguæ Sanscriticæ Professor 1881* [Gift of E.B. Cowell, Fellow and Professor of the Sanskritic language].

Edward Byles Cowell (1826–1903), of Ipswich, was one of the greatest Oriental scholars. Coming from Magdalen Hall, Oxford, he was Principal of the Sanskrit College, Calcutta, 1859–64, first Professor of Sanskrit at Cambridge in 1867, and first gold medallist of the Royal Asiatic Society. He became the first married Fellow of Corpus in 1874; Fellows were still not allowed to marry but he ingeniously got round the ban through having been married before entering Oxford, where it had already been abolished. He founded the Cowell Scholarship (later Cowell Prize). This modest and kindly man was famed for his generosity, his uncanny grasp of difficult languages, his magnificent beard, and his lifelong dependence on his learned and enthusiastic wife. The College has his portrait.

This gift seems never to have been used.

18.7 Scissors

1923 (Sheffield f). 6.9 by 2.2 in. All silver.

Blades half-interlock [to catch whatever has been cut]. Handles elaborately foliated and decorated.

Crest (on boss covering hinge): *pheasant.*

Maker's mark: W&H in rectangle, for Walker & Hall.

Bequeathed by Aubrey Bateman, probably for use in initiation ceremonies for new Fellows.

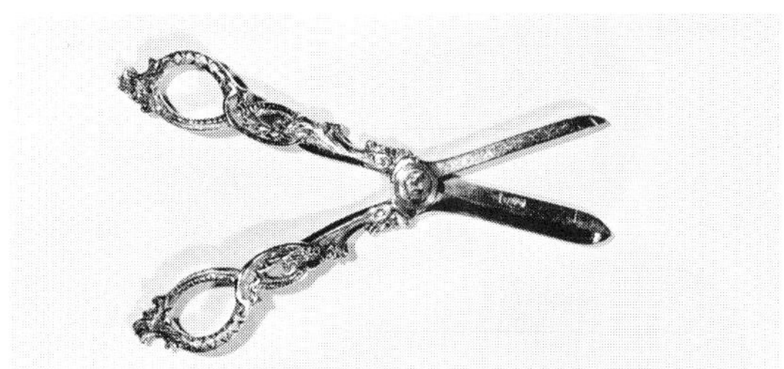

18.8 Scoops & Spades

Why not call a spade a spade?

A proverb

Bone-marrow, from long bones 'sent down to be grilled' after the meat had been eaten, was a characteristic part of human diet from the Palæolithic until the early 20th century. The earliest record at Corpus is the purchase of 8*d*. worth of marrow at Christmas 1457. Originally the bones were smashed, and maybe they still were in the 16th century, when no College feast was complete without half-a-dozen 'marybonys'.* By the 18th century elegant tools, consisting of two channelled scoops of different diameters joined by a handle, had been devised for getting at the marrow. At the time of writing marrowbones had to be smuggled from Calais owing to the supposed risk of Bovine Spongiform Encephalitis.

*CC(A): *LiberAlbus* f. 76v.; *College Accounts 1469–1510*; Book of Beadles' Feasts 1517 onwards.

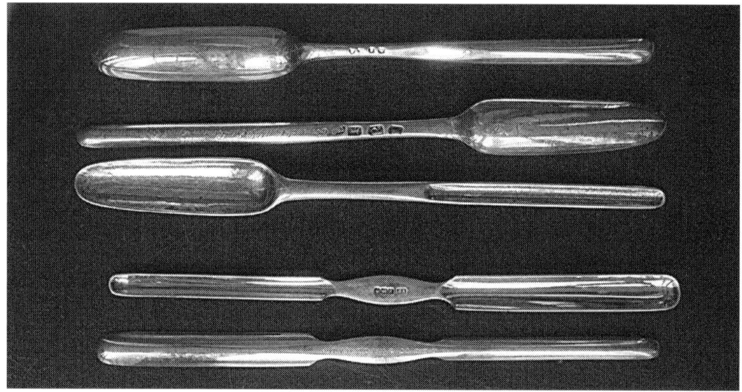

Marrow-Scoops: Beacon pair; Bateman; Pickthorn-Thomson

18.8.1 Two Beacon Marrow-Scoops

1739 (London d). 9.3 in.

Inscription: *Corp. X*^{ti}. *Coll. D.D. Edv. Beacon* $^{A.M.}$ *ejusd. Coll. nuper Soc.* (Given to Corpus Christi College by Edward Beacon, lately Fellow of the same College.) \ *N°. 1* \ *N°. 2*

Maker's mark: *J. King* in oval, for Jeremiah King, active 1739–.

Given by Edward Beacon in 1742 (see Beacon Punch-ladles, §18.5.1, 2).

18.8.2 [Bateman] Marrow-Scoop

1800 (London E). 9.1 in. No inscription or maker.

Bequeathed by Aubrey Bateman.

18.8.3 Wallis Spade

1822 (London g + King's head). 10 in.

Rectangular spatulate end; fiddle-pattern handle. College arms + pelican pseudo-crest.

Inscription: COLL: CORP: CHRISTI CANT. ED DN [*sic*] ARNOLD JOS: WALLIS, SOC: 1883.

Maker's mark: WE WF in rectangle, for William Eley II & William Fearn (§18.2.3).

Donor: Arnold Joseph Wallis, see Wallis Butter-knife (§18.3.12).

Supposed to be for digging Stilton. This noble blue-veined cheese, made in Leicestershire and marketed at Stilton (Huntingdonshire), used to come in huge squat cylinders, and was excavated with a tool like this, leaving a shell of rind. To judge by the condition of the blade, it contained a lot of sand.

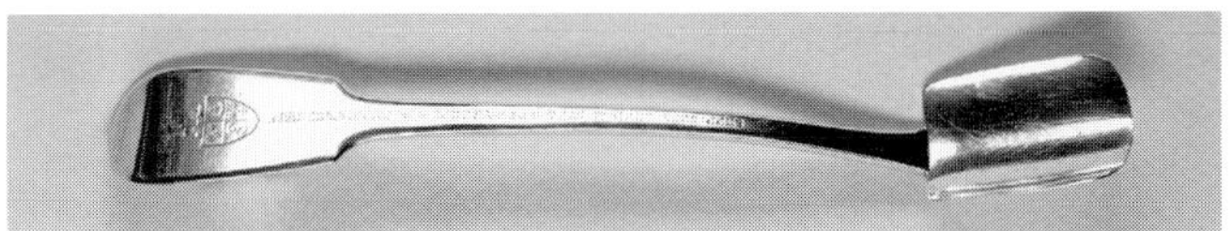

18.8.4 Six Pickthorn and Six Thomson Marrow-Scoops

1828 (Sheffield e). 9.1 in.

Inscriptions: *C.C.C. ET B.V.M. D.D. K.W.M.P.*
C.C.C. ET B.V.M. D.D. C.P.T. [error for G.P.T.]

Maker's mark: HA in rectangle, for Henry Atkins (died 1835).

These commemorate two very distinguished men. Kenneth William Murray Pickthorn (1892–1975), historian, son of a sailor, was a Scholar of Trinity. He was a Fellow of Corpus from 1914 for the phenomenal term of 61 years; fought in World War I; was Tutor 1927–35; was Burgess (that is, University M.P.) 1935–50; was M.P. for Carlton (Notts) 1955–64; Litt.D. 1936; Parliamentary Secretary to the Ministry of Education 1951; Baronet 1959; Privy Councillor 1964. These could be his wedding fine of 1924.

For Sir George Paget Thomson see the Thomson Rosewater Bowl (p. 272).

18.8.5 Two Bates Crumb-Scoops

1886 (London L). 12.3 in.

King's pattern handle (decorated on both sides with scrollwork and shells – a rare type in Corpus).

College arms, with pelican pseudo-crest.

Inscription: *MAGISTRO \ ET SOCIIS \ COLL. CORP. CHRISTI ET B.V.V.* [*sic*] *CANTABRIGIÆ \ D. D. \ S. E. BATES, A. M. \ COLLEGII \ ALUMNUS \ A. S. MDCCCLXXXVII* (S.E. Bates, M.A., Old Member of the College, gave [me] to the Master and Fellows of the College of Corpus Christi and the Blessed Virgin [Mary] at Cambridge in the year of grace 1887).

On belt round arms and text: *SIGNAT AVIS CHRISTUM QUI SANGUINE NASCIT* [*sic*] *ALUMNOS LILA* [*sic*] *VIRGO PARENS INTEMERATA REFERT* (The bird signifies Christ, who feeds his dependants with [his] blood; the lilies refer to the undefiled Virgin-Parent [Mary].)

Maker's mark: JA TS in quatrefoil, for John Aldwinckle (?–1894) and Alfred Thomas Slater (1856–1904), part of Holland, Aldwinckle & Slater 1883–*c*.1922.

Donor: Sydney Eggers Bates, admitted 1869.

This tool was used in genteel households for removing crumbs from the tablecloth after the meal, instead of shaking the cloth in front of the birds as less refined persons do. Its predecessor was the *voider*, into which page-boys used to scrape the trenchers, as laid down in medieval books of etiquette.

18.8.6 Nine Anonymous Marrow-scoops

Electroplate.

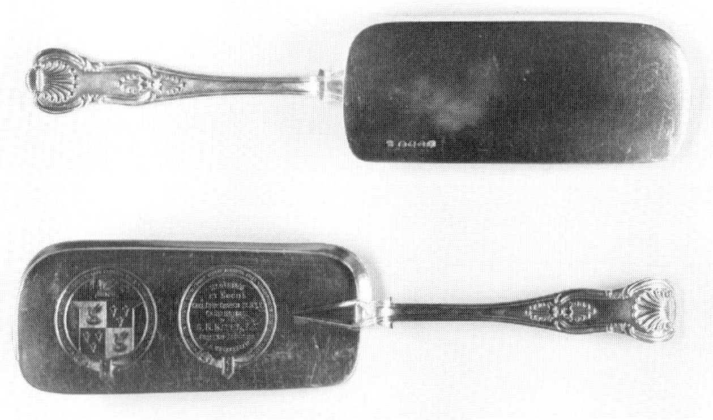

18.9 Strainers

Ye blind guides, which strain at a gnat, and swallow a camel.

St Matthew **23** 24

Strainers of various kinds, for removing tea-leaves from coffee etc., go back to the mid-18th century.

18.9.1 Wine Strainer

1792 (London r with George III's head for 1792). Bowl 3.35 × 1.45 in., spout 3.4 long.

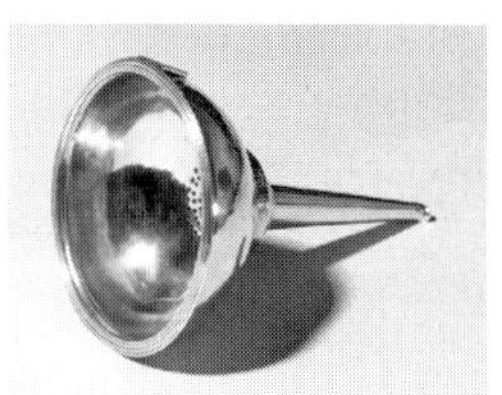

Hemispherical bowl pierced with about 100 holes, inside a collar; flat ribbed rim with a hook at one side. Spout is a push-fit to the collar; has asymmetric end.

Inscription: *C.C.C.C.* on both parts.

No maker's mark.

Has been much used, to judge by the rubbed state of the marks.

18.9.2 Small Pierced Ladle (Strainer)

1830 (London p). 5.4 in.

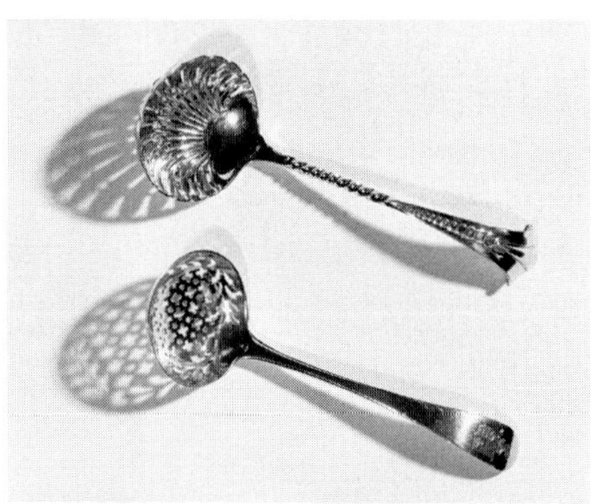

Strainers of 1867 and 1830

Flattish-bottomed bowl pierced with foliage, crosses, roundels; Old English handle with drop at its root. College arms + pelican pseudo-crest.

Maker's mark: W.S in oval, unidentified (many with these initials).

18.9.3 [Bateman] small Pierced Ladle (Strainer)

1867 (Sheffield Z). 5.6 in. Thinly gilt inside.

Deep round bowl pierced with rows of dots and dashes, fluted between; curved, twisted stem; handle decorated with rings.

Maker's mark: HA in rectangle, for Atkin Brothers.

Bequeathed by Aubrey Bateman.

18.9.4 [Bateman] Strainer

1897 (London b). 6.2 by 4.0 in.

Bowl pierced with holes, in wide flat *repoussé* surround, with hole for hanging it up. Ornamented with 5 *putti*, one conducting from music, the others playing trumpet, French horn, double flute, violin.

Marked F for Foreign. Maker's mark, BM in rectangle, denotes Franz Carl Berthold Müller of Hanau, active in London 1892–1922.

Bequeathed by Aubrey Bateman.

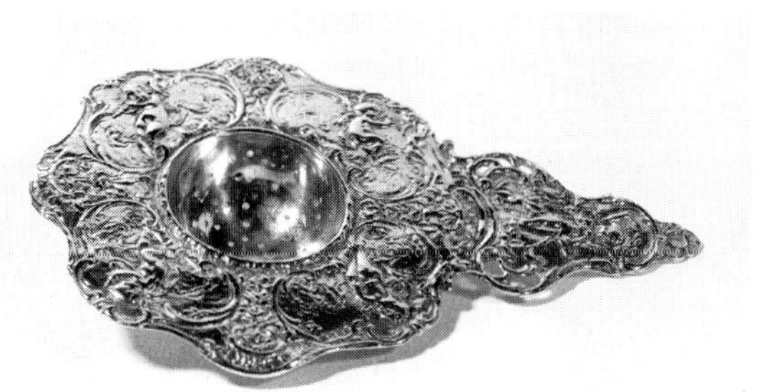

18.10 Tongs

> Then flew one of the Seraphim unto me, having a live coal in his hand, which he had taken with the tongs from off the altar.
>
> *Isaiah* **6** 6

This noble instrument no longer forms part of the Chapel plate, but is demoted to sugar-lumping and the pursuit of asparagus.

Tongs are of two kinds: the pattern with a hinge like scissors, and the 'sheep-shear' type in which the blades are connected by a strip of metal which forms a spring. The small tongs, 6 in. long or less, like a conjoined pair of teaspoons, were for picking up lumps of sugar cut off a sugar-loaf with that formidable instrument the *sugar-nippers*. They begin in the mid-18th century. The big ones, 9–10 in. long, were for picking up cooked asparagus, a slippery herb, hence the serrated blades.

18.10.1 'VCC' Sugar-Spring-Tongs
(not illustrated)

1808 (London N). 5.6 in.

Sheep-shear pattern; ending in very small plain spoon ends. *VCC* monogram

No maker's mark.

18.10.2 Robinson Sugar-Spring-Tongs

?1810 (?London P) 5.6 in.

Sheep-shear pattern; ending in very small plain spoon ends.

Crest: *a hart* between C.C. and C.C.

Inscription: *E dono Sirmor Robinson Soc. Com.* (Gift of Sirmor Robinson, Fellow-Commoner).

Maker's mark: TS in ellipse, ?for Thomas Streetie, active 1794–*c*.1822.

Probably given by S.W.K. Robinson of Durham, who also gave spoons (§18.1.13).

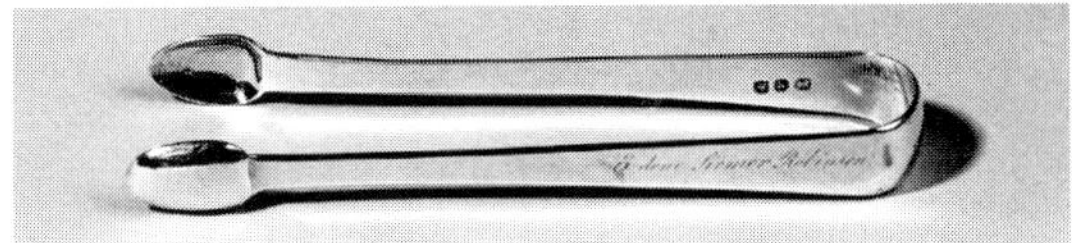

18.10.3 Josselyn Asparagus-Spring-Tongs

1841 (London 𝕱 + Victoria's head). 10.3 in.

Sheep-shear-pattern; flat blades, one with lip; rectangular loop (with two screws) limits travel; blades pierced with foliation and stars, reeded edges to handles and blades.

Inscription: E DONO JOANNIS JOSSELYN ESSEXIENSIS HUJUS COLLEGII SOCII COMMENSALIS. 1841 (Gift of John Josselyn of Essex, Fellow-Commoner of this College, 1841).

Maker's mark of the spooner George William Adams (§18.1.26).

18.10.4 [Bateman] Shell Tongs
(not illustrated)

1897 (Sheffield 𝔢). 3.9 in.

Scissor-pattern with loop handles; shell-shaped outsides of grips, concave insides.

Maker illegible.

Bequeathed by Aubrey Bateman.

18.10.5 [Bateman] Spring-Tongs
(not illustrated)

1897 (London b). 10.0 in.

Sheep-shear-pattern, asymmetric, with loop limiting outward travel.

Marks mainly illegible.

Bequeathed by Aubrey Bateman.

18.10.6 [Bateman] Croc-Tongs

Undatable. 9.9 in.

Sheep-shear-pattern; upper jaw raked like a crocodile's, ribbed, with downturn at end; lower jaw plain; rectangular loop with two screws. Crest: *steed's head*.

Marks: poorly struck, illegible.

Possibly bequeathed by Aubrey Bateman: his mini-saucepan has a similar crest.

18.10.7 Anonymous *Cannabis*-style Tongs

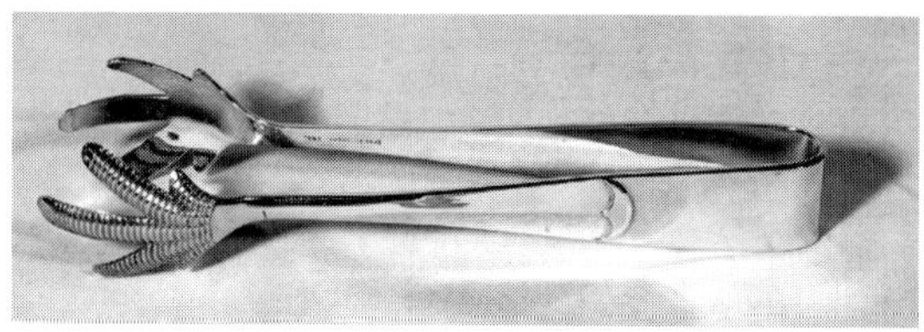

Undated. 6.5 in. Plated base metal.

Sheep-shear-pattern; symmetric blades in likeness of a 5-part palmately divided leaf with scale-like ornamentation; handles cusped like a Hanoverian spoon.

Marks: EPNS . A1. SHEFF. ENG | BS 5577 | 40 in oval.

18.10.8 Anonymous Spring-Tongs

Undated. 8.8 in. Plated brass.

Sheep-shear-pattern; asymmetric, curved rectangular blades, patterned piercing; fan-like mouldings on handles; bolt limits travel.

Marks: Ro. 164212 | sun | 𝔐𝔅 | crown.

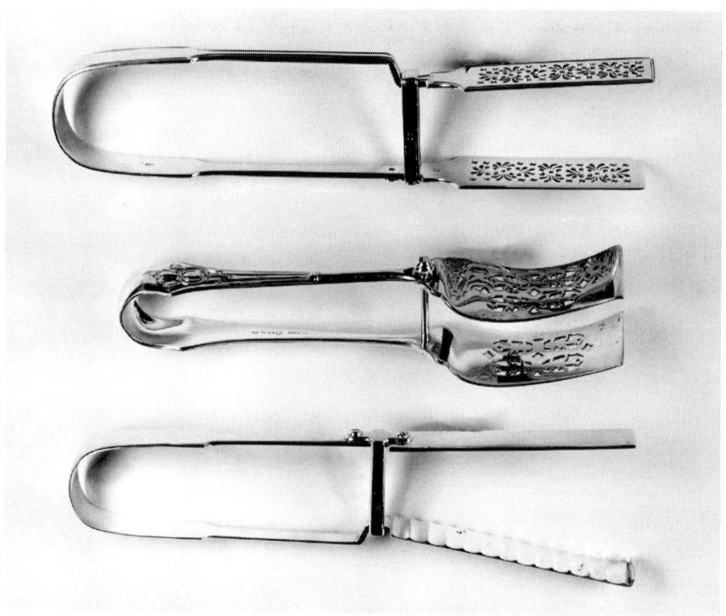

Tongs: Josselyn; Anonymous Curved; Bateman Crocodile

19

Instruments of Tobacconing

We perfume and aire our bodies with *Tabacco* smoake (by drying) preseruing them from Putrifaction.

Henry Butts [later Master of the College, p. 101], *Dyets Dry Dinner*, 1599

Many in this Kingdome have had such a continuall vse of taking this vnsauorie smoke, as now they are not able to forbeare the same, no more than an olde drunkard can abide to be long sober . . .

[James I], *Covnterblaste to Tobacco*, 1604

Before the meat come smoking to the board, our gallant must draw out his tobacco-box, the ladle for the cold snuff into the nostril, the tongs and priming-iron, all which artillery may be of gold or silver, if he can reach the price of it.

Dekker, The Gull's Horn-book, *1609*

(The tongs and priming-iron would have been for ignition.)

Cats may have had their goose
Cooked by tobacco-juice*
Still, why deny its use
  thoughtfully taken;

We're not as tabbies are,
Smith, take a fresh cigar,
Jones, the tobacco-jar
  Here's to thee, Bacon!†

C. S. Calverley, Ode to Tobacco, *1862*

* Evidently refers to recent animal experiments.
† The chief supplier of tobacco to Cambridge for over a century.

Tobacco is the dried, powdered or shredded leaves of the narcotic herbs *Nicotiana tabacum* and *N. rustica.* It was used by many American Indian nations as a hallucinogen on sacred and ceremonial occasions. The Cubans gave it to Columbus in 1492, but he ignored it, and it did not catch on in Europe until Jean Nicot, French ambassador in Lisbon, persuaded Catherine de Medici to grow tobacco in France *c.*1560. It reached England in about 1570. Torn from its liturgical and spiritual context, it lost its hallucinogenic properties and much of its subtlety, degenerating into a recreational hard drug.[1]

Tobacco has a special significance for Corpus because Richard Fletcher, ex-Fellow, smoked himself to death by 1596, apparently the earliest identifiable victim anywhere in the world (p. 91). His and other cases provoked James I, eight years later, to write *A Counterblaste to Tobacco,* which in the writer's childhood was held up as an example of the superstitious ignorance of that benighted age. There was a lively debate about whether tobacco should be banned as a menace to public health: indeed it was banned (on pain of death) by Murad IV, Sultan of Turkey. However, it was probably not so toxic then as it became much later with mass-produced cigarettes.

Tobacco was self-administered in six ways, all of Native American origin. In Europe each gave rise to characteristic silver artefacts.

(1) By chewing a ***plug*** of compressed leaf, and discharging the product into a ***cuspidor*** or ***spittoon***, of which we unfortunately have no identifiable example (although the Perowne Bowl (§21.2.4), among others, would serve).

1 For tobacco lore see: J Goodman 1993 *Tobacco in History: the cultures of dependence* Routledge, London.

(2) By snorting the powder, called ***snuff*** or ***smutchin***, scented and flavoured with other herbs. Snuff was rather unstable and was stored in an airtight ***snuff-box*** or ***snuff-mull***. This was the happiest, most civilized and subtle form of tobacco, the most widespread (especially in Scotland and France and among coal-miners) and the longest persisting.[2]

(3) By means of an enema of tobacco smoke or juice, using a gadget called a ***clyster***. This was popular mainly in France; we have no recognized example of the instrument.

(4) By igniting shredded leaves (using tongs and a live coal, or a match from a ***match-case***) in a ***pipe*** of stone, clay, hollowed-out corn-cob, or hard wood (silver only in Japan) and sucking the smoke. Pipe-tobacco was stored in an airtight ***tobacco-box*** or a silver ***tobacco-barrel***.[3] Pipe-smoking grew into a sociable and civilized art in Turkey, Persia, and India, whose apparatus for passing the smoke through scented water, the ***huqqa*** or ***narghilé***, never caught on in Cambridge.

(5) By ingesting smoke from smouldering leaves rolled into a cylinder called a ***cigar*** or ***stogie***, which was stored in a tight-fitting ***cigar-box***, initialized with a ***cigar-cutter***, and inflamed using a ***lighter***; the debris was discarded into a shallow receptacle called an ***ashtray***.

(6) By inhaling fumes from smouldering shreds of tobacco compressed in a tube of maize-husk or paper, called a ***cigarette*** or ***fag***, taken from a ***cigarette-box***, and mounted in a ***cigarette-holder*** provided by the smoker; the debris was discarded into an ***ashtray*** provided by the host, or, failing that, on the carpet. An ashtray is recognized by notches or lips on the rim, on which abandoned cigarettes would be left reeking to create the smoky atmosphere, perhaps a relic of the original hallucination hut, in which important decisions were taken. Early cigarettes were filled with scrap tobacco or recycled cigar-ends,[4] but in the 19th century a special 'mild' or 'bright' type of tobacco was developed – an addictive and malodorous kind which made tobacco the most deadly of drugs.[5]

Tobacco was consumed in Cambridge from late Elizabethan times until the end of the Space Age, but mostly between 1870 and 1970, to judge by the artefacts. The Earl of Rutland, ex-Fellow-Commoner of Corpus (p. 97), had a silver tobacco-box in 1600. In 1607 the Vice-Chancellor forbade smoking, especially at night, in Great St Mary's Church, and in college halls. In 1620 provisions for the Audit feast included three ounces of tobacco and two dozen 'tobaccopips'.[6]

The earliest physical evidence among the plate is the Castle box of 1728. The artefacts suggest pipe-smoking down to the mid-19th century, snuff in the 1870s and 1880s, then an overwhelming change to cigars, and some reversion to pipes in the 1950s.

In the 1960s all methods except cigarettes became unfashionable and were seldom used in the College except at feasts. Cigarettes, though the most dangerous method of administering tobacco, lingered for some twenty years more, but fell into disfavour because of their evil smell and ruinous effects on the user's health. At the time of writing the implements were disused, except for occasional use of the cigar-lighter and snuffhorn.

A Seventeenth-Century Pipe by Graeme Lawson

In 1980 a clay pipe bowl was found in a building trench in the Bursar's Garden with some tobacco still in it, preserved in the airless mud. Excavated pipe bowls often contain a little carbonized leaf, the remains presumably of their last smoke, but a substantial plug is rare.

The small egg-shaped bowl and large-bore stem mark this as a 17th-century pipe. It has a wheel-made decoration round the mouth. Almost indistinguishable pipes have been found all over Britain and the Netherlands and their colonies in North America.

Clay pipes were made in millions, and their indestructible fragments are everywhere. They ruined the smoker's lips, palate (when he bumped into a door), and teeth (by some startling dental wear).

2 Dr Bushnell, my predecessor, used to point out that it was the only kind of tobacco that might properly be administered in a church, though not during the Canon of the Mass.

3 Clare College has a fine 18th-century example of the latter: Jones *Cambridge* plate XIV.

4 H Mayhew (1851) *London Labour and the London Poor* London ('Of the Cigar-end Finders', **2** pp. 145f.).

5 For cigarette manufacture see G Bizet & P Mérimée (1875) *Carmen*.

6 Glanville (1990) p. 365; University Archives Coll. Admin. 11A ff69v–70; Lamb p. 164.

As time went on bowls got bigger and stems narrower, which may derive from tobacco getting cheaper and from changes in its preparation and combustion rate.

19.1 The Caldwell Snuff-Horn

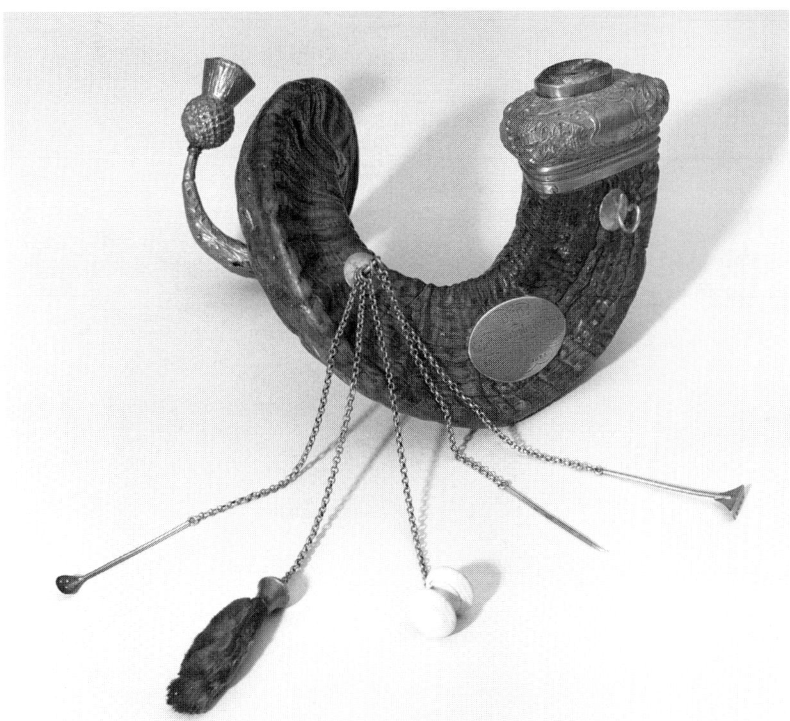

9.8 × 5.5 in. No date-letter.

This jolly object never fails to amuse. It is a coiled sheep's horn, stuffed with some inert material, leaving a cavity for the snuff in the big end. It is set with these paraphernalia:

(1) Silver finial in shape of a thistle (*Cirsium vulgare*, the badge of Scotland). Its foliage grips the end of the horn. The thistle's florets are represented by a piece of glass-like material, coloured green by rusting of the copper alloy beneath.
(2) Silver boss underneath, set to allow the horn to stand firmly on a table.
(3) Lid, *repoussé* and chased with thistles, set with another piece of glass, coloured brown by decay of glue;[7] arms of College; marked with a thistle (a Scottish standard-mark) and PW in rectangle.
(4) Rim of cavity, hinged by a ball-joint to lid.
(5) Silver plate inscribed *D.D. Robertus Townley Caldwell. SOCIUS ET SENESCALLUS.* [Fellow and Bursar] *3. JAN. 1883.*
(6) Ring with five silver chains bearing:
    (i) Silver awl (for dispersing any crust formed by damp or mould on the snuff powder).
    (ii) Silver rake (for levelling surface of snuff).
    (iii) Ivory mallet (for compacting surface of snuff).

7 Dr David Dewhirst writes: I suppose the stone is to be taken as a Cairngorm (= a naturally coloured Quartz), sometimes called Scotch topaz . . . I doubt even that it *is* a Cairngorm, but suspect a shaped piece of glass with a piece of colour-varnished tin foil under it.

(iv) Tiny silver spoon pierced with holes (for sprinkling a portion of snuff in the hollow of the taker's left wrist).
(v) Silver-mounted foot of a rabbit or hare (for wiping off remaining snuff from the wrist).
(The expert use of these tools was demonstrated by the late Dr Geoffrey Bushnell.)
(7) Silver hook to stow implements.

This is a fine example of the Scottish Baronial style, redolent of Balmoral and the Highland Games, but it perpetuates a genuine tradition, going back to the 1600s. Snuff, often home-made, was the favourite form of tobacco in Scotland. By the mid 18th century 'the "sneeshin-horn", with the spoon and hare's-foot attached to it by chains' was the standard equipment of the stage Scotsman.[8] Balliol College, Oxford has such a snuff-horn, less elaborate than ours but with identical tools, given by Sir William Hamilton in 1807. [9] There is another in St John's College, Cambridge.

This horn is not extreme. Serious snuffers snuffed from a snuff-stuffed sheep's skull, or a ram's whole woolly head. The top of his brain-pan hinged back to reveal the contents, and he ran round the table on three little wheels, under each horn and under his chin. Three such were exhibited at the Great Exhibition in 1851 – each horn of one was said to be 3 feet 5 in. long – and a Ram's Head presides at feasts of the High Constables of Perth.[10]

Robert Townley Caldwell (1843–1914), son of a Gordon Highlander from Barbados, mathematician, soldier and Freemason, was admitted in 1862. In three years he became a Fellow. As Bursar from 1871 to 1899, his 'unwearied exertions' saw the College through the agricultural depression. He was one of the first Fellows to marry (this piece appears to be his wedding fine); the College's first lay Master (1906–14); the first Master allowed to dine in Hall without the Fellows' permission; and the founder of Caldwell Scholarships. He was laird of Inneshewen (Aberdeenshire), which was his undoing, for he was killed in a car crash there, and magnificently piped to the grave.[11] (In legend he was the first Scottish victim of motoring: he had the misfortune to run into the other motor-car in Scotland.)

19.2 Mander Lighters

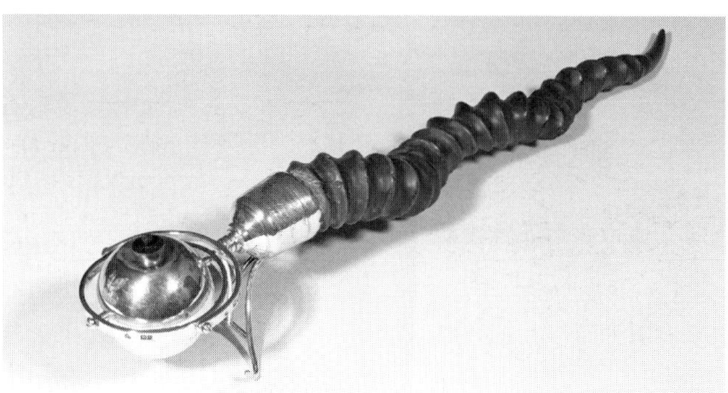

1898 (London c).
Two lighters (one disused) for setting fire to cigars, 21.2 and 20.2 in. long. A small globular spirit-lamp is mounted on gimbals so that it always stays upright. The handle is the spiral horn of an antelope, probably Indian black-buck (*Antilopa cervicapra*).

The socket at the end of the handle is inscribed: *Carolus Tertius Mander A.M. summus Wolverhamptoniensium magistratu per quadriennium functus Collegio suo Corp. Chr. et B.M.V. in usum conviviorum d.d. die Commemorationis A.S. MDCCCXCVIII.* (Charles Tertius

8 *Report of the Jurors of the Great Exhibition* 1851 [vol. 5] p. 674.
9 Moffatt Plate V.
10 Information from Dr Dewhirst (to whom I am indebted for particulars of the Great Exhibition) and from the Rev. W.F. Harris.
11 Bury pp. 119–36.

Mander, M.A., having officiated as Mayor of the Wolverhamptonians for a four-year term, gave this gift to his College of Corpus Christi and the Blessed Virgin Mary for the use of feasters on Commemoration Day A.D. 1898.)

Maker's mark JB in an ellipse, for Joseph Braham, active *c.*1886, died 1918; founder of Padgett & Braham.

Sir Charles Tertius Mander was an undergraduate from 1870; High Sheriff of Staffordshire 1903–4; made Baronet 1911.

19.3 Selwyn Cigar-Cutter

1909 (London o).
Silver box with steel works. 3.9 in. × 2.4 × 2.7 high.

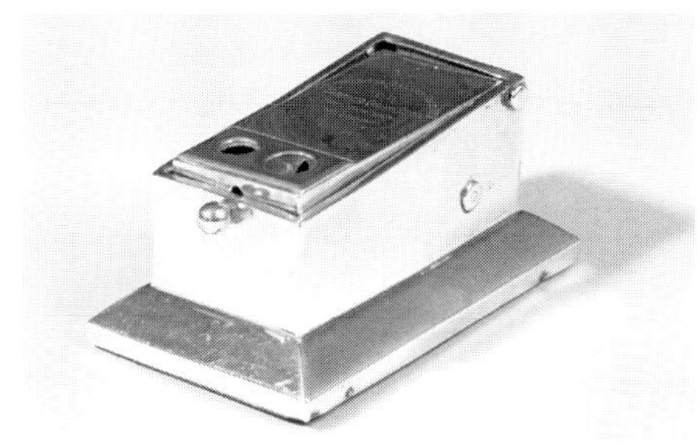

Cigars were often supplied unfinished and had to be initialized by the smoker, drawing a knife or using this gadget. The box has a hinged top; pressing it down actuates spring-loaded blades inside. The mouth end of the cigar was placed in one hole to be notched; the fire end was placed in another hole to be truncated.

Inscription: COMMENSALIBUS COLL. CORP. CHR. ET B.M.V. D.D. EDWARDUS GORDON SELWYN PRID. NON. SEXT. MDCCCCX. (Edward Gordon Selwyn gave [this] to the High Table Members of the College ... on 4 August 1910.)

Edward Gordon Selwyn (1885–1959), D.D., of Liverpool, Captain of Eton College and Scholar of King's, was a distinguished Classicist and later theologian. He was a Fellow of Corpus 1909–14, Dean of Winchester 1930–58, Honorary Fellow 1942–59.[12]

19.4 Boxes

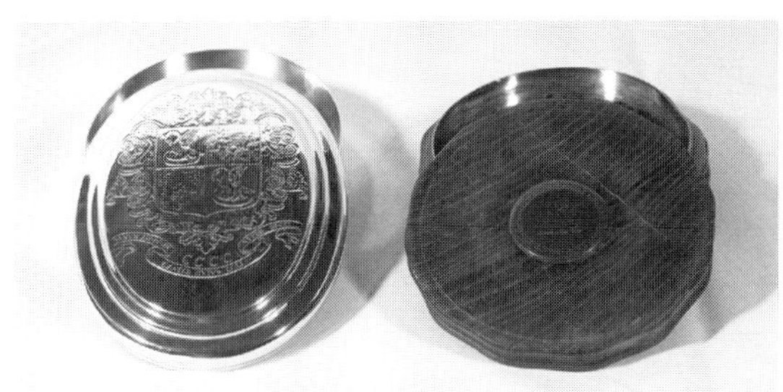

Castle (left) and Greene Tobacco-Boxes

19.4.1 Castle Pipe-Tobacco-Box

1729 (London O, poorly struck[13]). 5.3 in. × 4.1 × 1.3 high (too big for a snuff-box).

Flat box, between a rectangle and an ellipse in shape, with a push-on lid. College arms, on a baroque scrolled and foliated cartouche, take up most of lid.

Inscriptions: CCCC and DONVM EDMVNDI CASTLE HVIVS COLL: NVPER SOCII [Gift of Edmund Castle, lately Fellow of this College]. On base: 8^{oz} : 5^{dwt} 1730 [present weight 7.8 ounces].

Much used: nearly 6% of the metal has been cleaned away. Maker's mark illegible.

Edmund Castle (1698–1750) came from Kent to Corpus as Parker Scholar in 1716; Fellow 1722–9; B.D. 1745; elected University Orator 1726 in defiance of Nicholas Bentley, the notorious Master of Trinity; left his Fellowship to become Vicar of Elm and of Emneth (Isle of Ely), and gave this piece to mark the occasion. He returned as Master of the College 1744–50, which he combined with Dean of Hereford 1748–50. He had a reputation for old-fashioned integrity: 'a man more

12 Bury pp. 239f.
13 The piece appears in the inventory of 24 Sept. 1728, so the letter cannot be Q for 1731.

adorned with Learning and with Simplicity of Manners Antiquity never produced' (Henry Fielding).

19.4.2 Greene Tobacco-Box (*illustrated on previous page*)

c.1824. Round dugout oaken box, with similar lid, brass-lined. No silver. 4.3 in. diameter, 1.4 high.

On lid is a brass roundel with College arms, pelican pseudo-crest, and inscription FRATRIBUS CONSOCIATATIS [*sic*] DO THOMAS GREENE MDCCCXXIV (I, Thomas Greene, give [this] to the brethren of the Societety, 1824).

Thomas Greene (?–1868) of Huntingdonshire, grandson of Thomas Greene, Master of Corpus, was admitted as Scholar in 1808; Fellow 1814–35; as Bursar (1822–8) he handled the finances of building the New Court. In 1835 he left to become priest of the obscure College living of Fulmodeston-cum-Croxton, Norfolk. He was an Honorary Canon of Norwich Cathedral; Evangelical churchman; noted for holiness, sincerity, virtue, and self-sacrifice.

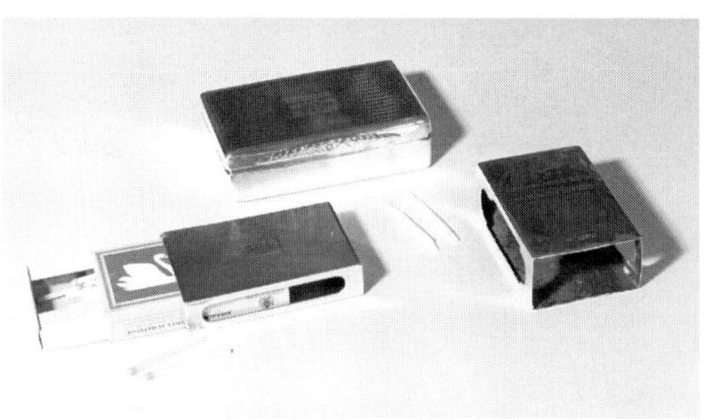

Left to right: Carter Match-case, Fanshawe Box, Archdall Match-case

19.4.3 Fanshawe Snuff-Box

1873 (London 𝔖). 4.0 in. × 2.55 × 1.0 high.

Flat rectangular box with piano-hinged lid. Top and bottom striped with hatching; sides and ends ribbed; front edge of lid with cast foliage and flowers. Traces of gilding inside.

Inscribed: SOCIIS ET AMICIS SUIS D.D. SOCIUS EMERITUS H.E.F. (Retired Fellow H.E.F. gave [me] to his Fellows and friends.)

Maker: Edward Charles Brown, active 1867–83, founder of Richards & Brown.

Henry Ernest 'Fanny' Fanshawe (1844–1913), son of a Durham seaman, was admitted as Scholar in 1862. He became Fellow 1866; in 1874 disqualified himself by marrying; returned in 1882 when married Fellows were legitimatized. He was Tutor 1892–1912, and squire of Dengie Hall, far away in Essex. He was famous for Classical learning, Conservatism, taste in port, good stories, feud with 'Charlie' Moule (p. 238), and refusal to take up 20th-century technology; he founded the Fanshawe Prize.

This box is surprisingly worn with long use. Probably meant for snuff, it now contains toothpicks.

19.4.4 Bateman-Jolliffe Cigar-box

1893 (London S). 8.0 in. × 3.3 × 2.0 high.

Like most cigar-boxes, this is made of tropical softwood, encased in silver except underneath, with a movable partition for different sizes of cigar. The lid is attached by a piano-type hinge, with a rib for lifting.

The lid bears the badge of a womanly Irish harp, royally crowned, with shamrock leaves, surrounded by garter inscribed 4TH BATT: ROYAL IRISH REGT. Inscription: *Presented to Captain Jolliffe by Lt. Colonel Trant & Officers 4th Battn. Royal Irish Regiment July 22nd 1893.*

Bequeathed by Aubrey Bateman, who had it from a military relative.

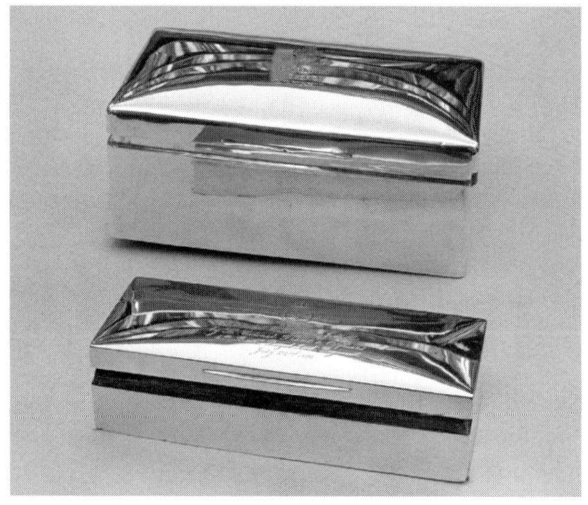

S.J.S. (above) and Bateman-Jolliffe Cigar-boxes

19.4.5 Archdall Match-case

1911 (Chester *K*). 2.8 × 2.0 × 1.0 in., made to fit a then customary size of match-box. Open sides enabled a match to be extracted from the box and ignited.

Inscribed: COMMENSALIBUS COLL. CORP. CHR. ET B.M.V. D.D. HENRICUS KAROW ARCHDALL A.D. VI. ID. DEC. MDCCCCXI (Henry Karow Archdall gave [me] to the Commoners of College of Corpus Christi . . . 8 Dec. 1911)

Presumably given by Henry Kingsley Archdall (1886–1976), divine, when he became a Fellow in 1911. (The discrepancy of name is unexplained.) He came from Sydney University to Trinity College and then to Corpus as Fellow and later Dean of Chapel. He had a later career in Australia, New Zealand, Oxford, and North America, and as Principal of St David's College, Lampeter, 1938–53.[14]

19.4.6 S.J.S. Cigar-Box

1922 (Birmingham W). 9.0 in. × 5.6 × 3.5 high.

Silver, gilt inside lid, enclosing a box (in poor condition) of some light broadleaved softwood (e.g. tulip-tree), with divider.

Inscription: CORPUS CHRISTI COLL. CAMB. EX DONO S.J.S. MCMXXII. College arms with pelican pseudo-crest.

Donor and maker (W.B.S.) unidentified.

19.4.7 Forbes Cigar-box

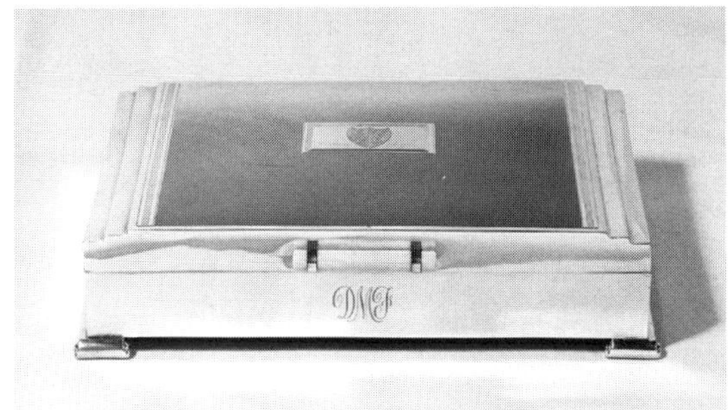

Dated 1935. 6.8 in. × 4.5 × 1.5 high.

Box of cigar-box wood (a light, ring-porous wood), scored for a divider, encased (save underneath) in silver box; cylindrical ivory handle on lid; four scrolled silver feet. Lid has stepped profile, hatched surface, rectangular cartouche.

College arms; inscription FOUNDED A.D. 1352. Monogram *DMF*.

Birmingham Jubilee hallmark with L for 1935. Maker illegible.

A note on the base used to say 'Presented to the College by Mrs Beatrice Forbes mother of D.M. Forbes died March 19 1955'. Donald Murray Forbes came as an undergraduate in 1935, the year this piece was made.

19.4.8 McCrum Pipe-Tobacco-Box

1962 (London *J*). Britannia silver. 2.9 × 1.1 in.

Flat circular box with push-fit lid. In middle of lid a medallion with pelican and inscription *DOMUI DUPLICI IN UNO CORPORE IUNCTAE* ∗ [To the double house joined in one body – alluding to the founding in 1961 of Leckhampton House, intended as a sub-community forming part of the College.]

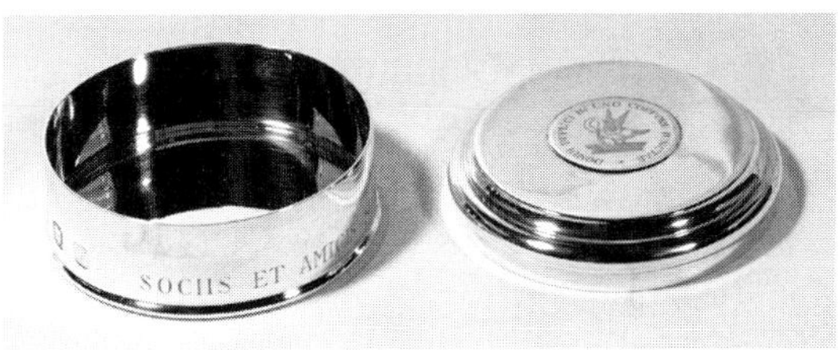

Inscription: *SOCIIS ET AMICIS SUIS D.D. SOCIUS M.McC. A.D. MCMLXII* (M.McC. gave [me] to Fellows and friends A.D. 1952)

Made by Gibson & Co.

Given by Michael William McCrum, Fellow and later Master (p. 118).

In the 1960s this box would pass round the Combination Room table until it reached Dr George Carter, who would empty it into his wooden pipe called Great Tom and reach for:

19.4.9 Two Carter Match-cases

1964 (London *i*). 3.1 in. × 2.0 × 0.6 high.

Flat silver box, made to fit round a box of 'Swan' strike-anywhere matches (a type of match much used

14 Bury p.243; Woodhead pp. 15f.

in the cigarette period). One end open, slot at other end and on each of the narrow sides. Top and bottom hatched.

Inscription: *d.d. G.S.C.* and *1965*.

For George Stuart Carter (1893–1969) see his mug (§10.2.7).

19.5 Ashtrays

The College had no fine ashtrays, and used cheap glass ones.

Two Bateman Ashtrays

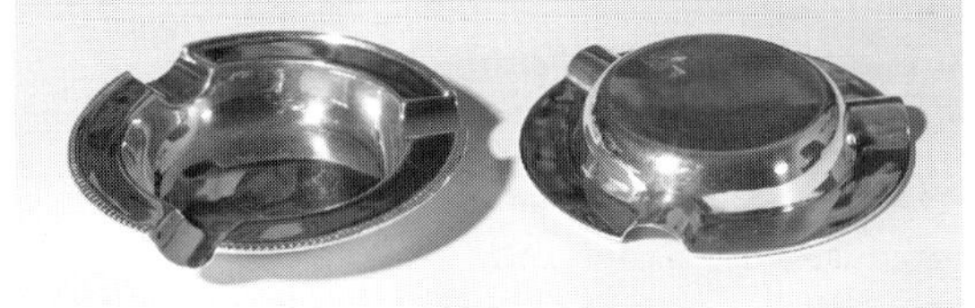

1926 (Sheffield i). 3.8 in. diameter.

Flat-bottomed vessel with flat rim on which are three lips for smouldering small cigars. Gadrooned edge.

Bequeathed by Aubrey Bateman.

20

Sporting Plate

> The science of rowing is studied by as many men with as much ambition and perhaps with as much seriousness as either Classics or Mathematics.
>
> *Students' Guide, 1863* [quoted by Bury (1952)]

Trophies, originally the property of the various sports clubs, tend to find their way into College custody. They are handed over to the College for safe-keeping and are overlooked by the next generation of undergraduates, or are forgotten when the sport or the club itself dies.

20.1 Wilkinson Sculls

1859 (London d). Two silver oars, 5.1 in. long; silver plates with lists of winners; oak box with two brass hinges and silver plate.

Oars with band round blade; maker's mark for Charles Edwards. Maker's mark GR . . (fragmentary).

List of winners for 1859–98; supplementary list 1899–1906.

Box lined with blue velvet; shield inscribed THE Wilkinson Sculls *Presented* 1859.

Donor: probably Thomas Boston Wilkinson (?–1872); of Norfolk; admitted 1849; Scholar; Fellow 1854–72; Dean 1865–71; musical.

In the 19th century serious rowing was not limited to eight-oared boats. A scull was a boat made for one rower pulling two oars. The winner in 1906 was Thomas Batterby; his portrait, rowing a scull, appears on his Wooden Spoon for 1907 (Appendix 4).

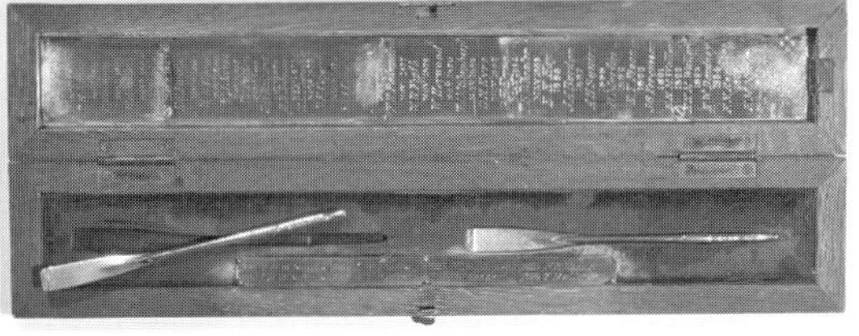

20.2 Corpus Christi College Billiard-Cue

1876 (London A). Silver billiard-cue 12.0 in. long; wooden box with silver mounts; silver plates with lists of winners.

The cue is a tapering cylinder, one flat side at big end. Big end is matt with spiral band bearing inscription.

Box of oak, veneered with tropical hardwood, silver plate on lid, silver hinges. List of winners 1867–93; supplementary list 1898–1905.

Inscription on cue: CORP: CHR: COLL: CHALLENGE BILLIARD CUE. On lid-plate: Corpus Christi College CHALLENGE BILLIARD CUE [College arms] Presented by SUBSCRIPTION 1866.

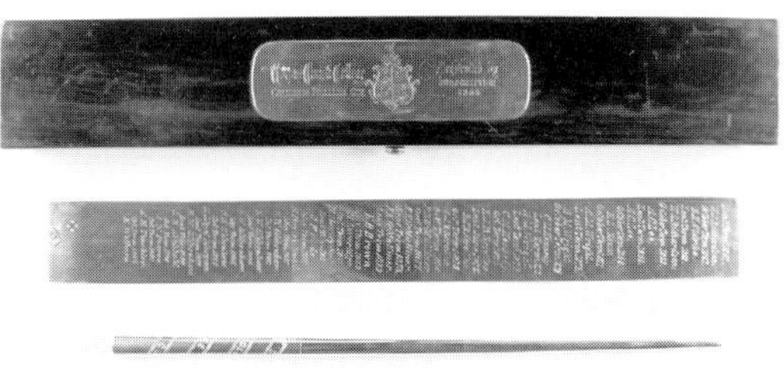

Marks on cue, box, lid-plate: JNM GW in cottage loaf shape, for John Newton Mappin & George Webb, partners 1863–.

Something must have happened to the original cue, this being a replacement: no assay office has A for 1866.

20.3 Rowlandson Bow and Stroke Oars

1873 (London s). Each silver oar is 12 in. long. Two separate oak boxes, each with brass hinges and silver plate, and two silver lists of winners.

The two oars have representations of leather rubbers and band round blade. Inscribed BOW and STROKE.

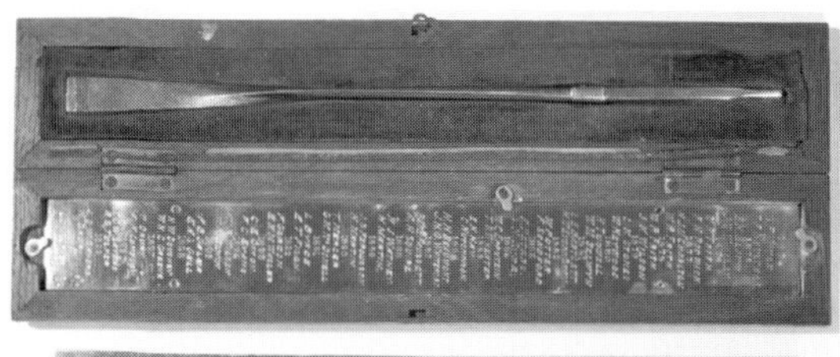

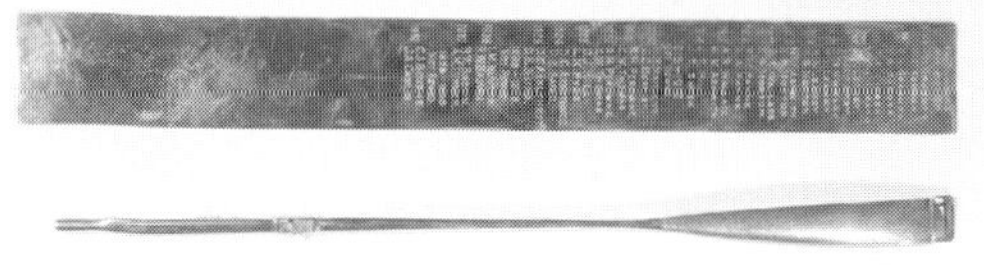

Lists of winners, for 1874–1900, are fully hallmarked. Supplementary lists for 1904–14, 1920–5, 1936–7, and 1957.

Boxes are lined with blue velvet (bow) and green velvet (stroke); plates inscribed C·C·B·C The Rowlandson Pairs 1874.

Tiny hallmarks. Bow oar made by GR . . , stroke oar and other silver parts by ECB (for E.C. Brown).

Donor: presumably William Henry Rowlandson (?–1907); admitted 1861; Scholar, winner of many prizes for Hebrew and Greek; opposed admission of non-Christians to the University; Fellow 1874–5; parson of College living of Great Braxted (Essex) 1875–1907.

A pair is a boat made for two rowers each pulling one oar. The winner in 1907 was Thomas Batterby of the Wooden Spoon (above).

20.4 Heywood Sculls

1879 ([London] D + Victoria)
Two silver oars, 5.7 in. long; oak box with silver shield, two silver plates with lists of winners.

Oars with band round blade. Marked with CE in oval cartouche with point, for the maker Charles Edwards, active 1868–.

List of winners for 1879–1924; supplementary list 1925–60.

Box lined with blue velvet; shield inscribed CCCBC The Heywood Freshmans Sculls PRESENTED May 1879, no marks.

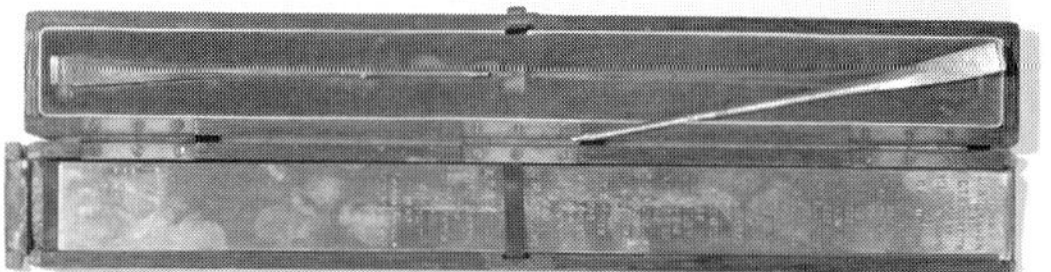

Donor uncertain. A William Heywood was admitted 1875, and a James Brettell Heywood in 1876.

Another of the trophies which adorned Thomas Batterby's brow.

20.5 Dalby Cup

1873 (inscription). Base metal, silver-plated, thinly gilt inside. 4.9 by 3.35 by 7.35 in. high. 8.04 oz = 250 g.

Egg-shaped. Beading on foot & knops; engraved strapwork and bands. Two oval cartouches chased with elaborate foliage etc. Cast griffin-head handles.

College arms. Inscribed: *CORPUS CHRISTI COLLEGE \ 1 MILE RACE WON BY W.B.S.* Dalby *TIME 5 MN: MARCH 1873*

Medal: base metal, in shape of University shield-of-arms, inscribed: *C.U.A.C. 1 MILE HANDICAP WON BY WBS Dalby (70 YDS) 4 MIN* $32\frac{4}{5}$ *SEC: LENT TERM 1874*

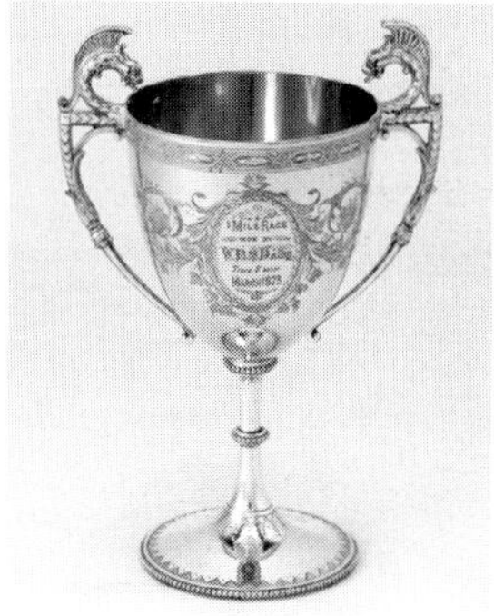

William Bramley Sayle Dalby (1853–1920), of Sharrington (Norfolk), went to Norwich Grammar School, like Archbishop Parker and the writer. Scholar 1872; M.A. 1884; Athletics Blue. He was Rector of Kelling with Salthouse (Norfolk) 1896–1915, and of Goadby Marwood (Leics.) 1915–20.

Men now run the mile in a little under 4 minutes; the first known to have done so was Sir Roger Bannister in 1954.

20.6 Chess Club Cup

1924 (London i). 6.2 in. greatest diameter, 3.9 diameter at mouth, 7.2 in. high.

Globular bowl on a rounded torus above a trumpet-shaped base. Three curved handles, each of which splits at both ends into two foliated finials. Hammer finish.

Arms: College, overlain by shield with a cruciferous flower and three 'red' and 'white' angular Cs.

Inscription: *On the hundredth anniversary of the Corpus Christi College Chess Club 19 June 1971 / President J.S. Edwards / Secretary P.S. Millard*

Marks: C . . . C^{O}. L^{D}. | REGD 37340 GOLDSMITHS & SILVERSMITHS COMPANY $L^{\underline{TD}}$ 112 REGENT. ST.

The Corpus Christi 'Cheeser' Chess Club was founded in 1871 as a specialist society, whose rules forbade eating or smoking over the chessboard. In the 1880s it played more cards than chess; by the 1900s had given up sport altogether in favour of smoking, feasting, and May Balls (Bury 1952); liquidated for rioting and drunkenness *c*.1993; should be revived with a modest entry qualification in chess.

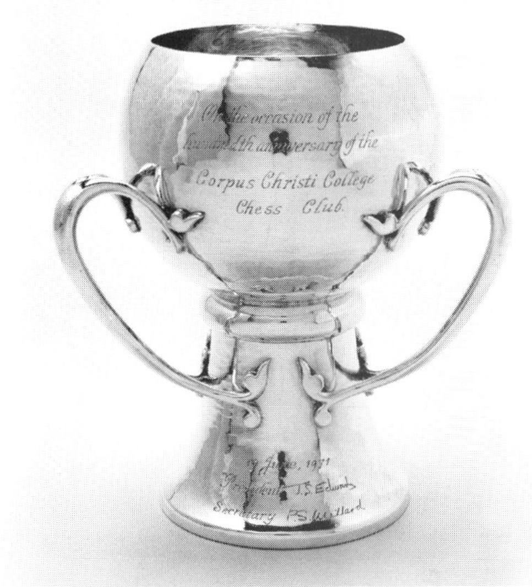

20.7 McCrum Two-Handled Bowl

1929 (London o). 7.0 by 4.7 by 3.5 in. high. Britannia silver.

Half-barrel-shaped, integral foot. Cast double-C handles. Chased with likenesses of fantastic birds and flowers in *chinoiserie* or *art-nouveau*-ish style. Blank cartouche-like space. Knobs on handles in likeness of exhibited heads.

Inscription: SODALITATE ATHLETARUM C.C.C.C. ET B.M.V. MICHAEL M^{C}CRUM TUTOR MCMLXII ⋆ BIBITE [To the Sports Syndicate of the College of Corpus Christi and the Blessed Virgin Mary, Cambridge. Michael McCrum, Tutor, 1962. Drink!]

Made by J.H. Stockwell.

Given by Michael McCrum, later Master, giver of several other items (p. 118).

Although this vessel was evidently intended as a loving-cup (p. 44), the shape is known as a *porringer*, pot versions being used for eating porridge.

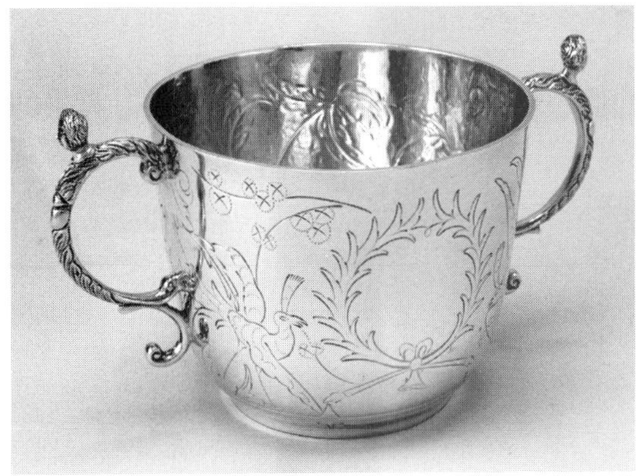

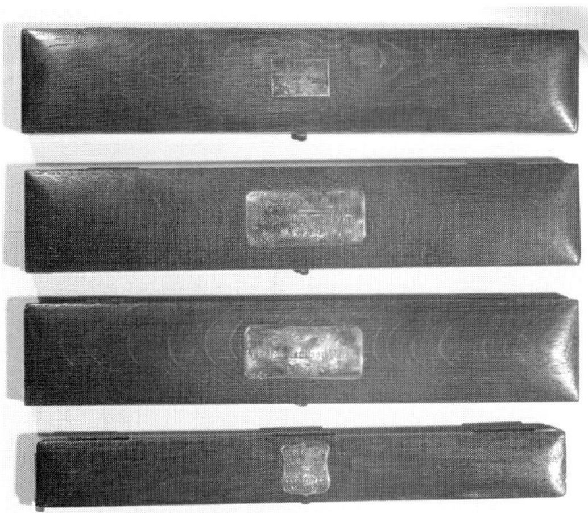

Boxes for Oars: *Wilkinson*
Rowlandson
Rowlandson
Heywood

21

Things Useful and Extravagant

21.1 Baskets

And out of the basket of unleavened bread, that *was* before the LORD, [Moses] took one unleavened cake, and a cake of oiled bread, and one wafer . . .

Leviticus **8** 26

[*rite of consecrating the high priest*]

CAKE-BASKETS AND EPERGNES . . . are objects of considerable importance in the plate-collections of the [eighteenth] century, and great taste and skill were expended upon their production. Most of them were made between 1730 and 1780.

Cripps (1891) p. 328

Silver baskets go back to Elizabethan times (the British Museum has a French one of 1629–30), but probably not in Cambridge before the rococo period. Either they were not needed – real baskets being good enough for the table – or such delicate objects disintegrated under rough usage (as ours demonstrate). Our baskets, though fine, are not overdone: the extreme of the fashion is the Clare College *Épergne*, a kind of Adamesque tree whose boughs bear nine baskets, dated 1777.

Most baskets are really silver bowls with the sides pierced to give the illusion of a basket. This was often done after the hallmarks were struck, so that the marks were partly cut away in the piercing. This technique, a revival of a favourite Anglo-Saxon craft, was also used on coasters and some mustard-pots.

21.1.1 Bateman (Blank Shield) Basket of 1769

1769 (London O). 13.3 in. × 11.7 × 3.6 high excluding handle.

Rococo. Elliptical plan, hinged handle. Central plate with blank shield surrounded by chased flowers. Sides pierced in 20 panels, alternately squares-&-quatrefoils and almond-shapes. Beaded, shallowly indented rim.

Altered to efface previous ownership. A blank shield has been added to cover an earlier coat-of-arms. Underside has been deeply scraped, as if to deface an inscription. Central plate much scratched; handle mended.

Date-letter partly cut away by piercing. Maker's mark, *TJ* in oval, unidentified, but known on other baskets of the period (Grimwade 1990).

Bequeathed by Aubrey Bateman.

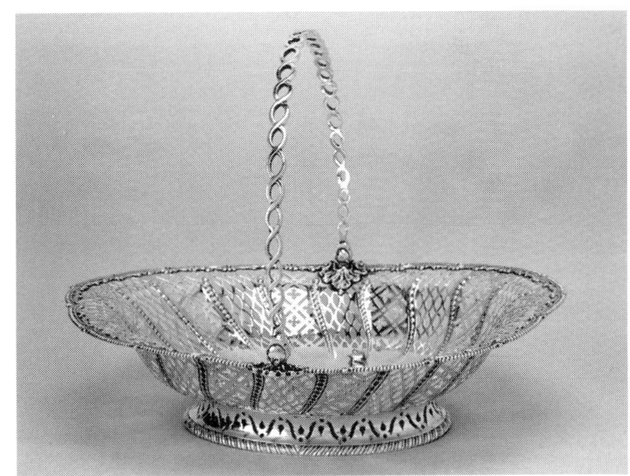

21.1.2 John Page Basket

1778 (London C – could be 1818). 13.4 in. × 11.0 × 4.1 high excluding handle.

Adamesque. Elliptical plan, hinged handle. Pierced interlacing Gothic ogees and circles; narrow band of stylized foliage engraved next to beaded rim. Central plate plain; three punch-marks for setting-out on underside. Foot engraved in abstract patterns.

Inscription (underneath): *Joannes Page Socio Commensalis D.D. C.C.C.C.*

Maker's mark: W·P in rectangle, probably for William Potter, known 1777–8. (William Plummer, prolific London basketmaker, used a punch with a curved outline.)

John Page of Middlesex was admitted FC 1769.

Several mends, including five in handle.

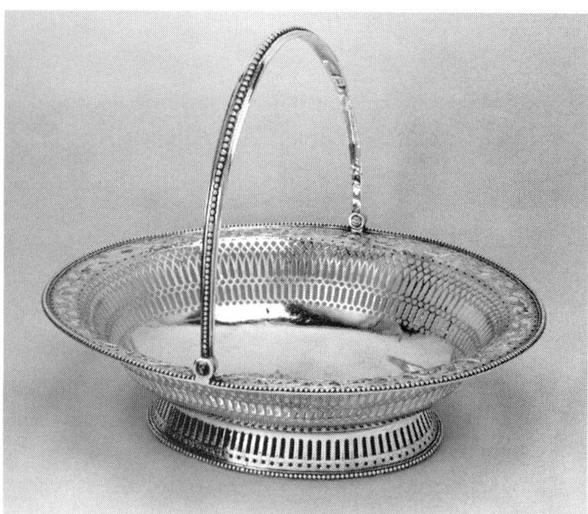

21.1.3 Woodhead Basket

*c.*1780. Silver with (broken) blue glass liner. 3.4 in × 3.55 high.

Adamesque. Mainly cast work, no piercing. Half-ovoid body is a cage of 16 vertical wires with attached swags and six medallions, one having a *repoussé* relief of a draped arm and another of a vase. Hinged, twisted handle.

Inscription: COLL: CORP: CHR: ET BMV DD GALFRIDUS WOODHEAD SOC: AD . MCMXLIX .:. (Geoffrey Woodhead, Fellow, gave [me] to the College . . . AD 1949.) Graffiti: 7/81 6/191 6/191.

Arthur Geoffrey Woodhead (1922–), of Nottinghamshire, is a Classical scholar. He was Scholar 1940; BA 1946; Fellow 1948–; FSA 1958–; President and historian

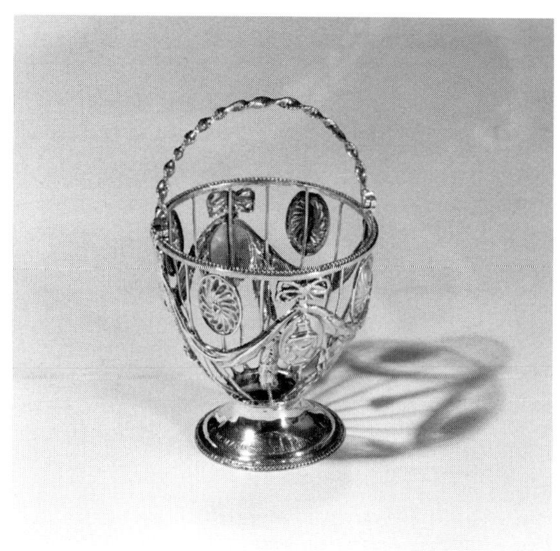

of the College; and giver of much help to the author of this book. This piece is his wedding fine.

21.1.4 Two Cheney Baskets

1912 (London r). 6.8 in. × 2.8 high.

Circular, slightly convex bottom. Sides pierced in lozenges, foot pierced in triangles. Three rows of cast beading.

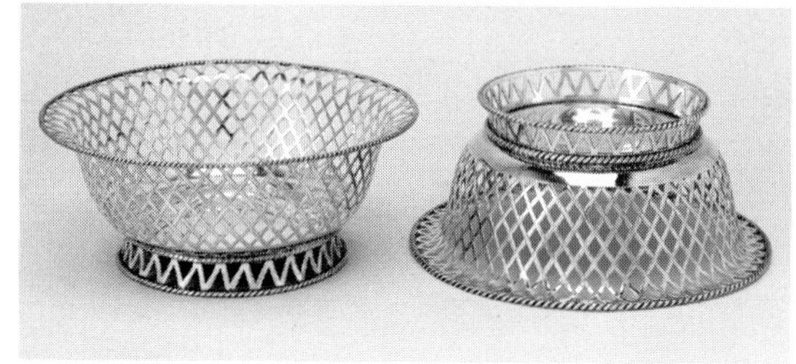

Inscription: *d.d. C.R. Cheney Socius MCMLXXII* (C.R. Cheney, Fellow, gave [me] 1972). Graffiti (on one only): 7 + 10 N 4217 PP/3/d CC/3 Each

Mark: C.S & H[S] in skull-shaped cartouche, for Charles Stuart Harris & Sons.

Christopher Robert Cheney (1906–87), medieval historian, from Banbury, after a distinguished career at Oxford, London, and Manchester was a Fellow of Corpus from 1955 to 1987, and Cambridge Professor of Medieval History. *Cheney's Handbook of Dates* lies at the author's elbow.

21.1.5 Two Large and Three Small Bateman Baskets of 1927

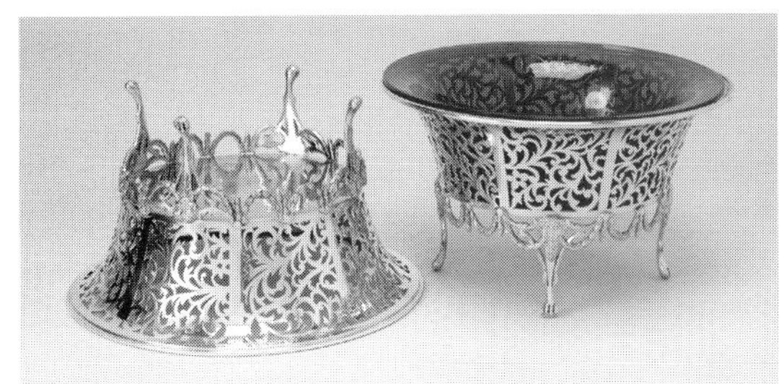

1927 (London m). Large: 10.9 in. × 5.5 high. Small: 8.3 × 4.6 in. high. Identical except in size.

Circular; animal-claw feet; animal masks at top of legs; cast swags hang underneath. Blue glass liners (one of which is pale blue and a poor fit).

Graffito (on one large basket): 9/244.

Made by Harris & Sons, as above. Large baskets marked also by LAKE, SILVERSMITH, EXETER.

Bequeathed by Aubrey Bateman. A fourth small basket was given to St Catharine's College in recognition of their hospitality during rebuilding of Corpus's kitchen, 1980.

21.2 Bowls

Or ever the silver cord be loosed, or the golden bowl be broken . . .

Ecclesiastes **12** 6

Bowls – open vessels, hemispherical or shallower, usually without lids – cover many shapes and functions: basins, punchbowls, porringers, quaichs, cuspidors (p. 231), monteiths, etc. etc. There were several silver bowls in the Roman hoard of Mildenhall, and ten among the East Anglian royal plate of Sutton Hoo.

Bowls other than rosewater basins appear slowly in post-medieval Cambridge. The 'bowles' in early inventories would now be called cups (p. 99). The earliest survivor is probably the 'Toy Basin', 1645, in Sidney Sussex College. Another is Magdalene's magnificent Norris Bowl of 1669. Corpus has none until well into the 18th century.

Sugar-bowls belong to the phase of sugar as a drug (pp. 187f.) and thus come rather late.

Some bowls form sets with *Coffee-Pots and Teapots* and are considered under them. For bowls with two handles and lid, see *Tureens*.

21.2.1 Bushnell Ecuadorian Bowl

18th century? 15.5 in. × 13.8 × 2.1–2.4 high.

Nearly flat-bottomed, everted concave rim; roughly shaped, with hammer-marked texture. Two loop-handles with gadrooned middle sections. No marks.

Inscribed: *Lancem hanc apud Ecuadorianos conquisitam in memoriam Galfridi coniugis sui quondam Coll. Corp. Chr. et B.M.V. socii d.d. Patricia Bushnell A.S. mcmlxxxiv* [Patricia Bushnell gave this bowl, acquired among the Ecuadorians, in memory of her husband, sometime Fellow of the College of Corpus Christi and the Blessed Virgin Mary, A.D. 1984].

Earlier inscriptions: **Luiza Silva** VAR [monogram]. Graffito: Pepa A m°.

Patricia Louise Egerton Bushnell is the widow of Geoffrey Hext Sutherland Bushnell (1903–78), of Hayling Island. He was an oil geologist, South American

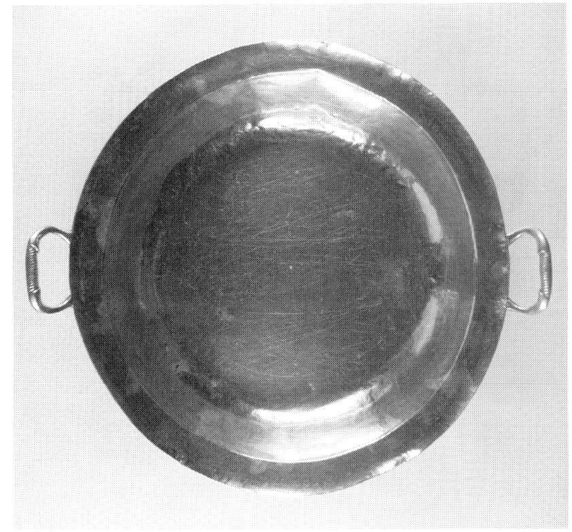

archaeologist, ecclesiologist; undergraduate of Downing College; Curator of the Museum of Archaeology and Ethnology 1948–70; Vice-President of Society of Antiquaries 1961–5; F.B.A. 1970–. He came to Corpus as Fellow in 1963; was Prælector 1969–73; the writer's predecessor as Keeper of Plate (p. xii).

This piece has seen hard service, with many dents and scratches, supposedly from uses such as baptizing infants. It is now intended as a rosewater basin.

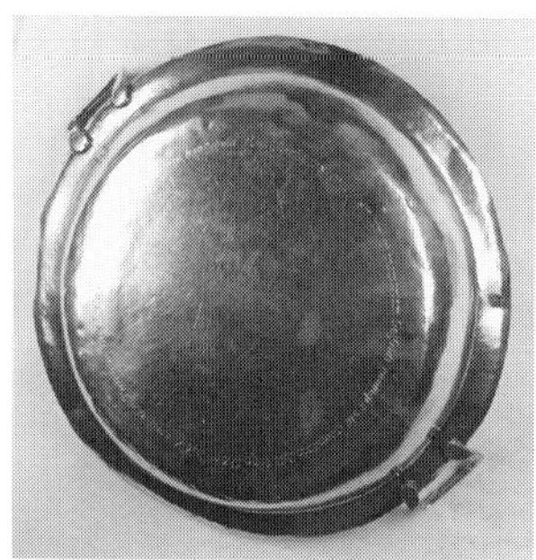

21.2.2 Two Dickens 2-Handled [Sugar-] Bowls

1780 (London e). 7.9 in. × 4.2 × 4.5 high.

Elliptical body and foot; saddle-shaped top. Gadrooned ornament. Foliated handle-attachments. Engraved College arms, hanging from ribbon, with COLL · CORP · CHRISTI on another ribbon.

Inscribed underneath one: *Dono dedit Joannes Dickens C.C.C. Socio-Commensalis 1781.*

Maker: WB in rectangle, for William Bennet, Walter Brind, or William Bromage.

John Dickens of Cambridgeshire was admitted Fellow-Commoner in 1779 or 1780. He gave also the Dickens Tureens, made also by WB.

The shape is rococo and old-fashioned by 1780; the engraving is Adamesque. Badly biffed.

21.2.2a Two Anonymous 2-Handled [Sugar-] Bowls

1779 (London d).

Identical (apart from damage) to above; same engraving.

Weight inscription: p^{r} 30‴0 [present weight 28: 22 ounces].

Maker: CW in rectangle, ? for Charles Wright, active 1754–90. The four evidently formed a set.

21.2.3 [Bateman] 2-Handled [Sugar-] Bowl

1804 (London I). 6.0 in. × 3.2 × 3.5 high. Gilded inside.

Elliptical shape, waisted, with foot, rising to 7-shaped handles. Pricked decoration: band of spirals and stylized flowers round top; band of rosettes in interlace round middle; mæanders round base; goes round hallmarks.

Maker's mark S·C, probably for Sebastian Crespel I (London, active 1760–1806). Graffiti: 7980 C8.12.

Bequeathed by Aubrey Bateman.

The shape of this piece is Adamesque. The decoration is incongruous and may be later (see Moule Cream-Jug).

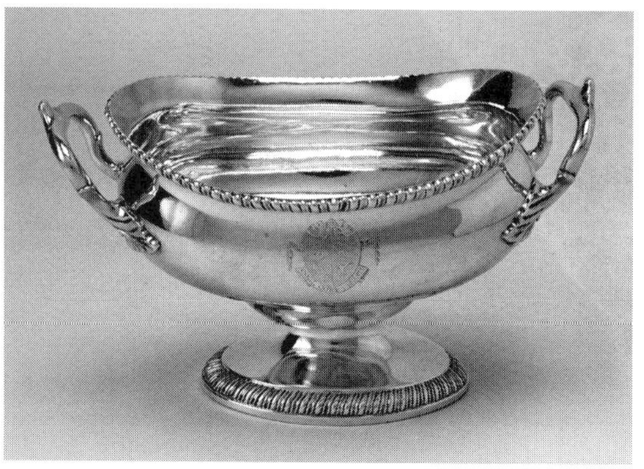

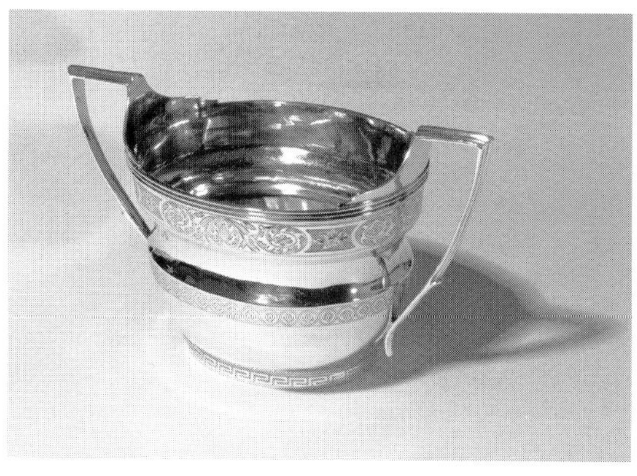

21.2.4 Perowne Bowl

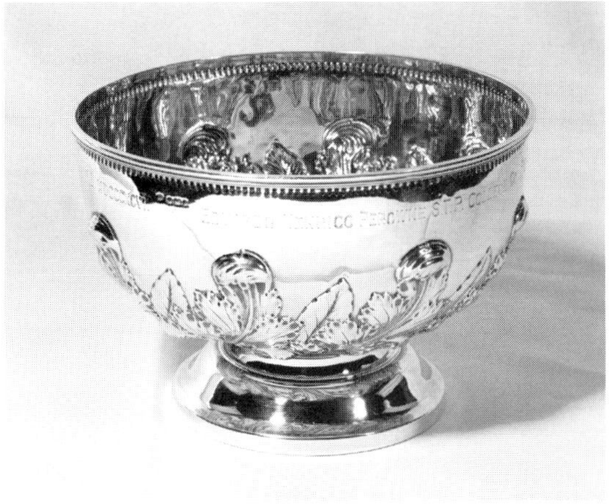

1895 (Sheffield date-letter 𝔠). 8.2 in. × 5.3 high. Rather light and thin.

Near-hemispherical. Reeding and tiny impressed leaves round rim. Lower part *repoussé* with spiral, vaguely marine-style leafage.

Inscribed: EDVARDO HENRICO PEROWNE S.T.P. COLLEGII CORP. CHR. ET B.V.M. MAGISTRO FRATRI DILECTO, FRATER NATU MAXIMUS EP'US VIGORNENSIS D.D. a.d. VII KAL: MAI. A.S. MDCCCXCVI. (The Bishop of Worcester, his eldest brother, gave this to his dear brother, Edward Henry Perowne, D.D., Master of the College of Corpus Christi and the Blessed Virgin Mary, on the day of 24 April in the year of grace 1896.)

Maker: JR in oval, for John Round & Son Ltd, 1874–, of Sheffield, 'The Largest Spoon and Fork Makers in the World'.

For the careers of J.J.S. and E.H. Perowne see their Bishop Green Cups (§10.4.3, 10.4.4).

21.2.5 Grammaticus Bowl

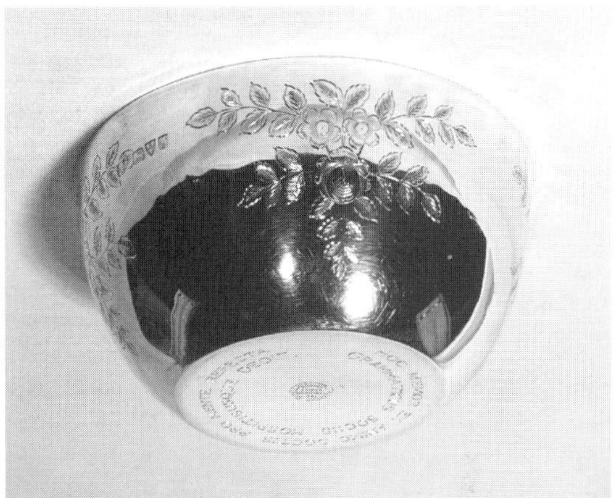

1907 (Chester *G*). 4.3 in. × 2.1 high.

Hemispheric, flat base, inverted rim. Chased with 4 panels of flowers and foliage.

Inscribed underneath: HOC MEMOR EX ANIMO DOCTIS PRO MENTE REFECTA GRAMMATICUS SOCIIS HOSPITIBUSQUE DEDIT. (A Grammarian, mindful from his heart, gave this to the Fellows and his hosts for a mind re-made.)

Maker: ALEXANDER CLARK · MANUFG. C°· 125 FENCHURCH STREET LONDON.

The Grammarian who gave this was presumably an early Schoolmaster Fellow-Commoner, spending a sabbatical term in the College, a category of Fellow-Commoner who happily still flourishes. (The list of regular Schoolmaster Fellow-Commoners goes back only to 1960 (Woodhead p. 286).)

21.2.6 'Leckhampton' Punch-Bowl

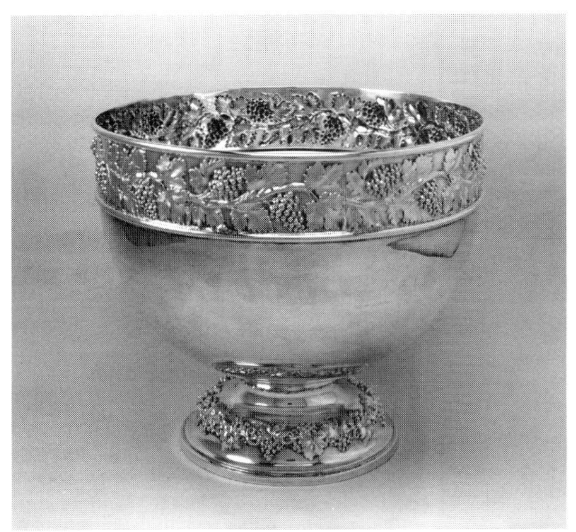

1911 (Sheffield t). 11.85 in. × 10.15 high.

Rim ornamented with *repoussé* vine-trail (leaves, tendrils, grapes), meant – very unusually – to be seen on both sides. Foot has similar but coarser, smaller-scale vine-trail cast into it.

Mark: JD & S, for James Dixon & Sons of Sheffield, active *c.*1823–, pioneers of the spin process (p. 9).

A massive object. For what a punch-bowl is see p. 222.

21.2.7 Great Bowl with Rings

Undated; silvered copper; 13.8 in. × 13.0 × 7.7 high.

Rim of bowl everted, undulated, with gadrooned margin. Flat plate on underside of foot. Two cast lions' masks with rings in mouths. Inscribed *Corpus Christi College Cambridge*.

Marks: SWS + coronet; SILVER PLATED ON COPPER MADE IN ENGLAND

Unknown origin; probably meant as a punch-bowl.

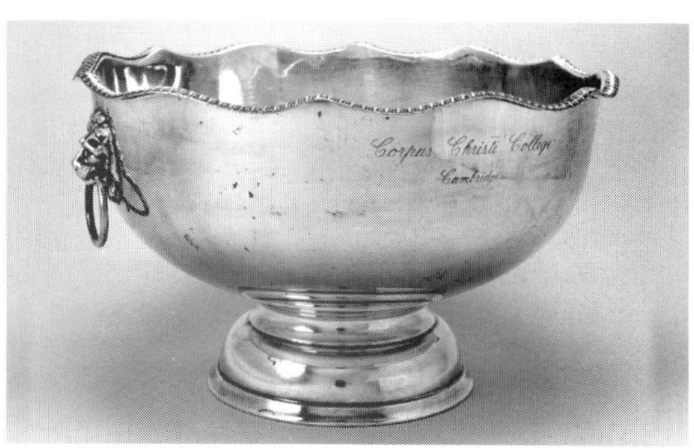

21.2.8 Lewis Quaich

1933 (Edinburgh *C*). 12.7 in. × 9.1 × 3.7 high.

Flat-bottomed bowl with two horizontal flat handles.

Inscription: PRESENTED BY DR AND MRS PETER LEWIS IN CELEBRATION OF THEIR GOLDEN WEDDING 12TH APRIL 1997. College arms on both handles.

Makers' mark and inscription: B&S in engrailed rectangle; BROOK & SON ST GEORGE ST EDINBURGH. Graffito: HA 6153 F/AB/.Y.

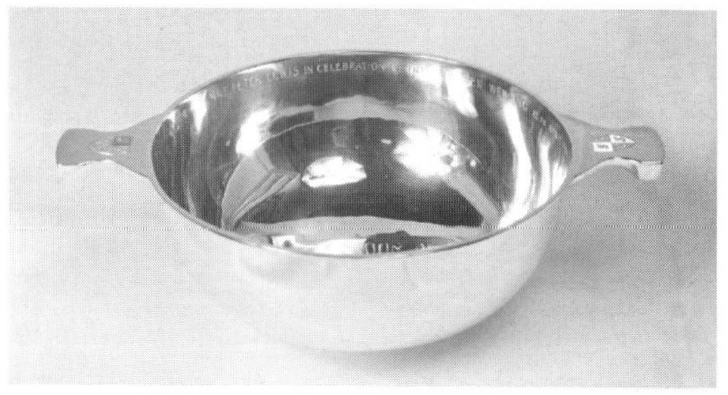

Peter Raymond Lewis (1924–), physiologist and famous teacher, of Leckhampton (Glos.), came from Oxford; he became a Fellow in 1960, Sc.D. in 1980; Bursar and Steward of Estates; founder-member of Leckhampton (Cambridge), preserver of the name Leckhampton; untiringly hospitable to Old Members, especially former medical students.

A *quaich* is a vessel, originally built of wooden staves, for the quaffing of whisky. The term implies a flat handle in the plane of the rim (a common Roman form). This exceptionally large one is used as a rosewater basin.

21.2.9 Braden Bowl

1945 (Sheffield C) 5.8 in. × 4.0 × 2.5 high.

Plain but for moulded handles and 3 reeds round foot.

Inscription: d.d. H.W.B. MCMLXXXIII. Graffiti: W T993 6.85

Maker: James Dixon & Sons.

Given by Harry William Braden of Edinburgh and Sydney: mathematician; Plumian Scholar of Corpus 1979; Research Fellow 1982–5; later at North Carolina, Durham, and Edinburgh Universities. This is his wedding fine.

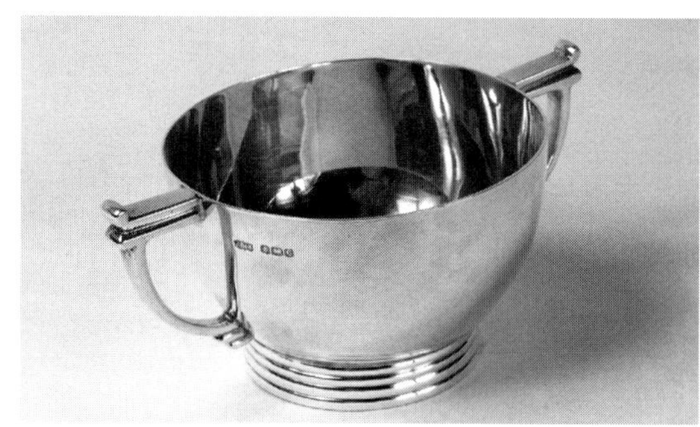

21.2.10 Kearton Son-of-a-Quaich

1973 (Sheffield 𝕰). 3.2 × 4.1 × 1.0 in. high.

Hemispherical bowl with flat bottom. One horizontal looped viperine handle:

> Look not thou upon the wine when it is red,
> when it giveth his colour in the cup...
> At the last it biteth like a serpent, and stingeth like
> an adder.
>
> *Proverbs* **23** 31f

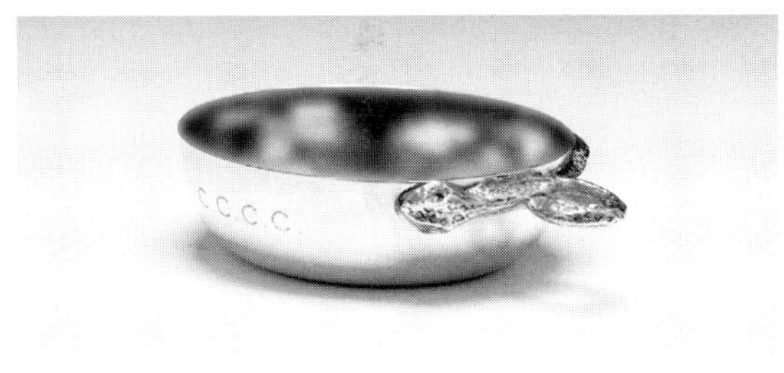

Inscription: C.C.C.C. | discessurus dd. CHERRY KEARTON SOC MCMLXXII MCMLXXVI [Cherry Kearton, Fellow 1972–6, gave this when about to leave].

Maker: CB & S in baroque shield, for Charles Boyton & Son Ltd, firm 1933–77.

Cherry Kearton (1945–); of Surrey, descendant of Cherry Kearton the naturalist, was Scholar of Corpus 1965, Foundation Scholar 1968; Caldwell Student; moved to Durham and became Reader in Mathematics 1991.

A small quaich-shaped vessel like this is also called a *wine-taster*, hanging round the neck of someone who haunts cellars and evaluates wines.

McCrum Bowl: see Sporting Plate
Haslam, Goodhart, Thomson, Small Thomson, Wilson Bowls: see Modernistic Plate

21.3 Boxes, Round, for Biscuits

These are for the biscuit called a Bath Oliver, which is $3\frac{1}{4}$ in. in diameter, hard and rather like a ship's biscuit. It was given to the world by Dr William Oliver (1695–1764), of Pembroke College, specialist in gout, founder of the Water or General Hospital, Bath. He bequeathed the recipe and ten sacks of flour to his coachman, who made a fortune.

21.3.1 Walker Biscuit-Box

?1871 (?Birmingham W: no assay office is given, but Sheffield has a different-shaped punch, London does not use W). 5.6 in. × 7.3 high.

Three-footed cylinder. Lid of smaller diameter than box, attached by small weak hinge; knob bolted to middle of lid. Body engraved with two cartouches for arms, with foliage, sprays of wheat and of short-awned two-rowed barley. Lid engraved with abstract swags. Two rings attached by fixtures resembling pelicans hanged by the neck.

Arms: College (with pelican pseudo-crest) and donor's: *A chevron sable between three rooks* [or similar birds]. Pseudo-crest: *a demi-horse carnivorous* [or similar beast] *facing dexter, per pale indented argent and vert.*

Inscription: *E dono Biyani* [*sic*] *Walker Nuper Socii* [Of the gift of Bryan Walker lately a Fellow].

Maker: HP & Co. below a crown, unidentified (many had these initials).

Parting gift of Bryan Walker (1840–87); son of a Yorkshire miller; Scholar and Fellow of Trinity Hall; distinguished mathematician, classicist, divine; Fellow of Corpus 1866–71; Rector of Landbeach 1871–87; historian of Landbeach and restorer of the church.

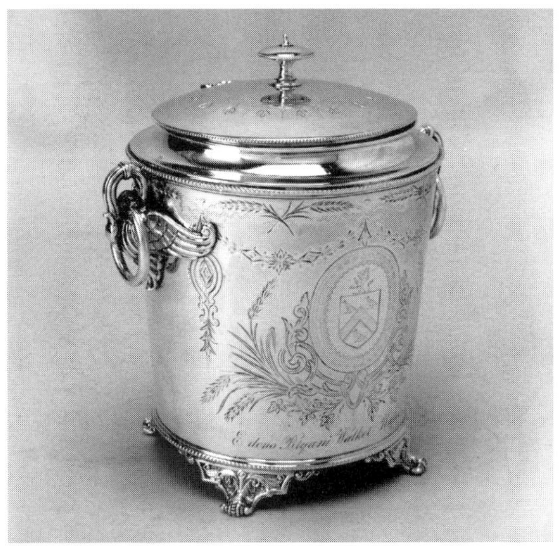

Couve de Murville Biscuit-Box *see* Modernistic Plate

21.4 Coasters

Dirty British coaster with a salt-caked smoke stack,
Battling through the Channel in the mad March days
John Masefield 1903

The term *coaster* is a nickname for a bottle-slider: a gadget for sliding wine decanters about the Combination Room table after dinner without scratching the table. It is presumably a successor to the salver; it is said to be named because it battles round and round the table like Masefield's coaster. Usually it has a round wooden hull padded with cloth underneath, with silver sides.

These objects are often too delicate for the rough-and-tumble of Combination Room use. Like baskets, they are often difficult to date or identify because the sides were marked first and then pierced into tracery, cutting away part of the hallmarks.

Gorged Heron *Ungorged Heron*

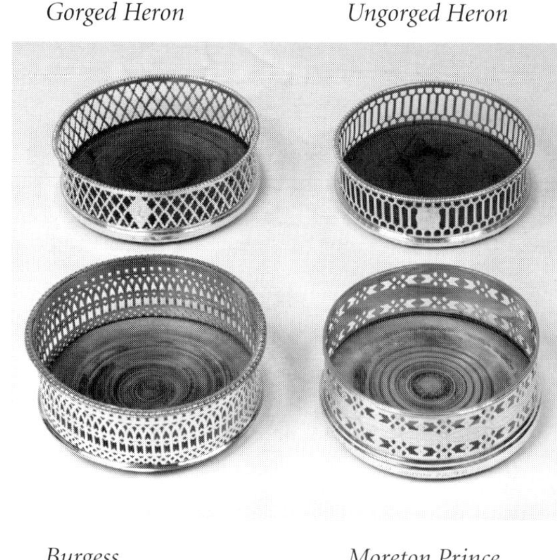

Burgess *Moreton Prince*

21.4.1 Four ?Storer 'Ungorged Heron' Coasters

1770 (London 𝔓). 5.0 in. × 1.45 high.

Plain hardwood base. Sides pierced to form upright straps, leaving small area for crest; plain moulded lower rim, cast gadrooned upper rim. Crest of *a heron.*

Remains of mark HCAG in quatrefoil, which would be for Charles Aldridge & Henry Green, supposedly entered 1775.

These may be the College's earliest coasters, 'Mr Storer's Bottlesliders', put into use in 1771. Anthony Morris Storer, a Jamaican, was admitted, probably as Fellow-Commoner, in 1764. (CC(A): Plate and Library log-book, 25 June 1771.)

21.4.2 Two Mosse 'Gorged Heron' Coasters

1783 (Sheffield 𝔅). 5.1 in. × 1.55 high.

Base of hard wood having large vessels, turned on topside with elaborate circles; underside grooved to receive edge of baize underlay. Sides delicately pierced in a diamond pattern of cusped lozenges; beaded upper, moulded lower rim.

One bears crest of *a heron's head and neck emerging from a coronet* [not of a recognized form], *gorged with a like coronet.* The other inscribed: ***C.C.C. – B.M.V. D.D., W.E. Mosse, Nuper Socius*** [lately Fellow].

Maker's mark: incuse DH, for Daniel Holy of Sheffield.

Werner Eugen Emil Mosse (1918–), of Berlin, fled the wrath of Hitler in 1933; admitted to Corpus as Scholar 1936; BA 1939; Research Fellow 1945–8; gave these on leaving; later Professor of European History, University of East Anglia.

21.4.3 Four Douglas Coasters

1789 (London o). 4.8 in. × 1.4 high.

Hardwood base, turned with concentric circles on top, grooved underneath for edge of baize covering. Solid sides look like plated brass, but hallmarked as silver; plain moulded rim and bottom edge.

Pseudo-crests of a *pelican* and of a *winged human heart royally crowned gules.* Inscribed: *R Douglas Socio Commensalis Dono dedit. C.C.C.C.*

Maker's mark, W.P, could be William Pitts, silver basketmaker, active 1781–*c*.1810. William Pinder, entered 1770, or William Peavey, entered 1773, are less likely.

Given by Robert Douglas of Essex, Fellow Commoner 1787 (see his Argyle, §11.8). The heart is that of Robert the Bruce, king of Scotland, which Sir James Douglas in 1327 was commissioned to extract and bury in Jerusalem.

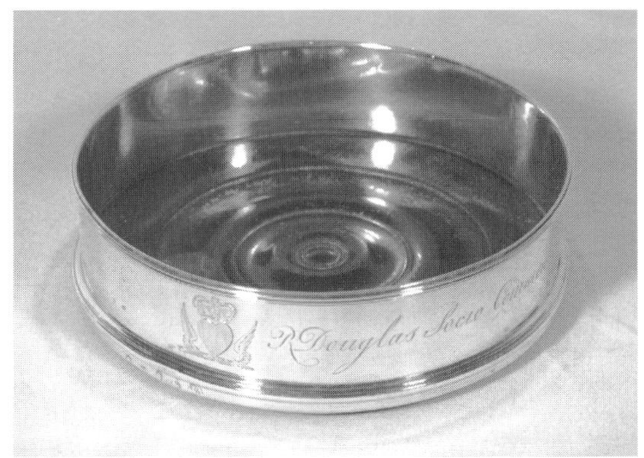

21.4.4 Four Bateman Coasters

Date-letter fragmentary, could be London 𝕯 for 1839. 8.2 in. × 2.6 high.

Silver floor and sides, low foot, base of tropical hardwood. Sides of interwoven reeded straps. Rim with vine-leaves and bunches of grapes. Floor with eight radial ribs. Reeded decoration on rim, floor, and foot. On central plate is the crest of *a pheasant* and the motto NEC PRECE NEC PRETIO.

Maker's mark: . . . M & ISH, for ?John Mortimer (successor to Paul Storr) and John Samuel Hunt, active 1839–*c*.1860, of Hunt & Roskell firm 1843–.

Bequeathed by Aubrey Bateman.

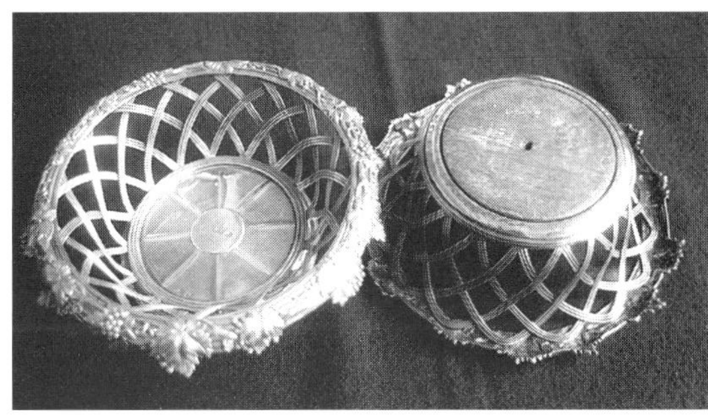

21.4.5 Two Morton Prince Coasters (*illustrated on facing page*)

1919 (Sheffield b). 5.0 in. × 1.9 high.

Beechwood base, turned with circles in middle. Silver sides pierced with two bands of strapwork, chased with interlacing curves.

Inscription (on both): *SOCIIS COMMENSALIBUS COLLEGII CORPORIS CHRISTI ET B.M.V. D.D. MORTON PRINCE* (Morton Prince gave [me] to the Fellow Commoners of the College . . .).

Maker's mark TB &S in shield, for Thomas Bradbury & Sons, active 1831–1943.

I am unable to trace the donor, presumably a Fellow-Commoner.

21.4.6 Two Medical Coasters

1814 if London, 1816 if Sheffield (no assay office shown). 5.0 in. × 1.6 high. Maker unknown.

Made of oak (both from the same tree), of dugout construction, turned on a lathe, with narrow gadrooned silver rim. A boss like a print (p. 56) in the middle bears a pelican pseudo-crest.

Inscription: *DONO DEDERVNT E SOCIETA-TE BRITANNICA MEDICINA PLERIQVE DOCTISSIMI MENS: IVN: A.D. MCMXLVIII* Χαῖρε καὶ πῖνε [Given by several very learned members of the British Medical Association in the month of June, A.D. 1948. Réjouissez et buvez.]

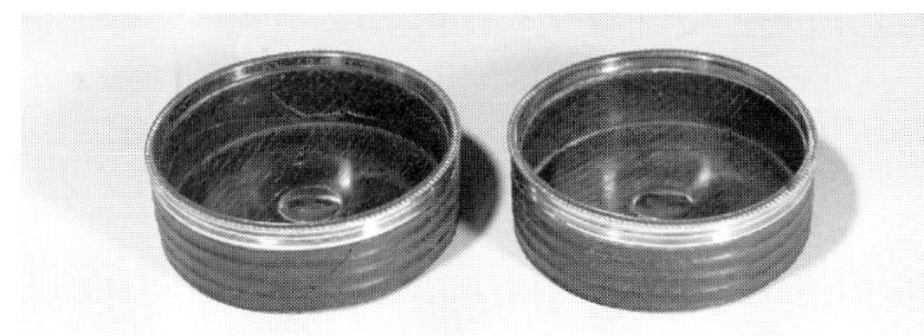

'In 1948 the college housed a number of doctors who were in Cambridge for a meeting of the British Medical Association . . . The doctors . . . generously subscribed to enable the College to purchase one or more pieces of plate in memory of their visit.' (Bury p. 170.)

21.4.7 Four Malcolm Burgess Coasters (*illustrated on facing page*)

Sheffield plate, undated. 5.2 in. × 2.2 high.

Hardwood base, turned with concentric circles on top, grooved underneath for edge of baize covering. Sides pierced with interlaced Gothick arches etc.

Given by Malcolm Archer Sheridan Burgess (1926–78) of King's School, Canterbury; Parker Exhibitioner 1945; Foundation Scholar; linguist; Lecturer in Slavonic Studies 1962–; Fellow of Corpus 1974–8; authority on Ali Pasha, tyrant of Ioánnina, NW Greece. A splendid theatrical designer, he was responsible for the decorations in the Hall, New Combination Room, and Chapel. He gave also a cup (pp. 135f.).

21.5 Dishes, Dishlets, and Shells

I was begot
After some gluttonous dinner: some stirring dish
Was my first father...

Middleton, *The Revenger's Tragedy*, 1607

I include all manner of shallow receptacles, except the big flat ones which are *Salvers* and those with three lips on the rim which are *Ashtrays*. The many types have more or less whimsical names related to their supposed functions.

Shells were fashionable shapes in the rococo period. Among the College's sad, self-inflicted losses were the 'Hon[l] Fred & Wm Herveys 12 Shells', as described when we melted them down in 1817 (CC(A): Inventory, 1817). These young aristocrats were the third and fourth sons of the Earl of Bristol, undergraduates in 1747 and 1751. Unusually for their rank, they both took degrees, William achieving his M.A. in the suspiciously short time of two years. Frederick became Bishop of Londonderry and then succeeded to the earldom, being celebrated as traveller and *bon viveur;* the various Bristol Hotels are named after him. Their noble pseudo-medieval park still survives at Ickworth, Suffolk.

21.5.1 Two Almond-Shaped [Bateman] Dishlets ('salt-cellar stands')

1798, 1804 (London C, I). 5.1 × 3.2 in.

Plain, slightly raised ends, ribbed margins, no pedestal or feet.

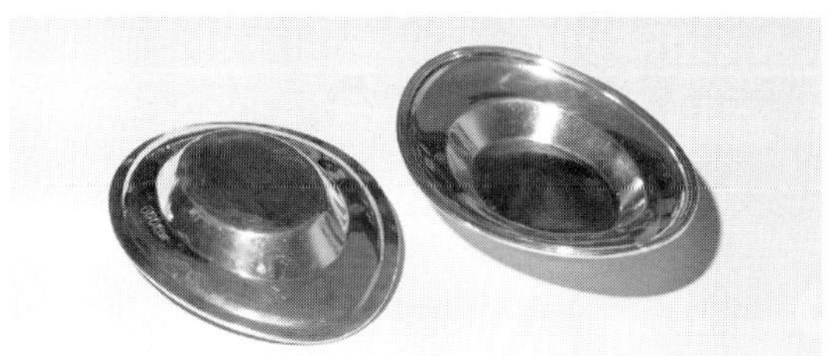

Graffiti (on earlier dish): WJ 457 7″18 *Du/ ap* [and another erased graffito].

Maker's mark: J.E in cottage loaf, for Joseph Emes, active 1786–*c*.1808.

Bequeathed by Aubrey Bateman.

21.5.2 Three Entrée Dishes and Four Lids

1816 (barely legible London a) and 1823. Body 11.9 in. × 8.7 × 1.9 high. Lid 10.9 × 7.7 × 1.8.

Rectangular with rounded corners; gadrooned edges. Lid similar, with a second row of gadrooning round edge of top. Bayonet-type socket for a lost handle. College arms, repeated in larger size on lid.

Inscription (body & lid): *Coll. Corp. Xti Cantab 1817.* Maker's mark (body and lid): *TR* in bifoil, for Thomas Robins from Somerset, active 1794–*c*.1820, specialist in *entrée* dishes.

This applies to one body and two lids; there was a second body until the 1930s. The other two bodies and lids are identical but dated *1823* and numbered *No. 3* and *No. 4*. They are by a different, illegible, maker.

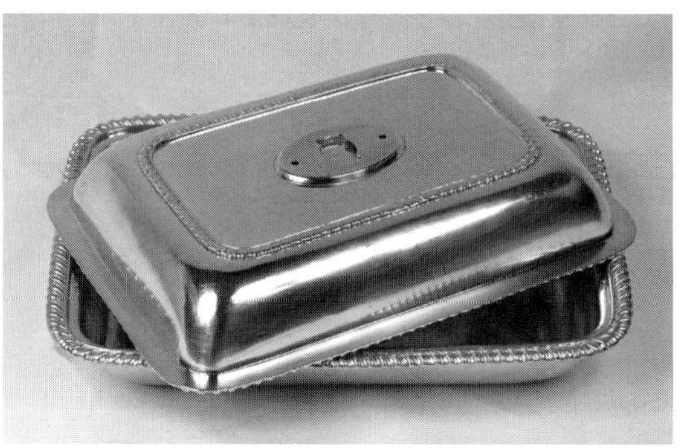

In the expansive days of yore, the term *entrée* presumably meant the preliminary to a proper meal (in Australia it still does). Later it was used for the third course, between the fish and the joint. In a still later, more austere age it had become the main course.

Dishes wrecked by constant use.

21.5.3 Four Shell-shaped Bateman Dishes

1848, 1849 (Sheffield E, F). 5.6 in. × 5.2 × 1.6 high. Two almost identical pairs.

Shaped as the shell of a scallop, *Pecten maximus* (like a pilgrim's souvenir of Santiago de Compostella, or as in Botticelli's *Venus*) on three spiral feet.

Crest (on dishes 1 and 2): *a pheasant.* Numerous graffiti.

Maker's marks: TI NC in square; later TJ NC in square. Made by Thomas Jones & Nathaniel Creswick of Sheffield, manufacturing silversmiths 1819–52; these variants of their marks are apparently not otherwise recorded.

Bequeathed by Aubrey Bateman.

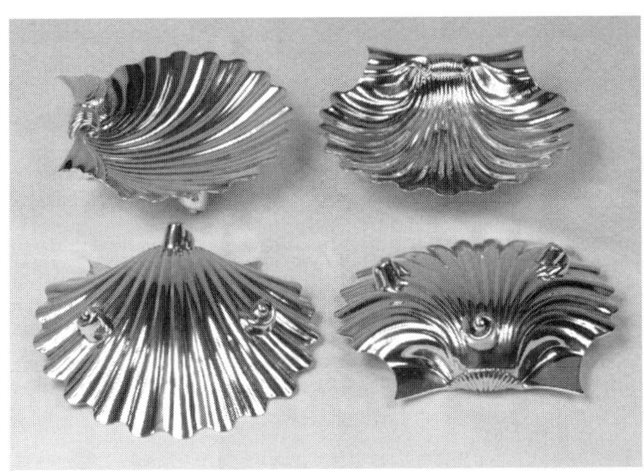

21.5.4 Bateman Boat ('Bon-bon Basket') with Handle

1898 (Sheffield f for 1898). 6.2 in. × 4.6 × 2.5 high.

Almond-shaped, on pedestal, bucket-type handle. Margin ribbed.

Crest: *a pheasant.*

Maker's mark: HA, for Henry Atkins, founder of

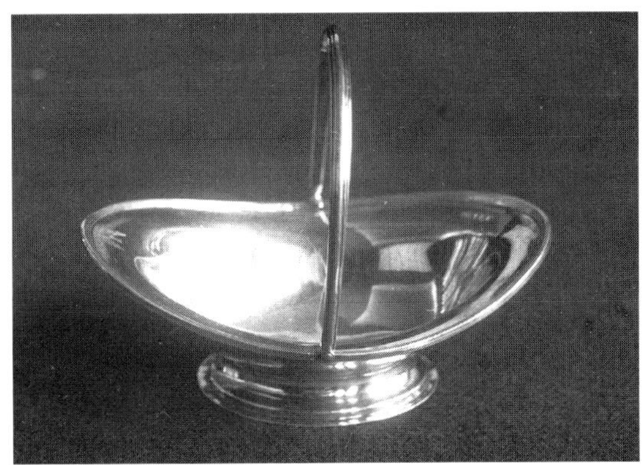

Atkins Brothers of Sheffield, large manufacturing silversmiths 1853–.

Bequeathed by Aubrey Bateman.

21.5.5 Five 'Dutch Bonbon Dishes'

1910? 3.15 in. × 1.9 high.

Octagonal, on a foot. Sides *repoussé* with four panels of stylized flowers and fruit alternating with four Dutch canal scenes.

Foreign pieces bearing London hallmarks as well as their own German ones: London p for 1910 | horseshoe and .925 in ellipse (London mark for imported silver) | BM in rectangle (twice) | n in heater-shaped shield | crown over nine pellets.

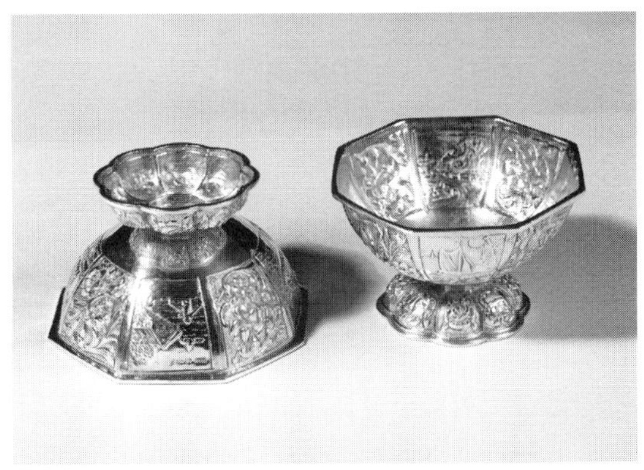

21.5.6 Six [Bateman] Dishlets

1927 (London m). 4.2 × 3.2 × 4.6 in. high.

Plain, on pedestal, with two loop handles.

Maker's mark: H A & S in hexagon, for Holland, Aldwinkle & Slater, active 1902–.

Bequeathed by Aubrey Bateman.

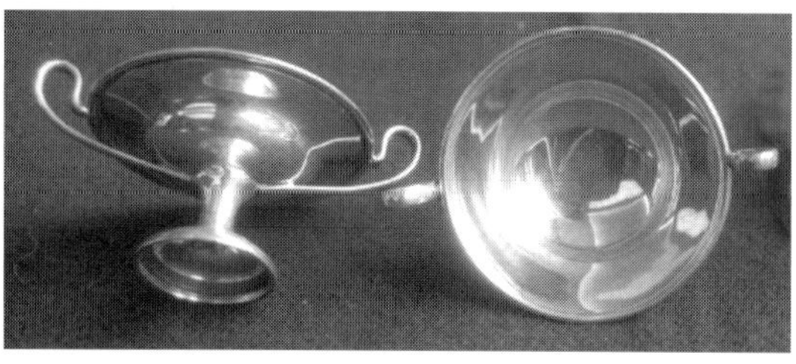

21.5.7 Seven Shells

Probably silver, but unmarked and undated. 4.8 × 4.0 × 0.7 in. high.

Vaguely scallop-shaped, with horizontal loop handle and bar to form a stable base.

Inscription: monogram ***AEP*** [?] C.C.C. One bears 48 in lozenge.

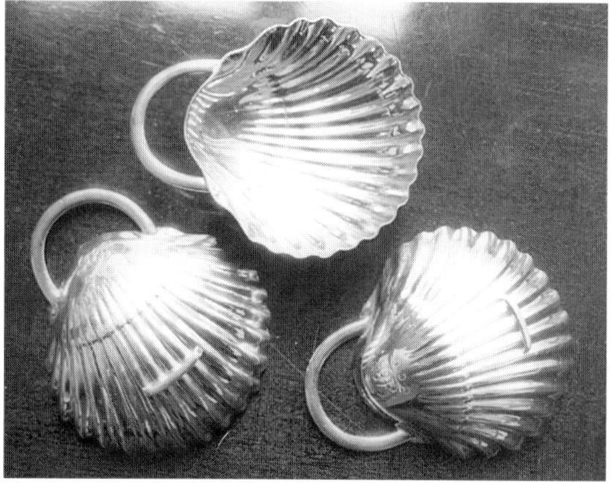

21.5.8 Gross Dish

1977 (London C). Britannia silver. 6.7 × 1.0 in. high.

Flat-bottomed bowl, domed in middle, broad rim with four grooves round it.

Inscription: *Hyman Gross Fellow 1977–1978.*
Marked with Britannia; also PS in trefoil and PAYNE & SON OXFORD – firm of silversmiths active since 1907.

Given by Hyman Gross (1929–) of New York; barrister; Goodhart Professor of Law; Fellow 1977–8 and 1980–92. It commemorates his year as a Professorial Fellow of Corpus, before migrating to Oxford.

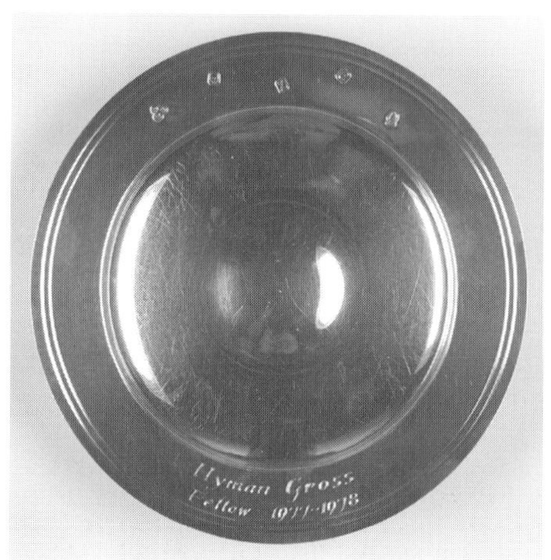

21.6 Elephant

Elephant ivory. 4.8 in. long × 5.0 high. 20th century.

Indian elephant richly caparisoned for a procession, with a small *stupa* or shrine upon his back. His trappings and toenails look like gold adorned with sapphires, pearls, and a ruby.

This jolly little beast is associated with Colonel T. Shamsher Singh, of Baroda, who came to the College in 1933 or 1934 and read Law. He is remembered as a loyal member of the College and a cheerful and welcome guest in later years. (Information from Geoffrey Woodhead.)

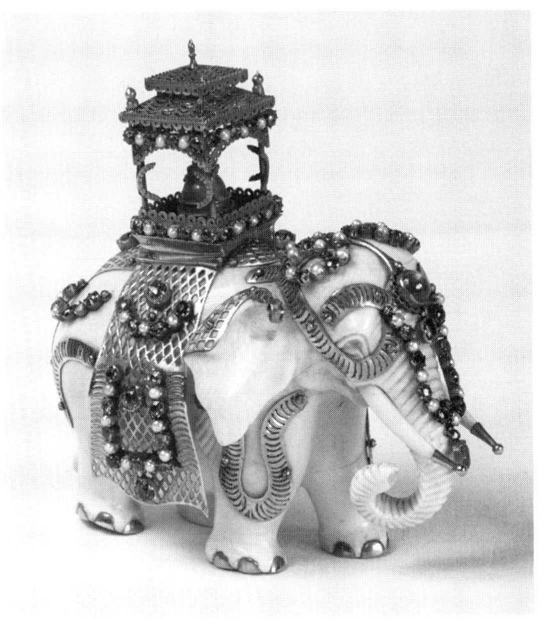
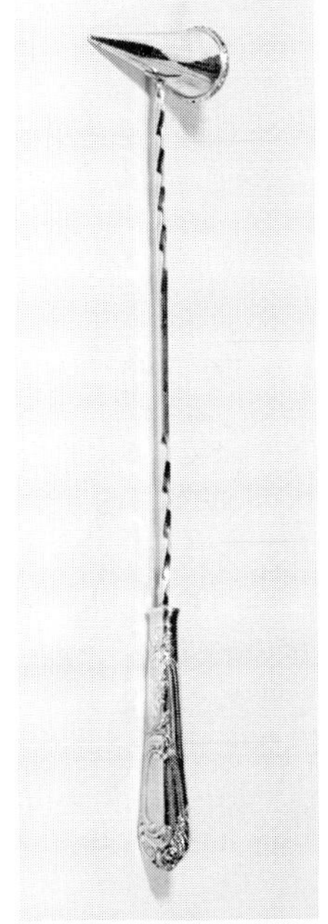
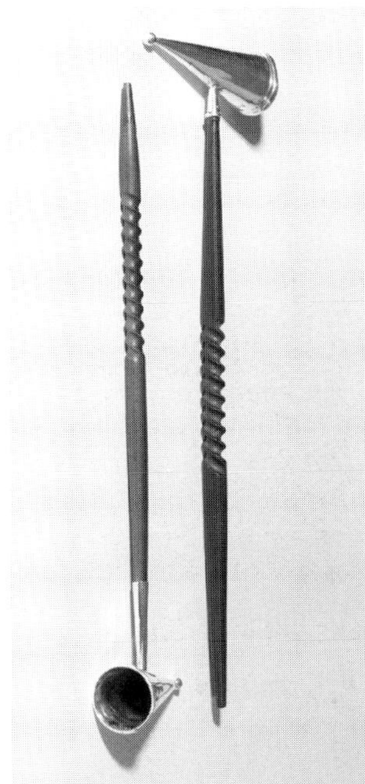

Elephant and three Extinguishers

21.7 Extinguishers

To put out a candle one has to choose between scattering wax over the table or burning one's fingers. The extinguisher (not to be confused with a snuffer) was invented to avoid this dilemma. Sometimes it is attached to the candlestick (see §11.21).

21.7.1 Anonymous Extinguisher

All silver, but unmarked and undated. 12.5 in. total length.

Cone with gadrooned rim, no finial, triangular attachment. Stem is a square silver rod, straight in middle, both ends twisted. Handle like that of a fish-knife, elliptical in section, decorated with rococo foliage and two blank cartouches.

21.7.2 Extinguisher

1960 (Birmingham *L*). Silver cone with handle of black ?horn. 11.7 in. long.

Cone with knob on end, prolonged into point. Long socket for handle. Round-section handle with carved twist. Traces of glue for missing silver finial.

Maker's mark: HU in bifoil.

21.7.3 Taylor Extinguisher

1977 (Birmingham C + Queen's head). Silver cone with handle of black ?horn. 11.7 in. long.

Cone with knob on end, moulded rim, silver socket and pin for handle. Handle of flattish section with twist carved into it. Traces of glue for missing silver finial. Inscription: d.d. C.J.T. MCMLXXVII.

Maker's mark: BE SC in shield.

Given by Christopher John Taylor (1943–97); of the Isle of Man; Scholar 1962–5; Fellow 1976–86. As Treasurer and Bursar he supervised renewal of the kitchens and making of Botolph Court, and planned the redevelopment of King's Parade. This is his wedding fine.

21.8 Jugs with Hinged Lids

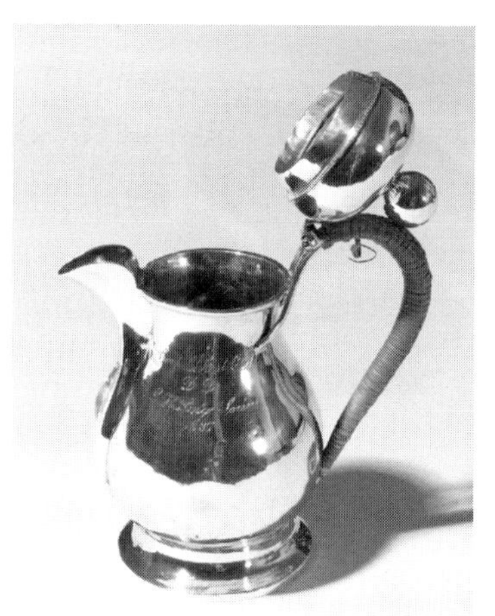

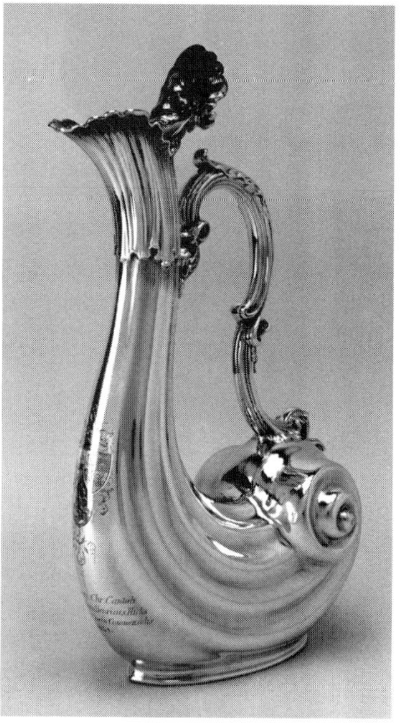

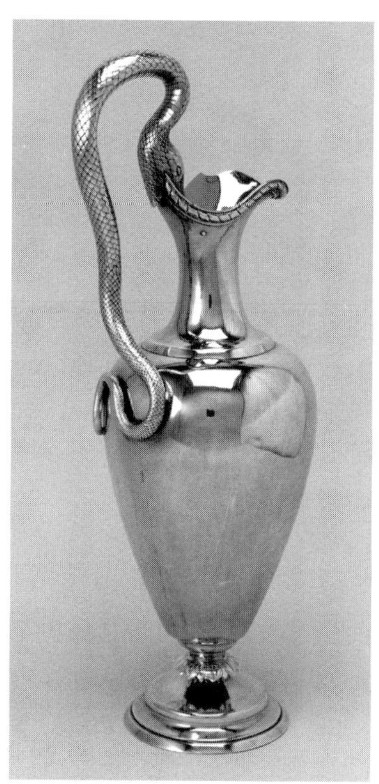

21.8.1 Sing Jug

*c.*1800. 5.6 in. × 3.2 × 6.2 high.

Bulbous base with large plain foot; large half-hexagonal lip; handle bound with cane, ending above in two tails; onion-shaped lid with spherical knob, attached to handle by flimsy hinge.

College arms with pelican pseudo-crest.

Inscription: ***Corp. Christ. Coll. DD G.H Sing Socius 1887*** (G.H. Sing gave [me] to CCC 1887). Graffito: M/oD 44.

Marks are said to be Venetian. Two are foreign symbols; the third is the planet Saturn with seven stars and the number 2 in a heptagonal cartouche.

Leaving gift from George Herbert 'Jorrow' Sing (1856–1901) of Liverpool; Classical scholar; undergraduate at Christ's College; Fellow 1879–87; lecturer on joy and sorrow; first Tutor of Selwyn College; Rector of Stalbridge, Dorset (Corpus living) and other places.

A fragile piece. Several old dents and solder mends; cane loose; knob cracked.

21.8.2 Hicks Claret-Jug

1851 (Sheffield H). 7.8 in. × 4.7 × 13.1 high. Contains 1.55 l = 2.73 pints, or more than 2 modern wine-bottles.

Voluted, vaguely marine-style shape; S-rococo handle; foliage engraved on rump. Shell-like hinged lid with shell thumbpiece. Finial to lid in form of vine-leaves and grapes, attached by wing-nut,.

College arms and donor's: *gules a bar wavy or between three fleurs-de-lis.*

Inscription: Coll: Corp: Chr: Cantab DD Gulielmus Henricus Hicks Norfolciensis Socio Commensali 1851. (William Henry Hicks of Norfolk gave [me] to CCC 1851). Graffito: Peters & Son Cambridge

The Rev. William Henry Hicks was undergraduate 1847, Fellow Commoner 1851.

Metal wine-jugs are impractical objects; it would be difficult to verify what was happening inside and whether any plate-powder was getting into the wine.

21.8.3 Chrystal Serpent Claret-Jug

1879 (Edinburgh W).

5.5 in. by 4.8 by 15.2 high. Silver, treble-gilt inside and both sides of lid. Contains 1.40 l = 2.46 pints = 2 modern wine-bottles.

Egg-shaped, long narrow neck with spout; foot connected to base by a rosette; tiny weighted hinged lid. Loop handle in form of non-venomous serpent trying to swallow jug, beginning at the edge. Rope-moulding round top and spout. Rosette in shape of two rows each of 8 bracts.

College arms, with pelican pseudo-crest.

Inscription: D. D. G. C. 1879 [on belt with buckle] | *SIGNAT AVIS CHRISTUM QUI SANGUINE PASCIT ALUMNOS LILIA VIRGO PARENS INTEMERATA REFERT* [for translation see p. 227].

Maker: J & C in rectangle.

George Chrystal (1851–1911), of Aberdeenshire, mathematician and physicist, went to Aberdeen University and Peterhouse; Second Wrangler 1871; Fellow of Corpus 1875–9; Professor of Mathematics, St Andrews 1877–9, Edinburgh 1879–1911; 'a great teacher and kindly and sympathetic'.

Such jugs could be made for tea or coffee, with an insulating handle: there are several examples in the Victoria & Albert Museum.

21.9 Jugs without Lids

not directly associated with teapots or coffee-pots

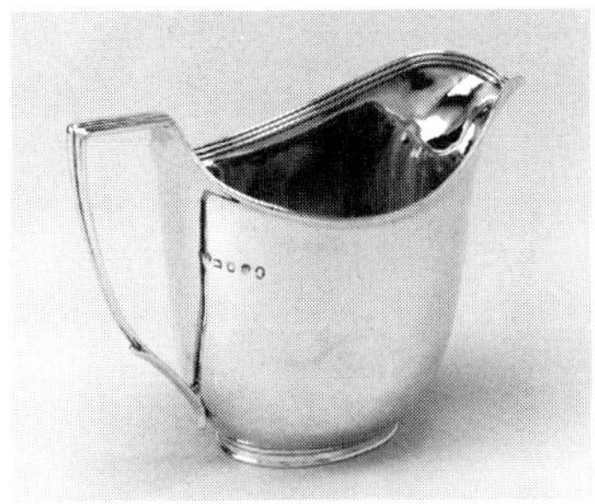

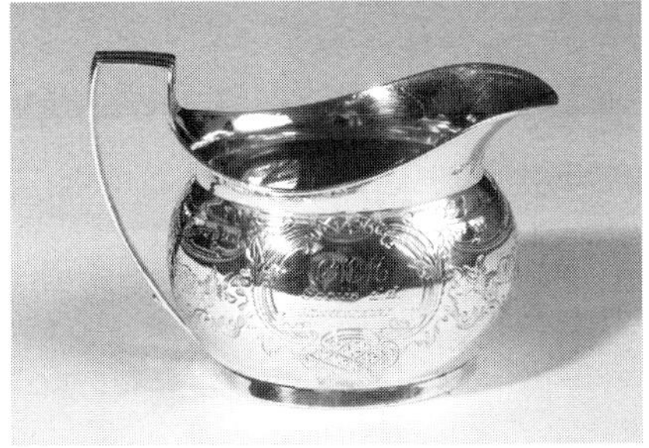

21.9.1 [Bateman] Jug

1803 (London H). 5.2 in. × 2.9 × 3.6 high.

Helmet-shaped, no distinct spout. Reeded on handle and round top.

Maker's mark: JE in quatrefoil, for John Emes. Graffito: 11 = 4

Bequeathed by Aubrey Bateman.

The helmet shape was invented in the late baroque.

21.9.2 Moule Cream-Jug

1803 (London H). 5.5 in. × 3.3 × 3.5 high. Gilt inside.

Oval body engraved with foliage, flowers, and two cartouches for arms and inscription. College arms with pelican pseudo-crest.

Inscription: *CWM Sociis d.d. MDCCCLXXXVI.\ Convivus gratos grate conviva salutat. Domus irrupto nostra sodalitio.* (C.W.M. gave [me] to the Fellows 1886. A married messmate thankfully salutes the thankful. Our house, to unbroken fellowship.)

Maker's mark illegible. Graffito: 9% het

Chasing seems to be added later, fitted round preexisting hallmarks, perhaps contemporary with the inscription (cf. Walpole Coffee-Pot, Bateman Sugar-Bowl).

Charles Walter Moule (1834–1921) of Dorset, son of a parson, was admitted 1853; Scholar 1854; Fellow 1858–61 and 1863–1921; Librarian, Tutor, and President; famous for Classical learning, for Low-Church Evangelicalism, and for his feud with Fanshawe (p. 236). He was one of the first Fellows to marry and remain a Fellow; this piece probably commemorates his wedding in 1885 at the age of fifty-one. [Did he and his bride toast the Fellows in a potation of cream?]

Whitbread Jugs *see* Modernistic Plate

21.10 Mini-Saucepan

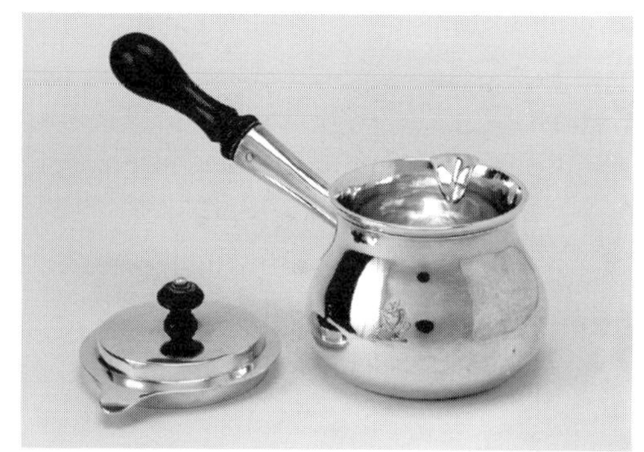

1741 (London f). 8.1 in. × 3.8 × 4.0 high.

Silver saucepan with wooden end to handle and separate silver lid. Said to be for heating brandy (for firing Christmas puddings?).

Cylindrical with lip, concave bottom; handle attached by heart-shaped escutcheon. Handle and knob on lid are of some tropical hardwood.

Crest: *a Steed's Head bridled.*

Maker's mark: Gothic-cursive JS in oval, for John Swift, active in Southwark from 1728.

Bequeathed by Aubrey Bateman.

21.11 Mirror

Plateau or Horizontal Mirror

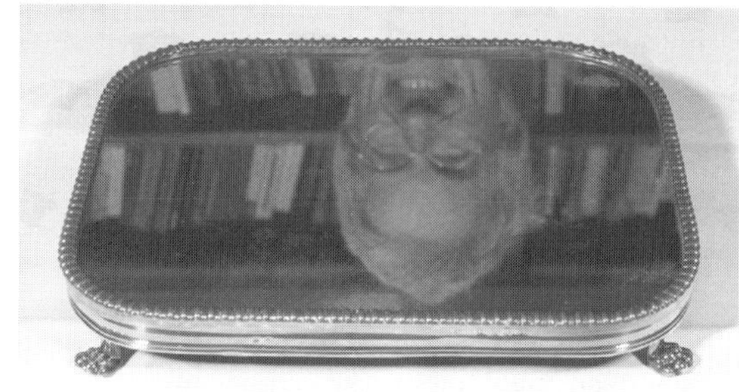

1814 (Sheffield W). 12.0 in. × 10.0 × 1.5 high.

Silvered glass, silver frame, tropical hardwood back.

Heavy frame, gadrooned and reeded; attached by 4 silver clips to backing; 4 leonine feet set into backing. Inscribed 1814. Graffito on clip: Job 75 4

Maker's mark: IK·IW & C° in rectangle, for Kirby Waterhouse & Co.

Mirror is starting to decompose.

21.12 Sauce-Boats

> Speed, bonnie boat, like a bird on the wing,
> 'Onward', the sailors cry...
>
> H.E. Boulton, *Skye Boat Song*, 1908

Sauce or gravy was presumably originally contained in saucers. The sauce-boat, as invented in the baroque period, was a boat-shaped vessel, with pouring lips at bows and stern and a handle on each side amidships. It was more practical, for passing from hand to hand round the table, than the modern shape which became standard from the rococo period onwards. Our earliest known sauce-boats were the pair given by Kenrick Clayton in 1733 and recycled forty years later into the Kenrick Cruet-frame.

Let not the humble sauce-boat be despised. In 1761 Norwich Corporation melted down Archbishop Parker's rosewater ewer and basin, one of the grandest pieces of plate in England, in order not to be without them (p. 73).

21.12.1 Lister Sauce-Boat

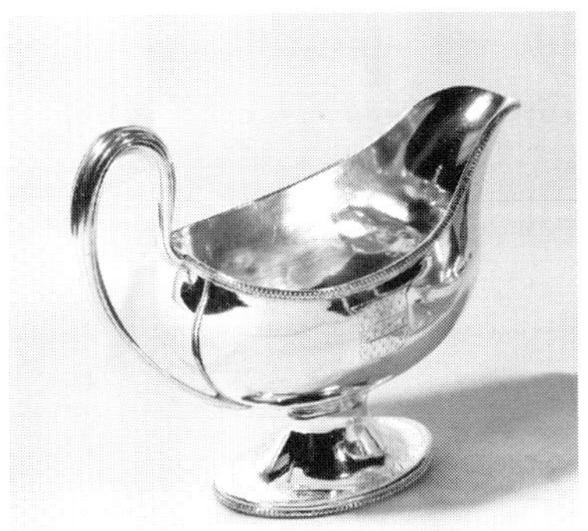

1793? 7.3 in. × 3.8 × 5.8 high.

High, on trumpet foot, with loop handle. Beading round rim and rim of foot; ribbed handle. College arms and donor's: *Ermine on a bar sable three estoiles argent, in chief a fleur-de-lys.* No marks, though genuine silver.

Inscription: *Georgius Lister LL.B. Lincolniensis D.D. Coll: Corp. Xti Cantab.* (George Lister, Bachelor of Laws, from Lincoln, gave [me] to the College . . .) He came to the College in 1787 and took this degree in 1793.

Battered condition.

21.12.2 Two Brodhurst and two Porcher Sauce-Boats

1816 (London a). 9.5 in. × 4.6 × 4.8 high.

Large, low, with strongly downturned spout; three feet; scrolled C-handle. Rim heavily gadrooned. Feet elaborately 'rococo', with shells. College arms.

Inscriptions: *Thomas Brodhurst A.B. Bedfordensis D.D. Coll. Corp. Xti Cantab. 1817.*

Henricus Porcher A.B. Modiasicensis D.D. Coll. Corp. Xti Cantab. 1817. (Henry Porcher, B.A., of Madras, gave [me] to the College of Corpus Christi, Cambridge 1817).

Maker's mark: *TR* in oval, for Thomas Robins, from Bruton (Somerset), worked in London 1801–.

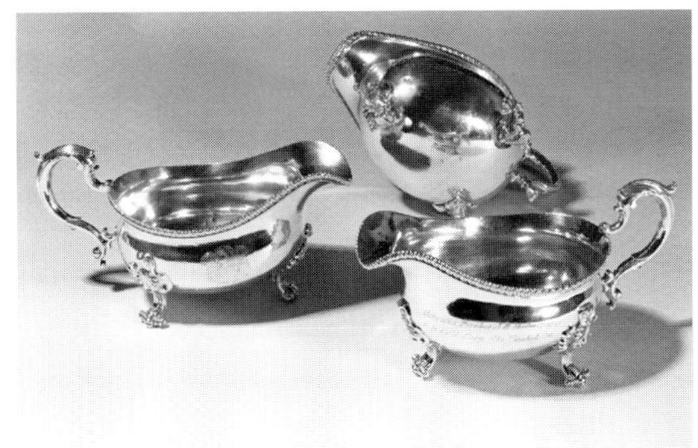

Thomas Brodhurst of Bedfordshire was admitted 1813. Henry Porcher of Madras entered 1811; MA 1819; later MP for Clitheroe, Lancashire.

Somewhat battered, the feet biffed in.

21.12.3 Two Bateman Sauce-Boats

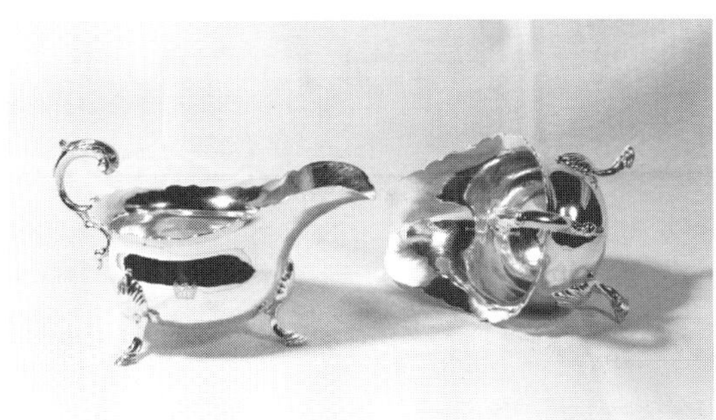

1898 (London c). 7.5 in. × 4.2 × 4.3.

Long, rather squat, with bulbous bow. Plain card-cut cusped edges. Three feet with moulded bases and grass-moulded attachments.

Crest: *demi-pheasant.*

Mark: AJH in butterfly outline, for Alfred James How, active 1897–*c*.1925.

21.12.4 Mini-Sauce-Boat (*not illustrated*)

1915 (London u). 3.8 in. × 2.1 × 3.0 high.

Card-cut body with big spout; 3 hoofed feet arising from shells. No maker's mark. Derelict.

21.12.5 Anonymous Sauce-Boat

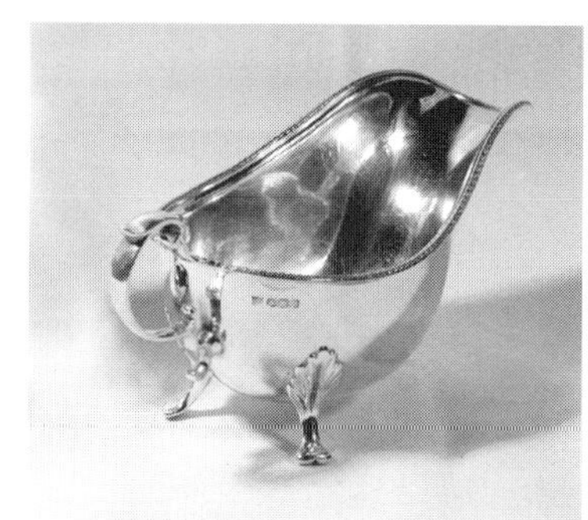

1924 (Sheffield g). 8.7 in. × 3.9 × 3.8 high.

Three feet, vestigial spout. Gadrooned rim. Foliated attachments to feet.

Mark: F B[S]. L[TD], for Fenton Brothers Ltd; this mark entered 1896.

21.12.6 AP Sauce-Boat (*not illustrated*)

Undated. Brass, heavily silver-plated. 8.8 in. × 4.2 × 5.2 high.

On base with narrow stalk. Vestigial foliation on handle.

Inscriptions: ***C.C.C.*** | *AP* on underside

Mark: 51 in lozenge

Very worn inside and where it touches the table. 'C.C.C.' worn down to brass as though by someone trying to erase it.

21.13 Spirit-Lamp ('Tommy's Kettle')

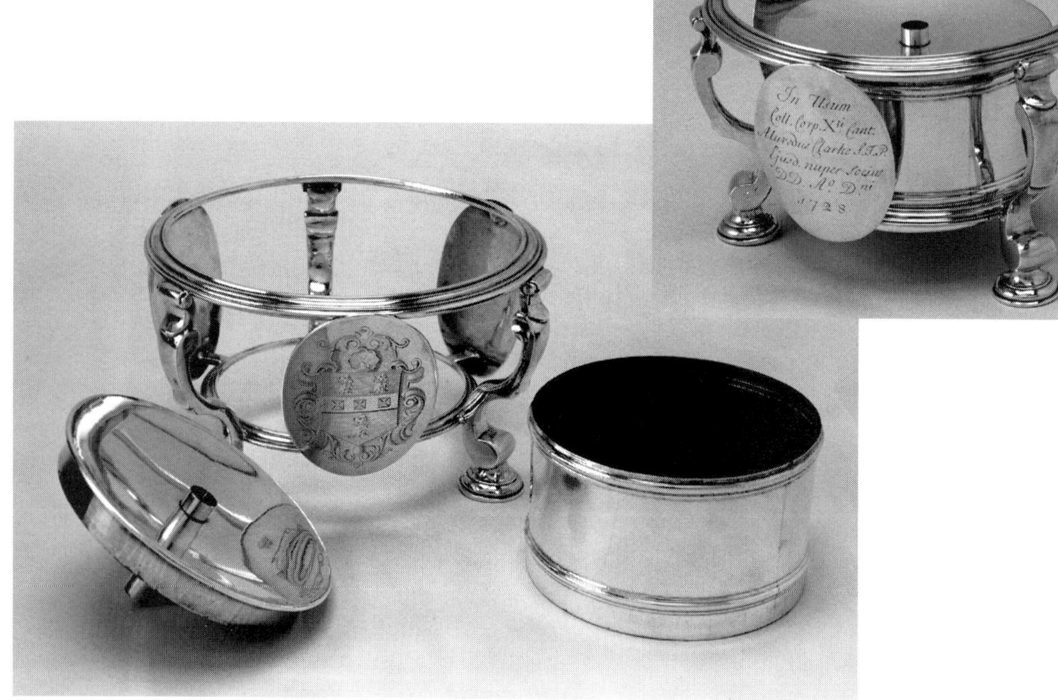

1728 (inscription). 5.2 in. diam. × 3.1 high.

A cylindrical container of silvered base metal fits snugly into a silver cage. Its tight-fitting lid is slightly depressed, with a central orifice for a wick. The cage consists of 2 horizontal circles joined by three cabriole legs and three oval cartouches.

Donor's arms on first cartouche: *Azure three crosses patée gules on a fess or between three griffins' heads erased.* College arms in foliation on second cartouche.

Inscription: *In Usum Coll. Corp. X^ti^ Cant. Aluredus Clarke S.T.P. Ejusd. nuper Socius D.D.A^o^ D^ni^ 1728.* (For the use of the College of Corpus Christi, Cambridge, Alured Clarke, D.D., lately Fellow, gave [me] A.D. 1728.)

No marks. Described in inventory for 1728 as 'A Stand for a Dish'.

This rare object is derived from a type commoner in the 1700s and 1710s, a teapot with a spirit-lamp made to fit under it. There are three examples in the British Museum.

Alured Clarke (1696–1742) of Huntingdonshire was admitted 1713, and was Fellow 1719–24 (successor to Stephen Hales, physiologist). He was Rector of Chilbolton (Hampshire), Chaplain-in-Ordinary to Georges I and II, and Dean of Exeter; he was prebendary of, and buried in, Westminster Abbey. He founded an hospital for the sick and lame at Winchester. (The College has a portrait of his brother, Sir Charles Clarke, judge, who is remembered for dying of gaol fever (typhus) while doing his judicial duty.)

> He held in utter contempt the practice (too common) of heaping up wealth from church preferments to raise a family, and determined to spend the whole surplus of his annual income in works of charity or hospitality, and never to have in reserve, how great soever his income might be, more than a sum sufficient to defray the expences of his funeral.
>
> *Masters (1753)*

21.14 Stand

c.1814. 10.3 × 7.3 × 5.2 in. high. Silvered copper.

A horizontal elliptical hoop stands on four cabriole-like legs with lionish feet, connected by curved stretchers. Hoop has moulded lower rim, flat gadrooned top edge. Legs attached by foliated capitals.

College arms. No marks.

Inscription: *Jacobus Crook Clements A.B. Socius Commensalis Dono dedit C.C.C.C. 1814* (James Crook Clements, B.A., Fellow Commoner, gave [me] to the College . . . 1814).

J. Cooke Clements (so spelt in Lamb's *History*) of Middlesex was admitted 1809; B.A. 1813. A James Crook Clements was parson at Clapton (London?) in 1841.

This object is presumably the mortal remains of 'Mr Clements trifle dish & glass' inventoried in 1817.

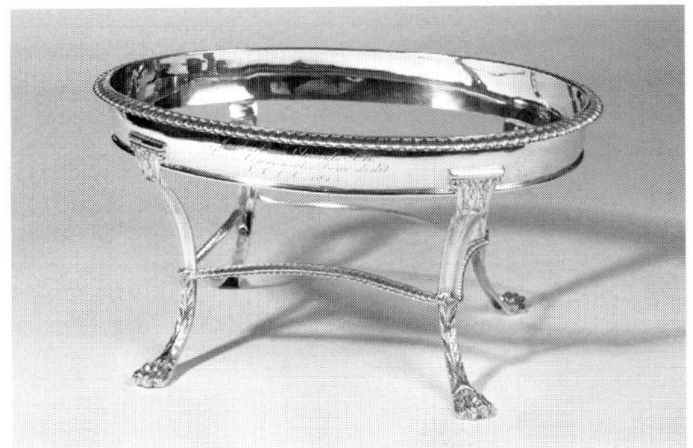

21.15 Toast-Racks

Two. 1898 (London f) 4.2 in. × 2.7 × 4.3 high.

Flat base; four ball feet; seven hoops; loop handle. *Pheasant* crest.

Maker's mark: M & W in very broad shield, inscription MAPPIN & WEBB LONDON.

Bequeathed by Aubrey Bateman.

Toast is sliced bread which has been singed to render it edible. It would be allowed to cool in these receptacles to acquire a suitably resilient texture.

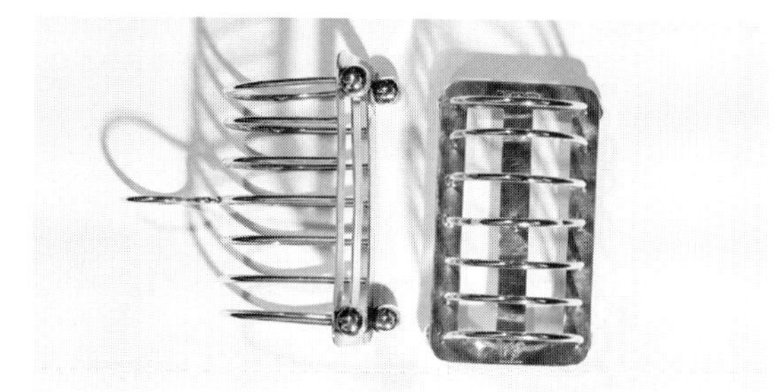

21.16 Top-Hat Brush *alias* Nib-Cleaner

1904 (Birmingham e) 3.0 in. diameter.

Bristle, bound with brass wire to wooden base, set in plaster and enclosed in silver shell.

Maker's mark: HCD, unidentified.

Bequeathed by Aubrey Bateman.

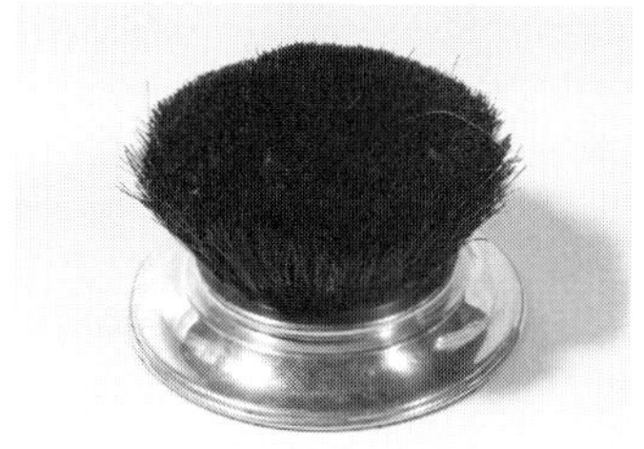

21.17 Tureens

Beautiful Soup, so rich and green,
Waiting in a hot tureen!

Lewis Carroll, *The Mock Turtle's Song*

A *tureen*, as its name implies (French *terrine*), is an earthen container for mock-turtle soup or similar hot liquid. From the mid-18th century onwards it was copied in silver, resulting in magnificent Adamesque and Regency pieces – which, however, conduct heat and are less practical than their humble originals.

21.17.1 Douglas Tureen and Lid

1809 (London O). Body 15.9 in. × 9.7 × 7.5 high, lid 10.8 × 9.6 × 5.3.

Bulbously rectangular body, cast loop handles. Convex, plain lid with handle mounted on a gadrooned plaque attached by a large bolt. Gadrooned border with shells at corners; gadrooned foot; body handles attached by card-cut plaques.

Arms: College, in elaborate border of nondescript foliage and vestigial strapwork. Donor's, on squarish shield: *Argent a human heart imperially crowned, on a chief azure three mullets.* Crest: *a human heart imperially crowned and winged.* Motto: *SPERO* [I hope].

Inscription: *Philippus Douglas Socius Commensalis Dono dedit C.C.C.C. A.D. 1809.* (Philip Douglas, Fellow Commoner, gave [me] AD 1809).

Marks are carelessly struck. The leopard is missing from the body; the leopard's face is twice shallowly struck on the body and missing from the lid.

Maker's mark: IE AH in rectangle, for James Ede & Alexander Hart, entered 1808: a surprisingly obscure pair to have made this ambitious piece.

Given by the Master, Philip Douglas (1758–1822) of Essex; admitted 1776; Fellow 1782; Tutor 1787–97; Doctor of Divinity 1795; Master 1795–1822; parson of Gedney (Lincs.) 1796; Vice-Chancellor 1795 and 1810. This massive piece (it weighs $3\frac{1}{2}$ kg) was presented in the year of his wife's death. Like Robert Douglas (§21.4.3) he claimed descent from the royal Douglases of Scotland, and bore the extracted heart of Robert the Bruce. He describes

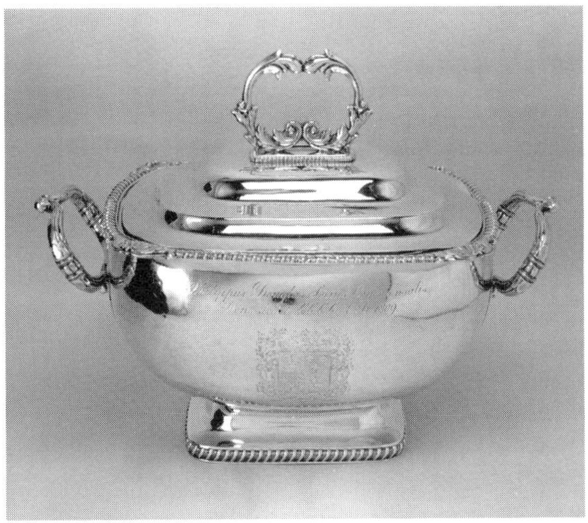

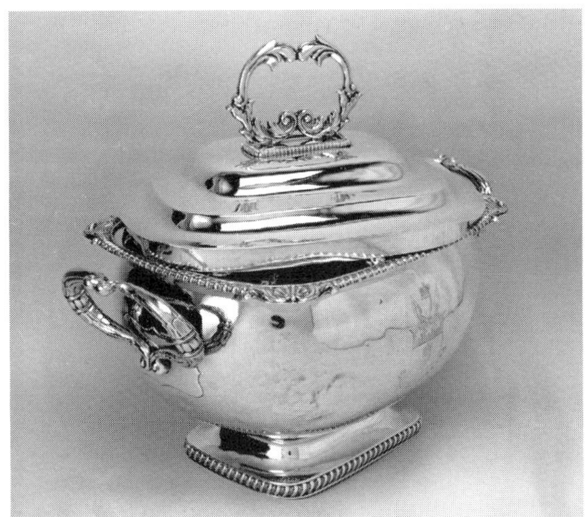

himself not as Master but as Fellow-Commoner. This was not a mistake: until 1906 the Master dined at High Table only by permission of the Fellows.

21.17.2 Four [Bateman] Tureenlets with Lids and Liners (*below*)

Bowls and 3 lids 1821, liners and No.4 lid 1822 (London f and g). 8.2 by 6.2 by 5.3 in. high (7.5 in. high including lid).

Massive two-handled bowl on pedestal with square base. Rim ornamented with beading and tongue-and-dart, below which are vine-leaves and grapes. Each handle is of two intertwined foliated ribbed stems. Six acanthus leaves below.

Plain liner with rounded bottom, two small scroll handles.

Lid with acanthus foliage and thistlehead-like knob.

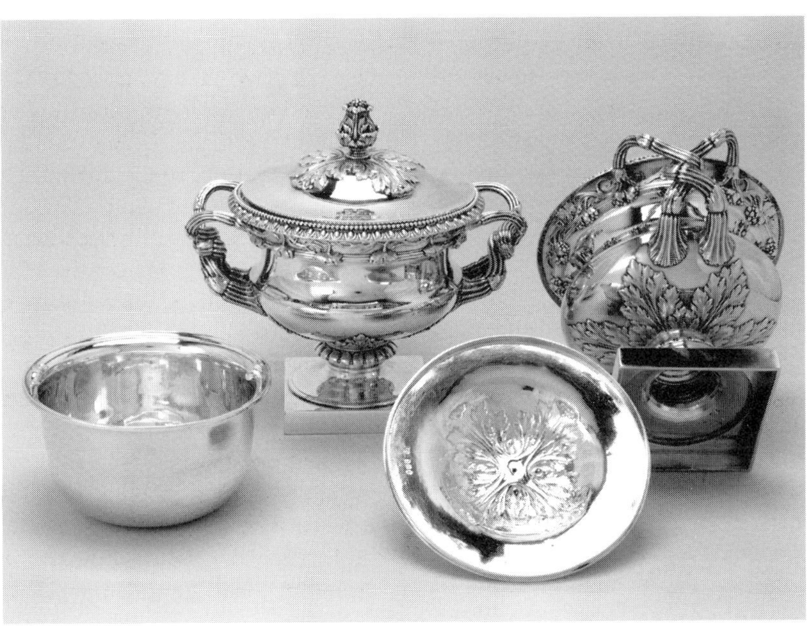

Weight inscriptions (under bowl; lid and liner bear number):

N°.1 41″15 [present weight of bowl and lid, but not liner = 41: 8] *N°*.2 [no weight]
N°.3 42″3 [41: 19] *N°*.4 42″8 [41.17]
The liners were therefore an afterthought, not included in the original weight.

Made by the famous Paul Storr (1771–1844), of Soho (London), active 1793–1839 (PS in bifoil).

Among the grandest objects bequeathed by Aubrey Bateman. This was a classic Regency design, inspired by the Warwick Vase, a giant Roman object published by Piranesi in 1744, or by its brazen copy now outside Cambridge Senate-House.

21.17.3 Two-Handled 'AEP' Tureen (*not illustrated*)

*c.*1900. Base metal, thickly silver-plated.

Bowl 16.75 in. × 9.25 × 10.75 high. Lid 12.7 in. × 9.3 × 4.6 high.

Deep, elliptical bowl with elliptical trumpet-foot. Loop handles bifurcated at top. Lid saddle-shaped, domed, flanged underneath; loop handle attached by wing-nut; peg in base of handle engages with hole in lid. Body beaded on top and bottom rims; handles gadrooned. Each end of lid handle terminates in the likeness of a twig torn off from its parent branch.

Inscription (twice on body and again on lid): ***AEP*** [owner's monogram] | C.C.C. | [on body only] 51 [in lozenge] 8388.

Provenance unknown.

21.18 Vases

21.18.1 Espy Vase

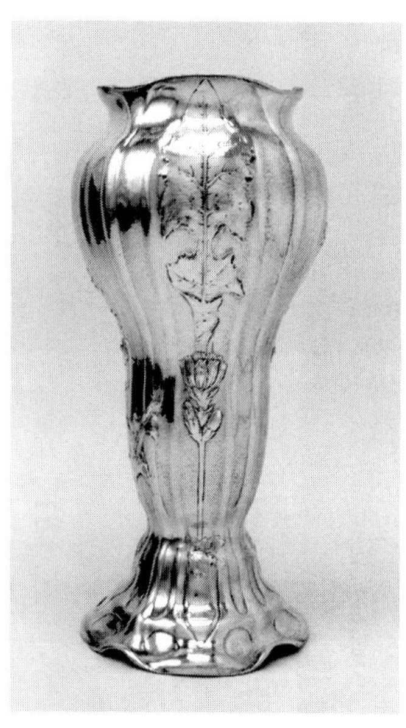

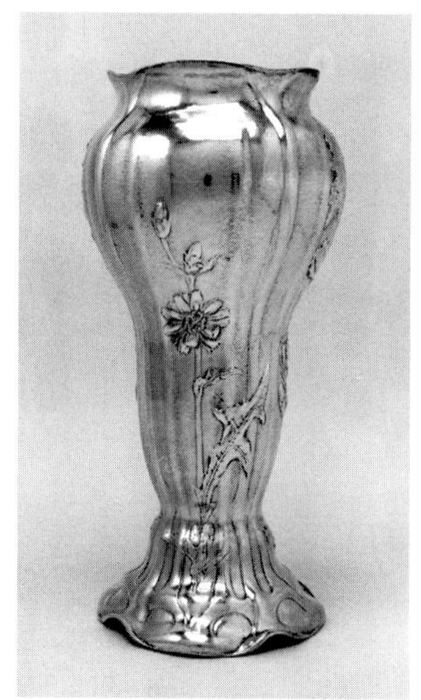

*c.*1890. 5.7 diam. × 12.7 high.

Upright gourd-shaped vessel. *Art-nouveau* decoration in *repoussé* work with four ribs alternating with chicory (*Cichorium intybus*) in bloom. Hammer-faceted texture.

Marks: word *Martelé* over outline of ?turkey-buzzard, beneath which are a lion passant, an anchor, and the letter 𝕲. Inscribed ·9584 I C Y GORHAM, INC. All these constitute the trade-mark of Gorham Manufacturing Co. of Providence, Rhode Island, founded 1831, and the 'largest firm of manufacturing silversmiths in the world' by 1881. The lion, anchor, and 𝕲 happen to resemble the Birmingham hallmarks for 1830 – Gorham did later have works in Birmingham, England, 1909–14. There is no sign of the date-symbol system developed by Gorham.

Graffito: H 26999 R–2

Inscription: *IN GRATEFUL RECOGNITION OF CORPUS CHRISTI COLLEGE CAMBRIDGE WALLACE SEELY ESPY 1926–1927 JAMES ESPY 1930–1931 OF CINCINNATI, OHIO. U.S.A.*

Wallace Seely Espy and James Espy were members of the College at those dates, but presumably not as undergraduates.

The College's best example of Art Nouveau style, and our only piece made in the United States (which had no hallmarking system). Gorham were noted for early Art Nouveau. The word Martelé refers not to the hammered texture but to the work of William Christmas Codman, English Art Nouveau designer, employed by Gorham 1885– (Rainwater 1975).

21.18.2 Four [Bateman] Vases

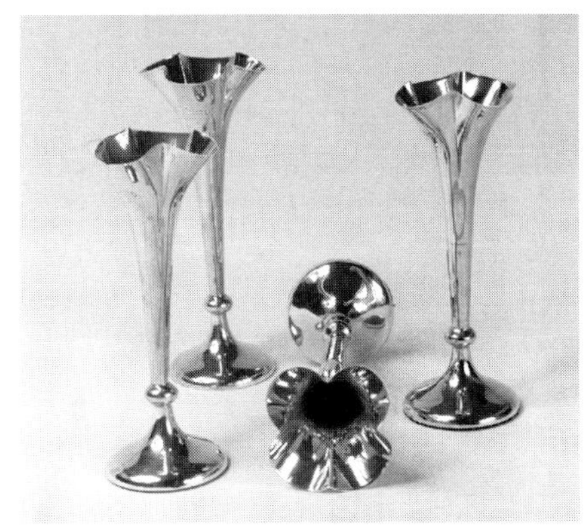

1899 (London d). 2.6 in. × 6.3. high.

Trumpet-shaped, mouth with four flutes, rim minutely serrate, knop near base, plain base stuffed with lead.

Maker's mark: H W&C^{o}. L^{D}. in cross, for Horace Woodward & Co. Ltd of Birmingham, active 1865–*c*.1919. It was said of their work:

> Some of these . . . will form historic pieces, and will be grand examples of the silversmith's art of the latter part of the nineteenth century at some future date, when the whole of the existing names in the trade shall have long been forgotten . . .

Bequeathed by Aubrey Bateman.

21.18.3 Four Bateman Vases

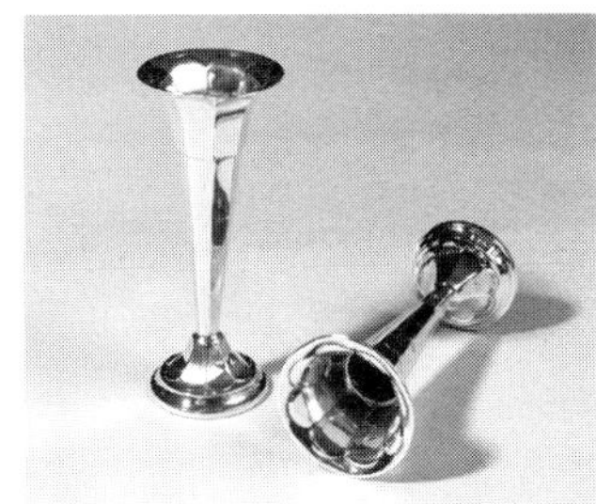

1917 (Sheffield з) 2.0 in. × 4.7 high.

Trumpet-shaped with offset in stem, octagonal with round mouth; bell-shaped base with round rim. Graffiti: RB.

Maker's mark: JD WD in shield, for John & William Pitchford Dakin of Sheffield, active 1880s and 1890s.

Bequeathed by Aubrey Bateman. Rare work of the First World War.

21.19 Wine-Labels

> The shipmates . . . would fain throw the whole guilt on the Ancient Mariner: in sign whereof they hang the dead [Albatross] round his neck.
>
> *Samuel Taylor Coleridge*, The Rime of the Ancient Mariner, 1798

These hang round the necks of decanters in the Combination Room, to identify dessert wines in poor light. Each label is normally a convex piece of metal, engraved or pierced with the name of the wine, suspended by a silver chain. They are a late Georgian invention, in a plain Adamesque style which lasted much longer than among other artefacts.

These dainty objects may not have marks. Where they do the marks are often incomplete or cut away by subsequent piercing of the letters.

The labels are a commentary on after-dinner drinking habits. Out of fifty-three, 19 are PORT or LISBON, 17 are MADEIRA, 12 are CLARET or BORDEAUX, four XERES or SHERRY, and one BRANDY. By the 1960s the balance had shifted towards port. At the time of writing much less port is drunk, very little Madeira, and some claret: dessert sherry is unheard-of; but Australian, German, and Rumanian dessert wines are much appreciated.

Rectangle with lug, reeded border

PORT, 1802 (London G), 1.5 × 0.9 inches, EM in rectangle

Inscription: d.d. L.E. FREEMAN BUTLER 1946–58. Given, no doubt, by the Butler on retirement.

Cut-corner rectangle, pierced letters, plain

MADEIRA, 1805 (London K), 1.8 × 1.0, JK in rectangle

Cut-corner rectangle, reeded border

CLARET, 1808 (London N), maker T.P. E.K in quatrefoil

MADEIRA, 1827 (London m), 1.4 × 0.7, maker doubtful

Inscription: d.d. W.S. & D.T.S. MCMX.

Sir Will Spens (1882–1962) of Glasgow, Scholar of King's College, joined Corpus Christi as Director of Studies in Natural Sciences, 1906, and became a Fellow 1907, Tutor 1910, Master 1927–52, and Vice-Chancellor 1931–3. In World War I he published the Black List of the Foreign Trade Department. He was knighted in 1939. In World War II he served as Regional Commissioner (a sort of Viceroy) for the Eastern Region. A celebrated Anglo-Catholic, he revived the academic fortunes of the College, and is credited with originating many of its 'ancient and laudable' customs. This (and its seven companions) must be his fine for marrying Dorothy Theresa Selwyn in 1912.

The College's smallest independent silver artefact, weighing $6\frac{1}{2}$ grams (0.2 oz.).

Kidney-shaped, plain or reeded border

MADEIRA, 1810 (London P), 2.0 × 1.0, rather C-shaped, reeded border, T.J in rectangle (Thomas James, active 1804–).

Inscribed for Will and Dorothy Spens, see above.

BORDEAUX, 1822 (Birmingham y), 1.8 × 1.0, SB&S L[D]

Four LISBON, 1822 (Birmingham y), 1.8 × 1.0, SB&S L[D]

Two MADEIRA, 1822 (Birmingham y), 1.8 × 1.0, SB&S L[D]

XERES, 1822 (Birmingham y), 1.8 × 1.0, SB&S L[D]

LISBON, 1829 (Birmingham 𝔉), 1.8 × 1.0 in. JW in engrailed oblong (Joseph Willimore)

XERES, 1829 (Birmingham 𝔉), 1.8 × 1.0 in. JW in engrailed oblong (Joseph Willimore)

BORDEAUX, 1830 (Birmingham 𝔊), 1.8 × 1.0 in., T&P in oblong (unidentified)

Oval-oblong, plain

MADEIRA, date cut away (1786 × 1819), 1.7 × 1.0, SM unidentified.

Rectangle, reeded border

MADEIRA (pierced letters), 1816 (London a), 1.6 × 0.8, D.H in rectangle

PORT, 1819 (London d, 17 × 0.9, I.R in rectangle; ?military badge of crowned Garter

Both are inscribed for Will and Dorothy Spens, see above.

Rectangle or oblong, pierced letters, gadroon border

MADEIRA, 1815 (London U), 1.7 × 1.0, TP ER JP in rectangle

CLARET, 1827 (London m), 1.8 × 1.2, R.E. E.B in bifoil

This and the previous are inscribed for Will and Dorothy Spens, see above.

CLARET, date cut away (1820 × 1837), CR in rectangle (Charles Rawlings, active 1817–*c*.1850)

CLARET, date cut away, 1.8 × 1.0, CR in rectangle (same)

Rectangle with 2 lugs, pierced letters, gadroon border

CLARET, ?1827 (?London m), 1.7 × 1.3 in., RE RB in quatrefoil (Rebecca Emes & Edward Barnard I)

Inscribed for Will and Dorothy Spens, see above.

Oval, pierced letters, elaborate *repoussé* vine-leaves and grapes

PORT, 1834 (London t), 2.5 × 1.9, W.K.R. in bifoil
Inscribed for Will and Dorothy Spens, see above.

Oblong, bordered with *repoussé* foliage and shells

MADEIRA, 1897 (Birmingham x), 2.1 × 1.2, GU in rectangle (George Unite & Sons, active 1825–)
Inscription: d.d. L.E FREEMAN BUTLER 1946–58.
SHERRY, 1963 (London *h*), 2.3 × 1.5, *NJ* in bifoil
PORT, London *e*, 2.4 × 1.6 in., DSS in trefoil
PORT, London *g*, 2.4 × 1.6 in., FH in circle
CLARET, unmarked, 2.2 × 1.5
CLARET and PORT, unmarked, 2.2 × 1.5, jejune lettering
Six MADEIRA, unmarked, 2.2 × 1.5
Five PORT, unmarked, 2.2 × 1.5

Ellipse or almond-shape, beaded edge

MADEIRA, 1896 (London a), DW JW in baroque shield
Two CLARET ditto (one repaired)
PORT ditto
CLARET and PORT ditto but almond-shaped
All these are inscribed *d.d. S.H.P. 1956*. For Stewart Henry Perowne see the Perowne Cup (§11.4.10)
MADEIRA and PORT, unmarked, 1.7 × 1.0 in.

Cusped rectangle, reeded edge, foliated corners

SHERRY, silvered brass, 2.2 × 1.1

Cut-out letters on chain, repoussé foliage

B.R.A.N.D.Y, unmarked, 2.8 × 0.7 in.

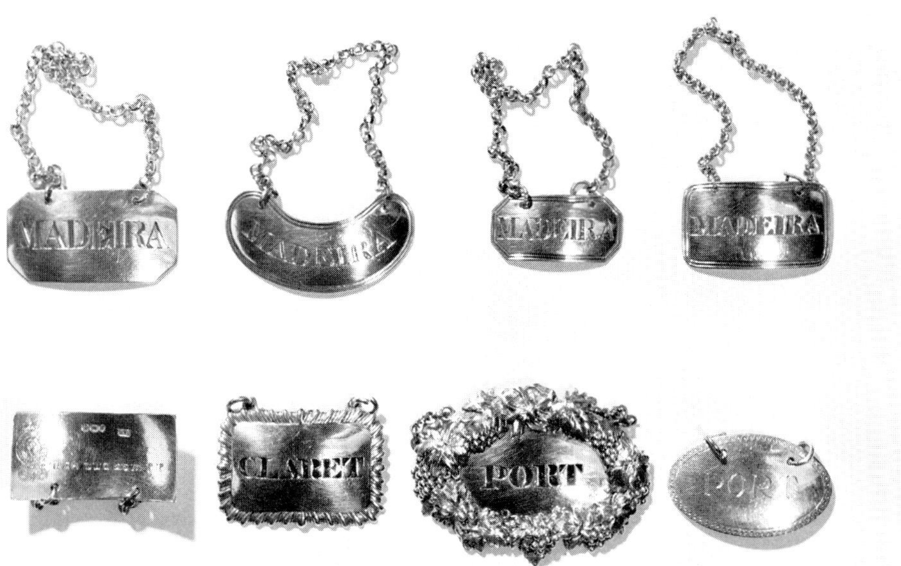

Examples of the different types of wine-label

22

Modernistic Plate

> The trend in Britain is clear: it is towards more elaborate, more decorative, and less useful pieces in silver.
>
> *Graham Hughes, 1987*

Silver is perhaps the most successful medium of modernistic art. Since 1930 silversmiths have got ingenious new textures and even colours out of the metal, as well as inventing new forms and combining silver with other materials.

Silver is not immune from the practical problems of modernism, as the Burgess Coffee-pot shows. Some silversmiths have a predilection for plain shiny surfaces, which look better through the glass of a showcase than on pieces which are handled. However, unlike modernistic architecture, silver does not get dingy or dilapidated with time. Nor does yesterday's taste get so quickly dated: in 2000 it was still respectable to appreciate the forms and textures of the 1960s and 1930s.

See also the later items of Chapel Plate (Chapter 9).

22.1 **Haslam** (Danish) **Bowl**

*c.*1930. 6.4 in. × 5.4 high.

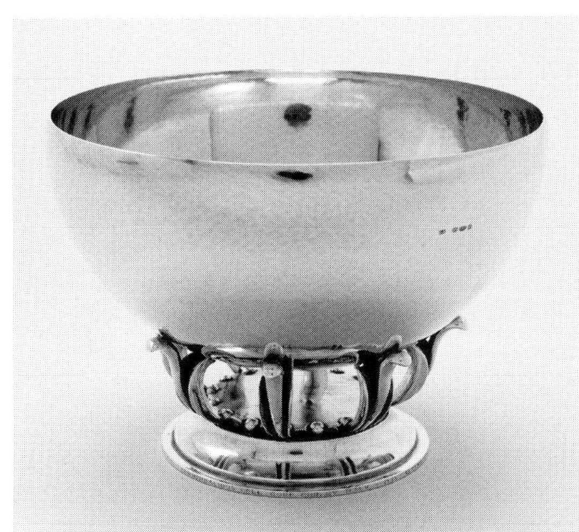

Hemispherical bowl supported by eight bifid feet from base. Hammered finish to outside of bowl.

Inscription: COMMENSALIBUS COLL. CORP. CHR. ET B.M.V. D.D. ALEXANDRUS HASLAM – 21 JUN. 1930. (Alexander Haslam gave this to the Commoners [i.e. members of High Table] of the College of Corpus Christi and the Blessed Virgin Mary, 21 June 1930).

Marks: GEORG JENSEN [crowned] DESSIN GP STERLING 584 DENMARK GI 925. No date.

Group Capt. the Rev. James Alexander Gordon Haslam (1896–1990), aviator, aeronautical scientist, priest, came from Rugby. He fought in World War I (M.C., D.F.C.), in Waziristan 1925 (Mentioned in Despatches), and in World War II. He was Fellow-Commoner 1925–30: studied airflow over aircraft in flight; University Lecturer in Aeronautics 1939–52; Fellow 1949–52; Rector of Sutton Benger, Wilts, 1958–64 (Bury 1952). No known Danish connexion.

The College's only example of *avant-garde*, one of the early modernist styles.

22.2 Morris Cup and Cover

1932 (London r). 5.8 in. × 12.8 high; lid 5.9 × 5.1 high.

Tall narrow body, angular handles, sharp-edged knop. Nearly flat lid with large keeled knob; finial in form of acute dodecahedron. Zigzag decoration on knop and finial. 2 masks at base of handles. Stepped moulding on handles.

Inscription: THIS LOVING CUP WAS PRESENTED TO THE CORPUS DINING CLUB BY GEOFFREY GRANT MORRIS. FROM ONE WHO HOPED HE WAS A SPORTSMAN TO THOSE WHO WERE. JUNE. 1934.

Marks: MC in bifoil MUNSEY, SILVERSMITH CAMBRIDGE Graffiti: 538 oz xx mtu.

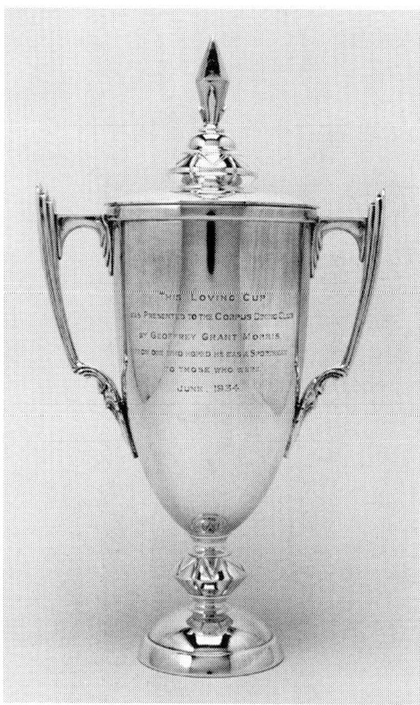

Geoffrey Grant Morris (1888–1938), of Eton College and Trinity, fine Classical scholar; was Fellow of Corpus 1919–37 and Bursar 1928–34; *bon viveur*, racegoer, opponent of women's degrees.

22.3 Goodhart Rosewater Bowl, Beaker, and Lid (*illustrated on facing page*)

1938. Bowl 18.3 in. × 2.5 high. Beaker 4.6 × 5.8 high. Lid 4.3 × 2.1 high.

Bowl: shallow, rising to a central boss; inward-sloping flange; wavy rim. Ornamented in *repoussé* with curved, raised radial ribs. Flange embossed with three wavy ribs. Dimpled texture, including underside, except rim and boss.

College arms boldly, slightly unconventionally engraved on boss.

Inscription: *The Gift of Arthur Lehman Goodhart formerly Fellow of this College 1920–1936*. On underside: *Designed by R. Gleadowe, made by Wakeley & Wheeler. June 1938.*

Marks: (large and bold) Sheffield C; maker *W & W* The date-letter is puzzling: C was the letter for London, not Sheffield, in 1938.

Beaker: ornamented inside and out with turbinate ribs to match those on bowl; short intermediate ribs near base. Four little flanges, applied to inside, sustain the lid. Texture as bowl. Marks as above.

Lid: low cone with thickened edge. Radial undulations intersected by two concentric ribs, all in *repoussé*. Texture as above. Knob of silver, ivory and mother-of-pearl attached by silver wingnut and bolt. Leopard hallmark on wingnut.

Arthur Lehman Goodhart (1891–1978) of New York, lawyer, came to Trinity College 1912. He was Fellow of Corpus 1919–35; Honorary Fellow 1942– (and of three other colleges); Professor of Jurisprudence, Oxford 1931–51; King's Counsel 1943–; Master of University College, Oxford 1951–63; President of the Pedestrians' Association for Road Safety 1951–63. He also gave the Goodhart Mug (p. 129).

This famous example of modernistic plate was our next rosewater bowl after the Parker Bowl. Gleadowe was art master at Winchester College and Slade Professor at Oxford, and one of the foremost silver designers of his time.

22.4 Adrian Triple Candlestick (*illustrated on facing page*)

1960 (London e). 9.4 in. greatest width by 3.0 high.

No base: three flat arms meet near ground level. Plain sockets and drip-trays.

Inscription: *C.C.C. R.H.A. 1960*

Made by AGB.

Donor: Richard Hume Adrian (1927–95) of Cambridge; son of Chancellor of the University; Scholar of Trinity College; physiologist; Fellow of Corpus 1955–60; as Dean of College had jurisdiction over the author; later Master of Pembroke College and Vice-Chancellor.

22.5 George Burgess Coffee-Pot (*illustrated on p. 272*)

1964 (London *i*). Originally 10.5 in. by 5.3 by 9.25 high. 33.8 oz = 1.05 kg.

Cylinder, narrowed to a neck, with black plastic handle and long single-curved spout. Original lid was of black plastic with silver rim, attached by disproportionately small hinge, no knob. No decoration apart from a hammer-marked finish. College arms. The shape closely resembles an invention of the Swedish silversmith Sigurd Persson, 1958 (Blair pp. 210f.).

Inscription: *In Memoriam G.F.A. Burgess Nat. A.C. MCMII, OB. A.C. MCMLXIII Alumni Vestrum Semper Memoris Memores Este* [In memory of G.F.A. Burgess, born in the Year of Christ 1902, DIED in the Year of

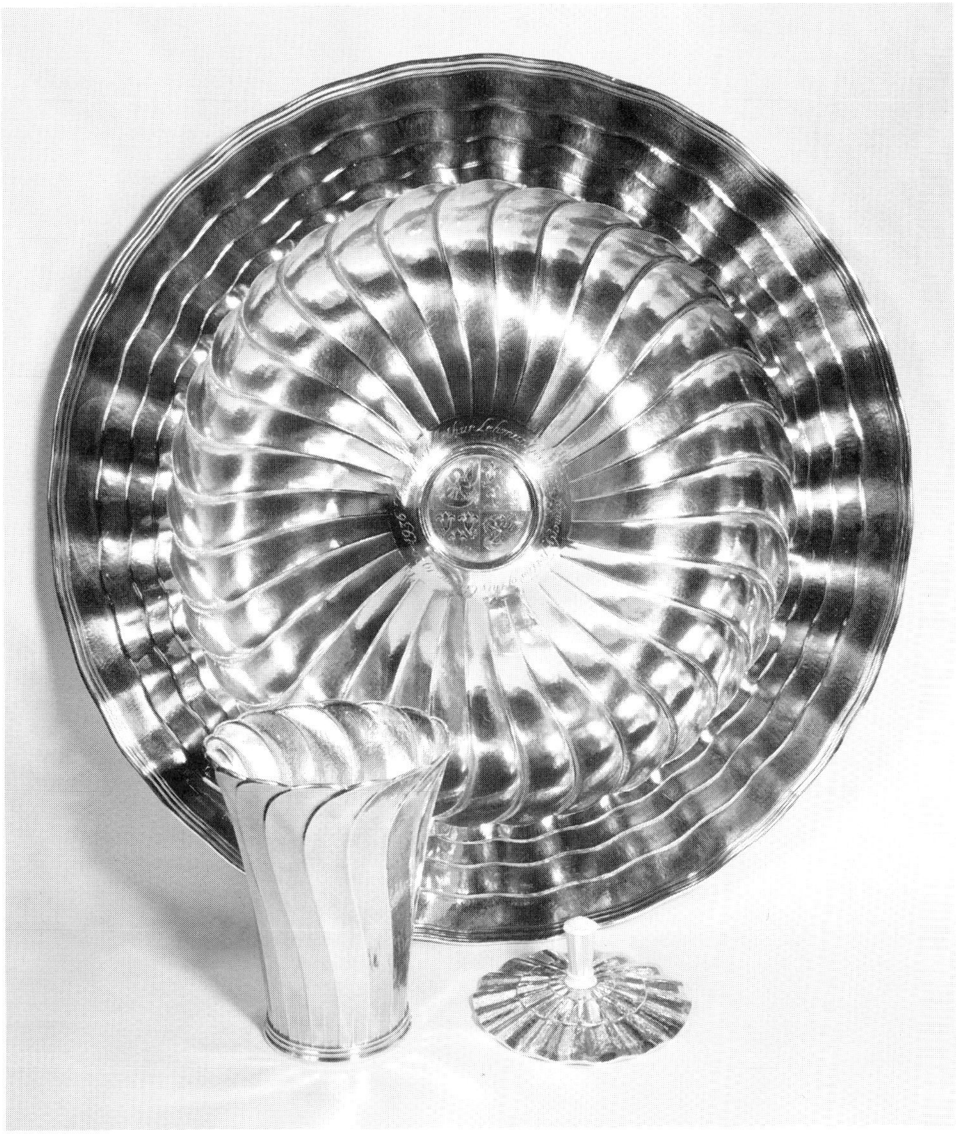

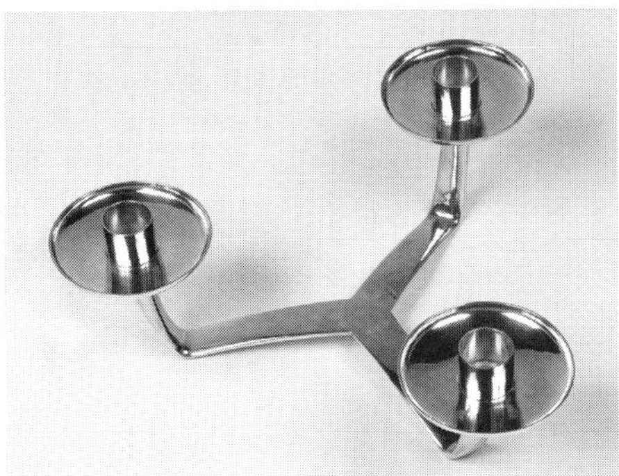

Christ 1963. Be mindful of your old member, who was always mindful of you.]

Maker's mark: RAB in barrel-shaped punch, for Andrew Bray.

The lid gave continual trouble owing to the weak hinge and insecure join between the silver and plastic parts. In 1996 it was replaced by a silver lid with octagonal stepped knob.

George Frederick Arthur Burgess (1902–63) came as undergraduate in 1921; actor and president of the Amateur Dramatic Company; later Chairman

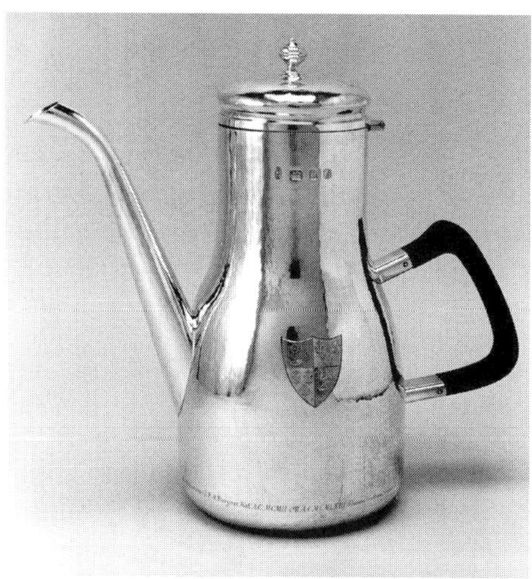

of the International Tin Research & Development Council.

22.6 Thomson Rosewater Bowl (*Plate 7*)

> Light behaves like waves on Mondays, Wednesdays, and Fridays, like particles on Tuesdays, Thursdays, and Saturdays, and like nothing at all on Sundays.
>
> *Attributed to Niels Bohr, atomic physicist*

1977 (Sheffield *c*). 14.0 in. × 6.4 high. No ewer.

Shallow bowl with flat flange and thickened rim. Middle of bowl rises into a column interrupted by a green and gilded disk. Above the disk the column continues with 6 wavy ribs, having a row of 7 balls on each rib. A second smaller gilt disk, patterned with concentric circles in green and gold, intersects the ribs. Edge of rim is ornamented with a pattern of waves and roundels. Column is held together by a bolt which ends beneath the bowl in a silver-gilt nut shaped like a double rose.

Inscription: GEORGE PAGET THOMSON, MASTER 1952–1962 DISCOVERER OF ELECTRON DIFFRACTION. On underside: *Commissioned by C.C.C. using a bequest from G.P.T.*

Maker: Hector Miller.

Commissioned from a specific legacy by Sir George Paget Thomson (1892–1975), mathematician, physicist, ship-modeller; son of Sir J.J. Thomson (Nobel Prize physicist and Master of Trinity); graduated from Trinity College in 1913; Fellow of Corpus Christi 1914–28; fought in World War I and did æronautical research; Professor at Aberdeen and Imperial College; Nobel Prize for physics 1937; Honorary Fellow of Corpus 1942–; Master of Corpus 1952–62; a chief originator of Leckhampton. The writer remembers his hospitality to undergraduates and his awe-inspiring brilliance when discussing science or philosophy. The College has his magnificent portrait by Edmund Nelson.

Thomson's Nobel Prize was awarded for his discovery of electron diffraction, which established that electrons, like light, had a dual nature as waves and particles. This piece symbolizes one of his classic experiments. In a cathode-ray tube he produced a beam of electrons, which passed through a very thin foil of gold. The crystal lattices in the gold acted as a diffraction grating, generating a diffraction pattern. (Ordinary light forms such patterns when it meets a diffraction grating of tiny parallel ridges, the kind that adorns ten-pound notes or the wing-cases of beetles.) The modified electron beam met a screen coated with willemite (zinc orthophosphate), a mineral which glows green where radiation strikes it. The pattern could there be viewed, as on a television screen, as a series of concentric rings.[1]

The central column represents a downward beam of electrons, shown in their particle aspect as spheres, impinging on a silver-gilt disk symbolizing the gold foil. Below the gilt disk the electrons, now shown in their wave aspect, go on to form a diffraction pattern of concentric green and gold rings on a plate representing the willemite screen. The irregular spacing of the rings is taken from one of Thomson's experimental photographs. The flange is decorated with waves and particles.

Thomson gave also the following, and the Thomson Marrow-Scoops (p. 227).

22.7 Small Thomson Bowl (Tazza)

1979 (London E). 7.65 in. × 5.15 high.

Shallow bowl with everted rim. Trumpet stem with cubical gilt knop. Bowl heavily gilt, minutely hammer-dented all over. Ungilt silver pelican on knop; a drop of blood, falling from its breast, is represented by a red stone set in silver.

1 GP Thomson 1927 'Experiments on the diffraction of cathode rays' *Proceedings of the Royal Society* **A 117** 600–9.
GP Thomson 1929 'Diffraction of cathode rays III.' *Ibid.* **A 125** 352–70, Plate 6A.
GP Thomson 1968 'The early history of electron diffraction' *Contemporary Physics* **9** 1–15.
I am indebted to Professor Haroon Ahmed (who briefed the designer) and Dr Tom Faber for help in tracing the source of the symbolism.

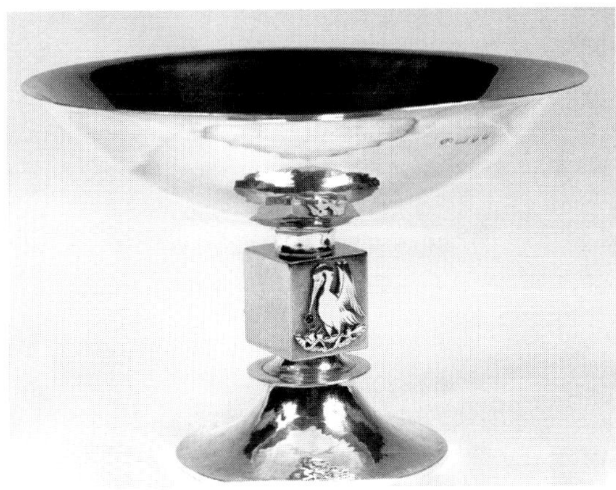

Inscription: *COMMISSIONED BY C.C.C.*

Maker's mark: SJ in ellipse.

Commissioned from the remainder of Sir George Thomson's bequest.

22.8 Couve de Murville Biscuit-Box

1983 (Birmingham *J*). 7.2 in. × 6.5 × 9.2 high. Silver body gilt inside, hinged silver lid with gilt finial, hardwood base.

Cylindrical body with flat rim, attached by bolt with silver nut. Skirt enclosing wooden base pierced with figurines of 12 cocks rampant. Flat lid with broad oval rim, one end with roughened finish to serve as handle. Finial in likeness of a cock statant on a 3-stepped pedestal, thinly gilded; secured by round hatched gilt nut inside lid.

Arms: See of Birmingham: *Per pale argent and purpure, a pallium proper with four crosses patée, in chief a cross potent [cross of St Chad] of the colours of the field counterchanged.* Impaling Couve de Murville: *argent three cocks hoppant purpure in a bordure engrailed of the second.* The arms overlie a patriarchal cross, under an Archbishop's hat of ten tassels a side. Motto: ALES DIEI NVNTIVS [Winged Herald of Day].

Inscription: *Mauritius Couve de Murville Archiepiscopus Birminghamiensis Mensae Hospitalis Comitatisque Haud Immemor DDD MCMLXXXIII* (Maurice Couve de Murville, Archbishop of Birmingham, not unmindful of [this] hospitable table and fellowship, gave this in 1983).

Maker's mark: A.E.J in ellipse.

Maurice Léon Couve de Murville was a High Table Member of Corpus when he was Roman Catholic Chaplain to the University (1977–82). He was Archbishop

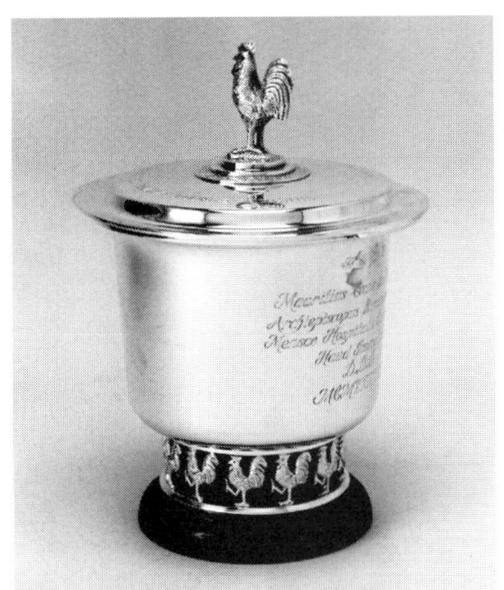

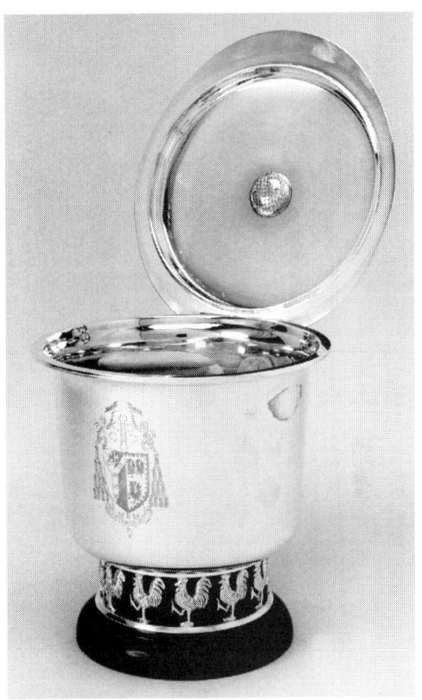

of Birmingham 1982–2000. This cheerful piece embodies the stately heraldry of a Roman Catholic prelate, alluding to the Archbishop's pallium and twenty-tasselled hat, and to the Gallic cock as totem of a distinguished family which includes a French Prime Minister. It is a container for Bath Oliver biscuits (p. 249).

22.9 Wilson Rosewater Bowl

1992 (London *S*). 19.1 in. diameter, 6.1 high. No ewer.

Deep bowl rising to boss in middle; broad, convex flange, thickened rim. On the boss is a pelican in

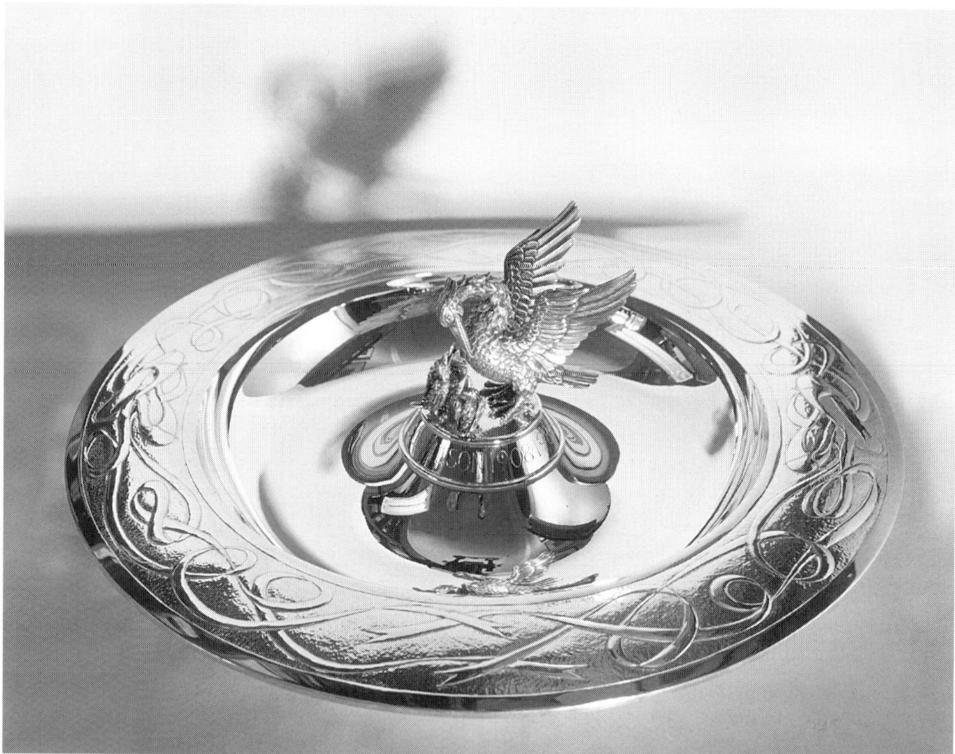

his piety, attached by a round nut with central rib. Flange embossed with two pairs of ballet shoes, whose interlaced ribbons form a pattern round the flange; hammered ground. The pelican (with three chicks) has a large bill, rather like an ornithological pelican; it is in a less reflective metal than the bowl, the crevices being filled with niello (black silver sulphide).

Inscription: d.d. G.B.L. WILSON 1908 · 1984 C. C. C. C. 1927 . 1930

Maker: Alex Brogden of Sheffield.

George Bulkeley Laird 'G.B.' Wilson (1908–84) was an undergraduate from 1927. He built up the Engineering collection in the Science Museum. He was a patron, photographer, and historian of ballet.

This splendid piece is the College's only example of the Post-Modernist style.

22.10 Four Whitbread Jugs

1998 and 2000 (London *y* and a). 8.3 in. handle to spout, 4.0 across mouth, 9.5 high.

Bulbous shape, everted rim and foot, baluster-like spout, double-curved handle with mouse climbing up. Thickened rim, ribs round base of spout, 2 bands of reeding round foot, card-cut cartouches round attachments of handle. Hammer-marked finish. Engraved with College arms.

Maker's mark: C OF H in rectangle.

Given by Mr Michael Whitbread in memory of his father, Colonel Billy Whitbread, undergraduate 1919–.

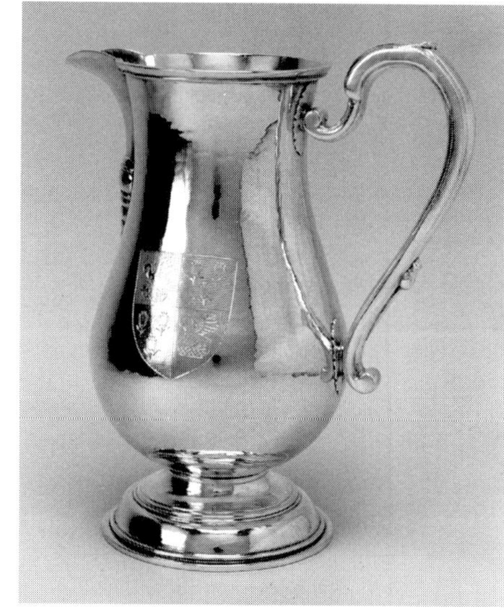

Appendix 1

Early Inventories of Plate

Oliver Rackham and Catherine Hall

Botener–Northwode Inventory, 1376–*c*.1390

This earliest inventory is in a little notebook, in poor condition. It survives because the blank pages and blank spaces within pages were later used by frugal Bursars for drafting College accounts. It consists of three quires of a distinctive ribbed paper, bound up with later quires of draft accounts on slightly larger later-medieval paper, to form a book now called the *Registrum Accounts.*

The original Inventory, as its author explains, was written by John Botener, Fellow, in 1376; it lists various categories of possessions, with long blank spaces left for further entries. It begins with a catalogue of the 64 books in the College library. It next cites 'the vestments and textiles belonging to the use of [St Bene't's] church which are the college's and not the parishioners', a long list which includes secular furnishings. Then there comes an extensive hoard of plate, in which sacred and profane are likewise mixed up.

Botener probably left the list unfinished. It was amended and completed by John Northwode, another Fellow, adding further items at the end and in the blanks (p. 47). There was still a good deal of blank paper, on which accounts were drafted, some in front of the beginning of the book dated 1385, others in different, somewhat later, hands overflowing from the later part of the book.

We are grateful for the help of Fred Ratcliffe and Christopher de Hamel, Parker Librarians, and of Mrs Gill Cannell, Library Assistant. The Botener-Northwode text was published by MR James 'The earliest inventory of Corpus Christi College' *PCAS* 62–3 (1912) 88–115.

Entries of plate

The translation of the text appears in column 2. This type-face represents Botener's hand, and this Northwode's. We have added reference numbers in column 1.

No.	Translation of text	Comments
	[f. 25]	
A1	Item one pyx of cop[per], gilt inside, and enamel, with a top on which four evangelists are depicted all round.	Survived until *c*.1545
	[f. 28]	
	The precious relics and jewels, that is, cups, chalices, bowls, spoons, and such-like.	
A2	First, two cruets of silver with silver tops, but one top is gilt, the other not.	For cruets see pp. 120, 187. Not heard of again
A3	2°. Three long knives in one sheath, of which the handles are of *digum* [unintelligible] for the table. [*Crossed out*]	Not heard of again
A4	3°. six spoons of silver . . . and on the end is a maiden's head with a hair-net veil (*crinile scleyre*) carved and gilt round each head. [*Crossed out*]	See p. 84. Not heard of again
A5	4°. one shallow bowl (*peluis plana*) and a shallow wash-basin, and the bowl is as big in circumference as a bushel (*modius*). [*Crossed out*]	See p. 73. Not heard of again
A6	Item one bowl in circumference on a pedestal with a convex wash-basin (lauacro gibboso). [*Crossed out*]	See p. 73. Not heard of again

(*cont.*)

Entries of Plate (cont.)

No.	Translation of text	Comments
A7	5°. one tabernacle of silver gilt in which the body of christ is used to be carried about on solemn days, and expecially on the day of corpus christi, and the value of it is twenty pounds of lawful money.	The Monstrance (p. 95). Survived until *c.*1535
A8	6°. one cup (*cowpa*) made of a vulture's egg, with a case of boiled leather (*clausura de guerbulie*, 'cuir-bouilli'), and this cup is called in English gripyshey, and it is with foot and lid silver-gilt with one silver-gilt ball in the middle of the foot. Given by h tangmer as in his last will.	Part underlined is in the hand of Peter Nobys, Master 1516–23. See pp. 91f. Survived until late 16th cent.
A9	7°. another cup similar to the first cup made of a vulture's egg in English grypishey, with silver foot and silver-gilt lid, and it does not have a case of boiled leather.	See pp. 91f. Survived until 1526
A10	8°. one shield[1] of silver and azure for the master, and twelve shields of lesser size of very similar construction for the fellows, and they are of the same metal; and seven more shields of the same metal and azure for the lesser clerics, and on each shield are depicted the weapons of the Passion of Christ, and at the end the arms of good henry duke of lancaster our founder who gave these shields and very many other goods, to whose soul God be favourable, Amen.	See p. 19. Survived until *c.*1535
A11	9°. one reli[quary] enclosed in silver-gilt and carved on the one side with an image of the cross of christ and on the other side with an image of st mary and there are contained about six holy relics but it is not known of whom.	Not heard of again
A12	10°. one great *birle*, spherical, round, and solid, and the size of it is like the size of a clenched hand, and it is white in colour in the manner of [rock-]crystal, and on its top there hangs a tongue of silver in a socket.	The mysterious 'Beryl'; lost *c.*1535
A13	*[f. 28v.]* 11°. one chalice [described] . . . assigned by Mr Thomas de eltisle senior to the use of the church of st benedict at the high altar and the paten was made at the expense of mr John Raysoun rector of the said church . . .	Eltisley, first Master, 1352–76. Raysoun was a Fellow as well as Rector
A14	12°. one cup [described] . . . given by lady alice de chaumberleyn . . . to carry the body of christ to the infirm parishioners of the church of st bened. . . .	Benefactress of the College
A15	13°. one *perapsis* of silver (~~in english a spiceplate~~) with a silver foot, ~~given to st benedict's church~~ by the said lady alice ~~for the offerings at the high altar of the said church~~, and in the middle of the *perapsis* is a boss of azure. [*Crossed out*]	A proto-salver (p. 169). Not heard of again (unless it is the same as A25)
A16	14°. one chalice and paten [described]	
A17	15°. one chalice and paten [described]	
A18	16°. one chalice and paten [described]	
A19	17°. one chalice and paten [described]	
A20	18°. one chalice and paten [described]	
	[f. 29] *The jewels pertaining to the use of the mas[ter] and fellows within the College.*	
A21	First, one great black cup, *in English Nut*, with a long foot of silver-gilt and a gilt lid.	Words *anglice Note* added in same hand. The present Coconut
A22	One great horn, in English *bugel*, with silver-gilt feet, and a silver-gilt head of an emperor on the tail, with a silver lid at the top of which are four gilt acorns.	Words *anglice bugel* added in same hand. The Horn

[1] The Latin *scutum* means a flat object, here some kind of badge carried by senior members of the Gild or College in the Corpus Christi procession.

Entries of Plate (cont.)

No.	Translation of text	Comments
A23	Item one silver piece in whose bottom is written this name *Jesus* and this name *Rich[ard] Wynkele* in golden letters, with a lid on whose top is an acorn with gilded oak-leaves.	Not heard of again. Wynkele is unknown
A24	Item one cup of ancient use with a long stem and broad foot of silver, and in the bottom of its bowl is a shield with three bears' heads with a lid with an identical shield in the middle.	Lost *c*.1535
A25	Item one silver *parapsis*, in english spiseplate, indented on the circumference, in the middle of which is a certain upright silver-gilt part, in which is a gilt lion with an indented foot.	Another prototype salver
A26	Item six silver spoons, of good weight, with heads of wom[en] gilt on their faces, which Mr Robert de Eltisle had made.	See p. 84
	[long blank space]	
A27	Item 1 maser with a narrow silver-gilt band on the circumference, and at the bottom an oblong silver-gilt plate engraved with an image of the mother of god with two angels with censers.	Added in blank space. See p. 61
A28	Item 4 great black masers, formerly left by brethren [of the Gilds], of which three are better and multiple-bound with plates of silver-gilt, but the fourth mazer is very decrepit.	Ditto
A29	Item one maser with lid, well harnessed with broad silver bands on the circumference and foot of the cup and on the top of the lid, of silver well gilt, and in the middle of the cup is a column of silver-gilt, on which sits a gilt swan, and it is made by experimental art, and this maser was of Mr Jo[hn] Northwode.	Swan Mazer. For fate of lid see p. 59
A30	Item one little maser with a lid of maser with a silver-gilt foot and with one silver-gilt knob on the lid, and a [picture of the] annunciation inside the lid . . . and this Mr Thomas Elteslee left . . .	Master 1352–76
	[one short line erased]	
A31	Item one maser with a broad silver-gilt band on the circumference, which . . . brought.	
A32	Item one lesser maser with a silver-gilt band which Mr Ric[hard] Bilingforth brought.	Master 1398–1432
A33	Item one lesser maser, very like the preceding, which Mr Jo[hn] Deueros brought.	
A34	Item one black maser with a silver band, . . . than either of the preceding, which Mr peter ffornham brought.	
A35	Item one black maser, smaller than the preceding, on the bottom of which, on a silver-gilt plate, is engraved the annunciation of the b[lessed] virgin, and Mr Thomas Trenche brought it.	

Date of the Inventory

Botener's part seems all to be of 1376 or very soon after. For some reason he did not finish the Inventory. Northwode completed it, and added other items as the College acquired them. The Horn, Coconut, and Swan Mazer were among the pieces inventoried early in Northwode's time, probably *c*.1380.

Northwode's additions are undated, except that one of his textile entries, inserted into a gap, he dates 1385. In another place he mentions John Kynne, Master of the College *c*.1377–*c*.1389.[2] Northwode himself wrote the accounts for 1388 and gives his own name among the Fellows, but is not listed in 1401.[3] Among donors, Billingford became Master in 1398 but may have been a Fellow for an unknown period previously. Trenche, Fornham and Deveros were said by Masters to have become Fellows in 1400, but he seems to have had no evidence for this other than their undated mentions in this document.

Two other lines of argument might be used to date Northwode's additions. In 1381 the College was sacked and plate stolen. In the list the sack is not mentioned,

2 f. 25v, 17v.

3 CC(A): *Registrum Accounts* f.48v. (8 Richard II), 109v., 115v.

and only four items of plate and a few other things are crossed out; so unless the whole list dates from before the sack the losses were exaggerated. (Most of the College archives, also, from before this incident still survive.) Alternatively, the attack could have stimulated Northwode to complete the inventory. Another factor is that after Thomas de Eltisle's death in 1376 his nephew Robert claimed and removed some of his uncle's plate.

Then there is the secondary use of the book for accounts. The order of the accounts is utterly confused, but there are two phases of them. The earlier phase, on blank pages preceding the first page of the Inventory, is dated 1385.[4] At this stage the Inventory was still a separate booklet. The later phase of the accounts begins on the later type of paper; the earliest date we can find is St Etheldreda's Day 1388. The earliest surviving date of that part of these accounts written in gaps in the Inventory itself is 1410–11.[5]

Northwode's part of the Inventory therefore dates mainly from the 1380s. He was adding to it at least as late as 1385, but shortly after then it was being treated as scrap paper. It had probably been superseded by 1390.

The *c.*1481 Inventory

This appears in the back of the College account-book, 1469–1510. It deals with pewter and kitchen equipment, such as '1 mostard querne' (a mustard-grinder) and '1 tancard' (probably not silver). The few pieces of plate are these:

	Comments
~~6~~ 5 *maserys* with gilt circles with 1 lid with 1 gilt knob	
~~18~~ 16 Silver spoons	
2 pieces with 1 lid	
. . . . . .	
In the pantry: *In primis* 3 maserys	These items are in English, in a different hand
Item 11 sponys of sylv^{r}	
. . . . . .	
4 salte salers wth ~~2~~ 1 cov'erys	

The date is not given, but the same page has rents received from Landbeach in 1481.

1510 Inventory

This comes in the back of the same account-book, and deals with pewter and kitchen tools as well as silver. Most of the plate was 'in the pantry' for daily use; the 'great plate' is not included.

4 *mccc^{o} lxxxv*, f.2.
5 12 Henry 4, f.12.

No.		Comments
B1	A candell styll of wyte plate	White plate, probably meaning ungilt silver
B2	It[em] sylvr sponys 14	
B3	It[em] a maser of the gift of Mr Tyard	Thomas Tyard, Fellow *c*.1478; this or one of the two others is probably the Mazer without Print
B4	It[em] a maser bowle of Sr J. Swayne exec[utors]	Unknown
B5	It[em] a maser wth a fote gylte [a]bowte of the executors of Mr Brocher	Richard Brocher, Fellow 1452–62. Probably the Cup of the Three Kings
B6	It[em] a cowyr [cover] for the same wth a knoppe of sylwyr and gyldyd	
B7	It[em] a maser of j. 1. Salysbery	Unknown
B8	It[em] 2 stondyng p[i]ec[e]s of sylvr w^t^ a covyr of sylvyr	
B9	It[em] a flatte pece of sylvyr chesyld [chiselled, *i.e.* chased] w^t^ cou[e]r	An early salver?

1513 Inventory

On the preceding page, dated 13 October 1513, is another list of more or less the same part of the plate, made by Thomas Crack, officer of the library.

No.		Comments
C1	First, 2 stondyng pecs of sylur w^t^ a cov^r^ of sylur havyng a crowne	= B8
C2	It[em] 3 salts of sylur wt on cour [cover] & a knopp gylte	
C3	It[em] 2 flat pecs of sylvr y^e^ on[e] hauyng a knopp in y^e^ botym w^t^out [without, i.e. outside] y^e^ odyr [other] hauyng a rose in y^e^ botym w^t^ynne [within]	= B9 (part)
C4	It[em] 14 sponys [spoons] of sylur	= B2
C5	It[em] on[e] stondyng mas^r^ w^t^ y^e^ foot gylt & a covr	= B5 Cup of the Three Kings?
C6,7,8	It[em] 3 masyrys [mazers] on[e] of y^e^ gyftynn [gifting] of mr tyard y^e^ od^r^ [other] bene of y^e^ executrs of p swayne ye od [other] of Thom' salysbery	= B3,4,7 One of these is the Mazer without Print?

1526 Inventory[6]

Hidden in a volume of Parker's private archive one of us (C.H.) found this document. Although the author is anonymous, the date places it in the retirement as Master of Peter Nobys, a deeply pious traditional Catholic who was much concerned to catalogue the College's duties and possessions in anticipation of the impending catclysm which he feared.

Certain words were crossed out and others (here underlined) added while the list was still current. Further additions written by Matthew Parker himself are in this typeface.

6 CC(L): MS 106, pp. 669–71 (red numbers). The document is one sheet of paper, folded and inserted into the book, and numbered in Parker's distinctive red crayon, but not bound in. O.R.'s translation from C.H.'s transcript of the Latin original.

No.		Weight given, ounces	Comments
	[*Annotation at top in Parker's hand*] Nearly all these were alienated and sold in the time of William Sowode, master, with the consent of the fellows, as they assert		
	Inventory made 27 day of the month december of the eighteenth year of the reign of k. Henry the eighth of all the silver utensils belonging to the College . . .		
D1	First, one monstrance (*le monstraunt*) of silver, wholly gilt, weighing	$78\frac{1}{2}$	Pre-1376 (A7) Not heard of again
D2–8	Item, seven pairs of chalices [and patens] . . . which are in the hands of the Master [and six named Fellows]		2 crossed out = A13, 14, 16–20
D9	Item, one stone of byrall weighing	15	Pre-1376 (A12) Not heard of again
D10	Item 13 great *stochynnys*[7] Enamelled weighing with their ribbons	$16\frac{1}{2}$	Pre-1376 (A10) Not heard of again
D11	Item 7 small *stochynnys* Enamelled weighing with their ribbons	$11\frac{1}{2}$	Pre-1376 (A10) Not heard of again
D12	Item the Common Seal of the College weighing	$2\frac{3}{4}$	Presumably pre-1376
D13	Item the seal of the master's office, with silver chains attached, weighing	$5\frac{1}{2}$	Otherwise unknown
D14	Item one salt with matching lid, ~~wholly~~ parcel-gilt and it really has on the outside many gilt pellets ~~the gilt letter F next the touch, of the gift of master Thomas Cosyn~~ and these two weigh	$19\frac{1}{2}$	Survived until after 1670
D15	Item two salts of one pattern, parcel-gilt, weigh	19	= C2
D16	Item ~~13~~ 12 new spoons having on the ends ~~gilt images of christ and the apostles~~ of the gift of ~~doctor Thomas Cosyn~~ and they weigh	21	Not heard of again
D17	Item 12 spoons with the acorns (*ly acornys*) of which one has the Image of Walstan, they weigh	$14\frac{1}{4}$	
D18	Item six other new spoons with the maids' heads (*ly madys hedys*) weighing	7	Not heard of again
D19	Item 12 spoons with the leopards' heads (*ly lebbardys hedys*)		Not heard of again
D20	Item one standing piece, wholly gilt, chased with a lid with knop matching the piece, of the gift of doctor Cosyn and it has t and c in the bottom inside, weighing together	32	Not heard of again
D21	Item one goblet with lid, wholly gilt, with a rose on top, by exchange for a silver piece called the griffin's egg (*ovo de ly grype*) and weighing	$25\frac{1}{2}$	Griffin's egg was pre-1376 (A9)
D22	Item one gilt piece with foot and lid, pounced, with a rose in the bottom and on the lid a leopard's head	$23\frac{1}{2}$	Not heard of again
D23	Item one piece with a foot, parcel-gilt, called the Bell, with a lid having *le garlonde* with flowers	$23\frac{1}{2}$	Not heard of again
D24	Item one standing piece, pounced, parcel-gilt, with lid having *le rownde knoppe*	17	
D25	Item one piece called the griffin's Egg (*le grypys Egg*') with foot and lid parcel-gilt, weighing	21	Pre-1376 (A8)
D26	Item *ly Blacke Notte* with foot and lid gilt outside	12	Pre-1376 (A21); the present Coconut
D27	Item one flat piece, whole-gilt, with lid, with a rose on one convex side and lilies on the other side, weighing	29	Not heard of again
D28	Item one small flat piece, whole-gilt, with a starlike rose in the bottom and with pounced whole-gilt lid, with a knop, weighing	$9\frac{1}{4}$	Not heard of again
D29	Item one silver piece, *powncyd*, having a gilt star with three falcon heads (*ly fawken hedis*) in the bottom	11	

No.		Weight given, ounces	Comments
D30	Item two pieces of one pattern, with gilt stars in the bottoms, of which one weighs $13\frac{1}{2}$ oz and the other weighs $13\frac{7}{8}$ oz . . .	$28\frac{3}{8}$ [*sic*]	Not heard of again
D31	Item Cup with lid called the [Coco]nut (*ly Notte*) Value 3*s*. 4*d*. per ounce and weighs in all	30	Not heard of again
D32	Item one small standing mazer (*mirra*) wholly gilt, on a foot, pounced with the Names of the kings of Cologne and with a lid	13	= B5 Cup of the Three Kings
D33	Item one mazer with a very similar lid called *ly swane*	$13\frac{1}{2}$	= A27 Swan Mazer
D34	Item one mazer with *ly Jhesus* in the bottom	$6\frac{1}{2}$	
D35	Item one small mazer with no symbol	$3\frac{1}{2}$	Not heard of again
D36	Item ~~four~~ three mazers of one pattern with bars (*ly barrys*), ~~of which one has a foot wholly gilt~~, weighing together	$32\frac{3}{4}$	
D37	three other older mazers, of which two are of the same pattern: and the third nearly twice as big		Not heard of again
	[*one or more lines have been cut off the bottom of the page*]		
D38	Item one great drinking-horn of bugle with Gilt attachments [*in margin*]		= A22 The Horn
	[*Additions by Parker on back*]		
D39	Item one salt, parcel-gilt, with lid with drops		
D40	Item two small salts of the same pattern		Not heard of again
D41	Item 12 new spoons with maidenh[ead]s	$16\frac{1}{4}$	
	Item [erased]	. . . $\frac{1}{4}$	
D42	Item one new mazer having a rose with bars		
D43	Item another mazer having the name Jesus		
D44	Item another mazer with a rose in the bottom		Rose Mazer
D45	Item another small mazer with a rose in the bottom		
D46	Item another standing mazer with a foot, having Warton in the bottom		

Inventory of *c.*1545[8]

On a loose sheet of paper. It was probably written early in Parker's mastership, after much of the pre-Reformation treasure had gone. The weights are added. Other additions are in this type-face; they refer to Andrew Peerson and Edmund Edwards, who became Fellows in 1542 and 1547.

No.	Weight given, ounces		Comments
E1	$28\frac{1}{2}$	Item a chalice with a patent [paten] parcel gilt	Not heard of again
E2		Item an other with a patent parcel gilt sold to buyld a doufhows [dovehouse]	Not heard of again
E3	$10\frac{1}{2}$	Item an other parcel gilt in ~~Mr persons kepyng~~ in the chu[r]che	Not heard of again
E4	7	Item ~~an other~~	Not heard of again
E5		Item ~~a monstrant~~ [monstrance] ~~in copper gilt~~	Not heard of again
		Item	
		Item	

(*cont.*)

8 CC(A): Misc. Documents no. 25.

(cont.)

No.	Weight given, ounces			Comments
E6	$12\frac{1}{2}$	Item a salt with y^{e} cover parcel gilt		
E7	13	Item a salt with out cover, Item an other salt without cover,		
		parcel gilt	buttry	
E8	$16\frac{3}{4}$	Item 12 sponis [spoons] of silver with gilt knoppes		
		In the hands of the master		
E9	$1\frac{5}{8}$	Item a great spone for y^{e} M[aste]r	In buttry	Not heard of again
E10	12	Item 12 sponis with acornes gylt	In buttry	Not heard of again
		Item		
E11	$25\frac{1}{2}$	Item a cup standyng with y^{e} cover holl [whole] gylt		
		~~in the M[aste]rs keying~~	In Mr Edwards kepyng	
E12		Item a goblet with y^{e} cover holl [whole] gylt.	In Mr ~~persons~~ kepyng	
E13	11	Item a pece of sylver without cover	buttry	
		Item		
E14	21	Item a cup set & stondyng in silver with y^{e} cover		
		ye cover cup in Mr Edwards keping		
E15	12	Item a nut set in silver with a cover gilt		The Coconut
E16		Item a olde broken maser		Not heard of again
E17	13	Item one maser stondyng in silver with a cover		Cup of the Three Kings
E18	$13\frac{1}{2}$	Item one maser Called the Swanne	in the M[aste]rs keping	Swan Mazer
		Item an other maser beyng y^{e} cover therfor		
E19	$41\frac{1}{2}$ [for 7 mazers]	Item one newe maser: with barris gilt		Not heard of again
		in the M[aste]rs keping		
E20		Item one other maser newe with barris gilt		Not heard of again
E21		Item one other maser with Jesus in y^{e} botom		Not heard of again
E22		Item one other maser with a rose in y^{e} botom		Rose Mazer
E23		Item one other maser with a flower in ye botom	the buttry	Not heard of again
E24		Item one great maser		Mazer Without Print?
E25		Item a very little maser	in the M[aste]rs keping	Not heard of again
		Item		
E26		Item a great bugle set in silver gilt		The Horn

Inventory of 1573/4[9]

The earliest inventory to record Parker's gifts, omitting those in which Parker (still alive) had a life interest (p. 70). Additions in another hand.

9 CC(A): Misc. Documents no. 34.

No.		Weight given, ounces	Comments
	Inventorie made & taken the 13 of Ffebruary An° 1573 . . . of all such moveable goods as be in the Treasurie hutche of Corpus Chri Colledge in Camebridge . . .		
F1	**Inprimis** a greate standing cup of silver, wth a Cover of the same gilt . . . of the gyft of Matthew Archbyshop of Cant'b	53	Parker Cup
F2	Itm a bugle tipped wth silver wth two feete of the same gilt		The Horn
F3	Itm one swan mazer, tipt wth silver & dubble gilt		Swan Mazer
F4,5,6	Itm 3 other mazers, tipt wth silver & dubble gilt one given to ye L keper		Lord Keeper, Nicholas Bacon (p. 59)
F7	Itm a pot wth a Cover of silv^{r} parcell gilt a mayden hed on ye top . . .		
F8	Itm a salt wth a Cover of silv^{r} dubble gilt . . .		Parker Salt
F9	Itm the blacke nutt wth a foote, barrs & cov^{r} of silv^{r} gilt		Coconut
F10	Itm the gripes egge, wtha Cover of silv^{r} parcell gilt		Tangmere Gripes-eye (A10)
F11	Itm a standinge mazer wth a foote of silv^{r} gilt & a Cover of woode painted painted wth a knob of silvr and gilt		Cup of the Three Kings
F12	Itm a standinge cup wth a cov^{r} silv^{r} & dubble gilt . . . wth an olde groat in the top of thinward side of the Covr	23	groat = small silver coin
F13	Itm a dossen [dozen] of spones mayden heds, knobs gilt in y^{e} Buttry		
F14	Itm two pownced potts wth on[e] cov^{r} of silv^{r} parcell gilt, of the gifte of Matthewe Archbish of Canterburie, wth his Armes on the botom eche pot & on the top of the Cov^{r}		Two Cups and One Lid
F15	Itm a Can wth a cover of silv^{r} dubble gilt & pounced, of the gifte of my L. Archbisshope of Canterburie, wth his Armes on the botom	$16\frac{1}{2}$	Parker Tankard
F16	Itm a gobblet wth a cover silv^{r} dubble gilt, wth a rose in y^{e} Cov^{r}	30	
F17	Itm a standing pece wth a covr silv^{r} dubble gilt wth LM	$31\frac{3}{4}$	LM was probably a donor's or maker's monogram
F18	Itm a standing pece wth a covr silv^{r} dubble gilt wth a rose in y^{e} top	31	Probably the cup given by John Aldrich, which the College covenanted never to alienate; not heard of again
F19	Itm 3 potts silv^{r} & gilt mr grenewood for 2, ye other mr dawson hath		Rodolphus Dawson, Fellow 1586–97
F20	Itm a pot wth a cov^{r} silv^{r} & gilt comonlie called the m[aste]rs pott		
F21	Itm a salt wth a cov^{r} silv^{r} & parcell gilt buttry		
F22	Itm a goblet wth a cov^{r} J A silv^{r} & dubble gilt		initials unidentified
F23	Itm a goblet wth a cov^{r} silv^{r} and dubble gilt	35	
F24	Itm a salt wth a cov^{r} silv^{r} parcell gilt but[tery]		
F25	Itm a salt wthout a cov^{r} silv^{r} parcell gilt but[tery]		
F26	Itm a silv^{r} pot parcell gilt but[tery]		
F27	Itm 6 spones silvr wth sharpe knobbs at thende [the end] buttery		
F28	Itm 6 spones silvr wth square knobbs gilt buttery		
F29	Itm 6 spones on[e] of them wth an apostle at ye ende gilt, ye rest round knobbs gilt		St Paul Spoon?
F30	Itm an olde silv^{r} goblet in Cheste		
F31	Itm an ould silv^{r} pot wth a cov^{r}		

Summary of Early Inventories

The symbol → means that the article was already there before the currency of the inventory. X means that the inventory records its disposal.

	1376–	1510	1513	1526	*c.*1545	1574	Later
Chalices & Patens							
Agnus Dei	→ A15			→ D2–X			
Hand	→ A16			→ D3–X			
Veronica	→ A17			→ D4	→ E1–X		
Star & Moon	→ A18			→ D5	→ E2–X		
Agnus Dei	→ A19			→ D6	→ E3		
Eltisley	A13			→ D7	→ E4–X		
Chamberleyn	A14			→ D8			
Ecclesiastical							
Pyx	→ A1				→ E5–X		
Cruets	→ A2						
Monstrance	→ A7			→ D1			
Reliquary	→ A11						
Birle	→ A12			→ D9			
Chamberleyn spiceplate	A15–X						
20 shields	A10			→ D10			
				→ D11			
Bowls							
Bowl & basin	→ A5–X						
Bowl	→ A6–X						
Rose & Lilies				→ D27			
Chargers							
Lion spiceplate	→ A25						
Flat with lid		→ B9	→ C3				
Rose			C3	→ D28?			
Drinking Vessels							
Gripes-eye	→ A9			→ D21–X			
Coconut	→ A21			→ D26	→ E15	→ F9	extant
Bugle	→ A22			→ D38	→ E26	→ F2	extant
Wynkele cup	→ A23						cover still there 1591?
3 Bears cup	→ A24	→ B8?	→ C1?				
Tangmere Gripes-eye + case	A10			→ D25	→ E14?	→ F10	replaced by Fletcher
Crown cup		→ B8	→ C1				
Cosyn cup				→ D20			
Leopard cup				→ D22			
Bell cup				→ D23			
Round knop cup				→ D24	→ E12?	→ F30?	
Falconheads cup				→ D29	→ E13?	→ F31?	
Gilt stars pair				→ D30			
Great coconut				→ D31			
Rose goblet				D21	→ E11	→ F16	
Maidenhead						→ F7	
Groat						→ F12	
Undescribed						→ F26	
LM + lid						→ F17	

(*cont.*)

	1376–	1510	1513	1526	c.1545	1574	Later
Second Rose						→ F18	
Three						→ F19	
Master's						→ F20	
JA goblet						→ F22	
35-oz						→ F23	
Great Parker						F1	extant
Parker 2 + lid						F14	extant
Parker tankard						F15	extant
Salts							
3 with gilt knobs			C2				
Cosyn				→ D14	→ E6?	→ F8	survived until after 1670?
2 parcel-gilt				→ D15	→ E7	→ F21	lost in 1590s?
						→ F25?	
Lid with drops				D39		→ F24	
2 small		[c.1481]		→ D40			
Mazers							
Gild black 1	→ A28						
Gild black 2	→ A28						
Gild black 3	→ A28						
Gild black 4	→ A28						
Virgin & Angels	→ A29						
Swan (Northwode)	A27			→ D33	→ E17	→ F3	extant
lid	A27			→ D33	→ E18	→ F4–X	
Annunciation (Eltisle)	A30						
Anon.	A31			→ D35?			
Billingford	A32			→ D37?			
Deveros	A33			→ D37?			
Fornham	A34			→ D37?			
Annunciation (Trenche)	A35			→ D36?–X			
Brocher		→ B5	→ C5	→ D32	→ E17	→ F11	Three Kings
lid		→ B5	→ C5	→ D32	→ E17	→ F11	
Tyard		→ B3	→ C6	→ D36	→ E24?	→ F6	Without Print?
Swayne		→ B4	→ C7	→ D36			
Salisbury		→ B6	→ C8	→ D36			
Jesus				→ D34	→ E21?		
Rose with bars				D41	→ E19?		
Jesus				D42	→ E25?		
Rose				D43	→ E22	→ F5	Rose Mazer
Small rose				D44	→ E23?		
Warton				D45	→ E20?		
Spoons &c							
3 knives	→ A3–X						
6 Veiled Maiden	→ A4–X						
6 Gilt Woman (Eltisle)	A26						
14		→ B2	→ C4				
12 acorn				→ D17	→ E10		
12 leopardshead				→ D19			
13 Cosyn apostle				→ D16–X			

(*cont.*)

(cont.)

	1376–	1510	1513	1526	*c*.1545	1574	Later
12 apostle				D16		→ F29 (1)	
6 maidenhead				→ D18			
12 maidenhead				D40	→ E8	→ F13	
1 large					→ E9		
6 sharp knobs						→ F27	
6 square knobs						→ F28	

Appendix 2

Analyses of Corpus Plate

By the Victoria & Albert Museum, 1975. Percentage composition

	Date	Silver	Copper	Lead	Gold	Bismuth	Iron	Antimony	Nickel	Laboratory no.
Swan Mazer	*c.*1380	88.50	10.20	0.63	0.37	—	0.20	0.05	0.05	106/80
Cup of Three Kings	*c.*1460	90.90	8.15	0.45	0.30	—	0.16	0.01	0.03	58/80
Lid of Parker 2-handled cup	1532	92.68	6.39	0.57	0.19	0.07	0.07	0.02	0.01	107/80
Parker 2-handled cup	1556	94.20	5.12	0.31	0.26	0.03	0.06	0.01	0.01	97/80
Parker Salt	1563	94.45	4.72	0.57	0.16	0.02	0.03	0.04	0.01	105/80
Great Parker Cup	1569	92.49	5.78	0.72	0.86	0.09	0.04	0.01	0.01	85/80
Ostrich Cup (base)	1593	95.06	4.15	0.55	0.08	0.07	0.06	0.02	0.01	86/80
Ostrich Cup (lid)	1593	94.02	5.22	0.47	0.18	0.04	0.05	0.01	0.01	95/80
Harrington Tazza	1607	93.82	5.36	0.65	0.10	0.03	0.02	0.02	—	102/80

Appendix 3

Comparative Table of Early Drinking Vessels and Spoons

	Great horns	Ostrich-eggs	Coconuts	Fine mazers	Fine spoons
Source	East Europe	N.Africa, Palestine, Arabia	India	England	England
Number recorded in England	12	>15	>30	*c*.600	many hundreds
Known number surviving in England	6 (+ 5 excavated)	4	*c*.25	*c*.80	few hundreds?
Range of dates in documents	55 BC–1534 AD	1251–1547	1259–1596	1064–1592	13th to 17th cent.
Range of dates of surviving examples	*c*.1320–*c*.1470 (excavated from *c*.600)	1592–1623	*c*.1340–*c*.1500	*c*.1340–1580	Roman to 17th cent.
Period of greatest popularity	Anglo-Saxon	1350–1450	1430–1490	1300–1530 (esp. 1440–80)	early 16th
Maximum number the College has had	one	2 in *c*.1520	2 in 1526	16 in 1526	54 in 1526
Date of College's surviving examples	*c*.1280	1592	*c*.1340	*c*.1380, *c*.1460, *c*.1460, 1521	1515 (one), 1566 (12)

Appendix 4

Wooden Spoons

From before 1803 until 1909 it was the custom to publish the results of the Mathematics Tripos, the University's premier degree-bearing examination, in order of merit, from the Senior Wrangler[10] at the top of the list down to the Wooden Spoon at the bottom.

The wooden spoon, the trophy of the least successful mathematician, was perhaps the most difficult Cambridge award to achieve; candidates who failed the examination did not get on the list at all. It was lowered from the Senate-House gallery on to the candidate's back as he knelt before the Vice-Chancellor to receive his degree.[11] In the hundred-odd years in which they were awarded, Corpus was much stronger in Wooden Spoons than in Senior Wranglers.[12] They seldom survive and are objects of great rarity.

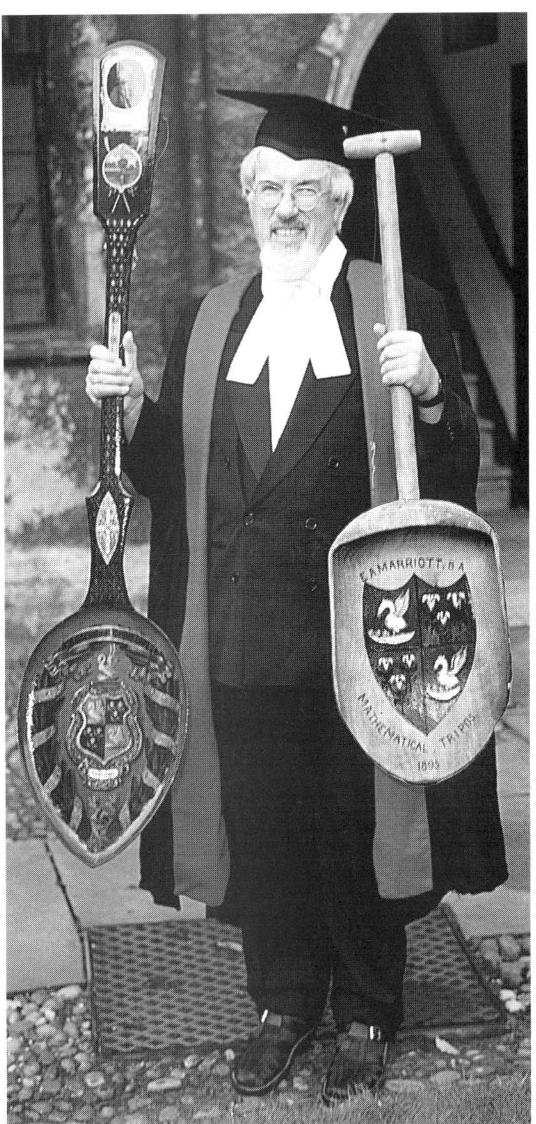

The Marriott and Batterby Wooden Spoons, held by one who is not much of a mathematician.

Marriott Wooden Spoon 1895

?Alder-wood, partly painted.

A rather crude object, probably adapted from a malt-shovel. Inscribed E.A. MARRIOTT B.A. MATHEMATICAL TRIPOS 1895. College arms, otherwise rough, include a good rendering of the lilies.

Edward Augustin Marriott had an ecclesiastical career, being Vicar of St Peter's, Harrow (Middlesex) from 1920 to his death in 1944.

Batterby Wooden Spoon 1907

57 × $12\frac{1}{2}$ in. Wood, painted and parcel-gilt.

10 On one famous occasion, a candidate was placed *above* the Senior Wrangler – women being then not legally members of the University, although they were in practice.

11 For a picture see E Porter 1969 *Cambridgeshire Customs and Folklore* Routledge, London, Plate 47.

12 Information from Dr K. Falconer, authority on wooden spoons (cf §17.3.9).

Fiddle-pattern spoon, bearing the following:

(1) Supposed portrait of 'Henry Duke of Lancaster, Founder of Corpus Christi Coll.', derived from the Ackermann engraving of him.

(2) Vignette of a man rowing a scull, doubtless illustrating the non-mathematical alternative wherein the Wooden Spoon had distinguished himself at Cambridge. (Batterby won the Wilkinson and Heywood Sculls and a Rowlandson Oar, Chapter 20).

(3) University motto *Alma Mater Cantabrigia* [Kind Ma Cambridge].

(4) 'Mathematical Tripos 1907'.

(5) On the bowl of the spoon, the winner's name, T. BATTERBY, with the College arms (and pelican pseudo-crest) surrounded by miniatures of the arms of all the Colleges including Corpus.

On the back are remains of attached ribbons in College colours of strawberry and white.

Label: A.W. CRISP & CO., Carvers, Gilders . . . Heraldic Painters, etc., etc. . . . Opposite Kings's College Chapel.

This, one of the last and most splendid of wooden spoons, is a triumph of signwriting. All the details relating to the individual must have been executed in the ten days (at most) between the publishing of the class-list and the conferring of the degree – and there were three co-equal Wooden Spoons that year!

Thomas Batterby, too, became a clergyman. He was Vicar of St Margaret's, Ipswich, from 1939 onwards; the writer often attended that church and must have sat under him. He was an Honorary Canon of St Edmundsbury from 1947 until his death *c*.1962.

Bibliography

of works often referred to in the text

BM	British Museum
BM	*Burlington Magazine*
CC(A)	Corpus Christi College, Cambridge: Archives
CC(L)	Corpus Christi College, Cambridge: Parker Library
G&C	Gonville & Caius College
LCA	*Letter of the Corpus Association*
SSJ	*The Silver Society Journal*

Age of Chivalry — J Alexander & P Binski (eds) 1987 *The Age of Chivalry: art in Plantagenet England 1200–1400* Royal Academy of Arts, London

Babees Book — FJ Furnivall 1865 *The Babees Book*... Trübner, London

Bennett — D Bennett 1988 *The Silver Collection, Trinity College Dublin* Trinity College Dublin Press

Blair — C Blair (ed) 1987 *The History of Silver* Little Brown, London

Bruce-Mitford — R Bruce-Mitford 1983 *The Sutton Hoo Ship Burial* BM Publications, London

Bury — P Bury 1952 *A History of Corpus Christi College Cambridge from 1822 to 1952* Corpus Christi Coll. Cambridge

Catling — HD Catling 1902 'Plate at the Cambridge Colleges No. II. Corpus Christi College Part II' *The Connoisseur* **4** (Oct. 1902) 86–92

Clifford — H Clifford 1997 'Archbishop Matthew Parker's gifts of plate to Cambridge' *BM* **139** 4–10

Cobban — AB Cobban 1993 'Commoners in medieval Cambridge colleges' Zutshi 47–64

Corpus Silver — C Ellory, H Clifford, F Rogers (eds) *Corpus Silver: patronage and plate at Corpus Christi College, Oxford* Needwood Press, England 1999

Cripps — WJ Cripps 1891 *Old English Plate, Ecclesiastical, Decorative, and Domestic: its makers and marks* 4th edn Murray, London

Culme — J Culme 1987 *The Directory of Gold & Silversmiths, Jewellers & Allied Traders 1813–1914* Antique Collectors' Club, Woodbridge

Forbes — JS Forbes 1999 *Hallmark: a history of the London Assay Office* Unicorn, London

Foster & Atkinson — JE Foster & TD Atkinson 1896 *An Illustrated Catalogue of the Loan Collection of Plate exhibited in the Fitzwilliam Museum May 1895* Deighton Bell, Cambridge

Gay — V Gay 1887, 1928 *Glossaire Archéologique du Moyen Age et de la Renaissance* Picard, Paris

Glanville 1987 — P Glanville 1987 *Silver in England* Unwin Hyman, London

Glanville 1990 — P Glanville 1990 *Silver in Tudor and Early Stuart England* Victoria & Albert Museum, London

Glanville 1996 — P Glanville (ed) 1996 *Silver* Victoria & Albert Museum, London

Goldsmith & Grape — C Blair 1983 *The Goldsmith & the Grape: silver in the service of wine* Goldsmiths' Company, London

Grimwade — AG Grimwade 1990 *London Goldsmiths 1697–1837: their marks and lives* 3rd edn Faber, London

Gunning — JH Gunning 1854 *Reminiscences of the University, Town, and County of Cambridge, from the Year 1780* London

Hall	CP Hall 1993 'The Gild of Corpus Christi and the foundation of Corpus Christi College: an investigation of the documents' Zutshi 65–91
Hayward	M Hayward 1999 'The storage and transport of Oxford silver' *SSJ* **11** 245–51
Hope	WH St John Hope 1887 'On the English medieval drinking bowls called Mazers' *Archaeologia* **50** 129–93
How & How	GEP & JP How 1952 *English and Scottish Silver Spoons, medieval to late Stuart, and pre-Elizabethan hall-marks on English plate* London
Jackson	I Pickford (ed) 1989 *Jackson's Silver and Gold Marks of England, Scotland, and Ireland* 3rd edn Antique Collectors' Club, Woodbridge
Jones *Camb.*	E Alfred Jones 1910 *The Old Plate of the Cambridge Colleges* Cambridge
Jones *Ch. Ch.*	E Alfred Jones 1939 *Catalogue of the Plate of Christ Church Oxford* Oxford
Jones *Magd.*	E Alfred Jones 1940 *Catalogue of the Plate of Magdalen College Oxford* Oxford
Jones *Merton*	E Alfred Jones 1938 *Catalogue of the Plate of Merton College Oxford* Oxford
Jones *Queen's*	E Alfred Jones 1938 *Catalogue of the Plate of The Queen's College Oxford* Oxford
Jones *Oriel*	E Alfred Jones 1944 *Catalogue of the Plate of Oriel College Oxford* Oxford
Jones *Russia*	E Alfred Jones 1909 *The Old English Plate of the Emperor of Russia* WH Smith, London
Josselyn	J Josselin *c.*1565 *Historiola Collegii Corporis Christi* ed JW Clark, Cambridge Antiquarian Soc. Octavo Publications **17** 1880
Kent	TA Kent 1981 *London Silver Spoonmakers 1500 to 1697* The Silver Society, London
Lamb	J Lamb 1831 *Masters' History of the College of Corpus Christi . . . with . . . a continuation to the present time* Murray, London
Masters	R Masters 1753 *History of the College of Corpus Christi and the Blessed Virgin Mary*
Moffatt	HC Moffatt 1906 *Old Oxford Plate* A. Constable, London
Palgrave	F Palgrave 1836 *The Antient Kalendars and Inventories of the Treasury of his Majesty's Exchequer* Commissioners of the Public Records
Penzer	NM Penzer 1960 'The steeple cup – III' *Apollo* June 165–70
Pinto	EH Pinto 1969 *Treen and other wooden bygones* Bell, London
Romilly	ME Bury & JF Pickles (eds) 2000 *Romilly's Cambridge Diary 1848–1864* Cambridgeshire Records Society
Smith	JJ Smith 1845 *Specimens of College Plate* Cambridge Antiquarian Soc. Quarto Publications **11**
Starkey	D Starkey (ed) 1998 *The Inventory of King Henry VIII* Harvey Miller, London
Taylor	G Taylor 1956 *Silver* Penguin, Harmondsworth
Thorold Rogers	JET Rogers 1865–87 *A History of Agriculture and Prices in England* Clarendon, Oxford
Venn	J Venn 1901 *Biographical History of Gonville and Caius College* Cambridge
Venn & Venn	J & JA Venn 1922–54 *Alumni Cantabrigienses* 10 vols Cambridge
Willis	R Willis (ed) 1859 *Facsimile of the Sketch-book of Wilars de Honecourt, an Architect of the Thirteenth Century* Parker, London
Woodhead	AG Woodhead *A History of Corpus Christi College Cambridge from 1952 to 1994* Boydell, Woodbridge
Zutshi	P Zutshi (ed) 1993 *Medieval Cambridge: essays on the pre-Reformation University* Boydell, Woodbridge

Index and glossary

Page numbers for biographical entries are in bold. Entries in bold italic include a description of the piece given by the individual named.

b: Butler or other on College staff
d: donor
dm: dining member
f: Fellow
fc: Fellow Commoner
m: maker (strictly, holder of the maker's mark)
mr: Master
s: student